sv agr	Error in subject-verb agreement **19.2**
sxl	Sexist language **9.11**
tf	Incorrect tense form **20.2**
tgl	Tangled sentence **16.2**
title	Error in form of a title **32.3**
trans bp	Transition needed between paragraphs **8.6**
t shift	Faulty tense shift within sentence **21.5**
wdy	Wordiness **9.12**
¶	New paragraph needed **8.1**
¶ *coh*	Paragraph lacks coherence or internal transition **8.3**
¶ *d*	Paragraph lacks direction **8.2**
¶ *em*	Paragraph lacks emphasis **8.4**
¶ *t shift*	Faulty tense shift in paragraph **21.6**
⊘	Faulty parallelism **14.4**
⌢, *conj*	Comma error with conjunction **26.2**
⌢, *cs*	Comma error between independent clauses **26.3**
⌢, *res*	Comma error with restrictive elements **26.6**
⌢, *ser*	Comma error in a series **26.8**
⌢, *d/a*	Comma error with date or address **26.11**
⌢, *bp*	Comma error between basic sentence parts **26.13**
;	Error with semicolon **27.2**
:	Error with colon **27.4**
.	Error with period **28.2**
?	Error with question mark **28.4**
!	Error with exclamation mark **28.5**
" "	Error with quotation marks **29**
—	Error with dash **30.2**
[ ]	Brackets needed **29.6**
. . .	Ellipsis dots needed **29.6**
/	Slash needed **30.4**
-	Hyphen needed **31.9**
'	Error with apostrophe **31.11**
×	Obvious error
∧	Something omitted
⊓	Transpose these two elements

WRITING
A College Handbook

THIRD EDITION

WRITING
A College Handbook

THIRD EDITION

James A. W. Heffernan
Dartmouth College
John E. Lincoln

W. W. Norton & Company
New York   London

Auden, W. H. From "Apothegms" from *W. H. Auden: Collected Poems*, ed. Edward Mendelson. Copyright © 1976 by Edward Mendelson, William Meredith, and Monroe K. Spears. Reprinted by permission of Random House, Inc.

Becker, Carl and Cooper, Kenneth S. From *Modern History*. Copyright 1958, 1977. Used by permission of Silver, Burdett & Ginn, Inc.

Bettelheim, Bruno. From "The Importance of Play." Copyright © 1985 by Bruno Bettelheim. Reprinted from A GOOD ENOUGH PARENT, by Bruno Bettelheim, by permission of Alfred A. Knopf, Inc. This essay originally appeared in THE ATLANTIC.

Broder, David. "Congress Needs Guts to Accept a Pay Raise." Copyright © 1988, Washington Post Writers Group. Reprinted with permission.

Chase, Alston. From GROUP MEMORY AND THE FUNNY MONEY SHEEPSKIN by Alston Chase. Copyright © 1980 by Alston Chase. By permission of Little, Brown and Company and the Wendy Weil Agency, Inc.

Dillard, Annie. From *Pilgrim at Tinker Creek* by Annie Dillard. Copyright © 1976 by Annie Dillard. Reprinted by permission of Harper & Row, Publishers, Inc.

Fromm, Erich. Specified excerpt adapted from pp. 57–58 from THE HEART OF MAN, by Erich Fromm, Volume XII of the RELIGIOUS PERSPECTIVES, Planned and Edited by Ruth Nanda Anshen. Copyright © 1964 Erich Fromm. Reprinted by permission of Harper & Row, Publishers, Inc.

Since this page cannot legibly accommodate all the copyright notices, p. 695 constitutes an extension of the copyright page.

Cover art: László Moholy-Nagy, *The Great Aluminum Picture (ALII)* (1926). Courtesy of Hattula Moholy-Nagy.

Cover design: Kevin O'Neill

ISBN 0-393-95951-1
ISBN 0-393-95953-8 *Instructor's Edition*

W. W. Norton & Company, Inc., 500 Fifth Avenue, New York, N.Y. 10110
W. W. Norton & Company Ltd., 10 Coptic Street, London WC1A 1PU

5 6 7 8 9 0

Contents

Preface   xxi

Acknowledgments   xxvii

Introduction   3
    Talking and Writing   3
    Standard English   4
    Grammar and Rhetoric   6
    Using this Book   7

Part 1
Writing Essays

1. Pre-writing   13
    1.1   Putting your Right Brain to Work   13
    1.2   Branching   16
    1.3   Choosing a Topic   19
    1.4   Making an Assigned Topic Your Own   21
    1.5   Pinpointing the Topic   22
    1.6   Triple-Viewing the Topic: Particle, Wave, and
          Field   23
    1.7   Dramatizing the Topic with Questions   24

1.8 Choosing a Basic Question to Define a Problem or Conflict 26
1.9 Getting Reactions to Your Question 27
1.10 Using Analogies 28
1.11 Working with a Nugget 29
1.12 Reading with a Purpose 29

2. Finding Your Aim 34
2.1 Thinking about Your Aim 34
2.2 Self-Expression 35
2.3 Directed Freewriting: Finding Your Way to a Thesis 37
2.4 Formulating a Thesis 40
2.5 Finding Your Tone 42
    2.5A Sounding Personal 42
    2.5B Sounding Impersonal 44
    2.5C Sounding Straightforward 45
    2.5D Being Ironic 46
2.6 Sample Theses on a Variety of Topics 47

3. Organizing Your Essay 49
3.1 Thinking about Your Readers 50
3.2 Arranging Your Major Points 53
3.3 Making an Outline 56
    3.3A Outlining with a Tree Diagram 56
    3.3B Outlining with a Vertical List 58
3.4 Introducing Your Essay 59
    3.4A Composing a Title 59
    3.4B Writing the Introduction 60
3.5 Shaping the Middle of Your Essay 64
    3.5A Using Your Outline and Making It Grow 65
    3.5B Thinking in Paragraphs 65
3.6 Ending Your Essay 67

4. Revising Your Essay 71
4.1 Reconsidering Your Aim 72
4.2 Reconsidering Your Tone 73
4.3 Reconsidering Your Structure 74

4.4   Developing Your Texture—Using Generalizations and Specifics *76*
4.5   Revising in Action *78*

5. Editing Your Essay   **88**

5.1   Making Your Sentences Rhetorically Effective *88*
5.2   Checking Your Choice of Words *90*
5.3   Checking Your Grammar *92*
5.4   Checking Your Punctuation *94*
5.5   Checking Your Spelling, Capitalization, and Apostrophes *94*
5.6   Proofreading Your Essay *97*
5.7   Preparing and Submitting Your Final Copy *98*

6. Methods of Development   **105**

6.1   Using Description *106*
      6.1A   External Description *106*
      6.1B   Analytical or Technical Description *107*
      6.1C   Evocative Description *108*

6.2   Using Narration *110*
      6.2A   Narrating Events in Chronological Order *110*
      6.2B   Narrating Events out of Chronological Order *111*

6.3   Combining Description and Narration *112*
6.4   Using Examples *113*
6.5   Using Analogy *115*
6.6   Using Comparison and Contrast *116*
      6.6A   Block Structure and Alternating Structure *117*
      6.6B   Writing an Essay of Comparison and Contrast *118*

6.7   Using Definitions *122*
6.8   Explaining by Analyzing—Classification and Division *124*
6.9   Explaining a Process *128*
6.10   Explaining Cause and Effect *130*
6.11   Combining Methods of Exposition *133*

7. Persuasion and Argument   **137**

7.1   What Is an Argument? *138*
7.2   Supporting Claims with Evidence *142*

7.2A   Giving Facts and Examples   *142*
7.2B   Citing Figures and Statistics   *142*
7.2C   Citing Sources and Authorities   *145*

7.3   Using Assumptions—Deduction and Induction   *147*

7.3A   Deduction and Validity—Drawing Necessary Conclusions   *148*
7.3B   Making Deductive Arguments Persuasive   *149*
7.3C   Induction—Drawing Probable Conclusions   *150*
7.3D   Making Induction Persuasive   *151*
7.3E   Placing Your Conclusion   *153*
7.3F   Combining Induction and Deduction   *153*

7.4   Avoiding Fallacies   *156*

7.4A   Arguing by Association   *156*
7.4B   Shifting the Meaning of a Key Term   *156*
7.4C   Begging the Question   *156*
7.4D   False Alternative   *157*
7.4E   False Analogy   *157*
7.4F   Personal Attack   *158*
7.4G   False Cause   *158*
7.4H   Irrelevant Conclusion   *159*
7.4I   Hasty Generalization   *159*

7.5   Using Argumentative Words   *161*
7.6   Reckoning with the Opposition   *162*

7.6A   Making Concessions   *162*
7.6B   Defining the Position You Will Oppose   *163*

7.7   Appealing to the Emotions   *165*
7.8   Constructing an Argumentative Essay   *167*

8. **Writing Paragraphs**   **172**

8.1   Why Use Paragraphs?   *172*
8.2   Direction   *176*

8.2A   Forecasting Your Main Point   *176*
8.2B   Signalling Turns—Transitions within the Paragraph   *178*

8.3   Coherence   *181*

8.3A   Using List Structure   *182*
8.3B   Using Chain Structure   *183*
8.3C   Combining List Structure and Chain Structure   *185*
8.3D   Strengthening Weak Connections   *186*

8.4   Emphasis   187

    8.4A   Using Repetition for Emphasis   187
    8.4B   Using Arrangement for Emphasis   188

8.5   Paragraphing in Action—Rearranging Sentences   189
8.6   Linking and Turning—Transitions between Paragraphs   193

9. Choosing Words   198

9.1   Choosing Your Level of Diction   198

    9.1A   Middle Level   198
    9.1B   High or Formal Level   199
    9.1C   Informal or Low Level—Colloquialisms and Slang   200
    9.1D   Mixed Levels—Pro and Con   200

9.2   Using the Dictionary   202
9.3   Choosing Words for Their Denotation   205
9.4   Choosing Words for Their Connotation   206
9.5   Choosing General and Specific Words   209
9.6   Using Words Figuratively—Simile and Metaphor   211
9.7   Avoiding Mixed Metaphor   214
9.8   Controlling Clichés   214
9.9   Using Idioms   216
9.10   Avoiding Jargon, Pretentious Words, and Euphemisms   217

    9.10A   Jargon   217
    9.10B   Pretentious Words   218
    9.10C   Euphemisms   218

9.11   Using Gender-Inclusive (Non-Sexist) Language   219
9.12   Avoiding Wordiness   221

    9.12A   Identifying the Most Important Words   222
    9.12B   Cutting Words You Don't Need   222

10. Reading in Order to Write   227

10.1   Subjective Response   227
10.2   Analytical Response   235

    10.2A   Catching the Tone   235
    10.2B   Finding the Writer's Main Point   239
    10.2C   Summarizing   243
    10.2D   Paraphrasing   245

10.2E   Judging the Supporting Points in an Essay *246*
10.2F   Writing an Interpretive Essay *248*

10.3   Imitative Response—Reading for Style *251*

Part 2
Writing Sentences

11. The Simple Sentence—Basic Parts   257

11.1   The Subject and the Predicate *257*
11.2   Writing the Predicate—The Role of Verbs *258*

    11.2A   Linking Verbs *258*
    11.2B   Intransitive Verbs *259*
    11.2C   Transitive Verbs *259*
    11.2D   Transitive Verbs and Voice *260*
    11.2E   Verb Phrases *260*

11.3   Writing the Subject *262*
11.4   Putting Subjects after the Verb *263*
11.5   Using Modifiers *264*
11.6   Using Compound Phrases *265*
11.7   Editing Mixed Constructions *267*
11.8   Editing Faulty Predication *268*
11.9   Adding the Possessive before a Gerund *270*

12. Modifiers   271

12.1   What Modifiers Do *271*
12.2   Using Adjectives and Adjective Phrases *272*
12.3   Overusing Nouns as Adjectives *272*
12.4   Using Adverbs and Adverb Phrases *273*

    12.4A   Double Negatives *274*

12.5   Misusing Adjectives as Adverbs *275*
12.6   Forming and Using Comparatives and Superlatives *275*

    12.6A   Comparatives *275*
    12.6B   Superlatives *276*
    12.6C   Special Forms *276*

12.7   Misusing Comparatives and Superlatives *277*
12.8   Using Appositives *277*

    12.8A   Placing Appositives *277*
    12.8B   Punctuating Appositives *277*

12.9   Using Participles and Participle Phrases *278*

    12.9A   Punctuating Participles *279*

12.10   Misforming the Past Participle *280*

12.11   Using Infinitives and Infinitive Phrases *283*

12.12   Avoiding the Split Infinitive *284*

12.13   Using Absolute Phrases *285*

12.14   Placing Modifiers *286*

12.15   Editing Misplaced Modifiers *288*

12.16   Editing Squinting Modifiers *288*

12.17   Editing Misplaced Restricters *288*

12.18   Editing Dangling Modifiers *290*

13. Coordination 1—Compound Sentences   **294**

13.1   Making Compound Sentences *294*

13.2   Compounding with Conjunctions *295*

    13.2A   Punctuation with Conjunctions *296*

13.3   Overusing *and* *296*

13.4   Compounding with the Semicolon *297*

13.5   Compounding with Conjunctive Adverbs *297*

    13.5A   What Conjunctive Adverbs Show *298*

    13.5B   Punctuation with Conjunctive Adverbs *299*

13.6   Editing Comma Splices *301*

13.7   Editing Run-on (Fused) Sentences *303*

14. Coordination 2—Parallel Construction   **306**

14.1   Why Choose Parallelism? *306*

14.2   Writing Parallel Constructions *307*

14.3   Using Correlatives with Parallelism *308*

14.4   Editing Faulty Parallelism *308*

15. Subordination—Complex Sentences   **312**

15.1   What Subordination Does *312*

15.2   What Subordinate Clauses Are *314*

15.3   Using Adjective (Relative) Clauses *315*

15.4   Choosing Relative Pronouns *316*

15.5   Placing the Adjective Clause *318*

15.6   Punctuating Adjective Clauses *319*

15.7   Overusing Adjective Clauses *321*

15.8   Using Adverb Clauses *322*

15.9   Choosing Subordinators *323*

15.10   Placing Adverb Clauses   *325*
15.11   Punctuating Adverb Clauses   *326*
15.12   Making Adverb Clauses Complete: Avoiding Faulty Comparisons   *327*
15.13   Using Noun Clauses   *329*
15.14   Placing Subordinate Clauses   *330*

16. Coordination and Subordination   **332**

16.1   Using Coordination and Subordination Together   *332*
16.2   Untangling Sentences   *336*

17. Complete Sentences and Sentence Fragments   **338**

17.1   What Is a Sentence Fragment?   *338*
17.2   Using and Misusing Sentence Fragments   *339*
17.3   Spotting and Editing Sentence Fragments   *340*

18. Using Pronouns   **345**

18.1   Using Pronouns with Antecedents   *345*
18.2   Using Pronouns without Antecedents   *346*
18.3   Using Pronouns Clearly   *346*
18.4   Avoiding Unclear Pronoun Reference   *347*

    18.4A   Ambiguity   *347*
    18.4B   Broad Reference   *347*
    18.4C   Muffled Reference   *348*
    18.4D   Free-Floating *they* and *it*   *348*
    18.4E   Indefinite *you* and *your*   *349*
    18.4F   Remote Reference   *349*

18.5   Making Antecedents and Pronouns Agree in Gender   *351*
18.6   Making Antecedents and Pronouns Agree in Number   *352*
18.7   Pronouns and Antecedents—Resolving Problems in Number   *352*
18.8   Avoiding Faulty Shifts in Pronoun Reference   *355*
18.9   Pronoun Case Forms   *357*
18.10   Using Pronoun Case   *358*

    18.10A   Subject Case   *358*
    18.10B   Object Case   *358*
    18.10C   Possessive Case   *358*
    18.10D   Reflexive/Emphatic Case   *359*

18.11   Using *who, whom, whose, whoever,* and *whomever*   360

18.12   Misusing Pronoun Case Forms   *360*

19. Subject-Verb Agreement   363

19.1   What Is Agreement?   *363*

19.2   Making Verbs Agree with Subjects   *364*

19.3   Making the Verb *be* Agree with Subjects   *365*

19.4   Avoiding Dialectal Mistakes in Agreement   *365*

19.5   Finding the Subject   *368*

19.6   Recognizing the Number of the Subject   *368*

     19.6A   Nouns Meaning One Thing   *369*

     19.6B   Nouns Meaning More Than One Thing   *369*

     19.6C   Pronouns Fixed in Number   *369*

     19.6D   Pronouns Variable in Number   *370*

     19.6E   Verbal Nouns and Noun Clauses   *370*

     19.6F   Nouns Followed by a Form of the Verb *be*   *370*

     19.6G   Modified Nouns and Pronouns   *371*

     19.6H   Compounds Made with *and*   *371*

     19.6I   Items Joined by *or, either . . . or,* etc.   *372*

     19.6J   Nouns Spelled the Same Way in Singular and Plural   *372*

     19.6K   Collective Nouns and Nouns of Measurement   *372*

     19.6L   Subjects Beginning with *every*   *372*

     19.6M   The Word *number* as Subject   *373*

     19.6N   Foreign Words and Expressions   *373*

20. Verbs—Tense   375

20.1   Tense and Time   *375*

20.2   Forming the Tenses   *376*

     20.2A   Forming the Present   *376*

     20.2B   Forming the Past   *376*

     20.2C   Forming Tenses with Auxiliaries   *376*

     20.2D   Forming the Progressive   *376*

20.3   Using the Present   *378*

20.4   Using the Present Perfect   *379*

20.5   Using the Past   *380*

20.6   Using the Past Perfect   *381*

20.7   Using the Future   *381*

20.8   Using the Future Perfect   *382*

20.9   Misusing Tenses   *383*
20.10   Managing Tense and Time with Participles and
        Infinitives   *383*
20.11   Forming the Principal Parts of Commonly Used
        Irregular Verbs   *384*

21. Verbs—Sequence of Tenses   388
21.1   Understanding Sequence of Tenses   *388*
21.2   Sequences in Compound Sentences   *389*
21.3   Sequences in Complex Sentences   *389*

   21.3A   Main Verb in the Present   *389*
   21.3B   Main Verb in the Present Perfect   *389*
   21.3C   Main Verb in the Past   *390*
   21.3D   Main Verb in the Past Perfect   *390*
   21.3E   Main Verb Indicating Future   *390*
   21.3F   Main Verb in the Future Perfect   *390*

21.4   Using Sequences in Paragraphs   *391*
21.5   Correcting Faulty Tense Shifts in Sentences   *392*
21.6   Correcting Faulty Tense Shifts in Paragraphs   *394*

22. Verbs—Active and Passive Voice   397
22.1   What Voice Is   *397*
22.2   Forming the Active and Passive Voice   *398*

   22.2A   Changing from Active to Passive   *398*
   22.2B   Changing from Passive to Active   *399*

22.3   Choosing the Active Voice   *399*
22.4   Choosing the Passive   *399*
22.5   Misusing the Passive   *401*

23. Verbs—Mood   405
23.1   What Mood Is   *405*
23.2   Using the Indicative   *405*
23.3   Using the Imperative   *406*
23.4   Using the Subjunctive—Modal Auxiliaries   *406*

   23.4A   Misusing Modal Auxiliaries   *408*

23.5   Using the Subjunctive—Special Verb Forms   *408*
23.6   Forming and Using Conditional Sentences   *409*

   23.6A   The Possible Condition   *410*
   23.6B   The Impossible or Contrary-to-Fact
           Condition   *410*

23.6C   Misusing *would have* in Conditional
Clauses *410*

24. Direct and Indirect Reporting of Discourse   **413**

24.1   Direct Reporting of Statements *413*

    24.1A   Using Tenses in Tags *414*
    24.1B   Quoting Extended Dialogue *414*
    24.1C   Quoting Several Lines of Prose or Poetry *415*

24.2   Indirect Reporting of Statements *415*
24.3   Direct Reporting of Questions *416*
24.4   Indirect Reporting of Questions *417*
24.5   Confusing the Direct and Indirect Reporting of
Questions *417*
24.6   Fitting Quotations into Your Own Prose *418*

    24.6A   Misfitted Quotations *418*

25. Invigorating Your Style   **420**

25.1   Vary Your Sentences *421*
25.2   Use Verbs of Action Instead of *be* *422*
25.3   Use the Active Voice More Often Than the
Passive *423*
25.4   Ask Questions *423*
25.5   Cut Any Words You Don't Need *425*

Part 3
Punctuation and Mechanics

26. The Comma   **431**

26.1   Using Commas with Conjunctions *431*
26.2   Misusing Commas with Conjunctions *432*
26.3   Misusing Commas between Independent Clauses—
The Comma Splice *432*
26.4   Using Commas after Introductory Elements *433*
26.5   Using Commas with Nonrestrictive Elements *435*
26.6   Misusing Commas with Restrictive Elements *436*
26.7   Using Commas with Coordinate Items in a
Series *438*
26.8   Misusing Commas with Coordinate Items in a
Series *438*

26.9   Using Commas to Prevent a Misreading *439*
26.10   Using Commas with Dates, Addresses, Greetings, Names, and Large Numbers *439*
26.11   Misusing Commas with Dates and Addresses *440*
26.12   Using Commas with Quotation Marks *441*
26.13   Misusing the Comma between Basic Parts of a Sentence *441*

27. The Semicolon and the Colon   **444**

27.1   Using the Semicolon *444*
27.2   Misusing the Semicolon *445*
27.3   Using the Colon *446*
27.4   Misusing the Colon *447*

28. End Marks   **449**

28.1   Using the Period *449*
28.2   Misusing the Period *450*
28.3   Using the Question Mark *451*
28.4   Misusing the Question Mark *451*
28.5   Using the Exclamation Point *451*

29. Quotation Marks and Quoting   **453**

29.1   Quoting Words, Phrases, and Short Passages of Prose *453*
29.2   Using Double and Single Quotation Marks *453*
29.3   Using Quotation Marks with Other Punctuation *454*
29.4   Quoting Long Prose Passages *458*
29.5   Quoting Verse *458*
29.6   Using Brackets and Ellipsis Dots to Mark Changes in a Quotation *459*
    29.6A   Using Brackets to Mark Words Added to a Quotation *460*
    29.6B   Using Ellipsis Dots to Mark Words Left Out of a Quotation *460*
29.7   Special Uses of Quotation Marks *461*
29.8   Misusing Quotation Marks *462*

30. The Dash, Parentheses, the Slash   **464**

30.1   Using the Dash *464*
30.2   Misusing the Dash *465*

30.3   Using Parentheses   *465*
30.4   Using the Slash   *466*

31. Spelling   469
31.1   Checking Your Spelling with a Computer
        Program   *469*
31.2   Listing Your Spelling Demons   *470*
31.3   Learning How to Add Suffixes   *471*
31.4   Learning When to Use *ie* and *ei*   *472*
31.5   Learning How to Add Prefixes   *472*
31.6   Recognizing Homonyms   *472*
31.7   Pluralizing Simple Nouns   *473*
31.8   Pluralizing Compound Nouns   *474*
31.9   Using the Hyphen   *476*
31.10   Using the Apostrophe   *478*
31.11   Misusing the Apostrophe   *479*

32. Mechanics   481
32.1   Using Capital Letters   *481*
32.2   Using Italics or Underlining   *483*
32.3   Titles   *484*
32.4   Using Abbreviations   *487*
32.5   Misusing Abbreviations   *488*
32.6   Using Numbers   *489*

Part 4
The Research Paper

33. Preparing the Research Paper   495
33.1   Choosing a Topic   *496*
33.2   Using the Library—The Reference Section   *499*
        33.2A   Learning What Your Topic Is Called   *499*
        33.2B   A Book-and-Article Bibliography   *501*
        33.2C   A Computerized Index   *502*
        33.2D   General Encyclopedias   *504*
        33.2E   Specialized Reference Works   *504*
        33.2F   Compilations of Facts and Statistics   *504*
        33.2G   Biographical Guides   *505*
        33.2H   Guides to Books   *506*

33.2I   Guides to Articles in Books *507*
33.2J   General Indexes to Periodicals *508*
33.2K   Specialized Indexes to Periodicals *509*
33.2L   Government Publications *510*

33.3   Finding Books—The On-Line Catalog and the Card Catalog *511*

33.3A   Using the On-Line Catalog *511*
33.3B   Using the Card Catalog *512*
33.3C   Getting Books Your Library Doesn't Have *514*

33.4   Finding Articles *514*
33.5   Keeping Track of Your Sources *515*

33.5A   Source Card for a Book *516*
33.5B   Source Card for an Article *516*

33.6   Using Microtexts *517*
33.7   Conducting an Interview *517*
33.8   Choosing Which Sources to Consult *520*
33.9   Examining Your Sources *522*
33.10   Taking Notes *523*

33.10A   Taking Notes with a Word Processor *523*
33.10B   Taking Notes on Index Cards *525*

33.11   Summarizing and Paraphrasing *526*
33.12   Quoting from Sources *529*
33.13   Formulating Your Thesis *531*
33.14   Filling Gaps in Your Research *532*

34. Writing the Research Paper **533**

34.1   Making an Outline *533*
34.2   Managing Your Sources as You Write *535*

34.2A   Citing Sources in the First Draft *535*
34.2B   Introducing Your Sources *535*
34.2C   Plagiarism *537*

34.3   Composing the Paper as a Whole *540*

35. Documenting the Research Paper **544**

35.1   Styles of Documentation *544*
35.2   Citing with Parentheses—The MLA Style *545*

35.2A   Citing and Listing—Basic Procedures *546*
35.2B   Citing and Listing Various Sources *549*
35.2C   Listing Various Sources—Further Examples *559*

36. Preparing the Final Copy of the Research Paper **566**

37. **Sample Argumentative Research Paper with MLA Parenthetical Style**   569

38. **Writing and Research across the Curriculum**   589

38.1   Three Disciplines Illustrated—Specialists Writing for Specialists   590

38.2   Asking the Question That Fits Your Discipline   593

    38.2A   Humanistic Writing—Focus on the Individual Work   593

    38.2B   Social Sciences—Focus on Social Groups   595

    38.2C   Natural Sciences—Focus on Physical Properties   596

38.3   Writing on Specialized Topics for Non-Specialists   597

38.4   Organizing a Research Paper in the Humanities   598

38.5   Documenting Sources in the Humanities   600

38.6   Organizing Research Papers in the Social Sciences   600

38.7   Documenting Sources in the Social Sciences—The APA Parenthetical Style   601

    38.7A   Writing APA Parenthetical Citations   602

    38.7B   Writing the Reference List—APA Style   603

38.8   Organizing Research Papers in the Natural Sciences   605

38.9   Documenting Sources in the Sciences   606

    38.9A   Citing Sources in the Natural Sciences—CBE Style   607

    38.9B   Writing the Reference List—CBE Style   608

38.10   Tables and Figures in Research Papers   609

    38.10A   Presenting Tables   610

    38.10B   Presenting Figures   610

Glossaries

Glossary of Usage   615

Glossary of Grammatical Terms   640

Appendices

Appendix 1 **Citing with Notes—MLA Style**   **659**

A1.1   Writing Footnotes and Endnotes *659*

A1.2   Writing Explanatory Notes *661*

A1.3   Writing Notes—First and Later References *661*

A1.4   Writing Notes for Various Sources *662*

A1.5   Writing the Bibliography *669*

A1.6   Sample Explanatory Research Paper with MLA Note Style *670*

Appendix 2 **Beyond Freshman English—Writing Examinations, Applications, and Letters**   **682**

A2.1   Writing Examination Essays *682*

A2.2   Applying for Admission to a School of Business, Law, Medicine, or Graduate Study—The Personal Statement *685*

A2.3   Applying for a Job—The Resumé and the Covering Letter *689*

A2.4   Writing a Business Letter—The Proper Format *691*

A2.5   Writing for Your Rights—The Letter of Protest *693*

Index   **697**

Preface to the Third Edition

The first two editions of this book set out to demonstrate that good writing is not simply the absence of grammatical error but the presence of rhetorical power. This remains our leading aim. We have tightened many sections and added a few new ones, but our basic approach remains unchanged. While identifying the mistakes commonly made in student writing and showing how to correct them, we emphasize what student writers *can* do rather than what they can't or shouldn't do. Above all, we try to show them how to generate the kind of writing that informs, excites, delights, and persuades the readers for whom it is written.

Since many teachers like to start by introducing students to the writing process as a whole, Part 1, "Writing Essays," begins with a five-chapter overview of that process. Users of the second edition will see that we continue to illustrate the writing process with various examples of student writing-in-progress, and with successive versions of one student essay as it evolves from brainstorming to final draft. But the first five chapters also incorporate several new features. Chapter 1 explains new ways of brainstorming for essay material with techniques such as branching and looping, and also shows students how to gather essay material by annotating what they read. Chapter 2 shows them how to find their way to a thesis by either of two ways: directed freewriting or using a general aim that leads to a specific one. It also shows them how to find a tone as they develop and formulate a thesis. Chapter 3 explains how to outline and organize an essay, but it begins with an expanded treatment of something every writer must learn to do in the planning stage of the writing process: think about the reader. Finally, as in the second edition, chapters 4 and 5 explain how to revise and then edit an essay, how to make large-scale changes and small adjustments.

The title of chapter 6, "Methods of Development," signals yet another change. Instead of accentuating the differences between description, narration, and various forms of exposition (such as defining and comparing), chapter 6 stresses the point that most essays combine at least two of these methods, and shows how they can be used to persuade as well as explain. Chapter 7 still treats the techniques of argumentation, but the new version clarifies the relation between logic and persuasion, expands the treatment of "hard" evidence (such a figures, statistics, and statements by authorities), and more fully explains fallacies. The rest of Part 1 incorporates minor changes. Chapter 8 still explains how to organize a paragraph, but now stresses the art of guiding readers from one sentence to the next. Chapter 9 still explains how to choose words, but includes a new section on how to avoid sexist language. Chapter 10 is virtually unchanged. As before, it shows how to turn reading into writing by using reading matter as a source of stimulation, as an object of analysis or interpretation, or as a model to be imitated.

Part 2, "Writing Sentences" maintains a positive approach to sentence construction even while showing students how to overcome their errors. Part 2 is keyed to a list of symbols for revision (found inside the front cover of the book) that guide the student to specific advice on error correction. But since this book was written to be read as well as consulted, most of the chapters in Part 2 begin by explaining and illustrating the rhetorical impact of a particular construction when it is correctly and effectively used. Before we attack the misplaced modifier, for instance, we show what a well-placed modifier can do; and before we identify the wrong ways of joining independent clauses (the run-on sentence and the comma splice), we show what coordination can do. Using lively examples from student essays as well as from the work of leading writers, we consistently aim to show students how they can exploit the rich, vital, and inexhaustible resources of the English language. Our chief aim in the whole of Part 2, in fact, is summed up by the title of Chapter 25: "Invigorating Your Style."

The emphasis on rhetorical effect in Part 2 is reinforced by the exercises. Instead of merely calling for the correction of errors, many of them ask for short sentences to be combined in more than one way so that students can see what rhetorical effects they can achieve with various constructions. Also, nearly all of the exercises in Part 2 now consist of consecutive sentences: sentences that work together to tell a story, build a description, or develop a point. Ranging in subject matter from bike-riding and modern consumerism to Greek myth, these exercises will help students see what the writing of an individual sentence can contribute to a paragraph.

Part 3, "Punctuation and Mechanics," is meant for reference. Users of the second edition will find that this part has been just slightly reorganized. (Brackets and ellipsis dots, for instance, are now treated in chapter 29, "Quotation Marks and Quoting.") The single most notable change is in the exercises. Nearly all of them in the new Part 3, like those in the new Part 2, consist of consecutive sentences.

We begin Part 4, "The Research Paper," by noting that a research paper may furnish an analytical argument about its topic or an explanatory survey of it. Then we trace the development of a particular argumentative paper from beginning to end. We explain how to use a library and (where available) its computerized resources, how to gather and keep track of sources, how to take notes in writing or with a word processor, and—something new in this edition—how to conduct an informative interview. We also explain how to organize a research paper and cite sources with the MLA style of parenthetical documentation, which is illustrated by a new sample argumentative research paper. (A sample explanatory research paper appears in Appendix 1.)

Part 4 ends with another new addition—a chapter called "Writing and Research across the Curriculum." Here we explain how humanists, social scientists, and natural scientists approach their subjects. We consider the kinds of questions that writers operating in different fields are equipped to answer; we explain how to organize papers in those fields; and to illustrate the documentation of sources in different fields, we briefly discuss the APA style (commonly used in the social sciences) and the CBE style (used for papers in biology). We aim to show that while some qualities are common to all good writing, a student doing a paper in a specified field such as sociology or biology needs to understand the conceptual framework of that field, the language proper to it, and the kind of writing expected of those who work within it.

Two glossaries—one on usage and the other on grammatical

terms—are now followed by two (rather than four) appendices. (Writing with a word processor, formerly the topic of Appendix 3, is now fully integrated into the text—starting with Chapter 1, which includes a brief explanation of how a darkened computer screen can facilitate pre-writing.) Teachers who prefer that students cite sources with notes rather than parentheses will find the MLA note style explained in Appendix 1 and illustrated by a sample paper, "Options for the Working Mother." Appendix 2 moves "Beyond Freshman English." With apt illustrations, it shows how to write an examination essay, a resumé and covering letter for a job application, a business letter, a letter of protest, and a personal statement for an application to a school of law, medicine, business, or graduate studies. Appendix 2 tries to demonstrate, in fact, that the ability to write well can have a real and lasting effect upon a student's life.

In addition to the changes in substance, this third edition differs from the second one in its look and feel: the text has been shortened somewhat and given a fresh design and smaller trim size. The result, we hope, is a more inviting handbook that is easier to handle.

Supplementary Materials

Many teachers may find that this book by itself serves all the needs of a beginning composition course. To help teachers and students in further ways, however, we have prepared a number of supplements.

For the student, *Writing—A College Workbook,* Third Edition, is a basic textbook on the writing of sentences and the handling of punctuation and mechanics. It parallels and supplements Parts 2 and 3 of the *Handbook* and includes basic instruction on sentence structure as well as abundant exercises—ranging from recognition and error correction to sentence-combining to revising and editing complete paragraphs—printed on tear-out pages that can be assigned as classwork or homework. An answer pamphlet is available to instructors on request.

A special version of *Norton Textra Writer 2.0* combines a powerful word processor and spell checker with a concise on-line version of *Writing—A College Handbook.* At a keystroke students can find grammatical and rhetorical advice in keeping with the positive approach of the *Handbook,* as well as cross-references to the book itself. *Norton Textra Writer 2.0* is available for IBMs and compatibles.

For the instructor, the *Instructor's Edition*, new with the third edition, combines the full text of the *Handbook* with a manual containing suggestions on how to use the *Handbook* in a composition course, a sample syllabus, suggested readings, and answers to exercises in the *Handbook*.

Lastly, a set of diagnostic tests is available in printed form and on disk for Macintosh and IBM PC and compatible computers. The diagnostic tests include fifty multiple-choice items on grammar, usage, punctuation, and mechanics, an administrator's manual, and diagnostic charts with cross-references to *Writing—A College Handbook*, Third Edition.

James A. W. Heffernan
John E. Lincoln

Acknowledgments

We have incurred many debts in the preparation of this book, and we are happy to acknowledge them here. It began as *The Dartmouth Guide to Writing*, by John E. Lincoln—a book of lessons and exercises issued by Dartmouth College for its students under a grant from the Lilly Foundation.

For help with the third edition, we are grateful, first of all, to the many teachers who took time to respond to our publisher's questionnaire: to Barbara Weaver, Anderson College, and to a small group of teachers who acted as on-going consultants on the entire manuscript: Lynn Dianne Beene, University of New Mexico; Diana DeLuca, University of Hawaii at Manoa; Judith Ferster, North Carolina State University; Jennifer Ginn, North Carolina State University; William Liston, Ball State University; and Richard Johnson, Mount Holyoke College.

We are also indebted to many others for various kinds of help: to William Cook, Charles Culver, Robert Fogelin, Ronald Green, Thomas Roos, and Robert Sokol, all of Dartmouth College; Harry Brent, Rutgers University, Camden College of Arts and Sciences; Barry E. Brown, Missouri Southern State College; Jean Brunk, Oregon State University—Corvallis; Alma G. Bryant, University of South Florida; Michael Cartwright, California State College—Bakersfield; Lynne Constantine, James Madison University; the late Gregory Cowan, Texas A & M University; Hubert M. English, Jr., University of Michigan; John J. Fenstermaker, Florida State University; Barbara Munson Goff, Cook College of Rutgers University; S. J. Hanna, Mary Washington College; James Hartman,

University of Kansas; Joan E. Hartman, College of Staten Island, City University of New York; Francis Hubbard, University of Wisconsin—Milwaukee; Naomi Jacobs, University of Missouri—Columbia; Craig Johnson, Hillsborough Community College—Ybor City Campus; Mildred A. Kalish, Suffolk County Community College; C. H. Knoblauch, Columbia University; James Mac-Killop, Onondaga Community College; Stephen R. Mandell, Drexel University; John C. Mellon, University of Illinois, Chicago Circle Campus; Susan Miller, University of Wisconsin—Milwaukee; James Murphy, California State University—Hayward; Karen Ogden, University of Manitoba; James F. O'Neil, Edison Community College; Andrew Parkin, University of British Columbia; Diana Pingatore, Lake Superior State College; Kenneth Roe, Shasta College; Ann Sharp, Furman University; Craig B. Snow, University of Arizona; Ken M. Symes, Western Washington State College; Keith A. Tandy, Moorhead State University; Mary Thysell, University of Waterloo; and Harvey S. Wiener, La Guardia Community College. We thank George Savvides, Charles Rice, Donald Murray, Charles Moran of the University of Massachusetts, and Ron Fortune, Illinois State University.

We must record here, too, our indebtedness to the many students who have contributed examples of what they do in their writing—in particular Mitch Arion, Barbara Clark, Sarah Watson, Robin Martinez, Erica Berl, Lisa Miles, James Mann, Timothy Boyle, Ken Oshima, Qiao Xing, David Lenrow, Sherri Hughes, Rick Kurihara, Daphne Bien, Scott Jaynes, Adam Usadi, Steven Arkowitz, David Leitao, Neil Okun, Jonathan Kulas, Vanessa Bernstein, and Leonard Chang. Thanks are due as well to Francis X. Oscadal and Lois Krieger, who gave us their expert advice on the use of library resources for research, and also to those who generously supplied us with material for appendix 2: Frances R. Hall of Dartmouth Medical School, Robert Sokol and Kenneth Shewmaker of Dartmouth College, and Andrew Vouras of the New England Telephone Company. We also thank Kathy Harp and Barbara Cunningham of the Dartmouth College English Department, who kindly helped us with the photocopying of material for this edition.

In addition, we wish to thank present and former members of our publisher's staff for their signal contributions. Ethelbert Nevin II and John E. Neill each played a part in persuading us to write the first edition of the book. John W. N. Francis and John Benedict gave superb editorial guidance for the first two editions, and our new editor, Julia Reidhead, has been equally effective with this one. We owe thanks to our first two copyeditors, Esther Jacobson and Marian Johnson, and now to our third, Margie Brassil, who copyedited this new edition. We also owe thanks to Barry Wade, James Jordan, Allen Clawson, and John Mardirosian. We especially thank Suzanne Bennett, our designer; Jennifer Schaeffer, our permissions editor; and Diane O'Connor, who supervised the production of this book.

We also wish to acknowledge our debt to the following books and articles: Monroe Beardsley, *Thinking Straight*, 4th ed. (New York: Prentice-Hall, 1975); Charles Bazerman, "What Written Knowledge Does: Three Examples of Academic Discourse," *Philosophy of the Social Sciences* 11 (1981), 361–87; N. R. Cattell, *The New English Grammar* (Cambridge, MA: MIT Press, 1969); Elaine Chaika, "Grammars and Teaching," *College English* 39 (March 1978), 770–83; Francis Christensen, "A Generative Rhetoric of the Sentence," "Notes toward a New Rhetoric," and "A Generative Rhetoric of the Paragraph," in *The Sentence and the Paragraph* (Urbana, IL: NCTE, 1966); Harry H. Crosby and George F. Estey, *College Writing: The Rhetorical Imperative* (New York: Harper & Row, 1968); George O. Curme, *English Grammar* (New York: Barnes and Noble, 1968); Bergen and Cornelia Evans, *A Dictionary of Contemporary American Usage* (New York: Random House, 1957); Charles Fillmore, "The Case for Case," in *Universals in Linguistic Theory*, ed. Emmon Bach and Robert T. Harms (New York: Holt, Rinehart and Winston, 1968); Linda S. Flower and John R. Hayes, "Problem Solving Strategies and the Writing Process," *College English* 39 (December 1977), 449–61; W. Nelson Francis, *The Structure of American English* (New York: Ronald, 1958); Robert J. Geist, *An Introduction to Transformational Grammar* (New York: Macmillan, 1971); William E. Gruber, " 'Servile Copying' and the Teaching of English Composition," *College English* 39 (December 1977), 491–97; A. S. Hornby, *A Guide to Patterns and Usage in English* (London: Oxford University Press, 1954); Darrell Huff, *How to Lie with Statistics* (New York: W. W. Norton & Company, 1954); Roderick A. Jacobs and Peter S. Rosenbaum, *English Transformational Grammar* (Waltham, MA: Blaisdell, 1968); Otto Jespersen, *Essentials of English Grammar* (London: George Allen & Unwin, 1959); James L. Kinneavy, *A Theory of Discourse* (New York: W. W. Norton & Company, 1980); Henriette Ann Klausen, *Writing on Both Sides of the Brain* (San Francisco: Harper & Row, 1987); Susan Peck MacDonald, "Problem

Definition in Academic Writing," *College English* 49 (1987), 315–31; Elaine P. Maimon et al., *Writing in the Arts and Sciences* (Cambridge, MA: Winthrop Publications, 1981); John C. Mellon, *Transformational Sentence Combining* (Urbana, IL: NCTE, 1969); Donald Murray, *A Writer Teaches Writing: A Practical Method of Teaching Composition* (Boston: Houghton Mifflin, 1968), and also various essays and lectures; Frank O'Hare, *Sentence Combining* (Urbana, IL: NCTE, 1973), and *Sentencecraft* (Lexington, MA: Ginn, 1975); Gabriele Lusser Rico, *Writing the Natural Way* (Los Angeles: J. P. Tarcher, 1983); Mina Shaughnessy, *Errors and Expectations: A Guide for the Teacher of Basic Writing* (New York: Oxford University Press, 1977); Harry Shaw, *Errors in English and Ways to Correct Them* (New York: Barnes and Noble, 1970); Stephen Toulmin, *The Uses of Argument* (Cambridge: Cambridge University Press, 1958); the *MLA Handbook for Writers of Research Papers*, Third Edition (New York: Modern Language Association, 1988); and the *Publication Manual of the American Psychological Association*, Third Edition (Washington, DC: American Psychological Association, 1983).

Lastly, we thank our spouses, Nancy Heffernan and Mary Lincoln, who contributed to the preparation of this book in ways too various to mention, and we thank our children—Andrew and Virginia Heffernan, and Chris, Peter, and Brian Lincoln—for supplying both vivid examples of their own writing and their own special brand of encouragement.

J.A.W.H.
J.E.L.

WRITING
A College Handbook

THIRD EDITION

Introduction

Talking and Writing

Talking is something most of us seem to do naturally. We learn to talk almost automatically, first imitating the words we hear and then imitating the ways in which people around us put them together. Well before we learn how to put words on paper, we unconsciously learn how to use them in speech.

But no one learns to write automatically. You cannot write even a single letter of the alphabet without a conscious effort of mind and hand, and to get beyond the single letter, you must be shown how to form words, how to put words together into sentences, and how to punctuate those sentences.

Writing, then, is a means of communication you must consciously learn. And part of what makes it hard to learn is that written words usually have to express your meaning in your absence, have to "speak" all by themselves. When you speak face to face with a listener, you can communicate in many different ways. You can raise or lower the pitch or volume of your voice to emphasize a point; you can grin, frown, wink, or shrug; you can use your hands to shape out a meaning when you don't quite have the words to do it; you can even make your silence mean something. But in writing you have to communicate without facial expressions, gestures, or body English of any kind. You have to speak with words and punctuation alone.

Furthermore, writing is a solitary act. When you talk, you normally talk to someone who talks back, who raises questions, who lets you know whether or not you are making yourself clear. But when you write, you work alone. Even if you are writing a letter to a friend, he or she will not suddenly materialize to prod or prompt you into speech, to help you fill in the gaps that so often occur when you try to tell a story or give an explanation off the

3

top of your head. To write well, you have to anticipate the reactions of a reader you cannot see or hear.

But writing does have one big advantage over speaking. It gives you time to think, to try out your ideas on paper, to choose your words, to read what you have written, to rethink, revise, and rearrange it, and most importantly, to consider its effect on a reader. Writing gives you time to find the best possible way of stating what you mean. And the more you study the craft of writing, the better you will use your writing time.

Standard English

This book aims to help you write effectively in English. But since there are many kinds of English, you should know which kind this book aims to teach—and why.

The language called "English" is used in many parts of the world. It is spoken not only in England but also in the British West Indies and in countries that were once British colonies—such as Canada, the United States, Australia, India, and Nigeria. These are all "English-speaking" countries, but they have different ways of using English. Sometimes, for instance, they have different words for the same thing:

    truck [U.S.] = lorry [Great Britain]
    pond [U.S.] = billabong [Australia]

Sometimes they have different ways of spelling or pronouncing the same word:

    labor [U.S.] = labour [Great Britain and Canada]
    recognize [U.S.] = recognise [Great Britain and Canada]
    laugh: pronounced "laff" in the U.S., "lahff" in Great Britain
    paint: pronounced "paynt" in the U.S., "pint" in Australia
    check [U.S.] = cheque [Great Britain and Canada]

Sometimes they use different grammatical forms:

    The jury has reached a verdict. [U.S.]
    The jury have reached a verdict. [all other English-speaking
      countries]

Probably you have already noticed differences such as these. Even if you have never traveled abroad, you have probably heard

British or Australian speech. When you did, you could undoubtedly tell after just a few words that what you were hearing was different from any kind of English commonly spoken in North America. The reason for the difference is that a living language never stands still. Like the people who speak it and the world they speak it in, it changes. And if English-speaking peoples live far enough apart, the English they use will change in divergent ways. That is why English sounds different in different parts of the world.

Just as English varies from one country to another, it also varies from one region of a country to another, and from one cultural or ethnic group to another. Consider these statements:

> She'll say I be talkin.
> She'll say I am talking.
>
> They ain't got no ponies; they got big horses: I rode one, real big uns.
> They don't have any ponies; they have big horses. I rode one, a really big one.
>
> I have three brother and two sister.
> I have three brothers and two sisters.

These statements illustrate four dialects—four kinds of English used in North America. The first statement in each pair illustrates a regional or ethnic dialect; the second illustrates Standard English. Each of these dialects has its own distinctive character and rules. But of them all, Standard English is the only one normally taught in schools and colleges, the only one normally required in business and the professions, and the only one widely used in writing—especially in print. Why does Standard English enjoy this privilege? Is it always better than any other kind? And if you were raised to speak an ethnic or regional dialect, must you stop speaking that dialect in order to learn the Standard one?

There is no easy answer to the first of these three questions. But the answer to the second one is no. Standard English is not always better than any other kind. In a spoken exchange, it can sometimes be less expressive—and therefore less effective—than a regional or ethnic dialect. Compare, for instance, the original version of a regional proverb with the Standard version:

> Them as has, gets; them as ain't, gets took.
> Those who have, get; those who do not have, get taken.

These two statements strike the ear in different ways. While the first has the expressive vitality of regional speech, the second—the Standard version—sounds comparatively stiff. The original packs more punch.

Part of what makes the original version so effective is the tradition that stands behind it, and because of that tradition, the answer to the third question we raised is also no. A regional or ethnic dialect is not just a way of speaking; it is the living record of a shared heritage and shared concerns. For this reason, no one who speaks such a dialect should be forced to give it up.

But if many people can learn more than one language, most people can learn more than one dialect, and whatever the dialect you were raised to speak, you can and should learn to write Standard English. Whether or not it is better than any other dialect for purposes of speech, it is what you will normally be expected to use in your writing. During college, it is what teachers will expect you to use in essays, exams, reports, and research papers. After college, it is what others will expect you to use in anything you write for business or professional purposes. For all of these reasons, Standard English is what this book aims to help you learn.

Grammar and Rhetoric

The grammar of a language is the set of rules by which its sentences are made. You started learning the rules of English grammar as soon as you started to talk. Well before you learned how to write, you could have said which of these two statements made sense:

> *Eggs breakfast fried I two for had.
> I had two fried eggs for breakfast.

The words in each statement are the same, but you can readily see that only the second arrangement makes sense. What you know about the English language tells you that some ways of arranging the seven words are acceptable and others are not. You may not be able to say just why the word order in the first arrangement is wrong, but you know that it is.

---

* From this point on, nonstandard constructions in this book generally are marked with a star. We also use asterisks to mark misspelled words in drafts of student essays.

Good writing requires a working knowledge of grammar, a basic command of the rules that govern the forming of a sentence. But good writing is more than the act of obeying grammatical rules. It is also the art of using rhetoric—of arranging words, phrases, sentences, and paragraphs in such a way as to engage and sustain the reader's attention.

The power of rhetoric can sometimes be felt in a single sentence. Patrick Henry said, "Give me liberty, or give me death." Franklin D. Roosevelt said, "The only thing we have to fear is fear itself." General George S. Patton said to his troops after a battle, "You have been baptized in fire and blood and have come out steel." Martin Luther King, Jr., said to a crowd of civil-rights demonstrators, "I have a dream." As these examples help to show, the sentence is at once the basic unit of writing and the basic source of its rhetorical effects. A good sentence not only takes its place with other sentences but also makes a place for itself, striking the reader with its own special clarity and force. One aim of this book, therefore, is to help you maximize the rhetorical impact of every sentence you write.

Yet you do not normally write single sentences in isolation. You write them in sequence, and rhetoric is the art of making that sequence effective—of moving from one sentence to another in a paragraph, and from one paragraph to another in an essay. It is the art of sustaining continuity while continually moving ahead, of developing a description, a narrative, an explanation, or an argument in such a way as to take the reader with you from beginning to end. The ultimate aim of this book, therefore, is to explain the rhetoric of the writing process as a whole.

Using This Book

You can use this book in one of two ways: as a textbook for a course in composition, or as a reference guide to help you with a large variety of writing tasks in college and afterward.

If you are using this book in a composition course, your teacher will undoubtedly assign certain chapters or sections to the whole class. In addition, after seeing what you individually have written, your teacher will probably assign certain sections and exercises specifically chosen to meet your needs. But since you may want to use this book on your own as well, you should know how it is organized.

We have divided this book into four main parts. Part 1, "Writing Essays," first guides you through the whole writing process from pre-writing to proofreading your final draft. Then it treats particular kinds of writing, such as exposition and persuasion, and particular parts of the writing process, such as paragraphing and choosing words. Part 2, "Writing Sentences," is designed chiefly to explain and illustrate the variety of ways you can use sentence structure. We explain the things you can't or normally shouldn't do, such as writing sentence fragments and misplacing modifiers. But we emphasize the things you can and should do, such as varying your sentence patterns, using modifiers of all kinds, organizing your sentences by means of coordination and subordination, enhancing coordination with parallelism, controlling emphasis by the way you arrange your words, and invigorating your style.† Part 3, "Punctuation and Mechanics," explains the rules of punctuation as well as spelling and the use of mechanical conventions such as capitals and italics. Part 4, "The Research Paper," explains how to prepare, write, and document a library research paper, and also how to write papers across the curriculum: in the sciences, the social sciences, and the humanities.

At the end of the book are two alphabetical glossaries. The Glossary of Usage explains many of the words or phrases that writers find troublesome or confusing; the Glossary of Terms defines the terms that are commonly used in discussions of writing. Although the terms we use are printed in **boldface type** in the text and defined where they first appear, you may find this glossary an additional aid.

Finally, the book includes two appendices designed to serve special needs. Appendix 1 explains how to cite sources in a research paper with footnotes or endnotes, and Appendix 2 explains writing in the world "beyond Freshman English," where you will have to compose such things as essay exams, personal statements for applications to professional schools, and covering letters for job applications.

Since this book is designed for ready reference as well as for steady reading, we have tried to make it as easy as possible for you to locate specific advice on every subject we cover. If you are seeking information on your own, the best places for you to start look-

---

†To illustrate various constructions, we often quote other writers, and we often italicize certain words in their sentences to stress particular points. In all such cases, the italics are ours, not the writers'.

ing are the summary on the back endpapers—which shows you the layout of the entire *Handbook* in chart form—and the table of contents at the beginning of the book. Both the summary and the contents list every major topic, so all you need to do is turn to the appropriate page. If you can't find the topic you want in either the summary or the table of contents, go to the index, which lists all topics alphabetically and gives the page numbers for each one.

In skimming through the book, you will notice various abbreviations and symbols (such as //). These are explained in the alphabetical list on the front endpapers: "Symbols for Revision." In this list, each abbreviation or symbol is followed by a brief explanation and a reference to the appropriate part of the text.

The abbreviations and symbols are intended for use by your instructor in marking your papers. If, for example, you see // on your paper, you can look for it on the front-endpaper lists. There you'll find that // refers you to the section explaining how to correct faulty parallelism.

Alternatively, your instructor may refer you to a specific topic by using one of the section numbers, which are listed on the back endpapers and in the table of contents. That is, instead of writing // on your paper, your instructor may write **14.4,** which refers to chapter 14, section 4, where we deal with faulty parallelism. Smaller points are treated in lettered subsections such as **22.2A,** "Changing from Active to Passive."

One other feature of this book that will help you find specific topics quickly is the reference box in the upper margin of each page. Inside the box, printed in boldface type, is the appropriate section number (e.g., **14.4**); above that, printed in italic type, is the chapter abbreviation (e.g., *coor/pc*); and underneath the box, whenever it is needed for reference, is the revision symbol (e.g., //). We hope these reference devices will help you find information conveniently both during your composition course and afterward.

Part 1
Writing
Essays

1
Pre-Writing

Where does writing begin? Where do writers find within themselves the energy and desire to generate words, to compose sentences, and to build paragraphs? How do essays originate?

To these questions we have no single answer. But since writing originates from somewhere in the mind, your first task is to find a way into your mind and then out again so that you can bring back the news locked up inside you, waiting to be broadcast and published. To begin with, then, this chapter aims to help you discover your own ideas.

What follows in this chapter is not so much a sequence of steps as a variety of suggestions. If any one of them leads you to discover in yourself the germ of an essay and prompts you to start writing one, then start. Don't feel obliged to take each section in order. You can experiment with different methods of getting started, and jump ahead to any method that you think will spur you on. (If you want to get started writing about something you've *read*, for instance, you can turn right now to section 1.12, and from there to chapter 10.) In this opening chapter, we have arranged the sections to guide you only so long as you need to follow their lead.

1.1 Putting Your Right Brain to Work

In recent years, psychologists have begun to define the human brain as a combination of two halves or hemispheres—a left brain and a right one. The left brain, they say, is verbal, analytical, logical, and systematic, taking things one step at a time; the right brain is visual, synthesizing, imaginative, and intuitive, making one big picture from many details. The hemispheric theory of the brain is not yet proved, and it will probably be debated for years to come. But whether or not the two different ways of thinking actually originate from separate halves of the brain, we all know from our own experience the difference between one kind of thinking and the other, and we can use the words "right" and "left" to name the difference.

The left brain, then, is what tells you now that you should read each section of this chapter in order, that writing an essay is a sequence of steps, that you must systematically move from topic to thesis to outline to introduction and so on until you reach the end. The right brain, however, can goad you to leap ahead, to see the germ of a whole essay in just one potent analogy, or to imagine all of its parts as the branches of a tree. Because of its power to visualize connections in this way, to see a pattern all at once, the right brain has sometimes solved problems that have stumped the systematic left one. It has broken through obstacles that could not be surmounted by any sequence of steps.

This does not mean that the best way to write—or to solve any problem—is to abandon all sequence. It means that the best writing, like the best thinking, comes from a brain in which both halves can freely talk to each other. If you tried to write with a right brain that never listened to the left, you would never learn how to put one word after another. But when the left brain silences the right one by refusing to look at its pictures or tolerate its sudden intuitions, the writer's world becomes a flat, gray map. To turn that map into a full-colored globe, you must learn to put your right brain to work.

The first step (there's the left brain talking, you see) is to turn down the voice of the left brain so that the voice of the right one can be heard. Turning down the voice of the left brain means forgetting for a time all the rules you ever learned about writing correctly, about arranging your thoughts in a systematic, orderly way. If you try to make each sentence perfect before moving on to the next one, if you stop after every few words to correct your spelling or grammar or punctuation, you will never tap the full creative power of your brain. But if you can temporarily silence the voice of analysis and correction, another kind of voice will begin to speak.

A word processor can help you stimulate this speech in a very simple way: turn down the contrast control so that the screen goes blank, and then start writing. Since you won't be able to see what you've written, you can't stop to correct anything, and the right brain will be free to create.

But whether or not you write with a word processor, you can also use a still more effective way of putting the right brain to work: drawing. Usually we think of drawing and writing as quite separate activities, and of writing as the superior one. We draw before we write, but once we start to write, most of us leave drawing behind. We think of it as doodling—a childish pastime to distract us from the grownup, intellectual task of writing. But if we truly want to hear what the right brain is saying, we have to realize that it often speaks *a language of pictures.*

Did you know that experienced writers sometimes make pictures to stimulate their powers of expression, and that you can do the same? Following is a page from the first draft of an essay in which a student named Andrea Lyle tells what happened when she and another young woman set out to explore an old copper mine. Andrea fills the margins of her draft with pictures of what she writes about: figures descending a jagged precipice at upper left, an aching hand and forearm just under it, a threaded length of pipe at bottom left, a gargoyle head at upper right. Notice too the star-shaped figure of white set in a dark circle in the right margin. As soon as Andrea drew this picture of the way the top of the mine appeared to her from a viewpoint far below it, she visualized the distant light as a star. Then she added the image of the star to the end of her sentence about the light.

Andrea happens to have a talent for drawing, but with or without such a talent, you can use pictures to generate words. If you know how to doodle, you already know how to draw from your right brain its powers of visualization: not just its ability to picture individual objects like a star-shaped opening, but its capacity to see patterns. The next section explains how you can use this capacity to generate patterns of thought.

1.2 Branching

Whether you realize it or not, your brain is an inexhaustible storehouse of what could be collectively called ideas: memories, opinions, perceptions, images, emotions, and facts. To write effectively about any one of those elements, you must not only find and name it, you must also connect it with related ideas and make patterns of meaning from the connections. One of the best ways of doing so is branching.`

ESCAPING FROM A MINE

Looking back, I guess it was pretty stupid. No climbing experience, nothing to climb with but a thin clothesline rope, and yet there we were in the middle of the old abandoned copper mine ~~slipping~~ crawling and sliding our way down to the bottom which Ellie had heard somewhere was over a hundred feet down. For awhile a great adventure, a colossel marvelous cave, outcroppings like gargoyle's all over the wall. But after about three hours, we were dirty and cut up from a few minor falls, and the Muscles in our fingers, our hands, and our arms all ached from climbing, so we decided to go back up. Then it hit us. On the way down we sort of ~~slid~~ slid rather than climbed ~~up~~ way down a 15 foot almost sheer precepice and nobody thought to leave a rope hanging there so we could climb back up. Now we tried ~~over and~~ again and again to scramble up the precepice but nJether of us could do it. It was scary. We looked up to the top of the mine where the light was but it seemed so far away. We felt ~~not much bigger~~ than a single star in a coal black sky. trapped. But we ~~wouldn't~~ weren't giving up. Not yet. We tried to find a way around the precepice and couldn't. Then we tried throwing the rope up to catch it somehow on the top of the precepice but that didn't work either. Finally on the ~~bottom~~ of the mine I found two old rusty pipes that were only about ~~eight~~ seven feet long, but Ellie noticed that the ends of each pipe were threaded, so we screwed the pipes together to make a long pole. Bracing the pipe on the ground beside the precepice ~~where~~ we helped each other climb the pole & get out of the mine.

Branching is the right-brain alternative to outlining. An outline is a list of points usually arranged under headings and subheadings, and it can show exactly the sequence of development that an essay will follow. (For more on this see section 3.3.) But unless you already know how your essay will develop its points, you can't very well list them in sequential order. What you can do, however, is put them on branches radiating from a single idea, and make the branches sprout more ideas. You can thus generate a picture of the ideas in your mind—a pattern of connections to look at.

Branching starts with a single word or phrase and grows from there by a process of association—but not free association. Since all main branches radiate from one key term, branching is a process of exploring its implications, of seeing the range and variety of thoughts it can evoke, of moving from the general to the specific. Branching allows the mind to wander to the detailed ends of an idea—the slenderest twigs of the tree—and then return to the source to develop a new main branch. So branching is a way of organizing as well as discovering your ideas—a way of brainstorming and patterning at the same time.

If you can draw with your computer, you can make a few branches on your screen, but the best equipment for branching is a sheet of unlined paper and a pen or pencil. Use colored pens or pencils if you want to color-code your branches. To start branching, write a key term in the middle of the sheet and circle it. Then add a main branch for each idea that grows directly from the circled one, a smaller branch for each idea that sprouts from a main branch, and so on. You will soon find that you have to turn the sheet around as you work. On the following page, for instance, is a branching diagram based on the term "writer's block."

Paradoxically, the very act of thinking about a writer's block can unblock a writer willing to think with the right brain, to make patterns and pictures such as the one of the locked door. The locked door may be a picture of the way you sometimes feel when you sit down to write: frustrated, balked, unable to penetrate your own mind. But as this diagram shows, branching can open the door of your mind and let you explore its passageways, let you see how one idea leads to another and how the return to the main idea stimulates you further.

This periodic return to the main idea is known as *looping.* Looping prefigures what an essay does, which is to create from a collection of various points a pattern of meaning organized around a central point. So in returning to the center of the branching dia-

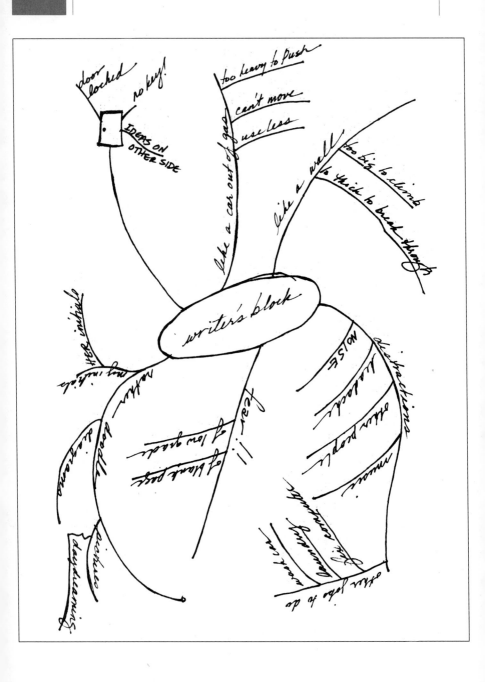

gram when you have thought your way to the end of a particular branch, you are actually beginning the work of organizing an essay.

Now try the following exercise to see what your right brain can do.

EXERCISE 1 Branching

Construct a branching diagram from a term of your choice or from any one of the following terms. See how many branches you can generate in ten minutes. (In later exercises we'll ask you to use this diagram.)

1. childhood
2. police
3. dancing
4. AIDS
5. supermarkets

1.3 Choosing a Topic

Branching will help you discover and organize your ideas on any topic. But if you're asked to choose a topic of your own and you have trouble doing so, here are five ways to find a good one:

1. Remember a moment that powerfully moved you. Was it the first time you gave a speech? Was it the day you broke your arm? Was it the first night you appeared in a play? Was it a funeral? Was it the time you were lost in the woods overnight, or capsized two miles from shore? If you search your memory, you can find at least one moment that is branded there forever by the sheer power of joy, grief, fear, guilt, or pain. Use your right brain to picture that moment again.

2. Explore a conflict. Since the richest moments of experience are often born out of conflict, suppose you recall a time when you were made or asked to do something you did not want to do. When and where did it happen? How did you feel about having to act against your will? How did you feel about the person who asked you to do so? What did you learn from the episode? Raising questions like these—and trying to answer them—will help you think more about the experience until you discover the point you want to explore in depth.

Alternatively, you can imagine a conflict of ideas—a debate about a question of current importance: Do smokers and non-smokers have equal rights in all public places? Should public schools teach Hispanic children in Spanish? Should any one course be required of all college students? Should handguns be federally regulated? Questions like these can provoke sharp dispute. If you picture the dispute as an argument between two people, you can write a dialogue, and thus generate the material for an essay.

3. <u>Spy on people</u>. Have you noticed the way some people (including you, perhaps) behave at rock concerts, at movies, in shopping centers, in department stores, in supermarkets, in classrooms, in restaurants, on sidewalks, on beaches, at parties? Does anything they do, say, or wear strike you as funny or strange or irritating? If so, why? And if you had the power to change their behavior, what would you do?

4. <u>Choose a topic you want to know more about</u>. Tap your curiosity. Investigate a subject that interests you. Go to the reference room of your college library and see what an encyclopedia can tell you about submarines, balloon flight, the cocaine industry, the history of photography, or the making of wine. As you learn about your topic, you will probably want to tell others about it—especially if the subject is one you have wondered about for some time. Look for the unexpected. Surprises will interest your readers as much as they interest you.

5. <u>Use your expertise</u>. Help others learn how to do something you do well. You may be an expert photographer, carpenter, guitar player, computer operator, cartoonist, salesclerk, or actor. What advice could you give others who would like to acquire your skill? What should they be prepared to do and sacrifice? What characteristics do they need to have? What obstacles will confront them? What kind of regimen should they follow?

EXERCISE 2 Choosing a Topic and Branching

Use any one of the methods explained above to choose a topic, and then use branching to discover and organize your ideas about it.

EXERCISE 3 Nonstop Writing

Using your branching diagram from exercise 1 or exercise 2 as a source of ideas, write nonstop for ten minutes. Don't worry about spelling, punctuation, or grammar; just keep following the points made on each of the branches (adding more points as they come to mind) and looping back to the main point. After ten minutes, read what you have just written, and underline anything that you discovered or remembered in the process of writing.

1.4 Making an Assigned Topic Your Own

If you're asked to write a paper on a specified topic that has been treated in a particular course, one good way of getting started is to consider how you might connect the topic to your own interests and experience. Suppose, for instance, you are asked to write about the free enterprise system for a course in economics. Your first thought may be of huge corporations: Du Pont, IBM, General Motors, Chrysler, AT&T. But big firms like these are far outnumbered by small ones such as pizza parlors, taxicab companies, barbershops, hairdressing salons, and drug stores. Lee Iacocca is a businessman; but so is the street vendor selling leather belts or costume jewelry at a busy intersection, and so is the ten-year-old behind a lemonade stand on a hot summer afternoon. If you've ever had a job, you've had the chance to see how someone else runs a business. If you've participated in Junior Achievement, you've helped to run a company yourself. And if you've ever sold anything of your own, whether goods or services (such as lawnmowing or babysitting), then you know what it means to run your own business, however small. Finally, if at different times you've worked for someone else and for yourself, you have firsthand experience of the difference between the predictability of a set wage and the unpredictability of profit, between security and risk, between earnings that are guaranteed but limited and earnings that are unguaranteed but limitless. Personal experience, then, can be just what you need to find your way into a topic, and you can use branching to help you discover your personal connections to it.

EXERCISE 4 Making a Topic Your Own

Describe a personal experience that you might use to make a point about any one of the following topics:

families	the selective service system	free enterprise
computers	crime	music
education	sports	transportation
farming	housing	drugs

1.5 Pinpointing the Topic

One of the biggest obstacles to the success of a short essay is an overly broad topic. If you try to write eight hundred words on the free enterprise system, you will probably find that you have room for only commonplace generalizations about it: big businesses don't pay their fair share of taxes; company executives are overpaid; workers are underpaid; the whole system takes from the many and gives to the fortunate few. When you fill up a paper with generalizations like these, you leave yourself no room to think and discover or to use your own experience.

If you can define a particular topic in terms of your own experience, you have already begun reducing it to a manageable size. But even as you connect it to your own experience, you should try to isolate and identify a piece of it, to make your topic as precise and specific as possible. Here are some examples:

GENERAL	SPECIFIC	MORE SPECIFIC
free enterprise	small business	running a small housepainting business
sports	college basketball	college basketball and grades
working mothers	working mothers with small children	working mothers with frequently sick small children
national elections	role of TV in national elections	role of TV in presidential campaign of 1988
nuclear waste	disposal of nuclear waste	burying nuclear waste vs. dumping it in the ocean
television commercials	women in TV commercials	changing roles of women in TV commercials
pollution	acid rain	effects of acid rain on trees
immigration	illegal aliens	employment of illegal aliens
drugs	drug testing	drug testing of college athletes
drugs	steroids	side effects of steroids

politics	college politics	campaigning for college offices

EXERCISE 5 Pinpointing the Topic

Take any one of the topics listed in exercise 4 and make it as specific as possible.

EXAMPLE

crime   shoplifting   punishment of shoplifters

1.6 Triple-Viewing the Topic: Particle, Wave, and Field

Once you have pinpointed your topic, you can begin to discover its possibilities by triple-viewing it, by seeing it in three different ways: as a particle, as a wave, and as part of a field.

1. To see the topic as a *particle* is to see it all by itself, self-contained and fixed, isolated for special scrutiny. If your topic is the roles that women play in television commercials, you would focus your questions on the commercials themselves. What kind of products do women help to sell on TV? Mainly food, cleaners, household appliances, and cosmetics? How often do women in commercials get to talk? How often do they simply appear while a man or a male voice-over does the talking? How do women respond to the men who appear with them? What sort of jobs are women represented as doing? What sort of problems do they care about? Anything more than headaches and dirty collars?

2. To see the topic as a *wave* is to see it as part of a process, to ask how it came to develop in time, and—if the topic is a historical situation or event—what resulted from it. The contemporary topic of women in television commercials leads to questions about its history: How long have women been making TV commercials? What kinds of products did they sell at first? Were they glamorous models or did they look ordinary? How did the problem-solution formula for detergent commercials originate? How much has the women's movement affected the roles women play in TV commercials? Are present-day commercials just a compromise between the old sexual stereotypes and the new feminist standards of equality? (To answer these questions you would probably need to do some reading, as explained in section 1.12.)

3. To see the topic as part of a *field* is to consider its relation to other topics that surround it. What's the connection between women in TV commercials and women in other media, such as printed advertising, movies, and TV news? How much do today's TV commercials reflect the way American women now live and work? How often do TV commercials deal with the problem of finding adequate day care—as distinct from the problem of getting shirts clean? How many American women hold the professional jobs that women in TV commercials usually have? How many American women live with husbands and children, like the women commonly shown in commercials? Do TV commercials reflect the way we live now, or do they take us on a nostalgia trip? And what's the relation between the women in TV commercials and the way we think about the products they sell?

> EXERCISE 6 Triple-Viewing the Topic
>
> Consider your topic first as a particle, then as a wave, then as part of a field. For each way of viewing the topic, write as many questions as possible, and put a parenthesized R (R) after any question that would have to be answered from reading in relevant source material.

1.7 Dramatizing the Topic with Questions

Another way of generating ideas about a topic is to dramatize it. If you think of your topic not as an object but as an action, you can dramatize it with six basic questions:

1. <u>What</u> happened? (the action)
2. <u>Who</u> was involved? (agents, spectators, and anyone else affected by it)
3. <u>When and where</u> did it happen? (the setting)
4. <u>How</u> did it happen? (the method)
5. <u>Why</u> did it happen? (the cause or motive)
6. <u>What effect</u> did it have? (the consequence)

To see how this dramatizing method works in practice, consider the questions raised by a student named Tim as he thought about the topic of scoring goals in hockey games:

What happens when I score a goal? What are the parts of the process? What goes through my mind as the puck goes past the goalie? What do I see? What do I feel? What do I hear?

Who besides me gets into the action? What about my teammates? What about the goalie? What about the coach? What about the crowd?

When and *where* do I score goals? How often? What is the moment of scoring like? Where am I when the puck goes into the net? What is the scene that surrounds me?

How do I score? Do I plan the shot, or is it just a lucky accident every time? How is my body positioned? Am I stopped or moving, hunched over or standing up straight?

Why do I love to score? Is it because I want to do my best for the team? Or because I love to hear the cheers of the crowd? Or because the coach will think I'm terrific? Or does it have something to do with just getting that puck past the goalie?

What effect does my scoring have? What does it do to the crowd? What does it do to my teammates? What does it immediately do for me?

The more questions you raise, the more deeply you will penetrate your topic. Suppose your topic is the effect of acid rain on trees. You can investigate it with questions like these:

What does acid rain do to trees? What happens to their leaves? What do their roots do? What happens to the bark and branches?

Who is responsible for acid rain? If it comes from the burning of high-sulfur industrial fuels, which industries are burning them? Who runs those industries? And who is affected by the damage that acid rain does to trees?

When and where does acid rain affect trees? What parts of the world or the country are most affected? How does a forest appear after an acid rainfall? How often does acid rain fall?

How does acid rain develop? How does the acid get to the clouds? How do the clouds carry the acid to the forests?

Why is acid rain threatening trees? Is it because we are burning too much fuel? Is it because we are using the wrong kind of fuel? Is it because we care more about promoting industry than protecting the environment?

What effect does the damage to trees have? How does it affect the timber supply? What does it do to birds and other wildlife? How does it affect people living near forests or elsewhere? Does acid rain reduce the capacity of trees to absorb carbon dioxide? If so, how much more global warming will result?

To answer all of these questions, you would need to do some reading and research—something we introduce in section 1.11. But when you dramatize your topic with questions, you are decisively beginning to investigate it.

EXERCISE 7 Asking Questions to Dramatize Your Topic

Using each of the six categories illustrated by the two examples given above, ask at least twelve questions about the topic you defined in exercise 5.

1.8 Choosing a Basic Question to Define a Problem or Conflict

All of the questions you ask can help you generate material, and a good deal of this material may find its way into your essay. But just as you need to define your topic as specifically as possible, you also need a basic question to help you define the key problem or conflict you will try to resolve. For Tim, the key question was *Why?* Why did he love scoring goals so much? Was it because scoring served the team—or because it served his own ego?

To focus on one basic question is also to see its relation to others. When Tim decided to concentrate on why he loved scoring, he knew that he would also have to say something about how he scored, about what he felt when it happened, about the people involved, about the scene and the moment of the shot, and about its effects. But he decided to make all of these other points secondary, to use them in answering the question *Why?* In choosing this question, he was taking a decisive step forward. He now had not only a specific topic, but also a definite purpose. (We show what Tim did with his basic question in section 2.3.)

Questions can bring out the conflicts inherent in any topic worth writing about, and once you move to topics outside your personal experience, you will often find conflicts of opinion or belief. In section 1.3 above, we have already cited some examples of such conflict, such as the clash between smokers and non-smokers. Another example appears in section 1.7 among the *Why* questions asked about acid rain: Is acid rain threatening trees because we care more about promoting industry than protecting the environment? This question clearly identifies a conflict between the value of our natural surroundings and the value of industry. Besides holding water, retaining soil, giving us beauty and shade, and absorbing carbon dioxide, trees furnish wood, pulp, resins, and many other products. But the industries that make rain acidic furnish jobs as well as goods and services, and all three may be threatened by the cost of environmental regulations. So we might ask the question another way: Should we regulate and penalize industry in order to protect our trees? Here is at once a question to be answered and a problem to be solved—the kind of problem that can generate an essay.

Once you've chosen the basic question you plan to pursue, you can choose other questions that will help you pursue it. The very first set of questions on acid rain—the *what* questions—concern the damage that acid rain does. To ask about the damage is to raise further questions about the cost of acid rain: what it costs us not just in beauty, shade, and water retention but also in all the raw materials that come from trees. The first set of questions, therefore, would help you to pursue the basic question, "Should we regulate and penalize industry in order to protect our trees?" This question cannot be answered without some reference to the costs of not protecting them.

EXERCISE 8 Choosing a Basic Question

Choose one of the questions you wrote for exercise 7 and briefly explain what conflict or problem it raises. Then make a list of other questions that could help you pursue the basic question.

1.9 Get Reactions to Your Question

One of the hardest things about writing is that you normally have to do it alone. Before you begin to write, therefore, find someone you can talk to about the basic question you plan to explore. If you already have some idea of how you might answer the question, your listener may give you a different answer. Hearing it will make

you more sensitive to the complexity of your subject, more skillful in anticipating possible misunderstandings or objections to your
point of view, and therefore more effective in explaining or defending it.

EXERCISE 9 Getting Responses

Explain to someone else the basic question you hope to explore and
also—if you can—your own ideas about how to answer it. Then (1)
record his or her response in writing and (2) comment on the response.

1.10 Using Analogies

An analogy is a comparison of something abstract or strange with
something concrete and familiar. An analogy answers the kind of
question we almost always ask about anything new to us: "What's
it like?" Because analogies let you translate abstract ideas or feelings into concrete terms, they can open your eyes to a whole new
way of looking at your topic. A freshman wrote recently that college first appeared to him as "a new mountain to be climbed."
Think of the questions this picture generates: Is he ready for this
mountain? Can he see the summit? Is he going to slip and fall?
What trail will he take? How much guidance will he have? Good
analogies turn thoughts into pictures. In the branching diagram on
p. 8, writer's block is literally pictured as a locked door, which
could mean either one of two things: the writer's imagination is
locked in, unable to break out and express itself, or the writer's
conscious mind is locked out, unable to enter the world of imagination. But analogy is one of the keys that can open the door, for
analogy is the work of the right brain: a way of picturing your
subject in words. Put your right brain to work for a moment on
acid rain. Picture yourself taking a shower in full-strength bleach.
What would that do to your skin? How would it make you feel? If
you can answer those questions, you can begin to describe vividly
what acid rain does to trees.

Of course no analogy can match your topic perfectly. To get
the most from your analogy, therefore, ask yourself not only how
it resembles but also how it differs from your topic. If going to
college is in many ways like climbing a mountain, how is it unlike
mountain climbing? This kind of question can help you under-

stand your topic clearly and explain it precisely. (For more on analogy, see section 6.5.)

EXERCISE 10 Using Analogies

Use an analogy to picture at least one aspect of the basic question you chose in exercise 4. Then write three questions about your picture.

1.11 Working with a Nugget

As you think about your topic, do you find yourself struck by a single word, phrase, idea, or example connected with it? If so, that may be your golden nugget, a rich source of further ideas. When Tim began thinking about scoring goals in hockey, the phrase that came to him was "freeze-frame." Once he thought of it, it captured for him the very moment of scoring, the instant when everything in a game of lightning speed and seemingly perpetual motion came to a sudden halt. A rich nugget—like a good analogy—usually calls up a picture, something your right brain can visualize. Once you have the picture in your mind's eye, you can use questions to discover all that it means.

EXERCISE 11 Working with a Nugget

Circle or underline the most suggestive word or phrase you can find in what you have written so far about your topic. Then use this item to generate a branching diagram.

1.12 Reading with a Purpose

Suppose you're writing about women in TV commercials. From a magazine article by Carol Caldwell ("You Haven't Come a Long Way, Baby: Women in Television Commercials," now reprinted in *The Commercial Connection*), you could learn that women have been making TV commercials since 1951, when the glamorous Betty Furness started advertising Westinghouse appliances; that the equally striking Julia Meade started advertising Lincolns on TV in 1956; and that beautiful women are still being used to sell cars on TV because they help to make the cars look sexy. You could also learn from *Ms.* magazine (Jan.–Feb. 1989) that 45 percent of car buyers are now women. Facts like these generate questions. Why do many TV commercials fail to reflect the ways in which women's roles have changed? How often do automobile commercials present women as workers—not just as consumers?

Besides reading for information and provocative facts that you can use in your writing, you will often be asked in college to write *about* a piece of assigned reading—such as a published essay. To prepare yourself for this kind of writing, you should first get *your own copy* of the reading matter, and then read it with a pen or pencil in your hand. (A colored marker is also handy for highlighting important passages.) As you read, you should *make the text your own.* Underline or highlight whatever seems important, and use the margin for annotations—questions or comments. Here's how a student named Sheila annotated a passage about the value of children's play:

What's this?

A four-year-old girl reacted to her mother's pregnancy by regressing. Although she had been well trained, she began to wet again, insisted on being fed only from a baby bottle, and reverted to crawling on the floor. All this greatly distressed her mother, who, anticipating the demands of a new infant, had counted on her daughter's relative maturity. Fortunately, she did not try to prevent her daughter's regressions. After a few months of this behavior, the girl replaced it with much more mature play. She now played "good mother." She became extremely caring for her baby doll, ministering to it much more seriously than ever before. Having in the regressed stage identified with the coming infant, she now identified with her mother. By the time her sibling was born, the girl had done much of the work needed for her to cope with the change in the family and her position in it, and her adjustment to the new baby was easier than her mother had expected.

Ok — it means turning yourself into a baby again

So play is a serious business for kids — a way of adjusting. But is all regression good? Is there any other way of adjusting?

In retrospect it can be seen that the child, on learning that a new baby was to join the family, must have been afraid that the baby would deprive her of her infantile gratifications, and therefore tried to provide herself with them. She may have thought that if her mother wanted an infant, then she herself would again be an infant. There would be no need for her mother to acquire another, and she might give up on the idea.

pleasures?

fantasy

Permitted to act on notions like these, the girl must have realized after a while that wetting herself was not as pleasant as she might have imagined; that being able to eat a wide variety of foods had definite advantages when compared with drinking only from the bottle; and that walking and running brought many more satisfactions than did crawling. From this experience <u>she convinced herself that being grown up is preferable to being a baby.</u> So she gave up pretending that she was a baby and instead decided to be like her mother: in play to be like her right now, in imagination to become at some future time a real mother. <u>Play provided the child and her mother with a happy solution to what otherwise might have resulted in an impasse.</u> —Bruno Bettelheim, "The Importance of Play"

key idea

right

The questions, comments, and underlinings here signify *active* reading. Finding in the very first sentence a word she doesn't recognize, Sheila circles it, and then discovers its meaning in the second sentence—without even checking her dictionary. More important than learning new words, however, is learning what the passage has to teach. By underlining and commenting on the author's most important points, the reader has learned something new and vital about the importance of play in growing up. She can now begin to think about how she would explore the author's ideas in an essay of her own, about the kinds of questions she would pursue. Is play a means of moving from fantasy (such as persuading her mother to give up pregnancy) to reality? Do older children and adults indulge in regression? If so, do they also use play to readjust to their responsibilities? And should kids be allowed to regress as often and as much as they want?

Active reading is so important to writing that we discuss it at length in chapter 10, "Reading in Order to Write." But for now, here are two exercises that will get you started on reading with an eye to your own writing.

EXERCISE 12 Using Information from an Article

Following is an excerpt from a newspaper article on China's one-child policy. Briefly explain how you would use the information it provides in an essay on population control or on family life.

BEIJING—They are China's pampered darlings.

Eight years after the world's most populous nation put its controversial family planning program into effect, limiting most couples to one child, one of the most conspicuous results has been the rise of a generation of "little emperors," which in the West would be known as spoiled brats.

The official press is full of stories about such children. Last year, the newspaper *China Youth News* published a 12-part series entitled "The Little Suns in Our Lives" that painted some disturbing portraits.

The parents of one third-grade boy, for example, bought him whatever he wanted. He dined on meat pies; his parents ate porridge. He spurned clothing that had been worn once. After his grandfather spanked him for starting a fight in school, the youngster took a pair of scissors and threatened to kill himself until the grandfather apologized and bought him a new toy.

A 7-year-old girl was asked by her parents to empty the chamber pot, but only emptied half because she said she was not the only one who had used it.

"What will be the outcome if parents allow this willfulness to continue?" the newspaper asked.

China has 337 million children under age 14. Of those, about 9 percent, or 30.5 million, are children without siblings, most of them concentrated at the younger grades, family planning officials said. Eight of every 10 first-graders come from single-child families. With the recent renewed emphasis on the one-couple, one-child policy, that ratio is likely to increase to 90 percent over the next five years, according to Liu Bin, vice minister of the State Education Commission.

Many only children are so doted upon by their families that they become timid, overbearing, lazy, self-indulgent or contemptuous of physical labor, officials said. Most only children have "weak points, such as (the) low ability to care for themselves, selfishness, willfulness and arrogance," Liu said.

"The only-children issue has caused social problems," said Zhou Huayin, a Beijing education official. Spoiled by their parents, these children often become "hot-tempered and pay little respect to parents and older generations," he said.

—Lena H. Sun, "China's One-Child Policy Produces Spoiled 'Little Emperors' "`

EXERCISE 13 Active Reading

Read and annotate the following passage with questions and comments, underlining any points that seem important. Then write three questions about the passage—questions you could explore in an essay.

Each sex has the same capacity to experience the pleasures and pains of romantic love. Women and men describe being in love in similar terms. This is surely as we would expect, since the deep impulses that give rise to love and the capacity to synthesize those impulses derive from our human nature; the potential for exaltation, transcendence, and transformation is not fundamentally altered by the accident of gender. In love we are more alike than different. Still, there are some important differences between women's and men's experiences of romantic love, particularly in the incidence of the different distortions to which love is prone.

The tapestry of an individual's love chronicles, his need for love, capacity for it, and specific vulnerabilities, is always woven of a complex mixture of social and psychological imperatives, penchants, and possibilities. Many of these are contingent on gender, and gender issues in turn have social and psychological, as well as biological, components. Although men and women face the same existential problems in life— death, aloneness, insufficiency, imperfection—they attempt to solve these problems in different ways and utilize love differently. Why? First, because there is a strong cultural component to love, and there are different cultural imperatives for the sexes. Second, the psychological development of each sex preordains different central problems and different strategies for resolving them. And finally, the ongoing cultural context locks in the pre-existing tendencies toward difference.

Because they are socialized in different ways, men and women tend to have different passionate quests—the passionate quest being that which constitutes the central psychological theme of a person's life. This passionate quest supplies the context for one's pursuit of self-realization, adventure, excitement, and, ultimately, transformation and even transcendence. The passionate quest is always a romance in the larger meaning of the word, but it is not always a quest for romantic love per se.

For women the passionate quest has usually been interpersonal, and has generally involved romantic love; for men it has more often been heroic, the pursuit of achievement or power. One might say that men tend to favor power over love and that women tend to achieve power through love. Socialization seems to be one of the factors that create the different dreams through which each sex shapes its narrative life.

—Ethel S. Person, "The Passionate Quest"

2
Finding
Your Aim

If you have tried all or even some of the methods explained in the previous chapter, you are probably ready to start writing. But two things may hold you back. One is the feeling that you aren't yet sure how to *organize* your thoughts—how to introduce your main point, develop it, and write a conclusion. The other is the feeling that you don't yet know what you *aim* to do in your essay besides somehow getting it written.

These problems should be faced one at a time. If you aren't yet sure how to organize your thoughts, don't worry. Organization will come in chapter 3. In this chapter we focus on the second problem—finding your aim.

2.1 Thinking about Your Aim

You can think of your aim in two ways: specific and general. Once you have written your essay, your *specific aim* is your **thesis**—the main point you express, explain, or try to prove. If you think you know now what your thesis is going to be, you can turn at once to section 2.4, which can help you to formulate it. But not every essay includes an explicit statement of its thesis, and not even published writers always know what the thesis of an essay will be when they start writing it. What they do know is what you should try to decide at this point: your general aim.

Everything you write involves you, your reader, and the world around you both. But your *general aim* depends on which of these three elements is most important:

1. If you're writing chiefly about yourself and your own experience, your aim is *self-expression.* You seek not so much to affect the reader or to explain the outside world as to express your personal thoughts, feelings, and experiences. This category includes personal narrative and recollection as well as essays in introspection. Self-expressive essays try to answer questions like, "What made my return to college so different from my first arrival?"

2. If your writing chiefly focuses on the outside world, your aim is *exposition.* You set out to explain something which, you assume, your reader does not yet know or fully understand. Expository essays try to answer questions like "What is the greenhouse effect?" and "Why is play so important to the development of children?" (For extended treatment of exposition, see chapter 6.)

3. If your writing seeks primarily to influence the reader, your aim is *persuasion.* You hope to make the reader share your opinion or belief. Persuasive essays try to answer questions like "Should handguns be regulated?" and "Did a meteor cause the extinction of the dinosaurs?" (For extended treatment of persuasion, see chapter 7.)

For certain kinds of essays you must know your specific aim—your thesis—from the outset. To start writing a persuasive essay, for instance, you must know what your main point is—what you want your readers to believe. But you have less need for a thesis when you start writing an expository or expressive essay. You have more freedom to discover your main point as you proceed. So long as you know your general aim, so long as you know whether you are mainly seeking to express your own feelings or to explain something in the outside world, you know enough to start writing.

2.2 Self-Expression

To see what you can produce by simply aiming to express your own thoughts, feelings, or recollections, consider the following passage. It's the first draft of what a student named Peter wrote in response to the question, "How did your return to college after the winter break differ from your arrival in the fall?"

As my brother turned the car to exit the highway and I first saw the college sign, my heart began to beat wildly. All summer I had been telling people how excited I was to be going to college, but the truth was that as the summer waned I really was rather frightened. For so many years college had seemed so far off, but yet all of a sudden it was there staring me in the face. A new mountain to be climbed.

When I saw Baker Tower looming over the college green for the first time as an actual student, it was breathtaking. It was beautiful, but yet it seemed foreign and uninviting. I still felt like an observer more than a student. The people that I saw walking around the campus that first day seemed older and more confident than me.

I arrived at my dorm and began to unload all my things that had been stuffed in the car for two days. There were nine days yet before classes began, but I was still surprised to find the dorm nearly uninhabited and entirely quiet. I felt like I shouldn't have been there. My brother helped me get my stuff to my room, said goodbye, and then left me in a room about as welcoming as a prison cell. I put my bags down on the hard wood floor and turned on the lonely light bulb in the middle of the ceiling. With absolutely nothing better to do, I unpacked my belongings as the blank walls watched. About one hour later, another freshman came to my door and introduced herself. Still frightened and extremely nervous, I remember continuously wiping sweat from my forehead and sideburns as I carried on a trivial conversation with her about freshman orientation.

Just a few days ago, I returned to the campus after winter break but my emotions and impressions were far different from the ones I experienced in September. As my brother and I once again exited the highway, the college sign made me all the more excited to see the friends that I had met in my first three months at the college. Like a frosted sheet cake with a huge candle in the middle, the snow-covered green and the enormous Christmas tree seemed to greet me and welcome me back. In every way but true temperature, the campus and its students were much warmer than they had been in September.

When I first arrived at the dorm, friends and acquaintances were in the halls exchanging winter break stories. The friendly faces that formed a sort of welcoming committee were a far cry from the empty corridors and bare walls that originally greeted me in September. When I opened the door to my room, it was entirely different from the empty room that I found in September. Instead, as I expected, it was wonderful to see my cozy, carpeted room, especially the posters and the pictures that make it such a home away from home. The absolute last thing that I wanted to do was to unpack. I dropped the bags in the middle of the floor and went to see all of the friends that I had missed so much over winter break.

This is a personal narrative that gradually finds its way as it proceeds. Though Peter never states the main point of the essay, he contrasts what he felt when he arrived at college with what he felt when he returned to it.

By simply recalling his own feelings on the two occasions and describing what prompted them, Peter clearly implies a thesis: because of the friends I had made during my first semester at college, returning to it was much more enjoyable than arriving at it. But he doesn't need to say this because the contrast he draws between returning and arriving speaks for itself. When he writes that his room first seemed "about as welcoming as a prison cell" and that he unpacked his gear "as the blank walls watched," he vividly evokes a cold emptiness; when he compares the Christmas tree on the snow-covered green to a "frosted sheet cake with a huge candle in the middle," he conveys a welcoming warmth. (For more on comparison and contrast, see section 6.6.)

Since Peter knew from the outset that he would be contrasting one experience with another, he had some notion of how he would shape his memories when he started to write. But suppose you have no idea how to shape your thoughts and feelings, and no idea what your thesis—your main point—will be. Suppose you know only that you want to explore your experience or your subject. In that case, you may be able to discover your main point in the very act of freewriting—as we explain next.

2.3 Directed Freewriting: Finding Your Way to a Thesis

Directed freewriting is writing that seeks the answer to a *specific question* but ignores all other constraints. You don't have to worry about an introduction or conclusion, about paragraphing, about spelling, or even about completing all of your sentences. Just let your right brain go to work on your basic question—as Tim Boyle did in this piece of freewriting:

Why score? For glory? For the good of the team? Maybe. But mainly I love the mind trip, the personal high I get from it—the feeling inside.* Especialy in hockey. The strange thing is, I know I'm going to score before I shoot. It's like getting up when the phone rings because I somehow *know* it's for me. I don't try and *analize why I know—I just *know*. A *wonder-full sensation. And that's what comes to me when I get ready to shoot. Peace. I relax and don't even consciously try to shoot, the shot just happens. Often I can't even remember looking at the puck, I'm so relaxed at this point I might not have. The feeling at this point is one of perfection. Everything is going right and I'm not even trying to do anything. Of course not every shot is like this, otherwise right now I'd be at the Bruins training camp on my way to hockey stardom instead of writing this. But since every shot is *not* perfect, and most of them end up looking like a third grader's and feeling like my body was working against itself, arms flailing one way and legs slipping the other, the ones that are perfect give me a wonderful sense of what the game should be like. And then there's the freeze-frame. Often I can't remember looking at the puck when I shoot, but I can always see it go into the goal. No matter how fast it goes or how far away I'm shooting from, I can always see the puck hitting the twine at the back of the net. And at that moment I see the whole world in a freeze-frame. I see where every other player is standing I even see the expressions of a face or two in the crowd. When the freeze-frame ends, the sense of power strikes. I realize then that the goalie tried his hardest but couldn't stop my shot. I was better than he was. For any human being in an intensely competitive situation that's a major high. Then the crowd begins to cheer, furthering the high. This is why I love to score goals. I don't want to sound selfish, and in all honesty I don't think I'm a selfish player. I don't try and hog the glory, and after a second or two of power trip, I come back to earth. But for that single moment I'm on top of the world looking down on it, and it's all mine.

This passage shows what you can do with freewriting. Writing at high speed, liberated from the need to worry about spelling or grammar or punctuation or paragraphing or organization, free from everything but the intense desire to re-create in words the experience of scoring, Tim discovered his thesis: he loved scoring because it gave him the sensation of power.

---

* Misspelled words in writing samples are marked with asterisks.

For one more example of what you can do with directed freewriting, consider again the passage by Andrea Lyle that was cited in chapter 1:

> Looking back, I guess it was pretty stupid. No climbing experience and nothing to climb with but a thin clothesline rope, and yet there we were in the middle of the old abandoned copper mine crawling and sliding our way down to the bottom which Ellie had heard somewhere was over a hundred feet down. For awhile a great adventure, a colossal marvelous cave. Outcroppings like gargoyles all over the walls. But after about three hours, we were dirty and cut up from a few minor falls, and the muscles in our fingers and hands and arms all ached from climbing, so we decided to go back up. Then it hit us. On the way down we'd sort of slid rather than climbed our way down a fifteen-foot almost sheer *precepice and nobody thought to leave a rope hanging there so we could climb back up. Now we tried again and again to scramble up the *precepice but *niether of us could do it. It was scary. We looked up to the top of the mine where the light was but it seemed so far away—not much bigger than a single star in a coal-black sky. We felt trapped. But we weren't giving up. Not yet. We tried to find a way around the *precepice and couldn't. Then we tried throwing the rope up to catch it somehow on the top of the precepice* but that didn't work either. Finally on the bottom of the mine I found two old rusty pipes. They were only about seven feet long, but Ellie noticed that the ends of each pipe were threaded, so we screwed the pipes together to make a long pole. Bracing the pole on the ground beside the *precepice, we helped each other climb the pole and get out of the cave.
>
> As I think back on this whole thing I'm not sure why we both felt so proud. We hadn't really done anything spectacular, and when we got home, nobody was surprised to see us. There was no celebration and no story in the paper. But maybe it was just that by working together, we figured our own way out of that place. We rescued each other. We had a problem that might have gotten really serious and we found a solution. Working together, depending on each other—there was nobody else—we found out what it means to be independent.

Once again, freewriting in response to a question leads the writer to her main point. As Andrea tells her story and tries to discover its significance, the memory of fear gives way to the memory of pride, and this memory in turn prompts her to ask why she felt proud. The answer is a point already implied by the story, but not made explicit until the end: in finding their way out of the cave, Andrea and her friend discovered what it means to be dependent and independent at the same time.

EXERCISE 1 Directed Freewriting

Using any of the methods described in sections 1.6 and 1.7, choose a basic question you might ask about the meaning of any personal experience you can vividly recall. Then do one half hour of freewriting to find the answer to this question.

2.4 Formulating a Thesis

As we said above, you can start a self-expressive essay without a thesis in mind, and you need not always make your thesis explicit in the essay itself. But you will sharpen the focus of your essay if you can formulate a thesis for it. Even if you need a session of freewriting to discover your thesis, and even if you write it out for your own guidance alone, it will help you to shape and unify your material. (Some teachers require a statement of thesis or statement of purpose to be submitted with each essay.)

A good statement of thesis expresses the main point of your essay by making a brief, precise assertion about the topic—usually in a single sentence. There are two ways to start formulating a thesis. If you think that you know—before you start to write—the answer to the basic question your essay will pursue, you can write out the answer at once. On the other hand, if you have used freewriting to discover your thesis, you can read what you have written and underline what you believe is your most important point. To become fully effective, however, the answer you've written or the point you've underlined must usually be rewritten—as Tim's was.

When Tim read over his freewritten material, he found his most important point in one set of words that jumped out at him as he read: *When the freeze-frame ends, the sense of power strikes.* There, he felt, was the answer to the question he had started with—*Why do I love scoring goals?*

Turning this set of words into a statement of thesis took a little more thought. If the underlined words held the answer to the question *Why*, Tim needed a statement that took the form of an answer, a statement that hinged on the word *because.* What he came up with was this:

> I love scoring goals because it gives me a sense of power.

Now he had a clear, definite, one-sentence answer to his basic question. But looking again at his freewritten material, he saw that his statement of thesis lacked something. It failed to indicate that the power trip lasted only "a second or two." So he added a qualifying word:

> I love scoring goals because it momentarily gives me a sense of power.

The addition of *momentarily* made the statement more precise. But Tim still felt something missing. His statement made no reference to any other reasons for his love of scoring, and therefore failed to indicate the unique importance of this one. He solved the problem by starting off with *Though:*

> Though many things make me want to score goals, I love scoring most of all because it momentarily gives me a sense of power.

This kind of statement not only announces the main point of the essay to come. By ranking that point above others, it also begins the work of organizing the essay. Thus it provides exactly what the writer needs for his first draft: a clear sense of direction. (For more examples of theses formulated gradually, in a succession of versions, see section 2.6.)

EXERCISE 2 Formulating a Thesis from Freewritten Material

First, underline the most important point you discovered about your topic in the process of freewriting. Second, using this point, write at least three versions of a sentence that could serve as a statement of thesis for the essay you plan to write. Third, say which version you think is best—and why.

EXERCISE 3 Formulating a Thesis from a Basic Question

Returning to the topic you pinpointed in chapter 1, exercise 5 (p. 23) and to the basic question you asked about it in exercise 8 (p. 27), write an answer to the question. Then rewrite the answer to make it as precise and specific as possible.

2.5 Finding Your Tone

The human voice always carries a tone. Imagine, for instance, how these two questions would sound if spoken aloud:

Would you mind putting out that cigarette?
Would you *mind* putting out that cigarette?

The words of both questions are exactly the same. Only the tone is different. The first question is polite; the second is insistent.

Though it is harder to hear the tone of a written word than the tone of a spoken one, the writer's attitude toward the reader and the topic determines the tone of an essay. Tim's thesis, for instance, catches the personal tone of his freewritten material. He sounds confident, open, and candid about himself—not at all afraid to say that a sense of power excites him. As you find your own aim, you should also try to find your tone. Will you sound earnest or playful? Will you sound calm or impassioned? Will you sound self-assertive or self-effacing? Will you sound authoritative or tentative? The more you can decide now about your tone, the better you will grasp your specific aim—your thesis.

How do you express a tone in writing? Part of the answer is content. To sound authoritative, you must be writing about what you know, and to sound convincingly impassioned, you must be writing about a subject of importance. But whatever your subject, you can strongly affect the tone of your writing by deciding 1) whether you want to sound *personal* or *impersonal,* and 2) whether you want to be *straightforward* or *ironic.*

2.5A Sounding Personal

Generally, writing sounds personal when the author is *I* speaking to the reader as *you.* When you write with a personal tone, you accentuate the fact that you are expressing your own feelings, opinions, observations, or beliefs. But a personal tone can be used in essays that serve any one of three major aims:

1. Self-expression

> As a man I spend most of my day in public, in a world largely devoid of speech sounds. So I am quickly attracted by the glamorous quality of certain alien voices. I am still gripped with excitement when someone passes me on the street, speaking in Spanish. I have not moved beyond the range of the nostalgic pull of those sounds.
>
> —Richard Rodriguez, *Aria: A Memoir of a Bilingual Childhood*

Rodriguez uses *I* repeatedly to underscore the point that he is expressing what he has personally experienced. The subject of every sentence he writes, in fact, is *I*.

2. Persuasion

> I believe that maturity is not an outgrowing, but a growing up: that an adult is not a dead child, but a child who survived. I believe that all the best faculties of a mature human being exist in the child, and that if these faculties are encouraged in youth they will act well and wisely in the adult, but if they are repressed and denied in the child they will stunt and cripple the adult personality. And finally, I believe that one of the most deeply human, and humane, of these faculties is the power of imagination: so that it is our pleasant duty, as librarians, or teachers, or parents, or writers, or simply as grownups, to encourage that faculty of imagination in our children, to encourage it to grow freely, to flourish like the green bay tree, by giving it the best, absolutely the best and purest, nourishment that it can absorb. And never, under any circumstances, to squelch it, or sneer at it, or imply that it is childish, or unmanly, or untrue.
>
> —Ursula Le Guin, "Why Are Americans Afraid of Dragons?"

Le Guin uses *I* repeatedly to stress the personal quality of her beliefs. She is expressing her own convictions, and the personal tone helps to give those convictions persuasive force.

3. Exposition

> Laughter comes in assorted shapes and forms. The nervous giggle, the cackle, the chuckle, and the guffaw are just a few of its many and strange variations. One friend of mine is known for a laugh that convulses anyone who hears it. Another friend laughs without making a sound, but her whole body shakes and heaves so violently that I sometimes wonder if

she'll come out of the laugh alive. Still another friend laughs so hard that his face wrinkles up like a raisin, his eyes squinch shut, and tears well out of the corners and trickle down his face. Why, I wonder, should laughter lead to tears? Why do we speak of "laughing to death"? —College student

This writer uses *I* and *mine* to stress the personal quality of her observations on laughter, and the personal tone gives her explanation the vividness of an eyewitness account.

A personal tone can enhance the effect of an essay by making your readers feel that you are talking directly to them. Nevertheless, you should use the personal tone with restraint. When overused in explanatory writing, it can make you sound impressionistic and self-absorbed—not a reliable guide to your subject. When overused in persuasive writing, it can make you sound merely self-assertive—not persuasive. For these reasons, you should know what the alternative is.

2.5B Sounding Impersonal

Your writing sounds impersonal when you make no reference to yourself or the reader, but merely focus on something distinct from you both:

Whenever two friends meet after a long separation, they go through a special Greeting Ritual. During the first moments of the reunion they amplify their friendly signals to super-friendly signals. They smile and touch, often embrace and kiss, and generally behave more intimately and expansively than usual. They do this because they have to make up for lost time—lost friendship time. While they have been apart it has been impossible for them to send the hundreds of small, minute-by-minute friendly signals to each other that their relationship requires, and they have, so to speak, built up a backlog of these signals.

This backlog amounts to a gestural debt that must be repaid without delay, as an assurance that the bond of friendship has not waned but has survived the passage of time spent apart—hence the gushing ceremonies of the reunion scene, which must try to pay off this debt in a single outburst of activity. —Desmond Morris, "Salutation Displays"

Like the student author of the passage on laughter just above (pp. 33–34), Morris reports on human behavior. But unlike the student, he makes no reference to himself as an observer. He writes not about *his* friends but about friendly behavior in general, using the third person "they" and such generalizing terms as the "Greeting Ritual" and "the reunion scene." His impersonal tone makes the writing sound factual, objective, and reliable.

A consistently impersonal tone suits lab reports and scientific articles written for specialists. But most good writing strikes a chord that combines the personal and the impersonal, that harmonizes "it is" with "I feel." Generally, therefore, you can enhance your writing by making some use of a personal tone, which simply reminds the reader that your essay has been written by a human being.

2.5C Sounding Straightforward

Straightforward writing sounds honest, direct, and sincere. But a straightforward tone can range from cool to impassioned, as you can see by comparing Morris's passage with this one:

> Anyone who knows that my husband Richard was one of the 53 American hostages in Iran for 444 days wouldn't be surprised to know that I still have nightmares.
>
> But my nightmares aren't over what might have happened in Iran.
>
> My nightmares are over what did happen four years earlier—right here in America—in a fast-food restaurant in Annandale, Va., where our 19-year-old son, Richard Jr., worked part time.
>
> One Friday night in March he didn't come home from work. That was unlike Rick. He was a happy and responsible young man. He loved his family, told us wherever he was going and never gave us reason to worry.
>
> The next morning, I went to the restaurant. I was told by police that my oldest son, my firstborn, had been murdered, shot in the back of the head, executed, blown away.
>
> A robber had hidden in the restroom past closing time. He was given all the available cash without resistance, but then he herded all four remaining employees of the Roy Rogers Family Restaurant (and one of their relatives) into the back freezer and made them all lie face down on the floor. They offered no resistance. None. But he emptied his handgun into the back of their heads. In case that wasn't enough, he reloaded and did it again. And then a third time.
>
> —Dorothea Morefield, "Gun Control California Style: A Victim Fights"

By itself, the subject matter here is shocking and brutal. But the writer conveys a passionate tone by repeating the word "nightmares" and by firing a volley of synonyms for the killing itself: "murdered, shot in the head, executed, blown away." Far more provocative than exclamation points would be, the repetitions re-enact the killer's repeated shootings and at the same time express the recurrence of the author's nightmares. Morefield repeats emotionally charged words and phrases to convey a passionate tone, and she uses the passionate tone to serve her persuasive aim: to argue for gun control.

2.5D Being Ironic

Irony emerges from a split between tone and content. Your writing is ironic when you pretend to sound sincere and earnest while approving or recommending something that is obviously bad, or while condemning something that is obviously good. Here is an example:

> Sitting down on our family's lop-sided sofa, I turned on the TV by remote control. After clicking my way through sitcoms, commercials, and movies, I settled on the 24-hour cable news channel, where the topic of the hour was the question of what America could do with its nuclear waste. I soon switched channels again, but the question lurked in the back of my brain as I watched two *Mission: Impossible* reruns and the first half of a *Roseanne* episode. All at once, during a commercial break in *Roseanne,* the answer came to me: marketing! To solve the problem of nuclear waste, the government should turn it into souvenir gift items and sell them to the American public.
>
> For purposes of marketing, nuclear waste could assume any number of forms. It could be molded, for instance, into the shapes of the fifty states, or put into bottles with labels such as "100% Pure Nuclear Waste from Oklahoma." Made into shavings, it could be placed into a transparent plastic bubble filled with water and containing a miniature city. When the bubble was shaken, an atomic snowfall would rain down upon the tiny city. This would make a great novelty item and, in addition, the water would help filter out some of the more harmful gamma rays.
>
> Of course it would take massive sales to reduce the vast amount of radioactive by-products now sitting in various dumps around the nation. But if a talented advertising agency took on the account, I believe it could start a run on nuclear

gifts that would rival the Cabbage Patch Doll craze of 1983. Furthermore, because the supply of nuclear waste may be limited, advertisers could legitimately claim that nuclear souvenirs would someday become collectors' items. It's quite possible, in fact, that a radioactive bubble on the living room coffee table would become the ultimate status symbol.

—College student

The irony here makes the writer's explicit thesis merely a disguise for his implicit one. While he pretends to recommend the conversion of nuclear waste into souvenir gift items, he is actually arguing that present methods of dealing with nuclear waste make no more sense than the method he proposes: a method based on the assumption that Americans can be persuaded to buy anything.

Irony can be hard to achieve and sustain because you must continually find ways to indicate that you mean something different from what you seem to be saying. But because irony prompts the reader to share your outrage or to laugh with you at whatever you find absurd, it can be a highly effective means of persuasion. (For more on how to catch the tone in what you read and also how to detect irony, see section 10.2A.)

EXERCISE 4 Finding Your Tone

a. If you have done exercise 1, do as follows with the freewritten material you produced: 1) Describe the prevailing tone of the material. 2) Indicate what features of the writing convey this tone. 3) Explain how this tone will help you realize your thesis or aim. 4) State whether you plan to keep or modify this tone for your essay.

b. If you have *not* done exercise 1, describe the tone you will use to develop your thesis or aim and explain why you are choosing this tone.

2.6 Sample Theses on a Variety of Topics

As the development of Tim's thesis shows (in section 2.4, above), a good thesis seldom comes quickly. Formulating it usually takes a good deal of thinking about various ideas, and especially about which idea is most important to the writer. Also, since the thesis sets the tone of the essay it will generate, the tone of the thesis itself requires careful thought. The following examples—all from the work of student writers—show what kind of thesis can develop from a succession of tries:

1. TOPIC: Women in TV commercials
   A. FIRST TRY: TV commercials often focus on housewives, unlike TV shows, which tend to glamorize women.
   B. SECOND TRY: Though TV shows often glamorize women, TV commercials typically present them as housewives—often in distress.
   C. FINAL VERSION: Though TV shows often glamorize women, TV commercials typically present them as housewives in distress so they can be rescued by the sponsor's product.
   TONE: skeptical, shrewd, impersonal

2. TOPIC: Escaping from a mine
   A. FIRST TRY: Escaping from a mine taught me something about myself.
   B. SECOND TRY: Escaping from a mine with my friend Ellie showed me how two friends can help each other out of a tight spot.
   C. FINAL VERSION: Escaping from a mine with my friend Ellie showed me how mutual dependence can lead to independence.
   TONE: thoughtful, self-confident, personal

3. TOPIC: Social competition in a small community
   A. FIRST TRY: The Shinnecook Indians are often divided among themselves but they can stand together when threatened from the outside.
   B. SECOND TRY: Though the five clans of the Shinnecook Indian Tribe sometimes don't get along, they stand together against outsiders.
   C. FINAL VERSION: Though the five clans of the Shinnecook Indian Tribe sometimes envy and resent each other, they stand together because they know that unity alone will keep their land from being lost.
   TONE: sympathetic, straightforward, impersonal

3
Organizing
Your Essay

If you have managed by now to formulate a statement of thesis that satisfies you, you have already started to organize your essay. You have given yourself a sense of direction by identifying your most important point. With this point firmly in mind, you can draw other points from the material you have produced in the pre-writing and freewriting stages and arrange those points in such a way as to support and develop your thesis.

But organizing your essay is not just a matter of arranging your points. It's also a process of turning your ideas into something your readers can grasp. Up to now, we've shown you chiefly how to write for yourself: how to explore the world of your own thoughts and feelings, how to express yourself in freewriting, how to discover your most important point. Now you should give special attention to your readers. To meet their needs and expectations, you must begin shaping the material generated by freewriting. You will still need your creative right brain to make further discoveries as you write and to help you visualize your ideas. But you will increasingly need the conscious, deliberate, analytical control that only the left brain can provide. In this chapter and the two that follow it, therefore, we explain how to shape, reshape, and refine your writing so that it will satisfy your readers.

3.1 Thinking about Your Readers

We said earlier (section 2.1) that most essays fall into one of three categories—self-expression, exposition, and persuasion. Since persuasive writing aims to influence the reader, it calls for more than usual attention to the reader's needs. But all good writers think about their readers, just as all good speakers think about their listeners. To organize an essay is to generate the answers to a series of questions that you can imagine the reader asking—questions such as these:

What are you talking about?	Introduction
What are you driving at?	Statement of thesis
Can you explain that?	Development
What's it all mean?	Conclusion

Different kinds of essays, of course, provoke different kinds of questions. If you're writing a persuasive essay, for instance, and you start by making a claim, you prompt a question such as "How can you say that?" (For more on the questions that persuasive essays try to answer, see chapter 7, pp. 126–27 and 131–32.) But to organize any kind of essay, you must think about answering general questions like these, and you must also consider the particular questions that might be raised by the readers you hope to reach. So the first question you must answer for yourself is "Who are my readers?"

The obvious answer is that your readers are your teachers, or *the* teacher of the course in which you are writing the essay. But writing well means learning how to write for different kinds of readers. For this reason, teachers of writing courses will sometimes assign not only a topic but an audience. You may be asked to explain a lab experiment to readers who know nothing about science, to re-create a personal experience for readers who know nothing about you, or to persuade a banker that you deserve a loan so that you can start a business. In assignments of this kind, the teacher is not so much your reader as your coach—helping you to reach the specified audience.

You can learn how to reach a specified audience by considering the following questions:

1. How much do your readers know about the topic? If you underestimate their knowledge, you will bore them by telling them things they already know; if you overestimate their knowledge, you may confuse them with unfamiliar terms or incomplete explanations.

Try to tell your readers only as much as they need to know in order to understand you.

How much do they need to know? This depends on both your topic and your audience. If you are writing a lab report for your chemistry professor, you can assume that he or she already knows the meaning of technical terms such as *fractionation*. But for readers unfamiliar with chemistry, you would have to explain such terms. (For more on this point, see section 38.3, "Writing on Specialized Topics for Non-Specialists.") The same is true for any terms that you cannot reasonably expect your readers to know. See how the student author of the following passage explains and translates the language of Brooklyn teenagers for the benefit of students living elsewhere:

> In my four months in Brooklyn I was mugged three times. Although such events may seem extraordinary to you, they are just a part of life in almost any minority neighborhood. It seems like everybody knows how to use some kind of weapon, whether it's a pair of nun-chucks (two round sticks attached by a chain) or an ice pick. As long as it will do the job, you can use it.
>
> In Brooklyn you fall into one of two categories when you start growing up. The names for the categories may be different in other cities, but the categories are the same. First, there's the minority of the minority, the "ducks," or suckers. These are the kids who go to school every day. They even want to go to college. Imagine that! School after high school! They don't smoke cheeb (marijuana) and they get zooted (intoxicated) after only one can of beer. They're wasting their lives waiting for a dream that won't come true.
>
> The ducks are usually the ones getting beat up on by the majority group—the "hard rocks." If you're a real hard rock you have no worries, no cares. Getting high is as easy as breathing. You just rip off some duck. You don't bother going to school; it's not necessary. You just live with your mom until you get a job—that should be any time a job comes looking for you. Why should you bother to go look for it? Even your parents can't find work.
>
> —Deairich Hunter, "Ducks vs. Hard Rocks"

Though Hunter assumes that his readers know the meaning of "mugged," he explains a number of other terms because they are not widely known.

2. How do your readers feel about the topic? Are they likely, first of all, to feel any desire to read about it? If you're writing about terrorism, abortion, or smoking, you can assume that most readers will be immediately interested in what you have to say. But if you're writing about chess for readers who may never have played the game, you can't assume much interest. You will have to stimulate it by explaining just what makes chess so interesting—even fascinating—to you.

If you *can* assume that your readers are interested in your topic, do they all feel the same way about it? And how strongly do they hold their views? If you want to write about smoking restrictions for an audience of fellow students, you have to realize that their attitudes toward smoking probably range from strong aversion to strong attachment. Even an expository essay may require some consideration for your readers' feelings. Explaining teenage life in Brooklyn to students who live elsewhere, Deairich Hunter admits that getting mugged three times in four months "may seem extraordinary to you."

3. How do your readers expect you to treat the topic? Sometimes this question is answered by the terms of an assignment, and you should realize that writing assignments are not limited to college courses. Professional writers—especially journalists—often work under instructions from editors who tell them not only what to write but also how to treat it. When you get a writing assignment, therefore, you should learn as much as you can about the approach you are expected to take.

In part that approach will depend on the rules of the game, the conditions under which you are writing. If your chemistry professor asks for a lab report, you are expected to record what the experiment showed, not what you felt when you performed it. But if your English teacher asks for an account of a personal experience and you decide to describe your first lab experiment, you will include your feelings, since for this assignment you are expected to describe what you felt. Students sometimes get conflicting advice about whether or not to start sentences with *I*, or whether to use *I* at all. The advice is conflicting because different readers have conflicting expectations. If the reader expects you to make personal experience a part of your essay, you should feel free to use *I*, just as Tim does in his essay on scoring goals. If the reader expects you simply to report facts and conclusions, you should avoid *I*. (For further guidance on what is expected in essays written for specialized fields in the humanities, sciences, and social sciences, see Chapter 38.)

4. How long is the finished essay supposed to be? Often, in college and afterward, you will be assigned a minimum or a maximum number of words or pages for your essay. Aim to make your first draft half again as long as the minimum. When you revise, you will probably find many words and even an idea or two that you want to cut out. Writing more than you will finally need gives you the chance to produce a finished essay in which every word will truly count.

REACHING YOUR AUDIENCE: IN BRIEF

How much do your readers know about the topic?

How do they feel about it?

How do they expect you to treat it?

How long is your essay supposed to be?

EXERCISE 1 Thinking about Your Readers

1. Suppose you are either *proposing* or *opposing* a Congressional bill that would ban smoking in all public places throughout the United States. Choose just one position, and then briefly explain how you would present it to each of the following: a) smokers, b) non-smokers, c) tobacco company executives.

2. Suppose you are explaining why a particular sport, hobby, or subject fascinates you. Write two sample paragraphs of explanation: one for readers who share your interest and knowledge, and one for those who don't.

3.2 Arranging Your Major Points

Once you have considered the kind of readers you will be writing for, you can select and arrange your major points. To do so, you should first make a list of all the points you have identified up to now. Tim did this simply by rereading his freewritten material and then jotting down the various points that he connected with scoring goals:

1. help the team
2. gain glory
3. take mind trip
4. feel relaxed
5. know I'm going to score
6. move smoothly, not awk- wardly
7. see world in freeze-frame
8. see puck going into goal
9. see players and crowd
10. feel sense of power
11. do better than goalie
12. hear crowd cheering
13. come back to earth after second or two

This, of course, is just a random list. But the advantage of making such a list before you make your outline is that it puts before you all of the points you have developed so far. You can then do what Tim did: underline the most important ones.

4. feel relaxed

7. see world in freeze-frame

10. feel sense of power

Your next task is to decide on the order or arrangement of your major points. To decide that, you must know what arrangements are possible and which are better than others for your particular topic, audience, and purpose. The following arrangements can be used with a variety of topics.

1. Chronological Order. This arrangement follows the order of events in time, and therefore works well in essays written to explain a procedure, such as pitching a tent, or a natural process, such as the migration of birds. (On explaining procedures and processes, see section 6.9). It is also commonly used in narrative (section 6.2), as well as in essays that use narrative, such as Peter's before-and-after comparison of his first arrival at college with his return to it (pp. 36–37).

2. Spatial Order. Spatial arrangement follows the order of objects in space and therefore works well in descriptive writing (section 6.1). Spatial order typically follows the movements of an imaginary eye surveying a scene—moving around a room, or across a landscape from left to right, or from foreground to background. It can also shift in scale, as when it moves from a comprehensive view to a close-up. Describing the town of Palatka, Florida, for

instance, Pat Jordan begins with a general view of its surroundings ("dense tropical foliage in limitless swamps") and then offers a close-up picture of weeds growing up between the bricks and through the cracks in the sidewalks (p. 109).

3. Cause and Effect Order. Cause and effect order allows you to explain one point as the reason for or as the result of another. In an editorial on why women work (pp. 130–31), the writer starts with the fact that more than 50 percent of women with young children are now holding jobs outside the home. Then he explains the reasons for this development. Likewise, in the first part of her freewriting on the cave, Andrea briefly presents the girls' predicament as a result of the way they came down (sliding and leaving no rope). In the final version of her essay, Andrea emphasizes causal order by starting with the girls at the bottom of the cave (see p. 61), and then backing up to explain how they got there. Thus she modified chronological order with causal order.

4. Climactic Order. When you order your writing climactically, you arrange points in order of ascending importance, rising from least important to most important. Climactic order sometimes corresponds to chronological order. In the first draft of Peter's essay on the contrast between arriving at college and returning to it (p. 36), the most important point—the pleasure of returning—is also the last in order of time. But in the passage from Dorothea Morefield's essay (p. 45), the most important point is what came first in time—the death of her son. To prepare us for the impact of this point, she puts it *after* her explanation of how—on the morning after his death—she set out to learn what had happened to him.

5. Oppositional Order. This arrangement opposes one point to another. It often works well at the start of a persuasive essay written for readers who are likely to resist the thesis. In arguing that top government officials deserve pay raises (pp. 167–69), David Broder begins by explaining the points that have been made against such raises, and then says why he favors them. (For more on this technique of concession, see section 7.6). You can also use oppositional order to compare and contrast two things, as shown in section 6.6, or just to highlight their differences.

6. Categorical Order. This order helps you to explain one large group as a collection of sub-groups. In the passage from Deairich Hunter's essay (p. 51), the author divides Brooklyn teenagers into two sub-groups or categories—ducks and hard rocks. He puts the ducks first because he is writing for those who would be called ducks if they lived in Brooklyn, namely for students at the Wilmington, Delaware high school he normally attends. (The essay first appeared in the high school magazine.) Only after explaining how ducks appear to hard rocks does he turn to the hard rocks themselves, who live by a code that most of his readers will find strange. Thus he presents the sub-groups in an order that suits his topic and his audience. (For more on the classification and division of sub-groups, see section 6.8.)

To see how you might use and combine some of these arrangements, consider what Tim did. Since he was writing for his fellow students, he decided to start with "help the team"—a common, readily understandable reason for wanting to score goals. Then, using oppositional order, he would shift to his own private reasons. These he would treat in climactic order, building up from the sense of relaxation through the freeze-frame effect—the sense of heightened awareness—to what for him was the most important reason for wanting to score: the sense of power.

EXERCISE 2 Arranging Your Major Points

Rereading your freewritten material and any other notes from the pre-writing process, make a random list of all the points you have so far accumulated for your essay in progress. Then underline the most important points, arrange them as well as you can, and identify the arangement(s) you have used.

3.3 Making an Outline

After deciding how to arrange your major points, you must decide what to do with the minor ones—or more specifically, how to connect them to the major ones. The best way to plan your connections is to make an outline, which may be either a tree diagram or a vertical list.

3.3A Outlining with a Tree Diagram

A tree diagram is a regulated, left-brained version of a branching diagram. Its branches are arranged to be read from left to right, and they spread out in one direction only—down from the thesis like the branches of a tree reflected in water. But because the tree is open ended, it leaves space for your right brain to visualize more

ORIGINAL DIAGRAM

THESIS: Though many things make me want to score goals, I love scoring most of all because it momentarily gives me a sense of power.

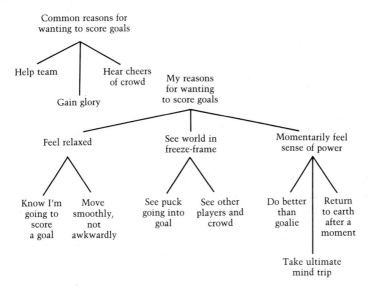

REVISED DIAGRAM

THESIS: Though many things make me want to score goals, I love scoring most of all because it momentarily gives me a sense of power.

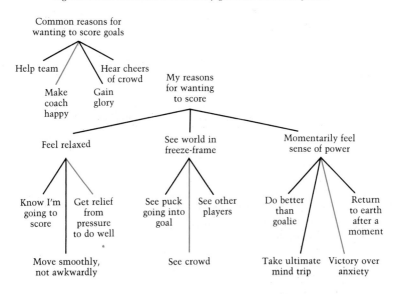

branches. So once you have drawn the tree to organize all your major and minor points, you can make it grow by adding more points as they come to mind.

The first tree diagram Tim drew appears on p. 57. As he studied this diagram, Tim discovered the need for more branches. When he asked himself, for instance, whether he had actually put down all the common reasons for wanting to score goals, he realized that he ought to mention pleasing the coach: a figure he had forgotten about, even though the coach did turn up in response to his original *Who* question (p. 25). Then Tim made more branches grow from the other headings. He realized that his sense of relaxation came partly from relief at the momentary lifting of pressure; he decided to separate his description of the crowd from his description of the players; and he saw how to reinforce his final point about power by adding "victory over anxiety"—something that "relief from pressure" had suggested to him. The result is the enlarged tree diagram on p. 57.

Because a tree diagram remains open-ended, it can be modified further as you write. Its great advantage is that *throughout the writing process*, you can use it not just as a record of your thoughts, but as a means of discovering them.

3.3B Outlining with a Vertical List

After you have produced some freewritten material, making a vertical outline of it is a good way to check the organization of your material—to see where the sequence and development are good, and also to spot any gaps where more information is needed. To outline your material vertically, write your thesis at the head of the page and then use headings and indented subheadings:

THESIS: Though many things make me want to score goals, I love scoring most of all because it momentarily gives me a sense of power.

   I. Common reasons for wanting to score goals
      A. Help team
      B. Gain glory
      C. Hear cheers of crowd
  II. My reasons for wanting to score goals
      A. Feel relaxed
         1. Know I'm going to score a goal
         2. Move smoothly, not awkwardly
         3. Get relief from pressure to do well

B. See world in freeze-frame
   1. See puck going into goal
   2. See other players and crowd
C. Feel momentary sense of power
   1. Do better than goalie
   2. Take ultimate mind trip
   3. Conquer anxiety
   4. Return to earth after a moment

Besides listing points in order of rising importance, this outline groups them under headings that show their relation to each other and to the thesis. Points that were at first jotted down in a random list have now become the skeleton of an essay.

EXERCISE 3 Outlining with a Tree Diagram

Following the example shown on p. 57, use a tree diagram to arrange all of your points. Then add whatever branches you think are needed.

EXERCISE 4 Outlining with a Vertical List

Using a vertical list with headings and subheadings, arrange your points in such a way as to clarify their relation to your thesis and to each other, and put them in an order that you think will best support the thesis.

3.4 Introducing Your Essay

3.4A Composing a Title

Every essay needs a title. It should be short but sharply focused on the main point of the essay. Compare the titles on the left with those on the right:

College	Where College Fails Us
Lawyers	When Lawyers Help Villains
The Mine	Finding a Way out of a Mine
First-Year Students	How First-Year Students Manage Money
College	Why Returning to College Beats Arriving
Hockey	Scoring Goals in Hockey

While the titles on the left merely identify a general topic, those on the right make the topic specific and pointed. A general title is better than none at all, but a sharply focused title tells your reader clearly what to expect. Also, if you can think of a good working title as you outline your essay, it can guide you through the writing of the essay itself. When you finish writing, you can reword the title if necessary to make it more precise. The last title in the column at right was the working title for Tim's essay. (His final title appears with the final version of the essay on p. 101.)

3.4B Writing the Introduction

The introduction comes first for the reader, but not necessarily first for the writer. Since you can't write a good introduction until you know what you're introducing, you may want to plunge immediately into the middle of your draft, write your way to a conclusion, and only then write your introduction. But whenever you write it, this section may help.

To write a good introduction, think about what strikes you when you start reading anything. What kind of opening bores you? What kind of opening seizes your interest and makes you want to read on? The better you understand that, the better your introductions will be.

A good introduction stirs the reader's interest by forecasting what is to come. You can forecast the rest of your essay by any one of the following means:

1. Lead up to an explicit statement of your thesis:

> THE TOWN DUMP
>
> The town dump of Whitemud, Saskatchewan, could only have been a few years old when I knew it, for the village was born in 1913 and I left there in 1919. But I remember the dump better than I remember most things in that town, better than I remember most of the people. I spent more time with it, for one thing; it had more poetry and excitement in it than people did. —Wallace Stegner

Stegner captures our attention with an opening sentence about a town dump. His second sentence makes us wonder *why* he remembers such a place. The third sentence answers that question by stating the provocative thesis of Stegner's essay: the town dump had more poetry and excitement than people did.

2. <u>Define a conflict, problem, or question you aim to resolve:</u>

THE CASE OF HARRY HOUDINI

When my grandfather was a boy he saw the wild-haired magician escape from a riveted boiler. He would remember that image as long as he lived, and how Harry Houdini, the rabbi's son, defeated the German Imperial Police at the beginning of the twentieth century. Hearing those tales and others even more incredible, sixty years after the magician's death we cannot help but wonder: What did the historical Houdini *really* do? And how on earth did he do it?

—Daniel Mark Epstein

While Epstein leads up to an explicit question, Andrea's introduction leads to an implicit question: how did she get out of the mine?

ESCAPING FROM A MINE

A slow, forbidding breeze chilled me as I watched Ellie struggling to get a grip on a rock wall that must have been at least fifteen feet high. She cursed. The breeze passed, but the chill on my face remained as I looked around again at where we were. The four rudely-cut walls that had held so much mystery and excitement for us a few hours ago now loomed threateningly over our heads. One hundred feet up was our salvation—the opening to the copper mine, looking not much bigger than a single star in a coal-black sky. The sharp overhangings and gargoyle-like outcroppings jutted harshly from the sides of the massive cave, ominously reminding us that we had climbed in, and now we had to climb out. But we couldn't. For at least an hour we tried to scale that one section of the mine wall, and couldn't see how to do it.

—Andrea Lyle

3. <u>Tell a story that illustrates the main point you will go on to make:</u>

DOUBLE VISION

When I was a little girl, my mother told me to wait for the light to turn green before I crossed the street and to cross always at the corner. This I did. Indeed, I was positive as a very young child that I would get mashed like a potato if I even so much as stepped a foot off the sidewalk while the light burned red. I followed my mother's advice until I realized that she herself jaywalked constantly, dodging in and out

of moving traffic—and pulling me with her. So after a while I
followed her example and not her advice.   —Lynn Minton

Minton tells a personal story to introduce the main point of her
essay, which is that adults are hypocritical.

4. Move from a generalization to a specific case:

> COLLEGE: DEPAUW
>
> American families differ greatly in their expectations
> about what going to college will mean in their children's lives.
> In the intellectual community to which my parents belonged,
> college was as necessary as learning to read. It was an intellec-
> tual experience and the gateway to the rest of life. All my life
> I expected to go to college, and I was prepared to enjoy it.
> —Margaret Mead

Mead starts with a generalization about college and family expectations. She then writes two sentences about her own family's
attitude toward college, and ends with a sentence about her personal expectations. She thus introduces an essay that will explain
how her first year of college actually disappointed her.

5. Indicate the method of your essay:

> HOW FAMILIES CREATE CULTURE IN EAST AND WEST
>
> Sociologists study the family because it is the basic unit
> of society. As a Chinese student who lived with an American
> family for six months, I had the opportunity to compare this
> family with my own in China. In so doing, I learned that the
> differences between the two countries are mainly created
> within the family. Though I was raised to tell my parents
> everything and to depend on others, each member of the
> American family had a private life, and the children were
> trained to be independent, to refuse help even when they
> needed it. The differences between my family and the Amer-
> ican one help to explain why Eastern and Western cultures
> have such different attitudes toward privacy, dependence, and
> independence.   —College student

This paragraph forecasts an essay in which the writer compares
one family with another in order to show something about the
differences between Eastern and Western cultures. Thus the introduction plainly defines the comparative method of the essay.

6. Challenge a widespread assumption or stereotype:

WHERE COLLEGE FAILS US

The case *for* college has been accepted without question for more than a generation. All high school graduates ought to go, says Conventional Wisdom and statistical evidence, because college will help them earn more money, become "better" people, and learn to be more responsible citizens than those who don't go.

But college has never been able to work its magic for everyone. And now that close to half our high school graduates are attending, those who don't fit the pattern are becoming more numerous, and more obvious. College graduates are selling shoes and driving taxis; college students sabotage each other's experiments and forge letters of recommendation in the intense competition for admission to graduate school. Others find no stimulation in their studies, and drop out—often encouraged by college administrators.   —Caroline Bird

In this two-paragraph introduction, Caroline Bird first describes the popular assumption that all high-school graduates should go to college. Then she challenges this assumption by introducing her main point: not everyone who goes to college belongs there.

7. To accommodate readers who may not agree with you, explain the position you aim to oppose:

THE CASE FOR TEST-TUBE BABIES

The mere mention of "test-tube babies" triggers instant repugnance in most of us. Visions arise, from Aldous Huxley's *Brave New World,* of moving assembly lines of glassware out of which babies are decanted at each terminus by a detached and impersonal technician. Procreation thus becomes reproduction in the full factory-like connotation of that word. And as we conjure up the distasteful (at the least) scene, words like *mechanization* and *dehumanization* reverberate through our neuronal networks.

Nevertheless, despite the offense to our sensibilities provoked by even the thought of artificial wombs, there is a valid case to be made for test-tube babies in the full Huxleyan image—not mass-produced on an assembly line, perhaps, but nevertheless wholly and "artificially" grown in a scientifically monitored environment without ever being carried in the uterus of a human mother. Such a case can be made (which does not mean that I personally advocate it) on the basis not merely of bizarre and exotic speculations but of purely humane, down-to-earth considerations having to do with the health of individual babies.   —Albert Rosenfeld

In the first paragraph, the writer shows that he understands the feelings of those who are horrified by test-tube reproduction. Only then does he begin to defend it. (For more on this kind of opening, see section 7.6B.)

Now that you've seen some of the ways in which a writer can effectively introduce a piece of writing, consider how Tim Boyle introduced his essay on scoring. He decided to start with a broad generalization about scoring goals—something that his readers (fellow students) would immediately understand. Then he narrowed the focus to what he had learned from his own experience in ice hockey. To write the introduction, he combined material from the upper left branches of his tree diagram with his statement of thesis:

WHY I LOVE SCORING GOALS

Anyone who plays on a team dreams of scoring goals. Why? Most people probably think that players long to score for the good of the team, or to make the coach happy, or to gain some glory: the cheers of the crowd, the smile of a cheerleader, and perhaps a headline in the school newspaper. But none of these things can fully explain the special *excitment of scoring, or more *specificly, the "high" I get from scoring in ice hockey. Though many things make me want to score, I love it most of all because it momentarily gives me a sense of power.

EXERCISE 5 Composing a Title and Writing an Introduction

Reviewing section 3.4A, compose a title for your essay. Then, using any one of the methods explained above, write an introduction.

3.5 Shaping the Middle of Your Essay

Whether you write your introduction before or after the rest of your essay, you will at some point have to shape the largest part— the middle. To do so, you must turn your outline into paragraphs.

3.5A Using Your Outline and Making It Grow

Shaping the middle of your essay calls for both invention and control. You need to follow your outline, but you should not be tyrannized by it. As you write, you will not only generate words, phrases, clauses, and sentences; you will think of new evidence, new strategies, even new points to be supported in their own right. If you write down everything that comes to mind, you will simply be freewriting again. But if you close your mind to new ideas, you may be putting the body of your essay into a strait-jacket. You need to do your shaping with a flexible hand.

So what do you do with a brand-new idea that comes to you as you write? Is it a gift or a distraction? Sometimes it can be hard to decide which. If the idea obviously supports the point you are developing in a particular paragraph, you can take it up right away. If it doesn't, and if you are using a tree diagram, see whether the new idea can be grafted onto a branch of the tree, for use later on. You can thus make your outline grow even as you follow its guidance.

3.5B Thinking in Paragraphs

To write a sentence is to work with words, phrases, and clauses; to write a paragraph is to work with sentences. Paragraphing is a deliberate act, the act of thinking about the connections and the differences between one sentence and another. To think this way is to think in paragraph form—the form good writing customarily assumes.

One way to think in paragraphs is to use each of the headings in your outline as a paragraph starter. Following the tree diagram shown on p. 57, Tim had already used the items clustered under the first heading—"Common reasons for wanting to score goals"— in his introductory paragraph. Reading from left to right across the diagram, he then turned to the items clustered under "Feel relaxed" for his next paragraph. Here is what he wrote:

> Scoring brings me a sense of relaxation. It begins even before I shoot, because even then I can see the puck going into a goal. I don't try to visualize the goal. The picture just flashes into my mind. The feeling is both *exhilerating and frustrating. When I see the picture a peacefulness fills me. I become relaxed and don't even consciously try to shoot. The shot just happens. Often I cannot remember looking at the puck, and I am so relaxed I might not have. The feeling at this point is

one of perfection. Unfortunately not every shot is like this, nor can every shot be made perfect. If I try to consciously *vizualise a goal, the shot feels forced. My body works against me rather than with me. When I unconsciously "see" a goal, I will always score, but if the effort to "see" a goal is conscious, I will not. This lack of conscious control is disturbing. I feel as if fate is controlling my shot and I can do nothing about it. I cannot make a goal happen. It happens almost by itself.

Scoring also gives me relief from pressure. In a competitive situation, players experience intense pressure to play to the best of their ability. Their parents, friends, schoolmates, teammates, and above all their coach expect a strong performance. So when I score, I feel a sense of relief. I have met the demands placed on me, and I can relax—for a moment anyway.

This is what Tim did in his first draft with the items clustered under "Feel relaxed" in the tree diagram. But he did not follow his outline slavishly; he modified it as he wrote. First, while developing the points about foreknowledge and perfection, he discovered a new point: making a perfect shot is "disturbing" because he feels as if fate is controlling him. Second, he wrote two paragraphs on relaxation instead of the one forecast by his diagram. Possibly because he felt the first paragraph was getting too long—especially with the new point added—he decided to treat "Get relief from pressure to do well" in a paragraph of its own. He then wrote two more paragraphs—one for each of the other two headings:

This moment of relaxation heightens my awareness of the world around me. Though I often cannot remember looking at the puck, I can always see it slide into the goal. No matter how fast the shot or how far away it was taken from, I can always see the puck hitting the twine at the back of the net. At this instant I see the world in a freeze-frame. Every other player seems caught, as if someone had suddenly stopped a fast-moving film. I can see the goalie down on the ice, the defensemen, the wingers cheering with their sticks in the air. Sometimes I can even catch the expressions of a face or two in the crowd.

In this frozen moment, the sense of power strikes. As I look at the goalie stretched out on the ice, I can see that he tried with every inch of his body to stop the puck, but couldn't because I shot it past him. For anyone driven by the urge to compete, this is a moment of pure triumph. *The ultimate mind trip. I have two victories now—one over the goalie, and one over the anxiety inside me, the fear that I will disappoint others. The crowd seems to cheer for me alone: not for the team or the coach or the school, but just for me. In that moment the world is mine.

Since this is only the first draft, it is not yet all it should be, and Tim has some revisions to make. But by turning the headings of his outline into paragraphs, he has already created the building blocks of which his essay will be made. (For a detailed discussion of paragraphing, see chapter 8.)

> EXERCISE 6 Drafting the Middle
>
> Using your outline as a guide, write one paragraph for each of its headings. If you find that a particular heading generates more or less than one paragraph, feel free to modify the outline. Remember that this is only a first draft.

3.6 Ending Your Essay

The ending of your essay is your last chance to clarify and emphasize your main point. But a fully effective ending does not simply summarize what the essay has said. It points beyond summary to reflection *on* the essay, or adds a final point that clinches the main one. To end an essay effectively, then, do any one of the following things:

1. Make the implications of your thesis explicit:

> We have found that violence on prime-time network TV cultivates exaggerated assumptions about the threat of danger in the real world. Fear is a universal emotion, and easy to exploit. The exaggerated sense of risk and insecurity may lead to increasing demands for protection, and to increasing pressure for the use of force by established authority. Instead of threatening the social order, television may have become our chief instrument of social control.
> —George Gerbner and Larry Gross,
> "The Scary World of TV's Heavy Viewer"

The authors restate their main point in the first sentence, and then connect it with the increased demand for protection. This point in turn leads to the explicit statement of what has already been implied: television may have become our chief instrument of social control.

2. Echo your introduction in terms that widen its significance:

> Poetry is seldom useful, but always memorable. I think I learned more from the town dump than I learned from school: more about people, more about how life is lived, not elsewhere but here, not in other times but now. If I were a sociologist anxious to study in detail the life of any community, I would go very early to its refuse piles. For a community may be as well judged by what it throws away—what it has to throw away and what it chooses to—as by any other evidence. For whole civilizations we have sometimes no more of the poetry and little more of the history than this.
> —Wallace Stegner, "The Town Dump"

Stegner's explanation of the poetry and excitement he found in a particular town dump leads in the end to a wide-ranging generalization: that all communities and even all civilizations may be judged by what they discard.

3. Recommend a specific course of action:

> The physically handicapped have the liabilities of a minority group. Shouldn't they be given the rights of a minority group? The answer is affirmative. It is time the action was also.   —Nancy Weinberg, "Disability Isn't Beautiful"

4. Answer a question posed by the introduction:

> What, then, can we conclude about mathematics and sex? If math anxiety is in part the result of math avoidance, why not require girls to take as much math as they can possibly master? If being the only girl in "trig" is the reason so many women drop math at the end of high school, why not provide psychological counseling and support for those young women who wish to go on? Since ability in mathematics is considered by many to be unfeminine, perhaps fear of success, more than any bodily or mental dysfunction, may interfere with girls' ability to learn math.
> —Sheila Tobias, "Who's Afraid of Math, and Why?"

5. Reflect on the experience that the essay records:

> We hadn't done anything spectacular, and when we got home, no one was surprised to see us. There was no celebration and no story in the paper. Yet looking back on our escape from the mine, I realize now why we both felt something more than relief. We felt proud that we had not panicked or simply given up and waited for help. We had faced a problem together, and we had finally found a solution. Paradoxically, by depending on each other—there was no one else—we discovered what it means to be independent. In a sense, we rescued each other.
> —Andrea Lyle, "Escaping from a Mine"

Having already explained how she and her friend escaped from the mine and thus solved the problem presented in her opening paragraph (p. 61), Andrea does not need to restate the solution. So she uses her final paragraph to reflect on her experience and explain what it taught her.

6. Reaffirm your thesis with a final telling example

To end an essay on the amount of garbage produced by New York City, Katie Kelley tells what she saw and heard at Fresh Kills, a Staten Island dumping site:

> "It sure has changed out here," one worker, who has been at Fresh Kills for years, told me. "Why, there used to be fresh natural springs over there." He gestured out over the hundreds of acres of garbage. Natural crab beds once flourished in the area. Now they, too, are gone, buried under tons of garbage.   —"Garbage"

The final paragraph clinches the point of the whole essay. The picture of the springs and crab beds buried under tons of garbage is far more effective than any final abstract statement about garbage could be.

Now that we've shown the variety of forms an ending can take, we return once more to Tim Boyle's essay in progress. He decided to end his essay by reaffirming his thesis in terms that widen its significance. Here is what he wrote:

> When the cheers subside, I lose my empire and become just another player again, reabsorbed by the game. But every time the moment of triumph comes, I learn once more why

scoring excites me so much. On or off the hockey rink or the playing field, life is frustrating. We miss shots; we reel from body checks; and sometimes we fall flat on our faces. To score is for one shining moment to conquer all frustration. Anxiety has been banished, and we rule the world. Ultimately, it is not for the team or the school or the coach that I love to score. It is for myself.

EXERCISE 7 Ending an Essay

First, turn to p. 120 and put a card or small sheet of paper over paragraph 6. Then turn to pp. 118–120 and read the first five paragraphs of the essay titled "Why Videotapes Won't Kill Movie Theatres." Finally—without looking at paragraph 6—furnish your own concluding paragraph for this essay.

EXERCISE 8 Comparing Endings

Read paragraph 6 on p. 120 and compare it with your own concluding paragraph. Then explain what each ending does and how well it works.

EXERCISE 9 Ending Your Own Essay

Write a paragraph to conclude the essay you have been writing in this chapter.

4
Revising
Your Essay

Revising literally means "looking again." To look at your essay again, the first thing you need is a copy of it on paper. If you have it only on a computer disk, you cannot see it as a whole. So anything you write with a word processor should be printed before you try to revise it. After you have marked it up by hand, you can make your changes on your disk.

If your instructor has asked to see your first draft and has returned it with suggestions for revision, as Tim Boyle's teacher did (see pp. 79–82), those suggestions will guide you. But outside of writing courses, most college instructors simply expect you to submit a final draft for a grade. Eventually, therefore, you should learn how to revise your essays *before* you submit them. That is, you should learn how to see for yourself what they need.

Seeing what they need does not simply mean making corrections in spelling, grammar, punctuation, or usage. That is small-scale revising, which we call *editing*. This chapter deals with large-scale revising, which means looking again at the whole of your essay: its tone, the development of its main point, and its appeal to the readers for whom it is written. The key to effective revision is this: *try to make big changes before turning to little ones.* If you try to do both at the same time, you may find yourself laboring over a particular sentence and then deciding to rewrite or cut out altogether the whole paragraph that contains it. So we suggest you revise and edit your essay in two stages. That is why we treat revising in this chapter and editing in the next.

4.1 Reconsidering Your Aim

As we said earlier in section 2.1, you can think about the aim of an essay in two ways—specific and general. Once the essay is written, its specific aim is to express, to explain, or to prove its main point—its thesis. Whether your thesis is explicit or implicit, you should now be able to say what it is and to see how well your essay develops it. But as you think about your thesis, ask yourself again about your general aim. Do you chiefly want to express your own feelings, to explain something outside yourself, or to persuade your reader?

You may decide to modify your general aim. When Andrea Lyle first wrote about her escape from the cave, she set out to write just a personal narrative expressing her own feelings. But in thinking about her escape, she discovered something beyond herself: the paradoxical relation between independence and mutual dependence. So she decided to explain what the escape taught her about that relation. The thesis she eventually formulated (given above in section 2.6) clearly reveals this shift from self-expression to explanation. While her first try at a thesis simply referred to herself, her final version went further: "Escaping from a mine with my friend Ellie showed me how mutual dependence can lead to independence."

If the thesis of your essay doesn't quite fit the general aim you have decided on, you may need to modify the thesis. When Tim Boyle reread the first draft of "Why I Love Scoring Goals" with the help of his instructor's comments (see below, section 4.5), he could see that his draft was purely expressive, solely the product of his personal feelings. The comments helped him see that what he had discovered about his own love of scoring might go beyond himself. So he decided to give his thesis a referential edge, to make it include all players. He revised it this way:

> ORIGINAL VERSION: Though many things make me want to score goals, I love scoring most of all because it momentarily gives me a sense of power.
>
> REVISED VERSION: Though many things make players want to score goals, my own experience in ice hockey leads me to think that we love scoring most of all because it momentarily gives us a sense of power.

Switching from "me" and "I" to "players" and "we," Tim adjusted the focus of his thesis. But he did not abandon his expressive aim.

On the contrary, he decided to explain why all players love to score by analyzing his own motives for scoring. In the next section, you will see what further revisions flowed from Tim's restatement of his aim.

EXERCISE 1 Reconsidering Your Aim

Do three things: 1) State the thesis of your essay in its present form. 2) State the general aim you have decided to pursue—whether self-expression, explanation, or persuasion. 3) If necessary, rewrite the thesis to make it fit the goal.

4.2 Reconsidering Your Tone

You can hear the tone of anything you read if you listen carefully enough to its words. But the best way to hear the tone of your first draft is to read it aloud to yourself, or ask someone to read it aloud to you. As you listen, consider these questions: Does the writing sound too personal for your topic and aim, or too impersonal? Is the tone consistent? Does it help you develop your thesis or realize your aim? To see how you might answer such questions, consider this opening paragraph of a student's first draft:

> Going to college for most people means the onset of new freedoms and many responsibilities. The acquisition of these new responsibilities helps to develop values and maturity in an individual. This makes the prospect of going to college appealing. Upon returning home for the Christmas holidays, I experienced new freedoms and respect from my parents.

The final sentence of this paragraph leads to a statement of thesis. But the detached, impersonal tone of the opening sentences, which refer to "most people" and "an individual," hardly prepares us for the personal tone of the final sentence. To bridge the gap between the two, the student made the middle sentences sound personal, so that the paragraph read this way:

> For most people, going to college means the onset of new freedoms and many responsibilities. In my first semester of college, new responsibilities helped me to develop values and maturity. This opportunity to mature is what drew me to

college in the first place, and I especially felt the change in myself when the semester ended. Upon returning home for the Christmas holidays, I experienced new freedoms and respect from my parents.

Now the paragraph moves from the impersonal tone of the opening generalization to a personal tone in the middle sentences, which lead the way to the distinctly personal statement of thesis. Thus the tone of the paragraph enhances its most important point. (For more on tone, see or review section 2.5.)

EXERCISE 2 Reconsidering Tone

Read the passage below and then say whether or not the tone is consistent. If not, identify the inconsistencies, and then revise the passage to make its tone consistent.

As Patrick Henry once delivered fiery speeches that roused American colonists to revolution in the 1770s, so Martin Luther King, Jr., inspired many Americans during the 1960s. Many people in this period struggled to bring blacks and whites together, but no one expressed the ideal of integration more movingly than King when he stood in front of the Lincoln Memorial and declared to the thousands of people gathered there, "I have a dream." King spoke straight from the heart. He didn't hide his feelings, as politicians often do. Of course the reason they hide their feelings is that they can't get elected any other way. That's the problem with straightforward speaking; it doesn't win elections. But I still like to hear an honest speech now and then. It's refreshing.

4.3 Reconsidering Your Structure

A well-structured essay first of all embodies *unity*. In a unified essay, all the objects described, the actions narrated, and the points made serve to introduce or develop a thesis—the main point of the essay as a whole. In Andrea's essay on her escape from the mine, for instance, the opening description of the mine and the narrative of her escape from it gradually introduce her main point, which is that mutual dependence can lead to independence. Whether stated or merely implied, a thesis should emerge from every essay you write. Even a personal narrative should strive to answer a basic question such as, "What did I learn from this experience?"

Besides unity, a well-structured essay displays *continuity* and *progression.* Continuity is a line of thought or a chain of association connecting all the elements of the essay from beginning to end. Progression ensures that every paragraph after the first one adds something new to the points already made.

To evaluate the unity, continuity, and progression in your essay, consider these questions:

1. Does your introduction announce your thesis or point toward it in some way? A good introduction leads up to your thesis directly, by stating it, or indirectly, by pointing toward it. If the introduction fails to indicate your thesis in any way, it is misdirecting the reader and thereby weakening the unity of your essay.

2. Can you state the main point or identify the most important image in each paragraph? If you can't do either, the paragraph lacks unity and must either be split up, reconstructed, or both. (For detailed discussion of how to revise a drastically disorganized paragraph, see section 8.4.)

3. Does the main point of each paragraph help to support and advance the thesis? If the main point of any paragraph departs from the topic or works against the thesis, you should first try to decide whether the material in that paragraph belongs in your essay at all. If you think the material can be linked to the topic, you must also find a way to make it support the thesis. To cut the paragraph altogether is to run the risk of oversimplifying your essay. But to keep it in without violating the unity of your essay, you must either change your thesis or reorganize the paragraph. Section 4.5 below shows how Tim Boyle turned a paragraph that worked against his thesis into a paragraph that worked for it.

4. From the second paragraph on, is the first sentence of each paragraph clearly connected to the last sentence of the one before? A well-structured essay has not only unity but also continuity, an unbroken line of development from one point to the next. The line breaks when the opening sentence of a new paragraph has no connection with the closing sentence of the one before it, and the line fades when a new paragraph begins by simply saying, "Another point to consider is X."

You can often generate continuity by improving the transition between one paragraph and the next, as explained in section 8.8. If you can't solve the problem that way, consider rearranging your paragraphs—that is, rearranging the order of your major points.

5. Does the main point of each new paragraph move beyond the main point of the one before it? Each new paragraph in your draft should move beyond the previous one by revealing something new about the topic. If a new paragraph mainly repeats the point made by the one before, your progression falters. To keep the essay moving, you should either cut the repetitive paragraph altogether or emphasize whatever is new in it.

6. Does the ending reaffirm, reflect upon, or extend the main point of the essay? The ending should reaffirm the main point of the essay as whole, and if possible explain its implications. If you've decided to change the thesis of your first draft, you will need to change your conclusion also.

4.4 Developing Your Texture—Using Generalizations and Specifics

Texture is something good writers create by interweaving general ideas with specific details. As you reread your own writing, therefore, you should alternately ask yourself two questions: (1) What piece of detail could I use to illustrate the general point I've just made? (2) What generalization can I draw from the specific point I've just mentioned? If the writing itself fails to answer these questions, it probably needs some work. Writing that lacks specific detail will strike the reader as thin, abstract, and empty, like a big square box made of clear plastic. Writing that lacks generalizations will seem unfocused and undefined, like a newspaper without headlines. But the combination of generalizations and specifics will help you develop your texture, as the following examples show.

1. GENERALIZATION: Free enterprise combines high risk with the possibility of high rewards.
   SPECIFIC EXAMPLE: To start my own summertime lawn-care service, I had to lay out all my savings—nearly two thousand dollars—on a used pickup, a used mower, a new fertilizer spreader, and a couple of big rakes. But by the end of the summer, I had cleared almost four thousand dollars, and I sold the pickup for fifteen hundred.
2. GENERALIZATION: Laughter takes many different forms.
   SPECIFIC DETAIL: The nervous giggle, the cackle, the chuckle, and the guffaw are just a few of its variations.
3. GENERALIZATION: In his first year as a pop musician, he had a hard time.

SPECIFIC DETAIL: He could not afford heat or hot water in his apartment, so he had to warm himself with heavy blankets and go to a public bathhouse for his showers.

As you revise your writing, you can develop your texture by doing two things:

1. Add specifics to make generalizations vivid and tangible:

> Religion has always been a major cause of persecution. An extreme example would be World War II, where religion was used in a discriminatory fashion.
> —Student essay, first draft

> REVISED: Religion has always been a major cause of persecution. During World War II, the German Nazis sent millions of men, women, and children to death in concentration camps simply because they were Jews.

2. Add generalizations to explain the significance of specific statements:

> As the team members dressed for the first day of practice, they said nothing to each other but "What's your name?" and "Where are you from?" Most of them dressed as fast as they could and finished the job while running out onto the field. One player said to me, "All of these guys are so much bigger than I am that I wonder if I've even got a chance of playing."
> —Student essay, first draft

> REVISED: On the first day of practice, competitiveness made us all tense and wary. While dressing we said nothing to each other but "What's your name?" and "Where are you from?" Most of the players dressed as fast as they could and finished the job while running out onto the field. They each wanted to be first. Everyone seemed to be looking at the rest of the team and measuring himself against the others. One player said to me, "All of these guys are so much bigger than I am that I wonder if I've even got a chance of playing."

EXERCISE 3 Recognizing Generalizations and Specifics

Identify the generalizations and specific details in Eugene Raskin's "Walls and Barriers," pp. 241–42.

EXERCISE 4 Furnishing Specifics

Add specific details or examples to the following generalization:

The sudden cry of "Fire!" panicked everyone in the store.

EXERCISE 5 Furnishing Generalizations

Suppose you are writing a booklet to be used in recruiting young people for the U.S. Army. What attractive generalization about the army could you make on the basis of the following details?

After completing basic training in obedience, privates are assigned to an advanced training unit, where they learn a particular specialty such as mechanics, radio operation, or infantry tactics. Privates who learn their specialties exceptionally well have the chance to become noncommissioned officers (NCOs) after training in leadership and supervisory skills.

EXERCISE 6 Revising with Specifics

Add specific details or examples to any passage in your first draft that leans too heavily on generalizations.

EXERCISE 7 Revising with Generalizations

Add one or more generalizations to any passage in your first draft that is not sufficiently clear in its overall significance.

4.5 Revising in Action

The foregoing suggestions, we hope, will help you to see what kind of revisions your first draft needs and how to make them. To see now the process of revision in action, consider once more the first draft of Tim's essay—this time with his instructor's comments on it. (The instructor is commenting only on large-scale matters at this stage, not on small-scale errors such as misspellings. Those will be corrected later.)

(1) Anyone who plays on a team dreams of scoring. Why? Most people probably think that players long to score for the good of the team, or to make the coach happy, or to gain some glory: the cheers of the crowd, the smile of a cheerleader, and perhaps a headline in the school newspaper. But none of these things can fully explain the special excitement of scoring, or more specifically, the "high" I get from scoring in ice hockey. Though many things make me want to score goals, I love scoring most of all because it momentarily gives me a sense of power.

Good introduction and statement of thesis.

(2) Scoring brings me a sense of relaxation. It begins even before I shoot, because even then I can see the puck going into the goal. The picture just flashes into my mind. The feeling is both exciting *exhilerating and frustrating. When I see the picture a peacefulness fills me. I become relaxed and don't even consciously try to shoot. The shot just happens. Often I cannot remember looking at the puck, and I am so relaxed I might not have. The feeling at this point is one of

Transition? What's the connection between this point and your thesis? Or the end of your first ¶?

What's the main point of this ¶? It seems to have two competing points:
1) scoring relaxes you,
2) scoring disturbs you.

perfection. Unfortunately not every shot is like this, nor can every shot be made perfect. If I try to consciously *visualise a goal, the shot feels forced. My body works against me rather than with me. When I unconsciously "see" a goal, I will always score, but if the effort to "see" a goal is conscious, I will not. This lack of conscious control is disturbing. I feel as if fate is controlling my shot and I can do nothing about it. I cannot make a goal happen. It happens almost by itself.

Is this the best transition you can think of?

(3) Scoring also gives relief from pressure. In a competative situation, players experience intense pressure to play to the best of their ability. Their parents, friends, schoolmates, teammates, and above all their coach expect a strong performance. So when I score, I feel a sense of relief. I have met the demands placed on me, and I can relax-- for a moment anyway.

Here you simply repeat the point already made. You seem to be going in circles.

(4) This moment of relaxation heightens my awareness of the world around me. Though I often cannot remember looking at the puck, I

can always see it slide into the goal. No matter how fast the shot or how far away it was
taken from, I can always see the puck hitting
the twine at the back of the net. At this instant I see the world in a freeze-frame. Every
other player seems caught, as if someone had
suddenly stopped a fast-moving film. I can see
the goalie down on the ice, the defensemen,
the wingers cheering with their sticks in the
air. Sometimes I can even catch the
expressions of a face or two in the crowd.

    (5) In this frozen moment, the sense of
power strikes. As I look at the goalie
stretched out on the ice, I can see that he
tried with every inch of his body to stop the
puck, but he couldn't because I shot it past
him. For anyone driven by the urge to compete,
this is a moment of pure triumph. *The
ultimate mind trip. I have two *victroies
now-- one over the goalie, and one over the
*anxiety inside me, the fear that I will
*disapoint others. The crowd seems to cheer
for me alone: not for the team or the coach
or the school, but just for me. In that moment,

Good! The tone is confident — even exultant.

It comes through strongly here.

the world is mine.

(6) When the cheers subside, I lose my empire and become just another player again, reabsorbed by the game. But every time the moment of triumph comes, I learn once more why scoring excites me so much. On or off the hockey rink or the playing field, life is frustrating. We miss shots; we reel from body checks; we sometimes fall flat on our faces. To score is for one shining moment to conquer all frustration. Anxiety has been banished, and we rule the world. Ultimately, it is not for the team or the school or the coach that I love to score, but for myself.

Very good! But since you use "we" in this ¶, couldn't you broaden your thesis and approach elsewhere to

make this more than just an essay of self expression?

On the whole, Tim found the comments encouraging. The teacher liked his introduction, his statement of thesis, his self-expressive aim, his tone of candid confidence, and his conclusion. But the question about his aim and the comments on the middle paragraphs showed that Tim still had work to do.

First, the question about his aim led him to revise his thesis as shown above in section 4.1 (p. 72). He then revised his introduction to fit the revised thesis:

> Anyone who plays on a team dreams of scoring goals. Why? Most people probably think players long to score for the good of the team, or to make the coach happy, or to gain some glory: the cheers of the crowd, the smile of a cheerleader, and perhaps a headline in the school newspaper. But none of these things can fully explain the special excitement of scoring, the "high" we players get from it. Though many things make us want to score goals, my own experience in ice hockey leads me to think that we love scoring most of all because it momentarily gives us a sense of power.

This revision of the introductory paragraph made it fit the newly formulated statement of thesis. But something more was needed to bridge the gap between the end of this paragraph and the beginning of the second, between "a sense of power" and "a sense of relaxation." Tim saw that he would have to either improve the transition between paragraphs 1 and 2 or rearrange his major points.

As for paragraph 2 itself, his teacher's comment made him see that it had not one main point but two competing points: (1) scoring relaxes me because I feel the shot will be perfect; (2) scoring disturbs me because I have no control over it. Coming at the end of the second paragraph, this second point seemed to push aside the first, and even seemed to undercut the thesis. If scoring made him feel manipulated by "fate," how could it end up giving him a sense of power?

Two more problems turned up in paragraph 3. Besides the comment on the weak transitional "also" at the beginning, the comment made at the end showed him something he had completely overlooked: the similarity between the end of paragraph 3 and the beginning of paragraph 2. By simply rounding back to the point that scoring brings relaxation, the draft had become repetitive and circular. It lacked progression.

How could he solve all these problems? Where could he begin? As a rule of thumb, the best way to start solving structural problems in an essay is to reconsider the structure of the essay as a whole—or more precisely, the arrangement of its major points. It makes no sense to reconstruct a particular paragraph before you've definitely decided where that paragraph should go.

In light of the basic principle that big problems should be solved first, Tim decided to see what would happen if he reversed the order of paragraphs 2 and 3—something easy to do with a word processor. With paragraph 3 *before* paragraph 2, he noticed, one problem suddenly disappeared: he no longer had a weak transition between the two. The echo or doubling-back effect that he got with the former arrangement became instead a link:

> END OF ¶ 2. (formerly 3) . . . I have met the demands placed on me, and I can relax—for a moment anyway.
> BEGINNING OF ¶ 3. (formerly 2) Scoring brings me a sense of relaxation.

He now had continuity, but he needed progression. What could he do with the point about relaxation? As he reread paragraph 3 in light of the new arrangement, it occurred to him that he could use **cause and effect** here (see section 6.10). He could move from the effect of relaxation to its original cause:

> END OF ¶ 2. . . . I have met the demands placed on me, and I can relax—for a moment anyway.
> BEGINNING OF ¶ 3. Strangely enough, the relaxation begins even before I shoot. It originates from a kind of *forknowledge, a feeling that I am *definately going to score, a *wierd hunch that everything I do will turn out perfectly.

With this new beginning of paragraph 3 before him, Tim had in hand the main point of the paragraph as a whole: the relaxation comes from a foreknowledge that makes him feel confident. But to unify the paragraph and to ensure that it supported his thesis, he had to do something about the other point—the one about his feeling disturbed by a lack of conscious control. He solved the problem this way:

> ¶ 3. Strangely enough, the relaxation begins even before I shoot. It originates from a kind of *forknowledge, a feeling that I am *definately going to score, a *wierd hunch that everything I do will turn out perfectly. The feeling is both frustrating and *exhilerating. On one hand, it bothers me that I can't control these moments of perfection. I can't control my shot. I feel instead that fate controls me. On the other hand, I feel all my usual awkwardness slip away. No longer working against me,

with arms flailing one way and legs slipping the other, my body works totally for me. I am so confident of my special power that I can see the puck sliding into the goal even before my stick touches it.

This revised version not only unifies the paragraph but also makes it clearly support the thesis of the essay as a whole. The point about being disturbed—the counter-point that worked against the thesis in the original paragraph—is now subordinated to a point that works for it. Tim has moved the counter-point from the end of the paragraph to the middle, so that he can end by reaffirming his main point, which is that a foreknowledge of scoring makes him feel confidently relaxed. He has also shrewdly managed to work into the last sentence the key word of his thesis: *power.*

At the same time, Tim has added specific detail. Even though he has compressed the paragraph to sharpen the focus on its main point, he has injected a phrase about arms and legs to illustrate his "usual awkwardness." Interestingly enough, he first used this detail in freewriting, skipped it in his draft, and then found a place for it in his revision.

Three other tasks remained. First of all, to ensure continuity between the new paragraph 3 and the old paragraph 4, he had to revise the opening of paragraph 4. He did so by once again using cause and effect, treating the mood of relaxation as a cause of heightened awareness:

END OF ¶ 3. I have met the demands placed on me, and I can relax—for a moment anyway.
¶ 4. The effect of this mood is a heightened awareness of the scoring moment. . . .

Secondly, he had to bridge the gap between his introductory paragraph and the one that would now follow it—the one about relief from pressure. He solved the problem by using reverse chronological order, moving backward in time:

END OF ¶ 1. . . . we love it most of all because it momentarily gives us a sense of power.
BEGINNING OF ¶ 2. Before the sense of power comes a sense of relief.

Finally, since Tim had changed his thesis, he had to revise his conclusion, which would now include all players, not just himself:

When the cheers subside, I lose my empire and become just another player again, reabsorbed by the game. But every time the moment of triumph comes, I learn once more why scoring excites me so much, and why, I believe, it so much excites anyone who scores. On or off the hockey rink or the playing field, life is frustrating. We miss shots; we reel from body checks; we sometimes fall flat on our faces. To score is for one shining moment to conquer all frustration. Anxiety had been banished, and we rule the world. Ultimately, it is not for our teams or our schools or our coaches that we players love to score, but for ourselves.

Since no two different drafts will ever present the same set of problems, the revisions Tim made in his draft can merely suggest what you might do with yours. Nevertheless, the specific things Tim did clearly illustrate a general point worth repeating. The key to effective revision is to look again at the whole of your draft and think big. Think not about commas or misspelled words but about the texture of your writing, about its tone, its aim, and its structure—the relation between the thesis and the paragraphs that are meant to support and develop it. You may find that you have to restate your thesis completely, rearrange your paragraphs drastically, or rewrite them extensively. But if you fully revise your draft, the result should be a definite improvement. (For the final version of Tim's essay, see pp. 99–103.)

EXAMINING YOUR ESSAY STRUCTURE: IN BRIEF

Does your introduction point toward your thesis?

Can you state the main point or central image in each paragraph?

Does the main point of each paragraph support the thesis?

Are transitions between paragraphs clear and smooth?

Does the main point of each paragraph move beyond the main point of the one before it?

Does the ending reaffirm or extend the main point of the essay?

EXERCISE 8 Reworking Your Structure

Following the suggestions made in section 4.3 and illustrated in section 4.5, rework the structure of your own draft to give it unity, continuity, and progression. Feel free also to make any further changes in texture, tone, and aim that you think will improve your draft. But do not worry now about correcting errors in spelling, grammar, or punctuation. Those can wait.

5
Editing
Your Essay

Editing is the final stage of writing. After you have drafted your essay and revised it, you must shift your focus from large units to small ones, from the substance and structure of your essay as a whole to the energy and structure of your sentences, to your punctuation, diction, and spelling. This chapter is designed to take you through those final steps—right up to the final copy of your essay.

5.1 Making Your Sentences Rhetorically Effective

Good writing is made of sentences that are not just grammatically correct but also rhetorically effective: vigorous, concise, emphatic, well-balanced, and varied. To achieve these effects with your own sentences, consider the following suggestions:

1. Use subordination to break the monotony of short, simple sentences and to emphasize your main points:

> Some working women find special ways to cope with resistance from their husbands. Take my mother's situation. She is a teacher. My father is a fine old Southern gentleman. He is opposed to her teaching. He was raised on old-fashioned beliefs. He thinks men should work and women should stay at home. He wouldn't object to her job if the family needed a second income. We don't need it. But my mother likes her job and won't give it up. So they've solved the problem by making

an agreement. He buys the necessities, and she buys the luxuries.

EDITED: Some working women find special ways to cope with resistance from their husbands. Take my mother, who teaches. My father, a fine old Southern gentleman, opposes her teaching because he was raised to believe that men should work and women should stay at home unless the family needed a second income. Though our family doesn't need a second income, my mother likes her job and won't give it up. To solve the problem, they've agreed that he buys the necessities, and she buys the luxuries.

By combining short sentences and using subordination, this passage clearly emphasizes the writer's main points. (For a full discussion of subordination, see chapter 15.)

2. Vary the length and construction of your sentences. Sentences of any length and any construction soon become monotonous if they are too much alike. To combat monotony, vary your sentences:

Ultimately, it is not for our teams, our schools, or our coaches that we players love to score, but for ourselves.
EDITED: Ultimately, it is not for our teams, our schools, or our coaches that we players love to score. It is for ourselves.

The contrast between a long, complex sentence and a short, simple one sharpens the impact of the final point. (For more on sentence variety, see section 25.1.)

3. Activate your verbs. Wherever possible, replace forms of the verb *be*—forms such as *is, are, was, were, has been,* and *had been*—with verbs that denote action:

On or off the hockey rink or the playing field, life is frustrating.
EDITED: On or off the hockey rink or the playing field, life breeds frustration.

The change of *is* to *breeds* energizes the sentence. (For more on this effect, see section 25.2.)

Activating your verbs also means changing the passive voice to the active voice (see section 22.3) whenever no good reason justifies the passive:

In modern Japanese families, all of the husband's salary is taken by the wife, and all household expenditures are managed by her.

EDITED: In modern Japanese families, the wife takes all of the husband's salary and manages all household expenditures.

4. Use parallel construction to enhance the coordination of two or more items:

To score is for one shining moment to conquer all frustration. Anxiety has been banished, and we rule the world.

EDITED: To score is for one shining moment to conquer all frustration, to banish anxiety, and to rule the world.

Since the three effects of scoring are coordinate—that is, equal in importance—the second sentence puts all three of them in the same form. (For more on parallel construction, see chapter 14.)

5. Cut unnecessary words:

There are many things that make me laugh.

EDITED: Many things make me laugh.

For more on eliminating wordiness, see section 9.12.

6. If a sentence is too tangled to be understood on the first reading, break it up and reorganize it:

Due to the progress in military weaponry over the years, there has been an increased passivity in mankind that such advancements bring as wars are easier to fight resulting in a total loss of honor in fighting.

EDITED: Since progress in military weaponry over the years has made mankind more passive and wars easier to fight, fighting has lost all honor.

To learn how to straighten out tangled sentences, see section 16.2.

5.2 Checking Your Choice of Words

It pays to choose your words with care. Words that muddy your meaning or suddenly change the tone of an essay can puzzle or annoy your readers. But well-chosen words can help your writing gain attention and respect. So as you edit your essay, we suggest you do as follows.

1. <u>Replace words too high or too low for your level of diction:</u>

> The faculty blew off the proposal.

The words "faculty" and "proposal" come from the middle level of diction, a level that suits most of the subjects you will be writing about and most of the readers you will be writing for. But "blew off" puts needless distance between the writer and the reader because it falls below the level of diction established by the rest of the sentence.

> EDITED: The faculty rejected the proposal.

For more on levels of diction, see section 9.1.

2. <u>Replace words that don't say precisely what you mean:</u>

> The decisions I make at college depend on the values I have incurred at home.

To *incur* (literally "run into") is to bring something upon oneself. We incur obligations, for instance. But since we don't incur values, *incurred* will make the reader wonder if the writer knows what he or she wants to say.

> EDITED: The decisions I make at college depend on the values I have learned at home.

For more on how to choose the right word for your meaning, see sections 9.2–9.4.

3. <u>Replace vague abstractions with concrete, specific, or figurative terms:</u>

> Going to college opens up a lot of interesting possibilities.

Since vague abstractions leave your reader uninformed, they should be replaced with words of more tangible meaning.

> EDITED: Going to college is like exploring a big city for the first time.

For more on concrete and specific words as well as on the effective use of abstract words, see section 9.5. For more on figurative language, see section 9.6.

4. Replace pretentious verbiage with words that plainly deliver your meaning:

> Upwardly mobile young lawyers often work in excess of seventy hours a week.

Upwardly mobile is sociological jargon for anyone who hopes to move up in wealth and status, and *in excess of* is a fancy way of saying "more than." Unless you're writing for readers who expect this kind of language, you should replace both phrases.

> EDITED: Ambitious young lawyers often work more than seventy hours a week.

For more on pretentious words as well as jargon and euphemisms, see sections 9.10–9.11.

5. Replace clichés:

> She earned the raise by keeping her nose to the grindstone.

Clichés are worn-out phrases that most readers have seen or heard far too often. For this reason, they should be replaced with single words or shorter phrases.

> EDITED: She earned the raise by working hard.

For more on clichés, see section 9.8.

5.3 Checking Your Grammar

It pays to check your grammar for the same reason it pays to check your choice of words. While grammatical weaknesses can damage the way your writing appears to a reader, grammatical correctness helps to make writing look polished and precise. As you edit your paper, therefore, watch for the following errors, which are explained in the designated section or chapter of Part 2.

1. The sentence fragment (chapter 17)

> Here at school, there is no one who regularly wants to know where I'm going and when I'll be back. *This being the biggest difference between my home life and my college life.
> EDITED: This is the biggest difference between my home life and my college life.

2. The dangling modifier (section 12.18)

> * After exercising, a swim was taken.
> EDITED: After exercising, we took a swim.

3. The misplaced modifier (section 12.15)

> * I thought about the speech I had to give in French class while sitting in the tub.
> EDITED: While sitting in the tub, I thought about the speech I had to give in French class.

4. The run-on (fused) sentence (section 13.8)

> * The quake struck without warning in minutes it leveled half the town.
> EDITED: The quake struck without warning, and in minutes it leveled half the town.

5. Unclear reference of pronouns (section 18.4)

> * When I took the Walkman back to the store, they told me I couldn't get a refund.
> EDITED: When I took the Walkman back to the store, the manager told me I couldn't get a refund.

6. Faulty shifts in pronoun reference (section 18.8)

> * When a college requires drug testing of their athletes, does it violate their rights?
> EDITED: When a college requires drug testing of its athletes, does it violate their rights?

7. Incorrect pronoun case forms (sections 18.9–12)

> * Him and I always disagreed.
> EDITED: He and I always disagreed.

8. Faulty agreement of subject and verb (chapter 19)

> * Anyone with small children know how demanding they can be.
> EDITED: Anyone with small children knows how demanding they can be.

9. Faulty tense shifts

> * As soon as I saw the coat, I recognize it.
> EDITED: As soon as I saw the coat, I recognized it.

5.4 Checking Your Punctuation

To spot your errors in punctuation, you will probably need the help of your teacher, who may refer you to a section of Part 3, "Punctuation and Mechanics." If your teacher finds punctuation errors in one of your papers, keep a list of those errors so that you can watch for them in future papers. Four of the most common errors involve the comma. They are as follows:

1. The comma splice (section 13.7)

> *Temperatures dropped below zero, the big pond froze for the first time in ten years.
> EDITED: Temperatures dropped below zero, and the big pond froze for the first time in ten years.

2. Misusing commas with restrictive elements (section 26.6)

> *Cars, equipped with air bags, can save the lives of drivers, who fail to wear safety belts.
> EDITED: Cars equipped with air bags can save the lives of drivers who fail to wear safety belts.

3. Commas after conjunctions (section 26.2)

> *We walked all over town, but, we couldn't find the record store.
> EDITED: We walked all over town, but we couldn't find the record store.

4. Commas separating the basic parts of a sentence (section 26.13)

> *Poisonous gas from a pesticide factory in India, killed more than two thousand people in 1984.
> EDITED: Poisonous gas from a pesticide factory in India killed more than two thousand people in 1984.

5.5 Checking Your Spelling, Capitalization, and Apostrophes

Most writers misspell from two to five words in a five-hundred-word draft, and they also make occasional errors in capitalization and the use of apostrophes. If you're using a word processor and you have a spelling-checker program, see section 31.1. But most such programs will miss any word that is simply misspelled for its context, as in *It's against the law to *steel*. So whether or not you use a spelling-checker program, you should check the following:

1. Your own spelling demons. These are the words you have trouble spelling correctly. Unless the spelling-checker catches them for you, you may need your teacher's comments to identify them in the first essay you submit:

> Strangely enough, the relaxation begins even
> before I shoot. It originates from a kind of
> *Sp.* for⌢knowledge, a feeling that I am defi⌢nately *sp.*
> going to score, a w⌢ierd hunch that everything *Sp.*
> I do will turn out perfectly. The feeling both
> frustrates and exhi⌢lerates me. On one hand, it *Sp.*
> bothers me that I can't control these moments

To find the correct spelling of the words marked *sp.*, look them up in a dictionary. Then make an analytical list of the misspelled words as explained in section 31.2, and correct the passage.

> EDITED: It originates from a kind of foreknowledge, a feeling that I am definitely going to score, a weird hunch that everything I do will turn out perfectly.

2. Apostrophes needed or misused (sections 31.10 and 31.11)

> * The towns police force consisted of the sheriff and his two retriever's.
> EDITED: The town's police force consisted of the sheriff and his two retrievers.

3. Capitalization needed or misused (section 32.1)

> * theodore Roosevelt became President of the United states when william McKinley was Assassinated in 1901.
> EDITED: Theodore Roosevelt became president of the United States when William McKinley was assassinated in 1901.

5.6 Proofreading Your Essay

Technically, proofreading is the reading of proof sheets—what the printer submits for the author's final corrections before a piece of writing is published. As you read your own essay once more, imagine that it is going to be published. Reread every word carefully, watching particularly for errors in grammar, spelling, and punctuation. If you make more than five corrections on a page, retype or reprint the page.

EDITING CHECKLIST

Does your essay show any weak spots when you read it aloud?

Sentence Rhetoric (5.1)

How often do you use the active voice?

How often do you subordinate one point to another?

How much do your sentences vary in length and structure?

Are any of your sentences confusingly tangled?

Word Choice (5.2)

Is any word too high or low for your level of diction?

Does any word fail to say just what you mean?

Sentence Grammar (5.3)

Does any sentence sound incomplete?

Does any part of a sentence seem out of place?

Does the form of each verb agree with its subject?

Is the reference of each pronoun clear?

Punctuation and Mechanics (5.4, 5.5)

Have you used commas where they belong, and only where they belong?

Are you sure that each word is correctly spelled?

Have you fixed all typographical errors?

EXERCISE 1 Proofreading

We have deliberately mutilated this passage from Mark Twain's
"Advice to Youth" so that it contains three misspellings, a sentence
fragment, and a comma splice. Find the errors and correct them.

   You want to be very careful about lying, otherwise you
are nearly sure to get caught. Once caught, you can never again
be, in the eyes of the good and the pure, what you were before.
Many a young person has injured himself pernamently through
a single clumsy and ill-finished lie. The result of carelessness   5
born of incomplete training. Some authorities hold that the
young ought not to lie at all. That, of course, is puting it rather
stronger than necessary; still, while I cannot go quite so far as
that, I do maintane, and I believe I am right, that the young
ought to be temperate in the use of this great art until practice   10
and experience shall give them that confidence, elegance, and
precision which alone can make the accomplishment graceful
and profitable.

EXERCISE 2 Proofreading

Following is a paragraph from the next-to-last version of the essay
by Andrea Lyle cited in earlier chapters. Correct any errors you find.

   For over half an hour we tried to snag the rope on an
overhanging rock. We never did make it. We tried other, longer
routes, giving each other boosts with our hands, but the top
layre of copper sediment was so thick. That what we thought
was a firm handhold would often crmble in our grasp. So we   5
couldnt trust the climbing surface. We even explored old mine
shafts in hopes that they would lead us out, they only led us
deeper into the mine. As we explored one shaft, however, we
stumbled over an eight-foot iron rod and then a six-foot metal
tube. With some dificulty, we found a way to fit the rod into   10
the tube, forming a crude but relativly sturdy pole of about
thirteen feet. Bracing the pole on the ground next to the pre-
cipece, we climbed it and made our way out of the cave.

ms   **5.7** **Preparing and Submitting Your Final Copy**   *ms*

The final copy of Tim Boyle's paper on pp. 99–103 illustrates a
format commonly used in the final copy of essays. Your teacher
may have additional or alternative instructions, and will tell you
whether or not you need a separate title page. Though some teachers may accept handwritten essays, most teachers expect them to
be typed or printed on one side only of standard-size (8½ by 11)
white sheets. If you use fanfold computer paper, separate the sheets
and remove the perforated strips before submitting your essay.

Format with title on first page of text

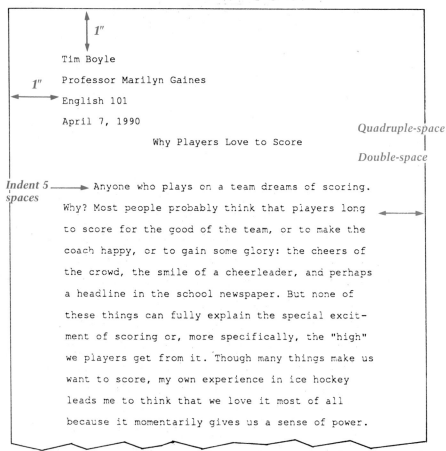

Format with separate title page

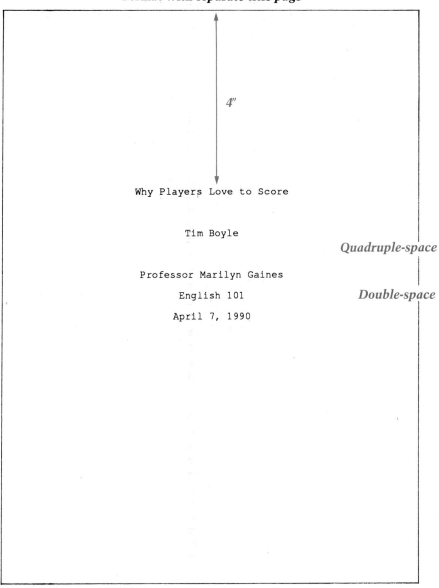

4″

Why Players Love to Score

Tim Boyle

Quadruple-space

Professor Marilyn Gaines

English 101

April 7, 1990

Double-space

First page of text following separate title page—note repeating title

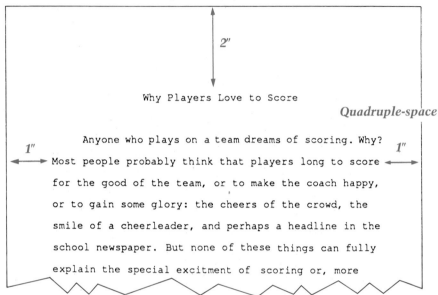

2"

Why Players Love to Score

Quadruple-space

1"

Anyone who plays on a team dreams of scoring. Why?
Most people probably think that players long to score
for the good of the team, or to make the coach happy,
or to gain some glory: the cheers of the crowd, the
smile of a cheerleader, and perhaps a headline in the
school newspaper. But none of these things can fully
explain the special excitment of scoring or, more

1"

Second and succeeding pages of text

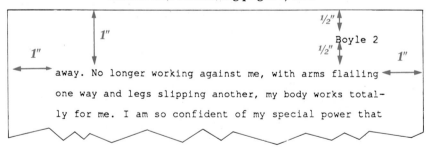

1"

1"

½"

½"

Boyle 2

1"

away. No longer working against me, with arms flailing
one way and legs slipping another, my body works totally for me. I am so confident of my special power that

Why Players Love to Score

Anyone who plays on a team dreams of scoring. Why? Most people probably think that players long to score for the good of the team, or to make the coach happy, or to gain some glory: the cheers of the crowd, the smile of a cheerleader, and perhaps a headline in the school newspaper. But none of these things can fully explain the special excitment of scoring or, more specifically, the "high" we players get from it. Though many things make us want to score, my own experience in ice hockey leads me to think that we love it most of all because it momentarily gives us a sense of power.

Before the sense of power comes a sense of relief. In a competitive situation, players feel intense pressure to do their best. Their parents, friends, schoolmates, teammates, and above all their coaches expect a strong performance. So when I score, I feel a sense of relief. I have met the

demands placed on me, and I can relax--for a
moment anyway.

    Strangely enough, the relaxation begins even
before I shoot. It originates from a kind of
foreknowledge, a feeling that I am definitely
going to score, a weird hunch that everything I do
will turn out perfectly. The feeling both
frustrates and exhilarates me. On one hand, it
bothers me that I can't control these moments of
perfection, that I can't control my shot. I feel
instead that fate controls me. On the other hand,
I feel all my usual awkwardness slip away. No
longer working against me, with arms flailing one
way and legs slipping another, my body works
totally for me. I am so confident of my special
power that I can see the puck sliding into the goal
even before my stick touches it.

    The effect of this mood is heightened awareness
of the scoring moment. No matter how fast the shot
or how far away it is taken from, I can always see
the puck hitting the twine at the back of the net.
At this instant I see the world in a freeze-frame.

Boyle 3

Every other player seems caught, as if someone had
suddenly stopped a fast-moving film. I can see the
goalie down on the ice, the defensemen, the wingers
cheering with their sticks in the air. Sometimes I
can even catch the expressions of a face or two in
crowd: a pair of eyes lit up with joy, a wide-open
grinning mouth.

In this frozen moment, the sense of power
strikes. As look at the goalie stretched out on the
ice, I can see that he tried with every inch of his
body to stop the puck, but he couldn't. I shot it
past him. For anyone driven by the urge to compete,
this is a moment of pure triumph, the ultimate mind
trip. I have two victories now--one over the goalie,
and one over the anxiety inside me, the fear that I
will disappoint others. The crowd seems to cheer
for me alone: not for the team or the coach or the
school, but just for me. In that moment the world
is mine.

When the cheers subside, I lose my empire and
become just another player again, reabsorbed by the
game. But every time the moment of triumph comes, I

Boyle 4

learn once more why scoring excites me so much, and
why, I believe, it so much excites anyone who scores.
On or off the hockey rink or the playing field,
life breeds frustration. We miss shots; we reel
from body checks; we sometimes fall flat on our faces.
To score is for one shining moment to conquer all
frustation, to banish all anxiety, to rule the
world. Ultimately, it is not for our teams or our
schools or our coaches that we players love to
score. It is for ourselves.

6
Methods of Development

A method of development is a way of achieving the aim that you set for yourself when you sit down to write. The various methods of development that we treat in this chapter—methods such as description, narration, and definition—are a succession of answers to *how* questions: How do you explore and articulate your feelings in an essay? How do you explain something in the world outside yourself? How do you persuade the reader to accept your opinion? Any one of the methods that we illustrate and explain below can help you write essays of self-expression, exposition, or persuasion.

Some of the methods discussed here may become ends in themselves. You can certainly set out to tell a story, to describe something, or to compare and contrast two things. But you will make the most of each method if you use it as a means to some purpose beyond the method itself, because your sense of that purpose will help you to organize and control your writing.

Take narration as an example. If you aim to explore your own feelings, you can tell a story that reveals them, such as the story that Andrea tells about her escape from a copper mine. A story told to reveal her feelings would show how they progressed from fear to relief and then to pride. But while Andrea recalls her feelings, she tells her story chiefly to make an explanatory point about human relations: to show how mutual dependence can lead to independence. Alternatively, she could have made her story serve a persuasive end. She could have used it to argue that young people should be allowed to take risks because of what they can learn by facing them.

In this chapter we explain various methods of development, show you some ways of combining them (most writing combines at least two of them), and periodically indicate how they can be made to serve the aims of self-expression, exposition, and persuasion. But since persuasion often requires not only methods of development but also special techniques of argumentation, we treat persuasion by itself in chapter 7.

6.1 Using Description

Description is writing about the way things appear, the way they are constructed, or the way they act. Description usually takes one of three forms: external, analytical, or evocative.

6.1A External Description

An external description enables the reader to visualize and recognize the object described. Suppose you are explaining automobile maintenance to readers unfamiliar with it, or trying to persuade those readers that they can easily learn how to service their own cars. For their information, you would need to describe such things as the electrode, which is—as one student writer described it— "the small open square of metal that sticks up out of the threaded tube at one end of the spark plug."

External description commonly focuses on the shape and color of objects and on their arrangement in space. But to describe any living creature, you should consider also the way it moves:

> Baby turtles in a turtle bowl are a puzzle in geometrics. They're as decorative as pansy petals, but they are also self-directed building blocks, propping themselves on one another in different arrangements, before upending the tower. The timid individuals turn fearless, or vice versa. If one gets a bit arrogant he will push the others off the rock and afterwards climb down into the water and cling to the back of one of those he has bullied, tickling him with his hind feet until he bucks like a bronco.
>
> —Edward Hoagland, "The Courage of Turtles"

Hoagland uses several images to help us visualize the turtles in motion. He uses "pansy petals" for their varieties of color, "building blocks" for the shapes they make in climbing on each other, and "bucks like a bronco" for the way one turtle throws another off its back. By revealing the energy and determination of baby turtles, this description serves the larger aim of the essay as a whole, which seeks to explain—as the title indicates—the courage of turtles.

EXERCISE 1 External Description

Briefly describe any object on your college grounds—such as a building, a tree, a playing field, or a statue—so that other students can recognize it. Then explain what your description shows about the college as a whole.

6.1B Analytical or Technical Description

An analytical or technical description enables the reader to understand the structure of an object. Consider this passage:

> The panda's "thumb" is not, anatomically, a finger at all. It is constructed from a bone called the radial sesamoid, normally a small component of the wrist. In pandas, the radial sesamoid is greatly enlarged and elongated until it almost equals the metapoidal bones of the true digits in length. The radial sesamoid underlies a pad on the panda's forepaw; the five digits form the framework of another pad, the palmar. A shallow furrow separates the two pads and serves as a channelway for bamboo stalks.
> —Stephen Jay Gould, *The Panda's Thumb*

Gould is describing the peculiar structure of the panda's paw. His language is precise, objective, technical *(radial sesamoid, metapoidal bones)*, and above all analytical. He focuses not on the furry surface of the panda's paw but on the framework of "thumb" and finger bones that underlie it. This analytical description serves an argumentative aim. Gould wants to show that the panda—which long ago had nothing but five fingers in its paw—gradually developed its radial sesamoid to do the work of an opposable thumb, to operate like a human thumb in grasping the bamboo stalks that pandas love to eat. Analytically described, the panda's paw helps Gould to substantiate the theory of evolution.

EXERCISE 2 Analytical or Technical Description

Describe in a paragraph any one of the following in such a way that the reader can understand its structure, design, or function:

a bicycle	a tire jack
a surfboard	the human foot
a solar house	the keystone arch
a rifle	the human hand
a trumpet	a pine tree
a skateboard	a peony

6.1C Evocative Description

Evocative description re-creates the impression made by an object:

> The coyote is a long, slim, sick, and sorry-looking skeleton, with a grey wolf-skin stretched over it, a tolerably bushy tail that forever sags down with a despairing expression of forsakenness and misery, a furtive and evil eye, and a long, sharp face, with slightly lifted lip and exposed teeth.
>
> —Mark Twain

Twain's words evoke both the visual effect of the coyote and the feeling that its appearance excites in him. All of the details work together to help us see the coyote as he sees it: *sick, sorry-looking, evil.*

Evocative description can appeal not just to the eye but to all the other senses:

> The heat of summer was mellow and produced sweet scents which lay in the air so damp and rich you could almost taste them. Mornings smelled of purple wisteria, afternoons of the wild roses which tumbled over stone fences, and evenings of honeysuckle. . . .
>
> In the heat of mid-afternoon the women would draw the blinds, spread blankets on the floor for coolness and nap, while in the fields the cattle herded together in the shade of spreading trees to escape the sun. Afternoons were absolutely still, yet filled with sounds.
>
> Bees buzzed in the clover. Far away over the fields the chug of an ancient steam-powered threshing machine could be faintly heard. Birds rustled under the tin of the porch roof.
>
> —Russell Baker, *Growing Up*

Baker's descriptive language appeals to the senses of smell, touch, taste, and especially hearing. In the last paragraph, *buzzed* and *chug* are onomatopoeic—that is, they actually sound like what they mean. An evocative description should always appeal to one or more of the senses. Compare these two descriptions of Palatka, Florida:

1. I couldn't stand Palatka. It was poor, seedy, smelly, and ugly, and the weather was always bad. I couldn't relate to the people either. My stay there was a nightmare.

2. Situated on the banks of the St. Johns River, Palatka was surrounded by dense tropical foliage in limitless swamps. It was always hot, and it rained daily. The town's main street, made of bricks, was called Lemon Street. Weeds grew out of the spaces between the bricks and out of the cracks in the sidewalks and at the bottom of the concrete buildings, so that to a stranger the vegetation appeared to be strangling the town. There was a paper mill in town. It supplied most of the blacks and poorer whites with employment. Each morning at six they were summoned to work by a whistle that woke the entire area. Shortly thereafter Palatka was blanketed by a lavender haze and filled with a terrible stench.   —Pat Jordan, *A False Spring*

In the first version, the writer gets between us and the town. He talks about his own feelings instead of showing us why and how the town affected him as it did. In the second version—which is what Jordon actually wrote—the descriptive details set the town before us. Nowhere does the writer say that Palatka is a dreary and decaying town, but every one of his details shows us that it is.

EXERCISE 3 Evocative Description

Write a one-paragraph description in which you re-create the impression that a particular person, place, or animal has made on you. Then explain how this description could be used to help illustrate a certain period of your life.

EXERCISE 4 Evocative Description

Using Pat Jordan's paragraph on Palatka as a model, write an evocative description of the neighborhood in which you grew up, or (if you moved around during childhood) of the neighborhood you remember most vividly. Assume that the reader has never seen this place, and describe as many sights, sounds, and smells as possible.

6.2 Using Narration

6.2A Narrating Events in Chronological Order

Narration or storytelling is writing about a succession of events. The simplest kind of narration follows chronological order: the order in which the narrated events actually occurred or could have occurred. Consider this account of an incident that helped to provoke the Boston Massacre in 1770:

> On Friday, March 2, a Boston ropemaker named William Green, busy with his fellows braiding fibers on an outdoor "ropewalk" or ropemaking machine, called to Patrick Walker, a soldier of the Twenty-ninth [Regiment] who was passing by, and asked if he wanted work. "Yes," Walker replied. "Then go and clean my shithouse," was Green's response. The soldier answered him in similar terms, and when Green threatened him, he departed, swearing to return with some of his regimental mates. Return he did with no less than forty soldiers, led by a big Negro drummer.
>
> —Page Smith, *A New Age Now Begins*

Here the writer reports events as they followed one another in time, and his use of dialogue—of Green's actual words—makes this moment in American history come vividly alive.

A short narrative or anecdote can readily serve an explanatory aim. The story above helps to explain the relations between American colonists and the British army in the years before the outbreak of the American revolution. The following anecdote helps to explain how Harry Houdini used the police to publicize his prowess:

> When he arrived in London in 1900 the twenty-six-year-old magician did not have a single booking. His news clippings eventually inspired an English agent, who had Houdini manacled to a pillar in Scotland Yard. Seeing that Houdini was securely fastened, Superintendant Melville of the Criminal Investigation Department said he would return in a couple of hours, when the escapist had worn himself out. By the time Melville got to the door, the magician was free to open it for him.
>
> The publicity surrounding his escape from the most prestigious police force in the world opened up many another door for him. . . .
>
> —Daniel Mark Epstein, "The Case of Harry Houdini"

EXERCISE 5 Narrating to Explain Personality

Write a short chronological narrative or anecdote that helps to explain
the personality of anyone you know, including yourself.

EXERCISE 6 Narrating a Fight

Using chronological order, give a brief narration of a fight or quarrel
you have seen or been involved in. Concentrate on how the fight or
quarrel got started.

6.2B Narrating Events out of Chronological Order

A short narrative can often follow chronological order with good
results. But strict adherence to chronological order in an extended
narrative can lead to a boring, meaningless string of "and thens."
To clarify the meaning of a sequence of events, the writer may
need to depart from chronological order, moving backward to
explain the cause of a particular event or jumping forward to identify its ultimate effect.

>   In June 1964 . . . two Italian fishing boats, working in
> tandem with a crew of 18, were dragging their nets along the
> bottom of the Adriatic. Toward dawn, as they pulled up the
> nets after a long trawl, the fishermen realized their catch was
> unusually heavy. . . . When they finally swung the nets inboard
> they saw an ungainly, prehistoric-looking figure missing both
> feet. It was, in fact, a 500-pound Greek statue covered with
> nearly 2,000 years of sea encrustations.
>   In November 1977, this life-size bronze fetched the
> highest known price ever paid for a statue—$3.9 million. The
> work is attributed to the fourth century B.C. Greek artist Lys-
> ippus. . . . Professor Paolo Moreno of Rome University, author
> of two books on Lysippus, identifies the statue as the portrait
> of a young athlete after victory and suggests that it may have
> been plundered by ancient Romans from Mount Olympus. The
> ship bearing the statue was probably sunk in a storm and there
> may well have been other treasures on board. Pliny the Elder
> tells us Lysippus made more than 1,500 works, all of them
> bronze, but it was doubted that any of the originals had sur-
> vived—until this one surfaced.
>   The fishermen stealthily unloaded the barnacle-cov-
> ered masterpiece in Fano, near Rimini, and took it to the cap-
> tain's house, where it was put on a kitchen table and propped
> up against a wall.   —Bryan Rosten, "Smuggled!"

The first paragraph tells the story of how a statue was discovered in June 1964. To explain what makes the story important, the writer flashes forward to 1977, when the statue was sold for nearly four million dollars. Then he flashes back to ancient times, when the statue was lost. After these forward and backward flashes, he returns to the original story in the third paragraph.

EXERCISE 7 Using Flashbacks and Flash-forwards

Using at least one flashback and one flash-forward, tell the story of one of the following:

your first day on a full-time job

your first day in college

your first meeting with someone who later became important in your life

the first time you felt that you were doing something wrong

6.3 Combining Description and Narration

Description and narration commonly go hand in hand. In his description of Palatka (p. 109), Pat Jordan tells us what happened there each morning: the whistle summoned workers at six, and soon the town was blanketed with haze. Conversely, this piece of narrative includes description:

> Everyone knows that a night relief is among the most difficult of infantry maneuvers. But we didn't know it, and in our innocence we expected it to go according to plan. We and the company we were replacing were cleverly and severely shelled: it was as if the Germans a few hundred feet away could see us in the dark and through the thick pine growth. When the shelling finally stopped, at about midnight, we realized that, although near the place we were supposed to be, until daylight we would remain hopelessly lost. The order came down to stop where we were, lie down among the trees, and get some sleep. We would finish the relief at first light. Scattered over several hundred yards, the two hundred and fifty of us in F Company lay down in a darkness so thick we could see nothing at all. Despite the terror of our first shelling (and several people had been hit), we slept as soundly as babes. At dawn I awoke, and what I saw all around were numerous objects I'd miraculously not tripped over in the dark. These

objects were dozens of dead German boys in greenish-gray uniforms, killed a day or two before by the company we were relieving. If darkness had hidden them from us, dawn disclosed them with open eyes and greenish-white faces like marble, still clutching their rifles and machine-pistols in their seventeen-year-old hands, fixed where they had fallen. . . . My adolescent illusions, largely intact to that moment, fell away all at once, and I suddenly knew I was not and never would be in a world that was reasonable or just.

—Paul Fussell, "My War"

This story of a night on the battlefield includes a vivid description of German corpses, and as the last sentence indicates, the author tells the story to express his personal feelings.

EXERCISE 8 Narrating Events In and Out of Chronological Order

This exercise has two parts. First, tell in strict chronological order the story of the most memorable trip you have taken. Then retell the story in non-chronological order, starting not with the beginning but with the part of the trip you remember best. Then work backward and forward from that point.

EXERCISE 9 Using Description in Narration

Use as much description as possible to expand the second version of the narrative you wrote for exercise 5.

EXERCISE 10 Using a Story to Make a Point

Tell a personal story that could be used to illustrate a general point about the experience of growing up. Then state the point itself.

6.4 Using Examples

You can develop almost any point by using examples. The author of the following passages uses a series of them to show that Canadians are much more law-abiding than Americans are.

When the great cattle drives of the American Midwest flowed north to railheads in Canada, cowboys adjusted to the shock of being asked to surrender their guns to the single policeman who met them at the border. One Mountie rode into Sitting Bull's camp a few days after the Battle at Little Big Horn, noted fresh American scalps and horses with U.S. cavalry brands, and advised Sitting Bull to obey Canadian laws or he, the Mountie, would deport the whole tribe. And Sitting Bull nodded.

During the Klondike gold rush of the nineties, the American town of Skagway in the Alaskan panhandle was run by a ruthless American gangster and gunfights in the streets were common. Across the border in Canada, Yukon mining towns were so law-abiding that a miner safely could leave his poke of gold in an unlocked cabin.

—June Callwood, "Portrait of Canada"

EXERCISE 11 Stating the Point Made by Examples

Each of the following passages offers one or more examples to explain or illustrate a point. State the point in a single short sentence, and briefly explain how the examples support it.

1. A hockey player rushing up ice travels at more than twenty-five miles an hour; a slap shot hurls a frozen rubber disc toward a goalie at one hundred miles an hour. Everything that happens in hockey—passing, stickhandling, checking, shooting—happens fast.   —Jeff Greenfield, "The Iceman Arriveth"
2. Curiosity is as clear and definite as any of our urges. We wonder what is in a sealed telegram or in a letter in which someone else is absorbed, or what is being said in the telephone booth or in low conversation.

—James Harvey Robinson, *The Mind in the Making*
3. Anyone who reads [ancient Greek stories] with attention discovers that even the most nonsensical take place in a world which is essentially rational and matter-of-fact. Hercules, whose life was one long combat against preposterous monsters, is always said to have had his home in the city of Thebes. The exact spot where Aphrodite was born of the foam could be visited by any ancient tourist; it was just offshore from the island of Cythera. The winged steed Pegasus, after skimming the air all day, went every night to a comfortable stable in Corinth. A familiar local habitation gave reality to all the mythical beings.

—Edith Hamilton, *Mythology*

EXERCISE 12 Using Examples

Develop the following point by adding a series of short examples to illustrate it.

Some of the most important things we need to know have to be learned outside a classroom.

6.5 Using Analogy

The first question we commonly ask about anything new and strange is "What's it like?" We ask the question because the only way we can understand what we don't know is by seeing its relation to what we do know. An **analogy** helps the reader to understand something vast, remote, abstract, or specialized by comparing it to something compact, familiar, concrete, or ordinary. Though a single analogy seldom extends to the length of a whole essay, it can be developed beyond a single sentence. Here are three examples.

1. The surface of the earth is like the skin of an orange, which cannot be spread out flat unless it is torn into strips. That is why flat maps of the whole earth always distort its appearance.
2. Starting college was like being a child in the middle of a candy store. Everywhere I turned I found an exotic treat, something I wanted to taste. But I couldn't taste everything, much less consume it all. A child who eats too much candy develops a stomach ache. A college student who joins too many clubs has too little time for course work, and must eventually suffer the pain of low grades. So I had to learn how to resist the sweet temptations of college life.
   —College student
3. Since the lattice-work molecular structure of metal normally vibrates, sending electrons through a copper wire by ordinary conduction is like shooting a bunch of pellets through a chain-link fence in the middle of an earthquake. Because the fence is shaking, some of the pellets hit the links or bounce off each other instead of passing through. But superconduction occurs when supercooling stops the vibration of the conductor. Superconduction, therefore, is like firing pellets through the fence when the earthquake is over. Because the fence stands still, all the pellets get through.

You can use analogy not just to explain, but to argue:

> Defenders of so-called "passive" euthanasia distinguish between killing a patient and letting one die. But whether euthanasia is morally right or wrong under any circumstances, allowing a preventable death to occur is morally no better than causing it. The practitioner of "passive" euthanasia is like a lifeguard allowing a man to drown. Let us suppose that the man is depressed or even suffering from an incurable disease, that he has asked the lifeguard to hold him under, and that the lifeguard has refused. If the lifeguard's duty is to save the lives of swimmers, letting the man sink to his death in deep water is not morally different from drowning him. Likewise, if a doctor's duty is to prolong the lives of patients, letting any one of them die is not morally different from giving a fatal injection.

Arguing by analogy takes special care. If the two things being compared don't correspond in essential ways, the argument will be misleading, unconvincing, or both. (For more on this point, see "False Analogy," section 7.4E.)

EXERCISE 13 Using Analogy

The federal government estimates that more than 26 million American adults are functionally illiterate, unable to read such things as recipes, warning labels, and want ads. Construct an analogy that begins, "To be functionally illiterate in our society is like . . ."

EXERCISE 14 Using Analogy

In the presidential campaign of 1988, one candidate proposed that no one should be granted a driver's license unless he or she had been tested for drugs. Construct an analogy that could be used to argue for or against this proposal.

6.6 Using Comparison and Contrast

While analogy connects two things that we normally think of as categorically different, such as an orange and the whole earth, comparison and contrast operate on two things that we normally think of as categorically alike: two cities, two schools, two board games, two means of transportation. The category containing the two things provides the *ground* of the comparison, and on this ground the writer draws lines of comparison: lines that connect the corresponding features of the two things. To plan an essay that would compare and contrast motorcycles with cars, for instance, you could begin by listing on separate lines such features as cost, convenience, safety, comfort, maneuverability, and contact with surroundings, and then noting on each line what different things are offered by cars and motorcycles.

Normally, writers compare and contrast two things in order to show what is distinctive about each of them. The following passage focuses on just one of the categories in which cars and motorcycles differ—contact with surroundings:

> You see things vacationing on a motorcycle in a way that is completely different from any other. In a car you're always in a compartment, and because you're used to it you don't realize that through that car window everything you see is just more TV. You're a passive observer and it is all moving by you boringly in a frame.
>
> On a cycle the frame is gone. You're completely in contact with it all. You're *in* the scene, not just watching it anymore, and the sense of presence is overwhelming. That concrete whizzing by five inches below your foot is the real thing, the same stuff you walk on, it's right there, so blurred you can't focus on it, yet you can put your foot down and touch it anytime, and the whole thing, the whole experience, is never removed from immediate consciousness.
> —Robert Pirsig, *Zen and the Art of Motorcycle Maintenance*

This is clearly more than a neutral account of contrasting features. Pirsig uses comparison and contrast not just to bring out differences, but to serve a persuasive aim: to show the reader—"you"—why riding a motorcycle is more stimulating than driving a car.

6.6A Block Structure and Alternating Structure

You can organize a comparison and contrast in either of two ways: in blocks or in regular alternation. In a block-structured comparison and contrast, each of the two things considered gets a block of sentences or an entire paragraph to itself. Pirsig, for instance, devotes most of his first paragraph to traveling by car and all of his second to traveling by motorcycle. But you can also compare and contrast two things by alternating back and forth between them. Consider this paragraph:

> Videotaped films offer many advantages over the celluloid kind. For one thing, they are often cheaper. If three or more people want to see a movie, they can usually rent a cassette version and a videotape machine for less than it would cost them all to go to a theater. Second, movie theaters offer nothing like the range of choice that videotapes provide. While the moviegoer has to take whatever the local theater happens to be playing, the videotape viewer can choose from hundreds of films, including foreign or X-rated items that will probably never find their way onto a local screen. Third, while movies are shown only at fixed times, videotapes can be seen whenever the viewer wants to see them, and just as often as he or she likes. Finally, videotapes allow the viewer a kind of privacy and comfort that no public movie theater can possibly furnish. The videotape viewer need not strain to hear a film over the buzz of the talkers sitting behind or to see it over the heads of the people sitting in front. Instead, he or she can enjoy it with just a few close friends at home.

Here the writer moves back and forth between the two things while also moving down a list of categories: cost, range of choice, timing, and privacy. But once again the writer is not simply listing differences. Comparison and contrast serve to explain the special attraction of videotape cassettes.

6.6B Writing an Essay of Comparison and Contrast

Because alternating structure continually reminds the reader that two things are being compared and contrasted, it can work well for the length of a paragraph. But steady alternation can become monotonous. For this reason, an essay that makes extensive use of comparison and contrast should combine alternation with block structure. The following essay not only illustrates this combination, but also shows how to use comparison and contrast in making an explanatory point:

WHY VIDEOTAPES WON'T KILL MOVIE THEATERS

[1] In the late forties and early fifties, when television first invaded American homes, self-appointed prophets grimly predicted the death of the movie theater. How could it possibly compete with TV? Why would people go out and pay to

see what they could get for nothing in their own homes? In recent years, the same kind of questions have been asked about videotape cassettes. Can movie theaters survive them? Can they compete with the more than five thousand commercial-free movies now available for home-viewing on videotape? The answer is yes, decisively. New movies continue to earn millions of dollars, and the most popular new ones earn hundreds of millions. The question, then, is not *whether* movie theaters can survive this latest threat, but *why* they are doing so.

[2] To see what they are up against, consider the advantages of videotape. First, it's frequently cheaper. If three or more people want to see a movie, they can usually rent a videocassette and recorder for less than it would cost them all to go to a theater, and if they happen to own a VCR, they can rent a cassette for less than the price of a single admission. Second, movie theaters offer nothing like the range of choice that videotapes provide. While the moviegoer has to take whatever the local theater happens to be showing, the videotape viewer can choose from hundreds of films, including foreign or X-rated items that will probably never find their way onto a local screen. Third, while movies are shown at fixed times only, videotapes can be seen whenever the viewer wants to see them, and just as often as he or she likes. Finally, videotapes allow the viewer a kind of privacy and comfort that no public movie theater can possibly furnish. The videotape viewer need not strain to hear a film over the buzz of the talkers sitting behind or to see it over the heads of the people sitting in front. Instead, he or she can enjoy it alone or with just a few close friends at home.

[3] Given all these advantages, why haven't videotapes already put movie theaters out of business? Why are theaters selling more tickets than ever before? Part of the answer is restlessness. Movie theaters offer us what no form of home entertainment—no matter how technologically sophisticated—will ever be able to provide: a chance to get out of the house, to get away from the kids, to leave behind the crumb-speckled carpet and the peeling wallpaper and the dirty dishes piled up in the sink. The fact that most people can make delicious dinners in the privacy of their own kitchens has not yet killed the restaurant business. Whatever we can eat, do, or see at home, all of us need an occasional night out.

[4] Movie theaters give us not only a night out but also a social experience. By forsaking the privacy of home, we escape its isolation. We go out to the movies in order to laugh, cry, and cheer with other people. Not every movie is like *The Rocky Horror Picture Show*, which invites us to dress up and act out

the film ourselves, but all movies shown in theaters do invite and excite a communal response. They make us feel part of a group.

[5] Besides getting us out of the house and into the company of others, movie theaters provide a visual experience far surpassing what videocassettes now offer. To the eye, a videotaped movie has two major drawbacks: scan lines and severe reduction. Television makes a video image by breaking down the subject into thousands of bits which are then transmitted across the screen in horizontal scan lines. These are always visible, especially at close range, and enlarging the screen simply enlarges the lines. The other thing that videotaped movies suffer from is contraction. Though older movies were made for near-square screens that are roughly proportional to those of television sets, the big, spectacular, wide-screen movies of recent years simply cannot fit on a TV screen. Lopping tops of heads and bottoms of legs, reducing long shots to medium shots and close-ups, cutting away material on either side of the central image, the videocassette literally shows only part of the movie. It cannot duplicate the original.

[6] For all of these reasons, I believe that movie theaters will survive the impact of videocassettes and video machines just as well as they have survived the impact of television. Nothing to be seen now on any television screen—no matter how big—equals the clarity, magnitude, and breadth of detail to be seen on the wide screen of a movie theater showing a good 35-millimeter print. Combined with the purely social attraction of moviegoing, this visual advantage will—for the time being anyway—keep movie theaters very much alive.

—Tony Walsh

This essay shows how comparison and contrast can be used to support the main point of an entire essay. In the introductory paragraph, the author clearly states his purpose, which is to show why movie theaters have successfully competed with videotaped films. To support this point, the author compares and contrasts the two kinds of film, using alternating structure to show the advantages of videotape (paragraph 2), then shifting to block structure for the social advantages of moviegoing (paragraphs 3 and 4) and the visual disadvantages of video viewing (paragraph 5). Since paragraph 5 also shows—by implication—the visual superiority of movie theater films, it nicely leads to the concluding paragraph 6, where the author summarizes the special advantages of moviegoing and thus completes his answer to the question originally raised.

EXERCISE 15 Comparing and Contrasting with Block Structure

Taking as a model the two paragraphs by Pirsig given on p. 117, use block structure to compare and contrast the two items in any one of the following pairs:

college/high school
good teaching/bad teaching
crime/terrorism
law/custom
typing/writing with a word processor
living with one's parents/living on one's own
pop rock/heavy metal

EXERCISE 16 Comparing and Contrasting with Alternating Structure

Taking as a model the example in section 6.6A (p. 118), use alternating structure to compare and contrast the two items in any one of the following pairs:

any small town/any large city
watching a movie/seeing a play
cycling/motorcycling
sculpting/painting
astronomy/astrology

EXERCISE 17 Using Comparison and Contrast to Explain a Point

Using comparison and contrast, write an essay that explains any one of the following:

1. why custom is sometimes more powerful than law
2. why growing up in a small town is better than growing up in a city, or vice versa
3. why video games are better than board games, or vice versa
4. why living on one's own is better than living with one's parents, or vice versa
5. why plays are more lifelike than movies, or vice versa
6. why running one's own business is better than working for someone else, or vice versa

6.7 Using Definitions

A definition explains a word or phrase. Definitions come in many different forms, and the least effective is the one that students most commonly use: quoting the dictionary ("Webster defines *freedom* as . . ."). Instead of quoting the dictionary, you can use one or more of the methods listed next.

1. Defining by synonym. A synonym is a word or phrase that means approximately the same thing as the word you are defining:

> *Apathetic* means "indifferent."
> *Prevaricate* means "lie."
> *Clandestinely* means "secretly."

The form of the synonym should correspond to the form of the word being defined. *Apathetic* doesn't mean "indifference," but "indifferent."

2. Defining by comparison, contrast, or analogy:

> The *plover* is a bird that lives on the shore, like the sandpiper. But the plover is usually fatter, and unlike the sandpiper, it has a short, hard-tipped bill.

> While burglary is the stealing of property from a place, *robbery* is the stealing of property from a person.

> A *lien* on a piece of property is like a leash on a dog. It's a way of legally attaching the property to someone who has a claim against the property owner.

3. Defining by function. If the word denotes a person or object, you can define it by saying what the person or object does:

> An *orthopedist* treats bone diseases.

> An *ombudsman* defends an individual in a conflict with an institution.

4. Defining by analysis. You can define a word by naming the class of the person or thing it denotes and then giving one or more distinctive features:

	CLASS	FEATURE
An *orthopedist* is	a doctor	who specializes in bones.
A *plover* is	a bird	that lives on the shore.
A *skylight* is	a window	set in the roof of a building.

5. Defining by example. You can define a word by giving examples after classifying the person or thing it denotes:

> A *crustacean* is a shelled creature such as a lobster, a shrimp, or a crab.
>
> A *planet* is a heavenly sphere such as Jupiter, Mercury, Mars, or Earth.

6. Defining by etymology. Etymology is the study of the roots of words. You can sometimes define a word by giving its root meaning and thus showing where it came from:

> *Intuition* comes from the Latin words *in* (meaning "in" or "into") and *tueri* (meaning "look" or "gaze"). Literally, therefore, it means a "looking inward."

A definition may use more than one of these methods, especially if it runs to a paragraph or longer. Here, for instance, is a definition of *interferon:*

> Interferon is a large hormone-like protein produced by the cells of all vertebrate animals. It was discovered in 1957 in Britain by virologists Alick Isaacs and Jean Lindenmann during their investigation of a curious phenomenon: people are almost never infected by more than one virus at a time. Seeking an explanation, the researchers infected cells from chick embryos with influenza virus. What they found was a substance that protected chick cells from both the flu and other viruses. Because it interfered with the infection process, it was dubbed interferon.   —*Time*, November 6, 1978

This definition combines analysis with comparison and with etymology of a sort—a little digging into the origin of the word. Interferon is a protein; that is its class. It is compared to hormones—described as "hormone-like"—and its name is said to have come from the word *interfere*.

You may want to use a word in a special or restricted sense. If so, you should clearly explain to your reader just what you mean by it. *Webster's New Collegiate Dictionary* defines *diagram* as "a line drawing made for mathematical or scientific purposes." But Kenneth Clark defines *diagram* somewhat differently—in order to explain how it functions in art:

> By "diagram" I mean a rational statement in a visible form, involving measurements, and usually done with an

ulterior motive. The theorem of Pythagoras is proved by a diagram. Leonardo's drawings of light striking a sphere are diagrams; but the works of Mondrian, although made up of straight
lines, are not diagrams, because they are not done in order to
prove or measure some experience, but to please the eye.
                              —Kenneth Clark, "The Blot and the Diagram"

Strikingly enough, Clark defines *diagram* not as a drawing but as
a "statement in a visible form," a way or proving or showing
something. Then he gives examples of what a diagram is and what
it is not. This definition is more than an incidental piece of clarification. It turns out to be essential to Clark's essay.

EXERCISE 18 Defining

Using at least two of the methods just described, define one of the
following words.

conservative	yuppie
suburbanite	rape
bigotry	sexism
feminist	holograph
ecology	neurotic
terrorist	gringo
hypocrite	amoeba

6.8 Explaining by Analyzing—Classification and Division

Probably you have been asked more than once to analyze a particular topic or problem. But just what does *analyze* mean? Essentially, analyzing a subject means breaking it into parts small enough
to handle. If you are asked to analyze democracy, for instance, you
can start by defining it as a system of government which depends
on the consent of the people. But in order to talk specifically about
"the people," you must separate them into categories or groups
such as voters and nonvoters, men, women, professionals, labor-
ers, industrial workers, farm workers, Southerners, Northerners,
Westerners, and the like. In so doing, you are using classification
and division.

Classification is the arrangement of objects, people, or ideas with shared characteristics into classes or groups. Whenever you speak of professors, sophomores, women, men, joggers, jocks, or grinds, you are grouping individuals together as a class because of one or more things they have in common. You can do the same with individual objects or ideas. You can classify motorcycles, cars, and trucks as "motor vehicles"; apples, pears, and oranges as "fruits"; monarchy, democracy, and plutocracy as "political systems." Classification is a way of imposing order on the hundreds of individual persons and things we have around us. We place these in general categories, just as we place ice cream, salt, coffee, chicken, cereal, milk, peanuts, tomatoes, eggs, lettuce, and Coke in one big shopping bag and speak of everything inside as "groceries."

Classification goes hand in hand with **division,** which is the act of cutting up one big group into several subgroups, If, for instance, you divide "fruit juices" into fresh, frozen, canned, and powdered, you have identified four different forms of juice. But instead of dividing the juices according to their forms, you could divide them according to their flavors: apple, orange, grapefruit, lemon, and so on. How you divide and classify depends on your purpose. When you come home with a bag of groceries, you commonly divide and classify them at first into just two groups: those that need refrigeration and those that don't.

In everyday living, then, everyone has to classify and divide in order to cope with a world of individual objects and people. And what is true in everyday living is also true in writing. Whenever you write about a group of people, objects, or ideas, you need a system of classifying and dividing them. Consider how the student author of this essay uses classification and division to explain Japanese society.

INSIDERS AND OUTSIDERS IN JAPANESE SOCIETY

[1] Many things about Japanese society puzzle Americans. But hardest of all for Americans to understand is the Japanese devotion to groups. Unlike Americans, the Japanese do not usually think of themselves as independent individuals. They act as members of a community, of a company, or at the very least of a family, which is the minimum social unit. Whatever the group, its very existence depends on the basic difference between insiders and outsiders. Understanding that difference is the key to understanding Japanese society as a whole, and the Japanese family in particular.

[2] The first thing to be understood about *insiders* and *outsiders* is that these are relative terms. Japanese society cannot be imagined as a tight little circle of insiders surrounded by a great big ring of outsiders. It is rather a world of bubbles. In each bubble is a group of people who think of each other as insiders and who look upon all the other people in all the other bubbles as outsiders. No one can be absolutely classified as either an insider or an outsider. To be inside one bubble is, inevitably, to be outside all the others.

[3] The system is complicated because one big bubble may sometimes contain many small ones. A big company, for instance, may include many departments or sections, and each of those sections is a bubble of insiders who work together closely, see each other often, and think of all other company workers as outsiders. Yet as soon as the insiders of a particular section think of their whole company in relation to a competitor, everyone who works for the company becomes an insider, and the outsiders are those who work for the competition.

[4] The opposition between insiders and outsiders becomes still more evident when we turn from Japanese companies to Japanese families. The Japanese family does not merge with other families, or with society at large. While American families often entertain large numbers of casual acquaintances, Japanese families seldom open their doors to anyone but insiders: family members or relatives. On the rare occasions when a close friend of the family is invited, he or she thereby becomes an insider—in effect, one of the family. Everyone else remains an outsider, and is literally kept outside the family home.

[5] The opposition between insiders and outsiders also explains why the actual structure of the Japanese family differs so much from the way it appears to the outside world, especially to Americans. Most Americans think the typical Japanese family is totally ruled by the husband, with the wife no more than a servant. In fact, the modern Japanese family is ruled by the wife. It is she who takes all of her husband's salary, oversees all household repairs and expenditures, and supervises the education of the children. Inside the family, she has absolute authority.

[6] Yet as soon as the family confronts an outsider, the husband plays the ruler. A perfect example of this switch is what happens when a Japanese family goes out to eat. Before the family leaves the house, the wife gives the husband enough

cash to pay the bill. When the family members sit down in the restaurant, the wife decides what the children will eat and often what her husband will eat as well, overruling him if she finds his choices too expensive. But as soon as the waiter arrives, the husband orders for the entire family as if he had made all the choices himself. In so doing, he represents the family for the eyes of an outsider, and so long as those eyes are watching, he is in charge. When he finishes paying the check with the money that his wife has allowed him, she and the children bow to him and say, "Thank you for a good meal, Father."

[7] To understand Japanese society, then, one must understand both the power of the group and the distinction between insiders and outsiders. Since all members of a group are insiders, they can act as individuals among themselves, arguing with each other until they agree or until one of them—the wife in the case of a family group—decides for all. But to outsiders they present a united front. Once they turn from confronting each other to confronting the outside world, insiders cease to be individuals and become part of a group which determines what their public roles will be.

—Rick Kurihara

Throughout this essay, the writer uses classification and division to explain Japanese society. The basic distinction between insiders and outsiders allows him to divide and classify all individuals in relation to groups, and thus to explain how group mentality in Japan governs individual action.

This essay also shows how different means of exposition can be made to work together. Besides classifying and dividing, the author compares and contrasts Japanese society with American society in paragraphs 1 and 4, uses the analogy of bubbles to explain Japanese groups in paragraphs 2 and 3, and illustrates Japanese family life with an example in paragraph 6.

EXERCISE 19 Using Classification and Division to Explain Yourself

Write an essay in which you (1) name any group to which you belong; (2) explain what the members of the group have in common; (3) divide the group into two or more subgroups; (4) explain each of the subgroups; (5) explain whether or not you belong to any one of them; (6) explain what this analysis reveals about you.

6.9 Explaining a Process

A **process** is a sequence of actions or events that lead or are supposed to lead to a predictable result. The way you explain a process depends on your purpose. If you want to teach someone else how to do it, you must be careful to give every step, as in this explanation of how to replace spark plugs:

> To replace worn plugs, you need three tools that you can buy at any automotive parts store: a ratchet wrench with a short extension handle, a spark plug socket, and a spark plug gauge.
>
> The most important thing to know about spark plugs is that you have to remove and replace them *one at a time.* If you take them all out at once, you will have to disconnect all of their wires at the same time, and you will probably not remember which plugs they came from. Since each plug has its own wire and since the car will not run if the wires are mixed up, you should never have more than one wire disconnected at any one time.
>
> The owner's manual for your car will tell you where the spark plugs are. Once you have located them, you must do five things with each plug in turn. First, disconnect the wire attached to it. Second, with the spark plug socket placed over the plug and the ratchet wrench in the socket, remove the plug by turning the wrench counterclockwise. Third, use the spark plug gauge to measure the size of the little gap in the electrode—the small open square of metal that sticks up out of the threaded tube at one end of the spark plug. If the gap is too big, the electrode is worn, and the plug must be replaced. Fourth, insert the old plug or a new one by turning it clockwise with your fingers until it sticks, and then using the wrench to turn it a quarter of a circle more. Fifth, reconnect the wire that belongs to that particular plug.
>
> —Jim Robb

This is a **teaching** explanation. It moves step by step, taking nothing for granted, and even anticipates possible missteps: *never have more than one wire disconnected at any one time.* The author also describes the *electrode* for readers who may not know what it is.

If you wish only to help your reader understand a process rather than perform it, your explanation need not cover all the steps. For example, here is an explanation of how a caterpillar becomes a butterfly:

> In contact with the proper food on leaving the egg, the caterpillar begins to eat immediately and continues until it has increased its weight hundreds of times. On each of the first three segments of the body is a pair of short legs ending in a sharp claw. These legs correspond to the six legs of the adult insect. In addition, the caterpillar has up to ten short, fleshy feet called prolegs, which are shed before it changes form. The insect passes its pupal stage incased in comparatively rigid integuments [layers] that form a chrysalis.
>
> Most butterfly chrysalides remain naked, unlike those of the moth, which have a protective cocoon. Breathing goes on through an air opening while the complete adult, or imago, develops. Wings, legs, proboscis, even the pigment in the scales, form in the tight prison of the chrysalis.
>
> At maturity, the chrysalis splits its covering and wriggles out as an imago, or perfect insect. Hanging from a leaf or rock, it forces blood, or haemolymph, into the veins of its wet wings, straightening them to their normal span. Soon the wings are dry, and the insect flies into a life of nectar drinking and courtship.
>
> —"Butterfly," *Funk & Wagnalls New Encyclopedia*

This is a **reporting** explanation. The writer describes the stages through which the insect passes, but does not explain everything about its transformation. The writer is trying to help us understand an overall process—not teach us how to become butterflies ourselves.

EXERCISE 20 Composing a Teaching Explanation

Write a teaching explanation of any simple process that you know well and that can be taught in writing—such as changing a tire, making a bed, frying an egg, or getting from one place to another. When you have finished, see if someone else can actually perform the process by following your instructions.

EXERCISE 21 Composing a Reporting Explanation

Write a reporting explanation of any process you know well, such as climbing a cliff, painting a picture, making a clay pot, taking or developing a good photograph. If you use any specialized terms, be sure to define them as you go along.

6.10 Explaining Cause and Effect

Since any situation or event can provoke questions about its causes, its effects, or both, one good way of explaining anything is to raise such questions. You can ask about causes, for instance. Why are more than 26 million adult Americans functionally illiterate? Why have the Republicans won all but one presidential election since 1964? Why have many states passed laws that make English an official language? Alternatively, or in addition, you can ask about effects. What has the succession of Republican presidents done for the United States? How does functional illiteracy affect an adult's life? If superconductors become commercially feasible, how will they change the way we live? What will happen if the "greenhouse effect" really is raising the temperature of the earth?

In the physical sciences, questions about causes and effects sometimes have simple, straightforward answers. Scientists know, for instance, that heat makes gases expand, that salt raises the boiling point of water, that chlorine disrupts ozone molecules, and so on. But inside as well as outside science, many questions about causes and effects in science and elsewhere elicit no single answer. For a particular situation or event there may be several causes, several effects, or both.

In such cases, however, you can strengthen your essay by connecting the causes or effects as much as possible. Consider this editorial on why the percentage of working women among mothers of children under one rose from 31 percent to 51 percent in the years from 1976 to 1987:

Most of Them Work Because They Must

[1] For many women with families, a job outside the home is nothing new. Those from lower-income families have always been under pressure to bring home a second income. What is new is the entry into the labor force of women who have young children and whose wages are not always necessary to keep the wolf from the door.

[2] Few educated Americans of either sex would choose to reverse this social revolution even if they could. It began as highly educated women with no financial need challenged social norms to join the white-collar elite. Their success has made it easier for middle-class women to break out of "women's work" and aspire to fulfilling careers.

[3] Equality is still far from real; women typically earn 20 to 30 percent less than men, even after adjusting for age, education and hours worked. But even the prospect of equality creates a benign impact on the culture of the work force.

[4] Even so, there are blunter reasons for millions of middle-class women having deserted housework for office and factory work. Their entry into the paid work force reflects the special obstacles young families must overcome to hold onto the middle-class living standard taken for granted by their parents. For these women and their families, the 1970's and 80's have been a time in which they have had to run just to stay in place.

[5] What explains their difficulties? The social acceptability of divorce plays a part. Divorced middle-class women, as well as poor women, often must assume financial responsibility for children. According to census figures, just half of all divorced mothers receive child support; and for those, the average annual payment in 1985 was a pitiful $2,500.

[6] But as Frank Levy, an economist at the University of Maryland and the author of "Dollars and Dreams," points out, the pressure on women to work also reflects deep problems in the economy. Between 1947 and 1973, the average worker's inflation-adjusted earnings rose 61 percent, reflecting a rise in productivity. Since 1973, however, productivity has stagnated and average earnings have fallen 15 percent. Family incomes have remained virtually constant only because many more women have joined the paid work force.

[7] Even these pre-tax figures mask some inequities imposed on women of child-bearing age. Social Security taxes have risen sharply, reflecting massive income transfers from young families to old. And younger families, who had not bought homes by the early 1970's, are being ravaged by housing costs. In 1973, mortgage payments represented 21 percent of an average 30-year-old male's income. In 1984, the figure was 44 percent.

[8] The explosive increase of wives and mothers in the labor force reflects a welcome change in social attitudes: Society is beginning to treat women as equals in the workplace. They can now aspire to work in any occupation because they want to. But that fact is harshly linked to another: Women who work, even in the most fulfilling professional jobs, do so because they have to.

—"Most of Them Work Because They Must." Editorial,
New York Times, 19 June 1988.

This editorial cites various causes and effects of the "new" situation defined in paragraph 1. The causes begin in paragraph 2, which indicates that financially secure, highly educated women joined the white-collar elite. As a result or effect of their success, middle-class women could "aspire to fulfilling careers" and—in paragraph 3—relish the prospect of economic equality. But paragraph 4 introduces a new set of causes. Young families have trouble maintaining the standard of living established by their parents, and this situation has causes of its own: divorce leaves many women ill-supported (paragraph 5); the average drop in earnings since 1973 has cut family incomes generally (paragraph 6); Social Security taxes and mortgage payments have both risen sharply (paragraph 7). The concluding paragraph draws all of these causes together into one general statement: "Women who work . . . do so because they have to."

EXERCISE 22 Explaining Cause and Effect

1. Identify what you believe are the causes of littering, and then explain how we could use our understanding of those causes to combat it.
2. Discuss the effects of drugs on American family life or on any segment of the American population.
3. Explain the causes or effects of any historical event that you know about.
4. The "greenhouse effect" is a global warming. It will occur when the sun's infrared radiation is trapped by increased levels of carbon dioxide in the atmosphere—an increase caused by the burning of fossil fuels. If the global warming occurs, the chart facing outlines what it will probably do to the Southeastern United States. Using this chart as a guide and stimulus, explain the effects of global warming in at least three of the six categories shown. Write one paragraph for each category discussed.

**PROJECTED GREENHOUSE EFFECTS ON THE
SOUTHEASTERN UNITED STATES**

Agriculture
Climate change could:
— decrease in corn and soybean yields in
  warmer areas; mixed results elsewhere
— decrease cultivated acreage
— increase need for irrigation, if rainfall
  declines
— increase pest infestations

Forests
Higher temperature could result in:
— significant dieback of southern forests
  in 30 to 80 years
— regeneration of species becoming
  difficult
— conversion of some forests to
  grassland
— forest declines evident in 30 to 80
  years

Water Resources
Increased temperature and changes in
precipitation:
— produce uncertain effects for water
  resource availability

— could affect water quality and flood
  risks
— cause levels in some recreational lakes
  to drop

Sea Level Rise
Rising sea level could result in:
— inundation of a significant proportion
  of the region's coastal wetlands
— flooding of some dry land areas
— significant costs for protecting coastal
  resources

Fisheries
— higher water temperatures and rising
  sea level could reduce fish and
  shellfish populations

Electricity
— higher temperatures will increase the
  demand for electricity

—Bill McKibben, "Is the World Getting Hotter?"
New York Review of Books, 9 December 1988.

6.11 Combining Methods of Exposition

When you are learning to write, you will find it useful to practice
the various methods of development separately. But good writing
usually combines several of them, as in the following essay:

WHAT IS PHOTOGRAPHY?

[1] Most of us think of the camera as an instrument of precision. It catches a scene in an instant, a gesture in a second, an expression in a moment, recording these with absolute fidelity for ever and ever—or so the advertisements would have us believe. But if the camera takes the picture, we have reason to ask whether photography can be an art, whether it actually requires anything more creative than the clicking of a shutter. Such questions bring us to the fundamental query: What is photography?

Explanation of process

[2] The answer has as many sides as a professional photographer can find in a face. To the beginner, it is simple and pedestrian: photography is a succession of petty details. First, he or she must choose and buy a camera from the seemingly infinite variety of models available; then decide on film, whether color or black and white; then learn how to load and wind, how to set the shutter, the exposure meter, and the lens for proper light and focus in each photograph; then snap the pictures, one by one, have them developed, and *finally* see the results. Some of the more ingenious new cameras have eliminated one or more of these steps, but for most beginners, this succession of petty, troublesome details is what photography is all about.

Comparison and contrast

[3] For all this trouble, in fact, the beginner and the ordinary amateur see the purpose of photography as primarily a matter of record. More observant than the human eye, they think, more tenacious than the human memory, the camera remembers baby as mother never could, meticulously transcribing every wrinkle of his little jowls and every bubble of his drool for the doubtful immortality of a family album. In this seizing of an instant, there seems to be scarcely more creativity (and possibly less) than is required of a Xerox machine. The beginner seldom thinks that photography is an art.

Classification and division

[4] And yet an art is precisely what photography can be—an art with its own rules, distinct from photo-copying and equally distinct from movie-making. For movie-making is an art compounded of many arts: writing, acting, and most especially editing—what Alfred Hitchcock once called "the putting together of pieces of film." But what Lessing said of poetry and painting may also be said of cinema and photography. Cinema is the movement of many pictures, and like poetry is essentially temporal, recreating the flow of time. Photography is the freezing of movement, and like painting is essentially spatial. It stops time.

[5] I speak, therefore, only of the individual picture—of one moment captured in time. And here we must remember that the camera is an instrument. The camera will not take a picture for us, any more than the carpenter's hammer will nail up a house for him. It is nothing more or less than a tool. While travelling through Europe some years ago, I bought in Paris a camera that functioned beautifully. But I was something less than a master of my newly acquired device. When I expected to get the facade of the Paris Opera House, I caught a piece of fire hydrant; when I expected to capture the unforgettable brilliance of the Côte d'Azur, I got a patch of gray and unidentifiable coastline; when I sought to record the lights of Florence reflected one evening on the River Arno, I got nothing.

Personal experience

Personal examples

[6] In part these were the blunders of a beginner, untutored in the technical subtleties of focus and exposure. But fundamentally they were failures in the discipline of form, shape, and arrangement that only a carefully ordered perspective can produce. Immanuel Kant is unintelligible to me most of the time, but I know what he means when he says that the eye creates what it sees. There is no such thing as a purely objective scene or landscape; there is only an odd collection of colors and forms, blended into a unified whole by the cohesive vision of the observer. It is he or she who creates the scene from his or her particular viewpoint, who fixes the relation between light and shadow, background and foreground, angle and curve.

Cause and effect

[7] This work of composition is what makes photography a creative art. Its instruments are admittedly more precise and more sophisticated than those of the painter, and they save a good deal of labor. But they can render no more than is actually seen or felt through the eye of the photographer, who catches with creative vision a moment of pain, fear, hatred, comedy, or pure beauty of form and light. Such captures are the products not of luck but of design, and in this the photographer is one with the artist of canvas and brush.

Comparison and contrast

—Tony Walsh

To begin with, the whole essay is a piece of definition—an attempt to define *photography*. But the writer uses a variety of methods to develop the definition. In paragraph 2, he explains the process of taking a photograph; in paragraph 3, he compares the camera to the human eye and memory; in paragraph 4, he classifies photography and painting as spatial arts, distinguishing them from the temporal arts, such as movie-making and poetry; in paragraph 5, he cites personal experience and several examples to show that the camera is only a tool; in paragraph 6, using cause and effect, he explains why the pictures he took were failures; and in paragraph 7, he uses comparison again to clinch the point that photography is a creative art.

EXERCISE 23 Combining Methods of Development

Using at least three of the methods of development that we have discussed in this chapter, write an essay in which you explain to a high school senior the operation of any team, club, or organization at your college.

7
Persuasion
and Argument

Up to now we have focussed chiefly on two kinds of writing—expressive and explanatory. Both require some attention to the reader. Once you move from freewriting to composing an essay, once you start to write for a reader rather than just for yourself, you must consider what the reader feels and what the reader needs to know.

Persuasion demands special attention to the reader's needs, for persuasion is the art of leading other people to do something or to believe something without compelling them to do so. So long as you think that your readers need only *information,* you will aim to explain. But once you realize that you are taking a side on a controversial question, once you realize that some of your readers may oppose, resist, or question what you affirm or recommend, you should aim to persuade. You should aim to make your reader see why one answer to a controversial or debatable question is better than another.

Everything that helps to explain can also help to persuade. Pat Jordan's description of Palatka (p. 109) could be used to persuade readers that Florida is anything *but* a tropical paradise; Paul Fussell's story of a night on a battlefield (pp. 112–113) could be used to show that war kills youthful idealism; Robert Pirsig actually uses comparison and contrast to show that motorcycling is much more exciting than driving a car (p. 117). So what does it mean to persuade? Persuading means earning the assent of your readers by appealing to their feelings, their reason, or both.

Advertising often makes a simple, straightforward appeal to the feelings. Over a big color picture of a farming family gathered around a tractor, a recent insurance ad proclaims:

There are people more famous we insure.
But none more important.

Under the picture the ad continues:

For over a hundred years, we've tried to keep personal insurance from becoming too impersonal.

When you do business with———, it's with one of our independent agents. So when you have a question about auto, health, home or life insurance, you deal with someone who is close to you and your situation.

You can easily find an independent———agent in the Yellow Pages.

———is one of the world's largest insurance companies, a size that doesn't diminish our big concern for the individual.

As in many ads, picture and text together seek to persuade readers that the advertiser cares about each of them. The means of persuasion are essentially emotional. With the family picture reinforcing the point, the reader is told that the company deals in "personal insurance," that the company agent will be "someone who is close to you and your situation." The tone is warm and reassuring; the statement is the verbal equivalent of a friendly handshake. The ad offers no evidence that the company cares about individuals. It simply tries to make you feel that the company cares.

Since feelings play a part in the formation of almost every opinion, you need to understand as well as you can the feelings of your readers. But you can seldom persuade readers by appealing to their feelings alone. If you respect their intelligence, you will also appeal to their minds. And to do that, you must construct an argument.

7.1 What Is an Argument?

We commonly think of an argument as a quarrel—a shouting match in which tempers flare and necks turn red. But strictly speaking, an argument is not a quarrel at all. It is simply a rational means of persuasion. It differs from exposition because it seeks to convince, not just to explain, and it differs from emotional persuasion because it seeks to convince by appealing to the mind. To see these differences more clearly, consider the following three passages:

1. The bear population of Maine is 7,000 to 10,000 animals, and the annual "harvest," or kill, averages 930. State wildlife biologists estimate that the number killed falls short by 120 of the "allowable harvest," i.e., "the harvest level that takes only the annual increase and does not affect the population size."
   —Jonathan Evan Maslow, "Stalking the Black Bear"

2. Every year, bloodthirsty hunters go into the Maine woods and ruthlessly shoot to death hundreds of bears. The hunters care nothing for the suffering they cause, for the blood they spill, or for the harm they do to creatures who have done no harm to them. Hunters kill for a thrill, and that is all they care about. No one seems to care anything for the bears.

3. Though some people may think hunting is nothing more than wholesale and wanton destruction of living creatures, hunters actually help to ensure the health and survival of wildlife. Take bear-hunting in Maine as a case in point. Out of the 7,000 to 10,000 bears that roam the Maine woods, hunters kill an average of 930 a year. State wildlife biologists estimate that this is 120 fewer than the annual population increase. If the bear population were allowed to grow unchecked, it would increase well over 1,000 a year, and the food available for any one bear would correspondingly decrease. By killing an average of 930 bears a year, hunters keep the annual increase down, and therefore help to ensure an adequate food supply for the bear population as a whole.

These three passages concern the same topic, but they treat it in fundamentally different ways. The first is **exposition;** it calmly explains the relation between the number of bears born and the number killed in Maine each year. The second is **emotional persuasion;** it tries to make the reader feel outrage at hunters and pity for bears. The third is **argument;** it tries to prove that hunting is beneficial to wildlife.

Consider first the difference between passage 2 and passage 3. Passage 2 relies on words like *bloodthirsty* to stir the reader's feelings; passage 3 relies on facts, figures, and authoritative estimates to gain the reader's agreement. Side by side, the two passages reveal the fundamental difference between emotional persuasion and argument. Purely emotional persuasion may well appeal to a reader who already tends to feel the way the writer does, but it is unlikely to change an opponent's mind. Words like *bloodthirsty* will simply antagonize the reader who likes to hunt. On the other hand, the argument of passage 3 is thought-provoking rather than antagonizing. It won't persuade all readers, but it will give even fervent conservationists something to think about. To combat such an argument effectively, conservationists would have to challenge its facts, figures, and estimates in a manner such as this:

> 4. Hunting advocates try to justify the killing of bears by arguing that it limits the annual increase in the bear population and thereby helps to ensure an adequate food supply for the bears that remain. But this argument rests on the assumption that wildlife biologists can reliably estimate the size of the population increase, which is said to be 120 more than the number of bears killed each year. Can we be sure it is? If estimates of the bear population range from 7,000 to 10,000, how can we accurately calculate the annual increase in that population? Do we even know how many bears die each year of natural causes? If we don't know that, we cannot determine what the net annual increase in the bear population would be in the absence of hunters. And even if we knew this figure exactly, it would not tell us just how well an unregulated bear population would manage to feed itself. Without hunters threatening them, bears might well become more venturesome and thus more successful in their quest for food. We can hardly be certain, therefore, that bears are better off with hunters than they would be without them.

This is an argument designed to combat the argument made in passage 3. Like passage 2, it aims to convince the reader that bear-hunting is unjustified. But unlike passage 2, it does not appeal to the reader's feelings. It does not try to stir pity for bears or outrage at hunters. Instead, it calmly exposes the weaknesses in the pro-hunting argument, and thus appeals to the reader's mind.

Just as argument differs from emotional persuasion, so also does it differ from exposition. In exposition, every statement is offered as a matter of accepted fact. In argument, only some statements are offered as matters of fact, and these are given as reasons to make us believe assertions or claims. For example, the assertion in passage 3 that "hunters actually help to ensure the health and survival of wildlife" is disputable and needs defending. Instead of assuming that we will believe it, the writer must give us reasons for doing so.

An effective argument, then, is the product of an imaginary conversation between the writer and the reader. In defending a claim, the writer imagines the questions that a skeptical reader might ask about it, and then proceeds to answer those questions. Questions thus help to generate the three basic parts of any argument:[†]

> 1. CLAIM: Hunters help to ensure the health and survival of bears.
>   QUESTION: How can you say that?
> 2. EVIDENCE: They limit the growth of the bear population.
>   QUESTION: So what?
> 3. ASSUMPTION: Fewer bears mean more food per bear.

Arguments originate from *claims*, which are statements that need defending. You have surely seen quarrels start this way: somebody makes a remark that somebody else challenges, and the first speaker then backs up the remark or backs down. But unlike the talker suddenly caught off guard, the writer of an argument anticipates questions and tries to answer them. To write an effective argument, in fact, the writer should imagine his or her readers as a live audience: an audience ready to ask for clarification, to demand specific facts, to call for explanations. As the above illustration shows, the answers to such an audience come in two basic forms: evidence and assumptions.

The *evidence* for a claim includes the specific facts or data on which the claim rests. The short sentence given as evidence in the above sequence is the barest statement of fact. To be accepted as true, it must be developed with the kind of detail provided in passage 3, which gives figures for a particular locality and cites authorities (wildlife biologists). But statements of fact can often be challenged, as passage 4 shows, especially when they depend on estimates rather than precise measurement. To build an effective argument, therefore, you must be sure of your facts.

---

† This analysis of argumentation comes in part from Stephen Toulmin, *The Uses of Argument* (Cambridge: Cambridge UP, 1958). But where Toulmin uses *grounds* we use *evidence*, and where he uses *warrant* we use *assumption*.

Besides evidence, most arguments require one or more *assumptions*, which are statements that the writer takes for granted. The assumption binds the evidence to the claim. It answers the second of two questions that can be asked about any piece of evidence: 1) Is it true? 2) Does it have any *connection* to the claim? When you've answered the first question, you may still have to answer the second—unless you can be sure that your readers already know the answer. If you were arguing, for instance, that birth-control pills can help underdeveloped countries, you might need to furnish only evidence that the pills had actually reduced the growth of certain populations. You might not need to state the widely shared assumption that limiting population growth increases the amount of food per person. But as passage 4 shows, environmentalists would probably question the corresponding assumption about bears and food. In such a case you would not only need to state your assumption; you might have to treat it as a claim and defend it.

Rational persuasion, then, depends on how well an argument is constructed: how firm the evidence for its claim is, how well the assumption binds the evidence to the claim, and how credible the assumption is. To show more clearly how arguments work, we will first consider the use of evidence and then (in section 7.3) the use of assumptions in arguments guided by the rules of logic.

7.2 Supporting Claims with Evidence

Effective arguments support general claims with specific evidence. The general claim or proposition is essential because it tells the reader what you are arguing for, what you want him or her to believe: solar power can solve the energy crisis; presidents should have longer terms; parents should share equally the responsibility for raising their children. But unless the reader is ready to accept your general claim at once, you will need to support it with evidence. Evidence includes specific facts and examples, figures and statistics, and the identification of sources and authorities. We treat each category of evidence in turn.

7.2A Giving Facts and Examples

Compare these three arguments—all written by first-term college freshmen:

1. My feeling is that all people are equal. Neither sex is superior to the other. In the times of today, men and women both have an equal opportunity for education. They can pursue any career that they are qualified for. Schools are now getting away from trying to make certain things for boys and vice versa. Children are growing up as equals.

2. Male athletes are stronger, faster, and tougher than their female counterparts. The men's record for the hundred-yard dash is about a full second faster than the women's. World records for the mile, marathon, high jump, discus, and all other track and field sports are much better on the male side than the female side. In tennis, a top male pro will always beat a top woman pro, and the same applies to swimming, skiing, basketball, hockey, and countless other sports.

3. There are differences between men and women, but none that make either sex inferior. Athletic performance is a case in point. A major study by a West German doctor has shown that because of different skeletal leverage in men and women, muscles of identical strength will produce about 5 percent greater apparent strength in men. In sports such as running and mountaineering, however, women show greater endurance and resistance to stress. Several years ago, when I assisted a friend running the Boston marathon, I noticed that although many of the male runners were literally collapsing at the finish or at least in need of help, the women rarely needed any help at all.

These three arguments reveal opposing points of view. While writers 1 and 3 claim that the sexes are equal, writer 2 claims that they are not. But these three writers differ in more than their objectives. They differ also in their argumentative methods.

Writer 1 makes general claims that are not supported by specific and relevant facts. The statement about equal opportunity in education—even if the reader accepts it as fact—does not necessarily support the claim that "all people are equal." The fact that women *may* attend colleges and professional schools does not prove that they do indeed attend such schools in the same numbers as men do or that they perform as well as men once they get there. Writer 2 is considerably more effective because, to begin with, his objective is much more specific. Instead of saying simply that men and women are equal or unequal, he limits the argument to athletics; and instead of saying simply that men are better athletes than women, he contends that they are "stronger, faster, and tougher," and then proceeds to cite specific evidence for this point.

Of course the evidence is not entirely convincing. By itself, the fact that the fastest male can outrun the fastest female does not really prove that men are generally faster than women, nor do the other world records cited answer this question. Nevertheless, this writer does give the reader something to chew on. Instead of dealing in unsupported claims, he offers specific facts as evidence.

The writer of passage 3 does likewise. Though there is hardly enough evidence here to prove that the sexes are equal, this claim for their equality is much better supported—and hence more convincing—than that of the first passage.

The persuasive force of an argument generally grows with the weight of evidence presented. See how this argument gathers power as it gathers facts and examples to support its opening claim:

4. Nuclear power plants are fundamentally unsafe. The history of nuclear power is a list of major accidents and near catastrophes. At Windscale, England, in 1957, a fire and a partial meltdown of a nuclear core spread radioactivity across miles of pastureland, and thousands of gallons of contaminated cows' milk had to be dumped. In 1966 another partial meltdown occurred at Unit One of the Fermi plant near Detroit. In 1970 fifty thousand gallons of radioactive water and steam escaped from the reactor vessel of the huge Commonwealth Edison plant near Chicago. At Browns Ferry, Alabama, in 1975, a single candle started a fire at a nuclear power plant that burned for seven hours, caused 150 million dollars' worth of damage and loss to the plant, and— according to some experts—very nearly caused a catastrophic release of radiation. Even after the Rasmussen report supposedly analyzed everything that could go wrong with a nuclear reactor, a malfunctioning water gauge led to yet another near meltdown at Three Mile Island, Pennsylvania, in 1979. Finally, in April 1986, an explosion and fire in the graphite core of a nuclear reactor at Chernobyl in the Soviet Ukraine caused more than 25 fatalities, spread radioactive dust over much of Europe, contaminated food supplies in Scandinavia, and may lead to more than 30,000 cancer-related deaths over the next 70 years. Taken together, all of these accidents show that the risks we run in operating nuclear power plants are intolerably high.

By themselves, facts will not always make an argument persuasive. As we explain below (section 7.3), you must know how to formulate an assumption that can link this evidence with your claim. But evidence is essential to the success of any argument, and the more you can make specific statements that are both reliable and relevant to your claim, the more persuasive you will be.

7.2B Citing Figures and Statistics

Figures and statistics help to make an argument persuasive by providing what appears to be "hard" evidence. If, for instance, you want to argue that hunters help bears, you can strengthen your case by stating that hunters hold the net growth of the bear population to 120 each year. If you want to argue that family life has significantly changed since 1950, you can state that the proportion of working women who are mothers of children under 6 rose from 11.9 percent in 1950 to 56.8 percent in 1987. If you want to argue that American highways have grown steadily more dangerous in the past forty years, you can state that auto fatalities in 1987 were 13,000 higher than they were in 1945.

But figures and statistics alone will not make your argument for you. If the figures on the bear population are only an estimate, this "hard" piece of evidence turns soft. If the number of automobile fatalities has risen since 1945, what about the number of cars and drivers on the road? If they've risen also—and they have—the number of fatalities doesn't tell the whole story. Other figures tell a different story: the *rate* of fatalities per 100 million vehicle miles actually *fell* after 1945, from 9.8 in 1946 to 2.5 in 1987. The meaning of the number of fatalities at Chernobyl must likewise be interpreted. If more than 25 persons were killed by the Chernobyl explosion, does this mean that every nuclear power plant is a disaster waiting to happen? Not necessarily, since (as a matter of fact) the design of the Chernobyl reactor is fundamentally different from the design of most commercial reactors in the West.

To make figures and statistics serve as evidence, then, you must clearly explain what they mean and you may also have to establish their reliability. Explaining what they mean requires showing how they support your claim, or what *connects* them to your claim. (For more on this point, see section 7.3 below.) Establishing their reliability often means citing the source or authority from which you got them, as shown next.

7.2C Citing Sources and Authorities

Some statements of fact can stand all by themselves. In argument 4, for instance, the statements made about specific accidents at various nuclear power plants are matters of public record readily available to all, and the worst accident mentioned is universally known through scores of reports. There is no need to cite any particular source for the basic facts about what happened, such as the fact that more than 25 persons were killed.

Statistics, however, are not matters of fact. They are products of calculation. Since they must be compiled by often complicated methods requiring special expertise, their reliability depends on their source, and their source should be cited along with the statistics themselves. You can *informally* cite a source in either of two ways.

> Source cited in passing:
> According to the U.S. Bureau of the Census, the proportion of working women who are mothers of children under 6 rose from 11.9 percent in 1950 to 56.8 percent in 1987.

> Source cited in parenthesis:
> The rate of fatalities per 100 million vehicle miles fell from 9.8 in 1946 to 4.24 in 1973 (National Safety Council).

For detailed guidance on *formally* citing a printed source, see Chapter 35.

Even more than statistics and figures, estimates and opinions depend for their reliability on who provides them. Named authorities carry more persuasive weight than unnamed ones. If "some experts" (in argument 4) say that a fire at a nuclear power plant "nearly caused a catastrophic release of radiation," how do we know they're right? How do we know that other experts would agree with them? When you cite estimates and opinions, you should consider these four questions:

1. Who is the authority? Is he or she an unnamed "expert" or a named, established specialist in a particular field? If you were writing an argument about infants born with spina bifida, for instance, and you cited the words of Dr. David G. McCone, they would carry the authority of a pediatric neurosurgeon who has treated hundreds of infants born with that disease. Likewise, if you were writing an argument about nuclear power plants and you cited the words of Norman Rasmussen, they would carry the authority of a professor of nuclear engineering at M.I.T.

2. Is the authority speaking on a topic in his or her field of expertise? If a specialist in the study of alcohol says that a driver with a blood alcohol content of .05 percent is twice as likely to have an accident as a driver who is perfectly sober, that statement carries the weight of special authority. But if the alcohol expert says that teenagers should not be allowed to drive until they are eighteen, he or she no longer speaks with special authority, because the topic has changed.

3. Given the facts available on a particular question, can any expert answer it with certainty? Predictions are notoriously unreliable, and experts on some subjects—the stock market, for instance—frequently miscalculate what will happen. No amount of authority can give to a prediction or an estimate the weight of an established fact.

4. Does any other expert agree with the one you cite? Experts often disagree. If the expert you cite is alone in his or her testimony, it will carry less weight than testimony backed by other experts.

CITING AUTHORITIES: IN BRIEF

You should consider these four questions:

1. Who is the authority?

2. Is the authority speaking on a topic in his or her field of expertise?

3. Can any expert answer the question at hand with certainty, given the available facts?

4. Does any other expert agree with the one you cite?

7.3 Using Assumptions: Deduction and Induction

Though all effective arguments combine one or more general claims with specific evidence, successful argumentation requires a basic understanding of **logic**. Logic is the art of drawing **inferences** or conclusions. Whether you realize it or not, you make inferences every day. If, for instance, you accidentally slide your finger along the edge of a piece of paper and then discover a thin line of dark red on the fingertip, you will probably infer that you have cut yourself. That is a logical inference because it is based on a credible set of *assumptions* (the edge of a paper can be sharp enough to cut; a dark red line on the fingertip is more likely to be blood than anything else) and a known *fact* (you have indeed run that fingertip along the paper's edge). Likewise, if every student you met on a given day happened to be suffering from the flu, you might infer that a flu epidemic had struck your school. That would be a generalization based on a number of specific observations.

If we all make inferences every day, why do we need logic? Why do we need rules of inference? We need them because it is all too easy to make mistakes in drawing inferences, and arguments based on mistaken inferences are like buildings resting on cracked foundations. At best they will totter; at worst they will fall.

Without logic to rein us in, we commonly jump to conclusions. How often have you heard two or three people complain about a proposal, and then concluded that *everyone* dislikes it? How often have you seen a member of a particular group do something odd or offensive and then concluded, "That's the way they all are"? If you are sensible enough to avoid such obvious mistakes in inference as those, you may nonetheless fall into more subtle traps. Suppose you were with the police at Berkeley in 1964 when they entered the office of President Emeritus Robert Gordon Sproul to remove student demonstrators who had broken into it during the Free Speech Movement. After the demonstrators were taken out, police found papers strewn all over the floor of Sproul's office. Surely, they thought, this was the work of the demonstrators. But in fact it wasn't. The papers had been strewn about by Sproul himself, who often liked to do his work on the floor.

To avoid subtle as well as obvious traps in the construction of your own arguments, you need to know something about inference. Inference is the process of drawing conclusions from assumptions and evidence. It commonly takes one of two forms—deduction or induction.

7.3A Deduction and Validity: Drawing Necessary Conclusions

Deduction is a form of inference that leads to necessary conclusions. In formal logic, deduction is sometimes illustrated by a **syllogism,** a set of categorical statements that looks like this:

MAJOR PREMISE: All those who limit the growth of the bear population help bears.
MINOR PREMISE: Bear hunters limit the growth of the bear population.
CONCLUSION (CLAIM): Bear hunters help bears.

In a syllogism, the claim supported by an argument appears last, as a conclusion. The conclusion is deduced or inferred from the major premise, which is commonly an assumption, and the minor premise, which is commonly a piece of evidence—a statement of fact.[†] When a deduction is *valid*, the conclusion follows *necessarily* from the premises. The above syllogism is valid because the minor premise puts bear hunters within the category of "all those who limit the growth of the bear population." Since what applies to *all* members of this category must apply to every group *within* it, the conclusion is validly drawn. But if this syllogism were to conclude that bear hunters help all animals, the conclusion would be invalidly drawn, for it would then have strayed outside the categorical boundaries established by the premises.

7.3B Making Deductive Arguments Persuasive

To be effective, a deductive argument must be valid. But validity alone will not make a conclusion true or an argument persuasive. The truth of a conclusion—like the truth of any claim—depends on the reliability of the evidence cited to support it (see above, section 7.2). Furthermore, the *persuasiveness* of a deductive argument depends on the *credibility* of its one or more assumptions.

In the deductive argument made by the syllogism in section 7.2, the assumption expressed by the major premise is questionable. If we don't know how many bears die each year from natural causes, how do we know that anyone who limits the growth of their population is helping them? So long as the assumption can be questioned in this way, any conclusion drawn from it will be questionable also. A conclusion validly drawn from premises that are questionable or false is like a route carefully followed in strict obedience to a faulty compass. The route is only as good as the compass that determines it, and the argument is only as credible as the assumption that stands behind it.

Consider the assumption made by this deductive argument:

> In spite of the widespread fear and resistance they often generate, nuclear power plants are fundamentally safe. From

---

[†]Here we describe only the simplest type of deductive argument. Not all deductive arguments follow this three-part form, and not all premises consist of an assumption and a statement of fact. Strictly speaking, the major premise is what contains the predicate term of the conclusion (in this case "help bears") while the minor premise contains the subject term (in this case "Bear hunters"). For a detailed account of deduction, see David Kelley, *The Art of Reasoning* (Norton, 1988).

1972 to 1975, a thorough study of nuclear power plants was made at a cost of four million dollars under the supervision of Norman Rasmussen, professor of nuclear engineering at M.I.T. Given the time, money, and expertise devoted to this study, its results must be reliable. And in fact they are not only reliable; they are also reassuring. After examining, identifying, and—with computer analysis—establishing the risk of every possible accident that could release radiation from a nuclear power plant, the Rasmussen study concluded that in any given year the odds against a single death from a nuclear plant accident are five billion to one. Obviously, therefore, nuclear power plants are at least as safe as anything on earth can be.

This argument rests on an assumption about authority: any prolonged, expensive study that is supervised by a recognized expert in the field being studied must be reliable. Since the Rasmussen study fits these requirements, the conclusion ("its results must be reliable") is validly drawn. But the conclusion is credible only if the assumption is credible. Can anyone—no matter how authoritative—reliably calculate the odds against a nuclear plant fatality? And even apart from accidents, what about the dangers caused by radioactive wastes?

To make such an argument persuasive, then, you would have to re-formulate the assumption on which it is based. Try this one: any enterprise that has functioned for more than thirty years without causing a single death or injury is fundamentally safe. If that assumption is credible—and it is certainly more credible than the assumption about authority—it could help to build a persuasive argument for the safety of nuclear power plants in the United States. (Such an argument would not have to explain the fatalities caused by the Chernobyl explosion, which occurred outside the United States—and after the Rasmussen study was made.)

7.3C Induction: Drawing Probable Conclusions

While deductive arguments draw *necessary* conclusions, as explained above (section 7.3A), inductive arguments draw *probable* conclusions, which are commonly generalizations based on specific examples. Thus, to support the claim that nuclear power plants are unsafe, the author of the argument on p. 144 cites six major accidents that have occurred at such plants since 1957. These examples do not prove that all nuclear power plants are unsafe, but they could help to make this general claim seem probable.

Likewise, the author of the following paragraphs uses inductive argument to persuade us that words used about women typically represent them as passive:

> One indication of women's passive role is the fact that they are often identified as something to eat. What's more passive than a plate of food? Last spring I saw an announcement advertising the Indiana University English Department picnic. It read "Good Food! Delicious Women!" The publicity committee was probably jumped on by local feminists, but it's nothing new to look on women as "delectable morsels." Even women compliment each other with "You look good enough to eat," or "You have a peaches and cream complexion." Modern slang constantly comes up with new terms, but some of the old standbys for women are *cute tomato, dish, peach, sharp cookie, cheese cake, honey, sugar,* and *sweetie-pie.* A man may occasionally be addressed as *honey* or described as a *hunk of meat,* but certainly men are not laid out on a buffet and labeled as women are.
>
> Women's passivity is also shown in the comparisons made to plants. For example, to *deflower* a woman is to take away her virginity. A girl can be described as a *clinging vine, a shrinking violet,* or a *wall flower.* On the other hand, men are too active to be thought of as plants. The only time we make the comparison is when insulting a man we say he is like a woman by calling him a *pansy.*
>
> —Alleen Nilsen, "Sexism in English: A Feminist View"

These two paragraphs help to support the generalization that words used for women identify them with passive objects. The paragraphs each work in two stages. The opening sentence—the topic sentence—introduces a general category of passive objects: food in the first paragraph, plants in the second. Then each paragraph goes on to show that specific items in the category are far more often associated with women than with men. Taken together, the general categories and the specific examples work inductively to make the generalization probable.

7.3D Making Induction Persuasive

The chief advantage of an inductive argument lies in the cumulative impact of successive examples. Because of this impact, an inductive argument can sometimes feel strongly persuasive, and the argument against nuclear power plants (above, p. 144) may feel that way to you. But would the argument persuade anyone who is not already opposed to nuclear power plants? Would it bring any new supporters to the no-nuke side, or merely bolster the morale of the old ones? To answer questions like these, you must not only weigh the impact of the examples but consider also the *unstated* assumption that links them to the claim that nuclear power plants are fundamentally unsafe.

Consider first the number of examples cited. Given all the nuclear power plants throughout the world, does a record of six accidents in thirty years really justify this claim? Behind the imposing facade of examples lurks an unstated and shaky assumption: if six nuclear power plants have suffered major accidents, all of them are unsafe. Is this any better than assuming that six defective washing machines make all washing machines defective?

Whether or not the writer states the assumption that stands behind an argument, he or she should know what the assumption is and how well it binds the evidence to the general claim. Is a fatal disaster at Chernobyl relevant to a general claim about the safety of nuclear power plants? Prior to the Chernobyl disaster, no one had been killed or injured in any of the accidents cited, and the Chernobyl accident was caused (as we have already noted) by a reactor fundamentally different from those in the United States. Given that difference, and given also the absence of any nuclear fatalities in the West, the unstated assumption does not adequately bind the evidence to the general claim.

Because inductive arguments commonly move from specific examples to general claims, it is easy to overlook the unstated assumptions that stand behind such arguments. But since inductive arguments cannot yield more than probable conclusions, you should be especially wary of assuming that any inductive argument can produce a certain result. To make an inductive argument persuasive, state your claim with caution, and be sure that your evidence can be linked to the claim by a credible assumption. The inductive argument about nuclear power plants, for instance, would be more persuasive if it were reformulated like this:

> CLAIM: It is probably impossible to guarantee the safety of nuclear power plants.
> EVIDENCE: Six nuclear power plants have suffered major accidents in the past thirty years.
> ASSUMPTION: If major accidents have repeatedly occurred at nuclear power plants, it is probably impossible to guarantee that no more accidents will occur.

7.3E Placing Your Conclusion

Whether the argument is inductive or deductive, the conclusion may sometimes be stated right at the beginning. If you want to prove inductively that nuclear power plants are unsafe, you can start by saying so, and then cite examples to support the point. If you want to prove deductively that nuclear power plants are safe, you can start by saying so, and then show how this conclusion is deduced. You may think that a conclusion should always come at the end of an argument, but in practice, a writer usually has some notion of the conclusion before he or she finds the examples or constructs the premises that are meant to prove it. In inductive reasoning especially, the conclusion often comes first. The writer begins with a claim and then gives examples to back it up.

However you reach your conclusion, where you put it is finally a matter of rhetorical choice. When you put it at the beginning, you tell the reader clearly what you intend to prove. When you put it at the end, you underscore the point that your assertion is a conclusion—the consequence of the facts or assumptions previously set out.

7.3F Combining Induction and Deduction

The main advantage of a deductive argument is that if its assumptions are credible, its statements of fact true, and its conclusion validly drawn, it must be accepted by any reasonable person. But meeting those three conditions can be hard. Just how do you establish a credible assumption about any subject worth arguing over? You may have to defend your assumption by using induction, as the author of this passage does:

> The Fortune 500 Company corporate executive directs a company whose sales in 1975 averaged almost $1.75 billion, whose assets totaled $1.33 billion, and which provided employment for almost 29,000 people. This executive directs the firm in a manner that allows it to earn an 11.6 percent return on its total investment. Such a rate of return is not guaranteed simply because a corporation is large. The opportunities to lose money are many; the managements of 28 of the 500 largest industrial corporations managed to show a loss in the recovery year of 1975. It is possible, moreover, to lose big: Singer reported a loss of $451.9 million in that year, and Chrysler $259.5 million. A chief executive who heads a management team that can avoid such losses and constantly suc-

ceed in earning a profit is obviously very valuable to the shareholders of a corporation. He is valuable not only to his employers but also to other corporations; thus his own firm pays him handsomely to retain his services.

—Robert Thomas, "Is Corporate Executive
Compensation Excessive?"

This passage is part of an essay which aims to show that chief executives of large corporations deserve the extremely high salaries they get. To support this point, the writer uses a deduction that may be stated in the following simplified form:

> MAJOR PREMISE (ASSUMPTION): Any chief executive who enables a large corporation to avoid losses and earn profits regularly is very valuable.
> MINOR PREMISE (FACT): The Fortune 500 Company corporate executive directs a huge company in such a way that it earns 11.6 percent return on its total investment.
> CONCLUSION: The Fortune 500 corporate executive is very valuable.

By itself, this deductive argument is fairly persuasive. But to make it more so, the writer defends his basic assumption with an inductive argument, with specific examples about the danger of losses that large corporations face.

Assumptions and evidence are equally important for almost any argument you want to make. Whether you use induction, deduction, or a combination of the two, you need to consider the assumptions that stand behind your argument. If you want to be persuasive, if you want to reach at least some of those who do not already agree with you, you must be able to formulate one or more credible assumptions that can link your evidence to your claim.

EXERCISE 1 Spotting Assumptions

Identify the assumptions made by each of the following arguments, and say how credible the assumptions are:

1. A woman's career threatens a marriage because it makes the woman financially independent of her husband. When a married woman depends on her husband for support, she is strongly motivated to stay with him. She knows that divorce would probably lead to a sharp reduction in her allowance and style of living, that she might have to move into smaller living quarters and give up many of the comforts and benefits she enjoys while married. But if she has her own career, she can comfortably support herself, so

she has no need for her husband. A two-career marriage, therefore, is far more likely to end in divorce than a marriage in which only the husband works.

2. Infants born with severe handicaps should be allowed to die rather than forced to endure lives of pain, privation, and constant dependence. An infant born with spina bifida, for instance, has a lesion in the spinal column that usually causes an accumulation of spinal fluid within the brain and thereby leads to mental retardation. In addition, some doctors predict that children born with spina bifida will never walk and will suffer gradually worsening problems of the bowels and bladder. In at least one well-publicized case—that of Baby Jane Doe on Long Island—the doctor in charge also predicted that the child would have a life of constant pain. For all these reasons, infants born with handicaps such as spina bifida should be allowed to die.

EXERCISE 2 Using Deduction

This exercise has three parts: 1) Formulate an assumption that could be used in a deductive argument which supports or attacks one of the following propositions; 2) write a syllogism containing the assumption; 3) write a short deductive argument based on the syllogism.

1. All college students should be required to study at least one foreign language.
2. No one convicted of a non-violent crime should be sent to prison.

EXERCISE 3 Using Deduction

This exercise has four parts: 1) make a general claim about any one of the topics listed below; 2) make a list of facts that could be used to establish the probability of the claim; 3) explain what assumption links the facts to the claim; 4) use this material to write a brief inductive argument.

music videos	smokers
Japanese cars	condominiums
U.S. senators	headache remedies
charter flights	part-time jobs

EXERCISE 4 Combining Induction and Deduction

Using induction to establish the probability of the assumption you formulated in exercise 2, expand the argument you made.

fal   **7.4 Avoiding Fallacies**   *fal*

To argue effectively, you should avoid **fallacies,** which are mistakes in reasoning. Following are the most common of them—the kind most likely to undermine the persuasiveness of an argument.

7.4A Arguing by Association

> It is well known that Senator Blank is a critic of the Chilean government. We also know that Latin American Marxists are critics of the Chilean government. It is clear, therefore, that Senator Blank is a Marxist.

Here a deductive argument is misused to promote guilt by association. Only if we assume that *all* critics of the Chilean government are Marxists must we conclude that any one critic of that government is.

7.4B Shifting the Meaning of a Key Term

> Criminals do everything possible to avoid and obstruct arrest, prosecution, and conviction. Likewise, liberal lawyers try in every possible way to obstruct the work of police. They are the ones responsible for things like the Miranda rule, which says that the police can't even interrogate anyone they've arrested until they tell the person what his or her rights are, and if they forget to do so, the case can be thrown out of court. Obviously, then, liberal lawyers are no better than criminals themselves.

This argument uses the word "obstructs" in two different senses. A criminal obstructs the police by hiding out, resisting arrest, or refusing to answer questions. Lawyers obstruct the police only insofar as they demand respect for the constitutional rights of the suspect, who—under the United States system of justice—must be presumed innocent until proven guilty. Since the writer uses the word "obstructs" to identify what lawyers and criminals have in common, the shift in the meaning of this key term invalidates the argument.

7.4C Begging the Question

> Women and men make up the human race. In this sense they are alike. They have feelings, expressed and unexpressed, due to their various upbringings in society. People have challenged men's superiority because women have begun to fend

for themselves and to seek a larger role in society. They are better able to cope with the difficulties of social acceptance and equality than men are because they have been allowed to express their feelings in the past. Men have it a bit harder. They have to learn to accept themselves as feeling human beings and to deal openly with their emotions instead of repressing them.

Men and women are emotional and intellectual equals. Neither sex is superior to the other.   —College freshman

The author of this passage makes a claim, but hardly realizes that the claim needs defending. She is not so much making an argument as expressing her feelings. If that is all she aims to do, she has succeeded. But if she hopes to persuade the reader that men and women are equal, she must give evidence for the claim. She cannot simply state it or "beg the question," as logicians say, and then go on to note the emotional differences between the sexes. What she says about those differences cannot support the claim that "men and women are emotional and intellectual equals."

7.4D False Alternative

Given the alarming number of immigrants to the United States who fail to learn English and speak it, the time has come for a constitutional amendment to make English the official language of the United States. If we fail to act, the diversity of languages will divide the country.

This writer assumes that a constitutional amendment is the only alternative to a national breakdown in communication. But even if foreign languages could overcome the dominance of English in America, which seems improbable at best, a constitutional amendment is hardly the only way of preventing a linguistic division of the country. To ignore other alternatives is fallacious.

7.4E False Analogy

A college has no right to fire a popular teacher. To do so is like throwing out of office a public official who has just been reelected by a majority of voters. Colleges that fire popular teachers violate the basic principles of democracy.

The problem with this argument is that a college is not a democracy. While teachers and college administrators like to know what students think of teachers—just as public officials like to know what voters think of them—teaching is not an elective office. Stu-

fal dents do not elect teachers, and therefore they cannot reelect them. The argument is faulty because it rests on a false analogy: it assumes a fundamental similarity between two things that resemble each other only in part.

We said earlier in this book that analogy may be used to explain. If you wanted to *explain* what teachers do, you might well compare them to public officials because both groups must be able to speak effectively to various audiences. But you cannot use analogy to argue unless the two things compared are essentially similar. (For more on this point, see section 6.5.)

7.4F Personal Attack

> A furor about the American funeral customs . . . has been created by Jessica Mitford's book *The American Way of Death*. [Pertinent here] are some facts about Jessica Mitford Treuhaft, which were reported in the November 5, 1963 issue of *National Review*. Several people "under oath before legally constituted agencies of both federal and state governments" have identified Jessica Mitford as a member of the Communist party. In fact, according to the *National Review*, both Mr. and Mrs. Treuhaft have a long record of Communist activities.
>
> Jessica Mitford's Communist connections are pertinent because they place her book in perspective as part of the left-wing drive against private enterprise in general and—in this case—against Christian funeral customs in particular.
> —Rev. Irving E. Howard, review of Jessica Mitford's
> *The American Way of Death*

Since Mitford's book argues that funeral directors are greedy and exploitative, some discussion of her Communist views may help to explain what prompted her to write it. But Howard tries to discredit her argument by discrediting her. This is an example of argument by personal attack (technically called argument *ad hominem*—"to the person"). Personal attack cannot persuade any fair-minded reader because it simply ignores what the person has argued. In the present case, the only effective way to disprove Mitford's argument is to cite evidence showing that funeral directors are considerate and fair.

7.4G False Cause

> Up until 1976, when Republican Gerald Ford left the White House, the U.S. enjoyed the friendship and support of Iran. Many Americans lived and worked there, and Iran sup-

plied us with much of our oil. But scarcely two years after Democrat Jimmy Carter became president, the Shah of Iran was driven out of his own country, and Americans were driven out after him. Clearly, then, the Democrats caused us to lose one of our most valuable allies in the Middle East.

This kind of argument equates sequence with causality: because Event A was followed by Event B, the first caused the second. (Technically this fallacy is called *post hoc, ergo propter hoc*—"after this, therefore because of it.") Since causes always precede their effects, we sometimes imagine or feel that *after* amounts to *because of*, especially when one thing *could* have caused another. In this case, President Carter could have played some part in the expulsion of the shah. But instead of presenting evidence that he did, the argument simply assumes that what followed his inauguration must have been his doing.

7.4H Irrelevant Conclusion

As everyone knows, the U.S. Constitution gives all American citizens the right to bear arms. Furthermore, there is far too much crime in the streets and subways of our major cities. So anyone faced with a mugger should have the right to kill the mugger on the spot.

After stating a fact and then a common opinion, this writer lurches to an irrelevant conclusion. Neither the right to bear arms nor crime in the streets gives anyone the right to shoot anyone else. To make a persuasive case for the right to retaliate against muggers, the writer should focus on life-threatening situations, which would allow him to introduce the highly relevant topic of self-defense.

7.4I Hasty Generalization

Keating won by a landslide, so it is obvious that everyone in the state supports his plan to reduce the deficit in the state budget. Regardless of complaints about what his plan will do to housing for the elderly and other state-supported welfare programs, Keating's plan is clearly what the people want.

In politics, winning by a "landslide" means winning by a decisive majority of the votes cast. Yet this writer tries to identify Keating's supporters with "everyone"—not just with all of the voters, but with all of "the people" in the state, whether or not they voted *fal*   at all (and whether or not they may be hurt by his plan). This argument would be more persuasive with a restricted claim, such as the claim that Keating's plan is supported by most voters. (We can probably assume that nearly all of those who voted for Keating support his plan.)

EXERCISE 5 Spotting, Explaining, and Eliminating Fallacies

Identify and explain the fallacy in each of the following statements. Then, if you can, eliminate the fallacy by revising the statement. If you can't salvage the argument, say so.

EXAMPLE
Since 1968, when a federal gun control act made it illegal to order a handgun by mail, the crime rate has risen substantially. So any attempt to regulate guns simply aggravates crime.
FALLACY: False cause.
EXPLANATION: This statement does not prove that the gun control act *caused* the increase in the crime rate, even though the increase followed the act. What the first sentence does show is that gun control laws are sometimes ineffectual. So a more workable version of the statement would look as follows:
REVISION: Since 1968, when a federal gun control act made it illegal to order a handgun by mail, the crime rate has risen substantially. Gun control laws, therefore, do not necessarily reduce crime.

1. Robert McNamara, former Secretary of Defense, opposes the so-called "Star Wars" defense system because he thinks it is technologically impossible to build an impenetrable shield against Soviet missiles. But the Soviets also oppose the "Star Wars" defense system. So McNamara is really a mouthpiece for the Soviets.
2. "If divorce becomes legal in Ireland, it will spread through the country like the radiation that started at Chernobyl and then covered all of Europe." (Archbishop of Dublin)
3. On December 7, 1941, shortly after the United States government received Japanese envoys who had come to discuss peace, the Japanese bombed the U.S. naval base in Pearl Harbor. That event plainly shows that a willingness to discuss peace simply encourages the enemy to attack.
4. The only way to make the tax law truly fair is to cancel all deductions and exemptions. Everyone knows that the government squanders billions of our tax dollars on expensive and unnecessary trips for legislators and their spouses, on lavish official par-

ties, and on military equipment for which the Pentagon is grossly overcharged. Something must be done to stop the waste in government spending.

5. Since we know that cigarette smoking has caused cancer in some cases, it is clearly dangerous to the health of the nation, and should be banned altogether.

7.5 Using Argumentative Words

Certain words signal an argument. *Therefore,* for instance, tells the reader that you are drawing a conclusion, that you are offering one statement as a reason for believing another:

> Hunters keep the growth of the bear population down and *therefore* help to ensure an adequate food supply for the bear population as a whole.

When you use a word like *therefore,* you are making an argumentative connection, and the reader will hold you responsible for it. If you introduce the word simply to fill the gap between two sentences, you will confuse your reader:

> Many college students have serious problems during their freshman year. *Therefore,* high school graduates should work for a year or two before starting college.

The word *Therefore* asks us to take one statement as a reason for believing another. But is the first statement in this passage a reason for believing the second? Would the problems of freshmen be eliminated if they came to college with a year or two of work behind them? There is no clear connection between these two statements, and filling the gap with *Therefore* is like trying to bridge a river with a six-inch stick. Before you connect two statements with an argumentative word, be sure that one statement actually does follow from the other.

Argumentative words include *for, since, because, so, consequently, therefore, hence,* and *accordingly.* Some of these words, such as *since, for,* and *because,* may be used not only to argue but also to explain:

> To Argue: American businesses should be allowed to stay in South Africa *because* they help to raise the standard of living for black people there.

To Explain: President Carter opposed U.S. participation in the Moscow Olympics *because* he wanted to protest the Soviet invasion of Afghanistan.

7.6 Reckoning with the Opposition

Persuasive writing never appears in a vacuum. It springs not only from the desire to defend a particular belief, but also from the recognition that others hold a contrary belief, that conflicting claims compete for public support—like rival products in the marketplace or rival candidates in a political campaign. If there is no room for disagreement, there is no need for persuasion. No reasonable writer would set out to argue the need for a reliable water supply because no reasonable person could doubt the need for it. But the very fact that a writer sets out to persuade means that there *is* room for disagreement on the topic chosen. If your topic is at all controversial and you can't be sure that all your readers will be sympathetic to your point of view, you must expect resistance and opposition.

How do you deal with opposition in a persuasive essay? To ignore it entirely is to risk antagonizing the reader or provoking objections that may undermine your argument. To argue effectively, you must first reckon with the opposition, and thereby anticipate objections. You can do this in one of two ways—by making concessions, or by fairly and honestly defining the position you plan to oppose.

7.6A Making Concessions

A concession is a point granted to the other side: an expression of concern for the feelings of those who may disagree with you, of respect for the reasons that prompt them to do so, or of clear-cut agreement with them on one or more aspects of the topic in dispute. To see the difference an opening concession can make, compare these two introductory paragraphs—both written by college freshmen:

1. No one should be admitted to college without a personal interview. What can admissions people tell from a piece of paper? They can't really tell anything. Only when they see a student face to face can they decide what kind of a person he or she is.

2. Admissions officers can tell some things from a piece of paper. They can tell how well a person writes and what he

or she is interested in, factors which go a long way toward determining if a student is capable of using the college resources to the fullest extent possible. However, there are things that an application cannot bring forth, things that can only be seen in a personal meeting. The way a person talks, answers questions on the spot, and reacts to certain pieces of information are all important signs of personality which cannot be found on a written piece of paper.

Both of these writers are arguing in support of the same point, that no one should be admitted to college without a personal interview by an admissions officer. But the first writer makes no concessions to the other side. He simply dismisses the idea that anything can be learned about an applicant from a piece of paper. The second writer concedes or admits that certain things can be learned from a written application, and then proceeds to show that certain other things can be learned only from an interview. The transitional word *However* marks the shift from concession to assertion. (For more on transitional words, see pp. 178–80).

Starting with concession is a good way to overcome the reader's resistance to an unpopular argument, to gain a hearing for even the most controversial point of view. (For more good examples of the concessive opening, see items 6 and 7 on p. 63.)

7.6B Defining the Position You Will Oppose

To begin with a concession is to express sympathetic concern for those you plan to disagree with, or even partial agreement with them. But if you see no reason for sympathetic concern or partial agreement, you can nonetheless begin your essay by fairly defining the position you aim to oppose, by letting the reader know that you understand and respect the views of your adversaries. One good way to introduce an argument, therefore, is to quote or paraphrase what your adversaries say:

> Ralph Nader stands at the end of a long line of critics who assail the high incomes of top corporate executives. Nader and his associates suggest that "in the absence of judicial limitations, excessive remuneration has become the norm." They observe that the average top executive in each of the fifty largest industrial corporations earns more salary in a year than many of the corporate employees earn in a lifetime. Salaries are only part (albeit the major part) of the compensation the top executives receive. Bonuses, lavish retirements, stock options, and stock ownership combine to swell the incomes

of corporate chief executives by another 50 to 75 percent of the executives' direct remunerations. Nader and his associates conclude that the top corporate executives receive "staggeringly large salaries and stock options."

—Robert Thomas, "Is Corporate Executive
Compensation Excessive?"

Before Thomas begins to defend the high salaries of corporate executives, he allows Ralph Nader—a leading consumer activist—to have his say. He does not call Nader an anticorporate nut who wants to cut executive salaries to the poverty level. Instead, quoting and paraphrasing the very words of Nader and his associates, he respectfully explains why they find the salaries of top executives "excessive." By thus defining his adversary's position, Thomas earns the right to a respectful hearing for his own.

By contrast, one of the biggest obstacles to effective persuasion is contempt for the opposing view. Consider these opening paragraphs of a newspaper column advocating gun control:

Logic, common sense and public opinion are on the side of gun control, but America's firearms fanatics are insufferably relentless. Now, for pete's sake, they want their own political party.

With their own blind, the gun lovers can offer us candidates promising not a chicken in every pot, but a pistol in every pocket. And carnage in every home. Someone else to vote against.

—Richard J. Roth, "Despite Evidence and Reason,
Pro-Gun Talk Won't Go Away"

To describe the opponents of gun control as "firearms fanatics" who promise "a pistol in every pocket" and "carnage in every home" is to antagonize any reader who is not already on the writer's side. This is not persuasive writing; it is a slapdash mix of invective and gross exaggeration. It will rouse the antigun faithful, but it is unlikely to make any converts.

EXERCISE 6 Making Concessions

Rewrite each of the following arguments in one of two ways: (1) support the writer's point of view but add one or more concessive sentences at the beginning, or (2) argue against the writer's point of view by first making a concession to it and then defending the other side. Whichever you choose to do, be sure to use a transitional word between your concession and the main point you are making.

1. Regional expressions are a hindrance to communication. Each part of the country has adopted many which cannot be found anywhere else. For instance, New England is the only part of the U.S. where you can order a "frappe" in a drugstore or ice cream parlor. Try ordering a frappe in Nebraska and see what kind of reaction you will get. The purpose of language is to make communication possible. By separating regions of the country from each other, nonstandardized forms of expression defeat this purpose.

—College freshman

2. American restaurants should abolish tipping and do what European restaurants do: add a service charge of 10 to 15 percent to every bill. The service charge would eliminate the worrying and wondering that goes into tipping: the customer worrying about how much to leave, and the waiter or waitress wondering how much is going to be left. Since the tip is always left at the end of the meal, not before, it can't really affect the quality of service provided, and shouldn't be left to chance.

EXERCISE 7 Defining a Position You Oppose

Choose from a newspaper, magazine, or any other printed source an essay written to defend a position that you oppose. Then, using Thomas's introduction (pp. 163–64) as a guide, write a paragraph defining this position.

7.7 Appealing to the Emotions

A working knowledge of argumentative technique is an indispensable tool for the writer who wants to persuade. But readers are seldom persuaded by rational arguments alone. For this reason the writer should try to understand the reader's feelings and appeal to them. Though excessive or exclusive appeal to the reader's feelings can weaken an argument, the combination of emotional appeal and rational support can be powerfully persuasive.

Consider the final paragraphs of Stephen Jay Gould's *Mismeasure of Man*. In the book as a whole, Gould demonstrates that biological determinism has no basis in fact, that no characteristics of anyone's parents can determine what he or she will become, and therefore that laws requiring the sterilization of children born to allegedly feebleminded parents are scientifically unjustified. After making this argument by strictly rational means, Gould ends his book by citing the case of Doris Buck, whose fifty-two-year-old mother had been judged to have a mental age of seven, and who was sterilized under a Virginia law in 1928. Gould writes:

> She later married Matthew Figgins, a plumber. But Doris Buck was never informed. "They told me," she recalled, "that the operation was for an appendix and rupture." So she and Matthew Figgins tried to conceive a child. They consulted physicians at three hospitals throughout her child-bearing years; no one recognized that her Fallopian tubes had been severed. Last year [1979], Doris Buck Figgins discovered the cause of her lifelong sadness.
>
> One might invoke an unfeeling calculus and say that Doris Buck's disappointment ranks as nothing compared with millions of dead in wars to support the designs of madmen or the conceits of rulers. But can one measure the pain of a single dream unfulfilled, the hope of a defenseless woman snatched by public power in the name of an ideology advanced to purify a race? May Doris Buck's simple and eloquent testimony stand for millions of deaths and disappointments and help us to remember that the Sabbath was made for man, not man for the Sabbath: "I broke down and cried. My husband and me wanted children desperately. We were crazy about them. I never knew what they'd done to me."

Given at the very end of a strictly rational, analytic, and mathematically supported argument, the story and the words of Doris Buck powerfully appeal to our emotions. They move us to see that biological determinism is not just scientifically unjustified, but unconscionably cruel.

EXERCISE 8 Using Emotional Appeal

From your own experience or the experience of anyone you know, tell a story or describe a situation that could lend emotional appeal to an argument made for or against any one of the following:

1. company-sponsored day-care centers

2. drug testing of anyone

3. TV commercials aimed at children

4. preferential treatment of women or racial minorities in hiring, granting of contracts, or offers of admission

5. preferential treatment of athletes applying for admission to college

6. the Scholastic Aptitude Test

7.8 Constructing an Argumentative Essay

To see how various methods of argumentation can work together, consider this essay:

Congress Needs Guts To Accept Pay Raise

[1] If ever a question arose in politics for which the simple, obvious answer is wrong, that issue is the pay for top government officials.

Claim announced indirectly

[2] To Ralph Nader, the consumer advocate, the proposal to increase the salaries of members of Congress, federal judges and top officials of the executive branch is simply a scheme by members of the "upper economic elite" to assure their domination of government. "Top federal officials now make . . . at least five times the average worker's wage," he says. "In a democracy, this is a sufficient distance between the political rulers and the ruled who pay their salary."

Concession #1: author defines position he will oppose

[3] The gut-level appeal of this kind of cockeyed populism is evident. Walk into any barroom or bowling alley and say, "I'm here to tell you that your poor congressman needs a raise 'cause he can't make it on $89,500 a year," and you'll be hooted down. The obvious response is, "Tough luck. Try making it on my take-home pay."

Concession #2: author describes feelings of those he will disagree with

[4] Members of Congress know this, so they have rejected or scaled back increases in their own salaries—and those of their counterparts in the other two branches of government—to the point that, in real, uninflated dollars, those salaries have declined by about one-third in the last 20 years.

Fact: Congressional salaries have declined

[5] A federal commission of distinguished private citizens, most with past government experience, has recommended a big catch-up raise for the top 2,500 government jobs, with comparable hikes for another 8,500 in senior supporting positions. The proposal goes to President Reagan, who has given informal signals through his former chief of staff, Howard H. Baker, Jr., that he will endorse most if not all of the raise in his final budget.

Authority cited: federal commission recommends big raises for government officials

[6] The pay boost will go into effect unless blocked by Congress, as many such proposals have been in the past. Why Congress is even voting on its own salary—an obvious conflict-of-interest—is a question some would like to address by taking the lawmakers entirely out of the process. But as long as they have a say, it's terribly tempting for the grandstanding politicians in the House and Senate to play Nader's populist tune by offering a resolution of disapproval. If the resolution comes to a vote, it passes, because few are brave enough to

Appeal to feelings: it takes bravery to raise your own pay

say, "A pay raise is good public policy, even if it benefits me."

[7] But the testimony to the salaries commission, headed by Washington lawyer Lloyd N. Cutler, is convincing evidence that the quality and integrity of government are being jeopardized by the diminishing rewards of public service.

[8] In the executive branch, Anthony S. Fauci, director of AIDS research at the National Institutes of Health (NIH), testified that because NIH salaries are capped at a level roughly half that of comparable positions in universities or industry, "Over the last decade, NIH has not been able to recruit a single senior research scientist from the private or academic sectors to engage in . . . a clinical or basic biomedical research program. . . . Not one."

[9] The problem may be particularly acute in scientific jobs. But headhunters for the incoming Bush administration also have a major stake in the pay-raise proposal. They must try to recruit able managers from high-salaried business and industry jobs—and, more important, hold them for more than the 18-month average for senior government positions, so they can make an impact once they know their jobs.

[10] In the judiciary, the number of resignations attests to the frustrations of non-competitive pay. Only six judges resigned between 1958 and 1973; in the comparable span from 1974 through this year, the number was 57. Conservatives justifiably worry how many of the Reagan appointees of recent years can afford to stay on the bench. But compelling testimony also came from a black judge, Robert M. Duncan, who quit in 1985, at age 57, to enter private practice.

[11] "The decision to leave the bench was agonizing," he said, but "after 11½ years of 60- to 65-hour work weeks," after enduring death threats to himself and his family members, "my wife was still working, we had not traveled outside the country, and I was unable to foresee how I could afford to send my youngest daughter to the university of our choice."

[12] As for Congress, the center of controversy in any pay-raise proposal, the Cutler commission is proposing a straight trade-off, endorsed by the leaders of both parties in the House and Senate. Give the members a substantial pay increase and, at the same time, require that they stop fattening their pay by picking up honorariums for speeches and visits to outside groups.

[13] The honorarium loophole is one through which House members can supplement their pay by 30 percent and Senate members by 40 percent. It is one of the ethical "black

Testimony cited

Fact: NIH salaries are half those paid elsewhere for comparable work

Fact: the NIH can't recruit senior research scientists

Assumption: if many judges resign judges must be underpaid

Fact: many judges have resigned

Appeal to feelings: picture of one overworked, underpaid judge

Authoritative proposal cited

holes" of Capitol Hill, a convenient trough through which lobbyists and interest groups can get money to legislators who lend a sympathetic ear to their causes.

[14] For all these reasons, the real heroes in this story will not be the self-righteous members of Congress who tell you they're leading the fight against raising their own pay. This is one battle where it takes more guts—and good sense— for Congress to "just say yes."   —David Broder

Fact: lawmakers can now supplement their pay with special-interest funds

Conclusion: direct statement of claim and final appeal to feelings

The author begins by announcing his claim indirectly. Before stating it directly, which he doesn't do until the end, he defines the position he will oppose and shows that he understands the feelings of the opposition.

The body of the argument includes two kinds of evidence: facts and the authoritative opinion cited in paragraph 5. Because the author treats several different kinds of government officials, several different assumptions—largely implied—link the facts to his claim. Paragraph 4, for instance, assumes that anyone whose salary has declined over the past twenty years deserves a raise. Paragraph 8 assumes that if any organization pays half the normal salary to its workers and is unable to recruit any new ones, its salaries must be raised; paragraph 10 explicitly assumes that low pay explains the growing number of judges who resign (an assumption justified by the example in paragraph 11), and implies that in order to keep them on the bench we must raise their salaries. Finally, paragraphs 12–13 implicitly assume that whenever any group of lawmakers must rely on money from special interest groups to supplement their salaries, their salaries must be raised.

Since all of the author's assumptions are credible, and since they effectively link his facts to his claim, the argument persuasively appeals to the reader's mind. But with the picture of the struggling black judge in paragraph 11 and the repeated references to the need for "guts" and "real heroes" (paragraphs 6 and 14), the author also appeals to the reader's feelings.

Because the author does not state his claim directly until his final paragraph, it comes across as a genuine conclusion to the argument as a whole. Of course he has long since told us indirectly where he stands. But before taking his stand openly, he leads us through the steps that brought him to it.

EXERCISE 9 Composing an Argumentative Essay

Using at least ten of the following items plus any others that you
can gather from printed sources, compose an argumentative essay
that defends or attacks the need for more gun-control laws. The
argument should be chiefly based on evidence and assumptions, but
you may reinforce it with one or more emotional appeals, and you
should reckon with the opposition before introducing your claim.

When you have written the essay, list all the assumptions it
makes—both explicit and implicit.

1. Lincoln, McKinley, and John F. Kennedy were all killed by guns.
   No American president has even been stabbed or clubbed to death.
2. Article II of the United States Bill of Rights says, "A well-regu-
   lated militia being necessary to the security of a free state, the
   right of the people to keep and bear arms shall not be infringed."
3. There are now almost 200 million guns in the United States, and
   50 million of those are handguns.
4. According to FBI statistics (as of 1981), 70 percent of the people
   who are killed or wounded by gunfire are shot by relatives,
   acquaintances, or themselves.
5. Rifle and shotgun barrels can be sawed off with a fifty-nine-cent
   hacksaw blade, and the resulting weapons are more lethal than
   most handguns.
6. John F. Kennedy, assassinated by rifle shots in 1963, was a member of the National Rifle Association who strongly believed in
   the citizens' right to bear arms.
7. Theodore Roosevelt, who was wounded by a pistol shot in the
   chest while making a speech, recovered from the wound and
   afterward joined the National Rifle Association, which he
   staunchly supported.
8. Guns are used in 250,000 crimes each year, and 20,000 of those
   are homicides.
9. A 1968 report by the National Commission on the Causes and
   Prevention of Violence says that for every burglar stopped by a
   gun, four gun owners or members of their families are killed in
   firearm accidents.
10. Hunters kill an estimated 200 million birds and 50 million other
    animals each year.
11. Public opinion polls show that 70 percent of Americans favor
    gun registration and slightly over 50 percent favor an absolute
    ban.
12. The worst mass murder on record in the city of Buffalo during
    this century was committed with a knife and hatchet.
13. John Wilkes Booth used a Saturday Night Special (a Derringer
    pistol) to assassinate Lincoln.

14. McKinley was also assassinated with a pistol.
15. Together with the federal gun control act of 1968, many state laws already regulate ownership of handguns. In the states of New York and Massachusetts, for instance, persons convicted of carrying unlicensed handguns—regardless of what they are carried for—must go to jail for a year.
16. Statistics indicate that 995 handgun owners out of 1,000 are safe, responsible, law-abiding citizens.
17. One advocate of national gun controls has proposed that every gun sold in the country—whether handgun, rifle, or shotgun—should be registered, that the buyer's criminal and psychiatric record should be investigated before the gun is handed over, and that every gun sold should be test-fired so that the spent shell and slug can be kept in police ballistic files along with buyer's name, photograph, and fingerprints.
18. Former President Reagan, a lifelong member of the NRA, favored a bill that would have imposed a national seven-day waiting period on all handgun purchases. This would allow local police to investigate the buyer.
19. In 1987, there were 166 times more handgun murders in the United States than in Canada, where the purchase and carrying of handguns is severely restricted.
20. In January 1989, a psychopath wielding an imitation AK-47 assault rifle killed five schoolchildren in Stockton, California.
21. High-powered semiautomatic rifles can fire 30 rounds in a clip. About 500,000 of these weapons in the United States are privately owned.

8
Writing
Paragraphs

Effective essays are made with paragraphs, blocks of sentences that help the reader follow the stages of the writer's thought. Though a paragraph is commonly part of an essay, it can and sometimes does serve as an essay in its own right, and the writing of one-paragraph essays will give you small-scale practice in organization. For that reason, much of this chapter deals with the single paragraph as a self-contained unit.

But just as you learn how to relate the separate sentences of a paragraph, you should learn also how to relate the separate paragraphs of an essay, and how to move from one paragraph to another. So this chapter shows you how to do both.

8.1 Why Use Paragraphs? ¶

A paragraph is usually a block of sentences set off by spacing or indentation at the beginning. Paragraphs come in many shapes and sizes—from the slim one-sentence models made to fit the narrow columns of a newspaper to the wide, many-sentenced model made for the pages of a book. But why use paragraphs of any kind? Why break up essays into blocks of sentences instead of just running all the sentences together?

Part of the answer is that an essay is like a long stairway. Unless it is interrupted now and then as if by a landing, a place to stop before continuing, the reader may simply get tired or bored.

Have you ever turned the page of a book or an article to find nothing but a solid block of print? Did you heave a little sigh, or a big one? That's because you expect to *see* paragraph breaks at regular intervals, especially where the writer's thought turns. Compare these two ways of presenting the same passage:

1. [At one time the migrants] had set forth in tribes. They wandered across the steppe or edged out of the forests down to the plains with wives and children and cattle in the long columns of all their possessions. Home was where they were and movement did not disrupt the usual order of their ways. It was quite otherwise in human experience when some among the Europeans of the sixteenth and seventeenth centuries migrated. Often it was a man alone, an individual, who went, one who in going left home, that is, cut himself apart from the associations and attachments that until then had given meaning to his life. Some inner restlessness or external compulsion sent such wanderers away solitary on a personal quest to which they gave various names, such as fortune or salvation.

2. [At one time the migrants] had set forth in tribes. They wandered across the steppe or edged out of the forests down to the plains with wives and children and cattle in the long columns of all their possessions. Home was where they were and movement did not disrupt the usual order of their ways.

   It was quite otherwise in human experience when some among the Europeans of the sixteenth and seventeenth centuries migrated. Often it was a man alone, an individual, who went, one who in going left home, that is, cut himself apart from the associations and attachments that until then had given meaning to his life. Some inner restlessness or external compulsion sent such wanderers away solitary on a personal quest to which they gave various names, such as fortune or salvation.

   —Oscar Handlin, *Race and Nationality in American Life*

In version 1, no indentation signals the end of one line of thought and the beginning of another. In version 2 the turn of thought is clearly marked. The first paragraph describes the movement of tribes, who carried their "home" with them. In contrast ("It was quite otherwise"), the second describes the movement of individuals, who cut themselves off from "home." The new paragraph marks a new stage in the development of the writer's thought and the reader's understanding.

EXERCISE 1 Dividing a Passage into Paragraphs

In the following passage from Loren Eiseley's "Man of the Future," we have deliberately run the author's original three paragraphs into one. Divide the passage into what you think were Eiseley's original three paragraphs, and state the main point of each.

There are days when I find myself unduly pessimistic about the future of man. Indeed, I will confess that there have been occasions when I swore I would never again make the study of time a profession. My walls are lined with books expounding its mysteries; my hands have been split and rubbed raw   5
with grubbing into the quicklime of its waste bins and hidden crevices. I have stared so much at death that I can recognize the lingering personalities in the faces of skulls and feel accompanying affinities and repulsions. One such skull lies in the lockers of a great metropolitan museum. It is labeled   10
simply: Strandlooper, South Africa. I have never looked longer into any human face than I have upon the features of that skull. I come there often, drawn in spite of myself. It is a face that would lend reality to the fantastic tales of our childhood. There is a hint of Wells' *Time Machine* folk in it—those   15
pathetic, childlike people whom Wells pictures as haunting earth's autumnal cities in the far future of the dying planet. Yet this skull has not been spirited back to us through future eras by a time machine. It is a thing, instead, of the millennial past. It is a caricature of modern man, not by reason of its   20
primitiveness but, startlingly, because of a modernity outreaching his own. It constitutes, in fact, a mysterious prophecy and warning. For at the very moment in which students of humanity have been sketching their concept of the man of the future, that being has already come, and lived, and passed   25
away.

EXERCISE 2 Building Paragraphs

In the following passage from a student's essay about a character in a short story, some of the paragraphs are too short. Combine them so that each new paragraph marks a turn in the writer's thought.

Humble Jewett reveals his love of natural beauty in several ways.

When he and Amarantha reach the crest of the hill, he kneels down and prays to the Creator. He is moved to worship by the sight of the sunlight lining the distant treetops.

He has a similar reaction later in the story as he is walking to Wyker's house. He is so awestruck by the splendor of the sunset that he doesn't notice the wound in his leg.

¶

The sight of human beauty also casts a spell. He wants to kiss Amarantha, yet he holds back, restrained by her loveliness. It's as if he chooses to keep such radiant beauty pure, within his sight but beyond his reach.

You have seen that paragraphing helps to mark the turns in a writer's thought. What else does it do? What other purpose does paragraph structure have? One way of answering these questions is to consider a set of sentences that obviously need paragraph structure:

> My life has been a very satisfying one so far. I've faced many challenges and attained some of the goals I've set. I am one of five children. I have two older sisters and two younger brothers. My father was a successful chef. He had a college degree in electrical engineering, but chose to study cooking instead. He traveled in Europe and worked with many different chefs. He had a great influence on all of our lives. He showed me what determination and hard work could do for a person. My mother was a good mother. She guided me in a very practical way. I was able to learn and grow under their supervision. At times, it's hard to attain confidence in some situations, but I think of my parents and continue on. I enjoy knitting and making things for others and I also love to cook. Preparing economical meals is a constant challenge. I like to read a lot. I also enjoy watching my son grow up. Children are a tremendous challenge. I read to him and try to let him be as creative as possible. I have also helped my husband go through his last year of college. It was a proud moment for me to watch him walk up and get his degree. I enjoyed working with him and learning as he did. You really get a good feeling when you've helped someone. Your rewards are twofold. Helping others is my goal in life. I enjoy people. So far, my life has been satisfactory to me. I've got future goals set to attain. I've got lots of hard work ahead of me. I just look forward to going day by day and getting further toward my one goal of a college education with a challenging job. —College student

The only thing that makes this set of sentences a "paragraph" is the indentation at the beginning. Every sentence here makes sense in itself, but reading these sentences one after the other is like trying to keep up with a kangaroo. The writer moves in short, sudden leaps, and the reader never knows where she will land next. She goes from goals and challenges to sisters and brothers, from parents to knitting and cooking, from helping others to helping herself. What point is she trying to make? She herself seems unsure. To reorganize a jumble like this, she must think about the con-

¶ *d* nections and the differences between her sentences. Only then can she write a paragraph that makes sense.

We will return to this paragraph and go to work on it after we have examined the three basic elements of paragraph structure: direction, coherence, and emphasis.

8.2 Direction ¶ *d*

A well-directed paragraph guides the reader from beginning to end. It follows the lead of its opening sentence and turns from that lead only after giving a clear signal. To write a well-directed paragraph, therefore, *forecast your main point and signal your turns.*

8.2A Forecasting Your Main Point

To forecast the main point of a paragraph, start with a **lead sentence**—a sentence that tells the reader where you are headed. The lead sentence is sometimes the **topic sentence** of the paragraph, the sentence that states its main point. But not every good paragraph begins with a topic sentence, and in some paragraphs the main point is merely implied. So a lead sentence can do its forecasting in any one of the following ways.

1. Stating the main point

> Ellie and I had come to the mine earlier that day for adventure. When we got there, the sun was shining on the remote dunes, stained red with copper sediment. An old, chillingly frank sign warned us "Danger: Keep Out!" Undaunted, I peered into the mine. The walls bulged as if they were going to fall down, blocking my view of the bottom. Ellie, who had been to the mine several times before, said she thought it was over a hundred feet deep. Carefully we worked our way down into the chasm, lowering ourselves inch by inch until we finally reached the bottom. We spent hours scaling the walls, exploring the caves, and marvelling at the vastness of the mine. —Andrea Lyle

2. Stating the topic

> I have grown fond of semicolons in recent years. The semicolon tells you that there is still some question about the preceding full sentence; something needs to be added; it reminds you sometimes of Greek usage. It is almost always a greater pleasure to come across a semicolon than a period.

The period tells you that that is that; if you didn't get all the meaning you wanted or expected, anyway you got all the writer intended to parcel out and now you have to move along. But with a semicolon there you get a pleasant little feeling of expectancy; there is more to come; read on; it will get clearer.

—Lewis Thomas, "Notes on Punctuation"

The lead sentence announces the topic (semicolons) and thus leads up to the main point, which comes at the end.

3. Asking a question

Can you remember tying on your shoes this morning? Could you give the rules for when it is proper to call another person by his first name? Could you describe the gestures you make in conversation? These examples illustrate how much of our behavior is "out of awareness," and how easy it is to get into trouble in another culture.

—Edward T. Hall, "The Anthropology of Manners"

The opening question initiates a series of questions that lead to the main point, which (once again) appears at the end.

4. Setting a new direction

. . . When my father sent love letters to my mother, my grandmother would open and hide them, and when my mother told her parents she was going to marry this man, my grandmother said if that happened, it would kill her.

Not likely, of course. My grandmother is a woman who used to crack Brazil nuts open with her teeth, a woman who once lifted a car off the ground, when there was an accident and it had to be moved. She has been representing her death as imminent ever since I've known her—twenty-five years—and has discussed, at length, the distribution of her possessions and her lamb coat. Every time we said goodbye, after our annual visit to Winnipeg, she'd weep and say she'd never see us again. But in the meantime, while every relative of her generation, and a good many of the younger ones, has died (usually nursed by her), she has kept making knishes, shopping for bargains, tending the healthiest plants I've ever seen.

—Joyce Maynard, "Four Generations"

Here the lead sentence forecasts the main point of the paragraph simply by setting a new direction. The main point of the paragraph is nowhere stated in a topic sentence but is nonetheless clearly implied: my grandmother knows how to survive.

¶ *d*   **8.2B Signalling Turns: Transitions within the Paragraph** *trans/wp*

Transitional words and phrases guide the reader through a paragraph by signalling turns in your thought, shifts in your viewpoint, or movement from one point to another. You can signal your turns in any of the following ways.

1. Marking time

> Technology makes life easier for everyone. *A hundred years ago* a man would have to take a horse-drawn carriage to deliver his produce to market. *Now* he can drive a truck.
>
> —College freshman

Other words that signal time are *previously, earlier, in the past, before, at present, nowadays, meanwhile, later, in the future, eventually.*

2. Marking addition

> Different as they were—in background, in personality, in underlying aspiration—[Grant and Lee] had much in common. Under everything else, they were marvelous fighters. *Furthermore,* their fighting qualities were really very much alike.   —Bruce Catton, *A Stillness at Appomattox*

Other words that signal addition are *besides, moreover, in addition.*

3. Pointing up conflict or contrast

> At many universities across the country, more than half the students in each entering class plan on entering med school. *But* there just aren't enough spaces for them.
>
> —College freshman

Other words that indicate contrast or conflict are *nevertheless, however, conversely, on the other hand, still, otherwise, in contrast, unfortunately.* You can also point up contrast by sharp variation of any kind:

> Most Americans have never had to live with terror. *I had to live with it all my life*—the psychological terror of segregation, in which there was a special set of laws governing your movements.
>
> —Mary Mebane, "The Back of the Bus"

4. Marking the shift from cause to effect ¶ *d*

> The world of religion and philosophy was shocked recently when Henry P. Van Dusen and his wife ended their lives by their own hand. Dr. Van Dusen had been president of Union Theological Seminary; for more than a quarter-century he had been one of the luminous names in Protestant theology. He enjoyed world status as a spiritual leader. News of the self-inflicted deaths of the Van Dusens, *therefore*, was profoundly disturbing to all those who attach a moral stigma to suicide and regard it as a violation of God's laws.
> —Norman Cousins, "The Right to Die"

Other words that indicate cause and effect are *hence, as a result, consequently, accordingly.* Don't use *thus* to mean *therefore; thus* means *in that manner.*

5. Marking likeness

> Geniuses have an uncanny power to defy physical handicaps. John Milton was blind when he wrote the greatest of English epics, *Paradise Lost. Likewise,* Beethoven was deaf when he composed some of his greatest symphonies.

Another word that indicates comparison is *similarly.*

6. Marking numerical order

> Churchill had many reasons for cooperating with Stalin during the Second World War. *For one,* Stalin was battling the Germans on the Eastern front and thus reducing German pressure on England. *Second,* Russia had power, and in the face of German aggression, England needed powerful allies. *Finally,* Churchill's hatred of Hitler consumed all other feelings. Though Stalin made him uneasy, Churchill said once that to destroy Hitler, he would have made a pact with the devil himself.

Among words that indicate numerical order are *first, second, third; in the first place, in the second place, in the third place; to begin with, next, finally.* But use these words and phrases sparingly. A succession of numbered sentences soon becomes boring.

7. Marking spatial order

> The once-a-year sale had apparently drawn just about everyone in town to Gerry's department store. *To the left of*

the main entrance, the three-acre parking lot was jammed with cars, motorcycles, and pickup trucks. *To the right,* a line of people stretched down Main Street for six blocks.

Other words that indicate spatial order are *nearby, in the distance, below, above, in back, in front.*

SHAPING EFFECTIVE PARAGRAPHS: IN BRIEF

Start with a <u>lead sentence</u> that tells the reader where you are headed. (8.2A)

Use <u>transitional words and phrases</u> to signal the turns in your thoughts. (8.2B)

Strengthen connections between your sentences by using <u>list structure</u> and <u>chain structure</u>. (8.3)

Emphasize your main point through selective repetition and strategic <u>arrangement</u> of key words and phrases. (8.4)

EXERCISE 3 Forecasting Your Main Point

In the following passage by a college freshman, we have deleted the opening sentence of paragraph 3. Write a sentence that forecasts its main point.

[1] Going to college for most people means the onset of new freedoms and many responsibilities. In my first semester of college, new responsibilities helped me to develop values and maturity. This opportunity to mature is what drew me to college in the first place, and I especially felt the change in myself when the semester ended. Upon returning home for the Christmas holidays, I experienced new freedoms and respect from my parents.

[2] Before I went to college, I lived under their watchful eyes. My father pried me from the TV set whenever he knew I had homework to do, and my mother made sure I ate something besides hamburgers and pizza at least once a day. They also took turns reminding me to wear whatever I needed to keep me warm and dry whenever it was wet or cold. Most important of all, they never let me out of the house at night without asking where I was bound and setting a time for my return.

[3] Since no one checked me in or out, I could stay up all night if I chose. I could eat pizza till I looked like one, and I could watch TV till my eyes glazed over. Starting college, in fact, was like being a child in the middle of a candy store. Everywhere I turned I found an exotic treat, something I wanted to taste. But I couldn't taste everything, much less consume it all. To get any work done, I had to learn how to say no to myself.

EXERCISE 4 Signalling Turns within the Paragraph

At one or more points in each of the following passages a transitional word or phrase is missing. Find the points and insert suitable transitions.

1. The group that led the campaign against gay rights in Florida held the belief that homosexuality is immoral and that, once allowed in an area, it would lead to a breakdown of the values of a society. Homosexuality has existed throughout the past. Some of the world's greatest geniuses have professed to be homosexuals. These men have made great contributions to society. Whether one agrees that their practices were immoral or not, one must respect the contributions of men such as Michelangelo and Tchaikovsky.
—College freshman

2. Higher education in America has recently hit a new low. In liberal-arts colleges, the abolition of many or even all specific requirements for graduation has left students to find their own way, which is too often a closed alley. Allowed to take any courses they want, many students concentrate on just one subject or specialized skill. They graduate with narrow minds.

3. Revolution and moderation seldom go hand in hand. In the early years of the French revolution, the moderate Girondists were outmaneuvered by the bloodthirsty Jacobins, who launched a reign of terror. Within months after the moderate Mensheviks launched the Russian revolution of 1917, the radical Bolsheviks seized power and established a government of ruthless repression.

4. In the seventeenth century, a voyage across the Atlantic took more than two months. A supersonic plane does the trip in three hours.

8.3 Coherence ¶ *coh*

Coherence is the verbal thread that binds one sentence to another. When a paragraph is coherent, the reader can see a continuous line of thought passing from one sentence to the next. When a para-

¶ *coh*   graph is incoherent, the sentences are discontinuous, and readers may lose their way.

If you know how to forecast your main point with a lead sentence and signal your turns along the way, you know almost all you need to know about paragraphing. But you can strengthen the coherence of your paragraphs by learning two simple ways of developing them: list structure and chain structure. We first explain how to use each structure separately, and then how to combine them.

8.3A Using List Structure

List structure is a sequence of sentences that use the same basic pattern to develop a general point with specific examples. In list structure, each new sentence becomes an item on a list:

> They were a diverse group. *There were* priests *who* had brooded over the problem of a world in eternity and made the startling discovery that a holy mission summoned them away. *There were* noblemen in the great courts *who* stared out beyond the formal lines of the garden and saw the vision of new empires to be won. *There were* young men without places *who* depended on daring and their swords and were willing to soldier for their fortunes. *There were* clerks in the counting-houses, impatient of the endless rows of digits, *who* thought why should they not reach out for the wealth that set their masters high? *There were* journeymen without employment and servants without situations and peasants without land and many others whom war or pestilence displaced *who* dreamed in desperation of an alternative to home. Through the eighteenth century their numbers grew and, even more, through the nineteenth.
> —Oscar Handlin, *Race and Nationality in American Life*

The lead sentence states the main point of the paragraph, and the following sentences develop this point by a series of examples. Additionally, the repetition of *there were . . . who* makes all the examples parallel in form.

In list structure paragraphing, you can use a particular structure repeatedly to generate a series of examples, as this paragraph shows:

> It is a misunderstanding of the American retail store to think we go there necessarily to buy. Some of us shop. There's

a difference. Shopping has many purposes, the least interesting of which is to acquire new articles. We shop to cheer ourselves up. We shop to practice decision-making. We shop to be useful and productive members of our class and society. We shop to remind ourselves how much is available to us. We shop to remind ourselves how much is to be striven for. We shop to assert our superiority to the material objects that spread themselves before us.

—Phyllis Rose, "Shopping and Other Spiritual Adventures"

After forecasting the main point in her opening sentences, Rose writes a list of her reasons for shopping. As you read along, you can almost feel the words *We shop to* generating each new sentence. (For another example of list structure, see the paragraph by Alice Walker in section 10.3, pp. 252–53.)

EXERCISE 5 Using List Structure

Develop the following paragraph by adding at least three more examples in sentences that repeat the underlined words.

As I jogged along the highway, *I thought* of all the different roads my friends were starting on. *I thought* of Ruth, *who* was headed for Syracuse to major in broadcast journalism.

8.3B Using Chain Structure

Another way of ensuring coherence is to make your sentences form a chain. As long as each new sentence is linked in meaning to the one before it, the reader can readily follow your line of thought:

The process of learning is essential to our lives. All higher animals seek it deliberately. They are inquisitive and they experiment. An experiment is a sort of harmless trial run of some action which we shall have to make in the real world; and this, whether it is made in the laboratory by scientists or by fox-cubs outside their earth. The scientist experiments and the cub plays; both are learning to correct their errors of judgment in a setting in which errors are not fatal. Perhaps this is what gives them both their air of happiness and freedom in these activities.

—Jacob Bronowski, *The Common Sense of Science*

¶ *coh*   The sentences in this paragraph are like the links in a chain:

LEAD SENTENCE: | The process of learning | is essential to our lives.

A. | All higher animals | seek (it) deliberately.

   B. (They) are inquisitive and (they) | experiment. |

      C. An (experiment) is a sort of harmless trial run of some action which we shall have to make in the real world; and this, whether it is made in the laboratory by | scientists | or by | fox-cubs | outside their earth.

         D. The (scientist) experiments and the (cub) plays; (both) are learning to correct their errors of judgment in a setting in which errors are not fatal.

           E. Perhaps (this) is what gives them both their air of happiness and freedom in these activities.

As the diagram indicates, only the second sentence is directly linked to the lead sentence; each of the others is linked to the one just before it.

For the writer, the advantage of chain structure is that each sentence tends to suggest or generate the next one. The idea of the process of learning leads to the idea of learners *(All higher animals)*; *animals* leads to a comment on what they do *(experiment)*; *experiment* leads to a definition of that term. When you use chain structure, you are not free to forget about the topic sentence entirely, but you are free to experiment, to pursue the trail opened up by your own sentences, and even to discover something you did not foresee when you wrote the topic sentence. When Bronowski started this paragraph with a sentence about the process of learning, did he expect to end it with a sentence about happiness and freedom?

EXERCISE 6   Using Chain Structure

Using chain structure, develop the following paragraph by adding at least three more sentences to it. Be sure that each new sentence is linked to the one before it.

LEAD SENTENCE: In the next hundred years, the exploration of outer space will undoubtedly change man's relation to the earth.

A. Earth will be just one of many places where man may choose to live.

8.3C Combining List Structure and Chain Structure

The following paragraph by a college freshman shows how list structure and chain structure can work together:

> Going home for the Christmas vacation gave me the chance to see my life at college in a new light. At home, relatives and friends asked me how I liked the school and my classmates. I answered most of their questions with one-word responses, but I also questioned myself. Had I made any real friends? Did I like the campus atmosphere? Did I enjoy my courses as well as learn from them? As I thought about these questions, I realized that every one of them had a two-sided answer. I had picked up many acquaintances, but I could not yet call anyone my friend. I liked the general atmosphere of the campus, but disliked its conservative air. I enjoyed my courses, but felt many self-doubts. I had to admit to myself that I had no settled opinion about anything at college. I was still finding my way.

Basically, this paragraph uses a chain structure with two lists attached to it—a list of questions and a list of answers:

LEAD SENTENCE: Going home for the Christmas vacation gave me the chance to see my life at college in a new light.

A. At home, relatives and friends asked me how I liked the school and my classmates.

 B. I answered most of their questions with one-word responses, but I also questioned myself.

 1. Had I made any real friends?

 2. Did I like the campus atmosphere?

 3. Did I enjoy my courses as well as learn from the m?

  C. As I thought about these questions, I realized that every one of them had a two-sided answer.

 1. I had picked up many acquaintances, but I could not yet call anyone my friend.

 2. I liked the general atmosphere of the campus, but disliked its conservative air.

 3. I enjoyed my courses, but felt many self-doubts.

  D. I had to admit to myself that I had no settled opinion about anything at college.

  E. I was still finding my way.

EXERCISE 7 Using List and Chain Structure Together

Expand the following paragraph by using a combination of list and chain structure to add supporting points. (Doing this exercise may require some reading.)

LEAD SENTENCE: The strongest weapon we can use in the war against AIDS is knowledge of the way it spreads.

A. For one thing, it can spread from a mother to her unborn child.
   1. If a woman is infected, her child has a 50 percent chance of inheriting the virus.
   2. So any woman who thinks that she could be infected should be tested for the virus before she becomes pregnant.
   B. Secondly, it can spread from a drug needle.

8.3D Strengthening Weak Connections

Separately or together, list structure and chain structure can help you develop a paragraph as well as hold it together. Most important, a little practice with each structure can help you gain a sense of coherence—the ability to see at once whether or not a set of sentences makes continuous sense. Consider this set:

> I enjoy watching my son grow up. Children are a tremendous challenge. I read to him and try to let him be as creative as possible.

A chain of connection runs from *my son* in the first sentence to *Children* in the second, with the writer moving from the particular to the general term. But the third sentence abruptly returns to the particular. To understand what *him* refers to, we have to jump back over the second sentence to the first. The link between *him* and *my son* is broken. How would you repair the link? One way is to rearrange the sentences:

> Children are a tremendous challenge. I enjoy watching my son grow up. I read to him and try to let him be as creative as possible.

Now *him* and *my son* are closely linked. But since *watching* is hardly a tremendous challenge, the link between the first two sentences is weak, and it cannot be repaired by any further rearrangement. In this case, the writer must *add* information to connect the idea of challenge with the son's growth and creativity. What does the writer do besides watching and reading to her son? Here's a possible answer:

> Children are a tremendous challenge. I try to answer all the questions my son asks. I read to him and encourage his creativity as much as possible.

Now there's a link between *challenge* and *try to answer* as well as between *son* and *him*. There's also a list of things the writer actively does: try to answer, read, and encourage. Whenever you can't repair a link by simply rearranging sentences, add whatever new material is needed to make your points cohere.

8.4 Emphasis ¶ *em*

Whether you are using list structure, chain structure, or a combination of both, you need to emphasize the main point of your paragraph. A paragraph without emphasis is baffling: we don't know how to look at it or what to make of it. Emphasis darkens certain lines, makes certain features stand out, and thus helps to define the paragraph as a whole.

How do you emphasize your main point? Aside from underlining or using italics (which should be used sparingly), the two most important ways of emphasizing a point are repetition and arrangement.

8.4A Using Repetition for Emphasis

You may have been told that you should never repeat a word or phrase when you write, that you should scour your brain or your thesaurus for synonyms to avoid using a word or phrase again. That is nonsense. If repetition gets out of control, it will soon become monotonous and boring. But selective repetition can be highly useful.

What is selective repetition? Consider the following paragraphs:

> As a student begins her last year of high school, she may start to wonder what college or university is right for her. She will usually apply to several schools for admission. At ———— College, the student actually exchanges information

¶ *em*

on herself through her application and other forms and interviews for information about the school. It is through a fair admissions process that ——— College and its candidates for entrance learn a lot about each other. This fair exchange of ideas and insight in the admissions process can be seen through the college's application for admission, the guidance counselor forms, and the alumni interview.　—College freshman

To me the interview comes as close as possible to being the quintessence of proper admissions procedure. It is a well-known secret (to use a paradox) that one can study for the achievement tests and the S.A.T. From personal experience I also know that schools "pad" grades and that students can receive marvelous grades without one iota of knowledge in a subject. One cannot, however, "fudge" an interview. One can buy a new suit and put on false airs, but 999 times out of 1,000 the interviewer can easily unmask the fraud and can thus reveal the true person.　—College freshman

Both of these paragraphs use repetition, but only one of them uses it selectively. In the first paragraph, repetition gets out of control. The writer uses *admission* twice, *admissions process* twice, *information* twice, *application* twice, *fair* twice, *exchanges* and *exchange*, *interviews* and *interview*. Using too much repetition is like underlining every word in a sentence or shouting every word of a speech. When everything is emphasized, nothing is.

The other writer makes repetition work by using it sparingly. *Grades* appears once too often, but the only word conspicuously repeated is the key term *interview*, which appears twice, along with *interviewer*, used once. This selective repetition keeps the eye of the reader on the writer's main point.

8.4B Using Arrangement for Emphasis

You can emphasize a word by putting it at the beginning or the end of a sentence. Likewise, you can emphasize a point by putting it at the beginning or the end of a paragraph. That is why the first sentence of a paragraph is a good place to state your main point and the last sentence is a good place to restate it—provided you don't simply repeat it. The last sentence of this paragraph, for instance, not only recalls the meaning of the first one but adds something new:

It seems to me that the safest and most prudent of bets to lay money on is surprise. There is a very high probability that whatever astonishes us in biology today will turn out to be usable, and useful, tomorrow. This, I think, is the established record of science itself, over the past two hundred years, and we ought to have more confidence in the process. It worked this way for the beginnings of chemistry; we obtained electricity in this manner; using surprise as a guide, we progressed from Newtonian physics to electro-magnetism, to quantum mechanics and contemporary geophysics and cosmology. In biology, evolution and genetics were the earliest big astonishments, but what has been going on in the past quarter century is simply flabbergasting. For medicine, the greatest surprises lie still ahead of us, but they are there, waiting to be discovered or stumbled over, sooner or later.

—Lewis Thomas, "Medical Lessons from History"

8.5 Paragraphing in Action—Rearranging Sentences

Now that you have seen how good paragraphs are put together, let's return to the one that needs major reconstruction—the one by the college freshman who is also a wife and mother:

[1] My life has been a very satisfying one so far. [2] I've faced many challenges and attained some of the goals I've set. [3] I am one of five children. [4] I have two older sisters and two younger brothers. [5] My father was a successful chef. [6] He had a college degree in electrical engineering, but chose to study cooking instead. [7] He traveled in Europe and worked with many different chefs. [8] He had a great influence on all of our lives. [9] He showed me what determination and hard work could do for a person. [10] My mother was a good mother. [11] She guided me in a very practical way. [12] I was able to learn and grow under their supervision. [13] At times, it's hard to attain confidence in some situations, but I think of my parents and continue on. [14] I enjoy knitting and making things for others and I also love to cook. [15] Preparing economical meals is a constant challenge. [16] I like to read a lot. [17] I also enjoy watching my son grow up. [18] Children are a tremendous challenge. [19] I read to him and try to let him be as creative as possible. [20] I have also helped my husband go through his last year of college. [21] It was a proud moment for me to watch him walk up and get his degree. [22] I enjoyed working with him and learning as he did. [23] You really get a good feeling when you've helped someone. [24] Your rewards are twofold. [25] Helping others is my main goal in life. [26] I enjoy people. [27] So far, my life has been satisfactory to me.

[28] I've got future goals set to attain. [29] I've got lots of hard work ahead of me. [30] I just look forward to going day by day and getting further toward my one goal of a college education with a challenging job.

Rereading these sentences in the light of what you know about paragraph structure, you may see that there is matter here for at least two paragraphs: one on the writer's childhood and the influence of her parents, the other on her life and goals as a wife, mother, and college student. This division in the material becomes obvious if you examine the links between the sentences. The first sentence looks like a lead sentence, and the second is connected to it, but the third sentence has nothing to do with *challenges* and *goals*, and not until sentence 15 does either of those words appear again. Sentences 3–13 are really a detour from the road that the first two sentences open up, and therefore need to be taken out and reorganized under a topic sentence of their own.

Sentences 3–13 can be used to make a paragraph because they all concern the same topic—the writer's childhood and her parents. But to develop a paragraph from these sentences, the writer will first have to identify one of them as a lead sentence, a sentence that can state or forecast the main point of the whole group. A likely candidate is sentence 12: *I was able to learn and grow under their supervision.* To make this sentence work at the beginning of the paragraph, the writer will have to change *their* to *my parents'.* She will then have the start of a paragraph:

I was able to learn and grow under my parents' supervision.

Now see how this lead sentence can help the writer organize the other sentences in the 3–13 group:

LEAD SENTENCE: I was able to learn and grow under my parents' supervision.

3. I am one of five children.
4. I have two older sisters and two younger brothers.
5. My father was a successful chef.
6. He had a college degree in electrical engineering, but chose to study cooking instead.
7. He traveled in Europe and worked with many different chefs.
8. He had a great influence on all of our lives.
9. He showed me what determination and hard work could do for a person.

10. My mother was a good mother.
11. She guided me in a very practical way.
13. At times, it's hard to attain confidence in some situations,
    but I think of my parents and continue on.

There are still some problems here. The lead sentence fore-casts a discussion of the writer's parents, but sentences 3 and 4 concern her brothers and sisters. Though the brothers and sisters are obviously related to the writer's parents, they are not con-nected with her parents' supervision of her, or—except in the phrase *our lives* (sentence 8)—with their influence on her. When sen-tences 3 and 4 are cut out, you actually begin to see a paragraph taking shape:

> I was able to learn and grow under ⌐my parents'⌐ supervision.
> 5. My (father) was a successful chef.

The writer now has a definite link between the topic sentence and the one that follows it. In fact, she has the beginnings of a para-graph combining list structure and chain structure:

LEAD SENTENCE: I was able to learn and grow under my par-ents' supervision. [formerly sentence 12]

> 1. A. My father had a great influence on my life. [8, with *all of our lives* changed to *my life*]
>   B. He showed me what determination and hard work could do for a person. [9]
>   C. He had a college degree in electrical engineer-ing, but chose to study cooking instead. [6]
>   D. He traveled in Europe and worked with many different chefs. [7]
>   E. He was a successful chef. [5]
> 2. A. My mother was a good mother. [10]
>   B. She guided me in a very practical way. [11]

CONCLUDING SENTENCE: At times, it's hard to attain confi-dence in some situations, but I think of my parents and con-tinue on. [13]

With the basic structure of the paragraph established, the writer can improve it further by adding transitional words and combining some of the sentences:

LEAD SENTENCE: I was able to learn and grow under my parents' supervision.

   1. A. My father had a great influence on me *because* he showed me what determination and hard work could do for a person.
      B. He had a college degree in electrical engineering, but chose to study cooking instead, traveling in Europe and working with many different chefs.
      C. He *thus became* a successful chef *himself.*
   2. A. My mother was a good mother *who* guided me in a very practical way.

CONCLUDING SENTENCE: At times, it's hard to attain confidence in some situations, but I think of my parents and continue on.

There is still room for development in this paragraph. To balance the chain of sentences about the father, the writer should say more about the mother, explaining how she gave guidance and what she taught. Specific statements here would enrich the paragraph and clarify the meaning of the topic sentence.

Shaping the rest of the original passage into paragraph form is harder. For one thing, there is no obvious lead sentence. Nearly all of the other sentences concern the writer's challenges and goals, but no one sentence on this subject forecasts the rest in the way that sentence 12 forecasts sentences 5–13. The writer speaks of past goals in sentences 1–2, 20–24, and 27, of present challenges and satisfactions in sentences 14–19 and 26, and of future goals in sentences 28–30. Most revealingly, she does not seem to know whether her main goal is helping others (sentence 25) or helping herself (sentence 30), or what the relation between these goals might be. Before she can write a coherent paragraph on her goals, she will have to do some more thinking and decide just what they are.

EXERCISE 8 Expanding a Paragraph

Expand the final version of the paragraph given above by inserting at least two sentences about the mother after sentence 2. A.

EXERCISE 9 Forming a Paragraph

Choose a lead sentence from the following list and rearrange the remaining sentences to complete a paragraph, combining them and adding words where necessary.

1. The announcement of this principle led scientists in the United States and Great Britain to test and prove it by various devices.

2. The zoetrope was a cylinder covered with images.

3. According to this principle, the human eye retains an image for a fraction of a second longer than the image is present.

4. The principle was announced in 1824 by a British scholar named Peter Mark Roget.

5. One of these was a toy known as a zoetrope.

6. These simple applications of Roget's principle eventually led to the development of the motion picture.

7. Motion pictures originated from the discovery of the principle known as the persistence of vision.

8. Another device was a small book of drawings that seemed to move when flipped by the thumb.

9. The motion picture is actually a rapid succession of still pictures put together by the persistence of vision in the eye.

10. The images merged into a single picture when the cylinder was rapidly spun.

8.6 Linking and Turning: Transitions between Paragraphs   *trans/bp*

A good essay is more than a collection of separate paragraphs. It is made up of paragraphs linked to each other not only by the substance of what they say but also by the transitions between them. We have already explained how to signal turns and transitions within the paragraph (see section 8.2B). There are various ways to link one paragraph with another, or to signal a turn as you begin the new one. Here are three ways to do so.

1. Use a transitional word or phrase:

> Boston today can still provide a fairly stimulating atmosphere for the banker, the broker, for doctors and lawyers. "Open end" investments prosper, the fish come in at the dock, the wool market continues, and workers are employed in the shoe factories in the nearby towns. For the engineer, the physicist, the industrial designer, for all the highly trained specialists of the electronic age, Boston and its area are of seemingly unlimited promise. Sleek, well-designed factories and research centers pop up everywhere; the companies plead, in the Sunday papers, for more chemists, more engineers, and

humbly relate the executive benefits of salary and pension and advancement they are prepared to offer.

But otherwise, for the artist, the architect, the composer, the writer, the philosopher, the historian, for those humane pursuits for which the town was once noted and even for the delights of entertainment, for dancing, acting, cooking, Boston is a bewildering place. . . .

—Elizabeth Hardwick, "Boston: The Lost Ideal"

The single word *But* nicely marks the transition from a paragraph about what makes Boston stimulating to a paragraph about what makes it bewildering. (Transitional words and phrases are listed and discussed in section 8.2B.)

2. Start a new paragraph by answering one or more questions raised in the one before:

Married or single, working or not working today, women must begin to think in terms of a basic choice: Public role and private role—which is the more important? In an emergency which would you sacrifice? If your child was sick or unhappy, would you leave him in someone else's care, as a man must do? If your husband's job took him to another country, would you give up a promising career to go with him? Would you go far away from friends and relatives for your career?

However important, responsible, and fulfilling a woman's work may be, the answer is quite predictable. Most women put their families first. And few will think them wrong. This is the choice women have been brought up to make and men have been taught to expect. It is the unusual woman, the woman wholly committed to her career or an impersonal goal, on whom criticism descends.

—Margaret Mead, "Women: A House Divided"

The first paragraph poses several questions stating choices women must make, and the second paragraph supplies an answer to those questions: *Most women put their families first.* The question-and-answer form makes the transition automatically, with no need for transitional words.

3. Start a new paragraph by echoing a key word or recalling a key idea from the one before:

There are days when I find myself unduly pessimistic about the future of man. Indeed, I will confess that there have been occasions when I swore I would never again make the study of time a profession. My walls are lined with books expounding its mysteries; my hands have been split and rubbed raw with grubbing into the quicklime of its waste bins and hidden crevices. I have stared so much at death that I can recognize the lingering personalities in the faces of skulls and feel accompanying affinities and repulsions.

One such skull lies in the lockers of a great metropolitan museum. It is labeled simply: Strandlooper, South Africa. I have never looked longer into any human face than I have upon the features of that skull. I come there often, drawn in spite of myself. It is a face that would lend reality to the fantastic tales of our childhood. There is a hint of Wells' *Time Machine* folk in it—those pathetic, childlike people whom Wells pictures as haunting earth's autumnal cities in the far future of the dying planet.

—Loren Eiseley, "Man of the Future"

Here the repetition of *skull* at the beginning of the second paragraph links the two paragraphs together and marks the transition from a general discussion of death to some thoughts about a particular skull.

You can also link paragraphs by recalling a key idea—by finding a word that summarizes or categorizes what went before:

... This is the choice women have been brought up to make and men have been taught to expect. It is the unusual woman, the woman wholly committed to her career or an impersonal goal, on whom criticism descends.

Up to the present the dilemma is one most women have managed to avoid. One way of doing it has been by defining their work as an adjunct to their personal lives. Even today, when over one third of the women living in husband-wife homes—about 15 million married women—are working, this remains true. The kinds of positions women hold and the money they are paid are, at least in part, a reflection of women's own definitions of the place of work in their lives and of the reciprocal belief among men that giving a woman a career job is a high risk.

—Margaret Mead, "Women: A House Divided"

trans/
bp   A *dilemma* is a difficult choice, and though *dilemma* itself does not appear in the previous paragraph, it echoes the sense of the key word *choice,* which does. It also supplies a shade of meaning that is important to Mead's discussion and that the neutral word *choice* does not have.

An effective paragraph, then, is a group of sentences that usually has both internal and external connections. Internally, the paragraph must be well-directed and coherent, with a line of thought leading from one sentence to the next. Externally, a paragraph that is part of an essay should look back to what has preceded it even as it breaks new ground. Thus it will serve to guide the reader from one point to another.

EXERCISE 10 Making Transitions between Paragraphs

1. In the following passage, one or more words at the beginning of the second paragraph have been deleted. Use a transitional word or phrase to clarify the shift between the two paragraphs.

As children growing up in a small town, my brother and I were the only ones whose father was "different." He couldn't sing the national anthem or remember the words of the Pledge of Allegiance and found it difficult to comprehend the intricacies of football and baseball.

. . . he was a very special parent. On rainy days he was always waiting for us at the school door, rubbers in hand; if we were ill he was there to take us home. He worked in town and was available to take us to music and dancing lessons or on little drives. When I was a small child he planted beside my window a beautiful oak tree that grew to be taller than our home.   —Janet Heller, "About Morris Heller,"
The New York Times, May 7, 1976

2. In the following passage, we have deleted the first sentence of the second paragraph and the first two sentences of the third. For each of those paragraphs write one or two opening sentences to clarify the transition from one paragraph to the next.

Outside, in our childhood summers—the war. The summers of 1939 to '45. I was six and finally twelve; and the war was three thousand miles to the right where London, Warsaw, Cologne crouched huge, immortal under nights of bombs or, farther, to the left where our men (among them three cousins of mine) crawled over dead friends from foxhole to foxhole towards Tokyo or, terribly, where there were children (our age, our size) starving, fleeing, trapped, stripped, abandoned.

. . . A shot would ring in the midst of our play, freezing us in the knowledge that here at last were the first Storm Troopers till we thought and looked—Mrs. Hightower's Ford. And any plane passing overhead after dark seemed pregnant with black chutes ready to blossom. There were hints that war was nearer than it seemed—swastikaed subs off Hatteras or the German sailor's tattered corpse washed up at Virginia Beach with a Norfolk movie ticket in his pocket.

. . . Our deadly threats were polio, being hit by a car, drowning in pure chlorine if we swam after eating. No shot was fired for a hundred miles. (Fort Bragg—a hundred miles.) We had excess food to shame us at every meal, excess clothes to fling about us in the heat of play.

—Reynolds Price, Permanent Errors

9
Choosing Words

To speak or to write is to choose words. In speaking and in the early stages of writing, you often choose them unconsciously. But to write effectively, you must think about the words you use, their shades of meaning, and their effect on your readers. That is what this chapter aims to help you do.

9.1 Choosing Your Level of Diction   *d*

Good writing is made of words that suit its subject and its expected audience. As you write, you constantly need to make choices among words that have similar meanings but different effects on people. The words you choose are called your **diction,** and the choices you make establish your **level of diction**—that is, your level of formality. This may be high, low, in the middle, or mixed.

9.1A Middle Level

To see how the middle level of diction is set and maintained, consider this passage from an essay written for a college course:

> Fears based on ignorance can sometimes be conquered by scientific fact. In 1938 a radio program called *War of the Worlds* actually terrified large numbers of Americans by pretending to report that the earth was being invaded by men from Mars. But as we now know from unmanned exploration of Mars itself, the idea that "Martians" could invade the earth is ———.

As is right for a piece on a serious subject aimed at an intelligent and somewhat critical audience (the instructor), this passage is formal rather than casual in tone. Words such as *conquered,* *d* *invaded,* and *exploration* establish a level of diction that is clearly above the colloquial. But the diction is not highly formal; this passage comes from a term paper, not a State of the Union address. It is written at the middle level of diction, the normal level for most college and professional writing, the level consistent with Standard English (as defined on pp. 4–6).

What, then, should the last word be? Here are some words that would fit the meaning of the passage. Choose one:

insupportable	silly
preposterous	false
incredible	crazy
ludicrous	loony
groundless	bull
absurd	

A quick glance down the list should make you see that these eleven words descend through several levels of diction, from the stately, many-syllabled formality of *insupportable* through the informality of *crazy* to the outright slanginess of *bull.* If you chose a word from the middle of the list—*ludicrous, groundless, absurd, silly* or *false*—you chose sensibly, for these words are all at the middle level of diction, and can fit into most contexts without seeming either coarse or pretentious, too low or too high. Slang words like *loony* and *bull* may be all right in conversation, but they do not suit a formal discussion of human fears, and the odds are they will not suit the audience either. So why not *insupportable,* from the top of the list? This word is impressively long, but its very length makes it carry more weight than most sentences can bear, and seasoned writers do not use long words just to impress their readers. In this case, the meaning of *insupportable* can readily be conveyed by a shorter word such as *groundless.*

As you move toward the middle of the list, choosing becomes harder. The words from *ludicrous* to *false,* all from the middle level of diction, differ not so much in formality as in the shades of their meaning, which are discussed below in section 9.3 (pp. 205–206).

9.1B High or Formal Level

Though the middle level of diction is the one to use in most of your college and professional writing, some occasions call for high formality. Consider this passage:

d

> We dare not forget today that we are the heirs of that
> first revolution. Let the word go forth from this time and place,
> to friend and foe alike, that the torch has been passed to a new
> generation of Americans—born in this century, tempered by
> war, disciplined by a hard and bitter peace, proud of our ancient
> heritage, and unwilling to witness or permit the slow undoing
> of those human rights to which this Nation has always been
> committed, and to which we are committed today at home
> and around the world.
>
> —John F. Kennedy, Inaugural Address

Kennedy's language is marked by stately words: *heirs, generation,
heritage, witness.* He is delivering a presidential speech on a cere-
monial occasion, and that requires language of high formality.

9.1C Informal or Low Level: Colloquialisms and Slang

Colloquialisms and slang are words commonly used in conversation and sometimes in writing. They often appear, for instance, in
sports reporting:

> Baker led off the ninth with a scorcher into the right-
> field corner, and took second when Bailey bobbled the ball.
> Muzio caught Lehmann looking at a slider on the outside cor-
> ner, but Tetrazzini clouted the next delivery into the upper
> deck. In the bottom of the inning Tom Stewart retired the Sox
> in order to ice the win.

Strictly speaking, slang is one step lower than colloquial diction.
While "led off" is colloquial, "ice the win" has the racy, untamed
flavor of slang. (Dictionaries use the word "informal" to designate
colloquialisms alone, and put slang in a separate category: see below,
section 9.2.)

9.1D Mixed Levels—Pro and Con

The passages in 9.1B and 9.1C show the extremes, and ordinarily
you should steer a middle course. But even when you are choosing
most of your words from the middle level of diction, you may
occasionally need a highly formal word, or—on the other hand—a
piece of slang:

> In Moulmein, in Lower Burma, I was hated by large
> numbers of people—the only time in my life that I have been
> important enough for this to happen to me. I was sub-divi-
> sional police officer of the town, and in an aimless, petty kind

of way anti-European feeling was very bitter. No one had the guts to raise a riot, but if a European woman went through the bazaars alone somebody would probably spit betel juice over her dress. —George Orwell, "Shooting an Elephant"

Guts is slang, but it is not hard to see why Orwell chose to use it in this passage of otherwise middle-level diction. Unlike the passage on the Martians, this one involves violent feelings. *Guts* therefore seems right here; it has bite and pungency. These qualities are reinforced by the word *spit*, which is not quite slang, but works together with *guts* to define and vivify the abstract phrase *anti-European feeling*.

One reason the slang is effective here is that Orwell has used it sparingly and with a specific purpose in mind. If you overuse slang, your writing will begin to sound like this:

When I got out of high school I figured I wouldn't start college right off because books were giving me bad vibes at the time and I wanted to get my head together first.

Just as bad is a sentence that suddenly lurches into slang with no good reason for doing so:

When I finished high school, I decided not to enter college immediately because academic work was giving me bad vibes.

In formal writing, therefore, use slang sparingly, or not at all:

When I finished high school, I decided not to enter college immediately because I just couldn't stomach any more academic work.

The verb *stomach* has plenty of force; you could also use *swallow* or simply *take*. None of these words is slang, but each of them gives most readers a stronger and more specific sense of the writer's feelings than does *bad vibes*. The more you write, the more you will find variety and power within the middle range of diction.

EXERCISE 1 Making Diction Consistent

Revise the following passage to eliminate any unjustified slang or excessive formality in its diction.

While I'm complaining, let me mention another gripe about New York. It's impossible to get a haircut here! When I inhabited a house in the town of Rye, I had a terrific barber, a person who, every month or so, would give me a straightforward trim for $3.50, a price which was reasonable in my opinion. He always cut my tresses exactly as I wanted him to, and he never suggested that a different style would be more beneficial. I like simple haircuts but have yet to get one in the five months I've been attending Columbia University, which is right here in New York City. It is my considered opinion that all of the barbers left town years ago, to be replaced by hair stylists, as they label themselves, men who use scissors on a man's locks in the way bad sculptors use their mitts to put soft clay into some kind of shape. If I present a request for a simple trim, these bums spray my head with water, comb my hair in every direction but the right one, grab tufts, and start hacking. They try to layer it in ways only a high-priced fashion model could ever want; and they leave the sideburns raw, claiming that's how men of taste want them. Then they plug in their damned hair dryers and blow up the mess they've made. In conclusion, they have the effrontery to submit a bill for a monetary sum in excess of $10. You can't win.

9.2 Using the Dictionary

You learn what words mean and how to use them by reading and listening to others speak. You can also learn about words by using a good dictionary—the indispensable tool of a good writer. To show you what a good dictionary can tell you about a word—even about a word you use often—here is a sample entry from *The American Heritage Dictionary*:

1. Spelling, syllable division, pronunciation. You already know how to spell and pronounce a one-syllable word like *cool*, but what about a longer word, such as *government?* The definition of this word begins "**gov·ern·ment** (gŭv'ərn-mənt)." With the word broken into three syllables, you can tell where to divide it when you need to hyphenate it at the end of a line. The version of the word in parentheses tells you to pronounce it with the accent on the first syllable (gŭv'). Here the word is spelled phonetically—that is, according to the way it sounds. The pronunciation key at the beginning of the dictionary (and at the bottom of each page) explains that ŭ sounds like the *u* in *cut* and ə sounds like the *e* in *item*.

2. Parts of speech. Like many other words, *cool* can be used in various ways. The abbreviation *adj.* tells you that it is being defined

Spelling   Pronunciation   Definition as adjective   Comparative and superlative forms

General usage

Slang usage

Informal or colloquial usage

Definition as verb

Verb forms

Definition as intransitive verb

Definition as noun

History of the word

Related forms

Distinctions in meaning between the word and others like it

cool (kōol) *adj.* ⌐cooler, coolest.⌐ **1.** Moderately cold; neither warm nor very cold. **2.** Reducing discomfort in hot weather; allowing a feeling of coolness: *a cool blouse.* **3.** Not excited; calm; controlled. **4.** Showing dislike, disdain, or indifference; unenthusiastic; not cordial; *a cool greeting.* **5.** Calmly audacious or bold; impudent. **6.** Designating or characteristic of colors, such as blue and green, that produce the impression of coolness. **7.** *Slang.* Having a quiet, indifferent, and aloof attitude. **8.** *Slang.* Excellent; first-rate; superior. **9.** *Informal.* Without exaggeration; entire; full: *He lost a cool million.* —*v.* cooled, cooling, cools. —*tr.* **1.** To make less warm. **2.** To make less ardent, intense, or zealous. —*intr.* **1.** To become less warm. **2.** To become calm. —cool it. *Slang.* To calm down, slow down, or relax. —cool one's heels. *Informal.* To be kept waiting for a long time. —*n.* **1.** Anything that is cool or moderately cold; *the cool of early morning.* **2.** The state or quality of being cool. **3.** *Slang.* Composure; *recover one's cool.* [Middle English *col,* Old English *cōl.* See gel-³ in Appendix.*] —cool'ly *adv.* —cool'ness *n.*

Synonyms: *cool, composed, collected, unruffled, nonchalant, imperturbable, detached.* These adjectives apply to persons to indicate calmness, especially in time of stress. *Cool* has the widest application. Usually it implies merely a high degree of self-control, though it may also indicate aloofness. *Composed* and *collected* more strongly imply conscious display of self-discipline and absence of agitation. *Composed* also often suggests serenity or sedateness, and *collected,* mental concentration. *Unruffled* emphasizes calmness in the face of severe provocation that may have produced agitation in others present. *Nonchalant* describes a casual exterior manner that suggests, sometimes misleadingly, a lack of interest or concern. *Imperturbable* stresses unshakable calmness considered usually as an inherent trait rather than as a product of self-discipline. *Detached* implies aloofness and either lack of active concern or resistance to emotional involvement.

first as an adjective; the entry then goes on to explain what it means when used as a verb (—*v.*) and as a noun (—*n.*).

3. Forms. For certain parts of speech several forms of the word are given. For example, *adj.* is followed by *cooler* and *coolest,* the comparative and superlative forms of the adjective *cool.*

4. Definitions. When a word can function in various ways (as adjective or verb, for instance), a separate set of numbered definitions is given for each. Some dictionaries begin with the earliest meaning of the word and then proceed in order to the latest ones, but most dictionaries—like the *American Heritage*—simply begin with the central, commonest meaning of the word.

5. Usage labels. These identify words or uses of words that are not part of current Standard English.

WORD	LABEL	MEANING
cool	Informal *or* Colloquial	entire, full
cool	Slang	composure
yclept	Archaic *or* Obsolete	named, called
calculate	Regional *or* Dialect	think, suppose
nowheres	Nonstandard	nowhere

The level of diction is often set by the sense in which a word is used. *Cool* is informal when used to mean "full" ("a cool million"), and slang when used to mean "composure" ("Don't blow your cool").

You will also find labels indicating words that are specialized and will therefore have to be explained for most readers:

WORD	LABEL	MEANING
ganef	Yiddish	thief, rascal
gamophylous	Botany	having united leaves

6. Transitive and intransitive use of the verb. A verb may be transitive (*tr.*), intransitive (*intr.*), or both. After —*tr.* in the sample entry are definitions for *cool* as a transitive verb, one that acts on a direct object (as in "The icy stream cooled the beer"). Under —*intr.* are definitions of *cool* as an intransitive verb, a verb without a direct object (as in "The beer cooled slowly"). Sometimes the abbreviations *v.t.* and *v.i.* are used instead.

7. Etymology. The etymology of the word being defined—its history or derivation—is given in brackets: [ ]. Some dictionaries put it at the beginning of the entry. In our sample it comes near the end of the first part; there we learn that *cool* can be traced to the Old English word *cōl*. "See **gel-³** in Appendix" means that under the heading **gel-³** in the Appendix to the dictionary (which is now published separately from the dictionary itself), you can find still older roots for the word *cool* in a prehistoric group of languages known as Indo-European. You can also find other words that come from the same roots (including *chill, cold, congeal, jelly,* and *glacier*), and you can sometimes find definitions of word roots. If you look up *calculate*, for instance, you will find that it comes from the Latin word *calculus*, which means "a small stone." (The ancient Romans used small stones for reckoning.)

8. Related forms. A related form is a variation on the form of the word being defined. For *cool*, the related forms include the adverb *coolly* (note the spelling) and the noun *coolness*. Sometimes these related forms have separate entries of their own.

9. Synonyms. In a standard dictionary, entries for some words include definitions of synonyms. These can help you choose the exact word for your meaning. (A thesaurus provides lists of synonyms, but does not usually define them.)

EXERCISE 2 Using New Words

Look up each of the following words in your dictionary, and then write a sentence containing it.

1. ingenuous   6. slake
2. clandestine   7. mordant
3. diffident   8. salacious
4. flagrant   9. spry
5. assiduous   10. venal

9.3 Choosing Words for Their Denotation

The **denotation** of a word is the specific person, object, sensation, idea, action, or condition it signifies or names. Consider again the final sentence about fear of an invasion from outer space:

But as we now know from unmanned exploration of Mars itself, the idea that "Martians" could invade the earth is ———.

We have said that the blank should be filled with a word from the middle level of diction—from the group of words falling between high formality and slang. But within this category are to be found all of the following: *ludicrous, groundless, absurd, silly, false.* How do you know which of these synonyms to choose? Just as the sky has different shades of blue, synonyms have different shades of meaning. To choose the right word for your purposes, you must know what each one means. From a good dictionary, you can learn the following:

Ludicrous means "worthy of scornful laughter."

Groundless means "unsupported by evidence." A *groundless* belief is not necessarily *silly, absurd,* or *ludicrous,* or even *false.* It simply has no basis in what is known.

Absurd means "irrational" or "nonsensical" but not "frivolous"; deadly serious people can sometimes have absurd ideas.

Silly means "frivolous," "foolish," or "thoughtless."

False means "not true." A statement may be *false* without being either *silly, ludicrous,* or *absurd.* It would be *absurd* to say that the first president of the United States was King George III, but merely *false* to say that the first president was Thomas Jefferson.

Learning just what every word denotes is not easy. A good dictionary will give you some help, or your instructor may be able to guide you. In any case, try to develop the habit of discriminating between words, of looking for the shades of difference between words with similar meanings. Then you will know exactly how you want to describe the idea that Martians could invade the earth. Only you can make that final choice. No one else can do it for you.

EXERCISE 3 Choosing Words for their Denotation

Using a good dictionary where necessary, answer each of the following questions.

EXAMPLE
Should you use *fatal* or *deadly* to describe a weapon that can kill?
ANSWER: deadly

1. If your meaning is "annoy continually," should you use *bother* or *harass*?

2. If your meaning is "defy," should you use *flaunt* or *flout*?

3. Should you use *toady* or *flatterer* to mean "someone who lavishly praises another for material gain"?

4. Is an impartial judge *uninterested* or a *disinterested* in the case brought before her?

5. If your meaning is "disapprove strongly," should you use *criticize* or *denounce*?

9.4 Choosing Words for Their Connotation

The **connotation** of a word is the feeling, attitude, or set of associations it conveys. To choose the word that best suits your needs in any given context, you must know how connotation can affect the meaning of a word.

Take for instance *house* and *home*. Both of these denote the same thing: a dwelling place or residence. But their connotations differ sharply. *House* connotes little more than it denotes—a place where people can live—while *home* normally connotes family affection, memories of childhood, and a reassuring sense of welcome.

Precisely because they involve feelings, the connotations of a word are sometimes too personal and variable to be defined. The connotations of *steak*, for instance, will be different for a vegetarian and for a Texas cattleman. Yet many words do have widely accepted connotations, and these determine the electrical charge of a word—positive or negative, favorable or unfavorable, generous or harsh.

Compare the adjectives in each of the following sentences:

> Ray is ambitious; Ralph is pushy.
> Ray is tough-minded; Ralph is ruthless.
> Ray is foresighted; Ralph is calculating.
> Ray is firm; Ralph is stubborn.
> Ray is self-respecting; Ralph is egotistical.
> Ray is persistent; Ralph is nagging.

Each pair of adjectives in these sentences is joined by denotation but split by connotation. The words describing "Ray" are generous, making him seem ideally suited for high responsibility in business or government. The words describing "Ralph" are loaded with negative connotations, making him seem all but disqualified for any responsibility at all. Loaded language appeals only to readers who themselves are already loaded with the prejudices of the writer. If you want to persuade readers who have various views, you should try to choose words with connotations that are fair to your subject. This does not mean that you must never describe anyone in terms like *pushy, stubborn,* or *ruthless;* it means only that before you use such words, you must be sure that you mean them.

EXERCISE 4 Recognizing Connotations

Following are groups of three words alike in denotation but unlike in connotations. Arrange the words so that the one with the most favorable connotation is first and the one with the least favorable connotation is last. If you have trouble arranging them, your dictionary may help you.

EXAMPLE
pushy   ambitious   aggressive
ambitious, aggressive, pushy

1. frugal	stingy	thrifty
2. scent	stench	odor
3. corpulent	fat	plump
4. call	scream	yell
5. firmly	harshly	sternly
6. prejudiced	partial	bigoted
7. slender	emaciated	skinny
8. retreat	flee	depart
9. mistake	blunder	error
10. dull	stupid	unintelligent
11. question	interrogate	ask

EXERCISE 5   Choosing Words by Connotation

Replace the italicized word in each sentence with a word of similar denotation but more favorable connotation.

EXAMPLE

After I showed him my receipt, the store owner admitted his *blunder.* mistake

1. Joe's decision to go skydiving reflects his *foolhardy* nature.
2. My uncle *reviled* me for treading on the flowers in his garden.
3. She has a *perverse* way of holding an umbrella.
4. The manager's *timidity* in discussing wages with employees is well known.
5. Professor Branch likes to *ridicule* her lab assistants about their rate of work.
6. Harold has been *shirking* his work at the laboratory.
7. After dieting for a month, Flora has begun to look *skinny.*
8. He dressed *sloppily* for the interview.

9.5 Choosing General and Specific Words

Words range in meaning from the most general to the most specific. If you want to identify something named Fido that runs, barks, and wags its tail, you can call it a *creature,* an *animal,* a *dog,* a *hound,* or a *basset.* Each of the words in this series is more specific than the one before, and each of them has its use:

> Fido is the most lovable *creature* I know.
> Fido is the first *animal* I ever liked.
> Fido is one of our three *dogs.*
> Fido is the fastest *hound* I've ever seen.
> We have three hounds: a dachshund named Willy, a greyhound named Mick, and a *basset* named Fido.

Almost everything can be classified in several different ways, with words ranging from the very general to the very specific. If someone moves, for instance, you can write that she *moves,* or more specifically that she *walks,* or still more specifically that she *struts.* The range from general to specific may be illustrated as follows:

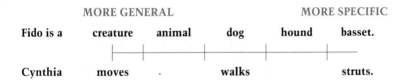

	MORE GENERAL				MORE SPECIFIC
Fido is a	**creature**	**animal**	**dog**	**hound**	**basset.**
Cynthia	**moves**	.	**walks**		**struts.**

A **concrete** or specific word names something you can see, touch, taste, smell, or hear. Examples are *fingernail, strawberry, sandpaper, smoke, whisper,* or *scream.* An **abstract** or general word names a feeling *(love),* a state of being *(misery),* an idea *(democracy),* a theory *(evolution),* a field of study *(biology),* or a class of things too broad to be visualized *(creature, plant, organism).* Abstract words sum up the total effect of many particular, concrete things, and can be powerfully used to label or categorize a collection of items, as in "She went to Mexico and returned with a vanload of *souvenirs.*"

When abstract words are misused or overused, however, they can turn writing into fog. If you write, "We experienced difficulty in that situation," you give the reader nothing to see. This is why good writing *combines* general and specific words. You need the color of particulars to help readers visualize your "situation," and you need the organizing power of abstraction to help them understand your main point. See how the general and the specific work together in this passage written by a college freshman:

> The cartilage in my ankle ripped painfully as I slammed onto the icy sidewalk. As I lay on my back, cursing myself for jogging in subzero weather, the chill of the morning wind made me shiver. I tried to raise my body but my ankle would not move, and all I could do was fall back on my concrete bed. I felt nothing but pain, cold, and dismay.

Dismay is an abstract word, but it perfectly sums up all the concrete details that come before it, and thus helps us to understand what the writer "experienced."

EXERCISE 6 Recognizing General and Specific Words

Following are groups of three words. Arrange the words in order, from the most abstract or general to the most specific.

EXAMPLE
walk   go   strut
go, walk, strut

1. sofa   property   furniture
2. poodle   animal   dog
3. whale   creature   mammal
4. dwelling   shelter   cottage
5. pitcher   athlete   ballplayer
6. automobile   Chevrolet   vehicle
7. run   move   sprint
8. meat   pork   food
9. literature   novel   book
10. pain   problem   toothache.

EXERCISE 7 Using Abstract Words

Use one abstract noun to sum up each of the following sets of three specific words.

EXAMPLE
kiss, smile, hug
affection

1. snarl, spit, scream
2. wheezing, stumbling, aching
3. pale, rigid, breathless
4. diamonds, marble, gold
5. laughter, singing, dancing

EXERCISE 8 Using Specific and Concrete Words

Replace the italicized word in each sentence with a word or phrase that is more specific or concrete.

EXAMPLE
Janet *spoke* to Tom.
whispered

1. Believing she could win with a strong finish, Harriet *ran* to the finish line.
2. In that climate people who fail to wear hats on a sunny day soon feel *uncomfortable*.
3. Cricket is becoming a popular *activity* in Canada.
4. After George III read a copy of the *paper,* he ordered his generals to suppress the rebellion.
5. I *looked* at the wad of five-dollar bills lying in the gutter.
6. During the race there were three *accidents*.
7. *Defects* in the pavement make driving difficult.
8. On a steaming hot day, nothing tastes so good as a *drink*.
9. On my first day of highway jogging, I stumbled over an *obstruction* and fell flat on my face.
10. Eight hours of heavy lifting made my *body* ache.

9.6 Using Words Figuratively—Simile and Metaphor *fig*

Figurative language enables you to compare something abstract or unfamiliar with something concrete or familiar or both, and thus *fig* to make your meaning vividly clear. Consider the following sentences:

1. Boston is like Philadelphia; it lives on its past.

2. My grandmother's house is older than my parents' house.

3. After the mole devoured its prey, it sank into the earth as a submarine sinks into the water.
   —Konrad Z. Lorenz, adapted

4. I was put into the game and stuck to my man like glue.
   —College freshman

5. A sleeping child gives me the impression of a traveler in a very far country.   —Ralph Waldo Emerson

6. The guide shooed his charges back along the gravel path as if they were chickens, which was what they sounded like.
   —Margaret Atwood

7. What does education often do? It makes a straight-cut ditch of a free, meandering brook.   —Henry David Thoreau

8. Every muscle in my body ached and cried for mercy.
   —College freshman

The first two sentences make ordinary comparisons between two things of the same kind: two cities, two houses. The rest of the sentences make figurative comparisons between two dissimilar things, such as a mole and a submarine.

Figurative comparisons help us visualize the unfamiliar and the abstract. By comparing a mole to a submarine, Lorenz shows readers who may never have seen a mole how quickly and effortlessly it can burrow into the ground. Likewise, by comparing education to ditch-digging, Thoreau makes us see what this abstract process often does. Figurative language gives the reader something to look at, touch, or listen to: a submarine, a traveler, a ditch, a cry, a flock of chickens.

Sentences 3–8 all make figurative comparisons. But you may have noticed a difference in the way those comparisons are made. In sentences 3–6, the writer says that one thing is *like* another, acts *as* another does, or gives the impression of another. This type of comparison is called a **simile.** In sentences 7 and 8, the writer says or implies that one thing *is* another: that education is a ditch-digger, a child's mind is a meandering brook, a muscle is a crying victim. Such a comparison, which is a compressed or intensified version of the simile, is called a **metaphor.**

How do you know when to use a simile and when to use a *fig* metaphor? The preceding examples can help to show you. See what happens, for instance, when sentence 3 is changed from a simile to a metaphor:

> SIMILE: After the mole devoured its prey, it sank into the earth as a submarine sinks into the water.
> METAPHOR: After the mole devoured its prey, it was a submarine sinking into the water.

Here the metaphor doesn't work because the earth is not mentioned. The reader cannot readily imagine what the mole was actually doing, and therefore cannot make sense out of the comparison. Now see what happens when sentence 8 is changed from a metaphor to a simile:

> METAPHOR: Every muscle in my body ached and cried for mercy.
> SIMILE: Every muscle in my body ached and was like a victim crying for mercy.

Here the simile breaks the flow of the sentence. Since the reader can easily imagine who might be crying for mercy, you don't need to specify *victim*. Using the shortcut of the metaphor, you can go straight to *cried*. When the reader cannot imagine a missing element, you have to mention it, and you will probably need a simile. But when the reader can supply the missing element, there is no need to mention it, and you can take full advantage of the intensity and compression that a metaphor provides.

EXERCISE 9 Using Figurative Language

In each of the following sentences, an abstract word or phrase is italicized. Make it specific by changing it to a simile or metaphor.

EXAMPLE
Life is *something to be organized.*
REVISED: Life is like a lump of clay; it is our task to mold it.

1. Travel books are *descriptions* of far-off places.

2. Entering a roomful of strange people is *frightening.*

3. The first week of college is *confusing.*

4. The fat man *moved awkwardly* across the street.

5. The child accepted the story *trustingly.*

cli

9.7 Avoiding Mixed Metaphor   *mix met*

A mixed metaphor is a set of two or more metaphors that do not mesh:

> * When the proposal was made, he smelled a rat, and he set out to nip it in the bud.
> * If we cannot get the deficit under control, the ship of state may soon come to the end of the road.

In the first example, a rat turns into a bud; in the second, a ship travels a road. To correct a mixed metaphor, make your metaphors consistent:

> EDITED: When the proposal was made, he smelled a rat, and he set out to trap it.
> EDITED: If we cannot get the deficit under control, the ship of state may soon capsize.

9.8 Controlling Clichés   *cli*

Clichés are the old coins of language: phrases that once made a striking impression but have since been rubbed smooth by repeated handling. We use clichés because they come readily to mind, because they can quickly fill up or fill out a sentence, and because many of them are figures of speech and therefore seem colorful or catchy. "Busy as a bee" sounds catchier than "busy" for the same reason that a foxtail on a radio antenna draws more attention than the antenna by itself does. But using worn-out phrases tells the reader that you have no imagination of your own, and instead of catching or stimulating your readers' interest, clichés will irritate them. Though all of us use clichés occasionally, overuse of them leads to passages like this:

> *At this point in time,* we should *let bygones be bygones, bury the hatchet,* and *put our shoulders to the wheel.* We cannot *stand idly by;* we must *make hay while the sun shines. In the final analysis,* if we fail, we will have *only ourselves to blame.*

When you spot a cliché in your writing, you can sometimes give it a new twist, as in *Halfway up the ladder of success, she found several rungs missing.* But if you can't give it a new twist, replace the cliché with a carefully chosen word or phrase:

* *At this point in time,* the national debt exceeds one trillion dollars.
EDITED: The national debt *now* exceeds one trillion dollars.

* In rural areas doctors are *few and far between.*
EDITED: In rural areas doctors are *scarce.*

* *Busy as a bee,* the cobbler worked from dawn to sundown every day.
EDITED: The *industrious* cobbler worked from dawn to sundown every day.

* Jerry's proposal *hit the nail on the head.*
EDITED: Jerry's proposal *solved the problem.*

EXERCISE 10 Replacing Clichés

Replace every cliché in the following sentences with a well-chosen word or phrase. If a sentence has no cliché, write *Correct.*

EXAMPLE
After the party, we chewed the fat until the wee hours of the morning.
EDITED: After the party, we talked until the early hours of the morning.

1. The Dean's report sent shock waves through the college.
2. It revealed that only half the students were putting their shoulders to the wheel.
3. The rest were just having a ball and painting the town red every night.
4. The president of the college said that all these students should be made to straighten up and fly right.
5. But she and the faculty couldn't see eye to eye on how to get this proposal off the ground.

EXERCISE 11 Replacing Your Own Clichés

Using as many clichés as possible, write a paragraph arguing that all thin persons in America should immediately go on a junk food binge. Then rewrite the paragraph and see if you can sweat every one of those clichés out of it.

9.9 Using Idioms

An idiom is an expression that cannot be explained by any rule of grammar but that native speakers of a language customarily use. Most English idioms include a preposition that varies according to the words that precede or follow it:

> bored *with* television
> tired *of* television
> dependent *on* others
> independent *of* others
> conform *to* the rules
> cooperate *with* the rules
> agree *with* the professor
> agree *to* the change
> agree *on* the terms

No general rule can explain why a particular expression requires one preposition rather than another. If *bored with television* is correct, you might expect that *tired with television* would be correct also, but it is not—simply because custom puts *of* after *tired*.

Though the use of a particular preposition often reflects no more than idiomatic custom, some phrases undergo a change in meaning when the preposition is changed. To differ *with* someone means to disagree with him or her; to differ *from* someone means to be unlike the person in one or more respects. (On this point and on the difference between *compare with* and *compare to,* see the Glossary of Usage.)

If you aren't sure what preposition to use in a particular phrase, check a good dictionary or ask your teacher. (Some dictionaries provide sample sentences containing idioms. One of the best is the *Oxford Advanced Learner's Dictionary of Current English* by A. S. Hornby. Written for students of English as a second language, it contains considerable guidance in the use of prepositions with various nouns, verbs, and adjectives.)

EXERCISE 12 Choosing Prepositions

Fill each blank with an appropriate preposition.

EXAMPLE
Some people always complain _____ the weather _____ anyone who will listen.
ANSWER: about, to

1. Crane's disgust _____ her country's racial policies and her hatred _____ its rulers drove her _____ self-imposed exile.
2. She had no confidence _____ the government's promises _____ gradual reform.
3. She could no longer cooperate _____ its demeaning laws.
4. Only _____ exile could she speak and write freely _____ them.
5. But she longed _____ the day when she could return _____ a country that would at last be free _____ oppression.

9.10 Avoiding Jargon, Pretentious Words, and Euphemisms

Jargon, pretentious words, and euphemisms can muffle the impact of a sentence or choke the flow of its meaning. For this reason, you should generally avoid all three.

9.10A Jargon *jarg*

Jargon is technical terminology. Technical terms belong in writings on specialized subjects, but they seldom suit essays on subjects of general interest, especially when ordinary words can be used in their place. Consider these examples:

> When I asked my parents if I could use the car, the *feedback* was *negative*.
> TRANSLATION: When I asked my parents if I could use the car, the answer was no. [or] When I asked my parents if I could use the car, they said no.

> *Upwardly mobile* young lawyers often work seventy hours a week.
> TRANSLATION: Ambitious young lawyers often work seventy hours a week.

If you are writing on a specialized subject for general readers, you can either explain the technical terms (as shown in section 38.3) or use them in such a way as to make their meanings clear. See how this passage enables us to understand the word *genomes*:

> If we became free of disease, we would make a much better run of it for the last decade or so, but might still terminate on about the same schedule as now. We may be like the genetically different lines of mice . . . programmed to die after a predetermined number of days clocked by their genomes.

If this is the way it is, some of us will continue to wear out and come unhinged in the sixth decade, and some much later, depending on genetic timetables.

—Lewis Thomas, "The Long Habit"

The technical term *genomes* is surrounded by words and phrases anyone would know: *die, clocked, wear out, come unhinged.* Even if you have never seen the word *genomes* before, you can figure out roughly what it means here: something inside you, probably having to do with your genes, that may determine how long you are going to live.

9.10B Pretentious Words *pret*

Pretentious words and phrases are too long and high-flown for the meaning they actually deliver. Substitute simpler words wherever possible:

Were it not for the *lucrative financial rewards,* she would have *tendered her resignation.*
TRANSLATION: Were it not for the money, she would have quit her job.

Large-size passenger vehicles utilize excessive quantities of fuel.
TRANSLATION: Big cars use too much gas.

Years of research have *impacted positively on* our understanding of cancer.
TRANSLATION: Years of research have improved our understanding of cancer.

9.10C Euphemisms *euph*

A **euphemism** is a word or expression that takes the sting out of an unpleasant reality. A euphemism for *dead* is *departed;* a euphemism for the MX missile is *peacekeeper;* euphemisms for *kill* include *eliminate* and *harvest.* Since euphemisms veil the truth instead of stating it openly, you should use them only when plainer words would needlessly hurt the feelings of those you are writing for or about.

But euphemisms should never be used to hide the truth or spare the feelings of those who have done wrong. George Orwell gives a telling example:

Defenseless villagers are bombarded from the air, the inhabitants driven out into the countryside, the cattle machine-gunned, the huts set on fire with incendiary bullets: this is called *pacification.*

No absolute rule can tell you that a particular euphemism is *sxl*
right or wrong. You must exercise your own judgment. Irrespon-
sible writers make free use of euphemisms to withhold vital but
unpleasant facts. Honest and responsible writers use euphemisms
only when plain words might needlessly offend or upset the reader.
Good writing is the art of being at once truthful and tactful.

EXERCISE 13 Translating Jargon, Pretentious Words,
and Euphemisms into Plain English

The following sentences are disfigured by jargon, euphemisms, or
pretentious words. Using your dictionary if necessary, translate each
sentence into plain English.

EXAMPLE
The very thought of flying made her paranoid.
TRANSLATION: The very thought of flying frightened her.

1. Young children need positive feedback regularly.

2. Nonsupportive articulations impact negatively on their development.

3. While interactiong with them, therefore, grownups should utilize
encouraging words as much as possible.

4. Also, children should be urged to verbalize their feelings, especially when they are sad.

5. A child whose mother or father has passed on, for instance, needs
a sympathetic listener.

9.11 Using Gender-Inclusive (Non-Sexist) Language *sxl*

Sexist language is language demeaning to either sex. It includes
not just such obviously insulting terms as *stud* and *bimbo* but also
any words and phrases that are condescending to women, that mark
women as inferior to men or restrict them because of their gender.
To make your writing fair to both genders, you should use language that includes both of them unless you have good reason for
excluding one. Specifically, we suggest the following.

1. Use gender-inclusive terms to designate any job or position that
can be held by a member of either sex:

Beverly Pepper is an American sculptress.
EDITED: Beverly Pepper is an American sculptor.

sxl

The stewardess checked her list of passengers.
EDITED: The flight attendant checked her list of passengers.

U.S. Congressmen are elected for two-year terms.
EDITED: U.S. Representatives are elected for two-year terms.

The chairman ruled the motion out of order.
EDITED: The chair ruled the motion out of order.

In words like those just above, you can change the *-man* ending to *-person*, as in *Congresspersons* and *chairperson*. But since the *-person* ending is awkward, use alternatives whenever possible: *letter carriers* (for mailmen), *business executives* or *business owners* (for businessmen), *meteorologists* (for weathermen), *fire fighter* (for fireman), and so on. A few gendered word forms, however—words such as *actress* and *waitress*, for instance—remain acceptable to most readers.

2. Whenever *man* or a *man*-word refers to both sexes, replace it with a genderless alternative such as *person, human,* or *people:*

Modern man takes electricity for granted.
EDITED: Modern people take electricity for granted.

Mankind as we know it first appeared about 40,000 years ago.
EDITED: Human beings as we know them first appeared about 40,000 years ago.

Voters seldom get the chance to choose the best man available.
EDITED: Voters seldom get the chance to choose the best person available.

3. When a pronoun refers to a word of unspecified gender, try to do one of the following:

a. Make the word and the pronoun plural:

BIASED: A doctor needs years of training before *he* is ready to operate.
FAIR: Doctors need years of training before *they* are ready to operate.

BIASED: Any student who thinks that *he* can easily pass organic chemistry is deceiving *himself.*
FAIR: Students who think that *they* can easily pass organic chemistry are deceiving *themselves.*

b. Use a feminine pronoun to balance the use of a masculine one:

BIASED: If we want the sergeant at *his* post on the DMZ in Korea or the lieutenant standing alert with *his* Strategic Air Command KC-135 refueling tanker to meet the high standards asked of those who wear our nation's uniform, the Senate must make that clear in the individuals it confirms for the position of secretary of defense.

FAIR: If we want the sergeant at *his* post on the DMZ in Korea or the lieutenant standing alert with *her* Strategic Air Command KC-135 refueling tanker to meet the high standards asked of those who wear our nation's uniform, the Senate must make that clear in the individuals it confirms for the position of secretary of defense. —Senator Sam Nunn

c. Eliminate the pronoun altogether:

BIASED: Everyone has *his* story to tell.
FAIR: Everyone has *a* story to tell.

If you cannot do any of the above, use double pronouns such as *he or she.* But use them sparingly, and avoid such hybrid forms as *s/he.* Also avoid using plural pronouns with singular antecedents. So long as you can write, "Everyone has *a* story to tell," there is no need to write, "Everyone has *their* story."

EXERCISE 14 Avoiding Sexist Language

Eliminate any sexist language that you find in the following sentences.

EXAMPLE
Firemen oppose the new regulations.
EDITED: Fire fighters oppose the new regulations.

1. Just as a nurse must know how to care for her patients, a lawyer must know how to defend his clients.
2. The jurymen will not be swayed by weak arguments.
3. But a strong one can lead to acquittal for the man on trial.
4. Policemen enforce the law, but only the courts can provide justice.
5. Justice is due to all mankind.

9.12 Avoiding Wordiness   *wdy*

Wordiness is verbal fat: words and phrases that add nothing but extra weight to sentences that could and should be leaner. To help *wdy* you cut away the fat, here is one general technique and several specific ones.

9.12A Identifying the Most Important Words

If you can't figure out how to improve a sentence that sounds wordy, do these two things: (1) Underline the most important words. (2) Make a sentence out of them, using a minimum of linking words. Here is an example:

> It is a matter of the gravest possible importance to the health of anyone with a history of a problem with disease of the heart that he or she should avoid the sort of foods with a high percentage of saturated fats.

> 1. It is a matter of the gravest possible importance to the health of <u>anyone</u> with a <u>history</u> of a problem with disease of the <u>heart</u> that he or she should <u>avoid</u> the sort of foods with a high percentage of <u>saturated fats.</u>
> 2. Anyone with a history of heart disease should avoid saturated fats.

9.12B Avoiding Specific Sources of Wordiness

1. Avoid repeating a word unless you need it again for clarity or emphasis:

> Of all the different *topics* of controversy, from politics to religion to environmental *questions,* nothing appears to get people so inflamed as those *questions* dealing with sex.
> EDITED: Of all the different *topics* of controversy, from politics to religion to the environment, nothing appears to get people so inflamed as the *topic* of sex.

The edited version cuts out the repetition of *questions,* a word that merely repeats the meaning of *topics.* But for clarity, *topic* is repeated just once, at the end of the sentence. Here is another example of effective repetition:

> A college experience that piles *option* on *option* and *stimulation* on *stimulation* merely adds to the contemporary nightmare.   —Caroline Bird

See also section 8.4A, "Using Repetition for Emphasis."

2. Avoid redundancy—using two or more words that mean essentially the same thing:

The defendant was accused of six *illegal crimes.*
EDITED: The defendant was accused of six *crimes.*

This particular problem has been ignored.
EDITED: This problem has been ignored.

3. In general, avoid starting sentences with *There is, There are,* or *There were:*

> *There are* many women who have to work.
> EDITED: Many women have to work.
>
> *It is* this that makes cities flourish.
> EDITED: This makes cities flourish.

Occasionally, however, *There is, There are,* or *There were* can be used with good effect to open a paragraph ("There are two reasons for acting now") or to line up the sentences in a list-structure paragraph (see p. 182).

4. Wherever possible, turn nouns into verbs:

> The crew had an *encounter* with an emergency.
> EDITED: The crew *encountered* an emergency.
>
> The reason for his *decision* to visit Spain was his *desire* to see a bullfight.
> EDITED: He *decided* to visit Spain because he *wanted* to see a bullfight. [or] He went to Spain to see a bullfight.

5. Wherever possible, get rid of adjective clauses like *who are, which was,* and *that had been:*

> Students *who are* in the band have to practice four times a week.
> EDITED: Students in the band have to practice four times a week.

6. Wherever possible, replace prepositional phrases with single words:

> She spoke *in regard to* water pollution.
> EDITED: She spoke about air pollution.
>
> We are *in need of* players *with intelligence.*
> EDITED: We need *intelligent players.*
>
> They were *in a state of noticeable confusion.*
> EDITED: They were *noticeably confused.*

wdy **7.** Avoid the verb *to be* in sentences like the following:

> Shakespeare is considered *to be* the greatest of all English playwrights.
> EDITED: Shakespeare is considered the greatest of all English playwrights.

> Gradual loss of memory may be *indicative of* Alzheimer's disease.
> EDITED: Gradual loss of memory may indicate Alzheimer's disease.

8. When possible, avoid *the fact that:*

> *The fact that* Redford appeared in the stands nearly caused a riot.
> EDITED: Redford's appearance in the stands nearly caused a riot.

> *Due to the fact that* my paper was wordy, I had to rewrite it.
> EDITED: Because my paper was wordy, I had to rewrite it.

For more on "due to," see the Glossary of Usage.

9. Avoid verbal detours:

> When we try to understand what God is, our first problem is *that of nonencounter at the level of vision.*
> EDITED: When we try to understand God, our first problem is that we cannot see him.

CHOOSING THE RIGHT WORDS: IN BRIEF

Is your level of diction suitable for your subject and audience? Is it consistent throughout your essay? (9.1)

Do your words convey the exact meaning you intend? (9.3)

Do they convey the feeling or attitude you want to express? (9.4)

Are they vivid and evocative? (9.6)

Have you reduced your clichés? (9.8) Have you cut out jargon, pretentious words, euphemisms, and wordiness? (9.10 and 9.12)

Are your words fair to both sexes? (9.11)

EXERCISE 15 Making Sentences Concise   *wdy*

The following sentences are wordy. Without dropping anything essential to their meaning, make each of them more concise.

EXAMPLE
The chipmunk who was hiding in the stone wall put his head out warily.
REVISED: The chipmunk hiding in the stone wall put his head out warily.

1. Photographers who worked in the nineteenth century faced many hardships and perils.

2. In their quest for pictures that would be perfect, some fell off mountains or buildings.

3. While engaged in photographing wildlife, they were attacked by elephants, rhinoceroses, lions, tigers, and, in addition, wild dogs.

4. But they were just as likely to die in the darkroom as they were to die in a jungle.

5. Darkrooms were dangerous due to the fact that the chemicals that were required for film processing in the nineteenth century were highly poisonous.

6. It is a fact that photographers had to breathe for several hours each day an atmosphere that was filled with noxious fumes.

7. In 1852 one photographer nearly experienced death from inhalation of mercury fumes.

8. Furthermore, there were some poisonous substances which penetrated the skin.

9. Worst of all were the hazards of consuming anything of a liquid nature in the darkroom.

10. In 1891, a Baltimore photographer who was well known mistook a solution of pyrogallic acid for a glass of whiskey and water.

11. As a resulting consequence, he died in three days' time.

12. For all these reasons, photography in the nineteenth century was considered to be an unhealthy occupation.

EXERCISE 16 Editing a Draft

The following passage illustrates weaknesses of wording common in many drafts. Improve the wording and cut any excess words you find.

A LIFE OF RESISTANCE

Black Boy is an autobiographical account of the childhood of Richard Wright. In the autobiography Wright describes how all the odds were stacked against him from his birth until the day many years later when he headed north to Chicago. The book portrays his struggle for success against these seemingly insurmountable odds, and the story illustrates in particular how his strong sense of justice allowed him to succeed. This sense of justice is shown partly in the way he responded when others tried to control his actions and behavior. Whenever someone tried to control him, his response depended on how he assessed the fairness of what they wanted him to do.

Richard would not agree to submit to a punishment he felt he did not deserve. Richard had encounters with this kind of punishment while he was living with his grandmother and one of his aunts. Her name was Aunt Addie, and she was mean to Richard, and she was a teacher at a church school. His aunt was continually trying to prove to the other students that she didn't favor Richard, who was her nephew. She tried to prove this by constantly punishing Richard for things he had not done. Finally she pushed him to the limit when she started attempting to punish him at home for things he had not even done at school. Richard assured her that he had not done the things she was accusing him of doing. This assurance only made her furious, angry. She threatened him and warned him she would beat him physically. Then Richard grabbed a kitchen knife to defend himself. He told Aunt Addie that he was not guilty of doing the things she said he had done. He said he would not accept her abusiveness just because she wanted to prove something to the other kids at school.

When Aunt Addie saw the knife, she became even more angry, and she told Richard he was crazy. However, from that point in time onward, she stopped accusing Richard of every little thing, and, in fact, she started ignoring him totally. She said he was a lost cause. Richard found that being on his aunt's lost cause list was quite enjoyable, and he was glad that he had defied her by not accepting the punishment that he felt, with his sense of justice, he did not deserve.

10
Reading in Order to Write

Reading generates writing in three basic ways. For a start, anything you read can stimulate a response—fascination, outrage, sympathy, bafflement, even just plain boredom. And as soon as you begin to respond to a piece of writing, you can begin to think and write about that response. In turn, the act of thinking and writing about your reaction can lead you to think and write about what prompted it: to **analyze** what you have read, to explain, amplify, attack, defend, or evaluate the writer's facts, ideas, opinions, or arguments. Finally, any piece of writing that you enjoy reading can show you something about how to write. It can give you something to **imitate.**

This chapter will consider each of these ways of reading in order to write. We concentrate on the reading of nonfictional prose rather than literature, and we focus sharply on the reading of argumentative prose, but much of what we say can be applied to anything you read.

10.1 Subjective Response

One way to get started writing about anything you read is to write about the way it feels to *you*. Do you like or dislike it? Why? Is it easy to understand or hard? Does it answer a question you've sometimes wondered about or tell you something you've never thought about before? Does it leave you with further questions? And how do you feel about the author?

These are all questions that call for personal, subjective answers. As soon as you get the answers down on paper, you are beginning to write as well as to think about what you have read. You don't have to justify or explain your responses to anyone else, or even use complete sentences. At this point, you're writing only for yourself.

You can begin to express a personal response to a piece of writing in any one of several ways. If you're reading from your own book or your own photocopied pages, you can annotate what you read, underlining passages and writing comments in the margin, as we explained in chapter 1 (pp. 29–31). You can also express your personal response in a piece of freewriting. Here, for instance, is a short passage from Carl L. Becker's *Modern History*, followed by one student's freewritten response:

> Students often say to me: "I don't know any history; I think it would be a good thing to learn some." What they seem to mean is that they have never had a "course" in history, or have never read Gibbon's *Decline and Fall of the Roman Empire*, or Mr. Rhodes's *History of the United States from the Compromise of 1850*, or other books similar to these. But they are greatly mistaken if they think they "don't know any history." Every man, woman, and child knows some history, enough at least to stumble along in the world.
>
> Suppose, for example, that you had awakened this morning totally unable to remember anything—all your other faculties working properly, but memory entirely gone. You would be in a bad way indeed! You wouldn't know who you were, or where; what you had done yesterday, or what you intended or other people expected you to do today. What could you do in that case? Wander about helplessly, seeing and hearing things, taking them in as altogether new, not at all knowing what they might mean in relation either to the past or the future. You would have to discover your little world all over again, much as you discovered it in childhood; you would have to "re-orient" yourself and get a new running start. In short, you would be a lost soul because you had ceased to have any knowledge of history, the history of your personal doings and associations in the past.
>
> For history is no more than things said and done in the past. It is as simple as that; and we might as well omit

the word "past," since everything said and done is already in the past as soon as it is said or done. Done, but not done *with*. We have to remember many things said and done in order to live our lives intelligently; and so far as we remember things said and done we have a knowledge of history, for that is what historical knowledge is—*memory of things said and done*. Thus everyone has some knowledge of history, and it is quite essential that everyone should have, since it is only by remembering something of the past that we can anticipate something of the future. Please note that I do not say *predict* the future. We cannot predict the future, but we can *antici-pate* it—we can look forward to it and in some sense prepare for it. Now if memory of some things said and done is neces-sary, it seems that memory of more things ought to be better. The more we remember of things said and done (if they be the right things for our purpose), the better we can manage our affairs today, and the more intelligently we can prepare for what is coming to us tomorrow and next year and all our lives.

Student response:

OK, OK. Knowledge and understanding of history is helpful and important. But not all *that* important. True it would be hard living every day without knowing what was said and done in the past but this could be an advantage.

We've learned a great deal socially through history that has proved beneficial but at times it seems history has not proved helpful. So maybe *no* knowledge of history could be an advantage. If we suddenly awakened and had no memory at all I believe many problems could be solved in social rela-tions. We wouldn't have knowledge of some of the evil or great things one minority had done, and so we wouldn't look at any one group above or below the others. We would have no knowledge of the feuds and wars that may have existed and possibly still exist between nations and minorities. Pres-ent and past discrimination and prejudice would be forgotten. Now I'm not saying this would make the world one giant, laughing, and incredibly happy place but I believe it would make the value of life much greater. Doubtless that people would still become angered with each other, but it would be for a reason of their own, not because of some hate he or his ancestors may have for that person's minority. The world would now not be divided among nations and minorities but by the quality of the people.

Something exciting happens here. Carl Becker's argument that we cannot live without history has prompted this student to take the opposite view: that we could live better without it because we would then be free of the prejudices and racial hostilities that our knowledge of the past gives us. The student does not have the whole truth, but neither does Becker. The point is that a few minutes of reading, and perhaps fifteen minutes of writing, have given the student a topic to think further about. Reading Becker has put him in touch with his own ideas.

If he wants to state those ideas persuasively, of course, he will need to do more thinking. Does he really want to say that *all* history is better forgotten? Or does he believe that we should not let our knowledge of the past tie our hands as we try to shape the future? Can he find examples to support his belief? Thinking about his point may bring him to a more persuasive as well as more polished formulation of it.

But polishing a personal response does not mean depersonalizing it. Here is the first part of a published essay in which the writer states her response to a book:

> There's a book out called *Is There Life after High School?* It's a fairly silly book, maybe because the subject matter is the kind that only hurts when you think. Its thesis—that most people never get over the social triumphs or humiliations of high school—is not novel. Still, I read it with the respectful attention a serious hypochondriac accords the lowliest "dear doctor" column. I don't know about most people, but for me, forgiving my parents for real and imagined derelictions has been easy compared to forgiving myself for being a teenage reject.
>
> Victims of high school trauma—which seems to have afflicted a disproportionate number of writers, including Ralph Keyes, the author of this book—tend to embrace the ugly duckling myth of adolescent social relations: the "innies" (Keyes's term) are good-looking, athletic mediocrities who will never amount to much, while the "outies" are intelligent, sensitive, creative individuals who will do great things in an effort to make up for their early defeats. . . . In contrast, the ex-prom queens and kings he interviews slink through life, hiding their pasts lest someone call them "dumb jock" or "cheerleader type," perpetually wondering what to do for an encore.
>
> If only it were that simple. There may really be high schools where life approximates an Archie comic, but even in

the Fifties, my large (5000 students), semisuburban (Queens, New York), heterogeneous high school was not one of them. The students' social life was fragmented along ethnic and class lines; there was no universally recognized, schoolwide social hierarchy. Being an athlete or a cheerleader or a student officer didn't mean much. Belonging to an illegal sorority or fraternity meant more, at least in some circles, but many socially active students chose not to join. The most popular kids were not necessarily the best looking or the best dressed or the most snobbish or the least studious. In retrospect, it seems to me that they were popular for much more honorable reasons. They were attuned to other people, aware of subtle social nuances. They projected an inviting sexual warmth. Far from being slavish followers of fashion, they were self-confident enough to set fashions. They suggested, initiated, led. Above all—this was their main appeal for me—they knew how to have a good time.

—Ellen Willis, "Memoirs of a Non-Prom Queen"

This writer's account of a book she has read is both objective and subjective. Objectively, she mentions its thesis—its main point—in her first paragraph, and she goes on in the next one to describe its contents. But the rest of her discussion is personal. She is judging this book about the effects of high school in the light of what she personally observed when *she* was in high school, of what she saw not just in herself but in others—especially in those who were popular.

Another way of turning a subjective response into a finished essay is to begin with a personal experience that *introduces* one of the basic themes in the book you are writing about. Here, for instance, are the opening paragraphs of a student essay on the theme of solitude in Thoreau's *Walden:*

The whirling snow and howling wind seemed determined to destroy me for trespassing on the sacred heights of Mount Washington in the middle of the winter. Spindrift poured down the Northern Gully like water from a faucet, but the screaming blasts of bone-chilling wind took my mind off the snow. With a cloud cover sitting on the mountaintop like a mother hen on her egg, I could see hardly anything of the steep, huge, icy headwall on which I perched. As I pressed upward, my modern steel ice tools seemed no more than thumbtacks. My arms felt like enormous sponges—full and heavy, yet also powerless. My calves burned, my feet froze, and my legs trembled like a mouse before a lion. The climb seemed endless. No rope bound me to anyone else; my climbing partner had turned back hours ago. There was only me and a wild, white, screaming world of perils. I have never in my life felt such solitude, and at the same time such freedom from loneliness.

To experience this kind of solitude is to understand one of the most important things that Thoreau discovered at Walden Pond. In *Walden*, Thoreau observes that many people fear or dislike solitude, that they cannot understand how he could bear to live alone for two years. To answer this question, Thoreau reveals in his book the difference between solitude and loneliness. While these two states may seem inseparable, Thoreau shows that they can be entirely independent.

This student responds to *Walden* by recalling a personal experience of solitude. In turn, the personal experience provides him with a way into Thoreau's book. It leads him to a thesis—a statement about the meaning of the book—and thus to the germ of an essay about it.

EXERCISE 1 Expressing a Subjective Response

This exercise has three parts. (1) Read the following essay by Lewis Thomas and record your immediate personal reaction to it—without worrying about sentence structure or form. (2) Compare Thomas's description of American health care to your own experience of it. (3) Use your personal experience of health care to introduce a statement of thesis about the meaning or value of Thomas's comments.

THE HEALTH-CARE SYSTEM

The health-care system of this country is a staggering enterprise, in any sense of the adjective. Whatever the failures of distribution and lack of coordination, it is the gigantic scale and scope of the total collective effort that first catches the breath, and its cost. The dollar figures are almost beyond grasping. They vary from year to year, always upward, ranging from something like $10 billion in 1950 to an estimated $140 billion in 1978, with much more to come in the years just ahead, whenever a national health-insurance program is installed. The official guess is that we are now investing a round 8 percent of the GNP in Health; it could soon rise to 10 or 12 percent.

Those are the official numbers, and only for the dollars that flow in an authorized way—for hospital charges, physician's fees, prescribed drugs, insurance premiums, the construction of facilities, research, and the like.

But these dollars are only part of it. Why limit the estimates to the strictly professional costs? There is another huge
marketplace, in which vast sums are exchanged for items
designed for the improvement of Health.   20

The television and radio industry, no small part of the
national economy, feeds on Health, or, more precisely, on disease, for a large part of its sustenance. Not just the primarily
medical dramas and the illness or surgical episodes threaded
through many of the nonmedical stories, in which the central   25
human dilemma is illness; almost all the commercial
announcements, in an average evening, are pitches for items
to restore failed health: things for stomach gas, constipation,
headaches, nervousness, sleeplessness or sleepiness, arthritis,
anemia, disquiet, and the despair of malodorousness, sweat,   30
yellowed teeth, dandruff, furuncles, piles. The food industry
plays the role of surrogate physician, advertising breakfast
cereals as though they were tonics, vitamins, restoratives; they
are now out-hawked by the specialized Health-food industry
itself, with its nonpolluted, organic, "naturally" vitalizing   35
products. Chewing gum is sold as a tooth cleanser. Vitamins
have taken the place of prayer.

The publishing industry, hardcover, paperbacks, magazines, and all, seems to be kept alive by Health, new techniques for achieving mental health, cures for arthritis, and   40
diets mostly for the improvement of everything.

The transformation of our environment has itself become
an immense industry, costing rather more than the moon, in
aid of Health. Pollution is supposed to be primarily a medical
problem; when the television weatherman tells whether New   45
York's air is "acceptable" or not that day, he is talking about
human lungs, he believes. Pollutants which may be impairing
photosynthesis by algae in the world's oceans, or destroying
all the life in topsoil, or killing all the birds are being worried
about lest they cause cancer in us, for heaven's sake.   50

Tennis has become more than the national sport; it is a
rigorous discipline, a form of collective physiotherapy. Jogging is done by swarms of people, out onto the streets each
day in underpants, moving in a stolid sort of rapid trudge,
hoping by this to stay alive. Bicycles are cures. Meditation   55
may be good for the soul but it is even better for the blood
pressure.

As a people, we have become obsessed with Health.

There is something fundamentally, radically unhealthy
about all this. We do not seem to be seeking more exuberance   60
in living as much as staving off failure, putting off dying. We
have lost all confidence in the human body.

The new consensus is that we are badly designed,

intrinsically fallible, vulnerable to a host of hostile influences inside and around us, and only precariously alive. We live in danger of falling apart at any moment, and are therefore always in need of surveillance and propping up. Without the professional attention of a health-care system, we would fall in our tracks.

This is a new way of looking at things, and perhaps it can only be accounted for as a manifestation of spontaneous, undirected, societal *propaganda.* We keep telling each other this sort of thing, and back it comes on television or in the weekly newsmagazines, confirming all the fears, instructing us, as in the usual final paragraph of the personal-advice columns in the daily paper, to "seek professional help." Get a checkup. Go on a diet. Meditate. Jog. Have some surgery. Take two tablets, with water. *Spring* water. If pain persists, if anomie persists, if boredom persists, see your doctor.

It is extraordinary that we have just now become convinced of our bad health, our constant jeopardy of disease and death, at the very time when the facts should be telling us the opposite. In a more rational world, you'd think we would be staging bicentennial ceremonies for the celebration of our general good shape. In the year 1976, out of a population of around 220 million, only 1.9 million died, or just under 1 percent, not at all a discouraging record once you accept the fact of mortality itself. The life expectancy for the whole population rose to seventy-two years, the longest stretch ever achieved in this country. Despite the persisting roster of still-unsolved major diseases—cancer, heart disease, stroke, arthritis, and the rest—most of us have a clear, unimpeded run at a longer and healthier lifetime than could have been foreseen by any earlier generation. The illnesses that plague us the most, when you count up the numbers in the U.S. Vital Statistics reports, are respiratory and gastrointestinal infections, which are, by and large, transient, reversible affairs needing not much more than Grandmother's advice for getting through safely. Thanks in great part to the improved sanitary engineering, nutrition, and housing of the past century, and in real but less part to contemporary immunization and antibiotics, we are free of the great infectious diseases, especially tuberculosis and lobar pneumonia, which used to cut us down long before our time. We are even beginning to make progress in our understanding of the mechanisms underlying the chronic illnesses still with us, and sooner or later, depending on the quality and energy of biomedical research, we will learn to cope effectively with most of these, maybe all. We will still age away and die, but the aging, and even the dying, can become a healthy process.

On balance, we ought to be more pleased with ourselves than   110
we are, and more optimistic for the future.

The trouble is, we are being taken in by the propaganda, and it is bad not only for the spirit of society; it will make any health-care system, no matter how large and efficient, unworkable. If people are educated to believe that they are   115 fundamentally fragile, always on the verge of mortal disease, perpetually in need of support by health-care professionals at every side, always dependent on an imagined discipline of "preventive" medicine, there can be no limit to the numbers of doctors' offices, clinics, and hospitals required to meet the   120 demand. In the end, we would all become doctors, spending our days screening each other for disease.

We are, in real life, a reasonably healthy people. Far from being ineptly put together, we are amazingly tough, durable organisms, full of health, ready for most contingencies. The   125 new danger to our well-being, if we continue to listen to all the talk, is in becoming a nation of healthy hypochondriacs, living gingerly, worrying ourselves half to death.

And we do not have time for this sort of thing anymore, nor can we afford such a distraction from our other, consid-   130 erably more urgent problems. Indeed, we should be worrying that our preoccupation with personal health may be a symptom of copping out, an excuse for running upstairs to recline on a couch, sniffing the air for contaminants, spraying the room with deodorants, while just outside, the whole of soci-   135 ety is coming undone.

— From Lewis Thomas, *The Medusa and the Snail*

10.2 Analytical Response

To analyze a piece of writing is to take it apart in order to show how it works. You identify its components so that you can explain their relation to each other and to the chief point the writer is trying to make.

Effective analysis begins with studying the writer's tone. Once you have identified that, you can find the writer's main point, test your understanding of this point by summarizing and paraphrasing the writer's words, and judge the supporting points.

10.2A Catching the Tone

Earlier, we discussed the ways in which you can convey a particular tone of voice in your own writing (see section 2.5). But tone is also part of what you experience when you read the writing of someone else. It affects the way you "take" what you read—the way you feel about it and hence the way you interpret it. When Carl Becker writes "Students often say to me," he reveals that he is probably a teacher, but we might also guess that from his lecture-room tone: "Please note that I do not say *predict* the future." Politely but firmly, he is treating us as students, carefully guiding us through his explanation. The tone tells us that he straightforwardly means what he says, so that we can take his words at face value.

But now consider this passage—the opening paragraphs of an essay:

WHY I WANT A WIFE

I belong to that classification of people known as wives. I am A Wife. And, not altogether incidentally, I am a mother.

Not too long ago a male friend of mine appeared on the scene fresh from a recent divorce. He had one child, who is, of course, with his ex-wife. He is looking for another wife. As I thought about him while I was ironing one evening, it suddenly occurred to me that I, too, would like to have a wife. Why do I want a wife?

I would like to go back to school so that I can become economically independent, support myself, and, if need be, support those dependent upon me. I want a wife who will work and send me to school. And while I am going to school I want a wife to take care of my children. I want a wife to keep track of the children's doctor and dentist appointments. And to keep track of mine, too. I want a wife to make sure my children eat properly and are kept clean. I want a wife who is a good nurturant attendant to my children, who arranges for their schooling, makes sure that they have an adequate social life with their peers, takes them to the park, the zoo, etc. I want a wife who takes care of the children when they are sick, a wife who arranges to be around when the children need special care, because, of course, I cannot miss classes at school. My wife must arrange to lose time at work and not lose the job. It may mean a small cut in my wife's income from time to time, but I guess I can tolerate that. Needless to say, my wife will arrange and pay for the care of the children while my wife is working. —Judy Syfers

On the surface, the writer's tone is direct, decisive, and assertive. She leaves no doubt about what she wants. Yet the second paragraph tells us that we can't take this essay at face value. A writer who calls herself "A Wife" and who also declares that she *wants* a wife must be playing some kind of game.

We soon discover that she is masquerading as a wife-hunting man: the kind of man who expects his wife to put him through school, satisfy all of his needs, serve him and his children in every possible way, and demand nothing in return. The real purpose of the masquerade becomes clear when we consider the sheer extravagance of these requirements. What the writer actually wants is to expose the egotism and insensitivity of men who think of wives as all-purpose servants.

The gap between tone and content here signals **irony.** If a writer sounds direct and decisive in stating demands that are grossly inconsiderate, or earnest and sincere in proposing something crazy, silly, or wildly inconsistent, you can be fairly certain that he or she is being *ironic.*

Now consider the tone in this passage:

> Home for Christmas my first year in college, I spoke to my best friend from high school. Elizabeth and I stayed on the phone for 45 minutes, but we had nothing very much to say to each other. After the conversation, I was upset. I remember wanting to tell my mother, who asked what the matter was, about the weirdness of discovering that this woman and I, who had talked every school day for five years, no longer had anything in common. All I could do was cry.
>
> Except for a brief, awkward visit to my house a month later when my father died, a church wedding where Elizabeth married a man I'd gone out with in seventh grade, and two short stopovers in southern New Jersey, I don't remember ever seeing or speaking to her again.
>
> We used to spend hours talking about our relationships with boys. We never discussed our relationship with each other. Except for the few minutes with my mother, who told me she thought Elizabeth and I never had anything in common, and my once making a distinction between acquaintances and friends, I'd never spoken about what I considered a real friendship.
>
> Many people have expressed agreement with Cicero that "friendship can only exist between good men." I'm not one of them. As a 30-year-old woman who has had friends since grade school, I have been very concerned with those friendships. Yet only in the last few years have such relationships been acknowledged as being as important as they've always been.
>
> It was always commonplace for girls in my high school to spend a great deal of time together. It was also common-

place for a girl to spend Saturdays with another girl listening to Johnny Mathis albums, trying on clothes to find something that fit right, or babysitting and then having the evening that was planned together usurped by some boy calling up for a date. When this happened to me, I felt betrayed. I never said anything. It didn't occur to me that this wasn't the natural order of things. I didn't know anyone who complained, nor do I remember anyone who ever turned down a boy because she'd already made plans with a girl.

—Susan Lee, "Friendship, Feminism, and Betrayal"

Here the tone is neither didactic nor ironically assertive. The writer is neither telling us plainly what we ought to think ("Please note . . .") nor pretending to say the opposite of what she really means. Instead, her tone is confiding. As candidly as possible, she is striving to recall the conflicts she experienced in her adolescent friendships with other women.

EXERCISE 2 Recognizing Tone

Read the following passage and then briefly describe (1) the author's attitude toward his audience, (2) his tone, and (3) his intention.

Being told I would be expected to talk here, I inquired what sort of talk I ought to make. They said it should be something suitable to youth—something didactic, instructive, or something in the nature of good advice. Very well. I have a few things in my mind which I have often longed to say for the instruction of the young; for it is in one's tender early years that such things will best take root and be most enduring and most valuable. First, then, I will say to you, my young friends—and I say it beseechingly, urgingly—

Always obey your parents, when they are present. This is the best policy in the long run, because if you don't they will make you. Most parents think they know better than you do, and you can generally make more by humoring that superstition than you can by acting on your own better judgment.

Be respectful to your superiors, if you have any, also to strangers, and sometimes to others. If a person offends you, and you are in doubt as to whether it was intentional or not, do not resort to extreme measures; simply watch your chance and hit him with a brick. That will be sufficient. If you shall find that he had not intended any offense, come out frankly and confess yourself in the wrong when you struck him; acknowledge it like a man and say you didn't mean to. Yes,

always avoid violence; in this age of charity and kindliness,
the time has gone by for such things. Leave dynamite to the
low and unrefined.　　　　—Mark Twain, "Advice to Youth"

10.2B Finding the Writer's Main Point

The first place to look for a writer's main point is the first sentence you read. Consider this paragraph:

> People feel safer behind some kind of physical barrier.
> If a social situation is in any way threatening, then there is an
> immediate urge to set up such a barricade. For a tiny child
> faced with a stranger, the problem is usually solved by hiding
> behind its mother's body and peeping out at the intruder to
> see what he or she will do next. If the mother's body is not
> available, then a chair or some other piece of solid furniture
> will do. If the stranger insists on coming closer, then the peep-
> ing face must be hidden too. If the insensitive intruder contin-
> ues to approach despite these obvious signals of fear, then there
> is nothing for it but to scream or flee.
>
> 　　　　　　　—Desmond Morris, *Manwatching:*
> 　　　　　　　*A Field Guide to Human Behavior*

The first sentence of this paragraph states its main point and the
rest of the sentences illustrate this point.

Though the first sentence is the first place to look for the
writer's main point, you will often have to look further. For
example:

> The movement has many faces: from sweet ladies
> handing out red roses and right-to-life cookbooks, to demon-
> strators brandishing bottled fetuses and hoodlums attacking
> medical clinics. It has many voices as well: from righteous
> ministers preaching the sanctity of unborn souls, to editorials
> raising the specter of the holocaust, to crowds screaming
> "murderer" at elected officials who take a different position.
>
> This is the anti-abortion movement, a cause that refuses
> to yield. Six years ago, the U.S. Supreme Court ruled that the
> right to have an abortion is beyond the reach of government.
> Since then, public-opinion polls have consistently shown that
> a majority of Americans favor making abortion a matter for
> patient and doctor to decide. Despite these developments, the
> subject is more politically explosive today than ever before.
> Opposition to abortion has become the most implacable, and
> perhaps the nastiest, public-issue campaign in at least a half
> century.
>
> 　　—Roger M. Williams, "The Power of Fetal Politics" (1979)

The first paragraph speaks of a "movement." But since no sentence in this paragraph tells us openly what the movement is, we are driven onward to the next paragraph. Here we find out what the movement is, and here also we find the writer's main point about it: "Opposition to abortion has become the most implacable, and perhaps the nastiest, public-issue campaign in at least a half century."

How do you know that this sentence states the main point? The answer is that this sentence contains, so to speak, all the other sentences in both paragraphs. Each of the other sentences specifically shows that the anti-abortion movement is either nasty or implacable. The Supreme Court ruling and the public opinion polls are cited simply to show how implacable the movement is, how stubbornly it resists both the judgments of the Supreme Court and the court of public opinion.

Sometimes no one single sentence states the writer's main point. Consider this passage:

> I once choked a chicken to death. It was my only barefaced, not to say barehanded, confrontation with death and the killer in me and happened on my grandparents' farm. I couldn't have been more than nine or ten and no firearms were included or necessary. I was on my knees and the chicken fluttered its outstretched wings with the last of the outraged protest. I gripped, beyond release, above its swollen crop, its beak gaping, translucent eyelids sliding up and down. . . . My grandfather, who was widely traveled and world-wise, in his eighties then, and had just started using a cane from earlier times, came tapping at that moment around the corner of the chicken coop and saw what I was doing and started gagging at the hideousness of it, did a quick assisted spin away and never again, hours later nor for the rest of his life, for that matter, ever mentioned the homicidal incident to me. Keeping his silence, he seemed to understand; and yet whenever I'm invaded by the incident, the point of it seems to be his turning away from me.   —Larry Woiwode, "Guns"

The last sentence tells us that the point of the incident was the grandfather's turning away. But this sentence merely implies the real point of the paragraph: the grandfather's turning away made the writer recognize himself as a killer.

In an extended piece of writing, the main point of the whole may not be immediately apparent. That is, a point developed in the early paragraphs may lead up to another, more important point.

Here are the opening paragraphs and the concluding paragraph of
an essay:

WALLS AND BARRIERS

My father's reaction to the bank building at 43rd Street
and Fifth Avenue in New York City was immediate and definite: "You won't catch me putting my money in *there!*" he
declared. "Not in that glass box!"

Of course, my father is a gentleman of the old school, a   5
member of the generation to whom a good deal of modern
architecture is unnerving; but I suspect—I more than suspect,
I am convinced—that his negative response was not so much
to the architecture as to a violation of his concept of the nature
of money.   10

In his generation money was thought of as a tangible
commodity—bullion, bank notes, coins—that could be hefted,
carried, or stolen. Consequently, to attract the custom of a
sensible man, a bank had to have heavy walls, barred windows, and bronze doors, to affirm the fact, however untrue,   15
that money would be safe inside. If a building's design made
it appear impregnable, the institution was necessarily sound,
and the meaning of the heavy wall as an architectural symbol
dwelt in the prevailing attitude toward money, rather than in
any aesthetic theory.   20

But that attitude toward money has of course changed.
Excepting pocket money, cash of any kind is now rarely used;
money as a tangible commodity has largely been replaced by
credit: a bookkeeping-banking matter. A deficit economy,
accompanied by huge expansion, has led us to think of money   25
as a product of the creative imagination. The banker no longer
offers us a *safe;* he offers us a *service*—a service in which the
most valuable elements are dash and a creative flair for the
invention of large numbers. It is in no way surprising, in view
of this change in attitude, that we are witnessing the disap-   30
pearance of the heavy-walled bank. The Manufacturers Trust,
which my father distrusted so heartily, is a great cubical cage
of glass whose brilliantly lighted interior challenges even the
brightness of a sunny day, while the door to the vault, far
from being secluded and guarded, is set out as a window dis-   35
play.

Just as the older bank asserted its invulnerability, this
bank *by its architecture* boasts of its imaginative powers. From
this point of view it is hard to say where architecture ends
and human assertion begins. In fact, there is no such division;   40
the two are one and the same. . . .

To repeat, it is not our advanced technology, but our

changing conceptions of ourselves in relation to the world that determine how we shall build our walls. The glass wall expresses man's conviction that he can and does master nature 45 and society. The "open plan" and the unobstructed view are consistent with his faith in the eventual solution of all problems through the expanding efforts of science. This is perhaps why it is the most "advanced" and "forward-looking" among us who live and work in glass houses. Even the fear of the cast 50 stone has been analyzed out of us.   —Eugene Raskin

This essay begins by talking about banks, and the main point of the first four paragraphs is that since tangible money has been largely replaced by credit, the banker now offers not a heavy-walled safe, but a bright, open, inviting service. This point is a kind of landing place to which the first three paragraphs lead, step by step:

1. My father won't put his money in a glass-walled bank.
2. A glass-walled bank violates his concept of money.
3. People of his generation think of money as a tangible commodity that must be heavily protected.
4. However, since tangible money has been largely replaced by credit, the banker now offers not a heavy-walled safe, but a bright, open, inviting service.

The fourth point is the main point of the first four paragraphs, but not of the whole essay. In the fifth paragraph, the point about bank design gives way to a more general point about architecture as a whole. The contrast between old banks and new ones illustrates the contrast between traditional and modern architecture, and that contrast in turn supports the main point of the whole essay: architecture reflects the way we think about our relation to the outside world.

EXERCISE 3 Identifying the Main Point

In each of the following passages, one sentence expresses the main point. Identify that sentence.

1. The history of Florida is measured in freezes. Severe ones, for example, occurred in 1747, 1766, and 1774. The freeze of February, 1835, was probably the worst one in the state's history. But, because more growers were affected, the Great Freeze of 1895 seems to enjoy the same sort of status in Florida that the Blizzard of '88 once held in the North. Temperatures on the Ridge on February 8, 1895, went into the teens for much of the night. It is said that

some orange growers, on being told what was happening out in the groves, got up from their dinner tables and left the state. In the morning, it was apparent that the Florida citrus industry had been virtually wiped out.   —John McPhee, *Oranges*

2. In early human history a Stone Age, a Bronze Age, or an Iron Age came into unhurried gestation and endured for centuries or even millennia; and as one technology gradually displaced or merged with another, the changes wrought in any single lifetime were easily absorbed, if noticed at all. But a transformation has come about in our own time. A centenarian born in 1879 has seen, in the years of his own life, scientific and technological advances more sweeping and radical than those that took place in all the accumulated past. He has witnessed—and felt the personal impact of—the Age of Electricity, the Automobile Age, the Aviation Age, the Electronic Age, the Atomic Age, the Space Age, and the Computer Age, to name but a few of the "ages" that have been crowding in upon us at such an unprecedented rate, sometimes arriving virtually side by side. Let us use the shortcut designation the "Age of Science" to encompass them all.

—Albert Rosenfeld, "How Anxious Should Science Make Us?"

EXERCISE 4 Identifying the Main Point

Reread the essay given in exercise 1, pp. 232–35, and identify its main point.

10.2C Summarizing

Summarizing a piece of writing is a good way to test and show your understanding of it. How you summarize will partly depend on whether you are dealing with a narrative or with an essay.

The summary of a narrative or a drama is usually called a plot summary; it may be sequential or comprehensive. A **sequential** plot summary follows the order in which the main events of a narrative or drama are presented in the original work. A sequential plot summary of *Moby-Dick*, for instance, would begin as follows:

Discontented with his life on land, a young school-teacher who calls himself Ishmael decides to go to sea on a whaling ship. He travels to New Bedford, where he meets and strikes up a friendship with a harpooner named Queequeg. Then the two men go to Nantucket and sign on board a ship named the *Pequod*. . . .

Because this is a sequential plot summary, it starts with chapter 1 and follows the order of the original in retelling the events. But that is not always the order that best expresses what happens. Instead of starting with the first chapter of a book or the first scene of a play, you can start with a **comprehensive** statement about the chief action of the book or play, and then give the chain of events making up that action:

> *Moby-Dick* is the story of Ahab's relentless quest for revenge against a white whale that has taken his leg and that eventually takes his life. Ahab is the captain of a whaling ship named the *Pequod*, and the story of his quest is told by one of the seamen who serves on his ship—a man who calls himself Ishmael. Discontented with his life on land, Ishmael decides to go to sea on a whaling voyage, so he signs on the *Pequod* along with a new-found friend named Queequeg. Shortly after the ship embarks, Ahab announces that the sole purpose of the voyage is to catch and kill Moby-Dick, the great white whale that has cut off Ahab's leg. . . .

A comprehensive summary such as this gives a clearer account of the book as a whole than a sequential summary does. While a sequential summary simply recounts one event after another without saying which is the most important, a comprehensive summary immediately identifies the central action to which all other actions must be referred.

The summary of an essay should begin by stating the main point of the essay as a whole, and then proceed to the chief supporting points. A good summary preserves the relative importance of each point mentioned, and thus avoids overemphasizing any subordinate point. Here, for instance, is a summary of Eugene Raskin's "Walls and Barriers" (pp. 241–42):

> Architecture reveals the way we think about our relation to the outside world. While the heavy walls of traditional architecture express a fear of that world, the glass walls of modern architecture express confidence that human beings can master the outside world and eventually solve all of its problems.

This summary begins with the main point of the whole essay, and the second sentence states the chief supporting point. Most of the summary is drawn from the final paragraph, which clearly states the essay's main point, and is often the best place to look for such a statement.

EXERCISE 5 Summarizing

Summarize the essay given in exercise 1, pp. 232–35.

10.2D Paraphrasing

Paraphrasing is restating a short passage in your own words. Besides demonstrating your understanding of what you read, paraphrasing enables you to discuss texts without quoting every word of them and thus to avoid interrupting your essay with long quotations. If you plan to analyze a particular passage in detail, you should quote it in full. But if you simply want to convey the essential point of the passage, you can paraphrase all or part of it. Consider these two ways of treating a passage in Thoreau's *Walden:*

> QUOTATION: According to Thoreau, the legendary Kouroo artist spent hundreds of years making a perfect staff because, "having considered that in an imperfect work time is an ingredient, but into a perfect work time does not enter, he said to himself, 'It shall be perfect in all respects, though I should do nothing else in my life.' "

> PARAPHRASE: According to Thoreau, the legendary Kouroo artist spent hundreds of years making a perfect staff because he believed that time had nothing to do with perfection, and he was willing to spend his whole life pursuing it.

While the quotation makes an awkward bulge in the writer's sentence, the paraphrase fits nicely. Slightly compressing the original, it clearly expresses Thoreau's essential point. When paraphrasing, be sure to acknowledge your source. (If you don't, you will be guilty of plagiarism, as explained in section 34.2C.)

EXERCISE 6 Paraphrasing

Restate each of the following passages in one sentence, using your own words:

1. "Most people who bother with the matter at all would admit that the English language is in a bad way, but it is generally assumed that we cannot by conscious action do anything about it."
   —George Orwell

2. "A good city street neighborhood achieves a marvel of balance between its people's determination to have essential privacy and their simultaneous wishes for differing degrees of contact, enjoyment, or help from people around." —Jane Jacobs

10.2E Judging the Supporting Points in an Essay

To summarize an essay, you must be able to identify its main point and its chief supporting points. To analyze an essay, you must also be able to judge the relevance and strength of each supporting point. You should therefore try to answer these questions:

1. Are the supporting points facts or opinions? A fact is a statement that can be indisputably verified. An opinion is a statement that may be impossible to verify but can be supported by facts—and usually needs such support in order to make an impression on the reader.

Since an opinion cannot stand on its own feet, you should take a hard look at what is said to support it. Sometimes there is no supporting statement at all, and sometimes the supporting statement turns out to be nothing but another opinion. When a writer says that "young people no longer work seriously" to persuade us that the nation is declining, the supporting statement is mere opinion. It cannot be verified until we know who the "young people" are, what their "work" is, and how to measure their seriousness.

Between fact and opinion stands another kind of statement: the questionable number. Suppose you read that there are eight million rats in New York City. This looks like a statement that can be checked and verified—a fact. But who can actually count the number of rats in New York? Contrary to popular belief, numbers have no special authority over words. The figures a writer cites are only as reliable as the methods used to get them or the source from which they come.

In general, therefore you should read with a question mark between you and the page. Be on the watch for deceptive exaggeration, "figures" that come out of thin air, and editorial opinion masquerading as reportorial fact. Life is too short for you to check out every unsupported claim or surprising new "fact" for yourself; usually you must trust the writer. But you can reasonably ask that a writer earn your trust—by respecting the difference between fact and opinion.

2. Are there enough supporting points? In the paragraph on barriers (p. 239), Desmond Morris's main point is that "people feel safer behind some kind of physical barrier," and he supports this point by describing what a child does when confronted by a stranger. But Morris's paragraph on the child is merely the opening of a chapter in which he describes the barrier signals that grownups use, the subtle movements and postures with which adults continue to shield themselves in unfamiliar company. By citing specific examples of adult as well as child behavior, Morris convincingly supports his point in the chapter as a whole.

Supporting points should cover a representative sample of the people or objects that the main point refers to. If a writer wants to show that blacks have become increasingly successful in American politics, the argument need not cite examples from all fifty states, but it should certainly cite examples from more than one state, and from states in different parts of the country. The more varied the examples are, the more convincing the argument will be.

3. Has the writer considered opposing points? To be wholly convincing, an argument must recognize the major points that can be set against it. (See section 7.6, "Reckoning with the Opposition.") When you read a completely one-sided essay on a subject you know has at least two sides, you may be sure that the argument is slanted.

4. Are there any fallacies in the writer's argument? Fallacies are mistakes in reasoning, such as arguing that if a team played better after getting new uniforms, the uniforms must have caused the improvement. (For discussion of this and other common fallacies, see section 7.4, "Avoiding Fallacies.")

READING ANALYTICALLY: IN BRIEF

Tone (10.2A)
What is the writer's attitude toward the subject?
Can the writing be taken at face value, or is it ironic?

Main point (10.2B)
What is the writer's main point?
Where is it stated?

Supporting points (10.2E)
Are the supporting points facts or opinions?
Are they relevant to the main point?
Has the writer considered opposing points of view?
Are there any fallacies in the writer's argument?

EXERCISE 7 Analyzing a Paragraph

Read the following paragraph and answer these questions: (1) What is the main point? (2) What are the supporting points? (3) Are any of the supporting points not strictly relevant to the main point? (4) Which are the facts and which are the opinions?

[1] Today Japan is the world's foremost economic power. [2] Last year the Japanese manufactured one and a half times as much per capita as Americans. [3] While for the first time in decades our exports of industrial goods fell behind our imports, Japan exported $75 billion more of industrial goods than it imported. [4] Japan's investment rate, as well as its GNP growth rate, is more than twice ours and its research and development efforts are growing much more rapidly than our own. [5] Its workers, contrary to our old stereotype, are effectively better paid than our own. [6] And its performance in educating the population, minimizing disparities of income, reducing the crime rate, and increasing the length of human life is substantially ahead of America's. [7] These differences will have far more profound consequences than we have begun to imagine.   —Ezra Vogel, "The Miracle of Japan: How the Post-War Was Won"

EXERCISE 8 Analyzing and Judging an Argument

Analyze and judge Lewis Thomas's argument about the health-care system (exercise 1, pp. 232–35).

EXERCISE 9 Using Facts in an Argument

Explain whether or not the facts stated by Thomas could be used to support a positive conclusion about the state of American health care.

10.2F   Writing an Interpretive Essay

To interpret a piece of writing is to explain what it means. Though interpretation calls for many of the analytical skills we have discussed above, it commonly aims not so much to evaluate as to elucidate, not so much to judge the effectiveness of arguments as to reveal the significance of works that do not usually make overt arguments: works of literature.

The interpretation of poetry, drama, and literary prose requires a number of specialized skills that we do not have space to explain fully here. But essentially, interpretive writing aims to construct an argument *about* the meaning of a literary work, to show that the work as a whole or some element of it—a character, a theme, a recurrent image, a scene, or a chapter—has a particular meaning. Here, for instance, is an interpretive essay written by a college freshman:

THOREAU'S TREATMENT OF TIME IN *Walden*

Henry David Thoreau's *Walden* is an account of the author's attempt to remove himself from society and live a life of self-sufficiency at Walden Pond. Yet strangely enough, Thoreau seems highly preoccupied with one of the very things that dominate the society he has left behind: time. If he is truly independent of society, if he has really forsaken the world of clock-watching business managers and wage-earners, why is he so concerned with measuring time? Why does he have so much to say about it? The answer, I think, is that Thoreau measures his life at Walden not by clock time but by nature's time: not in hours and minutes but in mornings, evenings, seasons, deaths, and births.

Introduction: topic leads to question; question leads to statement of thesis

Thoreau is sufficiently free from conventional notions of time that he can imagine a life without any time at all. He illustrates such a life with the story of the Kouroo artist who set out to make the perfect staff, and who devoted hundreds of years to the project because he believed that time had nothing to do with perfection, and he was willing to spend his whole life pursuing it. "As he made no compromise with Time," says Thoreau, "Time kept out of his way, and only sighed at a distance because he [Time] could not overcome him" (216). This story represents the ideal state that Thoreau would like to achieve. For him, the ultimate achievement would be to make time stand still.

Supporting point #1: story of Kouroo artist shows the ideal of freedom from time

But Thoreau knows that time cannot be stopped. At Walden, therefore, he decides to regulate his life not by the clock time that mechanically runs society but by the natural cycles that govern every living thing on earth, and even the earth itself. The morning of each new day at Walden marks the beginning of a new life, just as spring marks the awakening of the pond from its long winter's death. Thoreau measures his life at Walden by these natural patterns of cyclic renewal. Though he actually spent two years at Walden Pond, he compresses the story of his sojourn into just one complete cycle that begins with the building of his house in the spring and ends—after summer and fall and the chill of winter—with the glorious return of spring. "As every season seems best to

Supporting point #2: Thoreau was reborn each morning and in the spring

us in its turn," he writes, "so the coming in of spring is like the creation of Cosmos out of Chaos and the realization of the Golden Age" (207). The calendar might say that he was one or two years older, but Thoreau feels reborn when spring returns.

Supporting point #3: story of bug illustrates triumph over time

In Thoreau's concept of time, hours and minutes give way to the immeasurable rhythms of nature and life itself. He ends *Walden* with the story of the bug that suddenly emerged from the wood of a table. Many years before, its egg had been deposited in the tree from which the table was made; one day it gnawed its way out, "hatched perchance by the heat of an urn" (221). With no knowledge of how many years it had been buried and no desire to find out, it simply appeared because it had reached at last the peak of its life-cycle. In *Walden*, then, Thoreau urges us to disregard the years in which we have imprisoned ourselves and to stop measuring our existence by the clock and calendar. Instead, he shows us how to measure existence by the number of times we experience a renewal of our lives.

Conclusion

Works Cited

Thoreau, Henry David. *Walden*. Ed. Owen Thomas. New York: Norton, 1966.

This analysis of *Walden* illustrates a good way of organizing an interpretive essay. The author begins with a specific topic (Thoreau's concept of time), defines a problem (the conflict between a desire for freedom and a preoccupation with time), and then proposes a solution in the form of a thesis to be developed. To develop the thesis, he writes three paragraphs on three specific things from the text: the story of the artist, the passage on spring, and the story of the bug. In each of these paragraphs he quotes from *Walden* but only enough to make his points. He uses paraphrase to keep down the amount of material quoted and thus to keep the reader's eye on the line of interpretation he develops.

For further advice on writing about works of literature, see section 38.2A. For guidance on writing research papers about literary topics, see sections 38.4–38.5.

EXERCISE 10 Introducing an Interpretive Essay

Following the model shown above, write the introductory paragraph for an interpretive essay on any work chosen by you or your teacher. Your paragraph should (1) identify a topic, (2) define a problem, and (3) propose a solution in the form of a thesis to be developed.

EXERCISE 11 Writing an Interpretive Essay

Using the thesis generated for the previous exercise, write an interpretive essay in which you specifically refer to at least three passages from the work you have chosen. Include at least three quotations from the work.

10.3 Imitative Response—Reading for Style

In writing, as in any other art, you learn by studying and imitating styles you admire. If you read a sentence or a paragraph that excites you, make it your own. Write it down or memorize it. Then quote it when you get the chance, or imitate its style in a sentence of your own.

Conscious and formal imitation of a writer with a distinctive style can be an excellent exercise. Start by reading aloud to yourself this passage from Mark Twain's *Autobiography:*

> As I have said, I spent some part of every year at the farm until I was twelve or thirteen years old. The life which I led there with my cousins was full of charm and so is the memory of it yet. I can call back the solemn twilight and the mystery of the deep woods, the earthy smells, the faint odors of the wild flowers, the sheen of rain-washed foliage, the rattling clatter of drops when the wind shook the trees, the far-off hammering of woodpeckers and the muffled drumming of wood-pheasants in the remoteness of the forest, the snapshot glimpses of disturbed wild creatures scurrying through the grass—I can call it all back and make it as real as it ever was, and as blessed. I can call back the prairie, and its loneliness and peace, and a vast hawk hanging motionless in the sky with his wings spread wide and the blue of the vault showing through the fringe of their end-feathers. I can see the woods in their autumn dress, the oaks purple, the hickories washed with gold, the maples and the sumachs luminous with crimson fires, and I can hear the rustle made by the fallen leaves as we plowed through them. I can see the blue clusters of wild grapes hanging amongst the foliage of the saplings and I remember the taste of them and the smell. I know how the wild blackberries looked and how they tasted; and the same with the pawpaws, the hazelnuts, and the persimmons; and I can feel the thumping rain upon my head of hickory-nuts and walnuts when we were out in the frosty dawn to scramble for them with the pigs, and the gusts of wind loosed them and sent them down.

You may not think you could ever write like this. But you can—right now. In your own descriptive writing you can immediately use the two simple techniques illustrated here: starting with a memory statement *(I can call back, I can see)*, and filling each sentence with specific memories—sights, sounds, smells, and feelings.

Here, for instance, is a description of working on an asparagus farm written by a student who was deliberately imitating Twain:

> I can still remember changing pipe in nothing but gym shorts and tennis shoes, with swarms of bees humming all around me in the fern and never once was I stung. I remember disturbing countless quail and pheasants, and once in a while catching a brief glimpse of a coyote or jackrabbit. I remember freezing hands in early spring, when frost covered the pipes in the early morning, and burning hands in late summer, when a line had lain in the hot sun for a day or so. I know the sweet taste of grapes liberated from the next field, and the bitter taste of raw potato from another neighboring unit. I know how to grab a handful of wheat and rub off the chaff, leaving only the crunchy grain, and how good it tastes after a hard day's work. I can call back the ringing in my ears after driving a tractor all day, nonstop, and how good it would have felt to have had some earplugs. I remember the shimmering sun baking us to a golden brown as we lay snoozing on the ground after the pipes were changed, and how once in a while the boss would find us in that position. He never appreciated our attitude towards work.

Though you can easily recognize Twain's two basic techniques, you can also see that this is creative imitation. The student does not copy Twain's words. Rather he uses Twain's techniques to summon up personal memories, to generate a description of his own experience.

A passage of any length can be a model for you to imitate. Here, for instance, is a short paragraph:

> When we are children, growing up in our parents' care, we await the spark from the outside world. Sometimes our parents provide it—if we are lucky—sometimes it comes from another source far from home. We sit, paralyzed, surrounded by our anxiety and dread, hoping we will not have to grow up into the narrow world and ways we see about us. We are hungry for a life that turns us on; we yearn for a knowledge of

living that will save us from our innocuous lives that resemble death. We look for signs in every strange event; we search for heroes in every unknown face.

—Alice Walker, "The Civil Rights Movement:
What Good Was It?"

With the main part of the first sentence—*we await the spark from the outside world*—Walker establishes the pattern that dominates the style of this paragraph. Repeatedly starting sentences with *we*, she builds a list of parallels that gather force as she proceeds: *we await, we sit, we are hungry, we yearn, we look for signs, we search for heroes.* (On list-structure paragraphing, see section 8.3A.)

EXERCISE 12 Imitating Style

1. Drawing on your own memories of a specific period or experience in your life, write an imitation of Twain's passage. Begin at least one of your sentences with *I can still see*, at least one with *I can still hear*, and at least one with *I can still feel.*
2. Using Walker's paragraph as a model, explain what your own hopes and expectations are right now.

EXERCISE 13 Explaining and Imitating the Style of a Passage

Copy out a brief passage by any writer whose work you admire, and then (1) explain why you admire its style, and (2) imitate its style in a passage of your own.

Part 2

Writing Sentences

11
The Simple Sentence

BASIC PARTS

The sentence is a fundamentally human creation. Like the human beings who write them, sentences come in a seemingly endless variety of shapes and sizes: some stretch out for line upon line; others stop short after two or three words. Yet the sentence has a basic structure. Despite the variety in sentences, there are certain things we can say about the structure of *the* English sentence, the structure that most of us use whenever we write or speak.

How much do you need to know about this structure in order to write well? If you can speak and write English, you already know a good deal about the structure of the English sentence. But to improve the construction of your own sentences, you may need to know more. To help you make your sentences both grammatically correct and rhetorically effective, this chapter explains the basic parts of the simple sentence.

11.1 The Subject and the Predicate

A sentence normally has a subject and a predicate. The **subject** identifies a person, place, or thing. The **predicate** tells what the subject does or is, where it is, what it has, or what is done to it:

257

SUBJECT	PREDICATE
Helen	is laughing.
The movie about lions	started at eight.
Some economists	have predicted a recession in the textile industry.
Our economics professor	is a former member of the Federal Reserve Board.
The path to the observatory	is steep.
All of our photographers	are now in China.
The auditorium	has new seats.
Two tenants	are being evicted.

Every sentence combines at least one subject and one predicate; such a combination is called a **clause.** In this chapter we consider chiefly the one-clause sentence (known as the **simple sentence**) because all other sentences are based on this structure.

11.2 Writing the Predicate—The Role of Verbs

The predicate always includes a verb, and a verb is one of three types—linking, intransitive, or transitive.

11.2A Linking Verbs

A **linking verb** is followed by a word or word group that identifies, classifies, or describes the subject:

SUBJECT	PREDICATE	
	LV	SUBJECT COMPLEMENT
John Marshall	was	the fourth Chief Justice of the United States.
Pyrite	is	a mineral chiefly used as a source of sulphur.
The primaries	are	testing grounds for the candidates of both political parties.
Susan	became	sleepy after driving for six hours.

The most widely used linking verb is a form of *be,* such as *is, are, was,* or *were.* Other linking verbs include *seem, become, feel, sound,* and *taste.*

The word or phrase that follows a linking verb is called a **subject complement** because it completes the meaning initiated by the subject and linking verb. If the subject complement is a noun, such as *mineral,* it is called a **predicate noun.** If the subject complement is an adjective, such as *sleepy,* it is called a **predicate**

adjective. (For more on nouns, see section 11.3; for more on adjectives, see section 12.2.)

11.2B Intransitive Verbs

An **intransitive verb** names an action that has no direct impact on anyone or anything named in the predicate:

SUBJECT	PREDICATE
	INTR V
Children	*giggle.*
The glacier	*is moving* toward the sea.
All symptoms of the disease	*vanished* overnight.
The volcano	*could erupt* at any time.

11.2C Transitive Verbs

A **transitive verb** names an action that directly affects a person or thing mentioned in the predicate. The word or word group naming this person is called the **direct object** (DO) of the verb.

SUBJECT	PREDICATE	
	TR V	DO
Hurricane Hugo	*hit*	Charleston.
Gamblers	*lose*	money.
She	*wrote*	a song about unemployed miners.
A fungus	*is threatening*	maples in the region.

Some verbs can be intransitive or transitive:

> INTRANSITIVE: The child *spoke* slowly.
>
>   DO
> TRANSITIVE: The child *spoke* the truth slowly.

Some transitive verbs can have two objects: a direct object, as already shown, and an **indirect object** (IO), which comes between the verb and the direct object:

>   IO   DO
> The president *gave* his staff a stern warning.

You could also write:

>   DO
> The president *gave* a stern warning to his staff.

WRITING THE PREDICATE: THE ROLE OF VERBS   259

If you want to stress the one *for* or *to* whom something was done, you can use a phrase:

The president gave a stern warning to *his staff.*

But the use of an indirect object lets you highlight the direct object by putting it last:

The president gave his staff *a stern warning.*

Verbs that give you this option include *make, give, send, offer, show, write,* and *tell.*

Another kind of transitive verb usually calls for an **object complement** (OC), a word or word group that immediately follows a direct object and identifies or describes it:

SUBJECT	PREDICATE		
	TR V	DO	OC
Many scientists	*consider*	the experiment	a disaster.
We	*named*	our puppy	Fern.
Ray	*thought*	the lyrics	meaningless.

Object complements follow such verbs as *name, elect, appoint, think, consider, judge, find* (in the sense of "judge"), and *make* (as in "What *makes* some people stars?").

11.2D Transitive Verbs and Voice

A transitive verb can be in either the active or the passive voice. A verb is in the **active voice** when the subject performs the action named by the verb:

Farmers *plough* fields.

A verb is in the **passive voice** when the subject undergoes the action named by the verb:

Fields *are ploughed* by farmers.

For a full discussion of voice, see chapter 22.

11.2E Verb Phrases

Predicates often contain a verb phrase, which consists of two or more verbs—a base verb and at least one "helping" verb called an **auxiliary:**

SUBJECT	PREDICATE		
	AUX	BASE	
Dreams	*can*	*revive*	old memories.
The early settlers	*would have*	*perished*	without help from the natives.
The comet	*will*	*be*	visible in October.

As these examples show, auxiliaries indicate such things as time, capability, and possibility. Other auxiliaries are *is, are, was, were, has, had, do, does, may, might, would,* and *should.*

In many questions the sentence begins with an auxiliary:

AUX	SUBJECT	BASE	
Did	the initiation rites	*include*	bloodletting?
Are	interest rates	*falling?*	

For a full discussion of verbs, see chapters 19–23.

TYPES OF VERBS: IN BRIEF

Linking verb:

> Some snakes *are* poisonous.

Intransitive verb:

> Slowly the mist *evaporated.*

Transitive verb with direct object (DO) alone:

>   DO
> Janet *wrote* a letter.

Transitive verb with direct object and indirect object (IO):

>   IO   DO
> Janet wrote *me* a letter.

Transitive verb with object complement (OC):

>   DO   OC
> We *found* the instructions confusing.

11.3 Writing the Subject

The subjects of a simple sentence can be a noun, a noun phrase, a pronoun, or a verbal noun.

1. A noun is a word naming one or more persons, creatures, places, things, activities, conditions, or ideas:

SUBJECT	PREDICATE
Children	thrive on loving care.
Freedom	entails responsibility.
Dinosaurs	became extinct some sixty-five million years ago.

2. A noun phrase is a group of words consisting of a main noun (MN) and the words that describe, limit, or qualify it:

SUBJECT	PREDICATE
MN *The price of gold*	has dropped sharply.
MN *Long-standing labor disputes*	can be difficult to settle.
MN *The sound of snoring in the audience*	distracted the performers.

3. A definite pronoun (PR) takes the place of a noun (N):

SUBJECT	PREDICATE
N Investors	have become cautious.
PR *They*	fear a recession.
N Traffic	moved briskly at first.
PR *It*	soon slowed to a crawl.

For a full discussion of pronouns, see chapter 18.

4. A verbal noun is a word or phrase formed from a verb and used as a noun:

SUBJECT	PREDICATE
To err	is human.
Splitting logs	takes muscle.

Verifying the testimony of wit- *nesses to an accident*	can be a time-consuming process.

Verbal nouns enable you to treat actions as things, and thus to get more action into your sentences. There are two types: the **gerund,** which ends in *-ing,* and the **infinitive,** which is usually marked by *to.*

Verbal nouns may also serve as predicate nouns (PN) and direct objects (DO).

PN

Their aim is *to obstruct justice.*

PN

The most common mishap of all is *breaking a test tube.*

DO

Gourmands love *to eat.*

DO

Few enjoy *my singing of the national anthem.*

11.4 Putting Subjects after the Verb

The subject of a declarative sentence—a sentence that makes a statement—usually precedes the verb. But the subject follows the verb in sentences like these:

There were *riots* in the occupied territories.
It is hard *to read small print.*

In these sentences *there* and *it* serve as introductory words or **expletives.** They are not part of either the subject or the predicate.

The subject also follows the verb when the word order is inverted:

In the center of the painting stands *a white unicorn with a golden horn.*

The inversion of subject-verb order gives special prominence to the subject, so you should use inversion sparingly—and only when you want this special effect.

In questions the subject follows the auxiliary verb, so that the predicate is divided:

P   S   P

Will   *the Red Sox*   ever win a World Series?

11.5 Using Modifiers

A modifier is a word, phrase, or clause that describes, limits, or qualifies another word or word group. The italicized words are all modifiers in this sentence:

SUBJECT   PREDICATE
The price *of gold*   has dropped *sharply.*

The words modifying *price* form part of the subject; the word modifying *has dropped* forms part of the predicate. Here are further examples:

       S   P
A negligent workman   spilled lye *over the oriental rug.*
            S   P
The equivocal statements *of the prime minister*   are sending *mixed* signals *to the opposition.*
                       S
The brightly painted masks *used in the hunting rituals*
               P
are *sacred* objects *representing tribal ancestors.*
    S   P   S
Grandfather   sat *in his rocker, watching the children play.*

For a full discussion of modifiers, see chapter 12.

> EXERCISE 1 Recognizing Subjects and Predicates
>
> In each of the following sentences, identify the subject and the predicate, using brackets around the complete subject and parentheses around each part of the predicate.
>
> EXAMPLE
> A fool's brain digests philosophy into folly, science into superstition, and art into pedantry.   —G. B. Shaw
> [A fool's brain] (digests philosophy into folly, science into superstition, and art into pedantry).
>
> What would my parents not do for their children's well-being?
>   —Richard Rodriguez
> (What would) [my parents] (not do for their children's well-being)?
>
> 1. The hills across the valley of the Ebro were long and white.
>   —Ernest Hemingway

2. At once a black fin slit the pink cloud on the water, shearing it in two.   —Annie Dillard

3. Florence Nightingale shrieked aloud in her agony.
                                                                —Virginia Woolf

4. Outside literature, the main motive for writing is to describe the world.   —Northrop Frye

5. It is not worth the while to go round the earth to count the cats in Zanzibar.   —Henry David Thoreau

6. A work of art expresses a conception of life, emotion, inward reality.   —Susanne K. Langer

7. There is nothing so exhilarating as to be shot at without effect.
                                                                —Winston Churchill

8. Who will compute the lonely nights made less lonely by your songs, or the empty pots made less tragic by your tales?
                                                                —Maya Angelou

11.6 Using Compound Phrases

Compound phrases help to turn short, meager sentences into longer, meatier ones. A **compound phrase** joins words or phrases to show one of the following things:

1. Addition

Presidential election campaigns have become long.
Presidential election campaigns have become expensive.
COMBINED: Presidential campaigns have become *long and expensive.*

The dancer was lean.
The dancer was acrobatic.
The dancer was bold.
COMBINED: The dancer was *lean, acrobatic, and bold.*

Ants crawled over the floor.
They crawled up the wall.
They crawled onto the counter.
They crawled into the honey pot.
COMBINED: Ants crawled *over the floor, up the wall, onto the counter, and into the honey pot.*

The witness blushed.
He cleared his throat.
He began to speak in a halting manner.
COMBINED: The witness *blushed, cleared his throat, and began to speak in a halting manner.*

2. Contrast

> Marketing U.S. products in Japan is difficult.
> But it is not impossible.
> COMBINED: Marketing U.S. products in Japan is *difficult but not impossible.*

3. Choice

> The government must reduce its spending.
> Or it must raise taxes.
> COMBINED: The government must *either reduce its spending or raise taxes.*

> The senator had not anticipated the setback.
> Her staff had not anticipated the setback.
> COMBINED: *Neither the senator nor her staff* had anticipated the setback.

For advice on punctuating the items in a compound phrase, see sections 26.7-26.8.

EXERCISE 2 Sentence Combining with Compound Phrases

Combine the sentences in each of the following sets by using compound phrases.

EXAMPLE
Proud nations have gradually fallen into dust.
Great civilizations have gradually fallen into dust.
COMBINED: Proud nations and great civilizations have gradually fallen into dust.

1. The painting was savage.
   The painting was sensuous.
   The painting was brilliant.

2. It cost the artist hundreds of hours.
   It demanded all of her skill.
   It left her exhausted.
   It left her elated.

3. She had feared the demands on her strength.
   She could not spare herself.

4. She devoted the summer to sketching.
   She devoted the winter to painting.
   She devoted the spring to rejoicing.

5. An artist must use her powers.
Otherwise she must lose them.

mixed

11.7 Editing Mixed Constructions *mixed*

A mixed construction is a combination of word groups that do not fit together grammatically or meaningfully.

1. *Taken from their homeland and enslaved in a foreign country

    are among the many hardships endured by the ancestors of American blacks.

The would-be subject of this sentence is *Taken from their homeland and enslaved in a foreign land.* But this group of words cannot serve as the subject because it is not a noun of any kind. It is a **modifying phrase.** To correct a sentence like this, you must furnish some kind of noun as the subject:

EDITED: Taken from their homeland and enslaved in a foreign land, the ancestors of American blacks

    endured many hardships.

2. *Fearful of the dark kept the child from leaving the bedroom.

The subject of a sentence should be a noun or a noun phrase. *Fearful* is an adjective. To correct the sentence, you could replace *fearful* with *fear.*

EDITED: Fear of the dark kept the child from leaving the bedroom.

Or you could keep *fearful,* make *child* the subject, and use a new verb:

EDITED: Fearful of the dark, the child stayed in the bedroom.

3. *The head of the shipbuilding company congratulated the achievement of the workers.

pred   An *achievement* cannot be congratulated; only people can be. To correct the error, change the verb or the object so that the two things fit together.

> EDITED: The head of the shipbuilding company congratulated the workers on their achievement. [or] The head of the shipbuilding company praised the achievement of the workers.

> 4. *Of the two hundred persons questioned, no correct answer was given.

The first part of this sentence leads us to expect that the second part will say something about the *persons questioned*. Since the second part says nothing about them, it leaves us confused.

> EDITED: Of the two hundred persons questioned, none answered correctly.

EXERCISE 3 Editing Mixed Constructions

In each of the following a word or phrase is misused in relation to other parts of the sentence. Edit the wording to produce an acceptable sentence.

EXAMPLE
*Raised in Wyoming has made Polly love the West.
EDITED: Raised in Wyoming, Polly loves the West.

1. By climbing with sneakers in subzero weather nearly froze my toes.
2. Numbed with the cold often made me stumble.
3. But on reaching a heated cabin before sundown restored circulation to my feet.
4. Loaned a pair of insulated boots helped me get back down the mountain safely the next day.
5. Out of all the trips in my experience, I was challenged most this time.

11.8 Editing Faulty Predication   *pred*

Faulty predication is using words after a linking verb that are not compatible with the subject:

> 1. *Another kind of flying is a glider.

The sentence classifies an activity (flying) as an object (a glider). *pred*
But an activity is not an object. To correct the sentence, make the
verb link two activities or two objects:

> EDITED: Another type of flying is gliding. (two activities) [or]
> Another type of aircraft is a glider. (two objects)

> 2.* According to the senator, his greatest achievement was
> when he persuaded the president not to seek reelection.

An achievement is not a time, a *when*. It is an act:

> EDITED: According to the senator, his greatest achievement
> was persuading the president not to seek reelection.

> 3.* The reason for the evacuation of the building was because
> a bomb threat had been made.

This sentence equates *reason* with *because*. Those two words are
related but not equivalent. *Reason* is a noun, and *because* is not.
To turn the group of words after a linking verb into a noun, change
because to *that:*

> EDITED: The reason for the evacuation of the building was
> that a bomb threat had been made.

Or you could recast the sentence:

> The building was evacuated because a bomb threat had been
> made.

This sentence contains an adverb clause; for more on adverb clauses,
see section 15.8.

EXERCISE 4 Editing Faulty Predication

Rewrite each of the following sentences to make the words after the
linking verb compatible with the subject. If the sentence is correct
as it stands, write *Correct.*

EXAMPLE
* A picnic is when you eat outdoors.
EDITED: A picnic is an outdoor meal.

1. Successful campaigning is where you attract a wide range of voters.
2. The main fault of Claghorn's speeches was how they offended
voters over sixty.

poss/g

3. Claghorn's worst mistake was when he recommended large cuts in Social Security payments.

4. The reason for the proposal was because he wanted to balance the federal budget.

5. Another cause of his unpopularity with older voters was his endorsement of mandatory retirement at age sixty.

11.9 Adding the Possessive before a Gerund   *poss/g*

Normally a noun or pronoun used before a gerund should be in the possessive case:

> * Jake winning surprised everyone.
> EDITED: Jake's winning surprised everyone.

> * Everyone was surprised by him winning.
> EDITED: Everyone was surprised by his winning.

The possessive shows that what concerns you is not the person but the action—the winning. When the gerund is followed by a noun, you can use *of* to clarify the meaning:

> Jake's winning of the marathon surprised everyone.
> Everyone was surprised by his winning of the marathon.

EXERCISE 5 Adding the Possessive before a Gerund

Revise each of the following sentences in which the writer fails to use the possessive case with a noun or pronoun followed by a gerund. If a sentence is correct as it stands, write *Correct*.

EXAMPLE
Helen shouting startled me.
EDITED: Helen's shouting startled me.

1. Davy Crockett defending the Alamo is one of the great heroic feats in American history.

2. Along with approximately 180 Texans, he chose to fight to the death against an army numbering in the thousands.

3. There was no chance of Davy emerging from the battle alive.

4. With the defenders refusing to raise the white flag, Santa Anna's soldiers would take no prisoners.

5. Since that fateful day in 1836, Americans faced with overwhelming odds have been inspired to hold firm by someone shouting, "Remember the Alamo!"

12
Modifiers

12.1 What Modifiers Do

A modifier is a word or word group that describes, limits, or qualifies another word or word group in a sentence. Consider what modifiers can do for this sentence:

> The stag leapt.

This is a bare-bones sentence. It has a subject (*stag*) and a predicate (*leapt*), but no modifiers (except *The*), no words to tell us what the stag looked like or how he leapt. Modifiers can show the reader the size, color, and shape of a thing, or the way an action is performed. Thus they can help to make a sentence vivid, specific, emphatic, and lively:

> *Startled and terrified,* the stag leapt *suddenly from a high rock, bounding and crashing through the dense green woods.*

Modifiers also let you add information without adding more sentences. If you had to start a new sentence for every new piece of detail, you would begin to sound monotonous:

> The stag leapt.
> He was *startled.*
> He leapt *suddenly.*
> He leapt *from a rock.*
> The rock was *high.*

Instead of serving up information in bite-size pieces like these, you can arrange the pieces in one simple sentence, putting each piece where it belongs:

> The *startled* stag leapt *suddenly from a high rock.*

12.2 Using Adjectives and Adjective Phrases

1. Adjectives modify nouns, specifying such things as how many, what kind, and which ones:

> *Complex* problems require *careful* study.

> Investors were *jubilant.*

> The prosecutor, *intense and aggressive,* jabbed her forefinger at the witness.

2. Adjective phrases begin with a preposition—a word like *with, under, by, in, of,* or *at.*

> History books *for children* are thus more contemporary than
>
> any other form *of history.*   —Frances Fitzgerald

> The city was *in debt.*

> It was Seymour, *with a big bottle of champagne in his hand, a mile-wide grin on his fat, jolly face,* and *a triumphant gleam in his eye.*

12.3 Overusing Nouns as Adjectives

A noun used before another noun often serves as an adjective:

> Cars may not travel in the *bus* lane.
> A *stone* wall surrounded the *dairy* farm.
> An orthopedist is a *bone* doctor.

But the overuse of nouns makes a sentence confusing:

> The fund drive completion target date postponement gave the finance committee extension contact time to increase area business contributions.

In this sentence, the nouns are simply thrown together, and the reader is left to figure out how they relate to one another. To clarify the statement, remove unneeded words and turn some of the nouns into ordinary adjectives or adjective phrases:

> Postponement of the final date of the fund drive gave the finance committee additional time to increase contributions from local businesses.

12.4 Using Adverbs and Adverb Phrases

An **adverb** tells such things as how, when, where, why, and for what purpose.

> The delegates cheered *loudly.*

> Two bolts were *dangerously* loose.

> Light travels *amazingly* fast.

> *Unfortunately,* [acid rain has *seriously* damaged many forests.]

To form most adverbs, you add *-ly* to an adjective. Thus *quick* becomes *quickly,* and *gruff* becomes *gruffly.* Exceptions are as follows.

1. A few words (such as *fast, far, well,* and *little)* keep the same form when they turn from adjectives into adverbs:

> We made a *fast* stop. [adjective]
> We stopped *fast.* [adverb]

2. Adjectives ending in *-y* must be made to end in *-ily* when they become adverbs:

> A *lucky* guess saved me. [adjective]
> *Luckily,* I knew the answer. [adverb]

3. Adjectives ending in *-ly* do not change their endings when they become adverbs:

> A *deadly* blow struck him. [adjective]
> He looked *deadly* pale. [adverb]

4. Some adverbs—such as *never, soon,* and *always*—are not based on adjectives at all and have their own special forms.

An **adverb phrase** begins with a preposition—a word such as *at, with, in,* or *like*—and works like an adverb, telling how, when, or where:

> *In 1885* a severe drought forced some farmers to increase their mortgages.
> The production of machine tools has fallen *behind schedule.*
> Tyson used his right fist *like a sledgehammer.*

12.4A Double Negatives   *d neg*

A double negative occurs when the writer uses two negative words to make one negative statement:

> *The patient didn't want no sleeping pills.

To correct a double negative, remove or change one of the negative words:

> EDITED: The patient did not want any sleeping pills.
> [or]
> EDITED: The patient wanted no sleeping pills.

Negative words include *not (n't), never, hardly, scarcely, barely, none, nothing, no one, no, neither,* and *nor.* Here are further examples of the double negative:

> *People sitting in the back rows couldn't hardly hear the speaker.
> EDITED: People sitting in the back rows could hardly hear the speaker.

> *The foreman didn't give me nothing but grief.
> EDITED: The foreman gave me nothing but grief.
> [or]
> EDITED: The foreman didn't give me anything but grief.

> *The other team didn't follow the rules neither.
> EDITED: The other team didn't follow the rules either.

For advice on *could care less,* see the Glossary of Usage.

12.5 Misusing Adjectives as Adverbs

When the adjective form differs from the adverb form, do not use the first in place of the second. In conversation you might say that a car *stopped quick* or that its driver *talked gruff*, but formal writing requires *stopped quickly* and *talked gruffly*. Most adverbs require the *-ly* ending. On *good* and *well*, *bad* and *badly*, *poor* and *poorly*, see the Glossary of Usage.

12.6 Forming and Using Comparatives and Superlatives

The **comparative** lets you compare one person or thing with another; the **superlative** lets you compare one person or thing with all others in a group of three or more:

> Jake is *tall*.
> Jake is *taller* than Steve. (comparative)
> Jake is the *tallest* man on the team. (superlative)

12.6A Comparatives

To form a comparative adjective, add *-er* to most short adjectives. A comparative adjective starts a comparison that normally must be completed by *than* plus a noun or noun equivalent:

> Dolphins are *smarter* than sharks.

To form the comparative of adjectives ending in *-y*, such as *risky*, change the *-y* to *i* before adding *-er*:

> Skiing is *riskier* than skating.

With a long adjective, form the comparative by using *more* rather than *-er*:

> Are women *more observant* than men?

Use *less* with an adjective of any length:

> Are the Iranians any *less hostile* now than they were a year ago?

To form a **comparative adverb,** use *more* before an adverb ending in *-ly;* otherwise, add *-er.* Use *less* before any adverb:

> The north star shines *more brightly* than any other star.
> Does anything move *faster* than light?
> Roberts campaigned *less effectively* than Johnson did.

12.6B Superlatives

To form a **superlative adjective,** add *-est* to most short adjectives:

> St. Augustine, Florida, is the *oldest* city in the United States.
> The blue whale is the *largest* of all living creatures.

With a long adjective, form the superlative by using *most* rather than *-est:*

> Forest Lawn Meadow Memorial Park in Los Angeles has been called "the *most cheerful* graveyard in the world."

Use *least* with an adjective of any length:

> According to the *Guinness Book of World Records,* the *least successful* author in the world is William A. Gold, who in eighteen years of writing earned only fifty cents.

Use *most* or *least* to form a **superlative adverb:**

> The *most lavishly* decorated float in the parade came last.
> Of all grammatical forms, the superlative adverb is perhaps the one *least commonly* used.

12.6C Special Forms

Some modifiers have special forms for the comparative and superlative:

	POSITIVE	COMPARATIVE	SUPERLATIVE
good	[adjective]		
well	[adverb]	better	best
bad	[adjective]		
badly	[adverb]	worse	worst
little	[adjective and adverb, for quantity]	less	least
much	[adjective and adverb]	more	most
far	[adjective and adverb]	farther	farthest

12.7 Misusing Comparatives and Superlatives

Do not use *-er* and *more* or *-est* and *most* at the same time:

> *Anthracite is more harder than bituminous coal.
> EDITED: Anthracite is harder than bituminous coal.

> *Mount Everest is the most highest peak in the world.
> EDITED: Mount Everest is the highest peak in the world.

FORMING COMPARATIVES AND SUPERLATIVES:
IN BRIEF

Positive	Comparative	Superlative
high	higher	highest
confident	more confident	most confident
anxious	less anxious	least anxious
carefully	more carefully	most carefully
commonly	less commonly	least commonly

12.8 Using Appositives

An **appositive** is a noun or noun phrase that identifies another noun phrase or a pronoun:

> Graduation, *the hush-hush magic time of frills and gifts and congratulations and diplomas,* was finished for me before my name was called. —Maya Angelou

> Could I, *a knock-kneed beginner,* ever hope to ski down that icy slope without breaking a leg?

12.8A Placing Appositives

An appositive is usually placed right after the word or phrase it identifies. But it may sometimes come just before:

> *A chronic complainer,* he was never satisfied.

12.8B Punctuating Appositives

Most appositives are set off by commas, as in all of the examples above. But you can set off an appositive with dashes if you want to emphasize it, and you should use dashes if the appositive consists of three or more nouns in a series:

> Ninety-foot statues of three Confederate leaders—Jefferson Davis, Robert E. Lee, and Stonewall Jackson—have been carved in the face of Stone Mountain in Georgia.

Use no commas when the appositive identifies the noun just before it and the noun is not preceded by *a* or *the:*

> Reporters questioned city employee *Frank Roberts* about the fire. (COMPARE: Reporters questioned a city employee, Frank Roberts, about the fire.)

> Film producer *Brenda Budget* is making a movie about the last woman on earth.

12.9 Using Participles and Participle Phrases

A **participle** is a word formed from a verb and used to modify a noun; it can enrich any sentence with descriptive detail:

> The *sobbing* child stared at the *broken* fire engine.

A **participle phrase** is a group of words based on a participle:

> Her father, *taking her in his arms,* promised to fix it.

Participles may be present, past, or perfect:

1. The **present participle,** formed by the addition of *-ing* to the bare form of the verb, describes a noun as *acting:*

> Athletes from fifty nations entered the stadium with *flaming* torches.
> *Building* contractors watch for *falling* interest rates.

Present participles can be expanded into phrases:

> *Planning every minute of the journey,* she studied maps and tourist guides.
> The prospector stared in disbelief at the gold dust *shining brightly in his palm.*

2. The **past participle,** commonly formed by the addition of -*d* or -*ed* to the bare form of the verb, describes a noun as *acted upon:*

> A *sculpted* figure graced the entrance to the museum.

Past participles can be expanded into phrases:

> Politicians *influenced by flattery* talk of victory at receptions *given by self-serving backers.*

In the last sentence, the past participle *given* ends in -*n* because it is formed from an irregular verb, *give.* The past participles of other irregular verbs have various other forms, such as *seen, bought, flung,* and *bred.* (For the past participles of commonly used irregular verbs, see the list on pp. 384–87.)

3. The **perfect participle,** formed with *having* plus a past participle, describes the noun as *having acted*—having completed some action:

> *Having struck a reef,* the supertanker dumped over ten million gallons of oil into the waters of Prince William Sound.

12.9A Punctuating Participles

Punctuate participles and participle phrases as follows:

1. Normally, use one or more commas to set off a participle or participle phrase from the word or phrase it modifies:

> *Stalking her prey noiselessly,* the cat crept up to the mouse.
> The mouse, *frightened,* darted off into a hole.
> The cat squealed, *clawing the hole in vain.*

2. Don't use commas to set off a single participle when it is part of a noun phrase or when it immediately follows a verb:

> A *raging* wind fanned the flames.
> The *exhausted* fighter sank to his knees.
> Let *sleeping* dogs lie.
> Steve walked *muttering* out of the room.

3. Don't use commas to set off a participle phrase when it restricts— that is, limits—the meaning of the word or phrase it modifies:

Students *majoring in economics* must take at least one course in statistics.

For more on restrictive modifiers, see sections 15.6 and 26.6.

12.10 Misforming the Past Participle

The past participle is misformed in these sentences:

* For lunch I ate nothing but yogurt and *toss* salad.
* *Prejudice* persons see no difference between one Chicano and another.
* The department heads *use* to meet every Thursday.

If you write this way, it may be because you speak this way, not pronouncing the final *-d* or *-ed* when they are needed. To hear the difference those endings make, see if you can make them audible as you read the following sentences aloud:

EDITED: For lunch I ate nothing but yogurt and *tossed* salad.
EDITED: *Prejudiced* persons see no difference between one Chicano and another.
EDITED: The department heads *used* to meet every Thursday.

PARTICIPLES: IN BRIEF

Present participle:	planning
Present participle phrase:	planning every minute of the journey
Past participle:	influenced
Past participle phrase:	influenced by flattery
Perfect participle:	having lost
Perfect participle phrase:	having lost the election

EXERCISE 1 Sentence Combining with Various Modifiers

Combine the sentences in each of the following sets by using the first sentence as a base and adding modifiers from the others. Some modifiers may have to be combined with each other before they can be joined to the base sentence. Combine the sentences of each set in at least two different ways. Then, if you prefer one of the combinations, put a check next to it.

EXAMPLE
The bird sailed.
He did so for hours.
He was searching the grasses.
The grasses were blanched.
The grasses were below him.
He was searching with his eyes.
The eyes were telescopic.
He was gaining height.
He was gaining it against the wind.
He was descending in swoops.
The swoops were mile-long.
The swoops were gently declining.

—Deliberately altered from a sentence by
Walter Van Tilburg Clark

COMBINATION 1: The bird sailed for hours, searching the blanched grasses below him with his telescopic eyes, gaining height against the wind, descending in mile-long, gently declining swoops.

—Walter Van Tilburg Clark

COMBINATION 2: Searching the blanched grasses below him with his telescopic eyes, gaining height against the wind, descending in mile-long, gently declining swoops, the bird sailed for hours.

1. Wally sang.
   He was soulful.
   He was swaying.
   He was sensuous.
   He was dressed in a skinsuit.
   The skinsuit was glittering.
   The skinsuit was white.
   The skinsuit was satin.
   He was stroking his guitar.
   The guitar was electric.
   He stroked with fingers.
   The fingers were long.
   The fingers were pink.
   The fingers were nimble.

2. The spotlight illuminated his form.
   The spotlight was dim.
   His form was slender.

The illumination was faint.
The spotlight drew him out of the darkness.
He looked like an apparition.
The darkness was clammy.

3. He sang about a woman.
The woman was young.
She was dressed in a raincoat.
The raincoat was shiny.
The raincoat was black.
She was standing on a streetcorner.
The streetcorner was in New York.
The streetcorner was crowded.
She was waiting for a bus.

4. She waited in a certain mood.
Her mood was restless.
She clutched a suitcase.
It was big.
It was white.
Stickers covered it.
They were marked "Broadway or Bust."

5. She had just arrived from a town.
The town was little.
It was in Oregon.
It was in the eastern part.
She was filled with ambition.
She was dreaming of a career.
The career would be great.
It would be in the theater.

EXERCISE 2 Sentence Expanding with Modifiers

Expand each of the following sentences by adding as many modifiers as possible. Let your imagination go.

1. The gorilla roared.
2. The flames crackled.
3. The clown danced.
4. The rock-climber slipped.
5. The building shook.

12.11 Using Infinitives and Infinitive Phrases

The infinitive (usually made by placing *to* before the bare form of the verb) can be used to modify various parts of a sentence:

> Civilization has never eradicated the urge *to hunt.*
> Most young artists are eager *to innovate.*
> Determined *to succeed,* she redoubled her efforts.
> In every situation Chester plays *to win.*

Infinitives can form phrases:

> *To write grammatically,* you must know something about sentence structure.
> On August 27, 1966, Sir Francis Chichester set out *to sail a 53-foot boat singlehandedly around the world.*

Infinitives with *have* and *have been* plus a past participle identify an action or condition completed before another one:

> The work to be done that morning seemed enormous.
> Sandra was glad *to have slept* a full eight hours the night before.
> But she was annoyed *to have been told* nothing of this work earlier.

EXERCISE 3 Supplying Infinitives

Complete each of the following sentences with a suitable infinitive or infinitive phrase.

EXAMPLE
The sheer will _____ brought him through the operation.
to live

1. Throughout history a compelling desire _____ the unknown has led men and women _____.
2. Almost eight hundred years ago Vikings sailed west _____.
3. In recent years adventurous explorers like Jacques Cousteau have developed special underwater equipment _____.
4. The wish _____ has taken astronauts to the moon, and may someday take others beyond the solar system.
5. In medicine, doctors needing _____ regularly use x-ray machines and other technological devices.
6. Even the tiny atom has been yielding its secrets to scientists determined _____.

si   **12.12 Avoiding the Split Infinitive**   *si*

When one or more adverbs are wedged between *to* and the rest of an infinitive, the infinitive is said to be **split:**

> Detectives needed special equipment *to thoroughly and accurately investigate the mystery.*

This sentence is weakened by the cumbersome splitting. The adverbs should go at the end of the infinitive phrase:

> EDITED: Detectives needed special equipment *to investigate the mystery thoroughly and accurately.*

Sometimes an infinitive may be split by a one-word modifier that would be awkward in any other position:

> The mayors convened in order to *fully* explore and discuss the problems of managing large cities.

A construction of this type is acceptable nowadays to most readers. But unless you are sure there is no other suitable place in the sentence for the adverb or adverb phrase, do not split an infinitive with it.

EXERCISE 4 Editing Split Infinitives

Each of the following contains a split infinitive. If you find the split awkward, revise the word order to get rid of it. If you find the split necessary, write *Correct.*

EXAMPLE
He was sorry to have rudely answered.
EDITED: He was sorry to have answered rudely.

1. The nurse took a deep breath before starting to gently remove the bandage from the child's stomach.
2. The child, in turn, began to with strong determination resist her.
3. He exercised all of his cunning to cleverly distract her attention from the task.
4. Then, after running out of distractions, he decided to at the last moment grab her hands and bite them.
5. To fully control him, she had to strap him down.

12.13 Using Absolute Phrases

An **absolute phrase** usually consists of a noun or noun phrase followed by a participle:

> Donna laughed, *her eyes flashing with mischief.*
> *Its fuel line blocked,* the engine sputtered to a halt.

The participle may sometimes be omitted:

> *Head down,* the bull charged straight at the matador.
> *Nose in the air,* she walked right past me.

You can form compounds with absolute phrases, and use them in succession:

> The factory, *its freshly painted walls gleaming in the sunlight and dazzling the beholder,* symbolized economic progress.

> The village was silent, *its shops closed, the streets deserted.*

> The skaters are quick-silvering around the frosty rink, *the girls gliding and spinning, the boys swooping, their arms flailing like wings.*   —College student

As the examples show, you can enrich almost any sentence by using an absolute phrase at the beginning of a sentence, in the middle, or at the end.

EXERCISE 5 Sentence Combining with Absolute Phrases

Combine the sentences in each of the following sets by using the first sentence as a base and turning the others into absolute phrases.

EXAMPLE
Finch dozed.
His chin was resting on his chest.
COMBINED: Finch dozed, his chin resting on his chest.

1. Janet rode the big wave.
   Her shoulders were hunched.
   Her hair was streaming in the wind.
   Her toes were curled over the edge of the board.

2. The board sped forward.
   Its slender frame was propelled by surging water.

3. Janet yelled with delight.
   Her heart was pounding.
   Her eyes were sparkling with excitement.

4. Meanwhile the lifeguard gripped the arms of his chair.
   His knuckles were white.
   His hair was standing on end.
   His stomach was heaving.

12.14 Placing Modifiers

One of the hardest things about writing an effective sentence is that unless you can plan it out completely in your head beforehand, you may not know at once the best way to arrange all of its parts. You know by habit, of course, that an adjective usually comes before the noun it modifies. You don't write *leaves green* or *fumes smelly* or *brass hot*; you write *green leaves, smelly fumes,* and *hot brass*. But the placing of other modifiers—especially modifying phrases—may call for some thought. Often, in fact, you will not be able to decide where to put a particular modifier until *after* you have written out the whole sentence in which it appears.

While you are writing a sentence, therefore, don't worry about where to place the modifiers. Just start with the base sentence and put the modifiers at the end, using one modifier to lead you to another. See how this sentence grows:

Mary traveled.

Where from?

Mary traveled *from Denver.*

Where to?

Mary traveled *from Denver to San Francisco.*

How?

Mary traveled *from Denver to San Francisco by hitchhiking.*

Did she hitchhike all the way?

> Mary traveled *from Denver to San Francisco by hitchhiking to the house of a friend in Salt Lake City.*

And how did she finish the trip?

> Mary traveled *from Denver to San Francisco by hitchhiking to the house of a friend in Salt Lake City and then borrowing his motorcycle to make the rest of the trip.*

Now, having written your base sentence and added as many modifiers as you want, you can think about where to place those modifiers. You may decide, for instance, that you want to put most of them up front instead of at the end. In that case, bracket the words you want to move and use an arrow to show where they are to go:

> Mary traveled from Denver to San Francisco [by hitchhiking to the house of a friend in Salt Lake City and then borrowing his motorcycle to make the rest of the trip.]

When you rewrite the sentence, it will look like this:

> By hitchhiking to the house of a friend in Salt Lake City and then borrowing his motorcycle to make the rest of the trip, Mary traveled from Denver to San Francisco.

Do you like this version better than the other? That's the kind of question you will have to answer for yourself. If you want to state a simple point and then develop it, you will lead with that point and then put the modifiers after it; you will first say where Mary went and then explain how she got there. But if you want to create suspense, if you want the reader to wait for the main point that is delivered at the end, you will put all or most of your modifiers first. In that position they signal that the main point is on its way, and the structure of the sentence leads the reader to expect this point at the end, where it gets special emphasis. (For more discussion of how to emphasize your main point, see sections 15.1 and 15.10.)

Placing a modifier well means connecting the modifier to its **headword**—the word or phrase it modifies. If the modifier doesn't clearly point to its headword, the modifier is *misplaced*; if the headword is missing from the sentence, the modifier *dangles*.

12.15 Editing Misplaced Modifiers *mm*

A **misplaced modifier** does not point clearly to its headword—the word or phrase it modifies:

> 1.*I asked her for the time while waiting for the bus to start a conversation.

The sentence seems to say that the bus was ready to start a conversation. To get the meaning straight, put the modifying phrase right before its headword—*I*.

> EDITED: To start a conversation, I asked her for the time while waiting for the bus.
>
> 2.*The College Librarian announced that all fines on overdue books will be doubled yesterday.

The sentence puts the future into yesterday, or yesterday into the future. Either way it makes no sense:

> EDITED: The College Librarian announced yesterday that all fines on overdue books will be doubled.

12.16 Editing Squinting Modifiers *sm*

A **squinting modifier** is one placed where it could modify either of two possible headwords:

> *The street vendor she saw on her way to school occasionally sold wild mushrooms.

Did she see the vendor occasionally, or did he sell wild mushrooms occasionally?

> EDITED: The street vendor she occasionally saw on her way to school sold wild mushrooms. [or] The street vendor she saw on her way to school sold wild mushrooms occasionally.

12.17 Editing Misplaced Restricters *mr*

A **restricter** is a one-word modifier that limits the meaning of another word or a group of words. Restricters include *almost, only, merely, nearly, scarcely, simply, even, exactly, just,* and *hardly.*

Usually a restricter modifies the word or phrase that immediately follows it: *mr*

1. *Only* the Fabulous Fork serves brunch on Sundays.
2. The Fabulous Fork serves *only* brunch on Sundays.
3. The Fabulous Fork serves brunch *only* on Sundays.

A restricter placed at the end of a sentence modifies the word or phrase just before it:

4. The Fabulous Fork serves brunch on Sundays *only*.

In each of these sentences, the writer places *only* just before or just after the item it is meant to modify. But if you place *only* carelessly, the result will be a confusing sentence:

*The Fabulous Fork only serves brunch on Sundays.

Is brunch the only meal it serves on Sundays, or is Sunday the only day on which it serves brunch? To make the meaning of this sentence plain, the writer must place *only* right next to *brunch* or *on Sundays*, as shown above in sentences 2, 3, and 4.

EXERCISE 6 Editing Misplaced Modifiers

Revise each of the following sentences that includes one or more misplaced modifiers, squinting modifiers, or misplaced restricters. If a sentence is correct, write *Correct*.

EXAMPLE
An article describes the way skunks eat in *Time* magazine.
EDITED: An article in *Time* magazine describes the way skunks eat.

1. Alvin Toffler states that young Americans are becoming consumers of disposable goods in a recently published essay.
2. After just keeping an item for a few months, children want to throw it out and get something new.
3. I have learned that this practice marks a change from conversations with my grandparents.
4. In their childhood, a girl only played with one doll for years.
5. Then, wrapped in tissue paper, she would put it away against the day when she would present it to a daughter or a niece with fond memories.
6. Likewise a boy would keep his electric train so that he could one day give it to his children carefully boxed.

dg

7. There are several reasons why children no longer keep toys in this way according to Toffler.

8. One is the impact of industrialization and in particular of mass production.

9. Most toys were made by craftsmen who devoted years to just mastering their trade and hours to carefully shaping each product by hand until the late 1800s.

10. Toys were expensive and hard to get as a result; but each was a treasure, a unique creation.

11. Today large machines make toys in seconds, and each looks just like all the others of its kind.

12. Most of these mass-produced toys only captivate children for a short time and then wind up in the trash.

13. Another reason why modern toys soon lose their appeal is that they are made of plastic commonly.

14. Plastic almost costs nothing to make; and when painted in bright, vivid colors, it can seem shiny and desirable.

15. But unlike such materials as leather and wood, plastic does not mellow with age.

16. Finally, children are pressured to be habitual disposers and consumers by advertising.

17. With TV and catalogues continually showing them new toys, how can they learn to cherish their old ones?

12.18 Editing Dangling Modifiers   *dg*

A modifier dangles when its headword is missing. Since a modifier always needs a headword, it will attach itself to a false one if the true one is not in the sentence:

> *After doing my homework, the dog was fed.

And any dog that can do your homework for you certainly deserves his food! But unless the dog is unusually clever, this sentence contains a dangling modifier. You can eliminate it by saying who actually did the homework:

> EDITED: After I did my homework, the dog was fed.

But this revision still doesn't tell us who fed the dog. It fails to do *dg* so because *The dog was fed* is in the passive voice and does not mention the agent—the one *by whom* the dog was fed. That agent should be named:

> The dog was fed by me.

Once you've named the agent, you can turn this sentence from the passive to the active voice:

> I fed the dog.

Now you can write:

> After I did my homework, I fed the dog.

Or you can drop the first *I* and change *did* to *doing:*

> After doing my homework, I fed the dog.

To correct dangling modifiers, you may often need to change a sentence from the passive to the active voice. For a full discussion of voice, see chapter 22.

Here is one more example:

> *Based on the gradual decline in College Board scores over the past twenty years, American high school education is less effective than it used to be.

This is a miscombination of two sentences:

> American high school education is less effective than it used to be. This conclusion is based on the gradual decline of College Board scores over the past twenty years.

So how can you combine these two sentences and not leave *Based* dangling? Our advice is to kick the *Based* habit altogether. To combine sentences like these, use *shows that, indicates that,* or *leads to the conclusion that:*

> EDITED: The gradual decline of College Board scores over the past twenty years indicates that American high school education is less effective than it used to be.

dg

EXERCISE 7 Editing Dangling Modifiers

Revise each of the following sentences that includes a dangling modifier. Either supply a suitable headword as best you can, or reconstruct the whole sentence. If a sentence is correct as it stands, write *Correct.*

EXAMPLE
After checking the figures, the new budget was rejected.
EDITED: After checking the figures, the voters rejected the new budget.

1. At six each morning, the ringing of my alarm clock stirs me from a sound sleep.
2. Crawling from my bed, my black wool cycling shorts are put on, along with my green and black shirt.
3. I grope my way into the kitchen and unlock the back door onto the breezeway connecting the house to the garage.
4. As I face the early morning light, my breath is visible, chilled by the cold air.
5. Hastily pulling on my shoes and tightening my helmet strap, no help from my brain seems to be needed by my hands.
6. My legs begin to wake up wheeling the bicycle out of the garage.
7. Once pedaling along the road, my circulation quickens, and I no longer feel the cold.

dg

8. Turning left at Bank Street and beginning the rapid descent to River Road, the air rushes through my helmet and causes my eyes to water uncontrollably.

9. My senses are fully awakened, and I hear the swishing sound made by the tires speeding over the damp pavement.

10. Exhilarated, my bike is pushed forward, eager to outrace the sun.

11. Sixty minutes later I am becoming tired, straining to push myself up every hill.

12. Reaching the top of a long rise, a short break is taken before turning back and heading home.

13. The morning sun has won the race, just as it always does when pedaling to the point of exhaustion.

EXERCISE 8 Editing Misused Modifiers

Edit the following passage by correcting all misused modifiers.

The *New York Times Magazine* publishes often striking advertisements. One example is an ad for Movado watches, which are made in Switzerland from a recent issue of the magazine. Standing in the center of a ten-by-fifteen-inch page, with pitch-black fur, the ad shows a cat focusing its bright golden eyes on a fishbowl filled with sand, water, and white coral. But the fishbowl contains no fish. Resting among the pieces of coral, it only contains two Movado watches. Below the fishbowl are a brief description of the watches and the words "Movado, a century of Swiss Watchcraft" printed in large white letters.

The ad designer has created an eerie effect by almost covering half the page in black, hiding the body of the cat in darkness, and only showing its head in a dim glow of light. Looking down at the fishbowl, the watches are being eyed by the cat as if they were fish. But the watches also look like the cat. Set in a gold case, one has a black face, while the other has a gold face set in a black case. Thus both watches match the colors of the cat's eyes and fur.

The ad succeeds because it catches the reader's attention. Leafing through the magazine, the mysterious looking cat will strike the average reader, and, submerged in a fishbowl, he or she will carefully examine the watches. The combination of gold and black under water will make them look like treasures discovered at the bottom of the sea.

13
Coordination 1
COMPOUND SENTENCES

To coordinate two or more parts of a sentence is to give them the same rank and role by making them grammatically alike. As we have noted in section 11.6, you can coordinate words or phrases to make a compound phrase. In this chapter we show how you can coordinate simple sentences to make a compound sentence. The very fact that two statements of roughly equal weight are joined in one sentence indicates a connection between them, and when a conjunction is used, it shows just what the connection is.

13.1 Making Compound Sentences

A **compound sentence** consists of two or more simple sentences joined together on the same level. When a simple sentence is thus joined to another simple sentence, each is called an **independent clause** because each could stand by itself as a complete sentence. You can join the independent clauses of a compound sentence in one of three ways: with a conjunction, a semicolon, or a conjunctive adverb.

COMPOUND SENTENCE

INDEPENDENT CLAUSE	JOINED TO	INDEPENDENT CLAUSE
1. They acquired horses	and	their ancient nomadic spirit was suddenly free of the ground. —N. Scott Momaday
2. History does not stutter	;	it rhymes.
3. The average age for women to marry in Ireland is 26	; in contrast,	women of India marry at an average age of 14.

13.2 Compounding with Conjunctions

Conjunctions include the set of words commonly known as "A. B. Fonsy": *and, but, for, or, nor, so,* and *yet.* They show the following relations:

1. Simple addition

The economists considered budget cuts, *and* the politicians thought of votes.

2. Addition of a negative point

Many of the settlers had never farmed before, *nor* were they ready for the brutal Saskatchewan winters.

3. Contrast

We are all in the gutter, *but* some of us are looking at the stars. —Oscar Wilde

All of the candidates claim to understand Europeans, *yet* none has ever lived in Europe.

4. Logical consequence

My father never attended the military parades in the city, *for* he hated war.

During World War II, Americans of Japanese descent were suspected of disloyalty, *so* they were placed in detention camps.

For introduces a reason; *so* introduces a consequence.

5. Choice

Nelson could keep his ships near England, *or* he could order them to attack the French in Egypt.

13.2A Punctuation with Conjunctions

A conjunction used between clauses normally needs a comma just before it, as shown by all of the examples above. But there are two exceptions.

1. You can omit the comma when the clauses are short:

Many are called but few are chosen.

2. You can replace the comma with a semicolon when there are commas elsewhere in the sentence:

On the morning of June 28, 1969, the weather finally cleared; but the climbers, wearied by their efforts of the previous days, could not attempt the summit.

You can use a comma without a conjunction when there are more than two clauses, but you should normally use a conjunction between the last two:

The sun shone, a stiff breeze ruffled the bay, the sails bellied out, and the bow cut the water like a knife.

13.3 Overusing *and*

Use *and* sparingly in compound sentences. A series of clauses strung together by *and* can become boring:

I was born in Illinois, and the first big city I ever saw was Chicago, and was I ever excited! I went there with my father and mother, and we stayed in a big hotel in the Loop, and I saw lots of interesting sights. We spent a whole day just walking around the city, and I got a stiff neck from looking up at the skyscrapers, and my feet got sore too from walking down so many streets. I was glad to go back to the hotel and take a long soak in the Jacuzzi.

To break the monotony of compounding with *and*, substitute other linking words—or other constructions:

> Since I was born in Illinois, the first big city I ever saw was Chicago. Was I ever excited! My father and mother took me to a big hotel in the Loop. On the day after our arrival, we spent eight hours just walking around the city to see the sights. It was exhausting. In fact, I got a stiff neck from looking up at all the skyscrapers, and sore feet from walking down so many streets. I couldn't wait to take a long soak in the Jacuzzi at our hotel.

For alternatives to the overuse of *and* constructions, see chapter 15.

13.4 Compounding with the Semicolon

A semicolon alone can join two independent clauses when the relationship between them is obvious:

COMPOUND SENTENCE

INDEPENDENT CLAUSE	JOINED TO	INDEPENDENT CLAUSE
Some books are unde- servedly forgotten	;	none are undeservedly remembered.
		—W. H. Auden
Too much, perhaps, has been said of his silence	;	too much stress has been laid upon his reserve.
		—Virginia Woolf

13.5 Compounding with Conjunctive Adverbs

A **conjunctive adverb**—sometimes called a **sentence adverb**—is a word or phrase that shows a relation between the clauses it joins, as a conjunction does. But a conjunctive adverb is usually weightier and more emphatic than a conjunction:

INDEPENDENT CLAUSE	JOINED TO	INDEPENDENT CLAUSE
The Iron Duke had complete confidence in his soldiers' training and valor	; furthermore,	he considered his battle plan a work of genius.

13.5A What Conjunctive Adverbs Show

Conjunctive adverbs indicate the following relations between one clause and another:

1. Addition *(besides, furthermore, moreover, in addition):*

> Some economists oppose legislation restricting foreign trade; *in addition,* they attack proposals to increase corporate taxes.

2. Likeness *(likewise, similarly, in the same way):*

> Many young Englishmen condemned the English War against France in the 1790s; *likewise,* many young Americans condemned the American War against North Vietnam in the 1960s.

3. Contrast *(however, nevertheless, still, nonetheless, conversely, otherwise, instead, in contrast, on the other hand):*

> Einstein's theory of relativity was largely the product of speculation; experiments made within the past fifty years, *however,* have confirmed many of its basic points.

4. Cause and effect *(accordingly, consequently, hence, therefore, as a result, for this reason):*

> Chamberlain made an ill-considered peace treaty with Hitler after the German invasion of Czechoslovakia; *as a result,* England was unprepared for the German invasion of Poland.

5. A means-and-end-relation *(thus, thereby, by this means, in this manner):*

> Florence Nightingale organized a unit of 38 nurses for the Crimean War in the 1850s; *thus* she became a legend.

6. Reinforcement *(for example, for instance, in fact, in particular, indeed):*

> Public transportation will also be vastly improved; a high-speed train, *for instance,* will take passengers from Montreal to Toronto in less than two hours.

7. Time *(meanwhile, then, subsequently, afterward, earlier, later):*

> At first, members of the audience were overtly hostile to the speaker; *later,* they cheered her as one of their own.

13.5B Punctuation with Conjunctive Adverbs

A conjunctive adverb normally takes punctuation on either side of it. The punctuation depends on where the conjunctive adverb is used.

1. When used between two independent clauses, the conjunctive adverb is normally preceded by a semicolon and followed by a comma:

> Townspeople consider the covered bridge a link to a golden age; *as a result,* they have voted funds for its restoration.

2. Some conjunctive adverbs (including *thus, then, still, otherwise,* and *hence*) may be used to begin a clause with no comma after them:

> The rise of the dollar against foreign currencies drives up the price of our exports; *thus* we lose customers abroad.

3. When used *within* the second clause, the conjunctive adverb is normally set off by commas:

> Jackson did not get the nomination; he managed, *however,* to win the votes of over one thousand delegates.

Exception: Some conjunctive adverbs, including *therefore, nevertheless, nonetheless, instead,* and those mentioned above in 2, may be used without commas when they are placed just before the main verb:

> The hole in the ozone layer is steadily growing; we must therefore stop sending fluorocarbons into the atmosphere.

JOINING INDEPENDENT CLAUSES: IN BRIEF

The independent clauses (IC) of a compound sentence must normally be joined in one of the following three ways:

1. Use ____IC____ ; ____IC____ when the relation between clauses is obvious.

2. Use ____IC____ , conjunction____IC____ to make the relation explicit.

3. Use ____IC____ ; conjunctive adverb, (placement optional) ____IC____ to make the relation emphatic.

EXERCISE 1 **Sentence Combining to Make Compound Sentences**

Using a semicolon, a conjunction, or a conjunctive adverb, combine the sentences in each of the following sets into a single sentence. Whenever you use a conjunction or conjunctive adverb, state in parentheses the relationship it shows.

EXAMPLE
We are all in the gutter.
Some of us are looking at the stars.
COMBINED: We are all in the gutter, but some of us are looking at the stars. (contrast)

1. In sixteenth-century England women with literary talent undoubtedly wrote.
   None was encouraged to publish her work.

2. Two hundred years later, Jane Austen earned little acclaim for her novels.
   Today they are considered masterpieces.

3. Some writers gain fame with their first major work.
   Others win fame later or possibly never.

4. Harriet Beecher Stowe became widely known with the publication of *Uncle Tom's Cabin* in 1853.
   Emily Dickinson remained unacclaimed until fifty years after her death.

5. James Joyce was a painstaking writer. *CS*
He once spent half a day on the composition of a single sentence.

6. Ernest Hemingway would have sympathized with Joyce.
Hemingway rewrote the last page of *A Farewell to Arms* thirty-nine times.

7. In his later years John O'Hara is said to have disregarded revision altogether.
He typed his pages and mailed them untouched to his publisher.

8. Fictions become reality for some writers.
Balzac's characters walked about on his desk, speaking, striving, suffering.

9. Georges Simenon used to impersonate his main characters before writing about them.
His wife had to cope with a series of strangers.

10. Joseph Conrad's native language was Polish.
He wrote his novels and short stories in English.

13.6 Editing Comma Splices *cs*

The **comma splice,** also called the "comma fault," is the error of joining two independent clauses—two possible sentences—with nothing but a comma:

> *One of the runners suffered from heat exhaustion, she collapsed two miles from the finish.

This sentence consists of two statements that are related but nonetheless distinct. Each of them could stand by itself as a sentence. If you read the whole sentence aloud, you will probably hear your voice drop with the word *exhaustion,* which ends the first of the two sentences.

When you use the comma to join or splice two distinct statements, you are probably trying to keep two related points together in one sentence. But the comma alone cannot do that for you. You should therefore do one of three things:

1. Put a conjunction after the comma:

> EDITED: One of the runners suffered from heat exhaustion, so she collapsed two miles from the finish.

cs

2. Replace the comma with a semicolon:

> EDITED: One of the runners suffered from heat exhaustion; she collapsed two miles from the finish.

3. Replace the comma with a period, making two sentences:

> EDITED: One of the runners suffered from heat exhaustion. She collapsed two miles from the finish.

Sometimes a comma splice occurs when the second clause in a sentence begins with a conjunctive adverb:

> * Most working people get at least one raise a year, nevertheless, inflation often leaves them with no increase in buying power.

Nevertheless is a conjunctive adverb, and a conjunctive adverb used between two clauses must be preceded by a semicolon:

> EDITED: Most working people get at least one raise a year; nevertheless, inflation often leaves them with no increase in buying power.

Alternatively, you can use a period, making two sentences:

> EDITED: Most working people get at least one raise a year. Nevertheless, inflation often leaves them with no increase in buying power.

EXERCISE 2 Editing Comma Splices

Some of the following entries contain a comma splice. If you find one, correct it. If the punctuation is correct, write *Correct*.

EXAMPLE
The chemicals lodge in soil, they also enter streams and ponds.
EDITED: The chemicals lodge in soil; they also enter streams and ponds.

1. The sculpture represents Don Quixote and his horse Rocinante, the Don is the most famous knight in Spanish literature.

2. The knight looks ready for adventure, perhaps he has spotted giants disguised as windmills.

3. His left hand is grasping a shield, his right hand holds a sturdy lance.

4. The appeal of the small work lies in its materials, they could have been the contents of a mechanic's trash can.

5. The sculptor has used bolts, screws, washers, and scraps of sheet metal, they are all painted a flat black.

6. Rocinante's head, neck, and muzzle are a single unit made from a small elbow joint; and her body is an L-shaped allen wrench, with the smaller part forming a tail.

7. Welded to the body are four legs, they are made from socket head cap screws.

8. Slanting outward and to the rear, they give an impression of movement.

9. The Don's body is a threaded carriage bolt, one end is welded to the back of Rocinante.

10. The top of the bolt is rounded, and it represents a Spanish sombrero.

11. The Don's arms are made from two allen wrenches, in fact, they curve around his back to create the image of shoulders.

12. Two more allen wrenches form legs. Bent at the knees, they end in small globs of welding rods, the rods are molded to resemble boots with tiny spurs.

13. The knight's shield is a thin metal plate, its rough edges and solder marks give it a battle-scarred look.

14. The lance is not particularly long, nonetheless, it looks like a potent weapon.

15. Supporting both the horse and the man is a hefty looking washer, the base of the piece.

13.7 Editing Run-on (Fused) Sentences *run-on*

A run-on sentence joins two independent clauses—two possible sentences—with no punctuation or conjunction between them:

> * Emily listened to the lobster boats chugging out to sea from the cove she watched the gulls sailing overhead.

Here the first independent clause simply pushes into the second one. We cannot tell for sure where the first one ends. Is its last word *sea* or *cove?*

*run-
on*   You make this error when your thoughts come in a rush, outrunning your hand. You are most likely to find the error by reading your sentences aloud, listening for the drop in your voice to tell you where one statement (or independent clause) ends and another begins. When you find that point and see no punctuation to mark it, do one of three things:

1. Use a comma and a conjunction between the two clauses:

> EDITED: Emily listened to the lobster boats chugging out to sea from the cove, and she watched the gulls sailing overhead.

2. Put a semicolon at the end of the first clause, in this case after *cove:*

> EDITED: Emily listened to the lobster boats chugging out to sea from the cove; she watched the gulls sailing overhead.

3. Put a period at the end of the first clause. You will then have two sentences:

> EDITED: Emily listened to the lobster boats chugging out to sea from the cove. She watched the gulls sailing overhead.

EXERCISE 3 Editing Comma Splices and Run-on (Fused) Sentences

In some of the following, the punctuation is faulty. Correct any mistakes you find, adding words where necessary. If a sentence is correct as it stands, write *Correct*.

EXAMPLE
Cloudy days tend to make us gloomy, sunny days, in contrast, make us cheerful.
EDITED: Cloudy days tend to make us gloomy; sunny days, in contrast, make us cheerful.

1. On the coast of Maine is the small town of Pirates Cove it resembles the old New England seaports depicted in paintings hanging in country inns or seafood restaurants.

2. The narrow streets are paved with irregularly shaped bricks these make walking an adventure.

3. Most of the buildings have a weathered look the shingles are gray and the blue of the shutters is faded from exposure to the salt air.

4. At the harbor picturesque rock formations glisten in the sunlight, *run-on*
and the hulls of freshly painted fishing boats bob in the waves.

5. Completing the scene is a welcome touch of wildness large white
gulls swoop over the boats and various clam shells lie on the sand.

14
Coordination 2
PARALLEL CONSTRUCTION

14.1 Why Choose Parallelism?

Parallel construction, also called "parallelism," helps to show that two or more ideas are equally important by stating them in grammatically parallel form: noun lined up with noun, verb with verb, phrase with phrase. Parallelism can lend clarity, elegance, and symmetry to what you say. For example:

> 1. I *came;*
> I *saw;*
> I *conquered.*   —Julius Caesar

Using three simple verbs to list the things he did, Caesar makes coming, seeing, and conquering all equal in importance. He also implies that for him, conquering was as easy as coming and seeing.

> 2. In many ways writing is the act *of saying I,*
>   *of imposing* oneself upon
>   other people,
>   *of saying listen* to me,
>   *see* it my way,
>   *change* your
>   mind.
>   —Joan Didion

Didion gives equal importance to saying *I,* imposing oneself, and voicing certain commands. Furthermore, she builds one parallel construction into another. Using a series of imperative verbs, she puts equal weight on *listen, see,* and *change.*

> 3. We look for signs in every strange event; we search for heroes in every unknown face.   —Alice Walker

Walker stresses our searching by making the second half of this sentence exactly parallel with the first.

14.2 Writing Parallel Constructions

To write parallel constructions, put two or more coordinate items into the same grammatical form:

> 1. I have nothing to offer but *blood, toil, tears,* and *sweat.*
>   —Winston Churchill

Churchill uses four nouns to identify what he offers the British people in wartime.

> 2. . . . and that government *of the people, by the people, for the people* shall not perish from the earth.
>   —Abraham Lincoln

Lincoln uses three prepositional phrases to describe the essential characteristics of American democracy.

> 3. On all these shores there are echoes *of past and future: of the flow of time, obliterating* yet *containing* all that has gone before.   —Rachel Carson

Carson uses two prepositional phrases about time, and then a pair of participles to contrast its effects.

> 4. *We must indeed all hang together,* or most assuredly *we shall all hang separately.*   —Benjamin Franklin

Franklin uses two parallel clauses to stress the difference between two equally pressing alternatives.

> 5. *A living dog* is better than *a dead lion.*   —Ecclesiastes

The likeness in form between the two phrases lets us clearly see how much they differ in meaning.

14.3 Using Correlatives with Parallelism

When using a pair of correlatives, be sure that the word or word group following the first member of the pair is parallel with the word or word group following the second. The principal correlatives are *both . . . and, not only . . . but also, either . . . or, neither . . . nor,* and *whether . . . or:*

> 1. Before the Polish strikes of 1980, *both* the Hungarians *and* the Czechs tried in vain to defy Soviet authority.
>
> 2. His speech *not only* outraged his opponents *but also* cost him the support of his own party.
>
> 3. Near the end of the story Daniel Webster threatens to wrestle with the devil *either* on earth *or* in hell.

EXERCISE 1 Recognizing Parallel Elements

Each of the following sentences contains one or more parallel constructions. Write down the parallel elements.

EXAMPLE
Crawling down a mountain is sometimes harder than climbing up.
Crawling down, climbing up

> 1. The cosmic ulcer comes not from great concerns but from little irritations.   —John Steinbeck
> 2. She was impervious to lies or foolish excuses or the insufferable plea of not knowing any better.   —Eudora Welty
> 3. I went to the woods because I wished to live deliberately, to front only the essential facts of life. . . .   —Henry David Thoreau
> 4. I open my eyes and I see dark, muscled forms curl out of water, with flapping gills and flattened eyes.   —Annie Dillard
> 5. What is written without effort is in general read without pleasure.   —Samuel Johnson

14.4 Editing Faulty Parallelism

When two or more parts of a sentence are parallel in meaning, you should coordinate them fully by making them parallel in form. If you don't, the **faulty parallelism** may confuse your reader. Here are some examples of this error and of ways to correct it.

> 1. * The Allies decided *to invade* Italy and then *that they would launch* a massive assault on the Normandy coast.

To edit this kind of sentence, make the coordinate elements parallel:

> EDITED: The Allies decided *to invade* Italy and then *to launch* a massive assault on the Normandy coast.

Here are further examples:

> 2. *I like swimming, skiing, and to hike in the mountains.
> EDITED: I like *swimming, skiing,* and *hiking* in the mountains. [or] I like to *swim, ski,* and *hike* in the mountains.
>
> 3. *Either we must make nuclear power safe or stop using it altogether.
> EDITED: Either *we must make* nuclear power safe, or *we must stop* using it altogether. [or] We must either *make* nuclear power safe or *stop* using it altogether.

In both the edited versions, each correlative goes immediately before one of the parallel items:

> 4. *They fought in the streets, the fields, and in the woods.
> EDITED: They fought *in the streets, in the fields,* and *in the woods.* [or] They fought in *the streets, the fields,* and *the woods.*

In a series of phrases beginning with a word such as *to* or *in*, repeat the word before each phrase or don't repeat it at all after the first one.

EXERCISE 2 Editing Faulty Parallelism

Revise each of the following sentences that is marred by faulty parallelism. If a sentence is correct as it stands, write *Correct.*

EXAMPLE
You can improve your performance if you master the fundamentals and by training daily.
EDITED: You can improve your performance by mastering the fundamentals and by training daily.

1. Ancient Greek myths often describe the exploits of heroes confronting threats from violent men, evil monsters, and the gods sometimes menace them as well.

2. The heroes seek undying fame, not to become wealthy.

3. They generally display their remarkable prowess at an early age both by performing difficult tasks and they show bravery in the face of danger.

4. The infant Hercules, for example, strangles not only two ven-omous serpents in his crib but laughs at the menace.

5. Young Theseus enters the dreaded labyrinth on Crete deter-mined either to slay the Minotaur or he will die in the attempt.

6. Besides demonstrating bravery and strength against deadly foes, heroes often undertake dangerous journeys.

7. A companion travels with the hero, and sometimes the compan-ion is not mortal but a god.

8. Athene, in perhaps the most famous story of all, guides young Telemachos not only during a voyage from Ithaca to Pylos but also helps him to win the regard of kings.

9. Even for heroes, meeting a challenge can be as dangerous as to play Russian roulette.

10. In a major test of strength and courage, Jason has to yoke a pair of fire-breathing bulls, seed a field with dragons' teeth, and there is a climactic battle to be won against armed men sprouting from the seeds.

EXERCISE 3 Sentence Combining

Combine the sentences in each of the following sets into a single compound sentence, using parallel construction where possible.

EXAMPLE
Much of the land was arid.
The presence of many rocks was another feature.
To the Moabites the land was beautiful.
They loved it passionately.
They fought to keep it.
COMBINED: Much of the land was both arid and rocky; nonetheless, the Moabites found it beautiful, loved it passionately, and fought to keep it.

1. Most tarantulas live in the topics.
   The temperate zone, however, is home to some species of them.
   A few species commonly occur in the southern United States.

2. Some tarantulas have large bodies.
   Their fangs are powerful.
   They can bite hard.
   They can cause deep wounds.
   But they don't attack human beings.
   Their bite harms only certain small creatures.
   These include insects.
   Mice can be harmed by their bite too.

3. Tarantulas come out of their burrows at dusk.
Dawn is the time of their return to their burrows.
At night the mature males look for females.
Sometimes they become intruders in people's homes.

4. A fertilized female tarantula lays several hundred eggs at one time.
Her next act is to weave a cocoon of silk to enclose them.
She does nothing more for her young.

5. When hatched, the young walk away.
They live alone.
They are unlike ants in this respect.
They also differ from bees.
They do not live in colonies.

15
Subordination
COMPLEX SENTENCES

15.1 What Subordination Does

Subordination enables you to show the relative importance of the parts of a sentence. To use **subordination** is to make one or more parts of a sentence depend on the part that is most important to you.

Suppose you want to describe what a dog did on a particular night, and you want your description to include the following points:

> The dog lived next door.
> The dog was scrawny.
> The dog barked.
> The dog was old.
> The dog howled.
> The dog kept me awake.
> I was awake all night.

What is the best way to arrange these isolated facts in a sentence? Part of the answer is to coordinate facts that are equally important to the point you want to make. So here is one way you might combine those sentences:

> The dog was scrawny and old, and he lived next door; he barked and howled and kept me awake all night.

This sentence puts all the facts together, but it lacks something. It fails to show which fact is most important to the writer—to you.

Which *is* the most important? That depends on the topic of your essay. If you're writing about yourself, for instance, the most important fact about the dog is that it kept you awake all night. To highlight that fact, you could rewrite the sentence like this:

> The scrawny old dog next door kept me awake all night by barking and howling.

This sentence emphasizes just one statement: the dog kept me awake. By turning all the other statements into modifiers of *dog* or *kept me awake*, it subordinates them to the point that is most important to you. You can stress this point even more by placing it at the end of the sentence—the stress position:

> By barking and howling, the scrawny old dog next door kept me awake all night.

Alternatively, you can subordinate all the other facts about the dog to the fact that it lived next door:

> The dog *that kept me awake all night with its barking and howling* lived next door.

The entire group of italicized words modifies *dog.* So all the other facts about the dog are now subordinated to the fact that it lived next door.

Finally, suppose you want to subordinate all of these facts about the dog to a brand-new fact. Suppose you mainly want to tell what happened to you *as a result* of that sleepless night. Then you might write a sentence like this:

> Because the barking and howling of the scrawny old dog next door had kept me awake all night, I fell asleep in the middle of the chemistry final.

Subordination helps to make a sentence fit its context. Consider these paragraphs:

> For me, the one big problem with dogs is noise. On the night before I had to take a final exam in chemistry, "man's best friend" turned out to be my worst enemy. I got to bed at eleven, but I didn't sleep a wink. *What kept me awake all*

night was the barking and howling of the scrawny old dog next door.

The Bible tells us all to love our neighbors, but I have always had trouble even liking most of mine. When I was about six years old, I climbed over the fence in our backyard, wandered into Mr. O'Reilly's flower garden, and sat down in the middle of some big yellow daffodils. Mr. O'Reilly came up from behind and whacked me so hard I can still feel it now. We've moved a few times since then, but I have yet to find neighbors that I love. On the contrary, many of the things I don't love seem to come from across a fence. In El Paso, for instance, *a scrawny old dog that kept me awake all night with its barking and howling lived next door.*

In the chemistry course I managed to do just about everything wrong. To begin with, I bought a used textbook at a bargain price, and then found out that I was supposed to buy the new edition. Trying to get along instead with the old one, I almost always wound up reading the wrong pages for the assignment and giving the wrong answers to quiz questions. I did no better with beakers and test tubes; the only thing my experiments showed is that I could have blown up the lab. But the worst came last. *Because the barking and howling of the scrawny old dog next door had kept me awake all night, I fell asleep in the middle of the final.*

The sentence about the dog is written three different ways to emphasize three different things: the noise it made, the fact that it lived next door, and the fact that something happened because of its noise. In each case, the methods of subordination make the sentence fit the particular paragraph for which it is written. The three ways of writing the sentence also illustrate three different kinds of subordinate clauses. We consider these in the next sections.

15.2 What Subordinate Clauses Are

A **subordinate clause,** also called a "dependent clause," is a group of words that has its own subject and predicate but cannot stand alone as a simple sentence. It must be included in or connected to an **independent clause**—one that can stand by itself as a sentence:

SUBORDINATE CLAUSE	INDEPENDENT CLAUSE
1. Before she spoke to reporters,	she conferred with her advisers.

INDEPENDENT CLAUSE	SUBORDINATE CLAUSE
2. Medical researchers have long been seeking a cure for a disease	that takes thousands of lives each year.

INDEPENDENT CLAUSE	SUBORDINATE CLAUSE	SUBORDINATE CLAUSE
3. Pavarotti was cheered	as he finished the beautiful aria	in which Rodolfo declares his love to Mimi.

A sentence containing one independent clause and at least one subordinate clause is called **complex.** Complex sentences are made with various kinds of subordinate clauses, and the rest of this chapter will explain how to use each kind. (For the sequence of tenses in complex sentences, see section 21.3.)

15.3 Using Adjective (Relative) Clauses

An **adjective clause,** sometimes called a "relative clause," normally begins with a **relative pronoun**—*which, that, who, whom,* or *whose.* The relative pronoun refers to a noun or noun phrase that is called its **antecedent.** The adjective clause modifies this antecedent, which normally appears just before the relative pronoun:

The dog *that* kept me awake all night lived next door.

An adjective clause usually says more about its antecedent than a single adjective can. Compare these two sentences:

Medical researchers have long been seeking a cure for a *fatal* disease.
Medical researchers have long been seeking a cure for a disease *that takes thousands of lives every year.*

The adjective clause tells more about the extent and effect of the disease than the one word *fatal* does.

An adjective clause also enables you to subordinate one set of facts to another set. See how these two sentences can be combined:

Amelia Earhart disappeared in 1937 during a round-the-world trip. She set new speed records for long-distance flying in the 1930s.

COMBINATION 1: Amelia Earhart, *who set new speed records for long-distance flying in the 1930s,* disappeared in 1937 during a round-the-world trip.

COMBINATION 2: Amelia Earhart, *who disappeared in 1937 during a round-the-world trip,* set new speed records for long-distance flying in the 1930s.

Combination 1 subordinates Earhart's record-setting to her disappearance; combination 2 subordinates her disappearance to her record-setting. Which combination the writer chooses depends on which fact the writer wants to emphasize in a particular context.

15.4 Choosing Relative Pronouns

The relative pronoun you choose depends chiefly on the antecedent—the noun or pronoun the clause modifies.

1. Use *who, whom, whose,* or *that* when the antecedent is one or more persons:

A cynic is a man *who* knows the price of everything and the value of nothing.   —Oscar Wilde

Millard Fillmore, *whom* almost nobody remembers, was president of the United States from 1848 to 1852.

Writers *whose* books turn into movies may suddenly find themselves rich.

Pedestrians *that* ignore traffic lights are living dangerously.

The case endings of *who, whom,* and *whose* depend on what the pronoun does in the clause it introduces. (For a full discussion of case endings, see section 18.11.)

2. Use *which* or *that* when the antecedent is one or more things:

A mind *that* is stretched to a new idea never returns to its original dimensions.   —Oliver Wendell Holmes

A team of shipwreck hunters recently found the wreck of the

S.S. Leopoldville, which was sunk by a German torpedo on Christmas Eve 1944.

We must preserve the freedoms for *which* our ancestors fought.

3. Use *which* when the antecedent is an entire clause—but only when nothing else can be mistaken for the antecedent:

Tim cackled maliciously, *which* infuriated Paul.

For more on this use of *which,* see section 18.4B.

4. Do not use *that* when the antecedent is a proper name:

* The world's greatest jumpers include Carl Lewis, *that* has cleared nearly twenty-nine feet.

EDITED: The world's greatest jumpers include Carl Lewis, *who* has cleared nearly twenty-nine feet.

* The Verrazano-Narrows Bridge, *that* links Brooklyn to Staten Island in New York City, has the longest suspension span in the world.

EDITED: The Verrazano-Narrows Bridge, *which* links Brooklyn to Staten Island in New York City, has the longest suspension span in the world.

A relative clause referring to a proper name is normally *nonrestrictive.* For more on this, see section 15.6.

5. You may use *whose* with any antecedent to avoid writing *of which:*

The children worked in a schoolroom *whose* windows were never opened. (COMPARE: The children worked in a schoolroom *of which* the windows were never opened.)

6. You may use *where* or *when* as a relative pronoun when the antecedent is a place or a time:

That morning we drove to the town of Appomattox Court House, Virginia, *where* Lee surrendered to Grant at the end of the Civil War.

Her favorite season was spring, *when* the earth seemed born again.

15.5 Placing the Adjective Clause

Place the adjective clause so that the reader can clearly see its connection to the antecedent of the relative pronoun. Observe the following guidelines.

1. Whenever possible, place the adjective clause immediately after the antecedent of the relative pronoun:

> Students *who cheat* poison the atmosphere of the college.
> Newhouse made a proposal *that nobody else liked.*

2. If an adjective phrase gets between the relative pronoun and its antecedent, you can sometimes turn the phrase into another adjective clause:

> * Mothers of small children who work must juggle conflicting responsibilities.
> EDITED: Mothers *who work and who have small children* must juggle conflicting responsibilities.

Alternatively, you can reconstruct the sentence:

> Working mothers of small children must juggle conflicting responsibilities.

3. If the adjective clause is long, you can move the antecedent to the end of the main clause so as to avoid a construction like this:

> Leonardo da Vinci, *whose knowledge of sculpture, painting, architecture, engineering, and science made him the intellectual wonder of his time,* painted the *Mona Lisa* in Florence about 1504.

If your next sentence deals with Florence or 1504 (e.g., "That was an important year for Da Vinci"), this is an effective construction. But since the long adjective clause drives a big wedge between the subject and verb of the main clause—between *Leonardo da Vinci* and *painted*—you should know what your alternatives are. To connect the two parts of the main clause, change the verb from active to passive and then put the adjective clause at the end:

> EDITED: The *Mona Lisa* was painted in Florence about 1504 by Leonardo da Vinci, *whose knowledge of sculpture, painting, architecture, engineering, and science made him the intellectual wonder of his time.*

For more on this use of the passive voice, see chapter 22.

EXERCISE 1 Placing Adjective Clauses

To each of the sentences add the adjective clause written within parentheses. Reword the sentence if necessary so as to connect the clause clearly to the italicized item.

EXAMPLE
Psychologists have been studying the mental effects of prolonged weightlessness. (who work for NASA)
NEW SENTENCE: Psychologists who work for NASA have been studying the mental effects of prolonged weightlessness.

1. Workmen are busy cleaning a *statue* in Cedar Park. (that was designed by Phidias Gold in 1953)
2. The *statue* has been discolored by pollutants emitted by motor vehicles and nearby cement factories. (which represents the American farmer)
3. City officials want to honor *Gold* with a parade and a banquet on Labor Day. (whose works have earned him a reputation for bold designs)
4. The sculptor recently described a *memorial* in an interview with reporters. (that will honor the astronauts killed in the explosion of the space shuttle *Challenger*)
5. The *Challenger* blew up within minutes of its launching on January 28, 1986. (whose crew included the first schoolteacher ever sent into space)

15.6 Punctuating Adjective Clauses

1. Use commas to set off an adjective clause only when it is **non-restrictive.** A nonrestrictive adjective clause has a well-identified noun as its antecedent:

Linda Watson, *who earned a cumulative grade-point average of 3.8,* was graduated with highest honors.

This adjective clause does not identify the antecedent, Linda Watson. The proper name by itself identifies the person in question; the clause provides extra information about her. Without the adjective clause, some details would be lacking, but the essential information would remain:

Linda Watson was graduated with highest honors.

Exception: When the antecedent is the proper name of a *group*, the clause may restrict its meaning and would therefore require no commas:

> Most Canadians *who speak French* live in the Province of Quebec.

Well-identified nouns include not only names of persons but also names of things, job titles, and any other phrases that plainly identify one of a kind:

> The Lincoln Memorial, *which was dedicated in 1922,* attracts visitors from all over the world.

> We attended a reception for the Dean of the Business School, *who will retire in June.*

> My youngest brother, *who seldom opened a book as a teenager,* has just been appointed head librarian of Wakefield University.

In all of these examples, the adjective clauses are nonrestrictive. They give information about the antecedents but do not identify them.

2. Do not use commas to set off a **restrictive** adjective clause—one that *does* identify the antecedent:

> Students *who earn a cumulative grade point average of 3.7 or more* will be graduated with highest honors.

This adjective clause restricts the meaning of the antecedent, specifying which students are eligible for highest honors. Without the clause the sentence would say something quite different:

> Students will be graduated with highest honors.

Since a restrictive clause is essential to the meaning of the antecedent and of the sentence as a whole, it must not be separated from the antecedent by commas. Here is one more example:

> Tree surgeons may have to remove the oak *that towers over the new greenhouse.*

15.7 Overusing Adjective Clauses

Do not use adjective clauses starting with phrases like *who is* and *which are* when you don't need them. Cut the excess words:

> * Some of the compact cars *that are sold by American companies* are manufactured in Japan.
> EDITED: Some of the compact cars *sold by American companies* are manufactured in Japan.

> * Joseph P. Kennedy, *who was the father of President John F. Kennedy,* made a fortune in banking and real estate.
> EDITED: Joseph P. Kennedy, *father of President John F. Kennedy,* made a fortune in banking and real estate.

EXERCISE 2 Sentence Combining with Adjective Clauses

Combine the sentences in each of the following pairs by turning one sentence into an adjective clause and using it in the other. Then underline the adjective clause and in parentheses state whether it is restrictive or nonrestrictive.

EXAMPLE
Employees of a certain kind will be fired.
Those employees arrive late.
COMBINED: Employees *who arrive late* will be fired. (restrictive)

1. On Interstate 70 in Colorado, a stretch offers tourists many attractive sights.
   The stretch extends from Idaho Springs to Glenwood Springs.
2. At Idaho Springs the countryside is dotted with the entrances to old silver mines.
   One hundred years ago, the mines were making people rich.
3. Farther along, the highway enters Vail.
   Vail draws thousands of skiers to its beautiful trails every winter.
4. Glenwood Canyon is another rewarding place.
   Its colorful walls rise steeply above a winding river.
5. Here, in the spring, men and women ride the rapids in rubber rafts.
   The men and women relish adventure and spectacular scenery.

EXERCISE 3 Sentence Combining with Adjective Clauses

Combine the sentences in each of the following sets by using one or more adjective clauses.

EXAMPLE
Ronald Reagan governed California for two terms.
Then he became president of the United States.
He first made his name in the movies.
COMBINED: Ronald Reagan, who governed California for two terms
and then became president of the United States, first made his name
in the movies.

1. Susan B. Anthony was arrested on a certain day in 1872.
   On that day she led a group of women to the polls in Rochester,
   N.Y.
   Women owe their voting rights to early feminists like Susan B.
   Anthony.

2. Feminism in the nineteenth century was also strongly promoted
   by Elizabeth Cady Stanton.
   She organized the first U.S. women's rights convention in 1848.
   She presided over the National American Woman Suffrage Association from 1890 to 1892.

3. In the early twentieth century, Carrie Chapman Catt led the fight
   for women's rights.
   She became president of the National American Woman Suffrage
   Association in 1900.

4. She achieved her goal in 1920.
   At that time Congress passed the Nineteenth Amendment.
   That amendment gave women the right to vote.

5. Since the 1960s, the spirit of feminism has been revived by the
   National Organization for Women.
   This organization has demanded for women certain rights and
   opportunities.
   Those rights and opportunities have been traditionally granted
   only to men.

15.8 Using Adverb Clauses

An adverb clause begins with a subordinator—a word like *when,
because, if,* and *although.* Modifying a word, phrase, or clause, it
tells such things as why, when, how, and under what conditions.
Normally it gives more information than a simple adverb does.

ADVERB
Then I hit the brakes.

ADVERB CLAUSE
As the deer leaped onto the road, I hit the brakes.

An adverb clause also enables you to subordinate one point to another.

ADVERB CLAUSE   INDEPENDENT CLAUSE
As he was being tackled,   he threw the ball.

The main point of this sentence is that the player threw the ball; the subordinate point is that he was being tackled at the same time. The sentence is designed to fit into a paragraph like this:

> The line wavered, and Keene knew it would break in seconds. But he dropped back, dancing around until he spotted a receiver. *As he was being tackled, he threw the ball.* Polanski made a leaping catch at the twenty-five-yard line, came down running, zigzagged past the Iowa safety, and crossed the goal line. The crowd went wild.

On the other hand, if the most important thing is not the pass but the tackle, the sentence should emphasize that:

> Keene looked desperately for a receiver, sensing the seconds ticking away. Suddenly his blocking broke down, and he was surrounded. *As he threw the ball, he was being tackled.* The pass went nearly straight up, then fell to earth behind him. The game was over.

Now the sentence highlights the tackle. In the structure of the sentence, as in the situation it describes, the tackle is more important than the pass that failed because of it. Once again, the adverb clause lets you indicate which of two actions is more important.

15.9 Choosing Subordinators

As noted earlier, an adverb clause starts with a **subordinator,** a word or phrase that subordinates the clause to whatever it modifies. A subordinator can be used to signal one of the following relations:

1. Time

> The factory closed *when* the owner died.
> *Until* the power lines were restored, we had to read at night by candlelight.

You can also signal time with *after, as soon as, as long as, before, ever since, as,* and *while.*

2. Causality

> Kate was happy *because* she had just won her first case.
> *Since* I had no money, I walked all the way home.

3. Concession and contrast

> Money cannot make you happy, *though* it can keep you comfortable.

The clause begun by *though* concedes a point that contrasts with the main point: money cannot make you happy. If you attach *though* to the other clause, you can reverse the emphasis of the sentence:

> *Though* money cannot make you happy, it can keep you comfortable.

You can also signal concession and contrast with *although, even though,* and *whereas:*

> *Although* the mosquitoes were out in force, we spent an enjoyable hour fishing before sundown.

> In my new car, I am averaging over thirty-five miles per gallon of gas, *whereas* I got only twenty in my old one.

While can signal concession and contrast as well as time:

> *While* Marian sang, Zachary played the piano. [time]

> *While* Finnegan himself never ran for any office, he managed many successful campaigns. [concession and contrast]

4. Condition

> *If* battery-powered cars become popular, the price of gas will drop.
> He ran *as if* he had a broken leg.

You can also signal condition with *provided that, unless,* and *as though.* (For more on conditional clauses, see section 23.6.)

5. Purpose

> I worked in a department store for a year *so that* I could earn money for college.

You can also signal purpose with *in order that* and *lest.*

6. Place

> *Where* federal funds go, federal regulations go with them.

7. Result

> We are *so* accustomed to adopting a mask before others *that* we end by being unable to recognize ourselves.
> —William Hazlitt

> She fixed the clock *so that* it worked.

8. Range of possibilities

> *Whatever* the president wants, Congress has a will of its own.

You can also signal general possibility with *whenever, wherever, whoever, whichever,* and *however:*

> I can't pronounce the name *however* it is spelled.

9. Comparison

> The river is cleaner now *than* it was two years ago.

The clause begun by *than* completes the comparison initiated by *cleaner.* (For more on writing comparisons, see section 15.12.)

15.10 Placing Adverb Clauses

An adverb clause normally follows the word or phrase it modifies. But when it modifies a main clause, it can go either before or after that clause. To be clear-cut and straightforward, lead with your main clause and let the adverb clause follow:

> The colonel ordered an investigation as soon as he heard the complaint of the enlisted men.

> I worked in a department store for a year so that I could earn money for college.

This kind of order has a brisk, no-nonsense effect, and you will seldom go wrong with it. But it is not always the best order. To create suspense, or to build up to your main point, put the adverb clause at the beginning and save the main clause for the end. Consider these two versions of a sentence spoken by Winston Churchill in 1941, when the Germans had occupied most of Europe and were threatening to invade England:

> We shall not flag or fail even though large tracts of Europe and many old and famous states have fallen or may fall into the grip of the Gestapo and all the odious apparatus of Nazi rule.

> Even though large tracts of Europe and many old and famous states have fallen or may fall into the grip of the Gestapo and all the odious apparatus of Nazi rule, we shall not flag or fail.

There is nothing grammatically wrong with the first sentence, which starts with a main clause and finishes with a long adverb clause. But this sentence has all the fire of a wet match. Because the crucial words *we shall not flag or fail* come first, they are virtually smothered by what follows them. By the time we reach the end of the sentence we may even have forgotten its main point. The arrangement of the second sentence—the one Churchill actually wrote—guarantees that we will remember. Precisely because we are made to wait until the end of the sentence for the main clause, it now strikes with telling effect.

15.11 Punctuating Adverb Clauses

Introductory adverb clauses are followed by a comma:

> *Even though I knocked loudly on the door,* the storekeeper would not open it.

> *When the gate opened,* the bull charged into the ring.

Ordinarily, an adverb clause coming at the end of a sentence is not preceded by a comma:

> The bull charged into the ring *when the gate opened.*

> A wall collapsed *because the foundation was poorly constructed.*

If the adverb clause at the end of a sentence is nonrestrictive—not essential to the meaning of the sentence—a comma may precede it:

> We planted the trees in the fall of 1984, *just after we bought the house.*

EXERCISE 4 Sentence Combining with Adverb Clauses *comp*

Combine the sentences in each of the following pairs by turning one sentence into an adverb clause and attaching it to the other. Be sure to begin the adverb clause with a suitable subordinator, and in parentheses state the relation that the subordinator shows.

EXAMPLE
I see roses.
Then my nose starts to itch.
COMBINED: Whenever I see roses, my nose starts to itch. (time)

1. Assume that commercial airlines will offer regular flights to the moon by the year 2000.
   The moon may become the new playground of the super-rich.

2. This prospect is unlikely.
   But scientists may eventually establish some kind of observatory on the moon.

3. The moon has no atmosphere.
   Therefore it affords a perfectly clear view of the stars.

4. Even without a lunar observatory, we may be able to put a telescope in a permanently orbiting space station.
   As a result, we will get an equally clear view.

5. We will be able to study the stars without the least interference from atmospheric disturbance.
   Then our understanding of them will dramatically increase.

15.12 Making Adverb Clauses Complete: Avoiding Faulty Comparisons *comp*

1. Do not use an incomplete adverb clause when a complete one is needed to make a comparison clear:

   *The river is as clean now as two years ago.

This sentence seems to compare the river with *two years*. To correct the faulty comparison, complete the adverb clause:

   EDITED: The river is as clean now *as it was two years ago.*

2. You may skip any words in a comparison that can be easily supplied by the reader:

   The exhaust system emits less sulphur dioxide *than the original system (did).*

Some writers think more about plot *than (they do) about characters.*
Ever since I began swimming every day, I have felt better *(than I did before I began swimming).*

3. Do not skip any word that is essential to a comparison:

*Roger moves faster *than any player on the team (does).*

You can skip *does,* but if Roger himself is a player on the team, this sentence seems to compare him with himself as well as others. To clarify the comparison, add the word *other:*

EDITED: Roger moves faster *than any other player on the team.*

*Tokyo's population is larger *than New York.*

This sentence seems to compare a population with a city. To clarify the comparison, rewrite the sentence in one of the following ways:

EDITED: Tokyo's population is larger *than New York's (is).*
[or]
EDITED: Tokyo's population is larger *than that of New York.*

EXERCISE 5 Correcting Faulty Comparisons

Each of the following sentences makes a comparison. Revise any sentence in which the comparison is not clear and complete. If a sentence is correct as it stands, write *Correct.*

EXAMPLE
The Federal Reserve Bank in New York City holds more gold than any bank in the United States.
EDITED: The Federal Reserve Bank in New York City holds more gold than any other bank in the United States.

1. The old house on the bay at St. Anthony's Island looks just as good as twenty years ago.
2. At that time, however, the sand was much whiter.
3. Also, the water in the bay was clearer than any bay in the islands.
4. Now the bay gets more sewage than any septic system on St. Anthony's.
5. And fishermen are not catching nearly as many cod and haddock as twenty years ago.

15.13 Using Noun Clauses

A **noun clause** is a clause used as a noun within a sentence. Normally it gives more information than a simple noun can. Compare the following:

> Government officials did not anticipate the *problem.*
>
> Government officials did not anticipate *that protestors would occupy the presidential palace.*

A noun clause can serve as subject, object, or predicate noun.

1. Noun clause as subject

> *What Sylvia did* amazed me.
>
> *Whoever wins the nomination* will be running against a popular incumbent.

2. Noun clause as object

> I feared *(that) we would never get out alive.*
>
> The police have not discovered *how the prisoner escaped.*
>
> No one knew *whether or not interest rates would rise.*
>
> We will plug the leaks with *whatever is handy.*
>
> Alexandra wondered *what marriage would do to her.*

The parenthesized word is optional.

3. Noun clause as predicate noun

> The main reason for the change is *that all in the company will benefit.*
>
> A computer with the brain of a genius is *what I need right now.*
>
> The most puzzling mystery of all is *why she abdicated at the height of her power.*

EXERCISE 6 Using Noun Clauses

Underline the noun clause(s) in the following sentences. Then write a sentence of your own that resembles the form of the original one.

EXAMPLE
I have sometimes wondered how automatic elevators respond to conflicting signals.
Children often ask how bears survive winter.

1. Whoever tries to resolve a conflict soon learns that nothing pleases everybody.
2. What solves one problem often causes another.
3. No one knows for sure whether the gains will be greater than the losses.
4. It soon becomes evident that progress is elusive.

15.14 Placing Subordinate Clauses

When you use more than one subordinate clause in a sentence, place each subordinate clause next to the word or word group that it modifies:

> *After he had made more than a thousand tries,* Edison found a filament *that would burn continuously.*

If you separate a subordinate clause from the word or word group it modifies, the result may be confusing:

> * Edison found a filament *after he had made more than a thousand tries* that would burn continuously.

EXERCISE 7 Sentence Combining: Review of Subordination

Combine the sentences in each of the following sets by using at least two of the three different kinds of subordinate clauses—noun clauses, adjective clauses, and adverb clauses. Then in parentheses state which kinds of clauses you have used. If one of them is an adverb clause, state also what relation it shows. Note that the sentences of each set may be combined in more than one way.

EXAMPLE
Frank Waters was a powerful man.
He could not lift the big stove.
It weighed over four hundred pounds.
COMBINED: Though Frank Waters was a powerful man, he could not lift the big stove, which weighed over four hundred pounds. (adverb clause of contrast, adjective clause)

1. The Sioux Indians settled down near the Black Hills in 1867.
   Soon after, the Black Hills were invaded by white men.
   The white men were searching for gold.

2. A U.S. treaty forbade white men to enter the Black Hills.
Army cavalrymen entered the Black Hills in 1874 under General George Custer.
Custer had led the slaughter of the Southern Cheyenne in 1868.

3. Red Cloud led the Sioux.
Red Cloud denounced Custer's invasion.
The invasion violated the treaty.

4. This violation led to disaster in 1876 at Little Bighorn River.
At that time the Sioux attacked Custer ferociously.
As a result, he and all his men were killed.

5. Custer's extraordinary exploits in the Civil War made him the youngest general in the Union Army.
But most people know only one thing about Custer.
He was the tragic hero of "Custer's last stand."

16
Coordination and Subordination

16.1 Using Coordination and Subordination Together

Using coordination and subordination together, you can arrange all the parts of a sentence according to their relative importance and the desired emphasis. For example:

1. No one had the guts to raise a riot.
2. But suppose a European woman went through the bazaars alone.
3. Somebody would probably spit betel juice over her dress.
COMBINED: No one had the guts to raise a riot, but if a European woman went through the bazaars alone somebody would probably spit betel juice over her dress.   —George Orwell

In the combined sentence, both sentence 1 and sentence 3 have become main clauses; they are on the same level of importance, coordinated with each other and joined by *but*. The result is a compound sentence. Within it, sentence 2 becomes a subordinate clause introduced by *if*. Here is another example:

Thus the essence of freedom of opinion is not in mere toleration as such, but in the debate which toleration provides; it is not in the venting of opinion, but in the confrontation of opinion.   —Walter Lippmann

Lippmann reinforces the coordination between two main clauses by repeating a parallel construction based on *not in . . . but in.* He also enriches the meaning of *debate* by using an adjective clause *(which toleration provides)* to explain what makes debate possible.

EXERCISE 1 Sentence Combining

This exercise tests your ability to use coordination and subordination together. If you feel uncertain about how to use coordination and subordination separately, review chapters 13, 14, and 15 before you begin this exercise. Using coordination and subordination together, make one sentence from each of the following sets of sentences. Include all the information given, but feel free to change the wording or arrangement of the sentences. Combine the sentences of each set in at least two different ways. Then, if you prefer one of the combinations, put a check next to it.

EXAMPLE
The snow melts in the spring.
The dirt roads in the region turn into muddy streams.
Certain people live in isolated houses.
Those people use old footpaths to reach Bridgeton.
Bridgeton has two grocery stores.
It has one gas pump.
COMBINATION 1: The snow melts in the spring, so the dirt roads in the region turn into muddy streams; certain people live in isolated houses, and those people use old footpaths to reach Bridgeton, which has two grocery stores and one gas pump.
COMBINATION 2: When the snow melts in the spring, the dirt roads in the region turn into muddy streams, so people who live in isolated houses use old footpaths to reach Bridgeton, which has two grocery stores and one gas pump.

1. According to some, the source of evil lies in society's institutions.
   These are said to nurture evil behavior in otherwise good people.
   According to others, the source of evil springs from human nature.
   This is said to be inherently corrupt.

2. William Golding states his opinion in a novel.
   The novel is called *Lord of the Flies.*
   He nowhere states his opinion directly.
   But the setting, plot, and characters of his novel clearly reveal it.

3. The action is set on a beautiful South Pacific island.
   It has a bountiful supply of fruit trees.

It has springs of fresh water.
It has wild pigs.
They run freely through the thick vegetation.

4. The only human inhabitants are a group of British school children.
The children survived the crash of a plane.
The plane was shot down during World War II.

5. Ralph is the leader of the boys.
Ralph summons them to meetings in a certain way.
He uses a large shell.
The shell makes a loud noise at a certain time.
He blows into it at that time.
The boys respond to the sound for a certain reason.
The shell is a symbol of authority.
It is also a symbol of order.

6. At first the older boys follow Ralph's lead.
They agree to perform certain tasks.
One task is to build shelters.
Another task is to care for the youngest.
A third is to keep a fire burning.
The fire burns on a hilltop.
Its purpose is to serve as an SOS signal for crews of passing ships.

7. But trouble develops shortly.
Ralph's leadership is challenged by Jack.
Jack has been a leader of choir boys.
He wants to be the chief again.
Then he can give orders.
He will not take them.

8. Jack forms his own band of followers.
They walk out on Ralph.
They want to stop working on the signal fire.
They want to hunt wild pigs.
They like the excitement of the chase.
They like the excitement of the kill.
They stab the squealing pig with a wooden spear.

9. Jack's followers attack Ralph's group one night.
They take Piggy's glasses.
They want the lenses for a purpose.
They will use the lenses.
The lenses will concentrate the sun's rays on firewood.
The lenses will make a fire.
The fire will cook the pig meat.

10. In the end, the boys are discovered by a strong naval officer.
The naval officer scolds the boys.

The boys look like savages.
The boys have been fighting amongst themselves.
Yet he has been fighting too.
He has come ashore from a warship.
The warship seeks to sink enemy warships and their crews.

EXERCISE 2 Writing One-Sentence Summaries

This exercise tests your ability to compress as well as combine a set of sentences by means of coordination and subordination. Using either one or both, write a one-sentence summary of each of the following passages.

EXAMPLE
More than ever before in American politics, language is used not as an instrument for forming and expressing thought. It is used to prevent, confuse and conceal thinking. Members of each branch and agency of government at every level, representing every hue of political opinion, habitually speak a language of nonresponsibility.
—Richard Gambino, "Through the Dark, Glassily"

ONE-SENTENCE SUMMARY: More than ever before, American politicians and government workers use language not to express thought but to prevent, confuse, and conceal it; they speak a language of nonresponsibility.

1. The average person has many worries, but there is one thing he does not generally worry about. He does not worry that somewhere, without his knowledge, a secret tribunal is about to order him seized, drugged, and imprisoned without the right of appeal. Indeed, anyone who worries overmuch about such a thing, and expresses that worry repeatedly and forcefully enough, would probably be classified as a paranoid schizophrenic.
—Hendrik Hertzberg and David C. K. McClelland, "Paranoia"

2. Every grown up person expects to pay a price for his pleasures, but seldom is the price as vast as the one endured "however happily" by most mothers. We have mentioned the literal cost factor. But what does that mean? For middle-class American women, it means a life style with severe and usually unimagined limitations; i.e., life in the suburbs, because who can afford three bedrooms in the city? And what do suburbs mean? For women, suburbs mean other women and children and leftover peanut-butter sandwiches and car pools and seldom seen husbands.
—Betty Rollin, "Motherhood: Who Needs It?"

tgl

3. Historically, clutter is a modern phenomenon, born of the industrial revolution. There was a time when goods were limited; and the rich and fashionable were few in number and objects were precious and hard to come by. Clutter is a 19th century esthetic; it came with the abundance of products combined with the rise of purchasing power, and the shifts in society that required manifestations of status and style.

> —Ada Louise Huxtable, "Modern-Life Battle:
> Conquering Clutter"

4. I have described imagination as the ability to make images and to move them about inside one's head in new arrangements. This is the faculty that is specifically human, and it is the common root from which science and literature both spring and grow and flourish together.   —Jacob Bronowski, "The Reach of Imagination"

5. To lie habitually, as a way of life, is to lose contact with the unconscious. It is like taking sleeping pills, which confer sleep but blot out dreaming. The unconscious wants truth. It ceases to speak to those who want something else more than truth.

> —Adrienne Rich, "Women and Honor: Some Notes on Lying"

16.2 Untangling Sentences *tgl*

It is sometimes hard to put several ideas into a single sentence without getting them tangled up in the process. Consider this sentence:

> *Due to the progress in military weaponry over the years, there has been an increased passivity in mankind that such advancements bring as wars are easier to fight resulting in a total loss of honor in fighting.

If you come across such a sentence in your own writing, you should first of all break it up:

1. There has been progress in military weaponry over the years.
2. There has been increased passivity in mankind.
3. Such advancements bring passivity.
4. The passivity is due to the progress.
5. Wars are easier to fight.
6. This results in a total loss of honor in fighting.

tgl

Once you have broken up the sentence into single ideas, you can use coordination and subordination to put them back together clearly:

> Since progress in military weaponry over the years has made mankind more passive and wars easier to fight, there has been a total loss of honor in fighting. [or] Since progress in military weaponry over the years has made mankind more passive and wars easier to fight, fighting has lost all honor.

EXERCISE 3 Sentence Untangling—A Challenge

This may well be the toughest exercise in the book. All of the following sentences were written by students who had a lot to say but who got into a tangle when they tried to say it. So you will probably have trouble even figuring out what the writers meant. But we're asking you to do just that—and more. We're asking you to untangle each sentence in the same way we untangled the sentence about weaponry in the preceding discussion. First, cut up each tangled sentence into a series of short, simple sentences; second, using coordination, subordination, or both, recombine these into one long sentence that makes sense.

1. Thoreau spent much of his time outdoors in nature, which he loved, so he saw no reason to keep it out of his cabin, and he symbolized a doormat as the mistake of avoiding natural things like dirt and leaves like his neighbors.
2. The bean field made him self-sufficient, which was one of his beliefs, and he could also see it as an extension of himself, through the bean field, into nature in returning to a natural state.
3. If something in one of your paragraphs is marked as being "wrong," one possibility is the teacher making a mistake, not you, although the possibility is seldom admitted, teachers being mostly sure they are always right.
4. The author of "The Cold Equations" is saying, in effect, that the main difference of life on the frontier for people living there after living in settled communities is that their lives are now ruled by the laws of nature instead of people making the laws.
5. For fifty years the people prospered under his rule; then, feeling a personal responsibility for the welfare of his subjects and their safety, the old king fought another monster which he was severely injured and soon died.

17
Complete Sentences and Sentence Fragments

Good writers usually make their sentences complete. They do so because complete sentences help the writer to sound well organized and the reader to grasp the writer's point. Sentence fragments often do just the opposite. Unless skillfully used, they give the impression that the writer's thoughts are incomplete or disorganized, and they may confuse the reader.

17.1 What Is a Sentence Fragment?

A sentence fragment is a part of a sentence punctuated as if it were a whole one.

1. Forgot to thank you for the book.
2. Charlie Chaplin.
3. To keep litterbugs from spoiling the beaches.
4. But always meeting ourselves.

Each of these examples *looks* like a sentence. Each begins with a capital letter and ends with a period, and each gives information. But none of them is complete. Fragment 1 lacks a subject; it could be turned into a sentence like *I forgot to thank you for the book.* Fragment 2 lacks a predicate; it could be turned into something like *Charlie Chaplin was the great tramp comedian of silent films.* The last three examples seem to have been cut off by their punctuation from their rightful place in a sentence. Thus Fragment 3 might be a part of a sentence like this: *The selectmen in Wellfleet have been discussing ways to keep litterbugs from spoiling the beaches.*

17.2 Using and Misusing Sentence Fragments

In conversation we use and hear sentence fragments all the time. Fragment 2, for instance, could be the spoken answer to a spoken question, such as *Who was the great tramp comedian of silent films?* Fragments also appear in various kinds of writing.

> Every life is many days, day after day. We walk through ourselves, meeting robbers, ghosts, giants, old men, young men, wives, widows, brothers-in-love. But always meeting ourselves.   —James Joyce

> For so many years college had seemed far off, but all of a sudden it was there, staring me in the face. A new mountain to be climbed.   —College student

Both passages end with a sentence fragment, but the meaning of each fragment is perfectly clear in its context. In fact, the fragments serve to emphasize points that might not have been made so effectively with complete sentences.

But sentence fragments must be handled with care. If you don't know how to use them sparingly and strategically, your writing will look disorganized:

> In conclusion I feel Falstaff proves to be a most likable and interesting character. Showing an ability to think quickly in tight spots. But above all he lends a comical light to the play. Which I feel makes it all the more enjoyable.
>   —College student

frag This passage includes two fragments—one after the first sentence and one at the end. In each of the two previous passages, there is only one fragment, and because it comes right after a long, abundantly complete sentence, it strikes with telling effect. But the two fragments in this passage are simply distracting. Alternating with sentences of about equal length, they seem improvised and arbitrary, as if the writer could only now and then form a complete thought.

To sum up, then, there is a place for sentence fragments in good writing, but they call for discretion. If you know how to use them effectively, do so. If you don't, or if your instructor will not accept any fragments at all, make sure all of your sentences are complete.

17.3 Spotting and Editing Sentence Fragments *frag*

To edit sentence fragments, you have to be able to spot them. How can you tell whether a particular word group is a sentence fragment? Here are some useful questions to ask if you aren't sure.

1. Does the "sentence" start with a subordinator or a relative pronoun?

> a. On Halloween night some years ago, a full-grown man with a sick sense of humor disguised himself as a ghost. *So that he could terrify little children.*

Because *So that* is a subordinator, the italicized word group is a fragment—cut off by a period from the sentence about the man in disguise. The subordinate clause should be joined to the sentence:

> EDITED: On Halloween night some years ago, a full-grown man with a sick sense of humor disguised himself as a ghost so that he could terrify little children.

> b. The British and French together developed a supersonic plane called the Concorde. *Which can fly from New York to London in three hours.*

The word group after the first period is not a sentence but a relative clause modifying *Concorde*. To connect the fragment with the sentence preceding it, change the first period to a comma:

EDITED: The British and French together developed a supersonic plane called the Concorde, which can fly from New York to London in three hours.

2. Have you skipped the subject of a sentence without realizing it?

Lancelot won fame as a knight because of his prowess in battle. * *Defeated the other great warriors in the kingdom.*
—College freshman

The fragment should have its own subject:

EDITED: Lancelot won fame as a knight because of his prowess in battle. He defeated the other great warriors in the kingdom.

3. Have you skipped a verb without realizing it?

* *Staying up all night to finish a paper.* That left me red-eyed in the morning.

The first word group is a subject without a predicate. There are two ways of eliminating the fragment. You can combine it with the sentence that comes next:

EDITED: Staying up all night to finish a paper left me red-eyed in the morning.

Or you can rewrite the fragment as a separate sentence:

EDITED: I stayed up all night to finish a paper. That left me red-eyed in the morning.

4. Have you skipped both subject and predicate?

a. Voters can sometimes defy expectations. * *As in the presidential election of 1948.*

The second word group is a modifier unattached either to a subject or a predicate. The writer thinks of the second word group as an extension of the first, but the two are in fact separated by a period. To revise a fragment of this kind, you can combine it with the sentence before it:

EDITED: Voters can sometimes defy expectations, as in the presidential election of 1948.

frag   Or you can attach the fragment to a new sentence.

> EDITED: In the presidential election of 1948, for example, voters gave Harry Truman a victory over highly favored Thomas E. Dewey.
>
> b. They went to a ski lodge. * *With a panoramic view of the Rockies.*

A period cuts off the phrase *(With a panoramic view of the Rockies)* from the clause *(They went to a ski lodge).* The phrase should be joined to the clause:

> EDITED: They went to a ski lodge with a panoramic view of the Rockies.
>
> c. *After inventing the telephone.* Alexander Graham Bell turned his attention to the phonograph.

Here the writer treats *inventing* as a main verb. But *inventing* is part of a prepositional phrase here, and the whole phrase belongs to the sentence following it:

> EDITED: After inventing the telephone, Alexander Graham Bell turned his attention to the phonograph.

Note the comma—customary after an introductory phrase.

SPOTTING SENTENCE FRAGMENTS: IN BRIEF

Word group starting with a subordinator:
> *So that* he could terrify little children.

Word group starting with a relative pronoun:
> *Which* can fly from New York to London in three hours.

Word group missing a subject:
> Defeated the other great warriors.

Word group missing a verb:
> Staying up all night to finish a paper.

Word group missing both subject and predicate:
> As in the presidential election of 1948.
> After inventing the telephone.

EXERCISE 1 Eliminating Sentence Fragments   *frag*

Each of the following passages includes several sentence fragments.
Make whatever changes are necessary to remove them.

EXAMPLE
line 3: self-confidence if they

1. The directors of social programs like Special Olympics make
   the accurate assumption. That mentally and physically dis-
   abled kids need to develop self-confidence. If they are going
   to function in society. According to Evelyn West, handicapped children need "to develop a strong, realistic sense   5
   of self." Society hinders this development. Children tease
   handicapped classmates. Separate facilities and special education classes are all clues to the handicapped. That they
   are different. Because they cannot succeed in regular classrooms or gyms. They feel incompetent. Now any child who   10
   feels incompetent is not ready to compete. This is where
   competitive programs fail. Wanting to foster confidence,
   Special Olympics demands it of the contestants. Who are
   already sure they are going to lose out. Because they lack a
   vital prerequisite for any competition. Confidence.   15
        The kids' lack of confidence is, ironically, nurtured
   by Saturday morning practices. For which the kids are
   unequally skilled. The qualifications for enrollment in Special Olympics are nebulous at best. Supposedly, only children with a ninety or lower on an I. Q. test are considered   20
   eligible. Few, however, are actually tested, and no one is
   turned away. Consequently, many mothers with several
   children send all of their brood to Saturday practices. For
   the free, supervised care. Some of these kids are barely
   handicapped. So that their competing with the severely dis-   25
   abled clearly loads the dice. With unfortunate consequences for all. The least handicapped kids—the winners—
   gain a feeling of superiority. Based on a false measure of
   their skills. The severely handicapped—the losers—feel
   shunned again. This time in their own program. None   30
   emerges with the sense of pride and respect for others. That
   the program's founders hoped to instill.

2. Most of the people who eat at a fast-food restaurant like
   McDonald's fall into one of four subgroups. The regulars,
   the families, the groups of kids, and the travelers. The
   members of these groups differ. In their liking of the food,
   their appearance, and their actions in the restaurant.   5
        The person who goes regularly to McDonald's is dif-

ferent from the others. In that he actually enjoys the food. While ordering his usual meal. He converses briefly with the clerk. He then walks slowly to the seat. Where he always sits. He eats his food deliberately. Placing the french fries one by one into his mouth and relishing each sip of the milkshake. He doesn't talk to other customers. His meal is an opportunity. To enjoy a tasty bite and to relax after a strenuous day on the job. When he has finished his meal. He crumples the empty styrofoam container. Which held his food. Drops it in the trash barrel and leaves with his appetite satisfied. He waves to the clerk. As he pushes open the door.

    . . . Among the kids who go to McDonald's are the members of a birthday party. They are usually about seven years old. One mother supervises the eight or nine children. Who all think that the Golden Arches is the best place to have a party. They sit at a table. While the mother orders nine identical meals. As they wait. The kids play with straws. Blowing them through the air and shooting the wrappers at each other. When the food is brought to the table. There is a big argument over who gets what. Even though the orders are basically the same. Each complains that he has fewer french fries than the others have. None of them, however, is able to finish his portion. During the meal they talk loudly despite the mother's efforts to control the volume. And stare at nearby adults. Who wish the kids had sat someplace else. Or in the parking lot. After the kids leave the restaurant. Everybody is happy. The mother especially.

18
Using Pronouns

A **pronoun** is a word that commonly takes the place of a noun or noun phrase:

> Brenda thought that she had lost the dog, but it had followed her.

She and *her* take the place of *Brenda,* a noun; *it* takes the place of *the dog,* a noun phrase. Pronouns thus eliminate the need for awkward repetition.

18.1 Using Pronouns with Antecedents

The word or word group that a pronoun refers to is called its **antecedent.** "Antecedent" means "going before," and this term is used because the antecedent usually goes before the pronoun that refers to it:

1. The old man smiled as he listened to the marching band. Its

spirited playing made him feel young again.

2. To build city districts that are custom-made for crime is

idiotic. Yet that is what we do. —Jane Jacobs

In the second example, the antecedent of the first *that* is *city districts*. The antecedent of the second *that* is a whole word group: *To build city districts that are custom-made for crime.*

The antecedent sometimes goes after the pronoun that refers to it:

> By the time he was three, Coleridge could read a chapter of the Bible.

18.2 Using Pronouns without Antecedents

Some pronouns have no antecedent, and others may sometimes be used without one.

1. Indefinite pronouns have no antecedents. Compare these two sentences:

> Ellen said that *she* wanted privacy.
> *Everyone* needs some privacy.

She is a **definite** pronoun. It refers to a particular person, and its meaning is clear only if its antecedent has been provided—that is, if the person has already been identified. But *Everyone* is an **indefinite** pronoun. Because it refers to someone unspecified, it has no antecedent. Other widely used indefinite pronouns include *everybody, one, no one, each, many,* and *some.*

2. The pronouns *I* and *you* have no antecedent because they are understood to refer to the writer and the reader or to the speaker and the listener.

3. The pronoun *we* sometimes appears without an antecedent, for example in newspaper editorials, where the writer clearly speaks for a group of people.

18.3 Using Pronouns Clearly

The meaning of a definite pronoun is clear when readers can identify the antecedent with certainty:

> People who saw the Tall Ships sail up the Hudson River in 1976 will long remember the experience. It gave them a handsome image of a bygone era.

The antecedent of each pronoun is obvious. *Who* clearly refers to   *pr ref*
People; It refers to *the experience; them* refers to *People who saw the Tall Ships.*

18.4 Avoiding Unclear Pronoun Reference   *pr ref*

The meaning of a definite pronoun is unclear when readers cannot identify the antecedent with certainty. The chief obstacles to clear reference are as follows.

18.4A Ambiguity

A pronoun is ambiguous when it has more than one possible antecedent:

> * Whenever Mike met Dan, he felt nervous.

Does *he* refer to *Mike* or to *Dan*? The reader cannot tell. The simplest way to eliminate the ambiguity is to replace the pronoun with a noun:

> EDITED: Whenever Mike met Dan, Mike felt nervous.

But to avoid repeating the noun, you can put the pronoun before it:

> EDITED: Whenever he met Dan, Mike felt nervous.

18.4B Broad Reference

Pronoun reference is broad when *that, this, which,* or *it* refers to a whole statement containing one or more possible antecedents within it:

> 1. * The senator opposes the bottle bill, which rankles many of his constituents.

Are they rankled by the bill or by the senator's opposition to it?

> EDITED: The senator's opposition to the bottle bill rankles many of his constituents.

> 2. * Some people insist that a woman should have a career, while others say that she belongs in the home. This is unfair.

pr ref   What is unfair? *This* could refer to the whole sentence that precedes it, to the first half, or to the second:

> EDITED: This contradictory set of demands is unfair.

18.4C   Muffled Reference

Pronoun reference is muffled when the pronoun refers to something merely implied by what precedes it:

> 1. A recent editorial contained an attack on the medical profession. *The writer accused them of charging excessively high fees.

Who is meant by *them?* Before using *them,* the writer should clearly establish its antecedent:

> EDITED: A recent editorial contained an attack on hospital administrators and doctors. The writers accused them of charging excessively high fees.
>
> 2. *Lincoln spoke immortal words at Gettysburg, but most of the large crowd gathered there couldn't hear it.

The writer is thinking of Lincoln's address, of course, but the word *address* is missing. It must be inserted:

> EDITED: Lincoln gave an immortal address at Gettysburg, but most of the large crowd gathered there couldn't hear it. [or] Lincoln spoke immortal words at Gettysburg, but most of the large crowd gathered there couldn't hear his address. [or]. . . couldn't hear them.

18.4D   Free-Floating *they* and *it*

They and *it* are free-floating when they are used as pronouns but have no definite antecedents:

> 1. *In the first part of the movie, it shows clouds billowing like waves.

What shows clouds? The pronoun *it* has no antecedent. The writer is probably thinking of the *it* that simply fills out a sentence, such as *It was cloudy,* meaning *There were clouds.* That kind of *it* (an expletive) needs no antecedent. But the pronoun *it* does. If you can't readily figure out a way to furnish one, reconstruct the sentence:

pr ref

EDITED: The first part of the movie shows clouds billowing like waves.

2. Traveling in Eastern Europe can be difficult. * At some checkpoints they hold foreigners for questioning.

The word *they* needs an antecedent. But instead of providing one, you can replace the pronoun with a noun:

EDITED: At some checkpoints the authorities hold foreigners for questioning.

Alternatively, you can use the passive voice:

EDITED: At some checkpoints foreigners are held for questioning.

18.4E Indefinite *you* and *your*

You and *your* are indefinite when used to mean anything but the reader. Though writers sometimes use *you* to mean "people in general," you will increase the precision of your sentences if you use *you* and *your* for your reader alone.

1. * You didn't have microphones in Lincoln's day.
   EDITED: There were no microphones in Lincoln's day.

2. One of Orwell's contradictions is the unperson, a man who existed once, but doesn't anymore, so he never existed. * But by defining someone as an unperson, you are saying that he once existed.
   EDITED: But to define someone as an unperson is to say that he once existed.

18.4F Remote Reference

Pronoun reference is remote when the pronoun is so far from the antecedent that readers cannot find their way from one to the other:

Bankers have said that another increase in the prime lending rate during the current quarter would seriously hurt their major customers: homeowners, small business personnel, and self-employed contractors using heavy equipment. * It would keep all of these borrowers from getting needed capital.
EDITED: Such an increase would keep all of these borrowers from getting needed capital.

RECOGNIZING OBSTACLES TO CLEAR PRONOUN
REFERENCE: IN BRIEF

Ambiguity (18.4A):

*Whenever Mike met Dan, *he* felt nervous.

Broad reference (18.4B):

*The senator opposes the bottle bill, *which* rankles many of
his constituents.

Muffled reference (18.4C):

A recent editorial contained an attack on the medical profession. *The writer accused *them* of charging excessively high
fees.

Free-floating *they* and *it* (18.4D):

*Travelling in Eastern Europe can be difficult. *At some
checkpoints *they* hold foreigners for questioning.
*In the first part of the movie, *it* shows clouds billowing like
waves.

Indefinite *you* and *your* (18.4E):

You didn't have microphones in Lincoln's day.

Remote reference: see example in section 18.4F.

EXERCISE 1 Editing Unclear Pronouns

In some of the following sentences, the italicized pronoun has been
used confusingly. Briefly diagnose what is wrong and then clarify
the sentence. If the sentence is correct as it stands, write *Correct.*

EXAMPLE
The boy and the old man both knew that *he* had not much longer to
live.
DIAGNOSIS: *He* is ambiguous; it can refer to either the boy or the
old man.
CURE: The boy and the old man both knew that the old man had
not much longer to live. [The ambiguous pronoun is simply replaced
by its antecedent.]

1. Archimedes discovered the principle of displacement while he
   was taking a bath. *It* made him leap out of the water with excitement.

2. Shouting "Eureka!" over and over, he ran naked through the
   streets of Syracuse. *They* must have been amazed to see him—
   or at least amused.

3. But in any case, Archimedes had found the solution to a problem assigned to him by King Hieron II. *He* would surely be pleased.

4. Hieron wanted Archimedes to investigate a crown that had been recently made for the king from an ingot of gold. The king wanted to know if *it* was pure gold.

5. The weight of the crown exactly matched the weight of the original ingot, *which* pleased the king.

6. But the goldsmith could have taken some of the gold for himself and added copper in *its* place.

7. Since the resulting alloy would look just like pure gold and weigh as much as the original ingot, *you* couldn't tell by appearance or weight what the goldsmith had done.

8. Gold, however, is denser than copper. So any given weight of pure gold takes up less space than the same weight of copper, or of gold mixed with *it*.

9. To learn whether or not the crown was pure gold, therefore, *they* had to see whether its volume matched the volume of a pure gold ingot that weighed the same.

10. But the crown was so intricately shaped that no way of measuring known in Archimedes' time could establish *it*.

11. Only when Archimedes got into the tub did a solution strike *him*.

12. By measuring the water displaced by the crown, and then measuring the water displaced by the ingot, he could easily tell whether or not *they* matched in volume, and thus whether or not the crown was pure gold.

18.5 Making Antecedents and Pronouns Agree in Gender *pr agr/g*

In English, gender affects only the singular definite pronoun, which is masculine (for example, *he*), feminine *(she)*, or neuter *(it)*, depending on the gender of its antecedent.

> When Marie Curie outlined the first steps of the award-winning research to *her* husband, *he* encouraged *her* to complete *it*. Though *he himself* was an eminent chemist, *he* wanted *her* to gain credit for *it*.

When the antecedent is a word of unspecified gender such as *doctor* or *lawyer*, you should use something other than a singular masculine pronoun. See section 9.11, "Using Gender-Inclusive (Non-Sexist) Language," item 3.

18.6 Making Antecedents and Pronouns Agree in Number

An antecedent is singular if it refers to one person or thing, and plural if it refers to more than one. A singular antecedent calls for a singular pronoun; a plural antecedent calls for a plural pronoun:

> The boy saw that he had cut his hand.

> The Edmonton Oilers believed that they could win the Stan-
>
> ley Cup in 1988, and they did.

18.7 Pronouns and Antecedents—Resolving Problems in Number   *pr agr/n*

Some antecedents can be problem cases—hard to classify as either singular or plural. Observe the following guidelines:

1. Two or more nouns or pronouns joined by *and* are usually plural:

> Orville and Wilbur Wright are best known for *their* invention of the airplane.

Nouns joined by *and* are singular only if they refer to one person or thing:

> The chief cook and bottle washer demanded *his* pay.

2. When two nouns are joined by *or* or *nor*, the pronoun normally agrees with the second noun:

> Squirrels or a chipmunk has left *its* tracks in the new-fallen snow.
> Neither Pierre LaCroix nor his boldest followers wanted to
>
> expose *themselves* to danger.

3. A noun or pronoun followed by a prepositional phrase is treated as if it stood by itself:

> In 1980 Canada, together with the United States and several other countries, kept *its* athletes from participating in the Moscow Olympics.

The antecedent of *its* is simply *Canada*. Unlike the conjunction *and*, a phrase like *together with* or *along with* does not make a compound antecedent. The antecedent is what comes before the phrase.

> The leader of the strikers said that *he* would get them a new package of benefits.

The pronoun *he* agrees with *leader*, just as if *of the strikers* was omitted and *leader* stood by itself. The antecedent of *them* is *strikers*.

4. Collective nouns can be either singular or plural, depending on the context:

> The team chooses *its* captain in the spring.

Since the captain is a symbol of unity, the writer treats *The team* as singular, using the singular pronoun *its*.

> The audience shouted and stamped *their* feet.

Since each person in the audience was acting independently, the writer treats *The audience* as plural, using the plural pronoun *their*.

5. Some indefinite pronouns are singular, some are plural, and some can be either singular or plural:

	ALWAYS SINGULAR	
anybody	either	one
anyone	neither	another
anything		
each	nobody	somebody
each one	none	someone
	no one	something
everybody	nothing	
everyone		whatever
everything		whichever
		whoever

	ALWAYS PLURAL		
both	few	others	several

	SOMETIMES SINGULAR AND SOMETIMES PLURAL	
all	many	some
any	most	

pr
agr/n

As this list indicates, *each* is always singular:

> Each of the men brought *his* own tools.

But when *each* immediately follows a plural noun, the pronoun after *each* must be plural also:

> The men each brought *their* own tools.

Though some writers treat *everybody* and *everyone* as plural, we recommend that you treat them as singular or simply avoid using them as antecedents:

> Everyone in the cast had to furnish *his* or *her* own costume.
> All cast members had to furnish *their* own costumes.

The number of a pronoun in the third group depends on the number of the word or phrase to which it refers:

> Some of the salad dressing left *its* mark on my shirt.

> Some of the students earn *their* tuition by working part time.

> Many of the customers do not pay *their* bills on time.

> Many a man learns to appreciate *his* father only after *he* has become one *himself*.

6. The number of a relative pronoun depends on the number of the antecedent:

> Mark is one of those independent carpenters who *want* to work for *themselves*.

> Marilyn is the only one of the gymnasts who *wants* to compete in the Olympics.

EXERCISE 2 Recognizing Correct Pronoun Agreement

Each of the following consists of two sentences. In one sentence the number of the pronoun matches that of its antecedent; in the other there is a faulty shift in number. Say which sentence is correct—and why.

EXAMPLE

(a) Twenty years ago, a woman who kept her own name after marriage was hardly considered married at all.

(b) Twenty years ago, a woman who kept their own name after marriage was hardly considered married at all.

Sentence (a) is correct because the singular pronoun *her* matches the singular antecedent *woman*.

1.(a) On the first day of summer, the members of the Smith family found a rude surprise behind its house.
  (b) On the first day of summer, the members of the Smith family found a rude surprise behind their house.

2.(a) The neighbor's dogs or a raccoon had left their tracks on the freshly painted deck in the backyard.
  (b) The neighbor's dogs or a raccoon had left its tracks on the freshly painted deck in the backyard.

3.(a) None of the boards was without their trace of the intruders.
  (b) None of the boards was without its trace of the intruders.

4.(a) Ordinarily Mr. Smith is one of those stoical types who controls his temper.
  (b) Ordinarily Mr. Smith is one of those stoical types who control their temper.

5.(a) But this time, he, along with his wife and two daughters, vented his rage.
  (b) But this time, he, along with his wife and two daughters, vented their rage.

6.(a) Everyone in the neighborhood has their own version of the uproar that followed.
  (b) Everyone in the neighborhood has his or her own version of the uproar that followed.

7.(a) But every animal within shouting distance of the Smiths' house was put in terror of losing its life.
  (b) But every animal within shouting distance of the Smiths' house was put in terror of losing their lives.

8.(a) For weeks, in fact, neither of the neighbor's two dogs would show its head.
  (b) For weeks, in fact, neither of the neighbor's two dogs would show their head.

18.8 Avoiding Faulty Shifts in Pronoun Reference
pr shift

Pronouns referring to the same antecedent should be consistent in number and person. Follow these guidelines:

1. Avoid using *they, them,* or *their* with a singular antecedent:

* No one should be forced into a career that *they* do not want
to pursue.

The plural pronoun *they* is inconsistent in number with the singular antecedent *no one.*

> EDITED: No one should be forced into a career that *he* or *she*
> does not want to pursue.

2. Avoid shifting the reference of a pronoun from one grammatical
person to another:

> * When one is alone, one is free to do whatever you want.
> EDITED: When one is alone, one is free to do whatever one
> wants.
> EDITED: When you are alone, you are free to do whatever you
> want.

For the correct use of *you,* see section 18.4E.

EXERCISE 3 Revising a Passage with Inconsistent
Pronoun Usage

Each of the following passages is marred by shifts in the number
and person of pronouns referring to the same antecedent. Make these
pronouns consistent in number and person.

1. The job of being a counselor in a girls' summer camp is not an
   easy one. You have to meet your responsibilities twenty-four hours
   a day, and all are important. Because of the demands on us, we
   sometimes become tired and even cross. At these times everybody wants a break—a chance to go someplace else and relax. In
   a well-run camp you can do this; the director gives everybody a
   day off. After that we resume our duties with a cheerful, positive
   attitude.
2. Our body language often expresses our emotions. Through gestures, posture, facial expressions, and other visible signs, we indicate our feelings. If you are elated, for example, you tend to speak
   with more tonal fluctuations and with more arm movement than
   when a person is depressed. In a good mood, our eyes sparkle, our
   posture is erect, and you smile a lot. When someone is angry,
   their body language tells the tale. Our faces scowl, our jaws are
   clenched, one's gestures look aggressive, and sparks flash from
   your eyes.

18.9 Pronoun Case Forms

The form of a pronoun referring to a person depends partly on its case—that is, on the role it plays in a sentence. Consider this passage:

> The Kiowas are a summer people; *they* abide the cold and keep to themselves, but when the season turns and the land becomes warm and vital *they* cannot hold still; an old love of going returns upon *them*. The aged visitors who came to my grandmother's house when I was a child were made of lean and leather, and they bore *themselves* upright. *They* wore great black hats and bright ample shirts that shook in the wind. *They* rubbed fat upon *their* hair and wound *their* braids with strips of colored cloth.
> —N. Scott Momaday, *The Way to Rainy Mountain*

They, them, their, and *themselves* all have the same antecedent, *Kiowas.* But these four pronouns differ in form because they play different roles: subject (*they* abide), object (upon *them*), reflexive object (bore *themselves*), and possessive (*their* braids). Because each form signifies a different case, the difference between one case form and another helps the writer show exactly what his pronouns mean.

Here is a table listing the case forms for all pronouns. In the next section we explain their uses.

CASE FORMS OF PRONOUNS

PERSONAL PRONOUNS

	I	*He*	*She*	*It*	*We*	*You*	*They*
Subject case	I	he	she	it	we	you	they
Object case	me	him	her	it	us	you	them
Possessive case	my, mine	his	her, hers	its	our, ours	your, yours	their, theirs
Reflexive / emphatic case	myself	himself	herself	itself	ourselves	yourself, yourselves	themselves

PRONOUNS USED IN QUESTIONS AND ADJECTIVE CLAUSES

	Who	*Whoever*
Subject case	who	whoever
Object case	whom	whomever
Possessive case	whose	

18.10 Using Pronoun Case

18.10A Subject Case

Use the subject case when the pronoun is the subject of a verb:

> When Adam and Eve were accused of eating the forbidden fruit, *they* each excused themselves; *he* blamed Eve for tempting him, and *she* blamed the serpent for tempting her.

18.10B Object Case

1. Use the object case when the pronoun is the direct or indirect object of a verb:

> Rolls-Royces are so expensive that only millionaires can afford *them.*

> One tycoon who admires his wife has given *her* two of the cars.

> A chauffeur drives *him* and *her* around their estate every evening.

2. Use the object case when the pronoun is the object of a preposition, a word like *to, against,* or *on:*

> When John F. Kennedy was assassinated, people from all over the world paid tribute to *him.*

3. Use the object case when the pronoun comes immediately before an infinitive:

> The recruiter asked Heather and *me* to send our resumés.

18.10C Possessive Case

1. Use the possessive case of the pronoun to indicate ownership of an object or close connection to it:

> I brought *my* drums to the party, and Sheila brought *hers.*

The apostrophe is never used with the possessive case of the personal pronouns.

2. Use the possessive case of the pronoun before a gerund—an *-ing* word used as the name of an action:

> Because I had already studied calculus in high school, the math department approved *my* taking of advanced calculus.

For more on this point, see section 11.9.

18.10D Reflexive/Emphatic Case

Use the reflexive/emphatic case of the pronoun when

1. the object of a verb is a pronoun referring to the subject:

While sharpening a knife, the butcher cut *himself.*

2. you want to stress the word before the pronoun:

The governor *herself* was opposed to the bill.

EXERCISE 4 Choosing Case Forms

Choose the correct form for the pronoun or pronouns in each of the following sentences, and explain the reason for each choice.

EXAMPLE
The coach watched Rosenberg and (I, me) run.
Me (object case) is correct because the pronoun is the direct object of the verb *watched.*

1. (Me, My) brother Frank and (him, his) wife Rhonda love to play poker; it's (them, their) favorite pastime.
2. (My, Mine) is pool.
3. Frank and (I, me) sometimes argue about which of the two is more interesting.
4. Since Frank and (me, I) seldom agree on anything, I don't expect (we, us) to settle this question soon—if ever.
5. Frank (him, himself) realizes that (him, his) arguing will never convince (I, me) and that the dispute between (we, us) may continue indefinitely.
6. But Frank and Rhonda don't realize what (them, they) are missing.
7. While poker takes only a good head, pool takes good hands as well. Every shot depends on (their, them) steadiness.
8. Though Frank will admit this, Rhonda always objects to (me, my) saying that poker is mainly a game of luck.
9. In reply, I point out to (they, them) that pool is a game of nothing but skill.
10. But that statement is never the last word. In fact, we would talk (us, ourselves) to exhaustion on this subject if Rhonda did not finally tell Frank and (I, me) to stop.

pr ca   **18.11 Using *who, whom, whose, whoever,* and *whomever***

The form you need depends on which role the pronoun plays in the sentence or clause that contains it. Observe the following guidelines.

1. Use *who* or *whoever* whenever the pronoun is a subject:

> Some people *who* attended the concert were lucky.
> Tickets were given away to *whoever* wanted them.

2. Use *whom* or *whomever* when the pronoun is an object:

> Some voters will support *whomever* their party nominates.
> They back a candidate *whom* others have selected.

A sentence like this last one can be tightened by the omission of *whom:*

> They back a candidate others have selected.

And if you find *whomever* stiff, you can replace it with *anyone:*

> Some voters will support *anyone* their party nominates.

3. Use *whose* whenever the pronoun is a possessor:

> The colt *whose* picked skeleton lay out there was mine.
> —Wallace Stegner

18.12 Misusing Pronoun Case Forms   *pr ca*

To avoid misusing the case forms of pronouns, observe the following guidelines.

1. Use the same case forms for pronouns linked by *and:*

> a. * Her and I went swimming every day.

Her is in the object case; *I* is in the subject case. Since they are linked by *and,* both should be in the same case. To see which case that should be, test each pronoun by itself:

> I went swimming every day.
> * Her went swimming every day.

I works; *Her* doesn't. So *Her* should be put in the subject case, *She:*   *pr ca*

> EDITED: She and I went swimming every day.
>
> b. * He and myself took turns driving.
> TEST: He took turns driving. * Myself took turns driving.
> EDITED: He and I took turns driving.
>
> c. * There was little to choose between them and we.
> TEST: There was little to choose between them. * There was
> little to choose between we.
> EDITED: There was little to choose between them and us.

2. Avoid using *me, him, myself, himself, herself,* or *themselves* as
the subject of a verb:

> * Me and Sally waited three hours for a bus.
> TEST: * Me waited three hours for a bus. Sally waited three
> hours.
> EDITED: Sally and I waited three hours for a bus.

3. Avoid using a *-self* pronoun as the object of a verb unless the
pronoun refers to the subject:

> * The director chose Laura and myself for two minor parts, and
> then cast herself in the leading role.
> EDITED: The director chose Laura and me for two minor parts,
> and then cast herself in the leading role.

4. Avoid using a *-self* pronoun as the object of a preposition:

> * The letter was addressed to myself.
> EDITED: The letter was addressed to me.
>
> * The director had to choose between Laura and myself.
> EDITED: The director had to choose between Laura and me.

5. Avoid using the forms * *hisself,* * *theirself,* or * *theirselves* under
any conditions in Standard English.

6. Avoid using *I, he, she, we,* or *they* as the object of a verb or
preposition:

> * My uncle always brought presents for my sister and I.
> EDITED: My uncle always brought presents for my sister and
> me.

pr ca   **7.** When a pronoun after *than* or *as* is compared with a subject, use the subject case:

> * Pete [subject] dribbles faster than me. [object case]
> EDITED: Pete dribbles faster than I (dribble).

8. Use the object case after *than* or *as* when the pronoun is compared to an object:

> * The manager pays a veteran like Bob [object] more than I [subject case].
> EDITED: The manager pays a veteran like Bob more than me.

9. Avoid confusing *its* and *it's*, or *their*, *there*, and *they're*, or *whose* and *who's*. See the Glossary of Usage.

EXERCISE 5 Editing Mistakes in Case

Each of the following sentences may contain one or more mistakes in case. Correct every mistake you find by writing the correct form of the pronoun. If a sentence contains a compound, test it as shown in section 18.12. If a sentence is correct as it stands, write *Correct*.

EXAMPLE
The argument between Paul and I is unimportant.
EDITED: The argument between Paul and me is unimportant.

1. Every spring my aunt Mary and me go fishing in the mountains.
2. We put two sets of camping gear in the truck—mine and her.
3. Sometimes a forest ranger shows us where to look for trout.
4. The rangers theirselves have never fished with us; they just want to help ourselves get our quota.
5. Once my cousin Roger asked if he could go fishing with Aunt Mary and I.
6. Aunt Mary had to decide who to take—him or myself.
7. There wasn't room for we two in the truck, and neither him nor me had a car.
8. That spring her and Roger caught the biggest trout she had ever seen.
9. I heard all about it when Roger arrived home; nobody talks more than him.
10. He can hardly wait until Aunt Mary and him go fishing again.

19
Subject-Verb Agreement

19.1 What Is Agreement?

To say that a verb **agrees** in form with its subject is to say that a verb has more than one form, and that each form matches up with a particular kind of subject. Here are three parallel sets of examples based on a verb in the common present tense:

	STANDARD ENGLISH	FRENCH	SPANISH
Singular	I live	je vis	(yo)[†] vivo
	you live	tu vis	(tú) vives
	he lives	il vit	(él) vive
	she lives	elle vit	(ella) vive
Plural	we live	nous vivons	vivimos
	you live	vous vivez	vivis
	they live	ils vivent	(ellos) viven
		[masc.]	[masc.]
		elles vivent	(ellas) viven
		[fem.]	[fem.]

In this example, Spanish has six different verb forms, French has five, and Standard English has just two: *live* and *lives*.

[†] In Spanish, when the subject is a pronoun, it is sometimes omitted.

sv agr   To write Standard English correctly, you need to know which form goes with each subject, where to find the subject in a clause, and whether the subject is singular or plural.

19.2 Making Verbs Agree with Subjects   *sv agr*

In most cases, the subject affects the form of the verb only when the verb is in the present tense. Except for the verb *be* (see section 19.3) and for subjunctive verb forms (see sections 23.4 and 23.5), the rules of agreement in the present tense are as follows.

1. With third-person singular subjects, add *-s* or *-es* to the bare form of the verb:

> Peggy *wants* to study economics.
> She *works* at the bank.
> It *serves* over two thousand depositors.
> Each of them *holds* a passbook.
> Marvin Megabucks *owns* the bank.
> He *polishes* his Jaguar once a week.

EXCEPTION: The verb *have* becomes *has:*

> Everyone *has* moments of self-doubt.
> Uncertainty *has* gripped all of us.

2. With all other subjects, use the bare form of the verb:

> Economists *study* the stock market.
>
> They *evaluate* the fluctuation of prices.
>
> Like the experts, we *want* to make profitable investments.
>
> My brother and his wife both *work* on Wall Street.
>
> I *do* other things.

3. Whatever the subject, use the bare form of any verb that follows an auxiliary, such as *does, can,* or *may:*

> Does she *play* the sax?
>
> She can *sing.*
>
> She may *become* famous.

19.3 Making the Verb *be* Agree with Subjects

1. When *be* is a main verb, its forms are as follows:

PRESENT TENSE		PAST TENSE	
I *am* cold.		I *was* busy.	
You *are* cold.		You *were* busy.	
She		She	
He		He	
It	*is* cold.	It	*was* busy.
Everyone		Everyone	
The student		The student	
We		We	
You		You	
They	*are* cold.	They	*were* busy.
Many		Many	
The students		The students	

2. When *be* is an auxiliary, its form depends on the subject, just as when *be* is a main verb:

> I *am annoyed* by most tax forms.
>
> The current one *is written* in incomprehensible language.
>
> The pages *are covered* with small print and confusing diagrams.
>
> What *were* the experts *thinking* of when they designed the form?

19.4 Avoiding Dialectal Mistakes in Agreement

The rules of agreement in Standard English differ from the rules of agreement in regional and ethnic dialects. To write Standard English correctly, observe the following guidelines.

1. If you're writing about what anyone or anything is doing now, make sure you add *-s* or *-es* to the verb:

> * My brother work for the post office.
> EDITED: My brother *works* for the post office.

> * He live with a couple of his friends.
> EDITED: He *lives* with a couple of his friends.

2. If you're writing about what you or they (any group of two or more) are doing now, use only the bare form of the verb:

> * I needs a job.
> EDITED: I *need* a job.

> * Politicians loves to make promises.
> EDITED: Politicians *love* to make promises.

> * They wants votes.
> EDITED: They *want* votes.

3. The only verb to use between *I* and a verb with *-ing* added is *am:*

> * I be taking calculus this semester.
> EDITED: I *am* taking calculus this semester.

4. If you're writing about what anyone or anything is, use *is:*

> * Veronica be my best friend.
> EDITED: Veronica *is* my best friend.

> * Chain-smoking be risky.
> EDITED: Chain-smoking *is* risky.

5. If you're writing about what two or more persons or things are, use *are:*

> * Banks be closed on holidays.
> EDITED: Banks are closed on holidays.

6. Use *has* after anyone or anything:

> * My sister have a job.
> EDITED: My sister *has* a job.

7. Use *have* after *I, you,* or any words naming more than one:

> * I has a lot of bills to pay.
> EDITED: I *have* a lot of bills to pay.

> * My feet has been hurting.
> EDITED: My feet *have* been hurting.

8. Before *been,* always use *has, have,* or *had:*

> * Everyone been hurt by the layoffs.
> EDITED: Everyone *has* been hurt by the layoffs.

> * I been studying chemistry.
> EDITED: I *have been studying chemistry.*

*I done been watching the news when the phone rang.
EDITED: I *had been* watching the news when the phone rang.

For more on the differences between Standard English and other dialects, see the Introduction, pp. 4–6.

EXERCISE 1 Using Correct Verb Forms

For each verb in parentheses, write down a verb form that agrees with the subject. The correct form will sometimes be the same as the one in parentheses. Use the present tense.

EXAMPLE
A cold drink (taste) good on a hot day when you (be) working outside.
tastes, are

1. In Charles Dickens's well-known tale, Scrooge (be) a cold-hearted miser.
2. He (drive) a hard bargain in business and (spend) less on food, lodging, and himself than any other inhabitant of London (do).
3. The needs of others (do) not concern him; in his opinion, the poor and the homeless may (find) shelter in the public workhouses or prisons.
4. Or they can (die) and thereby help to reduce the surplus population.
5. It (be) not surprising, therefore, that no one (like) to visit with him.
6. Nor (do) he enjoy the company of others; to his way of thinking, all their socializing (have) no value whatsoever.
7. Any moment not given to the making of money (be) misspent: nobody (get) rich if he or she (devote) even one moment in the day to speaking with friends, helping the needy, or caring for families.
8. Scrooge's outlook (be) vividly illustrated by his behavior on Christmas Eve.
9. He (make) his underpaid clerk work until dark, he (do) not contribute a penny to a subscription for the poor, he (chase) a caroler from the office, and he cannot (speak) a civil word to his only nephew, who (invite) Scrooge to spend Christmas Day with his family.
10. To the miser, all talk of a happy holiday (be) "humbug," and people (be) fools not to spend the hours making money.

19.5 Finding the Subject

You can find the subject easily when it comes right before the verb:

> s
> Alan Paton / has written movingly about life in South Africa.
>
> s
> Many readers / consider *Cry, The Beloved Country* a classic.

But the subject sometimes follows the verb in sentences of the following kinds:

1. Sentences starting with *There* or *Here:*

> s
> There was once / a thriving civilization in the jungles of the
> Yucatan.
>
> s
> Here is / a translation of *Popol Vuh,* the Mayan book about
> the dawn of life.

In sentences like these, *There* and *Here* are always introductory words, never subjects.

2. Sentences with inverted word order:

> s
> Visible near Monte Alban in southern / massive pyramids
> Mexico are   constructed over
> two thousand years
> ago.

3. Some questions:

> s
> Have / archeologists / identified the builders of the pyramids?

19.6 Recognizing the Number of the Subject

To make a verb agree with the subject, you must know whether the subject is singular or plural. Observe the following guidelines for various kinds of subjects.

19.6A Nouns Meaning One Thing

A noun meaning one thing is always singular, even if it ends in -*s:*

> The *lens* was cracked.
> According to some critics, *The Grapes of Wrath* is John Steinbeck's greatest novel.

19.6B Nouns Meaning More Than One Thing

A noun meaning more than one thing is always plural:

> The *lenses* were cracked.
>
> His *teeth* are crooked.
>
> *Women* deserve to be paid as much as *men* are.

19.6C Pronouns Fixed in Number

Most pronouns are fixed in number. They include the following:

ALWAYS SINGULAR

he	each	one
she	each one	another
it		
	everybody	somebody
this	everyone	someone
that	everything	something
anybody	either	whatever
anyone	neither	whichever
anything		whoever
	nobody	
	none	
	no one	
	nothing	

ALWAYS PLURAL

we	these	both	few
they	those	others	several

19.6D Pronouns Variable in Number

The pronouns *all, any, many, more, most, some, who, that,* and *which* are variable in number. The number of such a pronoun depends on the number of the word or phrase to which it refers:

Most of the sand *is* washed by the tide.

Most of the sandpipers *are* white.

Some of the oil *has* been cleaned up.

Some of the problems *have* been solved.

Titan is one of the fifteen known satellites that *revolve* around Saturn.

Titan is the only one of the satellites that *has* an atmosphere.

Many is singular only when used with *a* or *an:*

Many of the artists *visit* Florence.

Many an artist *visits* Florence.

Other pronouns are not affected in number by the phrases that modify them; see section 19.G below.

19.6E Verbal Nouns and Noun Clauses

Verbal nouns are always singular:

> *Reassembling the broken pieces of a china bowl* is difficult.
> *To fit the fragments together* takes considerable patience.

Noun clauses are always singular too:

> *What one also needs* is steady hands.
> *That the sun and other planets revolved around the earth* was widely believed.

19.6F Nouns Followed by a Form of the Verb *be*

When a noun or pronoun is followed by the verb *be,* the verb agrees with what comes before it, no matter what comes after it:

> *Newspapers* are his business.
> His *business* is newspapers.

19.6G Modified Nouns and Pronouns

Except for pronouns variable in number (see 19.6D), the number of a modified noun or pronoun usually depends on the noun (N) or pronoun (PR) itself—not on any of the modifiers (M) attached to it:

M N *A ship carrying hundreds of tourists* enters the harbor every Friday.

PR *Each of the tourists* has a credit card and traveler checks.

M M N *Any gold ornament, together with silver bracelets and earrings,* always attracts a crowd.

19.6H Compounds Made with *and*

1. Compound subjects made with *and* are plural when they are used before the verb and refer to more than one thing:

The lion and the tiger belong to the cat family.

2. When a compound subject made with *and* follows the verb, and the first item in the compound is singular, the verb may agree with that:

There was *a desk and three chairs* in the room.

Strictly speaking, the verb should agree with both items: There *were* a desk and three chairs in the room. But since *There were a desk* sounds odd, no matter what follows *desk*, the verb may agree with *desk* alone—the first item. If the first item is plural, the verb always agrees with it:

At the entrance stand *two marble pillars and a statue of Napoleon.*

3. A compound subject made with *and* that refers to only one thing is always singular:

> *The founder and first president of the college* was Eleazor Wheelock.

19.6I Items Joined by *or, either . . . or,* etc.

When items are joined by *or, either . . . or, neither . . . nor, not . . . but,* or *not only . . . but also,* the verb agrees with the item just before it:

> *Neither steel nor glass* cuts a diamond.
> *Not a new machine but new workers* are needed for the job.

19.6J Nouns Spelled the Same Way in Singular and Plural

A noun spelled the same way in the singular and the plural depends for its number on the way it is used:

> *A deer* was nibbling the lettuce.
>
> *Two deer* were standing in the middle of the road.
>
> *One means* of campaigning is direct mail.
>
> *Two other means* are TV advertising and mass rallies.

19.6K Collective Nouns and Nouns of Measurement

Collective nouns and nouns of measurement are singular when they refer to a unit, and plural when they refer to the individuals or elements of a unit:

> *Half of the cake* was eaten.
>
> *Half of the jewels* were stolen.
>
> *Statistics* is the study and analysis of numerical information about the world.
>
> *Recent statistics* show a marked decline in the U.S. birthrate during the past twenty years.
>
> *Fifty dollars* is a lot to ask for a cap.

19.6L Subjects Beginning with *every*

When a subject begins with *every,* treat it as singular:

> *Every cat and dog in the neighborhood* was fighting.

19.6M The Word *number* as Subject

The word *number* is singular when it follows *the,* plural when it follows *a:*

> *The number of applications* was huge.
> *A number of teenagers* now hold full-time jobs.

19.6N Foreign Words and Expressions

When the subject is a foreign word or expression, use a dictionary to find out whether it is singular or plural:

> The *coup d'etat* just completed has caught diplomats by surprise.
>
> The *Carbonari* of the early nineteenth century were members of a secret political organization in Italy.

EXERCISE 2 Correcting Faulty Agreement

In some of the following sentences the verb does not agree with its subject. Correct every verb you consider wrong and then explain the correction. If a sentence is correct as it stands, write *Correct* and add the explanation.

EXAMPLE
One of the insurance agents are a graduate of my university.
The verb should be *is* because the subject is *One,* a singular pronoun.

1. Members of the city's transportation department is seeking a solution to the traffic problem on Main Street.
2. There has been many complaints from merchants and shoppers.
3. An attorney representing five store owners are preparing to sue the city for negligence and economic harassment.
4. Each of the five companies have lost money in the last ten months.
5. A number of shoppers is circulating a petition calling for the resignation of the mayor.
6. She, along with the heads of the transportation department, are feeling the heat.
7. Three-quarters of the gripes is justified.
8. Thirty minutes are too long for any motorist to drive two blocks.

9. No one with important errands wants to spend most of a lunch hour looking for a parking space.

10. A new and improved means of traffic control need to be found.

EXERCISE 3 Correcting Faulty Agreement

This exercise will give you practice in dealing with subject-verb agreement in an extended passage. In the following paragraphs from Juanita H. Williams's *Psychology of Women,* we have deliberately inserted some errors in agreement. We hope you can spot and correct them.

EXAMPLE
lines 4–5: efficiency and level . . . are usually measured

Cognition is the process by which the individual acquires knowledge about an object or an event. It includes perceiving, recognizing, judging, and sensing—the ways of knowing. The efficiency and level of the acquisition of knowledge is usually measured in older children and adults by the use of tests which requires language. Studies of infant cognition, of what and how babies "know," have begun to appear only in the last decade, with the development of new techniques which provides insights into what and how babies learn.

In spite of the persistent belief that babies differ along sex lines—for example, that girl babies vocalize more and boy babies are more active—sex differences in cognitive functions in the first two years of life has not been demonstrated. (Maccoby and Jacklin, 1974). Measurements of intellectual ability, learning, and memory does not differ on the average for boys and girls. However, patterns of performances are different for the two sexes, as are the consistency (thus the predictability) of the measures as the infants get older. A longitudinal study of 180 white, first-born infants, 91 boys and 89 girls, each of whom were tested in the laboratory at four, eight, thirteen, and twenty-seven months, offers some evidence concerning these patterns (Kagan, 1971). One of the behaviors for which different patterns were observed for boys and girls were vocalization, the infant's response when aroused or excited by an unusual or discrepant stimulus.

20
Verbs

TENSE

If English is your native language, you probably have a good working knowledge of tenses. You know how to describe what someone or something did in the past, is doing in the present, or will do in the future. But you may not know just how to describe an action that doesn't fall neatly into one time slot. For instance, how do you describe the action of a character in a novel or a play? How do you describe an action that started in the past but is still going on now? How do you write about an action that will be completed at some time in the future? This chapter is chiefly meant to answer questions like those.

The chapter is limited to verbs in the indicative mood (the mood of fact or matters close to fact) and in the active voice (in which the subject performs the action, as in "Whales eat plankton"). For a full discussion of mood, see chapter 23; for a full discussion of voice, see chapter 22.

20.1 Tense and Time

The **tense** of a verb helps to indicate the time of an action or condition:

> PAST: The sun *rose* at 6:03 this morning.
> PRESENT: As I *write* these words, the sun *is setting*.
> FUTURE: The sun *will rise* tomorrow at 6:04.

tf   But tense is not the same as time. A verb in the present tense, for instance, may be used in a statement about the future:

> The bus leaves tomorrow at 7:30 A.M.

The time of an action or state is often indicated by a word or phrase like *tomorrow, next week*, or *last week*.

20.2 Forming the Tenses   *tf*

The tenses of all but a few verbs are made from the four **principal parts**. The principal parts of regular verbs are formed by the addition of *-ing* or *-ed* to the bare form, as shown here:

PRESENT (BARE FORM)	PRESENT PARTICIPLE	PAST	PAST PARTICIPLE
cook	cook*ing*	cook*ed*	cook*ed*
lift	lift*ing*	lift*ed*	lift*ed*
polish	polish*ing*	polish*ed*	polish*ed*

Verbs with some principal parts formed in other ways are called **irregular.** Here are some examples:

eat	eating	ate	eaten
write	writing	wrote	written
go	going	went	gone
speak	speaking	spoke	spoken

For the principal parts of commonly used irregular verbs, see section 20.11.

20.2A Forming the Present

With most subjects, the form of a verb in the present tense is simply the bare form:

> Seasoned traders *drive* hard bargains.
> I *polish* my shoes every day.

But after a singular noun or a third-person singular pronoun, such as *she, it, this, each*, or *everyone*, you must add *-s* or *-es* to the bare form of the verb:

> Helen *drives* a cab.
> She *polishes* it once a week.

For more on this point, see sections 19.1–19.4.

20.2B Forming the Past

The past tense of regular verbs is formed by the addition of -*d* or -*ed* to the bare form:

> Helen *liked* her work.
> She *polished* her cab regularly.

For the past tense of commonly used irregular verbs, see section 20.11.

20.2C Forming Tenses with Auxiliaries

Besides the present and the past, there are four other tenses. You form these by using certain auxiliary verbs, such as *will, has,* and *had:*

	REGULAR VERB	IRREGULAR VERB
Future:	She will work.	She will speak.
Present Perfect:	She has worked.	She has spoken.
Past Perfect:	She had worked.	She had spoken.
Future Perfect:	She will have worked.	She will have spoken.

20.2D Forming the Progressive

The **common** forms discussed so far indicate a momentary, habitual, or completed action. The **progressive** forms indicate that the action named by the verb is viewed as continuing:

> PRESENT: The president *is speaking* now.
> PRESENT PERFECT: The president *has been speaking* for twenty minutes.
> PAST: The president *was speaking* while photographers took pictures.

EXERCISE 1 Writing Principal Parts

For each of the following sentences write out the principal parts of the italicized verb, listing in sequence the present, the present participle, the past, and the past participle. Whenever you are unsure of a form, refer to your dictionary or to the list of irregular verbs in section 20.11.

EXAMPLE
The concert *begins* at 8 P.M.
begin, beginning, began, begun

1. In 1927 Charles A. Lindbergh *flew* nonstop from New York to Paris.

2. On his return New Yorkers *gave* him a hero's welcome.

3. Some spectators *had slept* on the sidewalk in order not to miss the parade.

4. No one who *witnessed* the triumphant procession ever *forgot* the spectacle.

5. The young American *had laid* to rest the fear of crossing the Atlantic in a plane. (For a full discussion of the verbs *lay* and *lie*, see the Glossary of Usage.)

6. He *had broken* a barrier with his record flight.

20.3 Using the Present

1. Use the common present:

a. To report what happens regularly:

I *run* two miles every day.
Leaves *change* color in autumn.

b. To state a fact or widely held belief:

Water *freezes* at 32° F.
Opposites *attract*.

c. To describe characters, events, or other matters in an aesthetic work, such as a painting, a piece of music, a work of literature, a movie, or a television show:

In *Jaws*, a man-eating shark *attacks* and *terrifies* swimmers until he is finally killed.

In the first chapter, Gabriel *sees* the beautiful Bathsheba, but she *does* not see him.

d. To say what a writer or a creative artist does in his or her work:

Many of Mary Cassatt's paintings *explore* the theme of a mother's love for her child.

In *The Wealth of Nations* (1776), Adam Smith *argues* that an "invisible hand" *regulates* individual enterprise for the good of society as a whole.

In his famous Fifth Symphony, Beethoven *reveals* the power and fury of his imagination.

e. To describe an opinion or idea:

In the Marxist vision of history, the ruling classes ceaselessly *oppress* the working class.

f. To indicate that a condition or situation is likely to last:

My sister *loves* chocolate ice cream.

g. To describe a future action that is definitely predictable:

The sun *rises* tomorrow at 6:04.

h. To report a statement of lasting significance:

"All art," *says* Oscar Wilde, "is quite useless."

2. Use the present progressive:

a. To indicate that an action or state is occurring at the time of the writing:

The sun *is setting* now, and the birches *are bending* in the wind.

b. To indicate that an action is in progress—even though it may not be taking place at the exact moment of the writing:

Suburban life *is losing* its appeal. Many young couples *are moving* out of the suburbs and into the cities.

20.4 Using the Present Perfect

1. Use the common present perfect:
a. To report a past action or state that touches in some way on the present:

I *have* just *finished* reading *Gone with the Wind.*
A presidential commission *has* already *investigated* the causes of one nuclear accident.

The words *just* and *already* are often used with the present perfect.

b. To report an action or state begun in the past but extending into the present:

> Engineers *have begun* to explore the possibility of harnessing the tides.
> Since the invention of the automobile, traffic accidents *have taken* many thousands of lives.

c. To report an action performed at some unspecified time in the past:

> *Have* you ever *seen* the Statue of Liberty?

2. Use the <u>progressive</u> form of the <u>present perfect</u> when you want to emphasize the continuity of an action from the past into the present, and the likelihood of its continuing into the future:

> Some man-made satellites *have been traveling* through space for years.
> The cost of medical care *has been growing* at a staggering rate.

20.5 Using the Past

1. Use the <u>common past</u>:

a. To report an action or state definitely completed in the past:

> Thomas Edison *invented* the phonograph in 1877.
> The city *became* calm after the cease-fire.

b. To report actions repeated in the past but no longer occurring at the time of the writing:

> The family always *went* to church on Sundays.

2. Use the <u>past progressive</u>:

a. To emphasize the continuity of a past action:

> His insults *were becoming* unbearable.

b. To state that one action was being performed when another occurred:

> I *was pouring* a glass of water when the pitcher suddenly cracked.

20.6 Using the Past Perfect

1. Use the common past perfect:

a. To state that an action or state was completed by a specified time in the past:

By noon we *had gathered* three hundred bushels.

b. To indicate that one past action or state was completed by the time another occurred:

By the time Hitler sent reinforcements, the Allies *had* already *taken* much of France.

I suddenly realized that I *had left* my keys at home.

By the age of thirty, she *had* already *had* seven children.

c. To report an unfulfilled hope or intention:

Mary *had planned* to travel as far as Denver, but her money ran out while she was still in Chicago.

2. Use the progressive form to indicate that the first of two past actions or states went on until the second occurred:

Before Gloria entered Mark's life, he *had been spending* most of his time with books.

20.7 Using the Future

1. Use the common future:

a. To report a future event or state that will occur regardless of human intent:

The sun *will rise* at 6:35 tomorrow morning.
I *will be* nineteen on my next birthday.

b. To indicate willingness or determination to do something:

The president has declared that he *will veto* the bill.

c. To report what will happen under certain conditions:

If you get up early enough, you *will see* the sunrise.

d. To indicate future probability:

The cost of a college education *will increase.*

In the preceding examples, the auxiliary *will* is used. Years ago, *will* generally went with *you, they, he, she, it,* and noun subjects, and *shall* was used with *I* and *we* to express the simple future. When *will* was used with *I* and *we,* it signified the speaker's (or writer's) determination: "We will stop the enemy." The use of *shall* with *you, they, he, she, it,* or a noun subject had the same function: "You shall pay the tax." But in current usage *shall* and *will* mean about the same thing, and most writers use *will* with all subjects to express the simple future. Some writers substitute *shall,* again with all subjects, to express determination or certainty: "We shall overcome."

2. Use the future progressive:

a. To say that an action or state will be continuing for a period of time in the future:

Economists *will be* closely *watching* fluctuations in the price of gold.

b. To say what the subject will be doing at a given time in the future:

Next summer I *will be teaching* tennis.

20.8 Using the Future Perfect

1. Use the common future perfect:

a. To say that an action or state will be completed by a specified time in the future:

At the rate I'm living, I *will have spent* all my summer earnings by the end of October.

b. To say that an action or state will be completed by the time something else happens:

By the time an efficient engine is produced, we *will have exhausted* our supplies of fuel.

2. Use the progressive form of the future perfect to say that an activity or state will continue until a specified time in the future:

> By 1995 the *Pioneer 10* probe *will have been traveling* through space for more than twenty years.

20.9 Misusing Tenses   *mt*

1. Avoid using the present progressive to describe what someone or something does regularly:

> * Usually my day *is starting* at 7:00 A.M.
> EDITED: Usually my day *starts* at 7:00 A.M.

2. Avoid using the past tense to say that one action was completed by the time another occurred:

> * By the time the game ended, many of the spectators *left.*
> EDITED: By the time the game ended, many of the spectators *had left.*

3. Avoid using the past tense for an action that continues into the present:

> * Ever since the steel plant closed, the town *suffered.*
> EDITED: Ever since the steel plant closed, the town *has suffered.*

20.10 Managing Tense and Time with Participles and Infinitives

Participles and infinitives have two tenses: the present and the perfect. The present consists of the present participle or the infinitive by itself: *dancing, to dance.* The perfect tense is made with *having* or *have: having danced, to have danced.*

1. Use the present tense when the action or state named by the participle or infinitive occurs at or after the time of the main verb:

> We spend hours in conference with individual students, hours *meeting* together and with counselors, *trying* to teach ourselves how to teach and *asking* ourselves what we ought to be teaching.   —Adrienne Rich

2. Use the perfect tense when the action or state named by the participle or infinitive occurred before the time of the main verb:

> *Having lost* his cargo during the hurricane, the captain faced bankruptcy when his vessel finally reached port.

> Several reporters are sorry *to have missed* the president's impromptu press conference.

EXERCISE 2 Using Tenses

In the following passage from Daniel Mark Epstein's essay "The Case of Harry Houdini," we have replaced nearly every verb with a blank and put the bare form of the verb in parentheses. Write out the passage with the appropriate tense of each verb.

EXAMPLE
When he _____(arrive) in London in 1900, the twenty-six year old magician _____(do) not have a single booking.
When he arrived in London in 1900, the twenty-six year old magician did not have a single booking.

In 1901, when Houdini _____(take) on the Imperial Police, he _____ (is) not _____(whistle) in the dark. By the time he _____(leave) America at the end of the nineteenth century he _____(dissect) every kind of lock he _____(can) find in the New World, and whatever he _____(can) import from the old one. Arriving in London, Houdini _ (can) write that there _____(are) only a few kinds of British handcuffs, "seven or eight at the utmost," and these _____(are) some of the simplest he _____ever _____(see). He _____(search) the markets, antique shops, and locksmiths, buying up all the European locks he _____(can) find so he _____(can) dismantle and study them.

20.11 Forming the Principal Parts of Commonly Used Irregular Verbs

Following is a partial list of irregular verbs—those with special forms for the past, the past participle, or both. When more than one form is shown, the first is more commonly used. For verbs not listed here, see your dictionary.

PRESENT (BARE FORM)	PRESENT PARTICIPLE	PAST	PAST PARTICIPLE
arise	arising	arose	arisen
awake	awaking	awoke, awaked	awoke, awaked, awoken
be†	being	was/were	been
bear [bring forth]	bearing	bore	born, borne
bear [carry]	bearing	bore	borne
beat	beating	beat	beaten, beat
begin	beginning	began	begun
bid [command]	bidding	bade	bid, bidden
bid [offer to pay]	bidding	bid	bid
bite	biting	bit	bitten
bleed	bleeding	bled	bled
blend	blending	blended, blent	blended, blent
blow	blowing	blew	blown
break	breaking	broke	broken
bring	bringing	brought	brought
buy	buying	bought	bought
catch	catching	caught	caught
choose	choosing	chose	chosen
clothe	clothing	clothed, clad	clothed, clad
come	coming	came	come
cost	costing	cost	cost
creep	creeping	crept	crept
dig	digging	dug	dug
dive	diving	dived, dove	dived
do	doing	did	done
draw	drawing	drew	drawn
drink	drinking	drank	drunk, drunken
drive	driving	drove	driven
eat	eating	ate	eaten
fall	falling	fell	fallen
feel	feeling	felt	felt
fight	fighting	fought	fought
find	finding	found	found
fly	flying	flew	flown
forbid	forbidding	forbade, forbad	forbidden, forbid
forget	forgetting	forgot	forgotten, forgot
freeze	freezing	froze	frozen

†In this case the bare form *(be)* is not the same as the present *(am, is, are).*

Present (Bare Form)	Present Participle	Past	Past Participle
get	getting	got	got, gotten
give	giving	gave	given
go	going	went	gone
grow	growing	grew	grown
hang [execute]	hanging	hanged	hanged
hang [suspend]	hanging	hung	hung
have	having	had	had
hear	hearing	heard	heard
hide	hiding	hid	hidden, hid
hit	hitting	hit	hit
hold	holding	held	held
keep	keeping	kept	kept
know	knowing	knew	known
lay	laying	laid	laid
lead	leading	led	led
learn	learning	learned, learnt	learned, learnt
leave	leaving	left	left
let	letting	let	let
lie [recline]	lying	lay	lain
lie [tell a false-hood]	lying	lied	lied
lose	losing	lost	lost
make	making	made	made
pay	paying	paid	paid
prove	proving	proved	proved, proven
ride	riding	rode	ridden
ring	ringing	rang	rung
rise	rising	rose	risen
run	running	ran	run
saw	sawing	sawed	sawed, sawn
see	seeing	saw	seen
seek	seeking	sought	sought
shake	shaking	shook	shaken
shine	shining	shone	shone
show	showing	showed	shown, showed
shrink	shrinking	shrank, shrunk	shrunk, shrunken
sing	singing	sang	sung
sink	sinking	sank, sunk	sunk, sunken
slay	slaying	slew	slain

PRESENT (BARE FORM)	PRESENT PARTICIPLE	PAST	PAST PARTICIPLE
sleep	sleeping	slept	slept
smell	smelling	smelled, smelt	smelled, smelt
speak	speaking	spoke	spoken
spin	spinning	spun, span	spun
spring	springing	sprang	sprung
steal	stealing	stole	stolen
stride	striding	strode	stridden
strike	striking	struck	struck, stricken
strive	striving	strove	striven
swear	swearing	swore	sworn
sweep	sweeping	swept	swept
swim	swimming	swam	swum
take	taking	took	taken
teach	teaching	taught	taught
tear	tearing	tore	torn
throw	throwing	threw	thrown
tread	treading	trod	trodden, trod
wake	waking	woke, waked	woke, waked, woken
wear	wearing	wore	worn
weave	weaving	wove	woven
wed	wedding	wed, wedded	wed, wedded
weep	weeping	wept	wept
wind	winding	wound	wound
work	working	worked, wrought	worked, wrought
write	writing	wrote	written

21
Verbs

SEQUENCE OF TENSES

21.1 Understanding Sequence of Tenses

When a passage has more than one verb, the relation between the tenses of the verbs is called the **sequence of tenses.** Various sequences are possible.

When all the verbs in a sentence describe actions or states that occur at or about the same time, their tenses should be the same:

> Whenever the alarm clock *rings,* I *yawn, stretch,* and *roll* over for another fifteen minutes of sleep. (all present tense)

> The prima donna *opened* her arms to the audience, *smiled,* and *bowed* deeply. (all past tense)

On the other hand, a sentence may describe actions that happen at different times. It will then have verbs in different tenses:

> Beth *had been working* on the research project for almost three years before she *made* the first discovery. (past perfect and past)

> Recently the largest bank in the area *lowered* the interest rate on loans; the directors *want* to stimulate borrowing. (past and present)

In the rest of this chapter, we explain some of the common sequences and show you how to keep your own sequence of tenses consistent.

21.2 Sequences in Compound Sentences

A compound sentence consists of two or more independent clauses. Since the clauses are independent, the tenses of the verbs in those clauses may be entirely independent of each other:

> In the past, most Americans *wanted* big automobiles, but now many *prefer* driving smaller economical models. (past and present)

> The number of finback whales *is decreasing;* as a result, they *will be added* to the list of endangered species. (present and future)

21.3 Sequences in Complex Sentences

A complex sentence consists of one independent clause and at least one subordinate clause (see chapter 15). In this kind of sentence, which often deals with two different times, many sequences are possible. Here are the common ones.

21.3A Main Verb in the Present

MAIN VERB	SUBORDINATE VERB
[verb of independent clause]	[verb of subordinate clause]
Some Americans *are* so poor	that they *suffer* from malnutrition. (present)
Most children *learn* to talk	after they *have learned* to walk. (present perfect)
Greg *likes* to boast about the marlin	that he *caught* last summer. (past)
Astronomers *predict*	that the sun *will die* in about ten billion years. (future)

21.3B Main Verb in the Present Perfect

MAIN VERB	SUBORDINATE VERB
Scientists *have studied* the rings of Saturn	ever since Galileo *discovered* them. (past)

SUBORDINATE VERB	MAIN VERB
Although drivers *have complained* about the heavy traffic, (present perfect)	the police *have done* nothing to alleviate the problem.

21.3C Main Verb in the Past

MAIN VERB	SUBORDINATE VERB
Centuries ago most people *believed*	that the sun *revolved* around the earth. (past)
Recently archeologists working in Egypt *opened* a tomb	that *had been sealed* in about 2500 B.C. (past perfect)

SUBORDINATE VERB	MAIN VERB
When the crewmen *saw* land, (past)	they *rejoiced.*

21.3D Main Verb in the Past Perfect

SUBORDINATE VERB	MAIN VERB
By the time Columbus *sighted* land, (past)	most of his crew *had lost* all hope of survival.

21.3E Main Verb Indicating Future

MAIN VERB	SUBORDINATE VERB
People *will buy* new homes	when interest rates *are lowered.* (present)
Students *will get* their diplomas	only after they *have paid* their library fines. (present perfect)
I *start* my summer job	just as soon as I *have taken* my exams. (present perfect)

As the examples show, the subordinate verb in this kind of sequence is never future in form:

> * The building will be demolished when the school year *will end.*
>
> EDITED: The building will be demolished when the school year *ends.* (You could also use *has ended.*)

21.3F Main Verb in the Future Perfect

MAIN VERB	SUBORDINATE VERB
Workmen *will have completed* repairs	by the time the airport *reopens.* (present)

SUBORDINATE VERB	MAIN VERB
Before a new SALT agreement *has been signed,* (present perfect)	the United States and Russia *will have spent* billions on the development of new weapons.

EXERCISE 1 Transforming Tenses

This exercise should help you understand how the tense of a subordinate verb is related to the tense of the main verb. In each of the
following, change the italicized verb to the past tense if it is in the
present, and to the present tense if it is in the past. Then make
whatever other tense changes have become necessary.

EXAMPLE
We *want* to take a walk before it starts raining.
TRANSFORMED: We *wanted* to take a walk before it *started* raining.

1. On April 9, 1865, when Lee's Army of Northern Virginia has
   already been defeated, Ulysses S. Grant *meets* Robert E. Lee at
   Appomattox Court House, Virginia.
2. Historians *believed* that this meeting ended the Civil War.
3. The Confederate government *struggles* to survive for a short time
   even after Lee formally surrenders to Grant.
4. But Grant and Lee both *know* that the war is over.
5. They *realize* that the time for peace has come.

21.4 Using Sequences in Paragraphs

A paragraph normally includes many verbs and often several different tenses. But you should shift tenses in a paragraph only when
you have good reason for doing so.

A well-written paragraph is usually dominated by just one
tense. Consider the following example:

   1. Before I *set* my world record, I *was* a great fan of *The Guin-
      ness Book of World Records* and *read* each new edition from
      cover to cover. I *liked* knowing and being able to tell others
      that the world's chug-a-lug champ *consumed* 2.58 pints of
      beer in 10 seconds, that the world's lightest adult person
      weighed only 13 pounds, that the largest vocabulary for a
      talking bird *was* 531 words, spoken by a brown-beaked
      budgerigar named Sparky. There *is*, of course, only a fine
      line between admiration and envy, and for awhile I *had been*
      secretly *desiring* to be in that book myself—to astonish
      others just as I *had been astonished*. But it *seemed* hope-
      less. How could a nervous college sophomore, an anony-
      mous bookworm, perform any of those wonderful feats? The

t shift

> open-throat technique necessary for chug-a-lugging *was* incomprehensible to my trachea—and I *thought* my head alone must weigh close to 13 pounds.
> —William Allen, "How to Set a World Record"

The author is describing a past condition, so the dominant tense here is the simple past, as in *was, read, liked, consumed, weighed,* and *seemed.* Midway through the paragraph the author shifts out of the simple past, saying that there *is* a fine line between admiration and envy, and that he *had been* secretly *desiring* to be in the Guinness book. He has good reasons for both of these shifts: *is* describes a general truth and *had been desiring* describes a condition that existed before the simple past, before the time described in the rest of the paragraph. Then the author returns to the simple past with *seemed, was,* and *thought.*

Now consider this paragraph:

> **2.** February 2, 1975. Wasps *begin* to appear in country houses about now, and even in some suburban houses. One *sees* them dart uncertainly about, *hears* them buzz and bang on window panes, and one *wonders* where they *came* from. They probably *came* from the attic, where they *spent* the early part of the winter hibernating. *Now,* with longer hours of daylight, the wasps *begin* to rouse and *start* exploring.
> —Hal Borland, "Those Attic Wasps"

This passage describes not a past condition but a recurrent one—something that happens every year. The dominant tense of the verbs, therefore, is the present: *begin, sees, hears, wonders, begin, start.* Since the presence of the wasps calls for some explanation, the writer shifts tense in the middle of the paragraph to tell us where they *came* from and where they *spent* the early part of the winter. But in the final sentence, *Now* brings us back to the present, and the verbs of this sentence, *begin* and *start,* are in the present tense.

21.5 Correcting Faulty Tense Shifts in Sentences
t shift

The shift of tenses in a sentence is faulty when the tense of any verb differs without good reason from the tense of the one before it, or when the tense of a subordinate verb is inconsistent with the tense of the main verb.

1. TENSES INCONSISTENT: The novel *describes* the adventures of two immigrant families who *enter* the United States at New York, *withstand* the stresses of culture shock, and *traveled* to the Dakota Territory to make their fortune.
EDITED: The novel *describes* the adventures of two immigrant families who *enter* the United States at New York, *withstand* the stresses of culture shock, and *travel* to the Dakota Territory to make their fortune.

2. TENSES INCONSISTENT: The president *announced* that he *will* not *seek* reelection.
EDITED: The president *announced* that he *would* not *seek* reelection.

3. TENSES INCONSISTENT: Marthe *likes* to display the miniature spoons she *had collected* since her marriage to an antique dealer.
EDITED: Marthe *likes* to display the miniature spoons she *has collected* since her marriage to an antique dealer.

EXERCISE 2 Correcting Faulty Tense Shifts in a Sentence

In some of the following sentences, the tense of one or more verbs does not properly correspond to the tense of the italicized verb. Correct those sentences. If a sentence is correct as it stands, write *Correct*.

EXAMPLE
A roll of thunder *announced* the coming of the storm; then drops of rain begin to pelt the earth.
EDITED: A roll of thunder *announced* the coming of the storm; then drops of rain *began* to pelt the earth.

1. Filters *are being installed* in water systems that had been threatened by pollutants from industrial wastes.

2. The pollutants *were* first *discovered* last July when inspectors from the city's water department have checked the systems.

3. At that time, inspectors *found* that pollutants have already made the water unsafe to drink.

4. The water *will be* drinkable again after the filters had been installed.

5. But until the installation was complete, residents *are drinking* bottled water.

¶ t
shift

21.6 Correcting Faulty Tense Shifts in Paragraphs
¶ t *shift*

The shift of tenses in a paragraph is faulty when the tense of any verb differs without good reason from the dominant tense of the paragraph. Consider two examples, the first a commentary on *Green Mansions,* a novel by W. H. Hudson:

> 1. [1] On his return to the once peaceful woods, Abel *is horrified* to learn that his beloved Rima *has been slain* by savages. [2] Rage and grief *swell* within him as Kua-kó *tells* how Rima *was forced* to seek refuge in a lofty tree and how the tree *became* a trap when the savages *sent* searing flames and choking smoke high into the branches. [3] As Abel *hears* of her final cry—"Abel! Abel!"—and fatal plunge to earth, he *fought* against a wild impulse to leap upon the triumphant Indian and tear his heart out.

Since the present tense is normally used in the summary of a literary work (see section 20.3c), the dominant tense is the present *(swell, tells,* and *hears).* There is one shift to the present perfect *(has been slain* in sentence 1) and four shifts to the past *(was forced, became,* and *sent* in sentence 2, and *fought* in sentence 3). The shifts in sentences 1 and 2 are correct; the shift in sentence 3 is not. In sentence 1, *has been slain* tells what happened before Abel is horrified to learn about it. In sentence 2, the past-tense verbs describe what happened shortly before Kua-kó *tells* about it. But in sentence 3, the verb *fought* tells what Abel does just at the time that he *hears* of Rima's death. *Fought* should therefore be *fights.*

> 2. [1] To understand Marx, we *need* to know something about the times in which he *lived.* [2] The period *was characterized* by revolutionary pressures against the ruling classes. [3] In most of the countries of Europe, there *was* little democracy, as we *know* it. [4] The masses *participated* little, if at all, in the world of political affairs, and very fully in the world of drudgery. [5] For example, at one factory in Manchester, England, in 1862, people *work* an average of 80 hours per week. [6] For these long hours of toil, the workers generally *receive* small wages. [7] They often *can do* little more than feed and clothe themselves. [8] Given these circumstances, it *is* little wonder that revolutionary pressures *were* manifest.
>
> —Deliberately altered from Edwin Mansfield,
> *Economics: Principles, Problems, Decisions*

In sentence 1 the writer correctly shifts from the present tense *(need)*, which signifies the writer's time, to the past tense *(lived)*, which signifies Marx's time. In the last part of sentence 3, he correctly returns to the present tense *(know)* to signify his own time, and then shifts back to Marx's time with the past tense *(participated)*. But in sentences 5, 6, and 7, the shifts to the present tense *(work, receive, can do)* are all wrong because they refer to actions in the past; the verbs should be *worked, received,* and *could do.* In sentence 8 both tenses are correct. The present tense *is* signifies the writer's time, while the past tense *were* signifies Marx's time.

¶ *t*
shift

EXERCISE 3 Correcting Faulty Tense Shifts in a Paragraph

Each of the following paragraphs is a rewritten version of a paragraph from the source cited after it. In rewriting each paragraph, we have deliberately introduced one or more faulty shifts in tense. Correct them.

EXAMPLE
line 3; manfully thrashes

1. However violent his acts, Kong remains a gentleman. Whenever a fresh boa constrictor threatens Fay, Kong first sees that the lady is safely parked, then manfully thrashed her attacker. (And she, the ingrate, runs away every time his back was turned.) Atop the Empire State Building, ignoring his pursuers, Kong places Fay on a ledge as tenderly as if she were a dozen eggs. He fondled her, then turned to face the Army Air Force. And Kong is perhaps the most disinterested lover since Cyrano: his attentions to the lady were utterly without hope of reward. After all, between a five-foot blonde and a fifty-foot ape, love can hardly be more than an intellectual flirtation. His forced exit from his jungle, in chains, results directly from his single-minded pursuit of Fay. He smashes a Broadway theater when the notion entered his dull brain that the flashbulbs of photographers somehow endanger the lady. His perilous shinnying up a skyscraper to have plucked Fay from her boudoir is an act of the kindliest of hearts. He was impossible to discourage even though the love of his life can't lay eyes on him without shrieking murder.
—Deliberately altered from X. J. Kennedy, "Who Killed King Kong?"

¶ *t*
shift

2. Since graduating from college, Susan has held a variety of political jobs. Her warm, friendly manner, together with her capacity for hard work, makes her an ideal employee. Three years ago, she managed the reelection campaign of a New England governor. She has to talk with people in all parts of the state, trying to build support. Soon after the election, which turns out successfully for the governor, Susan goes to Washington, D.C., to work for a senator. She had a high-paying position; but, being more interested in working creatively than in making money, she soon resigned, proclaiming, "Never have so many people done so little work for so much money." Because she has had so much experience, finding a new job was easy. She becomes an adviser to the New England Governors' Conference on Energy.

—Deliberately altered from Mark Bartlett,
"A Political Woman"

22
Verbs

ACTIVE AND PASSIVE VOICE

22.1 What Voice Is

The "voice" of a verb depends on the relation between the verb and its subject. When the subject of a verb *acts*, the verb is in the **active voice;** when the subject is *acted upon*, the verb is in the **passive voice.**

The active voice stresses the activity of the subject and helps to make a sentence direct, concise, and vigorous:

> The tornado *flattened* entire houses.

> Each man *kills* the thing he *loves.* —Oscar Wilde

The passive voice presents the subject as the target of an action:

> The barn *was struck* by a bolt of lightning.

> In Moulmein, in Lower Burma, I *was hated* by large numbers of people—the only time in my life that I have been important enough for this to happen to me. —George Orwell

In passive constructions, the performer of the action is called an **agent.** In the examples above, *a bolt of lightning* and *large numbers of people* are agents.

22.2 Forming the Active and the Passive Voice

Verbs in the active voice can take many forms: the bare form, the past tense form, the *-ing* form with *be,* and the form with *have:*

> My sisters often *chop* logs for exercise.
>
> But today they *are lifting* weights.
>
> Last week they *stacked* firewood for the stove.
>
> They *have done* wonders.

Verbs in the passive voice are formed from their past participle and some tense of *be:*

> The burglar alarms *were chosen* by a security guard.
>
> They *will be installed* next week.

22.2A Changing from Active to Passive

You can change a verb from active to passive only if it has a direct object (DO):

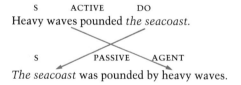

> S   ACTIVE   DO
> Heavy waves pounded *the seacoast.*
>
> S   PASSIVE   AGENT
> *The seacoast* was pounded by heavy waves.

In the passive version, the direct object of *pounded* becomes the subject of *was pounded:* it is acted upon. The subject of *pounded* becomes the agent of *was pounded.* But if the performer of an action is not important to your point, you don't need to mention the agent:

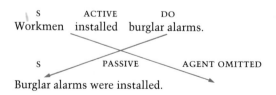

> S   ACTIVE   DO
> Workmen   installed   burglar alarms.
>
> S   PASSIVE   AGENT OMITTED
> Burglar alarms were installed.

22.2B Changing from Passive to Active

To change a verb from the passive to the active voice, turn the subject of the passive verb into the direct object of the active one:

      S   PASSIVE   AGENT

Pearl Harbor was bombed by the Japanese.

      S   ACTIVE   DO

The Japanese bombed *Pearl Harbor.*

If the passive version does not include the agent, you must either keep the passive or supply the agent itself before changing to the active:

> The city of Washington was planned in 1791. (passive, no agent)
>
> The city of Washington was planned in 1791 by Pierre Charles L'Enfant. (passive, agent supplied)
>
> Pierre Charles L'Enfant planned the city of Washington in 1791. (active)

22.3 Choosing the Active Voice

To make your writing forceful, direct, and concise, you should use the active voice frequently. Compare these sentences:

> Through her studies of child-rearing, personality, and culture, world fame was achieved by Margaret Mead. (passive)
>
> Through her studies of child-rearing, personality, and culture, Margaret Mead achieved world fame. (active)

The active version ditches the excess verbal baggage—*was* and *by.* Also, because it makes *Margaret Mead* the subject, the active version puts more stress on her achievement. To a great extent, the life and energy of your writing will depend on what the subjects of your sentences do.

22.4 Choosing the Passive

You should use the active voice as much as possible. But just as a good driver knows when to shift into reverse, a good writer knows when to shift into the passive. We suggest you do as follows.

1. Use the passive when you want to keep the focus on someone or something important that is acted upon:

> **a.** On August 13, 1927, while driving on the Promenade des Anglais at Nice, Isadora Duncan met her death. She *was strangled* by her colored shawl, which became tangled in the wheel of the automobile. —Janet Flanner

Here the writer shifts from the active *(met)* in the first sentence to the passive *(was strangled)* in the second sentence. The shift from active to passive enables the writer to keep the focus on a subject who is shown first acting, and then acted upon.

> **b.** Frederick Douglass learned to read while he *was owned* by Mr. and Mrs. Ault of Baltimore.

Here the writer moves from active to passive in one sentence. The shift keeps the focus on Douglass, who is shown at once acting (he *learned*) and acted upon (he *was owned*).

> **c.** If our heads swim occasionally, if we grow giddy with change, is it any wonder? We are urged to take our rightful place in the world of affairs. We are also commanded to stay at home and mind the hearth. We are lauded for our stamina and pitied for our lack of it. If we run to large families, we are told we are overpopulating the earth. If we are childless, we are damned for not fulfilling our functions. We are goaded into jobs and careers, then warned that our competition with men is unsettling both sexes.
> —Phyllis McGinley, "The Honor of Being a Woman"

The consistent use of the passive here helps the writer to keep the focus on women as acted upon, relentlessly subjected to pressures and demands. They *are urged, are damned, are goaded,* and so on.

2. Use the passive when the agent is unknown or unimportant to your point:

> Traces of the oil spill *were found* as far away as Newfoundland.

3. Use the passive when you want to put the agent at the end of a clause, where you can easily attach a long modifier:

> A secret mission to help thousands of starving Cambodians was organized in the summer of 1979 by Father Robert I.

Charlesbois, a forty-eight-year-old Catholic priest from Gary, Indiana, with twelve years of experience in the Vietnam war zone.

22.5 Misusing the Passive *pass*

Avoid switching from active to passive when you have no particular reason to do so:

Usually I run two miles in the morning, but that morning it *was decided* that a four-mile run *should be taken.*

Who made the decision?

EDITED: Usually I run two miles in the morning, but that morning I decided to run four.

The active voice makes the sentence snap into shape and keeps the focus on the one who is acting. You should switch to the passive only if it gives you a special advantage—such as keeping the focus on someone who is acted upon:

Usually I run two miles in the morning, but that morning I *was kept* in bed by the flu.

EXERCISE 1 Eliminating the Passive

Rewrite any of the following sentences in which you find the passive voice misused. If the passive voice is justified, write *Acceptable.*

EXAMPLE
Every year we cut a Christmas tree in the woods, and it is decorated by us on December 24.
EDITED: Every year we cut a Christmas tree in the woods and decorate it on December 24.

1. A conflict between a doctor and a child is dramatized by William Carlos Williams' short story "The Use of Force."
2. At the start of the story, the doctor enters the house of a blue-collar family knowing that a throat culture has to be obtained from a frightened girl.
3. No one in the family, however, gives him the cooperation that is needed by him.
4. His initial efforts to examine the girl are thwarted when his glasses are knocked to the floor by her.

5. The mother is visibly disturbed by the child's screams and lack of cooperation.

6. In addition, ambivalence over the examination is displayed by the father when his hold on his daughter's arms is first tightened and then loosened.

7. With no support from the family, the doctor wonders whether his visit should be ended.

8. He is troubled by his fear that he may lose his temper.

9. The idea of leaving is rejected, however, as his better judgment is overruled by his anger and wounded pride.

10. The child must be defeated; her resistance must be overcome.

11. An attack is launched with the aid of a metal spoon that is jammed between her teeth and pressed down hard like a lever.

EXERCISE 2 Gaining Vigor and Coherence with the Active Voice

In the following passage, passive verbs predominate, and since almost every sentence has a different subject, the writing is not only tedious but unfocused. Wherever you find the passive voice unjustified, make the verb active.

At the sound of a bell, the huge red building was entered by me along with hundreds of others. Just inside the entrance, instructions were being yelled at us by a mean-looking old lady. My lunchbox was clutched, and a crowd of six-year-olds was followed down a long hallway, up some steps, and down another corridor. Mrs. Nearing's room was being looked for by us. I knew our destination had been reached when I was greeted loudly by a tall, black-haired woman. I was asked my name by her. Then it was printed by her on a sticky tag, and the tag was pressed to my chest. Inside the room several other six-year-olds could be seen, some of them big. Finally the classroom door was closed by Mrs. Nearing, and a loud bang was made in the process. The small pane of glass near the top was prevented from shattering by a network of wires. To my imagination, the wires looked like the bars in a prison. I was back in school.

EXERCISE 3 Using Active and Passive Effectively Together

Following is a group of simple sentences, some with verbs in the active voice, others with verbs in the passive. Make one continuous

passage out of these sentences by combining some of them and *pass*
changing the voice of the verbs whenever such a change will tighten
a sentence or improve its focus. Underline all changes in voice.

EXAMPLE
1. As a prime minister of England from 1940 to 1945, Churchill led
   his country through World War II.
2. But immediately after the war people voted him out of office.
3. Later his position as prime minister was regained by him.
4. That office was left by him in 1955.
5. Great popularity for the rest of his life was enjoyed by him.
6. He died in 1965.
7. People acclaimed him as a national hero.

COMBINED: As prime minister of England from 1940 to 1945,
Churchill led his country through World War II, but immediately
after the war he was voted out of office. Later he regained his position as prime minister. After he left that office in 1955, he enjoyed
great popularity for the rest of his life, and when he died in 1965, he
was acclaimed as a national hero.

1. The political structure of modern China was largely created by
   Mao Zedong.
2. Mao led the Chinese Communist revolution.
3. The theory behind it was formulated by him.
4. China was virtually ruled by him from 1949 to his death in 1976.
5. Mao worked for revolution throughout much of his early life.
6. In 1911 the Nationalist armed forces of Hunan Province were
   joined by him in their revolt against the Manchu dynasty.
7. He was then eighteen.
8. In 1921 he helped to found the Chinese Communist party.
9. In the spring of 1928, the Fourth Chinese Red Army was organized by him and a fellow revolutionary named Zhu De.
10. In 1934–35, he and Zhu De led a six-thousand-mile march of
    Chinese Communist forces to northwest China.
11. There a new base of operations was established by the two lead-
    ers.
12. The new base was established against the Kuomintang.
13. That was the Nationalist political organization.
14. Generalissimo Chiang Kai-shek headed it.
15. Mao and Chiang joined forces during World War II in order to
    fight their common enemy, the Japanese.

pass

16. But in the summer of 1946 a full-scale civil war against the Nationalists was resumed by Mao.

17. Mao's forces won the war in three years.

18. On September 21, 1949, the establishment of the People's Republic of China was proclaimed by Mao.

19. A succession of increasingly powerful posts was then assumed by him.

20. The posts included chairmanship of the Government Council, chairmanship of the Republic, and, most important, chairmanship of the Chinese Communist party.

21. In effect, China was ruled by Mao for nearly thirty years.

22. For better or worse, a lasting change in that country was made by Mao.

23. People will long remember him as one of the most important revolutionaries of the twentieth century.

23
Verbs

MOOD

23.1 What Mood Is

The mood of a verb or verb phrase indicates your attitude toward a particular statement as you are making it. Do you think of it as a statement of fact? Then you will use the *indicative* mood. Do you think of it as a command? Then you will use the *imperative.* Do you think of it as a wish, a recommendation, or an imaginary condition? Then you will use the *subjunctive.*

23.2 Using the Indicative

The **indicative** mood is for statements of actuality or strong probability:

> Brian Mulroney *became* prime minister of Canada in 1984.
>
> The spine-tailed swift *flies* faster than any other bird in the world.
>
> The blizzard of '78 *was* not the worst in history, but it *did paralyze* Boston for a whole week.

Use *do, does,* or *did* with the indicative for emphasis.

23.3 Using the Imperative

The **imperative** mood is for commands and requests made directly:

1. Use the bare form of the verb for commands addressed entirely to others:

> *Vote* for Mulroney.
>
> *Fight* pollution.
>
> *Be* yourself.
>
> Kindly *send* me your latest catalog.

2. When a command or suggestion includes yourself as well as others, use *let us* or *let's* before the bare form of the verb:

> *Let us negotiate* our differences in a spirit of mutual trust and respect.
> *Let's cooperate.*

23.4 Using the Subjunctive—Modal Auxiliaries

The **subjunctive** mood is for statements of hypothetical conditions or of wishes, recommendations, requirements, or suggestions. To express the subjunctive, you often need one of the modal auxiliaries, which include *can, could, may, might, must, ought, should,* and *would.* Use them as follows:

1. Use can to express

> CAPABILITY: *Can* the Israelis and the Palestinians ever make peace?
> PERMISSION: Why *can't* Americans visit Cuba?

In formal writing, permission is normally signified by *may* rather than *can*, which is reserved for capability. But *can* may be used informally to express permission and is actually better than *may* in requests for permission involving the negative. The only alternative to *can't* in such questions is the awkward term *mayn't*.

2. Use could to express

> THE OBJECT OF A WISH: I wish I *could* climb Mount Everest.
> A CONDITION: If all countries of the world *could* set aside their antagonism once every four years, the Olympics would be truly international.

A DISTINCT POSSIBILITY: A major earthquake *could* strike California within the next ten years.

On the distinction between *would* and *could* in statements of wishing, see number 8 below.

3. Use *may* to express

A MILD POSSIBILITY: The next president of the United States *may* be a woman.
PERMISSION: Students who cannot afford tuition *may* apply for loans.

4. Use *might* to express

A REMOTE POSSIBILITY: Biogenetic experiments *might* produce some horribly dangerous new form of life.
THE RESULT OF A CONTRARY-TO-FACT CONDITION: If the Soviets had participated in the 1984 Olympics, they *might* have won several gold medals.

5. Use *ought* to express

STRONG RECOMMENDATION: The Pentagon *ought* to eliminate waste in defense spending.
LIKELIHOOD: The new museum *ought* to be ready by next fall.

Ought is normally followed by the infinitive.

6. Use *must* to express

AN ABSOLUTE OBLIGATION: Firemen *must* be ready for action at any hour of the day or night.
A FIRM CONCLUSION: William Bligh, who with eighteen other men and scant provisions sailed a small boat nearly four thousand miles, *must* have been an extraordinary seaman.

7. Use *should* to express

ADVICE: Students who hope to get into medical school *should* take biology.
EXPECTATION: By the year 2025, the population of the world *should* exceed eight billion.

8. Use *would* to express

THE RESULT OF A CONDITION OR EVENT: If a one-kiloton neutron bomb were exploded a few hundred feet over the earth, it *would* instantly kill everyone within a radius of three hundred yards.

THE OBJECT OF A WISH: Some people wish the federal government *would* support them for the rest of their lives.

Both *would* and *could* may be used to express the object of a wish. But "I wish you could go" means "I wish you were able to go"; "I wish you would go" means "I wish you were willing to go."

23.4A Misusing Modal Auxiliaries

Avoid putting two or more modal auxiliaries together:

> * He might could win the face.
> EDITED: He might win the race. [or] He could win the race.

EXERCISE 1 Supplying Modal Auxiliaries

Complete each of the following sentences with a suitable modal auxiliary. Then in parentheses identify the meaning it expresses.

EXAMPLE
Students who hope to attend medical school _____ take biology. Students who hope to attend medical school should take biology. (advice)

1. Helen _____ leave the hospital for the weekend; the doctor has just given her permission.

2. She _____, however, avoid going up or down stairs.

3. And she _____ limit her walking to no more than ten steps every two hours.

4. She _____ eat whatever she likes, provided she limits the size of the portions.

5. Although complications _____ develop, she _____ be strong enough to spend Thanksgiving at home with her family.

23.5 Using the Subjunctive—Special Verb Forms

The subjunctive mood is sometimes indicated by a special verb form instead of by a modal auxiliary.

1. The present subjunctive is the same in form as the bare form (infinitive form) of the verb. Use it to express a hope, a requirement, a recommendation, or a suggestion:

INDICATIVE	SUBJUNCTIVE
God *has* mercy on us.	God *have* mercy on us!
The queen *lives.*	Long *live* the queen!
A premed student normally *takes* biology.	The college requires that every student *take* freshman English.
The trustees' meetings *are* closed.	The students demand that those meetings *be* open.

The present subjunctive of the verb *be* is *be* with every subject.

2. The past subjunctive is the same in form as the common past, except that the past subjunctive of *be* is *were* with every subject. Use the past subjunctive to express a wish for something in the present:

INDICATIVE (FACT)	SUBJUNCTIVE (WISH)
I *have* five dollars.	I wish (that) I *had* a million dollars.
I *am* a pauper.	I wish (that) I *were* a millionaire.
I *am taking* Math 36.	I wish (that) I *were taking* Math 23.
I *live* in Ottawa.	I wish (that) I *lived* in Vancouver.

3. The past perfect subjunctive is the same in form as the common past perfect. Use it to express a wish for something in the past:

INDICATIVE (FACT)	SUBJUNCTIVE (WISH)
I *saw* the second half of the game.	I wish (that) I *had seen* the first. [or] I wished (that) I *had seen* the first.
I *was* there for the second half.	I wish (that) I *had been* there for the first.
I *had* no change with me.	I wish (that) I *had had* enough for the telephone.

23.6 Forming and Using Conditional Sentences

A conditional sentence normally consists of an *if* clause, which states a condition, and a result clause, which states the result of that condition. The mood of the verb in the *if* clause depends on the likelihood of the condition.

23.6A The Possible Condition

If the condition is likely or even barely possible, the mood is indicative:

> [condition] If another heat wave *strikes*, [result] I will buy an air conditioner.

23.6B The Impossible or Contrary-to-Fact Condition

If the condition is impossible or contrary to fact, the mood of the verb in the *if* clause is subjunctive, and the result clause usually includes a modal auxiliary, such as *would* or *might*. The tense of the verb in the *if* clause depends on the tense of the condition.

1. A condition contrary to present fact should be stated in the past subjunctive:

> If the federal government *spent* no more than it collected, interest rates would plunge.
>
> If I *were* a millionaire, I would buy an airplane.
>
> Carl Lewis runs as if he *were* jet-propelled.

The expression *as if* always signals a condition contrary to fact. Some writers now use *was* instead of *were* in sentences like the second and third, but in formal writing you should use *were*.

2. A condition contrary to past fact should be stated in the past perfect subjunctive:

> After the fight, the former champion looked as if he *had been put* through a meat grinder.
>
> If Montcalm *had defeated* Wolfe in 1759, the Canadian province of Quebec might now belong to France.
>
> If the Watergate scandal *had not occurred,* Gerald Ford might never have become president of the United States.
>
> If I *had had* the money, I would have taken a plane.

23.6C Misusing *would have* in Conditional Clauses

Avoid using *would have* to express a condition of any kind:

> * If I *would have* attended the meeting, I would have attacked the proposal.

Use *would have* only to express the *result* of a condition:

> EDITED: If I had attended the meeting, I *would have* attacked the proposal.

EXERCISE 2 Supplying Verbs in Conditional Sentences

Using the facts in brackets as a guide, complete each of the following sentences by supplying a suitable verb or verb phrase.

EXAMPLE
If Michael Dukakis _____ the presidential campaign of 1988, the Democrats would now control the White House as well as the Congress. [Michael Dukakis did not win the presidential campaign of 1988.]
If Michael Dukakis had won the presidential campaign of 1988, the Democrats would now control the White House as well as the Congress.

1. If high-speed trains _____ all major cities in the United States, Americans could travel much more often without their cars. [High-speed trains serve hardly any cities in the United States.]

2. If my father _____ five hundred shares of IBM in 1950, he would be a millionaire today. [Alas, my father never bought any shares of IBM.]

3. If the prime rate _____, unemployment may go up also. [The prime rate goes up and down regularly.]

4. After winning the match, Joan felt as if she _____ the world. [She did not actually conquer the world.]

5. If the Continental Army _____ to the British at Yorktown, George Washington might never have become president of the United States. [The Continental Army did not lose to the British at Yorktown.]

EXERCISE 3 Supplying Verbs in a Paragraph

For each of the blanks in the following passage, supply a suitable verb or verb phrase.

EXAMPLE
line 1: were

Many students wish that the Thanksgiving recess _____ one week long, or that the fall term _____ completely before

Thanksgiving, so that they could stay home between Thanksgiving and Christmas. But the students have not asked for either of those things. They have asked only that the Thanksgiving recess _____ on the Wednesday before Thanksgiving. If the recess _____ on Wednesday, students would have one full day to travel home before Thanksgiving Day itself. Many students need that time. If every student _____ rich, he or she could fly home in an hour or two. But most students are not rich.

24
Direct and Indirect Reporting of Discourse

Any statement, whether spoken or written, can be reported directly—by quotation of the actual words. Or it can be reported indirectly—by a paraphrase of those words. In this chapter we explain when and how to use each method of reporting discourse. (For special instruction in how to quote or paraphrase source material in a research paper, see sections 33.11 and 33.12.)

24.1 Direct Reporting

Use direct reporting when the exact words of the original statement are memorable or otherwise important. Enclose the words in quotation marks:

> "The vilest abortionist," writes Shaw, "is he who attempts to mould a child's character."

> Frost puts four stresses in his opening line: "The well was dry beside the door."

For a full discussion of how to punctuate quotations, see chapter 29.

24.1A Using Tenses in Tags

Since no statement can be reported until after it has been made, you should normally use the past tense for the verb in the accompanying tag:

> "I want to go to law school," she *said.*

> In 1782 Thomas Jefferson *wrote:* "There must doubtless be an unhappy influence on the manners of our people produced by the existence of slavery among us."

But use the present when you are quoting a statement of lasting significance or a statement made by a literary character:

> "In every work of genius," *observes* Emerson, "we recognize our own rejected thoughts."

> In the first chapter of *Huckleberry Finn,* Huck *says,* "I don't take no stock in dead people."

24.1B Quoting Extended Dialogue

In reporting an exchange between two speakers, you should first indicate clearly who is speaking and in what order. You can then omit tags until the dialogue ends or is interrupted. The speakers' remarks should be set off from each other with double quotation marks, and you should normally begin a new paragraph whenever one speaker gives way to another:

> "Our market surveys indicate," Hurts said, "that there are also a lot of kids who claim their parents don't listen to them. If they could rent a gun, they feel they could arrive at an understanding with their folks in no time."
>
> "There's no end to the business," I said. "How would you charge for Hurts Rent-A-Gun?"
>
> "There would be hourly rates, day rates, and weekly rates, plus ten cents for each bullet fired. Our guns would be the latest models, and we would guarantee clean barrels and the latest safety devices. If a gun malfunctions through no fault of the user, we will give him another gun absolutely free. . . ."
>
> "Why didn't you start this before?"
>
> "We wanted to see what happened with the gun-control legislation. . . ."   —Art Buchwald, "Hurts Rent-A-Gun"

24.1C Quoting Several Lines of Prose or Poetry

When you quote more than four lines of prose or two lines of poetry, you should indent instead of using quotation marks, as described in section 29.4, "Quoting Long Prose Passages."

24.2 Indirect Reporting of Statements

Use indirect reporting when the exact words of the original statement are less important than their content:

> Before he was elected, the president said that he opposed new taxes.

When reporting a statement indirectly, do not use quotation marks:

> ORIGINAL STATEMENT: I want you to get a good education.
> DIRECT REPORT (QUOTATION): My mother said to me, "I want you to get a good education."
> INDIRECT REPORT: My mother said that she wanted me to get a good education.

As this example shows, an indirect report does the following:

1. It refers to the speaker or writer.

2. It often puts *that* just before the reported statement. But *that* may be omitted:

> My mother said she wanted me to get a good education.

3. It changes the pronouns in the reported statement where necessary. In this example, *I* becomes *she,* and *you* becomes *me.*

4. It may change the tense of the verb in the original statement so that it matches the tense of the introductory verb. Thus *want* in the original statement becomes *wanted* in the indirect report. But if the original statement has continuing significance, the indirect report may keep the original tense:

> The president has said that he opposes new taxes.

Generalizations may be reported with the present tense for both verbs:

> Farmers say that rain before seven means sun by eleven.

EXERCISE 1 Transforming Reports of Statements

Each of the following consists of a statement, with the speaker and listener identified in brackets. Write a direct and an indirect report of the statement. Then put a check next to the version you think is more suitable, and say why you prefer it.

EXAMPLE
You will have to take a breath test. [*Speaker:* the policeman; *listener:* me]
DIRECT: "You will have to take a breath test," said the policeman to me.
√INDIRECT: The policeman told me that I would have to take a breath test.

(The content is more important than the exact words.)

1. You will have to earn your own spending money. [*Speaker:* my father; *listener,* me]
2. I do not mind lying, but I hate inaccuracy. [*Writer:* Samuel Butler]
3. I will pay you $3.50 an hour. [*Speaker:* the manager; *listener:* me]
4. You have been baptized in fire and blood and have come out steel. [*Speaker:* General Patton; *listeners:* the battle survivors]
5. Nothing in education is so astonishing as the amount of ignorance it accumulates in the form of inert facts. [*Writer:* Henry Adams]
6. Fanaticism consists in redoubling your efforts when you have forgotten your aim. [*Writer:* George Santayana]

24.3 Direct Reporting of Questions

To report a question directly, you normally use a verb of asking in the past tense:

> The Sphinx asked, "What walks on four legs in the morning, two legs at noon, and three legs in the evening?"

> "Have you thought about college?" my father asked.

Use the present tense when you are reporting a question of standing importance or a question asked by a literary character:

> The consumer advocate asks, "How can we have safe and effective products without government regulations?"

> The businessman asks, "How can we have free enterprise with government interference?"

When Tom Sawyer proposes to form a gang that will rob and kill people, Huck says, "Must we always kill the people?"

24.4 Indirect Reporting of Questions

To report a question indirectly, you normally introduce it with a verb of asking and a word like *who, what, whether, how, when, where, why,* or *if:*

> ORIGINAL QUESTION: Do you want to go to law school?
> INDIRECT REPORT: My father asked me if I wanted to go to law school.

As the example shows, you must change the word order, the punctuation, and the wording of the question: *Do you want* becomes *if I wanted.* Also, the question mark becomes a period.

Use the present tense for the introductory verb when reporting a question of continuing importance or a question asked by a literary character:

> The consumer advocate asks how we can have safe and effective products without government regulation.

> When Tom Sawyer proposes to form a gang that will rob and kill people, Huck asks whether they must always kill the people.

After a past-tense verb of asking, you must normally use the past tense in the reported question. But you may use the present tense if the reported question is essentially timeless:

> The Sphinx asked what walks on four legs in the morning, two legs at noon, and three legs in the evening.

24.5 Confusing the Direct and Indirect Reporting of Questions *quest*

Avoid confusing the direct and indirect reporting of questions:

> * The customer sat down at the counter and asked did we have any scruples?

The **direct report** of a question repeats its actual words and ends in a question mark:

EDITED: The customer sat down at the counter and asked, "Do you have any scruples?"

The **indirect report** of a question states that a question has been asked. The statement must introduce the question with a word such as *if* or *whether* and must end with a period:

EDITED: The customer sat down at the counter and asked if we had any scruples.

24.6 Fitting Quotations into Your Own Prose

What you quote should always make a complete, coherent sentence when it is combined with your own prose:

INTRODUCTORY PHRASE   INDEPENDENT CLAUSE
1. According to Phyllis Rose, "We shop to cheer ourselves up."

INDEPENDENT CLAUSE   COMPOUND PHRASE
2. Ambrose Bierce defines "the death of endeavor and the achievement as   birth of disgust."

INDEPENDENT CLAUSE   INDEPENDENT CLAUSE
3. Barbara Garson writes: "The crime of modern industry is not forcing us to work, but denying us real work."

24.6A Misfitted Quotations *m q*

A quotation is misfitted when it fails to combine with your own prose to make a complete, coherent sentence:

* According to Orwell, "When there is a gap between one's real and one's declared aims."

This would-be sentence lacks a main clause, and it leaves the reader guessing about what happens "when there is a gap." To correct the error, do one of the following:

1. Quote a complete sentence:

EDITED: According to Orwell, "When there is a gap between one's real and one's declared aims, one turns as it were instinctively to long words and exhausted idioms, like a cuttle fish squirting out ink."

2. Make the quoted matter part of a complete sentence:

> EDITED: According to Orwell, one resorts to obscure language "when there is a gap between one's real and one's declared aims."

EXERCISE 2 Fitting Quotations into Your Own Prose

Take a sentence from any printed source and do three things: (1) Copy it out verbatim, with the author's name in parentheses after it; (2) Write a sentence in which you quote it all; (3) Write a sentence in which you quote part of it.

EXAMPLE

1. "Both the victimization and the anger experienced by women are real, and have real sources, everywhere in the environment, built into society." (Adrienne Rich)

2. "Both the victimization and the anger experienced by women are real," writes Adrienne Rich, "and have real sources, everywhere in the environment, built into society."

3. According to Adrienne Rich, the causes of "the victimization and the anger experienced by women" are to be found throughout society.

25
Invigorating Your Style

Nearly all of the chapters in Parts 2 and 3 of this book aim to help you improve your style: to write not just correctly but cogently, to shape your sentences with coordination and subordination, to enhance them with parallel structure, to enrich them with modifiers, and to perfect them with well-chosen words. In this chapter, we focus specifically on what you can do to invigorate your style.

Good writing exudes vitality. It not only sidesteps awkwardness, obscurity, and grammatical error; it also expresses a mind continually at work, a mind seeking, discovering, wondering, prodding, provoking, asserting. Whatever else it does, good writing keeps the reader awake.

Unfortunately, much of what gets written seems designed to put readers asleep. Too many people write the way they jog, never changing the pace or skipping a beat, never leaping, zigzagging, or stopping to scratch the reader's mind. Does this mean that in order to be lively, you have to write like an acrobat? No, it doesn't. Different subjects call for different styles, and you shouldn't write about a problem in economics or history the same way you would write about a beach party or a New Year's Day parade. In most college writing you are expected to sound thoughtful and judicious. But no reader wants you to sound dull. To enliven your writing on any subject, here are five specific things you can do.

25.1 Vary Your Sentences

Nothing animates prose like variety, and the sentence is infinitely variable. It can stop short after a couple of words. Or it can stretch luxuriously, reaching over hills of thought and down into valleys of speculation, glancing to this side and that, moving along for as long as the writer cares to keep it going. You can vary its structure as well as its length. You can make it passive or active; you can arrange and rearrange its parts. Opening with a modifier, as we do in this sentence, you can hold your subject back. Or you can lead with your subject, as we do now, adding modifiers at the end. In structure and length as well as in meaning, English sentences admit of infinite variety.

How can you get some of that variety into your writing? Take a hard look at one of your paragraphs—or at a whole essay. Do all of your sentences sound about the same? If most are short and simple, combine some of them to make longer ones. If most are lengthened out with modifiers and dependent clauses, break some of them up. Be bold. Be surprising. Use a short sentence to set off a long one, a simple structure to set off a complicated one. Though you need some consistency in order to keep the reader with you (did you notice that all of our last five sentences are imperatives?), you can and should eschew the monotony of assembly-line sentences.

To see what you can do with a variety of sentences, consider this example:

> Someone is always at my elbow reminding me that I am the granddaughter of slaves. It fails to register depression with me. Slavery is sixty years in the past. The operation was successful and the patient is doing well, thank you. The terrible struggle that made me an American out of a potential slave said "On the line!" The Reconstruction said "Get set!"; and the generation before said "Go!" I am off to a flying start and I must not halt in the stretch to look behind and weep. Slavery is the price I paid for civilization, and the choice was not with me. It is a bully adventure and worth all that I have paid through my ancestors for it.   —Zora Neale Hurston

Among the many things that invigorate the style of this passage is the variety of sentence types that Hurston uses: simple, compound, complex, and compound with a subordinate clause.

1. SIMPLE: It fails to register depression with me.
                Slavery is sixty years in the past.
2. COMPOUND: The operation was successful *and* the patient
                is doing well, thank you.
                I am off to a flying start *and* I must not halt in
                the stretch to look behind and weep.

Note the compound phrase *(look behind and weep)* in the second
compound sentence.

3. COMPLEX: Someone is always at my elbow reminding me
                that I am the granddaughter of slaves.
                It is a bully adventure and worth all *that I have
                paid through my ancestors for it.*
4. COMPOUND WITH SUBORDINATE CLAUSE: Slavery is the price
                that I paid for civilization, and the choice was
                not with me.

Good writers know how to produce each sentence type and how
to make different types work together in one paragraph. If you want
to test the variety in a paragraph of your own, see how many different sentence types you have used.

Now consider this passage:

> This looking business is risky. Once I stood on nearby
> Purgatory Mountain, watching through binoculars the great
> autumn hawk migration below, until I discovered that I was
> in danger of joining the hawks on a vertical migration of my
> own. I was used to binoculars, but not, apparently, to balanc-
> ing on humped rocks while looking through them. I reeled.
> —Annie Dillard, *Pilgrim at Tinker Creek*

Dillard varies both the structure and the length of her sentences.
She moves from five to thirty-five words, then down to just two at
the end. When a very short sentence follows one or more long
ones, it can strike like a dart.

25.2   Use Verbs of Action Instead of *be*

Use verbs of action as much as possible. Verbs of action show the
subject not just *being* something but *doing* something. At times,

of course, you need to say what your subject *is* or *was* or *has been,* and these words can speak strongly when used to express equality or identity, as in *Beauty is truth.* But verbs of action can often replace verbs of being.

> Sheila *was the winner of* the nomination.
> Sheila *won* the nomination.

> Frederick's desire to learn reading *would have been a shock to* other slaveholders.
> Frederick's desire to learn reading *would have shocked* other slaveholders.

> Mr. Ault believed that learning *would be the ruin of* Frederick as a slave.
> Mr. Ault believed that learning *would ruin* Frederick as a slave.

25.3 Use the Active Voice More Often Than the Passive

Use the active voice as much as possible. Verbs that tell of a subject acting usually express more vitality than verbs that tell of a subject acted upon. While some sentences actually work better in the passive voice, overuse of the passive can paralyze your writing. This is a problem *to be seriously considered by anyone who has ever been asked* to write an essay in which a subject of some sort is *to be analyzed, to be explained, or to be commented upon by him or her.* That sentence shows what overuse of the passive will do to your sentences: it will make them wordy, stagnant, boring, dead. Whenever you start to use the passive, ask yourself whether the sentence might sound better in the active. Often it will. (For a full discussion of the active and passive voice, see chapter 22.)

25.4 Ask Questions

Break the forward march of your statements with an occasional question:

> He falls back upon the bed awkwardly. His stumps, unweighted by legs and feet, rise in the air, presenting them-

selves. I unwrap the bandages from the stumps, and begin to cut away the black scabs and the dead, glazed fat with scissors and forceps. A shard of white bone comes loose. I pick it away. I wash the wounds with disinfectant and redress the stumps. All this while, he does not speak. What is he thinking behind those lids that do not blink? Is he remembering a time when he was whole? Does he dream of feet?

—Richard Selzer, "The Discus Thrower"

Questions like these can draw the reader into the very heart of your subject. And questions can do more than advertise your curiosity. They can also voice your conviction. In conversation you sometimes ask a question that assumes a particular answer—don't you? Such a question is called **rhetorical,** and you can use it in writing as well as in speech. It will challenge your readers, prompting them either to agree with you or to explain to themselves why they do not. And why shouldn't you challenge your readers now and then?

INVIGORATING YOUR STYLE: IN BRIEF

Vary the length and structure of your sentences (25.1):

I was used to binoculars, but not, apparently, to balancing on humped rocks while looking through them. I reeled.

—Annie Dillard

Use verbs of action instead of *be* (25.2):

won
Sheila ~~was the winner of~~ the nomination.

Use the active voice more often than the passive (25.3).

Ask questions (25.4):

What on earth is *our* common goal? How did we ever get mixed up in a place like this? —Lewis Thomas

Cut any words you don't need (25.5):

He went
~~The reason for his decision to make a visit~~ to Spain ~~was his desire~~ to see a bullfight.

25.5 Cut Any Words You Don't Need

To make your writing lively, make it lean. Cut away the verbal fat that slows it down to a ponderous crawl.

> WORDY: During their tour of Ottawa, they saw the Parliament buildings, and they saw the National Art Center.
> EDITED: During their tour of Ottawa, they saw the Parliament buildings and the National Art Center.

> WORDY: The reason for his decision to make a visit to Spain was his desire to see a bullfight.
> EDITED: He decided to visit Spain because he wanted to see a bullfight. [or] He went to Spain to see a bullfight.

For a full discussion of how to eliminate wordiness, see section 9.12.

EXERCISE 1 Rewriting to Invigorate Style

Using verbs of action and the active voice as much as possible, asking at least one question, cutting all unneeded words, and varying the length and structure of your sentences, rewrite each of the following paragraphs to invigorate its style.

EXAMPLE

Mr. and Mrs. Ault were once the owners of Frederick Douglass. They were residents of Baltimore. At this time Frederick learned to read. He asked Mrs. Ault to help him learn. He felt safe in doing so. She thought of him more as a child than as a slave. Those of course were not the only alternatives. She could have seen him as a man. But at least he was more in her eyes than a piece of property. His request would have been a shock to other slaveholders. He would have been thrashed just for making it. But Mrs. Ault was not shocked by it. She was willing to help. Under her care the alphabet was learned by Frederick. He began to read simple verses in the Bible. Then there was intervention by Mr. Ault. He forbade his wife to continue the lessons. He believed that learning would be the ruin of Frederick as a slave. But fortunately Frederick had learned enough to teach himself more. Soon he became an excellent reader.

REWRITTEN: Frederick Douglass learned to read while he was owned by Mr. and Mrs. Ault of Baltimore. He felt safe in asking Mrs. Ault to help him learn, for she thought of him more as a child than as a slave. Those of course were not the only alternatives. Couldn't she have seen him as a man? But at least he meant more in her eyes than a piece of property. Though his request would have shocked other slaveholders, who would have thrashed him just for making it, it did not shock Mrs. Ault; she wanted to help him. Under her care Frederick learned the alphabet and began to read simple verses in the Bible. Then Mr. Ault intervened. He forbade his wife to continue the lessons because he believed that learning would ruin Frederick as a slave. But fortunately Frederick had learned enough to teach himself more, and he soon became an excellent reader.

1. The French culture is greatly respected by the French. No other culture, in their opinion, is even close to theirs in value, worth, or overall quality. And they want to keep things that way. Strenuous efforts are made to be sure there is protection against a loss of excellence from contamination. One of the greatest fears is the fear of words which are a threat to come into the country from American English. According to the defenders of French culture, it is a fact that the purity of the French language will be tainted if words used by the uncouth speakers of the American tongue are uttered by French men and women. Since 1945 many important electronic machines have been made by Americans, and given American English names. The computer is one such machine, and "computer" has become an important, widely-used word in American society along with many other related words. Among the French, however, there has been no willingness to use these American words, so French words have been created. A computer is called an *"ordinateur,"* software is called *"le logiciel,"* and data processing is called *"l'informatatique."* For the guardians of French culture, there must be a French sound to the words that are spoken and written by them.

2. Critics of detective stories have three complaints. First, there is too much senseless violence. Lots of characters are killed. Others are badly beaten. In *The Lonely Silver Rain* by John D. MacDonald over twenty people are killed. The violence and deaths are not "senseless," however. A purpose is served by them. Clues are furnished to the detective. Second, detective stories are said to be filled with old, lifeless plots. The age of the plots is a problem, but a youthful vitality is usually imparted to them by writing which is conducive to a dramatic effect with regard to both places and characters. Interiors are described in vivid detail by Rex Stout. In the dialogues of Ed McBain, the words spoken by his characters sound just like the words of real people. This vitality is ignored by critics. They have a third complaint. The detectives, they say, are cardboard cutouts. The characters are likened to wooden statues. In reality, fictional detectives are like real human beings. There are real problems in their lives. Agatha Christie's Hercule Poirot is faced with the problem of being an old man. A failed marriage is a haunting

memory in the mind of Ross MacDonald's Lew Archer. There is almost no end to the examples. So it may be asked whether the critics ever read the stories they criticize?

3. In the modern city there is no safety for decent people. They are in a situation of continual exposure to crime. But it is my belief that a solution to this problem is attainable. The solution may sound strange, even crazy. New ideas often sound that way. Here is my proposal. Criminals and law-abiding city dwellers must switch places—literally. Criminals should be released from prison. They will live in the perilous freedom of our cities. They will become victims of their own robberies, muggings, and killings. Eventually self-destruction will result. Meanwhile the prisons will be remodeled for all decent people. A cell will be allotted to each single person. Families will be housed in multicell units. With regard to those who prefer to live in solitude, applications for solitary confinement may be submitted on a first-come, first-served basis. Food and medical services will be available for the inmates. Educational programs will be broadcast to large TV screens in every cell. For entertainment there will be block parties. There will be games for children to play. Dances for adults will be arranged. At the end a movie will be shown. It will be about the bad old days. It will be a reminder of the dangers before the big switch.

4. In "The American Scholar" the wise use of books is discussed by Emerson. Unwise uses are also considered. The use is unwise, Emerson says, when the contents of books are taken as final truth by readers. They are deficient in their ability to see something. Truth in one period of time is not necessarily truth at a later time. There is another problem. Mistakes are made by authors. What is said in a book may be false to begin with. There is another unwise use. Some readers become bookworms. They enter the paper and binding of a book. No thought is given to its contents. But the behavior of wise readers is different. Emerson says that books can be studied by the wise reader for knowledge of history. They are also a source of scientific facts that can be absorbed. There is an additional good use. Inspiration can be gained from books. If books are used properly, they can be wonderful instruments for readers.

Part 3
Punctuation and Mechanics

26
The Comma

26.1 Using Commas with Conjunctions

1. Use a comma before a conjunction *(and, but, for, or, nor, so, yet)* linking two independent clauses:

> Canadians watch America closely, *but* most Americans know little about Canada.

> The prospectors hoped to find gold on the rocky slopes of the Sierra Madre, *so* they set out eagerly.

> Cowards never started on the long trek west, *and* the weak died along the way.

2. Use a comma before a conjunction linking the last two items in a series:

> She loved life, liberty, and the happiness of being pursued.

EXCEPTION: You may skip the final comma if the last two items are clearly distinguished:

> He shined his shoes, pressed his pants and carefully brushed his coat.

For more on conjunctions, see sections 13.2 and 13.3. For more on punctuating items in a series, see section 26.7.

, *cs*   **26.2 Misusing Commas with Conjunctions**   , *conj*

1. Do not use a comma before a conjunction within a series of just two items:

> *The manager was genial, but shrewd.
>
> EDITED: The manager was genial but shrewd.
> *She checked my weekly sales, and asked to speak with me.
> EDITED: She checked my weekly sales and asked to speak with me.

EXCEPTION: You may use a comma to set off a contrasting phrase:

> She liked running her own business, but not working on weekends.

2. Do not use a comma after a conjunction:

> *The speaker coughed, studied his notes, and, frowned in dismay.
> EDITED: The speaker coughed, studied his notes, and frowned in dismay.

> *He was scheduled to discuss Rembrandt. But, the notes treated the etchings of Picasso.
> EDITED: He was scheduled to discuss Rembrandt. But the notes treated the etchings of Picasso.

EXCEPTION: Use a pair of commas after a conjunction to set off a word, phrase, or clause:

> But, he sadly realized, the notes treated the etchings of Picasso.

26.3 Misusing Commas between Independent Clauses—The Comma Splice   , *cs*

Do not use a comma alone between two independent clauses:

> * The beams have rotted, they can no longer support the roof.
> EDITED: The beams have rotted; they can no longer support the roof.
> [or] The beams have rotted, so they can no longer support the roof.
> [or] Since the beams have rotted, they can no longer support the roof.

For a full discussion of the comma splice, see section 13.7.

EXERCISE 1 Using Commas with Conjunctions

Each of the following may require the addition or removal of a comma. Make any changes necessary. If an entry is correct as it stands, write *Correct*.

EXAMPLE
We can stop for the night in Moose Jaw or we can push on to Regina.
EDITED: We can stop for the night in Moose Jaw, or we can push on to Regina.

1. Odysseus longs to return to his home on the island of Ithaca but he does not reach it for ten years.
2. He blinds the son of the sea-god Poseidon so, he must endure Poseidon's avenging wrath.
3. Poseidon's son is a one-eyed giant named Polyphemus and he lives alone in a cave with herds of sheep, and goats.
4. Odysseus enters the cave with his men one day, for, he expects to find hospitality there.
5. Instead the giant blocks the exit with a massive stone, eats two of Odysseus' men, and threatens to devour the rest.
6. Odysseus and his men seem doomed but, Odysseus blinds the giant, and escapes with his men.
7. They escape by hiding under the bellies of rams for the giant does not see the men when he lets his herds out of the cave.
8. Odysseus then recklessly shouts his name to the giant so, the giant asks Poseidon to make Odysseus' homecoming as painful as possible.

26.4 Using Commas after Introductory Elements

1. Use a comma after an introductory clause, phrase, or word:

Whenever it rains hard, the roof leaks.

To stop the leak, we have been replacing old shingles with new ones.

Unfortunately, last night's thunderstorm showed us that we still have more work to do.

2. Use a comma after a conjunctive adverb (CA) at the beginning of a sentence or clause:

CA

The kitchen was drenched; in fact, an inch of water covered the floor.

CA

Nevertheless, the living room remained dry.

For more on conjunctive adverbs, see sections 13.5, 13.5A, and 13.5B.

EXCEPTION: To accelerate the pace of their sentences, writers sometimes skip the comma after an introductory adverb or short introductory phrase:

Today students protest individually rather than in concert.
—Caroline Bird

Throughout the 1930s the number of addicts remained about the same in both England and the United States.
—Edward Bunker

EXERCISE 2 Using Commas after Introductory Elements

Each of the following may require a comma after an introductory element. Add a comma if needed. If the sentence is correct as it stands, write *Correct*.

EXAMPLE
Furthermore an increase in property taxes would severely limit the number of young adults who could live in the area.
EDITED: Furthermore, an increase in property taxes would severely limit the number of young adults who could live in the area.

1. After Odysseus and his men escape from the giant's cave they sail to the island of Aeolus, god of winds.
2. From Aeolus Odysseus gets a bag of winds that is supposed to ensure his safe return to Ithaca.
3. Having sailed for nine days Odysseus and his men actually catch sight of Ithaca; nevertheless they are swept away by a storm when the men foolishly open the bag.
4. As a result they must sail on to further adventures.
5. On the island of Aiaia they find an enchantress named Circe.

6. When a group of Odysseus' men go to see her she turns them into pigs.

7. On learning of their fate Odysseus decides to see her for himself.

8. His remaining companions are terrified; in fact they fear that he will never return.

9. Fortunately he obtains a magic potion from Hermes.

10. With the aid of that, he withstands Circe's magic and persuades her to change the pigs back into men.

26.5 Using Commas with Nonrestrictive Elements

Use a comma or a pair of commas to set off **nonrestrictive** elements: words, phrases, and clauses that are not essential to the meaning of the sentences in which they appear. Compare these two sentences:

> Anyone *who publishes a book at the age of six* must be remarkable. (restrictive)

> Dorothy Straight of Washington, D.C., *who published her first book at the age of six,* was a remarkable child. (nonrestrictive)

In the first sentence, the *who* clause is essential to the meaning of the sentence because it restricts the meaning of *Anyone* to a certain person. The clause tells *which one* is remarkable. In the second sentence, the *who* clause is nonrestrictive and nonessential because it does not identify *Dorothy Straight*. She has already been identified by her name. Now compare these two sentences:

> At the microphone stood a man *wearing a green suit.* (restrictive)

> At the microphone stood the master of ceremonies, *wearing a green suit.* (nonrestrictive)

In the first sentence, the italicized phrase is restrictive because it identifies *a man.* In the second sentence, the italicized phrase is nonrestrictive because the man has already been identified by his title. The italicized phrase just adds further information about him.

The distinction between restrictive and nonrestrictive is commonly applied to adjective clauses, such as *who publishes a book at the age of six,* and participle phrases, such as *wearing a green suit.* Broadly speaking, however, nonrestrictive elements include anything that supplements the basic meaning of the sentence, anything not essential to that meaning. Here are further examples:

> The surgeon, *her hands moving deftly,* probed the wound. (absolute phrase: section 12.13)

> Fearful, *not confident,* he embarked on his journey. (adjective phrase: section 12.2)

> At midnight, *long after the final out of the game,* the losing coach was still shaking his head in disbelief. (adverb phrase: section 12.4)

> In October of 1987, *however,* stock prices plummeted. (conjunctive adverb: section 13.5B)

A single comma sets off a nonrestrictive element that comes at the end of the sentence:

> The tour includes three days in Toronto, *which must be one of the cleanest cities in the world.* (adjective clause: section 15.6)

> Celia stood in the wings, *waiting for her cue.* (participle phrase: section 12.9A)

26.6 Misusing Commas with Restrictive Elements $\bigodot$ *res*

Do not use commas with restrictive elements: with words, phrases, or clauses essential to the meaning of the sentences in which they appear:

> * All entries, *postmarked later than July 1,* will be discounted.
> EDITED: All entries postmarked later than July 1 will be discounted.

> * Plants, that aren't watered, will die.
> EDITED: Plants that aren't watered will die.

(Adjective clauses starting with *that* are always restrictive.)

> * No one, *without a ticket,* will be admitted.
> EDITED: No one without a ticket will be admitted.

> * Film director, *François Truffaut,* died of cancer in 1984.
> EDITED: Film director François Truffaut died of cancer in 1984.

A name that follows a common noun or noun phrase is restrictive and should not be set off by commas. But when the name comes first, the common noun that follows it is nonrestrictive and should be set off by commas:

> François Truffaut, *the film director*, died of cancer in 1984.
> (appositive phrase: section 12.8B)

EXERCISE 3 Punctuating Restrictive and Nonrestrictive Elements

Decide whether each of the italicized elements is restrictive or nonrestrictive, and add or remove commas where necessary. If a sentence is correct as it stands, write *Correct*.

EXAMPLE
All motorists, *who drive recklessly*, should have their licenses suspended for six months.
DECISION: restrictive
EDITED: All motorists who drive recklessly should have their licenses suspended for six months.

1. My brother's car *a 1979 Ford Fiesta* looks like a gooey red marshmallow.
2. The interior *which has never been cleaned* is sticky with grime.
3. Nobody could close the front ashtray *which is stuffed with bottle caps, Kleenex tissues, and wads of chewing gum.*
4. The dashboard, another disaster area, has all but disappeared beneath the dust *that has built up over the months.*
5. The speedometer is barely visible, and it's impossible for anyone, *with normal vision*, to read the fuel gauge.
6. The driver's seat *which is covered with a piece of worn vinyl* smells like a loaf of moldy bread.
7. The exterior *with its layers of grime, rust spots, and dents* looks no better than the inside.
8. The rear window *lacking a windshield wiper* looks like one of those gray boards, that *collect dust in the corners of old barns.*
9. The front windshield *on the other hand* has a clear spot, *made by an ice scraper.*
10. For the past month, my brother has been looking for a used car dealer, *who will take the car off his hands without charging him.*

, *ser* **26.7 Using Commas with Coordinate Items in a Series**

1. Use commas to separate three or more coordinate items in a series:

> Maples, oaks, and sycamores have been afflicted.

> The leaves shrivel, wither, and fall to the ground before autumn.

> Scientists are seeking to learn what is causing the blight, how it enters the trees, and whether it can be halted.

2. Use commas to separate two or more coordinate adjectives modifying the same noun:

> A big, old, dilapidated house stood on the corner.
> Its owner always spoke in a low, husky voice.

When items in a series are long or internally punctuated, use semicolons between them (see section 27.1, item 4). For more on punctuating items in a series, see section 26.1, item 2.

Misusing Commas with Coordinate Items in a Series , *ser*

1. Do not use a comma to separate adjectives when they are not coordinate—that is, when they do not modify the same word:

> * His deep, blue eyes stared at me.
> EDITED: His deep blue eyes started at me.

Deep modifies *blue; blue* modifies *eyes.* Coordinate adjectives can be reversed. A *low, husky* voice can become a *husky, low* voice. But *deep blue* eyes cannot become *blue deep* eyes.

2. Do not use a comma before a conjunction when there are just two items. (See section 26.2, entry 1.)

> EXERCISE 4 Using Commas with Items in a Series
>
> Each of the following may require the addition or removal of a comma or commas. Make the necessary changes. If an entry is correct as it stands, write *Correct.*

EXAMPLE
Under the circumstances, only an intelligent discreet and experienced official should be assigned to the case.
EDITED: Under the circumstances, only an intelligent, discreet, and
experienced official should be assigned to the case.

1. Last summer my brother, my father, and, I visited a busy, logging
   camp in a rugged, picturesque, largely uninhabited part of Maine.
2. From dawn to dusk, hardy skilled lumberjacks felled trees, cut
   them into logs, and cleared the thick, green underbrush.
3. Our guide was a slow-moving infirm old man with dark brown
   eyes; but he could still repair broken, or sputtering chain saws.
4. Dressed in his bright, red, flannel jacket, he had a sturdy, work-
   bench in a pleasant, shaded area next to the large, equipment shed.
5. Inside the shed were various things, including coils of thick heavy
   rope, stacks of wooden, axe handles, and bright, yellow, slickers
   for rainy days.
6. Our guide's worn, carpenter's chest contained pliers, screwdriv-
   ers with hard, rubber handles, a set of galvanized, steel, wrenches,
   two copper oil cans, and bolts of many different sizes.
7. Carefully expertly, and patiently he worked on each, broken chain
   saw until its motor coughed, wheezed, and, sputtered into life.
8. Then, with a deft, and clever adjustment of the carburet
   would soon have the motor purring like a cat stretched out
   a warm cozy fire.

26.9 Using Commas to Prevent a Misreading

Use a comma when you need one to prevent a misreading of your
sentence:

> * On the left walls of sheer ice rose over five thousand feet into
>   the clouds.
>   EDITED: On the left, walls of sheer ice rose over five thousand
>   feet into the clouds.

26.10 Using Commas with Dates, Addresses, Greetings, Names, and Large Numbers

1. Use commas to set off parts of dates and addresses:

> On the afternoon of July 1, 1963, the fighting began.
> The return address on the letter was 23 Hockney Street, Lex-
> ington, Kentucky 40502.

, d/a **2.** Use commas to set off the names of someone directly addressed in a sentence:

> A few weeks ago, Mr. Taplow, I spoke to you on the telephone about the possibility of a summer job.

3. Use a comma after the greeting in a friendly or informal letter, and after the closing in a letter of any kind:

> Dear Mary,   Sincerely,
> Dear Uncle Paul,   Yours truly,

4. Use commas to set off titles or degrees after a person's name:

> Barbara Kane, M.D., delivered the commencement address.

But *Jr., Sr.,* and *III* may be written without commas:

> Sammy Davis Jr. started his singing career at age four.

5. Use a comma after the last part of a proper name when the last part comes first:

> Lunt, George D.

6. Use commas to mark groups of three digits in large numbers, counting from the right:

> Antarctica is 5,400,000 square miles of ice-covered land.

26.11 Misusing Commas with Dates and Addresses , d/a

1. Do not use a comma to separate the name of a month from the day:

> * October, 22   * 15, May
> EDITED: October 22   EDITED: 15 May

2. Do not use a comma to separate a street number from the name of the street:

> * 15, Amsterdam Avenue
> EDITED: 15 Amsterdam Avenue

3. Do not use a comma to separate the name of a state, province, (,) *bp*
or country from the zip code:

> * Lebanon, New Hampshire, 03766
> EDITED: Lebanon, New Hampshire 03766

> * Toronto, Canada, M5S 1A1
> EDITED: Toronto, Canada M5S 1A1

4. Do not use a comma to separate the name of the month from
the year:

> * January, 1988   * 22 April, 1939
> EDITED: January 1988   EDITED: 22 April 1939

26.12 Using Commas with Quotation Marks

For a full discussion of how to use commas with quotation marks,
see section 29.3, "Using Quotation Marks with Other Punctuation."

26.13 Misusing the Comma between Basic Parts of a Sentence (,) *bp*

1. Do not use a comma between a subject and its predicate:

> * Voters with no understanding of the issue, should learn the
> facts.
> EDITED: Voters with no understanding of the issue should learn
> the facts.

2. Do not use a comma between a verb and its object:

> * For dessert we all had, strawberry shortcake.
> EDITED: For dessert we all had strawberry shortcake.

> * I could not understand, why she refused to see me.
> EDITED: I could not understand why she refused to see me.

○, *bp*

USING COMMAS: IN BRIEF

Generally, use a comma before a conjunction linking independent clauses (26.1):

> Canadians watch America closely, *but* most Americans know little about Canada.

Generally, do not use a comma after a conjunction (26.2):

> *The speaker coughed, studied his notes, and⊙ frowned in dismay.

Do not use a comma alone between two independent clauses (26.3):

> *The beams have rotted⊙ they can no longer support the roof.

Use commas after an introductory item (26.4):

> Whenever it rains hard, the roof leaks.
> Unfortunately, we haven't yet fixed it.

Use commas with nonrestrictive elements (26.5):

> Dorothy Straight of Washington, D.C., *who published her first book at the age of six*, was a remarkable child.

Do not use commas with restrictive elements (26.6):

> *Anyone⊙ who publishes a book at the age of six⊙ must be remarkable.

Use commas to separate three or more coordinate items in a series (26.7):

> We played cards, told stories, and sang old songs.

EXERCISE 5 Adding and Removing Commas—
A Review

In the following passage from Peter M. Lincoln's "Documentary Wallpapers," we have deliberately introduced some errors in punctuation. Remove all misused commas, add any that are needed, and leave any that are correctly used.

Many early American homes, were decorated with block-printed wallpapers. Imported from England, and France, the papers made the arrival of ships from abroad an exciting event for Colonial homemakers. Merchants, looking for sales, advertised that papering was cheaper than whitewashing, and, they urged would-be customers to examine the endless variety of brightly colored patterns. Indeed by today's standards the colors in many Colonial papers seem vibrant, intense, and, even gaudy. One wonders whether the citizens of Boston Massachusetts and Providence Rhode Island, yearned for bright reds, greens, and, blues because of the grey, New England winters.

The process of reproducing historic wallpapers, requires the finesse of a craftsman. To establish a particular paper's full pattern, the expert may have to fit together the fragments of surviving samples, that he finds in museums in the attics of old houses and even under layers of other papers. He determines the original hue of the colors in various ways: he runs chemical tests, or, he matches a fragment to a fresh original in some museum, even then he must be careful before proceeding to the next step printing the design. As a final precaution therefore he makes, a blacklight examination knowing it may reveal otherwise indistinguishable elements of the pattern.

One of the leading experts in America is Dorothy Waterhouse cofounder of Waterhouse Hangings. She first became interested in historic wallpapers in 1932 when she was restoring, an old house on Cape Cod Massachusetts. While stripping the walls in one room she got down to the eighth, and bottom layer of paper. She became very excited, she knew it had to be over 140 years old. That discovery was the first of many. Today she has a collection of some three hundred historic wallpapers, all carefully stored in her Boston home.

27
The Semicolon
and
the Colon

27.1 Using the Semicolon ;

1. Use a semicolon to join two independent clauses that are closely related in meaning:

> Insist on yourself; never imitate.   —Ralph Waldo Emerson

2. Use a semicolon to join two independent clauses when the second begins with or includes a conjunctive adverb:

> Shakespeare's plays are nearly four hundred years old; nevertheless, they still speak to us.

> Many of his characters resemble people we encounter or read about daily; a few, in fact, remind us of ourselves.

For more on semicolons and conjunctive adverbs, see section 13.5.

3. You may use a semicolon before a conjunction to separate two independent clauses that contain commas:

> By laughing at our faults, we can learn to acknowledge them graciously; and we can try to overcome them in a positive, even cheerful way, not grimly and disagreeably.

4. Use semicolons to emphasize the division between items that ⓢ
include commas:

> There were three new delegates at the meeting: Ms. Barbara
> Smith from Boulder, Colorado; Ms. Beth Waters from Omaha,
> Nebraska; and Mr. James Papson from Greenwood, Arkansas.

27.2 Misusing the Semicolon ⓢ

1. Do not use a semicolon between a phrase and the clause to which
it belongs:

> * The climbers carried an extra nylon rope; to ensure their safe
> descent from the cliff.
> EDITED: The climbers carried an extra nylon rope to ensure
> their safe descent from the cliff.

2. Do not use a semicolon between a subordinate clause and the
main clause:

> * Most of the crowd had left; before the concert ended.
> EDITED: Most of the crowd had left before the concert ended.

3. Do not use a semicolon to introduce a list:

> * The prophets denounced three types of wrongdoing; idolatry,
> injustice, and neglect of the needy.

Use a colon instead:

> EDITED: The prophets denounced three types of wrongdoing:
> idolatry, injustice, and neglect of the needy.

For more on colons, see the next section.

EXERCISE 1 Using Semicolons

Each of the following requires the addition or removal of one or
more semicolons. Make any necessary changes, adding other punctuation if necessary.

EXAMPLE
Some people give others take.
EDITED: Some people give; others take.

1. The Gateway Arch in St. Louis symbolizes opportunity, in particular, it represents the soaring aspirations of America's pioneers;
who ventured into unknown lands throughout the nineteenth
century.

2. The pioneers consisted of many subgroups; New England farmers
seeking richer soil, immigrants fleeing a nation's slums, shy trap-
pers from the north, lusty mountain men, failed merchants, and
adventurers with an eye for danger.

3. For all of these people St. Louis was a gateway, it was the entrance
to a new and prosperous life somewhere beyond the Mississippi
River.

4. Few of the pioneers realized how difficult their new lives would
be, on the contrary, they thought of the west as a vast land flow-
ing with milk and honey.

5. They would live high on the hog they would live like kings and
queens.

27.3 Using the Colon :

1. Use a colon to introduce a list coming at the end of a sentence:

Success depends on three things: talent, determination, and
luck.

2. Use a colon to introduce an example or an explanation related
to something just mentioned:

The animals have a good many of our practical skills: some
insects make pretty fair architects, and beavers know quite a
lot about engineering.   —Northrop Frye

3. Use a colon to introduce one or more complete sentences quoted
from formal speech or writing:

In the opening sentence of his novel *Scaramouche,* Rafael
Sabatini says of his hero: "He was born with the gift of laughter, and a sense that the world was mad."

4. Use a colon to follow the salutation in a formal letter:

Dear Mr. Mayor:
Dear Ms. Watson:
To Whom It May Concern:

5. Use a colon to separate hours from minutes when the time of day is shown in numerals:

    8:40   6:30   11:15

27.4 Misusing the Colon

1. Do not use a colon after *such as, including,* or a form of the verb *be:*

> *On rainy days at camp, we played board games such as: Monopoly, Scrabble, and Trivial Pursuit.
> EDITED: On rainy days at camp, we played board games such as Monopoly, Scrabble, and Trivial Pursuit.

> * One morning I woke up to find that someone had taken all of my valuables, including: my watch, my camera, and all of my money.
> EDITED: One morning I woke up to find that someone had taken all of my valuables, including my watch, my camera, and all of my money.

> * Still in my locker were: my toilet kit, my flashlight, and my wallet—now empty.
> EDITED: Still in my locker were my toilet kit, my flashlight, and my wallet—now empty.

2. Do not use a colon between a verb and its object or between a preposition and its object:

> * Before heading home, we stopped at: the supermarket, the hardware store, and the gas station.
> EDITED: Before heading home, we stopped at the supermarket, the hardware store, and the gas station.

> * We needed: pasta, a window screen, and ten gallons of gasoline.
> EDITED: We needed pasta, a window screen, and ten gallons of gasoline.

EXERCISE 2 Using Semicolons and Colons

In the following passage from Ismene Phylactopoulou's "Greek Easter," we have deliberately removed some of the author's punctuation. Add a semicolon or a colon wherever necessary.

⊙

EXAMPLE
line 1: 10:00

The events on Good Friday are tragic. At 10 00 a grim-looking priest conducts a solemn service Christ is removed from the Cross and placed in a tomb. All work ceases flags fly at half mast. Soldiers carry their rifles reversed as they do during funeral processions. Offices and shops close everyone goes to church. The church bells will toll all day long. After the service the young girls of the parish perform a bitter-sweet task they decorate the bier of Jesus with flowers from 11 00 to 1 00. By that time it is a mass of flowers.

Lunch consists of simple fare boiled lentils, which represent the tears of the Virgin, and vinegar, which represents the vinegar given to Christ on the Cross.

On Friday evening the church is filled to overflowing. All in the city are present old men and women, officials, husbands and wives, children. The songs of mourning are lovely in their sadness for example, in one of them Mary refers to her dead son as a child who was as sweet as spring. After the service, which usually ends at 9 00, a kind of funeral procession takes place. It follows a definite order first comes a band playing a funeral march next comes a priest carrying the Cross then comes the bier accompanied by girls in white, the Boy Scouts, and a detachment of soldiers then come the other priests. The people follow, each carrying a brown candle. The gathering has spiritual meaning it is also deeply human.

28
End Marks

28.1 Using the Period .

1. Use a period to mark the end of a declarative sentence, a mild command, or an indirect question:

> The days are growing shorter, and the nights are becoming cool.
>
> On some mornings a hint of frost chills the air.
>
> Nature is proceeding at her accustomed pace.
>
> Note her ways closely.
>
> You never know exactly what she will do next.

When typing, skip two spaces after the period before beginning the next sentence.

2. Use a period to mark the end of some abbreviations:

Dr. Boyle	Mr. G. H. Johnson
500 Fifth Ave.	Mrs. L. S. Allingham
N.Y., N.Y.	Ms. N. A. Stephens
Kate Fansler, Ph.D.	3 P.M.
	350 B.C.

Generally, you don't need periods with acronyms (words formed from the initials of a multiword title), with capital-letter abbreviations of technical terms, or with abbreviated names of states, agencies, and organizations:

CBS	ROTC	IBM
NATO	TVA	IQ
FM	ID	KP
NY	CIA	VISTA
CA		

But you do need periods with B.C. and A.D. as well as with abbreviations standing for the names of political entities:

U.S.A U.K. U.S.S.R.

For guidance, see your dictionary.

3. Use a period to mark letters or numerals used in vertical lists:

The handbook describes four kinds of cycles:
1. unicycles
2. bicycles
3. tricycles
4. motorcycles

If you give the information in a sentence, enclose the letters or numbers within parentheses and omit the periods:

The handbook has interesting descriptions of (1) unicycles, (2) bicycles, (3) tricycles, and (4) motorcycles.

28.2 Misusing the Period ⊙

1. In formal writing, do not use a period to separate the parts of a sentence. If you do, you will create a sentence fragment:

*Customers should be treated courteously. Even if they are rude.
EDITED: Customers should be treated courteously even if they are rude.

For more on sentence fragments, see chapter 17.

2. Do not use a period after another period or other end mark:

* To please our customers, we have ordered scarce materials from Home Supplies Company, Inc..

EDITED: To please our customers, we have ordered scarce materials from Home Supplies Company, Inc.

* We don't want customers saying, "Why don't you have what I want?".
EDITED: We don't want customers saying, "Why don't you have what I want?"

28.3 Using the Question Mark   ?

Use a question mark—
1. To mark the end of a direct question:

> Must the problems of farmers be ignored?
> To what agency can they go for legal aid?

2. To indicate uncertainty within a statement:

> Some exotic dish—pheasant under glass?—was served at the banquet.
> The host must have paid a lot of money (fifty dollars?) for each meal.

28.4 Misusing the Question Mark   (?)

Do not use a question mark at the end of an *indirect* question:

> * I wonder who wrote this song?
> EDITED: I wonder who wrote this song.

For more on punctuating indirect questions, see section 24.4.

28.5 Using the Exclamation Point   !

Use the exclamation point to mark an expression of strong feeling:

> What a spectacular view!
> Impossible!

Because exclamation points make a special appeal to the reader, you should use them sparingly.

EXERCISE 1 Using Periods and Question Marks

Improve the punctuation in the following paragraph by adding a period or question mark wherever necessary; also make any accompanying change in capitalization that may be required. As you make these corrections, write out the entire paragraph.

How do historians rate the contributions of Gen Gordon to his country their opinions differ some consider him a military genius, one of the greatest soldiers in British history others criticize him severely in their opinion C G Gordon, or "Chinese" Gordon as he was popularly known, acted impulsively he was rash he was dangerous he was not fit to hold a command did he seek death on Jan 26, 1885 historians give conflicting answers

29
Quotation Marks and Quoting

29.1 Quoting Words, Phrases, and Short Passages of Prose

Use double quotation marks (" ") to enclose any words, phrases, or short passages quoted from speech, writing, or printed matter:

> After the murder of the old king in Shakespeare's *Macbeth*, Lady Macbeth imagines there is blood on her hand and cries, "Out, damned spot!"

> "Look before you leap" is particularly good advice for divers.

> "An agnostic," writes Clarence Darrow, "is a doubter."

Quoted passages must normally be accompanied by identifying tags; see sections 24.1A and B.

29.2 Using Double and Single Quotation Marks

1. Use double quotation marks to enclose the words of speakers engaged in dialogue (conversation), and start a new paragraph each time the speaker changes:

> "How did the interview go?" Bob asked.
>
> "It's hard to say," said Helen. "At first I was nervous. Then I relaxed and spoke clearly. I even began to enjoy myself."
>
> "Well, it sounds as if you might get the job. If you do, let's celebrate."

2. Use single quotation marks (' ') to enclose a quotation within a quotation:

> At the beginning of the class, Professor Baker asked, "Where does Thoreau speak of 'quiet desperation' and what does he mean by this phrase?"

29.3 Using Quotation Marks with Other Punctuation

1. To introduce a quoted sentence with a *phrase,* use a *comma:*

> According to G. B. Shaw, "Economy is the art of making the most of life."

Like any other sentence, a quoted sentence always begins with a capital letter.

2. To introduce a quoted sentence with a *clause,* use a *comma* or *colon:*

> The professor said, "Let's consider what Carl Jung has claimed."
>
> In his first Inaugural Address, Lincoln asked: "Why should there not be a patient confidence in the ultimate justice of the people?"
>
> June Callwood writes, "Canadians are not Americans who live in a colder climate; they are different people."

Some writers use a comma after a short introductory clause and a colon after a long one. Others use a comma before quoting informal speech, and a colon before quoting formal speech or writing. We suggest you learn your teacher's preference.

3. To introduce a quoted *word* or *phrase,* use *quotation marks alone:*

> According to Jung, the "something greater" is the uncon-
> scious, which he defines as "a natural phenomenon producing
> symbols that prove to be meaningful."
> The professor said Jung's theories have been "seminal."

The quoted word or phrase begins with a lowercase letter unless it is a proper noun or proper adjective.

4. To end a quoted statement that is followed by a tag, use a *comma:*

> "It's time for you to leave," said Mimi.

But do not use the comma if the quoted sentence ends in a question mark or an exclamation point:

> "What's your problem?" John asked.
> "Get out!" she yelled.

The tag begins with a lowercase letter unless its first word is a proper name.

5. To set off an interruptive tag, use a *pair of commas:*

> "Ideas," writes Carl Jung, "spring from something greater than
> the personal human being."

The word "spring" is lower-cased because it simply continues the quoted sentence.

6. To end a quoted statement that ends a sentence, use a *period:*

> The governor stated, "I will not seek reelection."

7. A closing *comma* or *period* goes *inside* the closing quotation mark:

> "High school," writes Ellen Willis, "permanently damaged my
> self-esteem."

8. A closing *semicolon* or *colon* goes *outside* the closing quotation mark:

> The head of the union announced, "The new contract is a
> good one for management and labor"; then she left the room.

Later she told reporters that the new contract "has major benefits for women": payment for overtime, maternity leave, and seniority privileges.

9. A question mark or an exclamation point that *belongs* to the quotation goes *inside* the closing quotation mark:

Who wrote, "What's in a name?"

A new idea about the universe always prompts the scientist to ask, "What's the evidence for it?"

10. A question mark or exclamation point that does *not* belong to the quotation goes *outside* the closing quotation mark:

Suddenly he screamed, "Get out!"

QUOTATION MARKS WITH OTHER PUNCTUATION: IN BRIEF

1. To introduce a quoted sentence with a *phrase*, use a *comma:*

According to G. B. Shaw, "Economy is the art of making the most of life."

2. To introduce a quoted statement with a *clause*, use a *comma* or *colon:*

The captain said, "I need a volunteer."
The orders read: "Attack at dawn."

3. To introduce a quoted *word* or *phrase*, use *quotation marks alone:*

The paper said the team "looked weak."
The coach said she was "dismayed" by the article.

4. To end a quoted statement followed by a tag, use a *comma:*

"I'm leaving," said Gavin.

5. To set off an interruptive tag, use a pair of commas:

"In the first place," said Sally, "I need a job."

Should the United States support Latin American governments that it considers "moderately repressive"?

Yet the congressman simply dismissed the charge as "unimportant"!

11. To introduce a quotation with *that*, use *quotation marks alone* and no capital unless the quotation begins with a proper name:

> Margaret Atwood writes that "in fact, a character in a book who is consistently well-behaved probably spells disaster for the book."

For advice on fitting quotations smoothly into your own sentences, see section 24.6.

---

6. To end a quoted statement that ends a sentence, use a *period:*

Gavin said, "I'm leaving."

7. A closing *comma* or *period* goes *inside* the closing quotation mark:

"High school," wrote Ellen Willis, "permanently damaged my self-esteem."

8. A closing *semicolon* or *colon* goes *outside* the closing quotation mark:

She said she felt "vindicated"; then she left.
The company offered what it called "benefits": free parking, free coffee, and free uniforms.

9. A question mark or exclamation point that *belongs* to the quotation goes *inside* the closing quotation mark:

Who wrote, "What's in a name?"
Suddenly he screamed, "Get out!"

10. A question mark or exclamation point that *does not belong* to the quotation goes *outside* the closing quotation mark:

Just how freely given is a gift that is called "free"?

29.4 Quoting Long Prose Passages

To quote more than four lines of prose, use indentation instead of quotation marks, and follow the format shown here:

Vicki Hearne invokes the idea of artistry to explain why a horse is willing to jump a high fence: ◄————*Use a colon*

Indent—►There are various ways to talk about what could
10
spaces   possibly motivate a horse, or any animal, to such
    an effort. Fear certainly does not do it. Cour-
    age, joy, exaltation are more like it, but beyond
Double space   that horses have, some of the time, a strong
quoted matter
    sense of artistry. . . . When I say artistry, I
    mean that the movements of a developed horse,
    the figures and leaps, mean something, and an
    artistic horse is one who is capable of wanting
    to mean the movements and the jump perfectly.

Keep the punctuation of the original. For use of the ellipsis dots, see section 29.6B.

When quoting one or more paragraphs, follow this format:

At the end of his Inaugural Address, John F. Kennedy declared:

Indent ————►And so, my fellow Americans: ask not what your
13
spaces   country can do for you—ask what you can do for
Indent—►your country.
10
spaces   My fellow citizens of the world: ask not what
    America will do for you, but what together we
    can do for the freedom of man.

29.5 Quoting Verse

1. Quotations of verse must look like verse, not prose. Keep all capital letters that you find at the beginning of lines, and if you quote more than a line, use a slash (/), with a space on each side, to show where one line ends and another begins:

```
later poem, Sylvia Plath writes: "Mother to myself, I wake
swaddled in gauze, / Pink and smooth as a baby." This
preoccupation with herself and her own body characterizes
```

2. To quote more than three lines of verse, double-space them and indent each line ten spaces from the left margin:

```
William Blake's "The Tyger" begins with the lines:
      Tyger! Tyger! burning bright
      In the forests of the night,
      What immortal hand or eye
      Could frame thy fearful symmetry?
```

If the lines are long, you may indent fewer than ten spaces. If a single line is long, let it run to the right-hand margin and put the overflow under the right-hand side:

```
Ruefully alluding to his own ill-fated marriage, Byron
rhetorically asks,
      But—Oh! ye lords of ladies intellectual,
      Inform us truly, have they not hen-peck'd
                              you all?
```

For more on quoting verse, see section 35.2B, nos. 10–12.

29.6 Using Brackets and Ellipsis Dots to Mark Changes in a Quotation

To quote effectively, you must quote accurately, keeping every word of the original or plainly indicating any changes you have made. Use brackets to mark any words you have added, and ellipsis dots to show where you have left words out.

29.6A Using Brackets to Mark Words Added to a Quotation [ ]

1. Use brackets to insert a clarifying detail, comment, or correction of your own into a quotation:

> "In the presidential campaign of 1998 [1988], George Bush defeated Michael Dukakis."

> "When we last see Lady Macbeth [in the sleepwalking scene], she is obviously distraught."

> "Most remarkably, the Motherhood Myth [the notion that having babies is instructive and enjoyable] persists in the face of the most overwhelming maternal unhappiness and incompetence."—Betty Rollin.

When a misspelling occurs in quoted material, the Latin word *sic* ("thus") may be used to call attention to it, or the correct spelling may be given within the brackets:

> "There were no pieces of strong [*sic*] around the boxes," one witness wrote. [or] "There were no pieces of strong [string] around the boxes," one witness wrote.

If you're using a typewriter that has no keys for brackets, you can construct brackets by using the slash and underlining keys: [ ]

2. Do not use brackets when inserting comments into your own writing. Use parentheses or dashes. (See sections 30.1–30.3.)

For more on brackets, see section 33.12, no. 4.

29.6B Using Ellipsis Dots (. . .) to Mark Words Left Out of a Quotation

1. Use three spaced dots to signal the omission of a word or words from the middle of a quoted sentence:

> And so the writer . . . suffers, especially in the creative years of youth, every form of distraction and discouragement.
> —Virginia Woolf

In all cases, the material left out should be nonessential to the meaning of what is quoted. Here, for example, the words omitted are "Keats, Flaubert, and Carlyle."

In typing, leave one space before the first dot, between each pair of dots, and after the last one.

2. Use a period and three spaced dots—

    a. To show that you are omitting the end of a quoted sentence:

> Thoreau wrote: "We must learn to reawaken and keep ourselves awake, not by mechanical aids, but by an infinite expectation of the dawn. . . ."

The period follows the last quoted word without a space, and the fourth dot comes before the closing quotation mark. Normally you may cut off the end of a quoted sentence in this way only if what remains makes a complete sentence.

    b. To show that you have omitted one or more whole sentences:

> "In other words," as Percy Marks says, "the spirit of football is wrong. 'Win at any cost' is the slogan of most teams, and the methods used to win are often abominable. . . . In nearly every scrimmage the roughest kind of unsportsmanlike play is indulged in, and the broken arms and ankles are often intentional rather than accidental."

3. Use an entire line of spaced dots to signal that a line (or more) of poetry has been omitted.

> Under the cooling shadow of a stately elm
> Close sat I by a goodly river's side,
> Where gliding streams the rocks did overwhelm;
> . . . .
> I once that loved the shady woods so well,
> Now thought the rivers did the trees excel.
> And if the sun would ever shine, there would I dwell.
> —Anne Bradstreet

For more on ellipsis dots, see section 33.12, no. 3.

29.7 Special Uses of Quotation Marks

1. Use quotation marks to enclose certain titles, as explained in section 32.3.

2. Use quotation marks to define words:

> As a verb, *censure* means "find fault with" or "reprimand."

3. Use quotation marks to set off common words and phrases that you don't take at face value:

> When a man and woman decide to live together without being married, are they "living in sin"?

4. Use quotation marks to identify a word treated as a word:

> In America the word "liberal" has become a political insult.

You may also use italics or underlining for this purpose, as explained in section 32.2, no. 2.

29.8 Misusing Quotation Marks

1. Do not use quotation marks in indirect discourse:

> * The lieutenant said that "her platoon had finished ahead of schedule."
> EDITED: The lieutenant said that her platoon had finished ahead of schedule.

> * Clients are asking "when the rates will go down."
> EDITED: Clients are asking when the rates will go down.

For a full discussion of indirect discourse, see sections 24.2 and 24.4.

2. Do not use quotation marks for emphasis. Quotation marks can actually weaken a statement. For example:

> Joe's restaurant serves "fresh" seafood. [TRANSLATION: They say it's fresh, but I know better.]

EXERCISE 1 Punctuating with Quotation Marks

Use quotation marks and any other punctuation needed in the following sentences.

EXAMPLE
We are all strong enough wrote La Rochefoucauld to endure the misfortunes of others.
EDITED: "We are all strong enough," wrote La Rochefoucauld, "to endure the misfortunes of others."

1. What writer asked, Who has deceived thee so oft as thyself

2. Did Ambrose Bierce define a bore as a person who talks when you wish him to listen

3. Alexander Pope wrote, True wit is nature to advantage dressed, What oft was thought, but ne'er so well expressed

4. The history of the earth says Rachel Carson has been a history of interaction between living things and their surroundings.

5. *Continual* means going on with occasional slight interruptions. *Continuous* means going on with no interruption.

6. Perhaps the poet John Donne was right when he wrote: One short sleep past, we wake eternally / And Death shall be no more.

7. My roommate torments me by repeating trite sayings like better safe than sorry.

8. "This song, which was composed by Bailey in 1928 1930, reflects the influences of his five years in New Orleans." [The second date represents your correction of a mistake in a sentence written by someone else.]

9. "The most popular recording of the song featured Bix Dandy on the trumpit trumpet." [The second spelling represents your correction of a misspelling in a passage written by someone else.]

10. [The following sentence has been taken from George Orwell's "Politics and the English Language." Using ellipsis dots to mark the omission of words we have italicized, copy the rest of the sentence.] "Each of these passages has faults of its own, but, *quite apart from avoidable ugliness,* two qualities are common to all of them."

11. [The following sentences appear near the start of Orwell's essay. Select two successive sentences to copy, using ellipsis dots to mark the omission of words from the end of the first sentence you copy.] "Now, it is clear that the decline of a language must ultimately have political and economic causes; it is not due simply to the bad influence of this or that individual writer. But an effect can become a cause, reinforcing the original cause and producing the same effect in an intensified form, and so on indefinitely. A man may take to drink because he feels himself to be a failure, and then fail all the more completely because he drinks. It is rather the same thing that is happening to the English language."

30
The Dash,
Parentheses,
the Slash

30.1 Using the Dash —

1. Use a dash to introduce a word, phrase, or clause that summarizes or restates what comes just before:

> Terns, geese, and warblers—all migratory birds—fly hundreds of miles each year.

> But ideas—that is, opinions backed with genuine reasoning—are extremely difficult to develop.   —Wayne Booth

2. Use a dash to set off an interruption that is important to the meaning of the sentence but not grammatically part of it:

> It matters not where or how far you travel—the farther commonly the worse—but how much alive you are.
>   —Henry David Thoreau

Less important interruptions may be set off by parentheses (as explained in section 30.3).

3. Use dashes to set off a series of specific items:

> The wings of the natural extant flying vertebrates—the birds and the bats—are direct modifications of the preexisting front limbs.   —Michael J. Katz

4. Use a dash in dialogue to indicate an unfinished remark: ( )

> "You wouldn't dare to—" Mabel gasped in disbelief.
> "But I would," he said. "In fact, I—"
> "No!" she screamed.

When the dash is used to indicate an unfinished remark, it should be followed only by quotation marks, not by a comma or period.

5. If dashes set off a parenthetical remark that asks a question or makes an exclamation, put the question mark or the exclamation point before the second dash:

> During the American bicentennial of 1976, Canada's gift to the United States was a book of superb photographs of—what else?—scenery.   —June Callwood

6. In typing, make a dash with two hyphens (--) and leave no space on either side.

30.2 Misusing the Dash ⊖

The main misuse is overuse. Too many dashes can make your writing seem breathless or fragmented:

> Merryl's new designs looked stunning—do they ever look otherwise?—with their bold colors and daring lines. She was cheered by all of the regulars—the regular staff, that is—who work in the art department. One of them—I think it was Harry—did a cartwheel—what a surprise that was!—and then shrieked till he was blue in the face. I thought Merryl would die of blushing—she's really modest, you know.

30.3 Using Parentheses ( )

1. Use parentheses to enclose words, phrases, or complete sentences that offer a side comment or help to clarify a point:

> All this does not mean, what I should be the last man in the world to mean, that revolutionists should be ashamed of being revolutionists or (still more disgusting thought) that artists should be content with being artists.   —G. K. Chesterton

Why would parents want to go to such expense (treatment with biosynthetic hGH costs roughly $10,000 a year), cause their children pain (the shots hurt a bit), and risk unknown long-term side effects?   —Thomas Murray

Parentheses placed *within* a sentence do not change any other punctuation, and a parenthesized sentence within a sentence (such as *the shots hurt a bit*) does not need a capital or a period. But a freestanding parenthetical sentence needs both:

No Allied leader would have flinched at assassinating Hitler, had that been possible. (The Allies did assassinate Heydrich.)
—Michael Levin

2. Use parentheses to enclose numerals or letters introducing the items of a list:

Motherhood is in trouble, and it ought to be. A rude question is long overdue: Who needs it? The answer used to be (1) society and (2) women.   —Betty Rollin

3. Use parentheses to enclose numerals clarifying or confirming a spelled-out number:

The law permits individuals to give no more than one thousand dollars ($1,000.00) to any one candidate in a campaign.

Like material put between dashes, a parenthetical insertion interrupts the flow of a sentence. Parentheses make the interruption less emphatic than dashes do, but since they do in fact break up the sentence, you should use them sparingly.

30.4 Using the Slash /

1. Use a slash, or virgule, to indicate alternative words:

Every writer needs to know at least something about his / her audience.

Leave no space before or after a slash used in this way.

2. Use a slash to mark off lines of poetry when you run them on as if they were prose:

Coleridge introduces the mariner in the very first stanza: "It is an ancient Mariner, / And he stoppeth one of three."

Leave one space before and after a slash used in this way.

3. Use a slash in typing a fraction that is not on one of your typewriter keys:

2 1/2   5 7/8   15/16

EXERCISE 1 Using the Dash, Parentheses, and the Slash

Each of the following requires a dash or dashes, parentheses, or a slash. Using the comment in brackets as a guide, add the appropriate punctuation.

EXAMPLE
The asking price for the clock a whopping $500,000 has not deterred some collectors from attending the auction. [The explanatory phrase is important to the meaning of the sentence.]
EDITED: The asking price for the clock—a whopping $500,000—has not deterred some collectors from attending the auction.

1. An excellent production of *Antigone* the version by Jean Anouilh has reminded us how easily tyrants can justify their actions. [The explanatory phrase is important to the remark.]

2. The number of acres allotted to one family may not be less than twenty-five 25 nor more than fifty 50. [The numerals clarify the spelled-out numbers.]

3. The petitioner need not appeal directly to the governors unless he she wishes to speak in support of the request. ["He" and "she" are alternative words.]

4. The neighborhood lacks three important things: 1 paved roads, 2 traffic lights at every major intersection, and 3 adequate police protection. [The numerals introduce the items to a list.]

5. When we arrived in Warner it's about fifteen miles west of Concord we had the fan belt adjusted. [The interruption is relatively unimportant to the statement.]

6. Josephine Miles begins "Tally" with two lines describing a girl counting: "After her pills, the girl slept and counted Pellet on pellet the regress of life." [The two lines appear in a poem titled "Tally," and the second line begins with "Pellet."]

7. The pilot should tell the inspectors the facts of the accident at Edgeworth Airport whatever he knows to be the truth. [The clause starting with *whatever* restates the point made in the preceding words.]

8. In the third race the filly Hardtack the program listed her as belonging to Cranberry Stables set a track record. [The interruption is important to the rest of the sentence.]

31
Spelling

"I have no respect," said Thomas Jefferson, "for a man who can think of only one way to spell a word." Not many of us would ever have lost Jefferson's respect on this account. Some of the best writers have been notoriously bad spellers. They have struggled with a language in which the sound of a word frequently diverges from the way it is spelled, a language in which the same set of letters may be sounded several different ways in several different words. The letters *ough*, for instance, are sounded four different ways in the words *rough, through, bough,* and *thorough.* No wonder George Bernard Shaw could demonstrate the irrationality of English by spelling fish "ghoti." As Shaw noted, the *f* sound of *gh* in *rough,* the *i* sound of *o* in *women,* and the *sh* sound of *ti* in *diction* will together make a fish—or, he might have said, a very fishy word.

Yet in spite of all these difficulties, careful writers learn to spell their words correctly. They do so because they know that misspelled words can confuse as well as annoy the reader. The difference between *principle* and *principal,* for instance, is a difference in meaning as well as in spelling.

How can you learn to spell all of your words correctly? The simplest answer is a good dictionary. If you consult the dictionary whenever you aren't quite sure how to spell a word, you will certainly improve your spelling. You may also improve it by using one or more of the following methods.

31.1 Checking Your Spelling with a Computer Program

If you're writing with a computer and have access to a spelling-checker program, use it. The program will check every word in your essay against the words in its own dictionary; it will list or "flag" every word of yours that its dictionary doesn't have; and in some cases, it will tell you which words in its dictionary resemble yours. If you've written *complament*, for instance, the program will furnish two correctly spelled alternatives: *compliment* and *complement*.

Spelling-checker programs, however, *will not proofread your essay or correct your misspellings for you.* The programs can merely tell you which of your words does not appear in the program dictionary, and suggest one or more similar words that do. Also, spelling-checker programs can seldom identify a word misspelled for its context. If you write a *peace of pie*, most programs will accept the phrase—simply because each of its words appears in the program dictionary. Likewise, when the program suggests *compliment* and *complement* as correctly spelled alternatives to *complament*, you must still choose between these alternatives. If you don't know what they each mean, you will need to consult a printed dictionary or our Glossary of Usage.

Spelling-checker programs can save you time and help you spot misspellings that you might have overlooked. But since no such program is wholly foolproof, you should keep a good dictionary within easy reach of the computer screen. And to improve your spelling generally, you may also want to use one or more of the pre-electronic methods explained below.

31.2 Listing Your Spelling Demons

Keep an analytical list of your spelling demons—words you have trouble spelling. After your teacher has marked an essay, list all the words you misspelled in it. Beside each of the words, write out the correct spelling, as shown in your dictionary. Then, beside the correct spelling of the word, write the letter or letters involved in the error. Your list will look like this:

MISSPELLED	CORRECTLY SPELLED	ERROR
alot	a lot	al / a l
goverment	government	er /ern
defensable	defensible	able / ible
imovable	immovable	im / imm

31.3 Learning How to Add Suffixes

Learn how to add suffixes—extra letters at the end of a word.

1. Change final *y* to *i*. If the *y* at the end of a word follows a consonant, change it to *i* before adding a suffix:

> beauty + ful = beautiful
> bury + ed = buried
> tricky + est = trickiest
> carry + es = carries

EXCEPTION: If the suffix is *-ing,* keep the *y:*

> carry + ing = carrying
> bury + ing = burying

2. Drop silent *e.* If a word ends in a silent (unpronounced) *e,* drop the *e* before adding *-able* or *-ing:*

> love + able = lovable
> care + ing = caring

If any other suffix is added, keep the *e:*

> care = ful = careful

EXCEPTION: If the silent *e* follows *c* or *g,* keep the *e* before *-able:*

> change + able = changeable
> peace + able = peaceable

3. If the word ends in a single consonant after a single vowel *(forget)* and the accent is on the last syllable *(for get´)* double the consonant before adding *-ing, -ed, -or,* or *-er:*

> for get´ + ing = forgetting
> re fer´ + ed = referred
> bet´ + or = bettor

If the accent is not on the last syllable of the word, do not double the consonant:

> ham´ mer + ing = hammering

31.4 Learning When to Use *ie* and *ei*

Learn when to use *ie* and when to use *ei*. Some of the time, you can follow the rules of the jingle:

> Put *i* before *e*
> Except after *c*
> Or when pronounced *a*
> As in *neighbor* and *weigh*

Examples of *i* before *e* include *achieve, believe, grieve, relieve, grief,* and *niece.* Words with *ei* after *c* include *conceit, deceit, perceive,* and *receive.* Other words pronounced with an *a* sound as in *weigh* include *eight, sleigh,* and *vein.* Some words, however, have an *ei* combination that neither follows *c* nor is pronounced *a.* Examples are *either, neither, leisure, seize, weird, atheist,* and *sheik.*

31.5 Learning How to Add Prefixes

Learn how to add prefixes—extra letters at the beginning of a word. When adding a prefix, be careful to add all of its letters, and only those.

> dis + satisfaction = dissatisfaction
> mis + fire = misfire
> un + necessary = unnecessary

31.6 Recognizing Homonyms

1. Distinguish between homonyms—words that sound alike but have different meanings and different spellings—such as these:

bare	bear	
brake	break	
capital	capitol	
cite	site	sight
peace	piece	
principal	principle	
right	write	rite
there	their	they're

If you aren't sure how to spell a homonym, see your dictionary.

2. Distinguish between partial homonyms—words with syllables that sound alike but are spelled differently, such as these:

tol*e*rate   sep*a*rate
super*sede* ex*ceed* con*cede*
domin*ance* (think of domin *ate*)   exist*ence* (think of exist*en*tial)
incred*ible* (think of cred*it*)   irrit*able* (think of irrit*ate*)

31.7 Pluralizing Simple Nouns

1. Form the plural of most nouns by adding *s:*

book, books

2. Form the plural of nouns ending in *ch, s, sh, x,* and *z* by adding *es* (pronounced as a syllable):

church, churches   business, businesses   tax, taxes

EXCEPTIONS: crisis, crises; basis, bases; ox, oxen

3. Form the plural of nouns ending in *fe* by changing *f* to *v* before adding *s:*

wife, wives   life, lives

4. Form the plural of nouns ending in *f* by changing the *f* to *v* and then adding *es:*

leaf, leaves   thief, thieves

EXCEPTION: Some nouns ending in *f* need only *s* to become plural:

chief, chiefs   belief, beliefs   proof, proofs

5. Form the plural of some nouns ending in *o* by adding *es:*

hero, heroes

Most nouns ending in *o* need only an *s* to become plural:

piano, pianos
mosquito, mosquitos (*or* mosquitoes)
banjo, banjos (*or* banjoes)

6. Form the plural of words ending in a consonant plus *y* by changing the *y* to *ies:*

vacancy, vacancies   authority, authorities

Words ending in a vowel plus *y* need only an *s* to become plural:

day, days   attorney, attorneys

7. Form the plural of some nouns in special ways:

datum, data   criterion, criteria   woman, women

The forms *data* and *criteria* reflect the derivation of the words from Latin and Greek respectively.

8. Form the plural of numbers written as words by adding *s:*

They came by twos and threes.

9. Form the plural of figures, capitalized letters, undotted abbreviations, and isolated words by adding *s* or an apostrophe plus *s:*

the 1990s / the 1990's   three YMCAs / three YMCA's
four Cs / four C's   no *ifs* or *buts* / no *if's* or *but's*

10. Form the plural of lowercase letters and dotted abbreviations by adding an apostrophe and *s:*

six *s*'s and five *m*'s   three M.A.'s   two c.o.d.'s

11. Some nouns are spelled the same in the plural as in the singular.

deer, deer   fish, fish   barracks, barracks

31.8 Pluralizing Compound Nouns

Compound nouns are written as separate words (master chef), as words linked by a hyphen (self-esteem), or as one word (notebook). Here are guidelines.

1. If the compound is written as one word, pluralize the final word:

notebook   notebooks
blueberry   blueberries

EXCEPTION: passerby, passersby

2. If the compound is hyphenated or written as separate words, pluralize the major word:

mother-in-law   mothers-in-law
editor in chief   editors in chief

A few compounds have alternative plurals: *attorney general,* for instance, may be pluralized as *attorneys general* or *attorney generals.*

3. If the compound has no noun within it, pluralize the final word:

also-ran   also-rans

4. If the compound ends in *-ful,* add *s:*

mouthful   mouthfuls

EXERCISE 1 Spotting and Correcting Misspellings

In the following passage by Andrew Evans, we have deliberately misspelled some words. Make the necessary corrections.

    Mr. Bunten's farm is sucessful largely because he has kept the size within reason and because he is a skilful farmer. His heard is relatively small, consistting of only thirty-five milkers plus thirty more cows, including the heifers. When most farmers in the region expanded there operasion after   5 World War II by building expensive silos and milking systemes, Mr. Bunten kept his farm about the same size. Within a few years, many of his neighbors had gone into debt, and some had failed alltogether. It was a sad seen for just about everybody.   10
    We milk the cows in the mourning and at night. He gets up at 5:30, and I arive at 6 p.m. After geting down a dozen bales of hey, I dash around, feeding the cows and prepareing the milking machines. I literaly run to complete the chores in the shortest time posible. He never askes me to do them   15 quickly; however, if I should be moveing slowly, he'll say, "Geeze, boy, what took ya!" Usualy he doesn't have to say anything because he's the type of person one wants to please— some one on the go all the time. For a man of sixty-four he has unbeleivable endurance. Viewing his efforts as a chal-   20 lenge, I try to keep up and win his respect. Fortunetely, he gives me the benifit of the doubt much of the time.

31.9 Using the Hyphen

1. Use a hyphen to divide a long word at the end of a line:

> The long black centipede walked across the sand with an enor-
> mous limp.

Normally you divide a word at the end of a syllable. But do not put syllables of one or two letters on either side of a hyphen, as *i-tem* and *end-ed.* If you aren't sure what the syllables of a word are, see your dictionary.

2. Use a hyphen to show that two or three words are being used as a single grammatical unit:

> The older citizens don't want a Johnny-come-lately for mayor.
> But they don't want a stick-in-the-mud either.

3. Use a hyphen with a compound serving as an adjective and standing before the noun it modifies:

> Enrico Caruso was a world-famous tenor.
> I wouldn't touch cocaine with a ten-foot pole.
> John Kenneth Galbraith is a well-known economist.

4. Do not use a hyphen—
   a. between an adjective and a noun in a noun phrase:

> Not all twentieth-century writers were born in the twentieth
> century.

Twentieth-century is an adjective phrase; *twentieth century* is a noun phrase.

   b. in a compound serving as a predicate adjective that follows the noun it modifies:

> John Kenneth Galbraith is well known.

   c. in compounds made with a *-ly* adverb, such as *widely held*

   d. in compounds made with two nouns, such as *master chef* and *police officer.*

EXCEPTION: When the second noun is really a verb in disguise, the compound is usually hyphenated:

> A man-eater is an animal that eats human flesh.

When in doubt about using a hyphen with a particular compound, see your dictionary.

5. Use a hyphen to join a prefix to a capitalized word:

> un-American
> post-Renaissance

Do not use a hyphen when you join a prefix to an uncapitalized word:

> deemphasize
> nonprofit

6. Use a hyphen in a number written as two words, provided it is below one hundred:

> Twenty-five applicants have requested interviews.
> Two-thirds of the trees had been cut.
> One-half of the design is complete.

Do not attach a hyphen to the word for any number over ninety-nine:

> Some suits now cost over three hundred dollars.
> Some of the new "economy" cars cost more than eight thousand dollars.
> Thirty-five thousand spectators watched the game.

Thirty-five, which is below one hundred, is hyphenated, but no hyphen is attached to *thousand*.

EXERCISE 2 Using the Hyphen

Each of the following may require the addition of one or more hyphens. Add one as needed. If an entry is correct as it stands, write *Correct.*

EXAMPLE
The running of high speed trains between major cities in America would definitely reduce traffic on major highways.
EDITED: The running of high-speed trains between major cities in America would definitely reduce traffic on major highways.

1. The long distance runners looked buoyant as they passed the fifteen mile mark.

2. Organized by a well known sponsor, the race had attracted a

ν̷

number of world renowned athletes to compete before an all European audience.

3. Over three-quarters of the contestants were women from East Germany and Russia.

4. Many came from medium sized towns with populations ranging from twenty one thousand to over fifty five thousand.

5. All of the athletes ran so swiftly that overweight spectators had difficulty keeping up on their ten speed bicycles.

31.10 Using the Apostrophe ν̷

1. To form the possessive of nouns and abbreviations that do not end in *s*, use an apostrophe plus *s*:

a girl's hat	Bill's car	a team's mascot
NATO's future	the C.O.'s orders	Dr. T.'s patients
men's activities	children's toys	someone's coat

If a singular noun ends in *s* (as in *James*) you may form the possessive by adding an apostrophe plus *s* (James's apartment) or by adding just the apostrophe (James' apartment). Custom calls for the latter form with Zeus, Moses, and Jesus: Zeus' thunderbolts, Moses' staff, Jesus' teachings.

2. To form the possessive of plural nouns ending in *s*, add just an apostrophe:

players	players' uniforms
animals	animals' eating habits
the Joneses	the Joneses' car

3. To indicate that two people own something jointly, add an apostrophe, and *s* if necessary, to the second of the two nouns:

Ann and James' apartment

To indicate that two people own two or more things separately, use the apostrophe, and *s* if necessary, with both of the nouns:

Paul's and Marysa's cars

4. To form the possessive with singular compound nouns, add an apostrophe plus *s* to the last word:

my sister-in-law's career   the editor in chief's policy

5. To form the possessive of certain indefinite pronouns, add an
apostrophe plus *s:*

someone's coat   no one's fault   everybody else's jokes

With indefinite pronouns that do not take the apostrophe, form
the possessive with *of:* the plans of most, the hopes of many, the
cooking of few.

6. Use the possessive case with nouns or pronouns followed by
gerunds:

Sarah's running	the crowd's cheering	the men's arguing
the Joneses' celebrating	her protesting	our laughing

For more on this point, see section 11.9.

7. Use an apostrophe, and *s* when necessary, in common phrases
of time and measurement:

four o'clock	five dollar's worth
two week's notice	a day's work
our money's worth	a stone's throw

8. Use an apostrophe plus *s* to form the plurals shown above in
section 31.7, nos. 9 and 10.

9. Use an apostrophe to mark the omission of a letter or letters in
a contraction:

I have finished.	I've finished.
He is not here.	He's not here.
This does not work.	This doesn't work.
They will not stop.	They won't stop.
You should have written.	You should've written.

10. Use an apostrophe to mark the omission of numbers in dates:

the election of '88   the hurricane of '36

31.11 Misusing the Apostrophe

1. Do not use an apostrophe to form the plural of nouns:

* Five girl's went swimming.
  EDITED: Five girls went swimming.

* Two houses' need paint.
  EDITED: Two houses need
  paint.

(v) **2.** Do not use an apostrophe with the possessive forms of the personal pronouns:

> * This is our thermos; that one is their's.
> EDITED: This is our thermos; that one is theirs.

> * Ben's notes are incomplete; your's are thorough.
> EDITED: Ben's notes are incomplete; yours are thorough.

3. Do not confuse the possessive pronoun *its* with the contraction *it's*. Use *its* as you use *his*; use *it's* as you use *he's*.

> his success   he's successful
> its success   it's successful

4. Do not confuse the possessive *whose* with the contraction *who's:*

> Whose notebook is this?

> No one knows whose painting this is.

> Who's going to the concert?

> No one has heard of the pianist who's scheduled to play.

5. Do not use the apostrophe and *s* to form a possessive when the construction would be cumbersome:

> WEAK: Questions about the candidate's husband's financial dealings hurt her campaign.
> EDITED: Questions about the financial dealings of the candidate's husband hurt her campaign.

EXERCISE 3 Using the Apostrophe

Improve the punctuation in the following passage by adding or removing an apostrophe wherever necessary. As you make these corrections, write out the entire passage.

> Everyones talking about Frank Smiths novel. Its plot
> seems to be based on something that happened to him during
> his freshman year. Its weird to read about characters youve
> seen in class or in the students lounge. I dont think there are
> many of his classmate's who wont be annoyed when they dis-   5
> cover theyve been depicted as thugs' and moron's. Its as if
> Frank thought that his experiences were the same as every-
> ones—Juanitas, Murrays, and Mikes. That kind of thinking
> can be overlooked in someone whos in his early teen's, but it
> isnt all right for someone in his twenties'.   10

32
Mechanics

Mechanics are conventional rules such as the one requiring capitalization for the first word of a sentence. You need to follow the conventions so that your writing will look the way formal writing is expected to look.

32.1 Using Capital Letters   *cap*

1. Capitalize the first word of a sentence:

> The quick brown fox jumped over the lazy dog.
> Where do bears hibernate in the winter?

Here and elsewhere in the chapter, to *capitalize* a word means to capitalize its first letter.

2. Capitalize proper nouns and proper adjectives. Unlike a common noun, which names a *class* of objects, a proper noun names a *particular* person, place, thing, or event. Proper adjectives are based on common nouns. Here are examples:

COMMON NOUNS	PROPER NOUNS	PROPER ADJECTIVES
country	Canada	Canadian
person	Jefferson	Jeffersonian
state	Texas	Texan
river	Mississippi River	
revolution	the French Revolution	
party	the Communist Party	
east (direction)	the East (particular region)	

corporation	the Rand Corporation
economics	Economics 101
day	Wednesday

Do not capitalize words such as *a* and *the* when used with proper nouns, and do not capitalize the names of the seasons (fall, winter, spring, summer).

3. Capitalize a personal title when it is used before a name or when it denotes a particular position of high rank:

the president	President Eisenhower
	the President of the United States
	the Pope
the senator	Senator Nunn
the mayor	Mayor Young
the colonel	Colonel Templeton

4. Capitalize a term denoting kinship when it is used before a name:

my uncle   Uncle Bob

5. Capitalize titles as explained in section 32.3.

6. Always capitalize the pronoun *I:*

When I heard the news, I laughed.

EXERCISE 1 Using Capitals

Improve each of the following by capitalizing where necessary.

1. the grand canyon extends over 270 miles from east to west, measures 18 miles from rim to rim at its widest point, and reaches a depth of approximately 1 mile.

2. the canyon has been formed over billions of years by a combination of forces, including wind, erosion, and, in particular, the action of the mighty colorado river.

3. some of the canyon's most spectacular sights are to be found within grand canyon national park, which lies in northwestern arizona.

4. to protect the canyon from commercial development, president theodore roosevelt declared it a national monument in 1908; then in 1919 the congress of the united states proclaimed it a national park.

5. today the park attracts visitors from all of the fifty states as well as from countries far and near, including japan, south korea, france, and canada; the tourists prefer to arrive in july and august.

6. all who view the canyon marvel at the extraordinary rock formations, many of which have impressive names like thor temple, dragon head, and cheops pyramid.

7. according to one report, the canyon received its present name from major john wesley powell, who in 1869 was the first to travel through the canyon by boat. a brave man, he had lost part of an arm in the civil war.

8. he began the journey in wyoming with nine companions and four boats; he ended the journey three months later at the virgin river near lake mead with only three boats and six men.

9. modern tourists have an easier time, hiking along well-marked trails or riding in automobiles to scenic spots like powell memorial and hopi point.

10. Like the other national parks in the U.S.A., grand canyon national park is maintained by the national park service of the u.s. department of the interior.

32.2 Using Italics or Underlining *ital / und*

Use italics or underlining as explained below. (If you're writing with a typewriter or word processor that can print *italic type like this*, use italics. Otherwise use underlining.)

1. Use italics or underlining to emphasize a word or phrase in a statement:

```
There are just laws and there are unjust laws.
                    --Martin Luther King, Jr.
```

Use this kind of emphasis sparingly. When overused, it loses its punch.

2. Use italics or underlining to identify a letter or a word treated as a word:

```
The word suspense has three s's.

The poet uses eyes twice in the first stanza

and once in the second.
```

title

You may also use quotation marks to identify a word as such; see 29.7, no. 4.

3. Use italics or underlining to identify a foreign word or phrase not yet absorbed into English:

<u>au courant</u>   <u>Angst</u>   <u>Bildungsroman</u>   <u>carpe diem</u>

4. Use italics or underlining to identify the name of a ship, an airplane, or the like:

<u>Queen Elizabeth II</u> [ship]

<u>Spirit of St. Louis</u> [airplane]

<u>Apollo 2</u> [spaceship]

5. Use italics or underlining for titles as explained in section 32.3.

EXERCISE 2 Using Underlining

Each of the following may require the addition or removal of underlining. Make any necessary change. If an entry is correct as it stands, write *Correct*.

1. Carol and Alex have named their motorboat The Calex.
2. They wanted to call it Paradise, but couldn't agree whether the last consonant should be an s or a c.
3. They also argue about whether the drink known as a frappe is the same as the one called a frost.
4. But they do see eye to eye on some things, like *yoga* and *karate* classes, pasta and *pizza*, and the way to spell harassment.
5. When their first child was born, Alex gave Carol a dozen roses with a card explaining that the English word mother derives from the Middle English word moder and is akin to the Latin word mater.

32.3 Titles *title*

1. Capitalize the first and last word of a title, whatever they are, and all the words in between except articles (such as *a* and *the*), prepositions (such as *for, among,* and *to*), and conjunctions (such as *and, but,* and *or*):

```
Zen and the Art of Motorcycle Maintenance [book]

"Ode on a Grecian Urn" [poem]
```

2. Use underlining for the title of a book, scholarly journal, magazine, newspaper, government report, play, musical, opera or other long musical composition, film, television show, radio program, or long poem:

```
The Grapes of Wrath [book]

The American Scholar [journal]

Newsweek [magazine]

New York Times [newspaper]

Uniform Crime Reports for the United States [gov-
    ernment publication]

Hamlet [play]

Oklahoma [musical]

The Barber of Seville [opera]

Star Wars [film]

Roseanne [television show]

Morning Pro Musica [radio program]

Song of Myself [long poem]
```

3. Use double quotation marks for titles of works like these:

```
"Seal Hunting in Alaska" [magazine article]

"Bullfighting in Hemingway's Fiction" [essay]

"The Tell-Tale Heart" [short story]

"Mending Wall" [short poem]

"Born in the U.S.A." [song]

"The American Scholar" [speech]

"Winning the West" [chapter in a book]
```

title **4.** Change double to single quotation marks when the title appears within another title that needs quotation marks, or is mentioned within a quotation:

```
"Fences and Neighbors in Frost's 'Mending Wall'"

   [title of an essay on the poem]

"Frost's 'Mending Wall,'" said Professor Ains-

   ley, "is a gently disarming poem."
```

5. Do not use both underlining and quotation marks in a title unless the title itself includes an underlined title:

```
"Experience" [essay]

Gone with the Wind [novel]

"On Sitting Down to Read King Lear Again" [poem]
```

6. Do not use italics or quotation marks in a title of your own unless it includes a reference to another title:

```
What to Do with Nuclear Waste

Bull-fighting in Hemingway's The Sun Also Rises

Art and Sex in Pope's "Rape of the Lock"
```

EXERCISE 3 Writing Titles

Each of the following titles requires capitalization and may also require underlining or quotation marks. Make the necessary changes.

1. carmen [opera]
2. politics and leadership [speech]
3. my old kentucky home [song]
4. washington post [newspaper]
5. what freud forgot [essay]
6. 60 minutes [television show]
7. the will of zeus [history book]
8. john brown's body [long poem]

9. the mismatch between school and children [editorial]
10. natural history [magazine]
11. solutions to the energy problem [your report]
12. the role of fate in shakespeare's romeo and juliet [your essay]
13. imagery in the battle hymn of the republic [your essay]
14. barefoot in the park [play]

32.4 Using Abbreviations *ab*

Abbreviations occur often in informal writing, but in formal writing you should use them less often. We suggest you follow these guidelines.

1. Abbreviate most titles accompanying a name:

Dr. Martha Peters
Robert Greene Jr.
Ms. Elizabeth Fish
Joseph Stevens, M.D.

But use the full titles when referring to religious, governmental, and military leaders:

the Reverend Leonard Flischer
Senator Nancy Kassebaum
the Honorable Mario Cuomo, governor of New York
General George C. Marshall

2. Abbreviate terms that help to specify a date or a time of day:

350 B.C.	8:30 A.M.
A.D. 1776	2:15 P.M.

Note that A.D. precedes the date.

3. Abbreviate the name of a state, a province, or a country when it forms part of an address:

Austin, TX	Galway, Ire.
Long Beach, CA	Sherbrooke, Que.
Plains, GA	Quebec, Can.
Miami, FL	Manchester, Eng.
Washington, DC	Naples, It.

Abbreviate names of U.S. states and the District of Columbia with just two capital letters and no periods, as shown in the left column. Abbreviate names of foreign provinces and countries as shown in the right column.

4. You may use abbreviations in referring to well-known firms and other organizations:

NBC   YMCA
IBM   NAACP

5. If an abbreviation comes at the end of a declarative sentence, use the period marking the abbreviation as the period for the sentence:

The rocket was launched at 11:30 P.M.

If an abbreviation ends a question, add a question mark:

Was the rocket launched at 11:30 P.M.?

6. Most abbreviations must be marked by periods, but you need *no periods* to abbreviate the names of U.S. states and of well-known organizations, as shown above, or to abbreviate well-known phrases:

mph   mpg   cps

32.5 Misusing Abbreviations   (ab)

1. In formal writing, avoid using abbreviations for the days of the week and the months of the year:

Sunday   August

2. Avoid using abbreviations for the names of most geographical entities when they are not part of an address:

New England   the Snake River   Lake Avenue   Canada

Many writers now use *U.S.* and *U.S.S.R.* You may also use *Mt.* before the name of a mountain, as in *Mt. McKinley*, and *St.* in the name of a place, as in *St. Louis*.

3. Avoid using abbreviations for the names of academic subjects and the subdivision of books:

French 205   biology   chapter 10   page 45

EXCEPTION: In parenthetical citations of books and articles, "page" *num* is commonly abbreviated as "p." and "pages" as "pp."

4. Avoid using abbreviations for units of measurement (such as size and weight) unless the accompanying amounts are given in numerals:

> The new guard is six feet seven inches tall.
>
> This box must weigh over fifty pounds.
>
> A 50 lb. bag of fertilizer costs $24.50.

5. Avoid using any abbreviation that is not widely known without first explaining its meaning:

> * The MISAA was passed in 1978.
> EDITED: The Middle Income Student Assistance Act (MISAA) was passed in 1978.

After you have explained its meaning, you may use the abbreviation on its own. But beware of crowding too many abbreviations into a sentence or passage. If you don't keep them under control, your reader may end up drowning in alphabet soup:

> * In 1971 Congress established the BEOG program, and the EOGs were renamed SEOGs.
> EDITED: In 1972 Congress established the Basic Educational Opportunity Grant (BEOG) program, and the Educational Opportunity Grants (EOG) were renamed Supplemental Educational Opportunity Grants (SEOG).

If you aren't sure how to abbreviate a particular term, see your dictionary or ask your instructor. If you don't know whether you should abbreviate a term at all, don't. In formal writing, most terms should be spelled out in full.

32.6 Using Numbers *num*

When you refer to a number, you have to decide whether to use a figure or to spell it out as a word. In much scientific and technical writing, figures predominate; in magazines and books of general interest, words are common, though figures are also used. In this section, we offer guidelines for nontechnical writing.

num **1.** Spell out a number when it begins a sentence:

> Eighty-five dignitaries attended the opening ceremony.

Rearrange the sentence if spelling out the number would require three or more words:

> The opening ceremony was attended by 1,250 dignitaries.

2. Spell out a number that can be written in one or two words, except as noted in no. 4, below:

> A batter is out after three strikes.
> The firemen worked without relief for twenty-two hours.
> Twenty-five thousand people were evacuated.

A hyphenated number may be counted as one word.

3. Use numerals if spelling out a number would require more than two words:

> The stadium can hold 85,600 spectators.

4. Use numerals for addresses, dates, exact times of day, exact sums of money, exact measurements such as miles per hour, scores of games, mathematical ratios, fractions, and page numbers:

> 22 East Main Street   65 mph
> October 7, 1981   a ratio of 2 to 1
> 44 B.C.   5⅞
> 11:15 A.M.   page 102
> $4.36

However, when a time of day or a sum of money is given as a round figure, spell it out:

> Uncle Ben always gets up at six.
> He used to earn two dollars for ten hours of work.

5. Be consistent within a piece of writing. Use *either* words *or* figures but not both:

> *In the first inning, with a crowd of 35,000 looking on, the Tigers scored 5 runs on four hits, three walks, and 1 error.
> EDITED: In the first inning, with a crowd of thirty-five thousand looking on, the Tigers scored five runs on four hits, three walks, and one error.

EXERCISE 4 Using Abbreviations and Numbers

Each of the following may include incorrectly written abbreviations and numbers. Make any necessary changes. If an entry is correct as it stands, write *Correct.*

EXAMPLE

"Why," said the White Queen to Alice, "sometimes I've believed as many as 6 impossible things before breakfast."
—Adapted from Lewis Carroll
EDITED: "Why," said the White Queen to Alice, "sometimes I've believed as many as six impossible things before breakfast."

1. We plan to spend part of our vacation on a Miss. Riv. steamboat and the rest in the Cascade Mts.

2. 1st, however, we must attend a meeting of the Young Women's Christian Association that is expected to attract an audience of 25 hundred members in Alexandria, Virginia.

3. The Rev. Ann Proctor, Doctor of Divinity, will be one of the speakers; her talk is scheduled to begin at seven-fifteen P.M.

4. All of the speakers have said they will contribute ¾ of their honorarium to the Assoc.

5. The combined amounts should come to exactly seven hundred dollars and seventy-two cents,

6. Following the meeting, we will head west, being careful not to exceed the speed limit of sixty-five miles per hour.

7. If all goes well, we should arrive in St. Lou. on Fri., Aug. nine.

Part 4

The Research Paper

33
Preparing the Research Paper

Writing a library research paper is much like writing an ordinary essay. Both involve choosing a topic, asking questions to define and develop it, gauging the audience, finding a thesis, outlining the paper, writing it, and revising it. What makes a research paper different is that much of its material comes not from your own head but from printed sources, chiefly books and periodicals. Collecting raw material—by reading and taking notes—corresponds to the process of prewriting an ordinary essay.

A research paper may be one of two things. It may be an *explanatory survey* of facts and opinions available on a given topic, or an *analytical argument* that uses those facts and opinions to prove a thesis. While many research papers combine survey with argument, you should try to decide what your primary aim will be: to explain or persuade.

If you aim to explain your topic, you survey the facts and opinions on it, but you make little attempt to judge which opinion is worth more than another. Instead, through quotation, summary, or paraphrase, you try to report the available facts on your topic and the opinions it has evoked. You explain the pros and cons of various positions, but you don't side definitely with any one of them. (For a sample of an explanatory research paper, see Appendix 1, section A1.6.)

In an argumentative paper, you do considerably more. You do not simply quote, paraphrase, and summarize. You interpret, question, compare, and judge the statements you cite. You explain why one opinion is sound and another is not, why one fact is relevant and another is not, why one writer is correct and another is mistaken. Your purpose may vary with your topic; you may seek to show why something has happened, to recommend a course of action, to solve a problem, or to present and defend a particular interpretation of a historical event or a work of art. But whether the topic is space travel or Shakespeare's *Hamlet*, an argumentative research paper deals actively with the statements it cites. It makes them work together in an argument that you create—an argument that leads to a conclusion of your own. (For a sample argumentative research paper, see chapter 37.)

What follows will help you write either an explanatory research paper or an argumentative one. Whichever you choose, we have designed this chapter as a succession of steps to guide you systematically through the whole process of preparation. But you may well find, as you work your way into your topic and discover its potentialities, that you can't take the steps exactly in order.

Suppose, for instance, that you'd like to write about earthquakes but have no idea how to define the topic or what questions to ask about it. In that case, you might begin by reading an encyclopedia article, as explained in section 33.2D. That would help you to learn how to make the topic more specific (earthquakes in California, for instance) and might also provoke the kind of questions that could lead you to a thesis, or to further research that might help you discover one. But don't expect to find your thesis right away. Doing research—reading a variety of sources—is like listening to a long discussion and then suddenly realizing that you've formed an opinion of your own: that you know where you stand, that you're ready to speak. If you take this route to a thesis, you may be pleasantly surprised to see how much you have gathered along the way that will help you support it.

So treat the following sequence as flexible. If your topic is vague at the outset, let your research help you define it. If you can't think of a thesis, let your research help you discover one. Use whatever sequence works best for you.

33.1 Choosing a Topic

Choosing a topic for a research paper is in some ways like choosing a topic for an ordinary essay. But there are some differences. As you weigh your topic, ask yourself these questions.

1. Do you really want to know more about this topic? You will make the most of it only if you expect to learn something interesting or important in the process.

2. Are you likely to find many sources of information on this topic? You cannot write a research paper without consulting a variety of sources. If only one source, or none at all, is readily available, you should rethink your topic or choose another. If you pick a topic that is currently in the news, be sure it has been around long enough to generate substantial articles and books.

For this as well as other reasons, one good way to find a topic is to look in a textbook you are using in the course for which the paper is assigned. Steve Parini, the author of a paper on euthanasia, got the first idea for his topic from a textbook on medical ethics that he was using in his philosophy course: Ronald Munson, *Intervention and Reflection: Basic Issues in Medical Ethics*, 3rd ed. (1988). In reading this book, he was struck by the chapter on euthanasia—painless death—because it not only raised provocative questions but also included brief essays by various writers with sharply conflicting views. Since some of these writers made footnote references to books and other essays, he could see that there would be more than enough sources to consult.

3. Can you cut the topic down to manageable size? Be reasonable and realistic about what you can do in a period of two to four weeks. If your topic is "The Causes of the American Revolution," you will scarcely have time to make a list of books on your subject, let alone read and analyze them. Find something specific, such as "The Harassment of Loyalists after Watertown" or "The Role of Patrick Henry in the American Revolution." After you've done your research on a specific topic such as this, you could explain in your paper how it helps to illuminate the general topic you started with.

4. What questions can you ask about the topic itself? Questions help you get the topic down to manageable size, discover its possibilities, and find the goal of your research—the specific problem you want to investigate. Suppose you want to write about automobile safety. You could ask at least three or four pointed questions: How well can today's cars withstand collision? How often does speeding cause fatal accidents? How well are speed limits enforced? What about the national maximum speed limit of 55 mph? Why was it repealed? What does the repeal tell us about

American drivers? What effects has the return to 65 produced? Robin Martinez asked herself these questions as she started work on her paper. From time to time in this chapter and the next, we will see how she came to focus on one of these questions during the course of her research and how she found and used the sources that went into her paper.

THINKING ABOUT YOUR RESEARCH TOPIC: IN BRIEF

1. Do you really want to know more about this topic?
2. Are you likely to find many sources of information on this topic?
3. Can you cut the topic down to manageable size?
4. What questions can you ask about the topic itself?
5. Which question(s) will your paper answer?

EXERCISE 1 Writing Questions about Various Topics

Choose five of the following topics, and write two questions on each of them. Make the questions as pointed and specific as possible.

1. Solar energy
2. Viking explorations in North America
3. Censorship
4. French separatism in Quebec
5. Prayer in the public schools
6. Divorce
7. Sexual abuse of children
8. Oil spills
9. Acid rain
10. Prohibition
11. The political career of Pierre Trudeau
12. Adult illiteracy

EXERCISE 2 Writing Questions about One Topic

Think of a research topic that interests you, or take a topic you have been assigned, and write at least three specific questions about it.

33.2 Using the Library—The Reference Section

The best place to start systematically working on your research paper is the reference section of your college or university library. Here you can sometimes get access to computerized information about sources on your topic, and you can certainly find reference works of all kinds: encyclopedias, indexes, bibliographies, atlases, and dictionaries. Whatever your subject, a computerized database or a reference book will tell what has been written about it. To find your way to either of these guides, ask the help of the reference librarian, who will tell you of any orientation tours that may be available and will also do everything possible to help you find what you need.

In this section we start by explaining the quickest ways to learn about various sources on your subject, and then turn to more specialized routes. As soon as you've identified all the sources you think you need, you can skip to sections 33.3 and 33.4, where we explain how to find the sources you've identified.

33.2A Learning What Your Topic Is Called

If your library has an on-line catalog, it can give you a shortcut to some of the books on your topic. As we explain in section 33.3A, Robin Martinez started out by asking the on-line catalog to search for books on "Speed Limits," and it came up with four. But to find *any* item in an on-line file, you must remember one thing: *computers don't understand any word that is misspelled.* If you're looking for sources on "Speed Limits" and you accidentally type "Sped Limits," you'll be told there are 0 items in that file. So if any of your searches draws a blank in this way, make sure your search word or phrase is letter perfect before you give up.

You can also look for your topic in the subject catalog (see section 33.3B), where the cards will sometimes guide you; if you look up "Speed Limits," for instance, you might be told to *"See Traffic Regulations."* But if you aren't quite sure what your topic is called, you will need to learn the subject heading—or headings—under which it is normally listed.

Subject headings are the passwords to your sources. Suppose you decide to write about blacks in American business. To find material on this topic, you need to know that until 1976 the subject heading for books and articles on blacks was "Negroes" and is now "Afro-Americans." You can get this kind of information from the reference librarian or from the set of volumes called *Library of Congress Subject Headings*. When Robin Martinez looked up "Speed Limits" in these volumes, here is what she found:

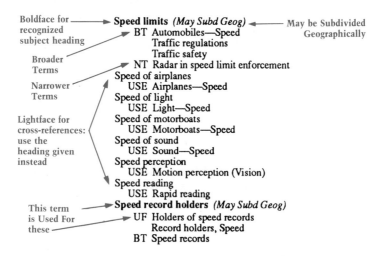

What does this entry mean? First of all, the boldface type for "Speed Limits" shows that this phrase is a recognized subject heading—one that Robin could use to find sources on her topic.[†] Under the boldface heading are Broader Terms (BT) and Narrower Terms (NT) that can be used. When UF appears under a boldfaced term, as it does under "Speed record holders," it means that the boldfaced term is Used For the one after it, so that if you were investigating holders of speed records, you would need "Speed record holders" to find your sources.

When a phrase appears in light print—as "Speed of airplanes" does—it is not a recognized subject heading. "USE Airplanes—Speed" means that you must use that phrase to find sources on this topic.

[†]The parenthesized note *May Subd Geog* means *May be Subdivided Geographically,* so that in some subject catalogs you may find separate headings for "Speed Limits—United States," "Speed Limits—England," and so on.

Once you know the subject headings for your topic, you can start looking for sources on it. (Though not all library catalogs and bibliographies use the Library of Congress subject headings, most do.) You'll usually find sources listed in one or more of the following works.

33.2B A Book-and-Article Bibliography

Before you look anywhere else, find out if there's a book-and-article bibliography on your topic—a guide to *both articles and books*. To locate such a bibliography, check your subject heading in the on-line catalog or the card catalog, or—since bibliographies are commonly kept in the reference room—ask a reference librarian to help you. When Steve Parini, for instance, asked the reference librarian about sources on euthanasia, he learned about the annual *Bibliography of Bioethics*, which describes books and journal articles on ethical problems in medicine. Here are three of the entries he found under the heading of "Euthanasia" in the 1987 issue:

> **Crisp, Roger.** A good death: who best to bring it? *Bioethics*. 1987 Jan; 1(1): 74-79. 8 fn. BE22712.
> *active euthanasia; family members; living wills; nurses; *physician's role; physicians; psychological stress; terminal care; terminally ill; *voluntary euthanasia
>
> The author supports the right of persons to terminate their lives when it would be in their "best interests" to do so. He considers cases in which persons are unable to kill themselves and request euthanasia or have requested it beforehand in a living will. Crisp rejects relatives, friends, and most phsicians as the agents to carry out the request because of the emotional trauma to the agents and the damage to the image of physicians as savers of lives. He proposes that the practice of euthanasia be part of "telostrics," an area of medicine specialization in the care of the terminally ill, and that these "telostricians" should perform voluntary euthanasia.

> **Donahue, M. Patricia.** Euthanasia: an ethical uncertainty. In   McCloskey , Joanne Comi; Grace, Helen Kennedy, eds. Current Issues in Nursing. Second Edition. Boston; Blackwell Scientific Publications; 1985: 1025- 1043. 26 refs. ISBN 0-86542-019-X. BE21569.
> *allowing to die; brain death; decision making; *ethical analysis; *euthanasia; extraordinary treatment; moral obligations; *moral policy; * nurses; *nursing ethics; *patient advocacy; prolongation

of life; rights; self determination; *terminally ill;
withholding treatment

Kuhse, Helga; Singer, Peter. Should the Baby Live?
The Problem of Handicapped Infants. New York:
Oxford University Press; 1985 228 p. Includes references. ISBN 0-19-217745-1. BE22782.
*active euthanasia; *allowing to die; case studies;
*congenital defects; costs and benefits; cultural
pluralism; *decision making; double effect

Unlike some bibliographies, which simply give titles and publication details, this one is *annotated,* which means that it offers
notes on each source listed. The first entry summarizes an article
that appeared in the January 1987 issue of *Bioethics;* the second
identifies an essay that appears in a book, *Current Issues in Nurs-
ing;* the third identifies a book about handicapped infants. All three
entries also cite the topics covered by each source, and the asterisk
before a topic such as "active euthanasia" indicates that this is a
subject heading for more entries elsewhere in the bibliography.

Other fields have their own bibliographies. If you're investigating a literary topic, for instance, you should consult *The MLA
International Bibliography,* published annually, an author-and-
subject index to books and journal articles on modern languages,
literatures, folklore, and linguistics. Though this bibliography is
not so thoroughly annotated as the one on bioethics, it does identify the chief subjects treated by each of the sources it lists. Until
1981, the "subjects" treated were usually the names of writers.
But since 1981, the bibliography has also included subjects in the
usual sense, such as "women in fiction."

Many bibliographies are issued annually, so if you check the
entries for your topic in the three or four most recent issues, you
can quickly learn about all the most recently published sources on
your topic.

Another good place to look for a list of books and articles on
your topic is a book on the topic itself. If you already know the
title of a book you plan to see, the library catalog will tell you
whether or not it has a bibliography (see 33.3B). If it does, you'll
find within it (usually at the end) a list that often includes articles
as well as books, and may well be annotated.

33.2C A Computerized Index

A computerized index (also called a database) is a computerized
file of sources in a particular field. Dialog Information Services,
Inc., has many such indexes. To use one, you will normally need

the help of a library technician and you may be asked to pay a small fee. But a computerized index can dramatically expedite your quest for sources because it's typically *cumulative,* covering all the years from a given year right up to the present one. The computerized version of the *MLA Bibliography,* for instance, covers all the years from 1964 on, which saves you the trouble of consulting a different issue for each year. For his study of euthanasia, Steve Parini was directed to the *Philosopher's Index,* which covers books and journal articles on philosophic subjects from 1940 to the present. Here is part of what he found:

```
THE ETHICS OF INFANT EUTHANASIA.
VARGA, ANDREW
THOUGHT, 57, 438-448,   D 82,
Languages: ENGLISH
Document Type: JOURNAL ARTICLE
Journal Announcement:   171
   THE PURPOSE OF THE ARTICLE IS TO EXAMINE THE ETHICAL QUESTIONS
OF LETTING DEFECTIVE NEWBORNS DIE BY OMITTING OR WITHDRAWING
THEIR TREATMENT.   THE OMISSION OR WITHDRAWAL OF THERAPEUTICALLY
USEFUL TREATMENT IS UNETHICAL. THE KILLING OF DEFECTIVE INFANTS
BY STARVATION OR DIRECT INTERVENTION CANNOT BE JUSTIFIED EITHER.
THE APPLICATION OF THERAPIES THAT ARE OUT OF PROPORTION AS TO
THE RESULTS THAT CAN BE EXPECTED IS NOT ETHICALLY OBLIGATORY.
   Descriptors: ETHICS; INFANT; EUTHANASIA; INFANTICIDE


INFANTICIDE AND THE VALUE OF LIFE.
KOHL, MARVIN (ED)
BUFFALO PROMETHEUS BOOKS   1978
Languages: ENGLISH
Document Type: MONOGRAPH
Journal Announcement: 144
   THE PURPOSE OF THIS ANTHOLOGY OF 18 ORIGINAL ESSAYS IS TO
UNDERSTAND WHAT CONDITIONS, IF ANY, WARRANT ALLOWING OR INDUCING
THE DEATH OF A SERIOUSLY DEFECTIVE INFANT.   PART I, ON RELIGIO-
ETHICAL ISSUES, CONTAINS PAPERS BY RICHARD BRANDT, JOSEPH
FLETCHER, IMMANUEL JAKOBOVITS, AND EIKE-HENNER KLUGE.   PART II
IS PRIMARILY CONCERNED ABOUT RELATED MEDICAL ISSUES AND PART III
ABOUT LEGAL QUESTIONS.   PART IV, ON SUFFERING AND THE VALUE OF
LIFE, INCLUDES PAPERS BY JOSEPH MARGOLIS, STEPHEN NATHANSON,
JOHN DONNELLY, AND MARVIN KOHL.
   Descriptors: ETHICS; INFANTICIDE; EUTHANASIA; BIRTH DEFECTS;
MEDICAL ETHICS; LIFE
```

The first entry is an article by Andrew Varga, "The Ethics of Infant Euthanasia," which appeared in the December 1982 issue of a journal called *Thought,* Volume 57, pages 438–48; the entry summarizes the article as well as citing it. The second entry is a book edited by Marvin Kohl, *Infanticide and the Value of Life;* the entry describes the contents of the book in detail.

33.2D General Encyclopedias

These give you an overview of virtually any subject in language that a nonspecialist can understand, and many encyclopedia articles end with a short list of books recommended for further reading on the subject. For this reason, an encyclopedia is a good place to start your research, though you should not expect to use it or cite it as a major source in itself. General encyclopedias include the thirty-volume *New Encyclopaedia Britannica* (1974), the thirty-volume *Americana* (revised annually), and the one-volume *New Columbia* (1975). Some encyclopedias can be scanned by computer. The 1988 edition of the *Academic American Encyclopedia*, for instance, is available on-line from Grolier Electronic Publishing, Inc., with updates added each quarter. If your library has this on-line encyclopedia, you can probably find it by asking the library computer to search the file called "ENCYCLOPEDIA." Then the on-screen instructions will tell you how to find the material you want.

33.2E Specialized Reference Works

These cover subjects in particular fields, such as art, education, history, literature, and psychology. To find the reference work for your subject, ask the reference librarian or see the *Guide to Reference Books* compiled by Eugene P. Sheehy (1976, with two supplements to date), which lists specialized guides to research in all fields, such as the *Encyclopedia of World Art* (1959–83), *The Encyclopedia of Education* (1971), *The Canadian Encyclopedia*, 2nd edition (1988), and the *International Encyclopedia of the Social Sciences*, ed. David L. Sills (1968–). (Note, by the way, that "Encyclopedia" is sometimes spelled "Encyclopaedia.")

EXERCISE 3 Using Encyclopedias

Read an article in a standard encyclopedia about the research topic you chose for exercise 2, and jot down any questions this article raises for you. Then find a specialized encyclopedia that contains an article on your topic. Explain how the second article differs from the first and whether or not the second answers all of the questions raised by the first.

33.2F Compilations of Facts and Statistics

These include such works as *Facts on File* (1904–), a "weekly news digest with cumulative index," which summarizes current events, and *Statistical Abstract of the United States,* which offers statistics on many subjects.

EXERCISE 4 Finding Facts and Statistics

Assume that you want to do research on oil spills at sea. Choose a six-month period taken from the past year, and from *Facts on File* and *Statistical Abstract of the United States* see what you can learn about oil spills during this period.

33.2G Biographical Guides

These give brief accounts of notable figures, sometimes with bibliographies. They include the following:

Chambers's Biographical Dictionary (1968) covers figures in all historical periods.

Who's Who covers living persons. Besides *Who's Who in the World* (1976), there are national volumes such as *Who's Who in America, Who's Who in Canada,* and volumes devoted to special categories such as black Americans, American women, and American politicians.

The *Dictionary of American Biography* (1928–) covers deceased Americans.

The *Dictionary of Canadian Biography* (1966–) covers deceased Canadians.

The *Dictionary of National Biography* (1885–) covers deceased Britons.

Notable American Women, ed. Edward T. James and Janet W. James (1971–80), covers American women from 1607 to 1950.

Dictionary of American Negro Biography (1982) covers deceased Afro-Americans.

Contemporary Authors (1967–82) covers chiefly living authors.

EXERCISE 5 Using Biographical Reference Works

If your topic concerns a particular person, consult one or more of the biographical dictionaries or *Who's Who* volumes mentioned above. Jot down at least two questions about the person, and then consult the *Biography Index* for the titles of two recent books or articles on your subject.

33.2H Guides to Books

These include the following:

1. The *Cumulative Book Index* (1898–) lists by author, title, and subject all books published in the United States from 1898 to the present.

2. The *Subject Guide to Books in Print* tells you what hardbound *and* paperbound books on your topic are currently in print.

3. The *Book Review Digest*, gives excerpts from book reviews. If, for instance, you wanted to know something about *The Dragons of Eden*, by Carl Sagan (1977), here is a sample of what the *Digest* would tell you:

> **SAGAN, CARL.** The dragons of Eden; speculations on the evolution of human intelligence. 263p il $8.95 '77 Random House
>
> 153 Intellect. Brain. Genetics
> ISBN 0-394-41045-9 LC 76-53472
>
> "What happens when an astronomer and space scientist turns inward to an exploration of the human brain? If the man is Sagan, he writes a rational, elegant, and witty book . . . . The second chapter is, as he acknowledges, difficult for even an initiated layman . . . [But] after that, the going is illuminating and frequently delightful. . . . No doubt some scientists will quarrel or quibble over some of Sagan's speculations. Many others will surely squirm with envy that one of their number can combine such clarity and charm of prose with a measure of humility."
> Robert Manning
> Atlantic 240:91 Ag '77 360w
>
> Choice 14:1386 D '77 180w
>
> "Like many non-specialist popularizers of psychology, Sagan overestimates our physiological knowledge and underestimates our psychological knowledge. . . . Though he knows how profoundly science can change our picture of the world, [he] seems not to realize that the psychological shift in outlook promises to be deeper, broader, and at times more difficult to accept than the Copernican and Darwinian ones were. Once again, people are to confront a science that challenges their egocentricity. . . . The intensity of their resistance is already apparent. . . . None of this surfaces in, or even ripples the surface of, Professor Sagan's book. He is asking his readers to change their minds about almost nothing, though doing so with grace, humor, and style." R. J. Herrnstein
> Commentary 64:66 Ag '77 2500w

These reviews appeared in 1977, the same year as the book. But some book reviews do not appear until the year after a book is published, so you should check the *Digest* for both years. Also, since the *Digest* favors books of general interest over academic and specialized works, it may not contain any reviews of a book in the latter category.

4. The *Book Review Index* and *Current Review Citations* (which ended in 1982) will tell you where to find reviews of the books you're interested in, though they don't print digests of the reviews themselves. Also, you can learn about reviews of scholarly books—which are usually not covered by the *Book Review Digest*—in these sources:

- **a.** For reviews of books in the *humanities,* see the *Combined Retrospective Index to Book Reviews in Humanities Journals, 1802–1974,* and the book review section of the *Humanities Index.*
- **b.** For reviews of books that are chiefly in the *social sciences,* see the *Combined Retrospective Index to Book Reviews in Scholarly Journals, 1886–1974,* and the book review section of the *Social Sciences Index.*

As their dates indicate, these indexes will not help you with any book published recently—partly because reviews of scholarly books sometimes appear several years after the publication date. So if the title and date of a particular book make it seem promising, you may simply want to get the book itself rather than tracking down reviews of it first.

5. The *MLA International Bibliography,* published annually, is an author-and-subject index to books as well as articles on modern languages, literatures, folklore, and linguistics. See above, section 33.2B.

6. The *RIE (Resources in Education)* summarizes virtually all books on educational topics. See p. 510.

EXERCISE 6 Using Book Reviews

Using the *Book Review Digest* and the *Book Review Index,* investigate reviews on *Time on the Cross,* a book about slavery written by Robert William Fogel and Stanley L. Engerman and published in 1974. What impression of the book do you get from the reviews?

33.21 Guides to Articles in Books

The *Essay and General Literature Index* lists the titles and authors of articles collected in books. Though it does not list articles from highly specialized books, it does cover a wide range of topics. Here,

for instance, is what you would find under "Nicaragua" in the
Essay and General Literature Index for 1983:

> **Nicaragua**
>
> **Foreign relations—United States**
>
> Gorostiaga, X. Dilemmas of the Nicara-
> guan Revolution. *In* The Future of Central
> America, ed. by R. R. Fagen and O. Pellicer
> p47-66

This tells you that X. Gorostiaga wrote an article titled "Dilem-
mas of the Nicaraguan Revolution" that appears on pp. 47–66 of a
book called *The Future of Central America,* edited by R.R. Fagen
and O. Pellicer. To make a note on this source, record the author
and title of the book as well as the article. You will need the book
title to find the book in the library catalog.

33.2J General Indexes to Periodicals

These include the following:

1. The *Reader's Guide to Periodical Literature,* issued every month
and cumulated quarterly as well as annually, is an author-and-subject index to articles of general (rather than scholarly) interest published in over a hundred American magazines. When Robin
Martinez looked up "Traffic Regulations" in the 1987 issue of the
Guide, here is part of what she found:

> **Traffic regulations**
> *See also*
> Traffic tickets
> 65 mph: America steps on the gas [Congress votes to
> change rural speed limit] il *U S News World Rep*
> 102:12 Mr 30 '87
> 65 mph: the time has come. S. Symms. *Car Driv* 32:27
> My '87
> 65—its for real! [speed limit] T. Orme. il *Mot Trend*
> 39:44 Jl '87
> Contrived concrete evidence! [55-mph speed limit] J.
> Dinkel. *Road Track* 39:40 O '87
> Fast talk [CNN debate with Rep. J. Howard on 55-mph
> speed limit] R. Ceppos. il *Car Driv* 33:26-7 Jl '87
> Speed-limit tutelage: is 65 enough? *Natl Rev* 39:18 Je
> 19 ' 87
> Step on it [Congress votes to increase the speed limit
> on rural interstate highways] *Time* 129:26 Mr 30 '87
> War stories [encounters with traffic police over 55-mph
> speed limit] P. Bedard. il *Car Driv* 33:164 Jl '87
> Wooden nickels [repeal 55-mph speed limit] R. Ceppos.
> il *Car Driv* 32:22 Ap ' 87

To identify and locate these sources, you have to know how to decipher the entries. First, the words *See also* direct you to other headings in the *Guide* that might give you other useful sources. Then comes the first item—an unsigned article titled "65 mph: America Steps on the Gas," which appeared in the March 30, 1987, issue of *U.S. News & World Report*, Volume 102, page 12. The letters "il" mean the article is illustrated, and if you don't recognize the abbreviated name of the periodical, the list of abbreviations at the beginning of the *Guide* will tell you what it means. If the title doesn't clearly indicate what the article is about, the bracketed words add a brief explanation, and the author's name follows unless the article is unsigned.

The first two items caught Robin's eye. She could see at once that the first would give her essential facts about the repeal of the 55 mph speed limit, and that the second would offer arguments for repeal. These two articles would begin to answer the questions she had raised about her topic. So she made a note on each, jotting down not only the titles of both and the author of the second, but also—just as important—the information about where and when each one appeared.

2. The *Magazine Index* lists chiefly by subject matter articles from over four hundred magazines. It's a microtext made to be used with a special viewer. The reference librarian will tell you if your library has one and where to find it.

3. The *New York Times Index* lists selected articles published in the *Times* from 1851–1912, and all articles published in the *Times* thereafter. Issued twice a month with quarterly cumulations and then bound into annual volumes, this index is a prime source of up-to-date information.

33.2K Specialized Indexes to Periodicals

These list articles in one or more specified fields. Here is a small selection:

1. The *Environment Index* lists articles as well as books and technical reports under subject headings such as "Oil Spills." Many of the articles are briefly summarized in a companion volume, *Environment Abstracts*.

2. The *General Science Index* lists articles under subject headings in fields such as astronomy, botany, genetics, mathematics, physics, and oceanography.

3. The *Humanities Index* lists articles by author and subject in fields such as archaeology, folklore, history, language, literature, the performing arts, and philosophy.

4. The *Social Sciences Index* lists articles by author and subject in fields such as anthropology, economics, law, criminology, medical science, political science, and sociology.

5. The *Bulletin of the Public Affairs Information Service (PAIS)* covers articles on public affairs and public policy as well as government documents and books.

EXERCISE 7 Making Notes on Articles in Periodicals

Using a general or specialized index to periodicals, find out about two articles on your topic and make a note on each. Be sure to note the name and date of the periodical in which each article appears.

33.2L Government Publications

The United States government produces a vast amount of printed matter on a wide range of subjects. Here is a sample of the guides to this material, which can often be found in the microfiche collections of many large libraries.

1. The *ASI (American Statistics Index)* consists of two volumes, *Index* and *Abstracts.* The first is a subject index to statistical documents produced by hundreds of government offices; the second describes the documents more fully.

2. The *CIS,* published by the Congressional Information Service, also consists of two volumes, *Index* and *Abstracts.* They index and describe working papers of Congress: reports, documents, and other special publications of nearly three hundred House, Senate, and joint committees and subcommittees.

3. The *Monthly Catalog of United States Government Publications,* indexed semiannually, lists government publications by author, title, and subject matter.

4. *Resources in Education (RIE),* issued monthly and indexed semiannually by the Educational Resources Information Center (ERIC), lists books, pamphlets, and conference papers on educational topics under subject headings, author, and title, and also *summarizes* every document it lists. Though *RIE* does not list journal articles on education, you will find these in the *Current*

Index to Journals in Education (CIJE), also produced by ERIC. Since these two sources together treat virtually all publications dealing with educational topics, they are indispensable to anyone working on a topic in the field of education.

33.3 Finding Books—The On-Line Catalog and the Card Catalog

If you have done some work in the reference section, you now have not only an overview of your topic but also a list of books and articles on it. But you don't yet know how many of those sources your library has. To find that out and then locate the books themselves, you need to consult one or more catalogs. This section explains how to find books through the catalog; section 33.4 explains how to find articles.

33.3A Using the On-Line Catalog

The on-line catalog is a computerized file of a library's holdings. Few such catalogs are now complete, but if your library has begun to compile one, it's the best place to start your search for the books you need. (If your library doesn't have an on-line catalog, skip this section and go on to section 33.3B.) To use the on-line catalog, ask any librarian for the location of the nearest terminal and follow the instructions listed beside it. You can then call up a specific book by author or title, or ask the computer to search its file for books on a given topic. Since no two computer systems are exactly alike, we can't tell you exactly what your library's system will do, but we can tell you what Robin Martinez got from the on-line catalog in her library. When she asked for books on "Speed Limits," the computer came up with four, starting with this one:

```
    Title : 55 : a decade of experience / [edited for TRB
            by Edythe Traylor Crump].
  Imprint : Washington, D.C. : Transportation Research
            Board, National Research Council, 1984.
   Series : Special report (National Research Council
            (U.S.), Transportation Research Board) ; 204.
 Location : Baker Stacks HE/5620/S6/A154/1984

 Subjects : Speed limits -- United States.
            Traffic accidents -- United States.
            Traffic safety -- United States.
```

From the title of this book, Robin figured that it had to be a study of the 55 mph speed limit, and therefore indispensable to her research. Her computer terminal was connected to a printer, so she went through the commands needed to print out the screen. But if there's no printer handy, you should make a note of the author (or in this case, the editor), the title, and the location—the library call number—of the book, as explained in section 33.5.

Since the computer came up with just four books under "speed limits," she wondered if there were more books on her topic lurking somewhere in the mainframe under different headings. There are two ways to get this kind of information. One is to note the "tracings" or subject headings under each book that comes up on the screen. Since the headings under 55 included not only "Speed limits" but also "Traffic accidents" and "Traffic safety," Robin could use both of those headings to find more books. The other way to find more headings is to check the *Library of Congress Subject Headings,* as explained above in section 33.2A. Since Robin had already learned from this guide that the usual heading for her topic was "Traffic Regulations," she tried that heading and came up with 31 items, including this one:

```
Author  :  Gardiner, John A., 1937-
 Title  :  Traffic and the police; variations in law-
           enforcement policy / [by John A. Gardiner].
Imprint  :  Cambridge, Harvard University Press, 1969.
 Series  :  Joint Center for Urban Studies. Publications.
Location :  Baker Stacks HE/371/M4/G36
```

Though she could see by the date of this book (1969) that it had appeared before the 55 mph speed limit began, she could also see that it dealt with a subject important to her topic—the question of enforcement. So she added this book to her printout file.

33.3B Using the Card Catalog

You will need the card catalog if your college library has no on-line catalog, and you may need it if the on-line catalog is incomplete. If it is incomplete, ask the reference librarian how far back its listings go. (Libraries usually enter the newest books first and then work backwards through their collections.) If all of the library's books published since 1960 are now on line, and you don't need anything published earlier than 1960, then you don't need the card catalog. But otherwise you should know how to use it.

Each book in the catalog is listed in three ways: by author, by title, and by subject. If you know the author of the book you want, check the author card. That will give you the title and a good deal more:

Library call number indicates where you can find the book

```
                                                              Author
                   Crump, Edythe Traylor◄──────────────── or editor
    HE             55 : a decade of experience / [edited
    5620               for TRB by Edythe Traylor Crump].  --
    .S6A154        ►Washington, D.C. : Transportation
    1984            Research Board, National Research
                    Council, 1984.                    ◄──── Size of
Place of            vii, 262 p. : ill. ; 23 cm. --          book
publication,       (Special report / Transportation
publisher, and     Research Board, National Research
date of            Council ; 204)                          The book
publication         Includes bibliographies.◄───────────── has a
                   ISBN 0-309-03664-X (pbk.) : $14.00       bibliography

                                                           Tracings
Number                1. Speed limits--United States--Cost list the subject
of                 effectiveness.                          headings under
pages                                                      which the book
                                                          ─is catalogued
```

If you know the title of the book you want, but aren't sure of the author, check the title card.

```
                   Fifty-five, a decade of experience.◄─ Title

    HE             55 : a decade of experience / [edited
    5620               for TRB by Edythe Traylor Crump].  --
    .S6A154        Washington, D.C. : Transportation
    1984            Research Board, National Research
                    Council, 1984.
                    vii, 262 p. : ill. ; 23 cm. --
                   (Special report / Transportation
                    Research Board, National Research
                    Council ; 204)

                    Includes bibliographies.
                    ISBN 0-309-03664-X (pbk.) : $14.00
```

If you have only a subject, check the subject card:

Subject heading ——————→ SPEED LIMITS--UNITED STATES--COST
EFFECTIVENESS.

```
HE          55 : a decade of experience / [edited
5620           for TRB by Edythe Traylor Crump].   --
.S6A154        Washington, D.C. : Transportation
1984           Research Board, National Research
               Council, 1984.
               vii, 262 p. : ill. ; 23 cm. --
               (Special report / Transportation
               Research Board, National Research
               Council ; 204)

               Includes bibliographies.
               ISBN 0-309-03664-X (pbk.) : $14.00
```

If a card has tracings, check them for possible leads. The author card for the Crump book, for instance, includes the tracing "Speed Limits—United States—cost effectiveness." Checking subject cards under this heading, Robin found several other books, including the one noted below in section 33.5A.

33.3C Getting Books Your Library Doesn't Have

If you can't find a particular book in the card catalog but would like to use it in your research, ask to see the person in charge of interlibrary loan. Provided you can wait at least a week for the book, your library may be able to borrow it for you from another library.

33.4 Finding Articles

The reference works described above in sections 33.2I–K will tell you about articles on your topic. Once you know what those articles are, you need to locate each of them in your library.

If the article appears in a book of articles or essays, find the call number of the book by looking up its title in the card catalog.

If the article appears in a periodical, ask the reference librarian where to find it. Some libraries list all periodicals under their titles (like book titles) in the card catalog; others list periodicals in a separate file, often called a "serials list." If the article you want is more than a year old, it may be in a bound volume with a library call number, and you can locate the volume just as you locate a book. If the article is less than a year old, you will probably find the issue that contains it in the periodical section of your library, where printed instructions or the person in charge will tell you where to locate the issue.

Since it always takes time for new issues to be bound at the end of each year, the issue you want may be neither on the shelf nor in the periodical room, but at the bindery. If you can't find the issue you want, ask the person in charge of the periodical section when and where it will be available.

Finally, if your library doesn't have the periodical you want, the reference librarian may be able to get a photocopy of the article from another library.

33.5 Keeping Track of Your Sources

As you learn about sources from various reference books, you should record the names of authors, titles, and other information (such as names and dates of periodicals) so that you can find the sources in your library. The simplest way to keep track of books is to print information directly from an on-line catalog entry. But if you can't make printouts, or find them too big and floppy to handle easily, you should fill out a 3-by-5-inch source card on each book you plan to consult, and you'll need a source card in any case for each article you plan to see. To illustrate, here are source cards for a book and an article.

a. *HE*
5620
.S6
U558
1980

b. Sostkowsi, R., D. Phillips, R. Monroe, and A. Pearson

c. Determining the Cost of Enforcing the National Maximum Speed Limit

d. Garthersburg, MD: International Association of Chiefs of Police, 1980

33.5A Source Card for a Book

This source card provides the following information:

    a. The library call number at upper left. This enables you to locate the book in the stacks, or to fill out a call slip for the librarian at the circulation desk.

    b. Author's name, last name first. If there is more than one author, the names of those after the first one go in normal order.

    c. Title and subtitle, if any. To distinguish books from articles, underline book titles.

    d. Place of publication, publisher, and date of publication. You'll need all three when you cite the book in your paper. If the book is a reprint, you should note both the date of the reprint and the date of original publication.

33.5B Source Card for an Article

If the periodical containing the article has a call number, put that number in the upper left **(a)**. You also need the author's name **(b)** if the article is signed, and the title of the article in quotation marks **(c)** to distinguish it from a book title. At the bottom goes the name of the periodical, the volume number, the page number(s), and the date **(d)**. Include the issue number also if it's given. (In this case it wasn't given by the *Reader's Guide*.) The final form of the citation may be a little different from what you put on the source card,

---

   a.   L 44.267

   b.   S. Symms

   c.   "65 mph: The Time has Come"

   d.   <u>Car & Driver</u> 32:27 May '87

---

depending on which style of documentation you choose (see chapter 35), but while taking notes just be sure to record all the information on each source.

Once you actually get a particular source, make sure that the information on your source card is accurate and complete. Checking all this information now can save you trouble later, when you may not have the source in hand but will have to cite it fully and accurately. When Robin got her hands on the Symms article, for instance, she learned that the author was U.S. Senator Steve Symms—something useful to know when she cited his words in her paper.

EXERCISE 8 Making Source Cards

Using the card catalog and the list of serials, get the call numbers of one book and of one periodical containing an article that you would like to use in your research. Fill out a card for each source as shown above.

33.6 Using Microtexts

Because of storage problems, libraries have increased their use of microtexts—printed material photographically reduced in size and readable only with the aid of mechanical viewers. Some excellent sources, such as complete files of major newspapers and magazines, may be available only in this form. When Robin looked up the Symms' article in *Car & Driver*, for instance, she found it on microfiche—a card on which reduced pages are arranged in rows. Robin also learned that some microfiche-reading machines can produce a full-size photograph of whatever appears on the screen. She was able to use such a machine, and in less than a minute she had her own complete copy of the article.

33.7 Conducting an Interview

An interview can enliven both the process of research and the finished product. Anyone with a special knowledge of your topic can be a living source of information that might not be readily available anywhere else. In addition, quotes and paraphrases from an interview can bring a special vitality to your paper.

To get as much as possible from an interview, we suggest that you follow these steps:

1. Find the right person to interview. If there is someone on your college faculty or living near the college who specializes in your topic, your teacher or a reference librarian can probably tell you. When Robin Martinez asked a reference librarian for help in finding sources on speed limits, she was advised to supplement printed sources by talking with a representative of the New Hampshire State Police—someone with first-hand experience of speed limits and their effect. So she telephoned the State Police headquarters in Concord, N.H., and got the name of a police captain who would be able to answer her questions.

2. Arrange the interview beforehand. Several days or more before you plan to conduct the interview, telephone the person to make an appointment for a specified period of time. A face-to-face interview is best, but if that's not possible, make an appointment for a telephone interview. And however you conduct the interview, you should get advance permission if you plan to use a tape recorder.

3. Prepare your questions. A good interviewer comes prepared with some preliminary knowledge of the topic gleaned from printed sources, and—most important—with a list of productive questions. Productive questions call for more than a "yes" or "no" answer, and also for more than a simple expression of personal feeling. They call for information. Compare these questions:

a. How do you feel about smoking in restaurants?
b. Should smoking be banned in restaurants?
c. If all restaurants are required to maintain separate sections for smokers and non-smokers, how will this requirement affect the restaurant business?

Question (a) invites a statement of personal feeling such as "I hate it," and question (b) invites a one-word answer: "yes" or "no." Only question (c) calls for the kind of information you need in a research paper.

Productive questions can be *open-ended* or *pinpointed*. An open-ended question stimulates a wide-ranging response, while a pinpointed question calls for a specific piece of information:

> OPEN-ENDED: How have tobacco companies responded to the growing body of evidence that links smoking to cancer?

PINPOINTED: At what point—at what number of cigarettes a day—does smoking begin to pose a serious danger to health?

4. Ask follow-up questions whenever you need to clarify a point. Though you should come to the interview with a list of questions prepared in advance, you should also be ready for surprises. If your interviewee says something unexpected or puzzling, ask a follow-up question. This is what Robin did in her interview with Captain Loomis, as shown by the following excerpt from her transcript of the interview:

> R.M.: I've read that an increase in average speed doesn't much affect the frequency of accidents. Is that true in your experience?
>
> Captain Loomis: In a sense, yes. The safest situation is a line of cars all traveling at the same speed. If the average speed is 55, a driver going 30 can be just as likely to cause an accident as one going 80—in good driving conditions, that is.
>
> Interviewer: What if conditions aren't good?
>
> Captain Loomis: Then it's different. You see—most drivers adjust their speed to the roads they're traveling on. In other words, they'll slow down after leaving an interstate highway for a secondary road. What they don't adjust to is *conditions*—like rain and ice and snow. Every year after the first snowfall, we get cars sliding all over the road. People don't realize how slippery things get in the winter, and all of a sudden you've got a demolition derby out there. Bad weather and high speed just don't mix.

The point about conditions was something Robin hadn't seen in her reading, and as page 7 of her paper shows (on p. 576), it helped her to buttress her argument. She also used the phrase "demolition derby" and the final statement about bad weather.

5. Take careful notes or tape the interview. The best way to record the whole interview is to get it on tape (with the permission of the interviewee) and then transcribe it. But if you don't have or can't use a tape recorder, make sure your notes are accurate and thorough.

6. Follow up the interview. If you quote from the interview in your paper, check with the interviewee to make sure that your quotations are accurate and consistent with the context from which they are taken. It's also courteous to send the interviewee a note of thanks and a copy of your paper.

EXERCISE 9 Preparing an Interview

Describe the kind of person you would most like to interview for your research paper and then make a list of at least six questions that you would ask.

33.8 Choosing Which Sources to Consult

As you work your way through reference books and catalogs, you will probably find more sources than you can manage in the time you have. You should therefore look for the following:

1. Works with obvious relevance to your topic. A title such as *55: A Decade of Experience* clearly promises a book important to anyone studying the history of the 55 mph speed limit. But once Robin decided to focus on speed limits, she felt no obligation to see all of the books in her library that dealt with automobile safety. She could skip over books such as Jeffrey O'Connell's *Safety Last: An Indictment of the Auto Industry* because that deals with the safety of automobiles themselves, not with the effect and enforcement of speed limits.

2. Works published recently. Most of the time you can safely assume that recently published works give you up-to-date information, which is valuable not just for current topics but for topics concerned with the past. A recent book on the American Revolution, for instance, may be more reliable and more informative than one published in 1862 or even 1962. Furthermore, a recent book will usually cite most or all of the important books on its subject that came before it, so that you may use it as a bibliographical source.

3. Works frequently cited. Any book or article that is cited frequently in other books or articles is probably important and influential. To learn how often a particular source has been cited in a given year, see one of these three: the *Science Citation Index*, published bi-monthly and cumulated every five years; the *Social Science Citation Index*, published three times a year and cumulated annually; and the *Arts & Humanities Citation Index,* published in the same way.

4. Classics. Some books stay alive long after they are published. Classics include not just enduringly great works of poetry, fiction, and drama, but also nonfiction works of lasting importance in various fields: in political theory, Alexis de Tocqueville's *Democracy in America* (1835); in biology, Charles Darwin's *Origin of Species* (1859); in psychology, Sigmund Freud's *Interpretation of Dreams* (1900); in physics, Albert Einstein's *Relativity* (1916); in economics, John Maynard Keynes's *General Theory of Employment, Interest, and Money* (1936). Unfortunately, catalogs won't tell you whether a particular library book is a classic in its field. But if you start your research by reading an overview of your topic, or a recent book on it, you are almost certain to find out what the classics in the field are.

5. Primary and Secondary Sources. *Primary* means "first," and a primary source is one on which later, or secondary, sources are based. Depending on the subject, primary sources may be more or less valuable than secondary ones.

There are two kinds of primary sources: informational and authorial. An *informational* primary source is any firsthand account of an experience or discovery—an Arctic explorer's diary of an expedition, a scientist's report on the results of an experiment, a news story on a disaster written by someone who has seen it. *Authorial* primary sources are the writings of the individual you are studying. If you were writing a paper on James Baldwin, for instance, Baldwin's novels, essays, and letters would be your primary sources, and the critical essays that have been written *about* Baldwin's work would be your secondary sources.

You need not always draw a line between primary and secondary sources, nor should you always feel obliged to start with primary ones. If you are investigating a particular author or thinker, you should normally start by reading at least some of what he or she has written and then see what has been written about that person's works. But if you are seeking information of an impersonal kind, you do best to start with secondary sources and let them lead you to the primary ones. Secondary sources are further than primary sources from what they describe, but for that very reason, they may give you a more detached, objective point of view.

6. Books with bibliographies. As already noted, the catalog tells you whether the book has a bibliography—a list of related books and articles. Because it focuses on a given topic, a bibliography can save you time—especially if it appears in a recent book.

Some bibliographies are annotated, supplying descriptions and evaluations of the works they list. So they can help you decide which sources are worth consulting.

33.9 Examining Your Sources

When you have gathered sources you plan to use, you are ready to examine them. As you read, of course, you will probably learn about other sources, and you should keep a record of these for later investigation. But your chief task now is to examine the materials you have on hand. Here are some suggestions about how to do so.

1. Organize your reading time. List in order of importance the books and articles you plan to consult, and set up a reading schedule. Plan to finish all your reading and note-taking a week before the paper is due. After you have done your reading and note-taking, you will need time to assimilate your sources, to make coherent sense out of them.

2. Read selectively. You can often get what you want from a source without reading all of it. Since you may have to consult many sources in a very short time, you should learn to read them selectively.

If your source is a book, read the preface to get an idea of its scope and purpose. Then scan the table of contents and the index for specific discussions of your topic. Then read any promising sections, watching for important facts and interpretations and taking notes.

3. Read responsibly. Respect the context of what you quote. Reading selectively doesn't mean reading carelessly or lifting statements out of context. To understand what you are quoting and to judge it adequately, you may have to read a good part of the section or chapter in which it appears—enough, at least, to familiarize yourself with the context.

4. Read critically. Critical reading is more important for an analytical research paper than for a survey, but in either case, you need to decide whether what you are reading is worth citing at all. Beyond that, you need to decide how reliable its evidence and arguments are. If the writer gives opinions without facts to support them, or makes statements of "fact" without citing sources, you should be suspicious. (For more on this point, see section 10.2E, "Judging the Supporting Points in an Essay.") You should also compare your sources. If you find one of them more reliable or more persuasive than another, you're already beginning to see how you will present them in your paper.

33.10 Taking Notes

You can take notes on your sources in a variety of ways: by writing on index cards, legal pads, or loose sheets; by photocopying the pages you need; or by typing them out with a word processor. Here we illustrate two of these methods.

33.10A Taking Notes with a Word Processor

If you can bring the books and articles you need to a word processor, you can use it for making all of your notes. (If you don't have a word processor, skip to section 33.10B.) Once you've typed a note into the word processor, you will be able to call it up for use anywhere in your paper without retyping it. Also, if you use headlines for each aspect of your topic, you can begin to organize your notes even as you take them. Below, for instance, is a portion of the notes Robin took for her paper on speed limits.

```
SPEED LIMITS PROVOKE OPPOSITION BECAUSE PEOPLE LIKE TO SPEED

"Plans to have general speed limits imposed arouse excited

opposition expressly because, among other things, the

pleasures of speeding are threatened. The 'speed demon'

often does not drive fast so much to reach some
```

destination as to enjoy the primitive sensation of speed

for its own sake. The speedster drives fast even when he

is in no hurry."

                                    Naatanen, Road 47

Comment: Could this be the real reason for the repeal of

55?

"If the limit is 55, where do such companies as Porsche,

General Motors, Ferrari . . . get off making cars that

will double the double-nickel without even breathing

hard?"

Auto ads increasingly show "cars flying down twisty rural

roads in dazzling exhibitions of cornering power and

acceleration."

"One patrolman . . . once told me, 'If I had to drive 55

all day, I'd go nuts.' "

                                    Yates, "Hypocrisy" 21

Comment: The excitement of speed--who can resist it?

Robin first wrote the headline for the note from Naatanen's
book. Then, when she took her notes on Yates's article, she realized that they would fit under this headline too. She used a
broken line to separate one note from the other, but the headline helped her to group them together. Her comments after each
note helped her to think about how she would use this material,
which gave her the substance of the second paragraph on page 15
of her paper (see p. 584).

     After each note or set of quotations, Robin wrote the author's
name, the first important item in the title (sometimes it's a number, such as 55), and the page number(s) of the material used. To

keep track of her sources, she created a file called "55SOURCE." There she entered each new source in alphabetical order by the last name of the author or editor. (For unsigned sources she used the first important item in the title.) So the two sources quoted above looked like this in her source file:

Naatanen, Risto, and Heikki Summala. Road-User Behavior and Traffic Accidents. Amsterdam: North-Holland Publishing Company, 1976.

Yates, Brock. "Hypocrisy on Board." Car & Driver, Vol. 32, No. 2. August 1986, page 21.

If you file each of your sources in this way, you'll end up with an alphabetical list that can be called up and inserted at the end of your paper after you've written it. (For detailed advice on documenting your sources, see chapter 35.)

Once you've taken all your notes with a word processor, make a back-up copy of the file on your disk and *print a hard copy* for reference when you're away from the terminal. You'll also find that a hard copy of your notes makes them easier to review all at once.

33.10B Taking Notes on Index Cards

If you don't have access to a word processor, the simplest way of taking notes is with a stack of index cards. Putting each note on a separate card considerably simplifies the task of *arranging* your notes when you start to organize your paper.

We therefore suggest that you use one whole card (4-by-6 or 5-by-7 inches) for each quotation, paraphrase, or summary. The larger size makes it easy to keep note cards separate from source cards and leaves room for comments of your own. (If a note is long, continue it on a second card, which can be stapled to the first.) At the end of each note, write the last name of the author or editor, the first important item in the title (it may be a number, such as 55), and the page number(s) of the material you have used. If the source is unsigned, just use the title word and page. But in any case, *be sure to note the source.* If you don't, you won't be able to cite the source in your paper, and if you use the material without citing the source, you will be guilty of plagiarism (see section 34.2C).

To illustrate note-taking by hand, here is one of Robin's notes as it would have looked on an index card:

SPEED VARIANCE

It may be impossible to raise speed limits while keeping speed variance down. For example, higher average speed creates more variance at intersections, where drivers have to slow down in order to enter and exit.

Crump, <u>55</u>, 241

So we can't really isolate speed variance from average speeds?

Unlike the notes on p. 524, this note has no quotation marks because—as explained in the next section—it summarizes and paraphrases its source rather than quoting it.

33.11 Summarizing and Paraphrasing

You need some quotations in your paper, as explained below in section 33.12. But if you quote too much, the reader may lose track of what you yourself want to say. Whether you take notes on index cards or on a computer screen, therefore, you should learn to summarize your sources occasionally and to paraphrase them as well, putting them into your own words. (On summarizing, see section 10.2C; on paraphrasing, see section 10.2D.) Summarizing and paraphrasing a passage are good ways of getting a firm grip on its meaning.

Take for example the note displayed just above. This note derives from a passage on page 241 of *55: A Decade of Experience,* edited by Edythe Crump. A source card on the book would like like this:

Crump, Edythe Traylor, Ed.

55: A Decade of Experience

Transportation Research Board
  Special Report 204

Washington, DC: National Research Council, 1984

Since the title page of the book presents it as a numbered report, the source card includes that fact along with the other information.

To see how Robin used the material from this book, compare her note with the original passage from _55: A Decade of Experience:_

> In addition, whether speed limits could be raised without simultaneously increasing speed variance is uncertain. It is uncertain which policy measures, such as minimum speed limits, might be used to constrain the speed variance, nor is it known what their likely impacts would be. Further, there are physical and behavioral constraints on how effective such policies could be. For example, wider variance in speed occurs at intersections where the minimum speed is defined by the slower speed necessary for exiting and entering traffic. Higher average speed would increase speed variance at these locations.

Robin's note (p. 526) does three things with this passage:

1. It gives the passage a subject heading that will help Robin decide how to use this note in her paper.

2. It catches the essential point of the passage in just two sentences. You can often summarize a writer's words in less time than it would take to copy all of them out (or even find your way to a photocopying machine), and when you summarize a passage, you prove to yourself that you understand it.

3. It clearly separates the source material from the response. If you don't clearly separate the two, you risk confusing them, and that may lead to plagiarism when you write the paper. (See section 34.2C.)

4. It records Robin's response. So even while taking notes, she's beginning to write her paper.

As you summarize or paraphrase, you should of course quote particular words or phrases that seem important. Compare the following paragraph from the Symms article (cited above, p. 516) with Robin's note on it.

> PARAGRAPH: The CHP [California Highway Patrol] deploys 85 percent of its officers on 55-mph roadways and spends $3 million a year for three airplanes and ground support to enforce 55. Despite the cost and effort, California is on the verge of losing federal highway funds because of high non-compliance rates. These expenditures—made primarily to avoid losing federal funds—are not only ineffective, but they are diverting resources away from more effective law-enforcement efforts, such as keeping drunk drivers off the road.

NOTE:

ENFORCING 55

The three million dollars California spends each year on enforcing 55 could be more effectively spent on "keeping drunk drivers off the road."

Symms, "65" 27

Was 55 really unenforceable? Was all that money wasted?

In this compressed version of Symms's paragraph, Robin quotes only what is most important to her, and the quoted phrase becomes part of her own sentence. (For more on fitting quotations to your own prose, see section 24.6.)

33.12 Quoting from Sources

You should quote rather than summarize a statement when it precisely and concisely expresses one of the author's fundamental views, when its language is notably vivid or eloquent, or when you expect to analyze it in detail. (See for instance the first of Robin's notes on page 523.) In quoting, observe the following guidelines:

1. Quote accurately. Be careful to avoid mistakes of any kind. After copying a passage, always proofread your version, comparing it with the original.

2. Use quotation marks to indicate the beginning and the end of quoted material. As the note card on p. 528 illustrates, you must always distinguish between quotation and paraphrase in your notes. For detailed advice on how to punctuate quotations, see chapter 29.

3. Use ellipsis dots (. . .) to indicate that you have deliberately omitted words in writing out the quotation. Be careful not to make an omission that distorts the original. You may leave out words only when they are not essential to the meaning of what you quote.

ORIGINS

"One cannot afford to be naive in dealing with dreams. They originate in a spirit that is not quite human, but is rather a breadth of nature. . . . If we want to characterize this spirit, we shall certainly get closer to it in the sphere of ancient mythologies, or the fables of the primeval forest, than in the consciousness of modern man."   Jung, "Approaching" 52

So dreaming is a kind of myth-making?

Compare the quotation on the note card above with the complete passage in Carl Jung's "Approaching the Unconscious," *Man and His Symbols*, ed. Jung and M.-L. von Franz (Garden City, NY: Doubleday, 1964):

> One cannot afford to be naive in dealing with dreams. They originate in a spirit that is not quite human, but is rather a breath of nature—a spirit of the beautiful and generous as well as of the cruel goddess. If we want to characterize this spirit, we shall certainly get closer to it in the sphere of ancient mythologies, or the fables of the primeval forest, than in the consciousness of modern man.

The researcher uses three ellipsis dots to indicate that the last part of the second sentence has been omitted; the fourth dot is a period. If the words before the omission did not make a complete sentence, the researcher would use just the three ellipsis dots and then finish the quotation: "One cannot . . . be naive in dealing with dreams."

What the researcher has omitted in this note is not essential to the meaning of the passage quoted. But see what happens to the passage when a quotation does leave out something essential:

> One cannot afford to be naive in dealing with dreams. They originate in a spirit that is not quite human, but is rather a breath of nature. . . . If we want to characterize this spirit, we shall certainly get closer to it . . . in the consciousness of modern man.

Jung is now made to say just the opposite of what he actually said. This is the worst possible way of quoting a source. (For more on ellipsis dots, see section 29.6B.)

4. If you underline anything that is not underlined in the original, say so in parentheses:

> Jung finds something mysterious in dreams. "They originate," he writes, "in a spirit that is <u>not quite human</u>" (emphasis added).

5. Use brackets to mark explanatory words added within a quotation. The note below derives from Erich Fromm's *The Forgotten Language* (New York: Rinehart, 1951). The brackets in the note indicate an insertion made by the note-taker to indicate who *He* is. (For more on brackets, see section 29.6A.)

```
┌─────────────────────────────────────────────────────┐
│                    FUNCTIONS                          │
│  "Not only do insights into our relations to others   │
│   or theirs to us, value judgments and predictions    │
│   occur in our dreams, but also intellectual          │
│   operations superior to those in the waking state.   │
│   ... The best known example of this kind of dream    │
│   is the one of the discoverer of the Benzine ring.   │
│   He [Friedrich Kekule] had been searching for the    │
│   chemical formula for Benzine ... and one night the  │
│   correct formula stood before his eyes in a dream.   │
│   He was fortunate enough to remember it after he     │
│   awoke."                                             │
│                          Fromm, Forgotten 45          │
│  So one function of dreams is problem solving.        │
└─────────────────────────────────────────────────────┘
```

For advice on how to *introduce* quotations within the paper itself, see section 34.2B.

33.13 Formulating Your Thesis

We said earlier that doing research is like listening to a long discussion and then suddenly realizing that you've formed an opinion of your own. If you plan to write an argumentative paper and you discover your thesis before you reach the end of your research, you may be ready to start writing as soon as you have finished reading and note-taking. But if you're still looking for a thesis, reviewing your note cards is a good way to find it.

Rereading your cards gives you a concentrated view of all your research, and thus helps you to decide—if you haven't decided already—what basic questions you will try to answer. As Robin reread her cards, she found herself questioning the arguments that had been made against the 55 mph speed limit. Was it really true, as critics said, that average speed had no effect on fatalities, so that speed limits made no difference? And was the limit really impossible to enforce? Since she had found evidence to contradict both of these points, she began to ask herself if there were other reasons behind the repeal of the national speed limit. These questions led her to a basic question: What does the repeal of a remarkably effective safety measure tell us about American motorists? That question led in turn to a tentative answer, a tentative statement of thesis: the repeal of the 55 mph speed limit shows that American motorists care less about saving lives than about making time.

33.14 Filling Gaps in Your Research

While you are rereading and sorting your notes, or even after you have decided what kind of paper you will write and what its thesis will be, you may discover that you need to know more about one or two things. You may suddenly discover that you have failed to consult an important source—one that several of your sources often refer to—or have failed to answer an important question. While sorting her own notes, Robin realized that she hadn't ever checked to see what had happened to annual automobile fatalities since the 55 mph speed limit was repealed. Were they up, down, or unchanged? By going back to the reference librarian, she learned that a book called *Accident Facts* would give her the answer to this question: an answer that would help to clinch the argument of her paper.

34

Writing the Research Paper

In every writing project there comes a time when you must shift from exploring your subject and gathering materials about it to writing a full first draft. Some students start writing as soon as they have headlined their notes in the computer, as shown in section 33.10A, or sorted their note cards into separate piles for each aspect of the topic they are writing about. If you believe that your headlines or your sorted notes will give you as much guidance as you need, then by all means start writing. But if you don't feel you're ready to start writing yet, you would do well to make an outline first.

34.1 Making an Outline

Once you have established the main subject headings of your paper, you must decide the order in which you will arrange the headings and the order in which, under each heading, you will present your materials. Most importantly, as we have said already in section 33.13, you need a framing question or a thesis. If you plan to write an explanatory research paper, you need a question that will frame or define the survey—such as the question of how working mothers can reconcile their conflicting obligations (see. p. 670). If you plan to write an argumentative research paper, you need a thesis, a statement you will defend.

In Robin's case, a basic question about the real reasons for the repeal of the 55 mph speed limit led to a thesis about what the repeal shows. Once Robin had formulated her thesis, she could devise an order or sequence in which to present the main headings of her topic. Since she had in her notes all of the material she would need, and since she had in her headlines all the points she would cover, she was able to draft a full-sentence outline:

> Thesis: The repeal of the 55 mph speed limit shows that American motorists will sacrifice anything—including life itself—for the convenience and pleasure of driving faster than 55.
>
> I. Speed limits do affect the number of annual fatalities.
>   A. Though other factors reduced fatalities from 1974 to 1987, the 55 mph speed limit by itself saved thousands of lives.
>   B. Though fatalities may be due more to speed variance than to speed itself, higher average speed makes speed variance higher, and thus makes fatalities higher too.
>   C. Annual fatalities have risen since the 55 mph speed limit was repealed.
> II. The costs of the 55 mph speed limit were fully justified by all the savings it generated, especially the saving of human life.
>   A. The limit required 350,000 hours of additional driving time each year for each life saved.
>   B. But it saved millions on fuel, maintenance, car repair bills, medical costs, and legal fees.
>   C. By sparing thousands from death or serious injury, it gave us the value of all they lived to produce.
> III. Though average speeds approached 60 mph in the last years of the 55 mph limit, it remained effective in keeping speeds down.
>   A. Most motorists regularly drove over the 55 mph speed limit in the mid-1980s.
>   B. Critics charged that money spent enforcing it was not justified by the results.
>   C. But the 55 mph speed limit kept average speeds well below what they had been before the law was passed.
> IV. Conclusion. Since the 55 mph limit actually reduced fatalities and injuries, repeal of the limit shows that American motorists equate speeding with freedom, and will not tolerate anything that keeps them from going faster than 55.

A full-sentence outline allows you to see exactly where you are headed from the beginning of the paper to the end. As an ordered structure of assertions that work together to support the thesis, this kind of outline plainly defines the writer's argumentative strategy.

34.2 Managing Your Sources as You Write

34.2A Citing Sources in the First Draft

In the final draft of your paper, you may be asked to use one of the methods explained below (see chapter 35) to cite your sources. But in writing the first draft, you can cite them simply by putting the following items in parenthesis after each use of a source:

1. author's last name
2. first important item in title
3. page number(s) of material used

Though you won't need all of these items for every reference in the final version of your paper, as explained in section 35.2, using them all in the first draft will ensure that you have all the information you may need on each source. Item 2, for instance, will prevent confusion in case you end up citing more than one source by the same author.

To illustrate, here is a passage from the first draft of Robin's paper:

> The NRC notes that during the first year of the 55 mph speed limit, "the percentage of drivers exceeding 65 mph on the rural Interstates declined from 50 to 9 percent. . . . As a result the variance of speeds on Interstate highways narrowed considerably" (Crump, *55* 24). Even some opponents of the 55 limit have recognized this point. "Lowering the limit," writes Alan Pisarski, "pushed those who normally traveled much faster down to speeds close to 55, while those who usually traveled at 55 continued to do so. This resulted in more vehicles traveling within a small range of speed—and thus safer roads" (Pisarski, "Deep" 16).

34.2B Introducing Your Sources

Whenever you use a source in any way, you should introduce it smoothly, either naming the author or clearly indicating the boundaries of your material. Quotation marks show when you are quoting, but whenever you summarize or paraphrase, you must *signal* that fact, showing precisely where your debt to a source begins and ends. In each of the following passages, the opening signal is italicized:

> *According to Senator Symms,* funds spent on the enforcement of the 55 mph limit in California could have been more effectively spent on "keeping drunk drivers off the road" (Symms, "65 MPH" 27).

> Even after allowing for the effects of reduced travel and safer overall driving conditions in 1974, *the National Research Council found* that the speed limit alone saved between 3,200 and 4,500 lives that year (Crump, 55 43).

> *As John A. Gardiner observes,* no police force can arrest everyone who violates a traffic law. "Limited resources and a multitude of other police duties, if nothing else, make it impossible" (Gardiner, *Traffic* 5).

> What finally brought repeal of the limit, however, was not so much the economic case against it as the argument that it could no longer be effectively enforced. *A California writer tells us* what happened in August 1985, when he drove a motorcycle for 30 miles in the slow right lane of a California freeway at exactly 55 mph. Thirty-seven vehicles came up from behind in that lane to go around him, and in nearby lanes he was passed by 170 cars before sheer boredom led him to stop counting ("Life" 18).[†]

EXCEPTION: You do not need an opening signal to introduce statements of fact when the source is cited immediately afterwards:

> Average speed on rural interstates in 1985 was 59.5 for the country as a whole, and over 60 mph in 23 states (Symms, "65 MPH" 27).

On fitting quotations into your own sentences, see section 24.6. On punctuating quotations, see chapter 29.

[†] The article cited here is unsigned, and is therefore cited by its title alone. (For more on this point see section 35.2A, no. 8.)

34.2C Plagiarism

Plagiarism is presenting the words or thoughts of another writer as if they were your own. You commit plagiarism whenever you use a source *in any way* without indicating that you have used it. If you quote anything at all, even a phrase, you must put quotation marks around it or set it off from your text; if you summarize or paraphrase an author's words, you must clearly indicate where the summary or paraphrase begins and ends; if you use an author's idea, you must say that you are doing so. In every instance, you must also formally acknowledge the written source from which you took the material.

You may use a source without formal acknowledgment only when you refer to a specific phrase, statement, or passage that you have used and acknowledged earlier in the same paper. But when you use new material from a source already cited, you must make a new acknowledgment.

We have explained above how to use sources honestly, how to draw the line between what is your own and what you have taken from others. Now here are examples of various kinds of plagiarism. In each instance, the source is a passage from p. 102 of E. R. Dodds's *The Greeks and the Irrational* (Berkeley, 1951; rpt. Boston: Beacon, 1957). First, here is the original note, copied accurately from the book:

FUNCTIONS OF DREAMS: FANTASY

"If the working world has certain advantages of solidity and continuity, its social opportunities are terribly restricted. In it we meet, as a rule, only the neighbors, whereas the dream world offers the chance of intercourse, however fugitive, with our distant friends, our dead, and our gods. For normal men it is the sole experience in which they escape the offensive and incomprehensible bondage of time and space." Dodds, *Greeks* 102

Fantasy— an obvious function, but nicely described.

And here are five ways of plagiarizing this source.

1. Word-for-word continuous copying without quotation marks or mention of the author's name:

> Dreams help us satisfy another important psychic need—our need to vary our social life. This need is regularly thwarted in our waking moments. If the waking world has certain advantages of solidity and continuity, its social opportunities are terribly restricted. In it we meet, as a rule, only the neighbors, whereas the dream world offers us the chance of intercourse, however fugitive, with our distant friends. We awaken from such encounters feeling refreshed, the dream having liberated us from the here and now. . . .

2. Copying many words and phrases without quotation marks or mention of the author's name:

> Dreams help us satisfy another psychic need—our need to vary our social life. In the waking world our social opportunities, for example, are terribly restricted. As a rule, we usually encounter only the neighbors. In the dream world, on the other hand, we have the chance of meeting our distant friends. For most of us it is the sole experience in which we escape the bondage of time and space. . . .

3. Copying an occasional key word or phrase without quotation marks or mention of the author's name:

> Dreams help us satisfy another psychic need—our need to vary our social life. During our waking hours our social opportunities are terribly restricted. We see only the people next door and our business associates. In contrast, whenever we dream, we can see our distant friends. Even though the encounter is brief, we awaken refreshed, having freed ourselves from the bondage of the here and now. . . .

4. Paraphrasing without mention of the author's name:

> Dreams help us satisfy another important psychic need—our need to vary our social life. When awake, we are creatures of this time and this place. Those we meet are usually those we live near and work with. When dreaming, on the other hand, we can meet faroff friends. We awaken refreshed by our flight from the here and now. . . .

5. <u>Taking the author's idea without acknowledging the source:</u>

> Dreams help us to satisfy another important psychic
> need—the need for a change. They liberate us from the here
> and now, taking us out of the world we normally live in. . . .

A final note: if there is anything about plagiarism you do not
understand, *ask your teacher.*

EXERCISE 1 Recognizing Plagiarism

Pick out the sentences, phrases, and key words that were taken from
Dodds in examples 1–3.

EXERCISE 2 Recognizing Plagiarism

Read this two-paragraph passage. Then read the summary that follows, and indicate whether any part of the summary—aside from
the word "motifs"—should be in quotation marks.

> And, speaking more generally, it is plain foolishness to
> believe in ready-made systematic guides to dream interpreta-
> tion, as if one could simply buy a reference book and look up
> a particular symbol. No dream symbol can be separated from
> the individual who dreams it, and there is no definite or   5
> straightforward interpretation of any dream. Each individual
> varies so much in the way that his unconscious complements
> or compensates his conscious mind that it is impossible to be
> sure how far dreams and their symbols can be classified at all.
> It is true that there are dreams and single symbols (I   10
> should prefer to call them "motifs") that are typical and often
> occur. Among such motifs are falling, flying, being persecuted
> by dangerous animals or hostile men, being insufficiently or
> absurdly clothed in public places, being in a hurry or lost in a
> milling crowd, fighting with useless weapons or being wholly   15
> defenseless, running hard yet getting nowhere. A typical
> infantile motif is the dream of growing infinitely small or
> infinitely big, or being transformed from one to the other—as
> you find it, for instance, in Lewis Carroll's *Alice in Wonder-*
> *land.* But I must stress again that these are motifs that must   20
> be considered in the context of the dream itself, not as self-
> explanatory ciphers.
> —Carl G. Jung, "Approaching the Unconscious," *Man and His*
> *Symbols,* ed. Jung and M.-L. von Franz (Garden City, NY:
> Doubleday, 1964) 53.

SUMMARY: According to Carl G. Jung in "Approaching the Unconscious," it would be just plain foolishness for anyone to think he or she could interpret dreams reliably by buying a ready-made reference book. No such guide has value because it is impossible to separate a dream symbol from the person who dreams it, and the unconscious of everyone is unique. Jung does admit that certain dreams and symbols come often to many. Calling these "motifs," he lists several, including falling, fighting with useless weapons, and running hard yet getting nowhere. But he emphasizes that even the motifs cannot be understood properly unless considered in the context of each dream itself.

34.3 Composing the Paper as a Whole

Composing a research paper is in many ways like writing an ordinary essay. You need to introduce your survey or argument, to develop it with the aid of your notes, and to conclude it. Beyond these general requirements, the writing of a research paper makes its own special demands. To help you meet them, we make these suggestions:

1. Introduce the paper by clearly announcing its topic and thesis, or its topic and framing question. If the outline is not quite firm as you start to write, you don't have to write the introduction first. You can write it after you've written the rest of the paper—when you know exactly what you're introducing. But whenever you write it, the introduction should clearly establish the topic of your paper and its thesis or its framing question.

Like any good introduction, the introduction to a research paper should also take account of the reader. If the paper is to be argumentative, the introduction should start by describing the views that the paper will challenge. Here, for instance, is Robin's introduction:

> In March 1974, a shortage of fuel precipitated by the Arab oil embargo led Congress to impose a temporary national speed limit of 55 miles per hour. When the number of highway fatalities dropped by some 9,100, from 55,511 in 1973 to 46,402 in 1974, the lifesaving benefits of the new speed limit became obvious, and Congress made it permanent (Crump 1, 15).† But even though it came to be recognized as "the great-

† For guidance on the parenthetical style of documentation illustrated here, see chapter 35 (pp. 544–65). For the complete text of Robin's paper, see chapter 37 (pp. 570–88).

est traffic safety measure ever instituted in our history"
(*National* 75), it did not last. Almost from the beginning, it
provoked an opposition that steadily grew and that finally
prevailed in March 1987, when Congress voted to let states
raise the limit from 55 to 65 on rural Interstates ("65 MPH"
12).

Critics of the 55 mph speed limit made many arguments against it. They claimed that speed was wrongly blamed
for causing fatalities. They cited the millions of hours and
dollars lost each year in extra time spent behind the wheel.
Most of all, they argued that the law grew unenforceable
because nearly everyone disobeyed it. But hard evidence shows
that the 55 mph speed limit did save thousands of lives. In
light of that crucial fact, what does repeal of the limit tell us?
It tells us, I believe, that American motorists will sacrifice
anything—including life itself—for the convenience and pleasure of driving faster than 55 miles per hour.

Robin begins by clearly identifying her topic, summarizing its history, and stating the arguments that her paper will challenge. Then
she presents her own position—the thesis she will defend.

The introduction to an explanatory research paper leads up
to a framing question rather than a thesis, but it can appeal to the
reader by describing general attitudes before focusing on a specific
problem. Consider the introduction to Erica Berl's paper, "Options
for the Working Mother" (starting on p. 670):

Everyone knows that women are no longer staying at
home. They have gone out into the world of paid work, filling
not only such traditionally feminine roles as secretary and
clerk, but also such typically masculine roles as lawyer, doctor, stockbroker, business executive, governor, and United
States senator. But statistics show that a growing percentage
of working women are mothers of preschool children. While
less than a third of these mothers held jobs outside the home
in 1970, the figure rose to nearly a half by 1978 and is expected
to keep on rising into the 1990s.[†] A crucial question of our
time, therefore, is how these women can reconcile the demands
of a career with the responsibilities of child-rearing. By examining various answers to this question, we can understand the
options open to American women.

[†] The source of this information is given in a note to the complete text of Erica's paper,
which appears on pp. 670–81. For guidance on documenting with notes, see Appendix 1.

Beginning with general observations about working women, this introduction moves to the particular problems faced by working mothers. The question raised in the next to last sentence identifies a conflict and thus clearly introduces a survey of possible solutions.

2. <u>Make your sources work together</u>. Writing the main part of a research paper is partly a process of weaving your sources into a coherent whole. You are responsible for showing your reader the relations among your sources, for explaining what they signify when taken together. Quote only as much as you need to make your point, and no more.

In general, your commentary on anything you quote should be at least as long as the quotation itself. If a lengthy passage is important enough to be quoted in full, you ought to have something important to say about it. If you don't have much to say about a passage, don't quote it at length, or at all. A long quotation followed by a single sentence of commentary usually tells the reader that the writer is dozing his or her way through the paper.

Remember, too, that quoting is not the only way of using the material in your notes. If you have summarized and paraphrased some of your material while taking notes on it, you already have in hand alternatives to quotation, restatements of your sources in your own words. You will find that when you use summaries instead of lengthy quotations, you can wield your sources much more effectively, that you can make them talk to each other instead of just stolidly filling up a page. Consider this passage from Robin's paper:

> What finally brought repeal of the limit, however, was not so much the economic case against it as the argument that it could no longer be effectively enforced. A California writer tells us what happened in August 1985, when he drove a motorcycle for 30 miles in the slow right lane of a California freeway at exactly 55 mph. Thirty-seven vehicles came up from behind in that lane to go around him, and in nearby lanes he was passed by 170 cars before sheer boredom led him to stop counting ("Life" 18). What he saw typified American driving in 1985. Average speed on rural interstates in 1985 was 59.5 mph for the country as a whole, and over 60 mph in 23 states (Symms 27). "By actual measurement," according to one report, "75 percent of the vehicles on monitored stretches of rural interstate highways were exceeding the limit" that year (Martz 14).

Robin cites three different sources in this paragraph, but they all work together to support its main point.

3. <u>End an argumentative research paper by reaffirming your thesis and stating its implications.</u> Here is Robin's last paragraph:

> We can indeed. We can readily imagine their impatience, their frustration, and their resentment of a law that kept them in harness when they longed to gallop, to show what all of their horsepower could do. But if we are going to indulge this lust for speed, we should at least be honest enough to recognize what comes with it. After all the objections to the 55 mph speed limit have been studied, after all the arguments for higher limits have been weighed, we must face the hard and simple fact that higher speeds mean more fatalities. Human life is the price we have already begun to pay for repealing the national speed limit.

This concluding paragraph restates the thesis but also points up its implications: we cannot evade the costly consequences of higher speeds.

4. <u>End an explanatory research paper by summarizing its findings and stating its implications.</u> Here is the concluding paragraph of Erica's paper on working mothers:

> It takes a gift for organization to manage both a job and a family. But given the variety of ways in which the demands of each can be met, a woman no longer needs to feel that she must sacrifice one for the other, must abandon her family for the sake of her job or give up her job for the sake of her family. Working women who happen to be mothers have made themselves an indispensable part of the workforce, and they are here to stay.

Noting "the variety of ways" in which a working mother can meet her conflicting obligations, Erica neatly sums up her survey. Then she states its implications: women are no longer bound to choose between motherhood and a career.

35
Documenting the Research Paper

In the final draft of your research paper, you must clearly identify all the sources you have quoted from, summarized, or paraphrased. For this purpose you will need a style of documentation.

35.1 Styles of Documentation

Styles of documentation are established by professional societies and journals to regularize the citing of sources in each field. Though each field has its own special requirements, scientists and social scientists generally cite their sources by parenthetical reference rather than numbered notes, and parenthetical citing has recently been adopted by many humanists also. This chapter explains just one kind of parenthetical citation: the MLA style, which has been recommended by the Modern Language Association for research papers on literature, philosophy, art, and other humanistic subjects. If your instructor expects you to cite your sources with notes, see Appendix 1. For brief comment on styles of documentation in the social sciences and sciences, see sections 38.7 and 38.8.

35.2 Citing with Parentheses—The MLA Style

Complete information on the MLA style appears in the third edition of the *MLA Handbook for Writers of Research Papers,* by Joseph Gibaldi and Walter S. Achtert (New York: Modern Language Association, 1988). Here we explain briefly how to use the MLA style with the kinds of sources you are likely to cite in a research paper written for a college course.

Citing with parentheses calls for two steps: citing each source in parentheses as you use it, and making a list of Works Cited at the end of your paper—an alphabetical list of all the sources you have used. In the finished paper, the list starts on a separate page and looks like this:

                                                    Martinez 10

Start entry
at margin   Works Cited

→   Accident Facts: 1987 Edition. Chicago, IL:

            National Safety Council, 1987.

      Baker, Robert F. The Highway Risk Problem:

            Policy Issues in Highway Safety. New York: *Double-*
                                                            space
            Wiley-Interscience, 1971.   *between and*
                                                            within
      Bedard, Patrick. "A Law We Can Live With." Car   *entries*

            and Driver Mar. 1985: 162.

      Cohen, John, and Barbara Preston. Causes and   *All lines*
                                                            after the
            Prevention of Road Accidents. London: Faber   *first in*
                                                            each entry
            and Faber, 1968.   *are indented*
                                                            5 spaces
      Crump, Edythe Traylor, Ed. 55: A Decade of

            Experience. Transportation Research Board

            Special Report 204. Washington, DC: National

            Research Council, 1984.

The simplest way to use parenthetical citation is to compile your Works Cited *while making parenthetical references in your paper.* Some software, such as *Norton Textra Writer,* offers a special Works Cited function. With other software, you can create a "Workcit" file for your Works Cited. Then split the screen each time you make a parenthetical reference, switch to the "Workcit" file, and write the full reference there, as explained in the following sections. If you keep the alphabetical order as you insert each new entry in the "Workcit" file, your list of Works Cited will be ready to print just as soon as you've finished writing the paper.

If you aren't using a computer or can't split the computer screen, make a source card for each work you cite (as explained earlier in section 33.5). When you've finished the paper, alphabetize the cards and then write the list according to the instructions given here.

Following are guidelines for parenthetically citing and then listing various kinds of sources. Most of what you need to know is *illustrated* by examples rather than explained by detailed commentary, so you should study each example carefully. We first explain the basic procedures for citing and listing in section 35.2A. Then we show how to cite and list various sources in sections 35.2B and 35.2C.

35.2A Citing and Listing—Basic Procedures

Place the parenthetical citation at the end of the material taken from a particular source. If you introduce the material without mentioning the author by name, give the author's last name and the page number(s) in parentheses:

> Writes one traffic analyst: "If the average speed
> of vehicles on a highway is 55 mph, a vehicle
> traveling at 40 mph has as great a chance of
> having an accident as one traveling at 70 mph,
> and the safest speed is 55 mph" (Baker 74).

No comma or p. before the page number

Punctuation follows the citation

If you use the author's name to introduce the material cited, give only the page numbers:

> As Senator Steve Symms has observed, therefore,
> "the decline in fatalities cannot be attributed
> exclusively to 55" (27).

1. Listing books in Works Cited:

```
Baker, Robert F. The Highway Risk Problem: Policy

    Issues in Highway Safety. New York: Wiley-

    Interscience, 1971.
```

Give the author's name (last name first) and the complete title—including subtitle, if any—underlined or in italics. Then give the place of publication, the name of the publisher, and the date—all of which you'll find on the front or back of the title page. If the publisher is a university press, use the initials U and P:

> Chicago: U of Chicago P
> Cambridge, MA: Harvard UP

2. Listing articles in Works Cited:

```
Symms, Steve. "65 mph: The Time Has Come." Car

    and Driver May 1987: 27.
```

Put the title of the article in quotation marks and underline or italicize the title of the periodical. For guidance in listing articles from various kinds of periodicals, see section 35.2B.

35.2B Citing and Listing Various Sources

1. Different works by the same author

Give a short form of the title—along with the page number(s)—each time you cite any one of his or her works:

```
Community colleges, says Astin, have tradition-

ally had a "disproportionate share" of minority

students (Minorities 141).
```

```
"On-campus work of up to twenty-five hours a week,"

says Astin, "can give students a sense of

involvement and help them persevere in their

studies" (Preventing 63).
```

Use no comma between the title and the page number. But if you introduce the cited material without using the author's name, put the name and a comma just before the title:

```
Modern dream researchers now accept the principle

that dreams express "profound aspects of person-

ality" (Foulkes, Sleep 184). But investigation

has shown that young children's dreams are in

general "rather simple and unemotional" (Foulkes,

"Dreams" 78).
```

CITING AND LISTING SOURCES IN MLA PARENTHETICAL STYLE: AN OVERVIEW

Works (books and articles) variously authored:

One-author work (in Basic Procedures)   546–47
Different works by the same author   547–49
Work with two or three authors   550
Work with more than three authors or editors   550–51
Anonymous work   552–53
Work with corporate author   563

Books with special features:

Book compiled by editor   551
Book with author and editor   551–52
Book in numbered series   561–62
Second or later edition   562
Reprint   562
Translation   562
The Bible   556
Work in more than one volume   552

Articles and other short works:

Article in journal   559

Works Cited

Astin, A. W. <u>Minorities in American Higher
Education: Recent Trends, Current Prospects,
and Recommendations</u>. San Francisco: Jossey-
Bass, 1982.

---. <u>Preventing Students from Dropping Out</u>. San
Francisco: Jossey-Bass, 1975.

Foulkes, David. "Dreams of Innocence."
<u>Psychology Today</u>. Dec. 1978: 78—88.

---. <u>The Psychology of Sleep</u>. New York:
Scribner's, 1966.

Article in periodical published monthly, weekly, or daily
559–60

Editorial   560

Article in reference book   560–61

Article or other short work from a collection   561

Poems, Plays, and Long Prose Passages:

Play with act, scene, and line numbers   553–54

Poem with numbered lines but no sections   554–55

Poem with sections and numbered lines   555

Poem without numbered lines   555

Prose passage long enough to be indented from your text   556

Verse passage long enough to be indented from your text   557

Nonprint sources (such as films, interviews, and works of art)   557–59

Other sources:

Government publication   563

Published or broadcast interview   563–64

Document from information service   563

Personal letter to researcher   563

Material quoted by your source 553

Arrange the works of each author alphabetically by title, but instead of repeating the author's name, use three hyphens followed by a period.

2. A work with two or three authors

If you cite a work with two or three authors, give all of their last names either in your text or in parentheses:

> According to Dickmeyer, Wessels, and Coldren, commuting students are often poorer than residents and are generally forced to take on more outside work (13).

or

> One study found that commuting students are often poorer than residents and are generally forced to take on more outside work (Dickmeyer, Wessels, and Coldren 13).

> Works Cited
> Dickmeyer, Nathan, John Wessels, and Sharon L. Coldren. Institutionally Funded Student Financial Aid. Washington: American Council on Education, 1981.

In your citation, give the authors' names in the order you find them on the title page, and invert only the first name of the series.

3. A work with more than three authors or editors

Give the last name of the first author listed plus "et al.," which stands for *et alia* ("and others"):

> Some critics argue that content cannot be separated from form. "A change in one," they say, "is a change in the other" (Eastman et al. 1207).

Works Cited

```
Eastman, Arthur M., et al., eds. The Norton
     Reader: An Anthology of Expository Prose.
     6th ed. New York: Norton, 1984.
```

If the work is a second or later edition, note that after the title.

4. A book compiled by an editor

```
     Even  after  allowing  for  the  effects  of
reduced  travel  and  safer  overall  driving  condi-
tions  in  1974,  the  National  Research  Council  found
that  the  speed  limit  alone  saved  between  3,200
and  4,500  lives  that  year  (Crump  43).
```

Works Cited

```
Crump, Edythe Traylor, ed. 55: A Decade of
     Experience. Transportation Research Board
     Special Report 204. Washington, DC: National
     Research Council, 1984.
```

If the book is part of a numbered series, note that after the title.

5. A book with an author and an editor

```
Mrs.  Hurstwood,  Dreiser  says,  "was  a  cold,  self-
centered  woman,  with  many  a  thought  of  her  own
which  never  found  expression,  not  even  by  so  much
as  the  glint  of  an  eye"  (104).
```

Cite the author—not the editor—of the material you are using. Cite the editor only if you are using material written by him or her:

```
Kenneth  Lynn  writes:  "In  the  slow,  measured  man-
ner  of  Hurstwood's  preparation  for  suicide,
Dreiser  reveals  to  us  the  essential  dignity  as
well  as  the  tragedy  of  man"  (xvi).
```

```
                    Works Cited

Dreiser, Theodore.  Sister Carrie. Ed. Kenneth S.
     Lynn. New York: Rinehart, 1959.
```

Put the author's name first if you've cited the author's text. If you've cited material written by the editor, put the editor's name first, then the title of his or her material (capitalized but not underlined), and, at the end, the pagination:

```
Lynn, Kenneth.  Introduction. Sister Carrie. By
     Theodore Dreiser. New York: Rinehart, 1959.
     v—xvi.
```

If you are citing both the author's text and the editor's material, list the book under both names, using the author's name for cross-reference:

```
Dreiser, Theodore.  Sister Carrie. Ed. Kenneth S.
     Lynn. New York: Rinehart, 1959.
Lynn, Kenneth S. Introduction. Dreiser v—xvi.
```

6. A work in more than one volume

```
"Having witnessed the corruption of the English
government at first hand," Smith writes, the colo-
nists who had visited England "were determined to
preserve America from exploitation and repres-
sion" (1: 151).
```

Here a colon separates the number of the volume (1) from the number of the page (151).

```
                    Works Cited

Smith, Page.  A New Age Now Begins. 2 vols. New
     York: McGraw-Hill, 1976.
```

7. An anonymous work

```
Almost from the beginning, it provoked an opposi-
tion that steadily grew and that finally prevailed
```

```
in March 1987, when Congress voted to let states
raise the limit from 55 to 65 on rural Inter-
states ("65 MPH" 12).
```

```
                    Works Cited
"65 MPH: America Steps on the Gas." U.S. News and
     World Report. 30 Mar. 1987: 12.
```

The work is cited, listed, and alphabetized by its title. If the title is a number, treat it as if it were a word—in this case, as if it were "Sixty-five."

8. Material quoted by your source

```
Robert G. Templin, Jr., Dean of Instruction at
Piedmont Community College in Virginia, says that
better-off students are "squeezing out the poor,
disadvantaged, and minority students who once
called the community college theirs" (quoted Wat-
kins 1).
```

```
                    Works Cited
Watkins, Beverly T.  "2-Year Colleges Told
     They're Becoming Institutions for Middle-
     Class Students." Chronicle of Higher Educa-
     tion. 11 Apr. 1984: 1.
```

Whether or not the original source of the quoted material is named, only the name of *your* source appears in the list of Works Cited. But if you find yourself making extensive use of material quoted from a printed source, you should obtain that source and draw your own quotations from it.

9. A play with act, scene, and line numbers

Don't cite page numbers. Use arabic numerals with periods between them to indicate act, scene, and line number(s):

```
In Shakespeare's Romeo and Juliet, Romeo sees
Juliet as "the sun" of his universe (2.2.3).
```

If you're asked to cite plays with roman numerals, use uppercase for the act, lowercase for the scene, and arabic numeral(s) for the line number(s):

```
Shakespeare's Romeo sees Juliet as "the sun" of
his universe (Romeo and Juliet, II.ii.3).
```

If you cite a play repeatedly, you don't need to repeat the author and title each time. After the first reference, just give the relevant numbers:

```
Juliet speaks of Romeo as "the god of my idola-
try" (2.2.114).
```

Works Cited

```
Shakespeare, William.  Romeo and Juliet. Ed. John
     E. Hankins. Baltimore: Penguin, 1970.
```

10. A poem with numbered lines but no sections

Cite it by the lines, not by page numbers:

```
In Robert Frost's "Death of the Hired Man,"
one character speaks of home as "the place
where, when you have to go there / They have
to take you in" (lines 118—19).
```

Use the whole word "line" or "lines." Once you've established that the parenthesized numerals mean line numbers rather than page numbers, just give the numbers:

```
But his wife calls home "something you somehow
haven't to deserve" (120).
```

Works Cited

```
Frost, Robert.  "The Death of the Hired Man." The
     Poetry of Robert Frost. Ed. Edward Connery
     Lathem. New York: Holt, 1969. 34—40.
```

Use quotation marks for the title of the poem and underline the title of the book. Put the page numbers of the poem at the end of the citation.

11. A poem with sections and numbered lines

> When Milton's Satan first sees Adam and Eve in
> their bliss, he cries out, "O Hell! what do mine
> eyes with grief behold!" (<u>Paradise Lost</u>. 4.353).

If the poem is divided into sections ("books," cantos, or parts) that each start at line 1, give in order the section number and the line number(s), using arabic numerals for both. If the lines are numbered continuously through all the parts, give just the line numbers:

> At the end of part 4 of Coleridge's "Rime of the
> Ancient Mariner," the mariner says that when he
> looked upon the watersnakes, a "spring of love"
> gushed from his heart (line 284).

Works Cited

Coleridge, S. T.   "The Rime of the Ancient Mari-
     ner." <u>The Norton Anthology of English Liter-
     ature</u>. Ed. M. H. Abrams et al. 2 vols. New
     York: Norton, 1962. 2: 181–97.
Milton, John.   <u>Paradise Lost</u>. Ed. Scott Elledge.
     New York: Norton, 1975.

12. A poem without numbered lines

A poem without numbered lines may be cited by its title alone:

> In "Cape Breton," Bishop speaks of mist
> hanging in thin layers "like rotting snow-ice
> sucked away / almost to spirit."

Works Cited

Bishop, Elizabeth.   "Cape Breton." <u>The Complete
     Poems</u>. New York: Farrar, 1969. 75–77.

13. The Bible

> When Jacob dreams he hears the voice of God
> promising to give him and his descendants "the
> land whereon thou liest" (Genesis 28: 12—13).

Cite Biblical passages by giving the name of the Biblical book (without underlining or quotation marks) followed by the chapter and verse numbers. If you do quote from the Bible, list the version or translation you have used.

Works Cited

The Bible. King James Version. Nashville: Thomas
  Nelson, 1972.

14. Prose passage long enough to be indented from your text
Put the citation two spaces *after* the final punctuation mark:

> In A Room of One's Own, Virginia Woolf goes on to
> speak about women in literature and history:
>
>> A very queer, composite being thus
>> emerges. Imaginatively she is of the
>> highest importance; practically she is
>> completely insignificant. She pervades
>> poetry from cover to cover; she is all
>> but absent from history. She dominates
>> the lives of kings and conquerors in
>> fiction; in fact she was the slave of
>> any boy whose parents forced a ring upon
>> her finger. (60)

Quoted prose of more than four lines should be indented from your text, as explained in section 29.4. When the quoted matter is *not* indented, the parenthetical citation goes *before* the final punctuation mark, as shown just above in entry 14.

15. Verse passage long enough to be indented from your text

Put the citation at the right end of the last line or (if it won't fit there) just under the right end of the last line:

```
In "New Hampshire," Frost writes:

        How, to my sorrow, how have I attained

        A height from which to look down criti-

            cal

        On mountains? What has given me assur-

            ance

        To say what height becomes New Hamp-

            shire mountains,

        Or any mountains?        (lines 313-17)
```

A poetic passage of more than three lines should be indented from your text, as explained in section 29.5. When the quoted poetry is *not* indented, the parenthetical citation goes *before* the final punctuation mark, as shown above in entry 11.

```
                    Works Cited
    Frost, Robert.  "New Hampshire." The Poetry of
        Robert Frost. Ed. Edward Connery Lathem. New
        York: Holt, 1969. 159-72.
    Woolf, Virginia.  A Room of One's Own. New York:
        Fountain, 1929.
```

16. Nonprint sources

Cite films, recordings, radio and television programs, computer software programs, machine-readable documents, performances, and works of art by the title or the name(s) of the person(s) chiefly responsible for the work cited, or both. Give pagination only for machine-readable documents:

Film

```
    In Atlantic City, Guare exposes the tawdriness,

    ruthlessness, and brutality that undermine the

    would-be revival of a fabled sea resort.
```

Recording

Frost's own reading of "Birches" fully exploits the resonance of its language.

Computer program

Computer programs such as Wayne Holder's The Word Plus allow the writer to see exactly which of the words in a computerized text may be misspelled.

Television program

"The Enlightened Machine" graphically revealed just what happens to the brain during an epileptic seizure.

Work of art

The vortex that became Turner's trademark first appeared in his Snow Storm: Hannibal and His Army Crossing the Alps.

Performance

A recent performance of Shakespeare's Much Ado about Nothing once again demonstrated how much his language can achieve theatrically without the aid of elaborate sets.

Interview

According to Captain Ernest Loomis of the New Hampshire State Police, most drivers fail to adjust their speed to changes in weather conditions.

Works Cited

"The Enlightened Machine." The Brain. Narr. George Page. PBS. WETK, Burlington, VT. 10 Oct. 1984.

Frost, Robert. "Birches." <u>Robert Frost Reads His</u>
    <u>Poetry</u>. Caedmon, TC 1060, 1956.

Guare, John, screenwriter. <u>Atlantic City</u>. Dir.
    Louis Malle. With Burt Lancaster, Kate Reid,
    and Susan Sarandon. Paramount, 1980.

Loomis, Ernest. Interview with the author. 22
    April 1989.

Holder, Wayne. <u>The Word Plus</u>. Computer Software.
    Oasis Systems, 1982. CP/M 2.2, disk.

Shakespeare, William. <u>Much Ado about Nothing</u>.
    Dir. Terry Hands. With Derek Jacobi, Sinead
    Cusack, and the Royal Shakespeare Company.
    Gershwin Theatre, New York. 19 October 1984.

Turner, J. M. W. <u>Snow Storm: Hannibal and His</u>
    <u>Army Crossing the Alps</u> (1812). The Tate Gal-
    lery, London.

35.2C Listing Various Sources—Further Examples

The above sections show how to *cite* all sources. (To cite any article, for instance, see pp. 546–48). But the following sources need
special handling when *listed* in the Works Cited:

1. An article in a journal

    Delbrück, Max. "Mind from Matter?" <u>The American</u>
        <u>Scholar</u> 47 (1978): 339–53.

The name of the journal is followed by the volume number, date,
and pages. If each issue in the volume starts from page 1, give the
volume and issue number with a period between:

    Posen, I. Sheldon, and Joseph Sciorra. "Brook-
        lyn's Dancing Tower." <u>Natural History</u> 92.6
        (1983): 30–37. .

2. An article in a periodical published monthly, weekly, or daily

    Beatty, Jack. "In Harm's Way." <u>The Atlantic</u> May
        1987: 37–53.

```
Strout, Richard L.  "Another Bicentennial."
    Christian Science Monitor 10 Nov. 1978: 27.
```

If the article you cite appears on nonconsecutive pages—starting on page 1, for instance, and continuing on page 11—cite just the starting page with a plus sign right after it:

```
Watkins, Beverly T.  "2-Year Colleges Told
    They're Becoming Institutions for Middle-
    Class Students." Chronicle of Higher Educa-
    tion 11 April 1984: 1+.
```

When the article is unsigned, begin with the title:

```
"The Vietnam War: The Executioner." Newsweek 13
    Nov. 1978: 70.

"Turnpike Trade-offs." Fortune 5 Jan. 1985: 103-
    4.
```

If the paper is divided into lettered sections (A,B,C etc.) that each start from page 1, give the section number before the page number, as shown below.

3. An editorial

```
"How to End Watergate." Editorial. New York Times
    10 Jan. 1979: A22.
```

You should identify an editorial as such to distinguish it from a news report.

4. An article in a reference book

Give the name(s) of the author(s), the title of the article, the title of the book, and the year of the edition. If the articles are alphabetically arranged, you don't need volume or page numbers:

```
Kilma, Edward S.  "Phonetics." Funk & Wagnalls
    New Encyclopedia. 1973 ed.
```

If the article is unsigned, start with its title:

"Pollution." <u>The Columbia Encyclopedia</u>. 1963 ed.

If the article is signed by initials, you will usually find the full name at the beginning of the volume, or—if the volume is part of a set—at the beginning of the first volume.

5. Article or other short work from a collection

Put the title of the work in quotation marks, underline the title of the book, and put the page numbers at the end:

> Hauptman, Arthur M. "Shaping Alternative Loan
> Programs." <u>Meeting Student Aid Needs in a</u>
> <u>Period of Retrenchment</u>. Ed. Martin Kramer.
> New Directions for Higher Education 40. San
> Francisco: Jossey-Bass, 1982. 69—82.
>
> Hemingway, Ernest. "The Short Happy Life of Fran-
> cis Macomber." <u>The Short Stories of Ernest</u>
> <u>Hemingway</u>. New York: Scribner's, 1938. 3—37.

If you are citing works by different authors from the same book, list the collection by the name of its editor and use that for cross reference:

> Hauptman, Arthur M. "Shaping Alternative Loan
> Programs." Kramer 69—82.
> Kramer, Martin, ed. <u>Meeting Student Aid Needs in</u>
> <u>a Period of Retrenchment</u>. New Directions for
> Higher Education 40. San Francisco: Jossey-
> Bass, 1982.
> St. John, Edward P., and Charles Byce. "The
> Changing Federal Role in Student Aid." Kra-
> mer 21—40.

6. A book in a numbered series

> Crump, Edythe Traylor, Ed. <u>55: A Decade of Ex-</u>
> <u>perience</u>. Transportation Research Board

```
Special Report 204. Washington, DC: National

    Research Council, 1984.
```

The capitalized name of the series (without underlining) goes right after the title.

7. A second or later edition of a book

```
Ornstein, Robert E.  The Psychology of Con-

    sciousness. 2nd ed. New York: Harcourt, 1977.
```

8. A reprint

```
Weston, Jessie L.  From Ritual to Romance. 1920.

    Garden City: Anchor-Doubleday, 1957.
```

The date of original publication follows the title; the date of the reprint follows the name of the publisher.

9. A translation

```
Flaubert, Gustave.  Madame Bovary. Trans. Francis

    Steegmüller. New York: Random House, 1957.
```

If you have cited the translator's introduction or notes, use this form:

```
Steegmüller, Francis.  Translator's Introduction.

    Madame Bovary. By Gustave Flaubert. New

    York: Random House, 1957.
```

If you use material from both the author's text and the translator's introduction, list both names and use the author's name for cross-reference:

```
Flaubert, Gustave.  Madame Bovary. Trans. Francis

    Steegmüller. New York: Random House, 1957.

Steegmüller, Francis.  Translator's Introduction.

    Flaubert v—xv.
```

10. A government publication

```
U.S. Bureau of Labor Statistics. Women in the
    Labor Force: Some New Data Series. Rept.
    575. Washington: GPO. 1979.
```

"GPO" is a standard abbreviation for "Government Printing Office." "Rept." stands for "Report."

11. A personal letter to the researcher

```
Achtert, Walter S.  Letter to the author. 2 Nov.
    1984.
```

12. A document from an information service

```
Heffernan, James A. W.  Getting the Red Out: Grad-
    ing without Degrading. ERIC, 1983. ed 229 788.
```

ERIC stands for Educational Resources Information Center, and the last item is the ERIC document number. If the source originates from a publisher other than ERIC, give the original publisher's name and date before the ERIC number:

```
Franklin, P.  Beyond Student Financial Aid: Is-
    sues and Options for Strengthening Support
    Service Programs under Title IV of the Higher
    Education Act. Washington: College Entrance
    Examination Board, 1980. ERIC Ed 185 913.
```

13. A work with a corporate author

```
Sloan Study Consortium. Paying for College: Fi-
    nancing Education at Nine Private Institu-
    tions. Hanover, NH: UP of New England, 1974.
```

14. Published or broadcast interview

Give the relevant information in the form appropriate for the source:

Gordon, Suzanne. Interview. <u>All Things Con-</u>
<u>sidered</u>. Natl. Public Radio. WNYC, New York.
1 June 1983.

Kundera, Milan. Interview. <u>New York Times</u> 18
Jan. 1982: sec. 3: 13+.

EXERCISE 1 Citing with Parentheses—MLA Style

Take the information given on each source, and use it to write two
entries in the MLA style: a parenthetical·citation as it would look
in the text, and the entry as it would appear in a list of Works Cited.

EXAMPLE
The source is a book by Paul Fussell entitled *The Great War and
Modern Memory.* It was published by the Oxford University Press
in 1975. The first place of publication listed is New York. Your reference is to material on pages 96 and 97. In the text you introduce
the material without mentioning Fussell's name. You are using no
other book by him.

PARENTHETICAL CITATION

(Fussell 96—97)

IN WORKS CITED

Fusssell, Paul. <u>The Great War and Modern Memory</u>.
New York: Oxford UP, 1975.

1. Your source is a book titled *A Literature of Their Own,* subtitled
British Women Novelists from Brontë to Lessing. It was published in 1977 by Princeton University Press, which is located in
Princeton, NJ. You refer to material on pages 121, 122, and 123,
and you use the author's name (Elaine Showalter) to introduce
the material.

2. The source is a book by Joseph Conrad entitled *Lord Jim.* It was
edited by Thomas C. Moser and published by W. W. Norton &
Company, Inc. in 1968. The place of publication is listed as New
York. Your reference, a direct quotation, is to something the editor states on page vi, and you mention him by name when introducing the quotation. You are using no other work edited or written
by Moser.

3. Your source is a book by Ngũgĩ wa Thiong'o. It is called *Decolon-
izing the Mind: The Politics of Language in African Literature.* It
was published in 1986 by Heineman Educational Books, Inc., in

London. You introduce the material without using the author's name, and the material comes from page 86.

4. The source is an essay by Stuart Levine entitled "Emerson and Modern Social Concepts." The essay is one of several essays by different authors in a book entitled *Emerson: Prospect and Retrospect*. The essay appears on pages 155 through 178 of the book. The editor of the book is Joel Porte. The book is number 10 in a series named Harvard English Studies. The book was published in 1982 by the Harvard University Press. The place of publication is Cambridge, Massachusetts. Your reference is to page 156 and you mention Levine by name in the text.

5. The source is an article by George F. Kennan entitled "America's Unstable Soviet Policy." It appears on pages 71 through 80 of *The Atlantic Monthly*, a monthly magazine published by The Atlantic Monthly Company. The place of publication is Boston, MA. Kennan's article is printed in the November 1982 issue. You quote two sentences on page 79, but do not mention Kennan. You are using another work by him, *The Nuclear Delusion*.

6. The source is Victor Hugo's *Les Misérables* in the translation by Norman Denny. The edition is in two volumes, each with its own pagination; that is, each begins with a page 1. The edition was first published by the Folio Press in 1976; then by Penguin Books in 1980. The place of publication of the Penguin edition, which is the one you are using, is listed as Harmondsworth, Middlesex, England. Your reference is to an episode Hugo presents on pages 210 through 214 of volume 2. You name Hugo in the text when making the reference.

7. The source is an editorial printed on page 15 of *The Christian Science Monitor* dated November 9, 1984. The editorial is unsigned; its title is "Polling Power." You give the name of the newspaper when introducing the source.

8. The source is a recording of a poem as read by the author, T. S. Eliot. The title of the poem is "The Love Song of J. Alfred Prufrock." It is one of several poems on a record entitled *T. S. Eliot Reading Poems and Choruses*. The manufacturer is Caedmon Records, Inc., of New York City. The catalog number is TC 1045. A note on the record states that the recording was made in 1955. Your reference is to Eliot's portrayal of Prufrock in the entire poem. You mention Eliot by name in your text, and you also mention the title of the recorded poem.

36
Preparing the Final Copy of the Research Paper

Following are generally accepted requirements for the final copy of a research paper. If your teacher has special requirements, you should of course follow those. But otherwise, we suggest you do as follows:

1. If you've written your paper with a word processor, be sure your hard copy is clear and readable and your page breaks are inserted where you want them. If you're typing your paper, use a fresh black ribbon on white, twenty-pound 8½-by–11-inch sheets. Don't submit your final copy on fanfold computer paper or erasable paper; make a photocopy on uncoated paper instead.

2. Use double-spacing throughout, leave one-inch margins all around the text (top, bottom, and both sides) and indent paragraphs as shown on p. 567.

3. Type on one side of the paper only.

4. If your instructor requires a title page, follow the second format shown in section 5.7. p. 99. If your instructor also wishes an outline, follow the format shown on p. 534 and put the outline between the title page and the first page of your paper.

5. If your instructor does not require a title page, follow the format shown below. Do not underline the title or put it in quotation marks.

6. On each page after the first, give your last name and the page number at upper right, as shown on p. 568.

7. Always keep a copy of what you have submitted.

Research paper: format with title on first page of text

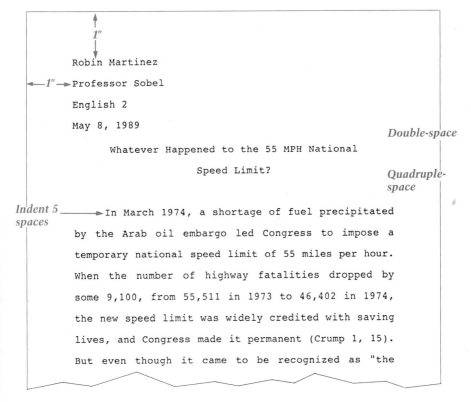

1"

Robin Martinez

◄—1"—► Professor Sobel

English 2

May 8, 1989

Double-space

Whatever Happened to the 55 MPH National

Speed Limit?

Quadruple-space

Indent 5 spaces ——► In March 1974, a shortage of fuel precipitated by the Arab oil embargo led Congress to impose a temporary national speed limit of 55 miles per hour. When the number of highway fatalities dropped by some 9,100, from 55,511 in 1973 to 46,402 in 1974, the new speed limit was widely credited with saving lives, and Congress made it permanent (Crump 1, 15). But even though it came to be recognized as "the

Research paper: second and succeeding pages of text

greatest traffic safety measure ever instituted in our history" (National 75), it did not last. Almost from the beginning, it provoked an opposition that steadily grew and that finally prevailed in March 1987, when Congress voted to let states raise the limit from 55 to 65 on rural Interstates ("65 MPH" 12).

As the following pages will show, critics of the 55 mph speed limit made many arguments against

37
Sample Argumentative Research Paper with MLA Parenthetical Style

The following argumentative research paper is documented in the MLA parenthetical style, with a list of Works Cited at the end. (For a sample explanatory research paper using the MLA note style, see Appendix 1.)

Robin Martinez

Professor Sobel

English 2

May 8, 1989

Whatever Happened to the 55 MPH National

Speed Limit?

In March 1974, a shortage of fuel precipitated by the Arab oil embargo led Congress to impose a temporary national speed limit of 55 miles per hour. *Writer explains the history of the 55-mph speed limit.* When the number of highway fatalities dropped by some 9,100, from 55,511 in 1973 to 46,402 in 1974, the new speed limit was widely credited with saving lives, and Congress made it permanent (Crump 1, 15). But even though it came to be recognized as "the greatest traffic safety measure ever instituted in our history" (National 75), it did not last. Almost from the beginning, it provoked an opposition that steadily grew and that finally prevailed in March 1987, when Congress voted to let states raise the limit from 55 to 65 on rural Interstates ("65 MPH" 12).

As the following pages will show, critics of

Martinez 2

the 55 mph speed limit made many arguments against
it. They claimed that speed was wrongly blamed for
causing fatalities. They cited the millions of hours
and dollars lost each year in extra time spent
behind the wheel. Most of all, they argued that the
law became unenforceable because nearly everyone
disobeyed it. But these arguments cannot overcome
clear evidence that the 55 mph speed limit saved
thousands of lives. In light of that crucial fact,
the repeal of the limit shows that American motorists will sacrifice anything--including life itself
--for the convenience and pleasure of driving faster
than 55 miles per hour.

Writer cites the arguments made against it.

Writer states her thesis: repeal of the limit shows willingness to sacrifice life for speed.

The 55 mph speed limit is admittedly just one
of several things that have helped reduce fatal
accidents during the past fifteen years. According
to the National Research Council, the striking drop
in highway fatalities for 1974--the first year of
the new speed limit--was due in part to "economic
conditions and fuel shortages that curtailed the
amount of driving" as well as to "improved vehicle
characteristics, safer highways, and increased

Writer con- cedes that drop in fatali- ties was not solely due to the limit,

Martinez 3

emergency medical services" (Crump 2). These last three developments have continued to push fatalities down. Though the NRC says that average speeds gradually rose above 55 after 1974 (Crump 57), statistics show that the rate of fatalities per 100 million vehicle miles gradually dropped--from 3.59 in 1974 to 2.5 in 1986 (Accident Facts 2). As Senator Steve Symms has observed, therefore, "the decline in fatalities cannot be attributed exclusively to 55" (27).

but shows that the limit saved thousands of lives.

Nevertheless, the 55 mph speed limit unquestionably saved a substantial number of lives. Even after allowing for the effects of reduced travel and safer overall driving conditions in 1974, the National Research Council found that the speed limit alone saved between 3,200 and 4,500 lives that year (Crump 43). Ten years later, despite "the partly offsetting effects of other safety improvements," the NRC estimated that "the lower and more uniform speeds" resulting from the national speed limit were continuing "to save 2,000 to 4,000 lives each year" (Crump 34).

Martinez 4

In the face of these findings and estimates, how can the repeal of the limit be justified? One answer is the disarming claim that speed alone does not matter. This claim was first made almost thirty years ago in a report published by the U.S. Department of Commerce. According to the report, "it is not so much the speed of a particular vehicle that matters as the variation in the speed of different vehicles" (Cohen and Preston 62). One traffic analyst gives an example: "If the average speed of vehicles on a highway is 55 mph, a vehicle traveling at 40 mph has as great a chance of having an accident as one traveling at 70 mph, and the safest speed is 55 mph" (Baker 74). This theory was tested by mathematical analysis of data on average speed, variation in speed, and fatalities for the years 1981 and 1982, and the analysis seemed to show that "speed, per se, had no effect on fatalities; it was only variance that mattered" (Lave 206). Predictably, opponents of the 55 mph limit embraced this conclusion. What it meant to them was succinctly

Writer considers argument that speed alone does not affect fatalities.

expressed in a headline for a magazine article about the official report on the analysis: "Official Report Says: Speed Doesn't Kill."

If that is true, we can raise speed limits without raising the death toll. Shortly before the 55 mph limit was repealed, Senator Symms declared: "Drivers are already driving 65 mph because they are comfortable driving at that speed. And when speed limits are posted at reasonable levels, speed variance is reduced, and driver comfort and safety are enhanced because more time is spent driving and less is spent 'looking out for Smokey'"(27). But this argument rests on the dangerously shaky assumption that we can control or even reduce speed variance while increasing average speed. There is actually no evidence that we can do either. Professor Charles A. Lave, who wrote the report that supposedly says "speed doesn't kill," frankly states in his own words: "It is not clear whether the variance of speed can be controlled independently of the average" (201).

On the contrary, it is clear that average speed

strongly affects variation in speed, and thus the number of fatalities. The NRC notes that during the first year of the 55 mph speed limit, "the percentage of drivers exceeding 65 mph on the rural Interstates declined from 50 to 9 percent. . . . As a result the variance of speeds on Interstate highways narrowed considerably" (Crump 24). Even one opponent of the 55 limit recognized this point. In an article urging repeal of the limit (it was titled "Deep-Six 55"), he acknowledged its lifesaving benefits. "Lowering the limit," he wrote, "pushed those who normally traveled much faster down to speeds close to 55, while those who usually traveled at 55 continued to do so. This resulted in more vehicles traveling within a small range of speed—and thus safer roads" (Pisarksi 16). Return to higher speed limits could have only the opposite effect. Even if most drivers would respect a "reasonable" speed limit of 65 mph, as Senator Symms implies, higher speed limits inevitably increase the difference between cruising speed and speed at intersections, where--as the NRC notes--drivers have to slow down

Writer shows that speed does affect fatalities.

in order to enter and exit (Crump 241). There is simply no way of raising average speed without also increasing variation in speed, and thus raising the death toll.

Three other points strengthen the link between higher speed limits and higher fatalities. First of all, according to Captain Ernest Loomis of the New Hampshire State police, most drivers fail to adjust their speed to changes in weather conditions, and when roads are wet or icy, higher speed only raises the chances of starting what Loomis calls a "demolition derby." As he went on to say in an interview, "High speed and bad weather just don't mix." Secondly, whatever the weather, high speed under any conditions makes a collision both more likely to happen and more likely to be fatal--for the simple reason that the faster a car is traveling, the longer it takes to stop. The NRC describes what would happen to two drivers traveling at 65 and 55 who suddenly see an overturned truck blocking the road at 290 feet ahead of them. While the driver traveling at 55 would be able to stop short of the truck, the driver traveling at 65 would hit the truck at 35 mph, "would certainly be injured . . . and could be killed" (Crump 38). The startling effect of the difference between speeds of 55 and 65 becomes still worse in light of the third point, which is that raising the speed limit to 65 pushes still higher the speed at which many cars actually move. Shortly before the national limit of 55 was repealed on rural Interstates, a spokesman for the Texas Highway Patrol declared, "If they do raise it, say to 65, you're going to start seeing speeds of 80 and 85, and we're going to see more traffic deaths" (quoted Martz 16).

The NRC emphatically agreed. Before repeal of the 55 mph limit, the NRC predicted that a return to 65 on rural interstates alone "might result in about 500 more fatalities each year" (Crump 11). Now we can test that prediction against the facts. In 1987, though the 55 mph speed limit was not repealed until late March of that year, highway fatalities stopped declining for the first time since 1980. Instead they rose--from 48,300 to 48,700

(Accident Facts 2). If it is fair to assume that highway fatalities would have continued declining without the change in the speed limit, we can only conclude that the first nine months of the new speed limit cost us more than four hundred lives.

Writer considers argument that 55 mph speed limit costs too much in time and money,

Can the cost be justified? Those who think so weigh the saving of life against the saving of time. According to the NRC, the 55 mph speed limit kept drivers on the road much longer than previous speed limits did, requiring "350,000 hours of additional travel time . . . for the saving of one life plus the avoidance of one serious, severe, or critical injury" (Crump 4). To some this seemed a bad bargain. Calculating that 350,000 hours of travel would be the equivalent of 120 people driving eight hours a day for a year, one commentator asked: "How much wealth could those 120 people be creating in a year if they weren't harnessed to the wheel?" ("Turnpike Trade-offs" 104). Furthermore, since rural Interstates are safer than other roads, the NRC estimated that a 55 mph speed limit on them necessitated 97 years of additional driving time for each life

Martinez 10

saved (Crump 123). At least some of this time can be directly translated into money. In the early 1980s, the Independent Drivers' Association calculated what the 55 mph speed limit was doing to owner-operators, who are paid by the mile and yet cannot legally drive for more than a specified number of hours each day. By reducing the distance they could travel each day, the 55 mph speed limit also reduced their earnings by as much as $15,000 a year (Crump 116).

When examined as a whole, however, the net costs of the 55 mph speed limit were clearly justified by the value of all that it saved. First of all, according to Alan Altshuler, chairman of the national committee appointed to study the 55 limit, the time it imposed on the average driver was just "seven additional hours per year" (quoted Bedard 162). Secondly, while the 55 limit may have reduced the daily earnings of individual truck drivers, it also cut considerably the cost of fueling and maintaining the trucks themselves (Crump 117). Third, it reduced not only fatalities but also property

but shows that net losses were clearly justified by savings.

damage and injury, cutting "serious, severe, and critical injuries" by about 2,500 to 4,500 a year (Crump 166). Thus it lowered medical bills, legal costs, and repair bills by $122 to $240 annually (Crump 88—91). Fourth, Altshuler says that the 55 mph speed limit produced "taxpayer savings for medical and welfare assistance programs worth $65 million a year" (quoted Bedard 162).

To all these savings we must add the incalculable value of the work done and the lives lived by the thousands of men and women who were spared death or serious injury because of the 55 limit. In view of all these benefits, can we be sure that the limit generated "a significant loss of productivity," as Senator Symms claimed (27)? Even in hard economic terms, can we be sure that it did not actually produce a net gain? So long as that question cannot be decisively answered, the economic case against the 55 limit cannot stand.

What finally brought repeal of the limit, however, was not so much the economic case against it as the argument that it could no longer be effectively enforced. A California writer tells us what happened in August 1985, when he drove a motorcycle for 30 miles in the slow right lane of a California freeway at exactly 55 mph. Thirty-seven vehicles came up from behind in that lane to go around him, and in nearby lanes he was passed by 170 cars before sheer boredom led him to stop counting ("Life in the Passed Lane" 18). What he saw typified American driving in 1985. The average speed on rural Interstates in 1985 was 59.5 mph for the country as a whole, and over 60 mph in 23 states (Symms 27). "By actual measurement," according to one report, "75 percent of the vehicles on monitored stretches of rural interstate highways were exceeding the limit" that year (Martz 14).

Writer considers argument that 55 mph limit was ineffective.

Besides citing this widespread evidence of noncompliance, critics of the 55 mph speed limit also complained that the task of enforcing it needlessly consumed the time and energies of state police forces. As John A. Gardiner observes, no police force can arrest everyone who violates a traffic law. "Limited resources and a multitude of

other police duties, if nothing else, make it
impossible" (5). Efforts to enforce the 55 mph speed
limit clearly illustrate this point. In North Carolina, for instance, where half of all traffic colli-
sions occur on the secondary roads, the task of
enforcing the 55 limit forced police to spend 75
percent of their time on the primary roads (Sostkowski et al. 172). In Oregon, state police spent a
third of their time enforcing the limit on freeways
even though only 6 percent of fatal accidents were
occurring there (Crump 159). In California, the
Highway Patrol used 85 percent of its officers to
enforce the 55 limit and spent $3 million a year on
the effort (Symms 27). Altogether, in fact, the
total cost of enforcing the 55 limit was about $118
million a year, with an additional $2 to $3 million
a year for federal monitoring of compliance (Crump
101—02). Critics thought we did not get our money's
worth. According to Senator Symms, funds spent on
the enforcement of the 55 limit in California, for
instance, could have been more effectively spent on
"keeping drunk drivers off the road" (27).

Martinez 14

Given a choice between eliminating drunk drivers and eliminating the 55 mph speed limit, few of us would hesitate to choose the first. But did we have to make the choice? Was enforcement of the 55 mph speed limit as ineffective and needlessly expensive as critics have claimed? As far as the cost of enforcement is concerned, the NRC found that virtually all of it could have been offset by fines (Crump 102). As for the effectiveness of the 55 mph limit, comparison tells a revealing story. In spite of the gradual increase in average speeds since 1974, average speed on rural Interstates in 1985 was still more than 5 mph less than it was in 1973, when--according to Highway Statistics--it stood at 65 mph (cited Crump 245). To conclude that a speed limit is ineffective because drivers exceed it by an average of less than 5 mph is unrealistic. As the NRC says, anything less than 5 mph over a given speed limit is "within the tolerance zone allowed by almost all traffic police" (Crump 157). In view of that point, the 55 mph speed limit was effective in keeping average speeds well below what they were

Writer shows that the limit kept average speeds down.

Martinez 15

before the limit was enacted. Now that the limit
has been repealed, average speeds have risen again,
and as I have shown already, annual fatalities have
risen with them.

The arguments against the 55 mph limit prevailed, I believe, not because they were truly convincing but because they allowed us to rationalize
our real motive for overturning it: our love of
speed. As two Dutch writers observe, general speed
limits provoke resistance because they threaten "the
pleasures of speeding. . . . The 'speed demon' often
does not drive fast so much to reach some destination as to enjoy the primitive sensation of speed
for its own sake. The speedster drives fast even
when he is in no hurry" (Naatanen and Summala 47).
TV auto ads exploit this lust for speed. As Brock
Yates notes, they increasingly show "cars flying down
twisty rural roads in dazzling exhibitions of cornering power and acceleration" (21). Speed is
exciting; speed limits are boring. The real reason
for the overturning of the 55 limit was once frankly

*Writer pre-
sents real rea-
son for repeal
of the limit:
love of speed.*

stated by a patrolman. "If I had to drive 55 all day," he said, "I'd go nuts" (quoted Yates 21).

Most Americans think of speeding as an inalienable right, especially when they live in the wide open spaces of the West. To Westerners in particular, the national speed limit of 55 mph finally came to seem yet another example of federal interference with states' rights and individual freedom alike. In 1986, shortly before the limit was overturned, a spokesman for Senator Chic Hecht of Nevada declared that repealing it was "the number-one issue out West. Nevada didn't even have speed limits until 1974 [when the national limit was enacted], so you can imagine how our voters feel about it" (quoted Holt 30).

We can indeed. We can readily imagine their impatience, their frustration, and their resentment of a law that kept them in harness when they longed to gallop, to show what all of their horsepower could do. But if we are going to indulge this lust for speed, we should at least be honest enough to

Martinez 17

recognize what comes with it. After all the objec-

Writer concludes by reaffirming thesis: repeal of the limit has already increased fatalities.

tions to the 55 mph speed limit have been studied, after all the arguments for higher limits have been weighed, we must face the hard and simple fact that higher speeds mean increased fatalities. Human life is the price we have already begun to pay for repealing the national speed limit.

Martinez 18

Works Cited

Accident Facts: 1988 Edition. Chicago, IL: National Safety Council, 1988.

Baker, Robert F. The Highway Risk Problem: Policy Issues in Highway Safety. New York: Wiley-Interscience, 1971.

Bedard, Patrick. "A Law We Can Live With." Car and Driver Mar. 1985: 162.

Cohen, John, and Barbara Preston. Causes and Prevention of Road Accidents. London: Faber and Faber, 1968.

Crump, Edythe Traylor, ed. 55: A Decade of Experience. Transportation Research Board Special Report 204. Washington, DC: National Research Council, 1984.

Gardiner, John A. Traffic and the Police: Variations in Law-Enforcement Policy. Cambridge, MA: Harvard UP, 1969.

Holt, Harvey. "Slow Death." National Review 21 Nov. 1986: 30.

Lave, Charles A. "Speeding and Highway Fatalities." Appendix C in Crump 200—208.

"Life in the Passed Lane." Road and Track Aug. 1985: 18.

Loomis, Ernest. Telephone interview. 22 April 1989.

Martz, Larry. "Does Speed Kill?" Newsweek July
    21, 1986: 14—17.

Naatanen, Risto, and Heikki Summala. Road-User
    Behavior and Traffic Accidents. Amsterdam:
    North-Holland, 1976.

The National Maximum Speed Limit: A Summary of Three
    Regional Workshops Conducted by the Interna-
    tional Chiefs of Police for the Department of
    Transportation. Washington, DC: National
    Highway Traffic Safety Administration, 1977.

"Official Report Says: Speed Doesn't Kill." Con-
    sumers' Research Dec. 1986: 29—31.

Pisarski, Alan E. "Deep-Six 55." Consumers'
    Research February 1986: 15—18.

"65 MPH: America Steps on the Gas." U.S. News and
    World Report 30 Mar. 1987: 12.

Sostkowski, R., D. Phillips, R. Monroe, and A.
    Pearson. Determining the Cost of Enforcing
    the National Maximum Speed Limit. Gaithers-
    burg, MD: International Association of
    Chiefs of Police, 1980.

Symms, Steve. "65 mph: The Time has Come." Car &
    Driver May 1987: 27.

"Turnpike Trade-offs." Fortune 5 Jan. 1985: 103—
    104.

Yates, Brock. "Hypocrisy on Board." Car and
    Driver Aug. 1986: 21.

38
Writing and Research across the Curriculum

Good writing does not stop at the borders of the English department. College courses in many different subjects require written work, and many of the qualities that make an essay on Shakespeare effective can also enhance a paper on the biology of adaptation or the influence of urban environment on family life. Whatever its subject, a good piece of writing is grammatically correct, lucid, precise, coherent, well focused on its main point, and—just as importantly—well designed to satisfy its readers, the audience for whom it is written.

But different disciplines (which is what academic subjects are called) require different kinds of writing. Even when a humanist, a social scientist, and a natural scientist examine the same object, they approach it from fundamentally different points of view. For this reason, a highly specialized study can sometimes seem to be written in a language of its own: a language that sounds strange and difficult to the nonspecialist reader.

So if you plan to write a paper in a specialized discipline, or even to read specialized books and articles, you will have to learn something about the methods, assumptions, and above all the language of that discipline. In what follows, we first consider the kind of writing specialists produce when they are writing for other specialists. Then we explain how you can begin to write in various disciplines yourself.

38.1 Three Disciplines Illustrated—Specialists Writing for Specialists

To see the difference between writing in the humanities, writing in the social sciences, and writing in the natural sciences, consider how specialists from each of these three different fields of study approach a common topic.

1. A literary critic writes about fictional treatments of cruelty to children:

> Any story will be unintelligible unless it includes, however subtly, the amount of telling necessary not only to make us aware of the value system which gives it its meaning but, more important, to make us willing to accept that value system, at least temporarily. It is true that the reader must suspend to some extent his own disbeliefs; he must be receptive, open, ready to receive the clues. But the work itself—any work not written by myself or by those who share my beliefs—must fill with its rhetoric the gap made by the suspension of my own beliefs.
>
> Even something as universally deplored as cruelty to children can be molded to radically different effects. When Huck's pap pursues him with the knife, or when the comic-strip father beats his child because he's had a bad day at the office; when Jim in "Haircut" and Jason in *The Sound and the Fury* disappoint the children about a circus; when Elizabeth Bowen's heroine experiences the death of the heart; when Saki's little pagan is punished by his aunt; when Medea kills her children; when Macbeth kills Lady Macduff's children; when Swift's Modest Proposer arranges to have the infants boiled and eaten; when Pip is trapped by Miss Havisham; when Farrington in Joyce's "Counterparts" beats his son; and, finally, when the child is beaten to death in *The Brothers Karamazov*, our reactions against the perpetrators range from unconcerned amusement to absolute horror, from pitying forgiveness to hatred, depending not primarily upon any natural relation between the bare events and our reaction but upon a judgment rendered by the author.
>
> —Wayne Booth, *The Rhetoric of Fiction*

Booth is writing for readers familiar with a wide variety of literary texts—with works ranging from *Huckleberry Finn* to *The Brothers Karamazov*. His object of study is "the work itself." He treats the individual work of literature as the source of meaning and value, as something that can make us react in a variety of ways to any theme—even cruelty to children.

2. A sociologist writes about the family as a social group:

> The implications of conflict theory might best be considered from the perspective of an alternative theory. According to conflict theory, power pervades both the interactional and the societal levels of social life. Bierstedt (1974) elaborated on the theory of *social organization* by defining power as latent force, and identifying the sources of power as resources, numbers (especially majorities), and social organization (including authority, or institutionalized power). By implication, social organization must be triadic, because authority entails command, either by a person or by a norm, and obedience; this points to the consensus of a majority, and a majority cannot exist in a detached dyad. Resources *per se* cannot influence social life unless they are given social definition (Bierstedt, 1974). The conception of the family as an institution holds that normative structures have crescively developed to meet the functional requirements of men, women, and children joined by ties of kinship. Women give birth and are more nurturant, children require a long·period of dependency, and males exhibit greater aggressiveness and dominance the world over (Maccoby and Jacklin, 1974). These universal features gave rise to the traditional consensus regarding family statuses and the norms attached to them, whether in the conjugal family today or in the patriarchal family of the past. In summary, the view we have outlined sees social organization as triadic and hierarchical, instead of dyadic and polarized, and points to the principle that each person acts where he or she is strong (Weaver, 1948).
>
> —Lawrence L. Shornack, "Conflict Theory and the Family"

Shornack writes for readers familiar with sociological terms such as *interactional* (relating to behavior between persons), *dyadic* (twofold), *triadic* (threefold), and *crescively* (increasingly). He distinguishes between two rival theories that could be used to explain the family: conflict theory, which treats all social structures in terms of a two-sided (dyadic) struggle between oppressive top dogs and powerless underdogs; and organizational theory, which treats social structures as triangular (triadic), with a peak of power resting on a base of majority consent. As a sociologist, Shornack focuses on social groups. While Booth describes the many different forms that child abuse can take in various fictional families, Shornack seeks to explain the social structure of *the* family—that is, the social structure common to all family groups.

3. A team of pediatricians and neurologists reports on a study of children who suffered minor head injuries:

INTRODUCTION

Minor head injury is a common problem in the pediatric population. Yet, despite the relative frequency, it remains a source of concern often raising the spectra of serious sequelae and long-term neuropsychological problems. Relatively few data are available on the outcome of minor head trauma. Published studies have emphasized a substantial functional and behavioral morbidity and an increased incidence of headaches [1–6]. In general, however, these abnormalities have been established by comparing information obtained from individuals following head trauma with expected outcomes in healthy subjects.

The purpose of this study is to expand our knowledge of the physical and behavioral morbidity experienced by children with minor head injuries by comparing this population with individuals who had minor injuries to other parts of the body. All children were followed prospectively by telephone interviews. Our results have identified several short-term behavioral sequelae in a pediatric population treated in an emergency room for minor injuries, whether injuries affect the head or other body parts. Physician awareness of specific transient functional deficits following minor injuries can result in a reduction of parental anxiety.

—Mychelle Farmer et al., "Neurobehavioral Sequelae of Minor Head Injuries in Children"

Dr. Farmer and her colleagues are writing for specialists in the fields of pediatrics and neurology—for readers familiar with terms such as *trauma* (wound), *morbidity* (illness), *sequelae* (abnormalities resulting from a wound), and *transient functional deficits* (short-term incapacities). They made their study to answer a specific question about a well-defined population: in children under 13, what special abnormalities can be expected to follow a minor head wound? To answer this question, they compared head-injured children with a "control group" of children suffering from other injuries. In this introduction to their report, they refer to what published studies have already shown; they explain the comparative method of their own study; and they note that what they have learned about minor head injuries can be used to reduce "parental anxiety."

Each of the three passages above considers children and the family—a topic everyone knows something about. Yet each is written in terms unfamiliar to most of us, because each is written to be read by specialists in a particular field. In addition, each also embodies a specialized way of thinking about its topic—a specialized kind of questioning. This we explain next.

38.2 Asking the Question That Fits Your Discipline

The key to generating an effective piece of writing in any field is *to ask the kind of question that the field is organized to answer.* To learn what kind of question this is, consider the different things that humanists, social scientists, and natural scientists focus on when they write.

38.2A Humanistic Writing—Focus on the Individual Work

Specialists in philosophy and religion study what real people think and believe, but most other humanists—in spite of their generic name—do not study human beings directly. They study works of literature, music, and art, and in the process, they often try to explain how particular works *represent* human beings. Also, humanists typically regard each work as unique, irreducible to any one formula. In passage no. 1 above (section 38.1), Wayne Booth shows that he thinks this way even though he is making a general point about works of fiction. According to Booth, all works of fiction are in a strict sense *rhetorical;* their authors try to persuade us to view and judge their characters in a certain way. This general theory of fiction brings to light what is distinctive about each fictional work. If the theme of cruelty to children can be "molded to radically different effects," made to enrage us in one work and to amuse us in another, what explains these differences? Only a detailed analysis of the rhetorical strategies used in particular works can answer the question. Even as he explains a general theory of fiction, therefore, Booth shows us how to discover the uniqueness of individual works, how to formulate the kinds of questions that can lead us to their meanings, such as "Why are we amused when Huck's pap pursues him with a knife?" or "What makes us sympathize with Medea even when she kills her own children?"

Humanists studying works of literature and art commonly classify them in terms of period, category, or both. Just as scholars

---

THINKING LIKE A HUMANIST

Consider a work of art or of literature with questions such as these:

1. What kind of work is it?
2. How is it related to other works of its kind or other works by the same person?
3. How does it differ from other works like it?
4. What is the relation of any one of its parts to the whole?

THINKING LIKE A SOCIAL SCIENTIST

Investigate social groups with questions such as these:

1. What is the correlation between event or condition X and event or condition Y within population Z?
2. What are the norms and values shared by a particular population?
3. What concept or theory will explain a particular form of behavior?

THINKING LIKE A SCIENTIST

Investigate the natural world with questions such as these:

1. What are the effects or causes of a particular physical condition or event?
2. What is the correlation between event or condition A and event or condition B?
3. If such a correlation may exist, what kind of experiment will confirm or disprove it?

---

writing about *Moby Dick* often connect it to other American novels of the nineteenth century, art historians writing about the paintings of Claude Monet often connect them to other examples of French impressionism. Humanists may also generalize about groups of works and recurrent types: about portraits and historical paintings, for instance, or about the typical hero of the detective novel. But in most studies of art and literature, discussion of general concepts—periods and categories—provides a background for analysis of the individual work or artist: the special ways in which *Moby Dick* combines epic form and novel form, or the qualities that distinguish Monet from such fellow impressionists as Camille Pissarro and Mary Cassatt. Seeking to understand the internal relations of an individual work or an individual career, the humanist typically asks what a particular image or character contributes to the meaning of the work as a whole, or what a particular work reveals about the development of a whole career.

Generally speaking, then, the humanities are organized to answer questions of this type about a work of music, literature, or art:

1. What kind of work is it?
2. How is it related to other works of its kind or other works by the same person?
3. How does it differ from other works like it?
4. What is the relation of any one of its parts to the whole?

38.2B Social Sciences—Focus on Social Groups

While humanists use categories and general terms to help them define something or someone unique, social scientists study groups, and they treat individuals only as members of groups. Shornack's approach to families differs from Booth's in two fundamental ways. He is not only writing about real families rather than fictional ones; he is also generalizing, as sociologists typically do, about *the* family. Even when he distinguishes "the conjugal family" of today from "the patriarchal family of the past," he is still dealing with groups, with social categories rather than individuals.

This generalizing viewpoint is particularly evident in the kind of essay he has written—a *review article* focusing on theories of the family rather than on any personal observation of actual families. In *case studies*, social scientists study individuals, and you may be asked to do the same. But you will study an individual as a *case*—that is, an example of a definable group, or of a particular stage of development. In a psychology course, for instance, you may be asked to observe a particular child at a daycare center in order to answer a question such as "What is the relation between language learning and socialization in three-year-olds?"

Professional social scientists use similar methods of investigation. A recent study of child development set out to explain the relation between child abuse and illness in children under three. By studying such a relationship in a randomly drawn sample of this population, investigators tried to learn whether illness is typically the cause or the effect of abuse.

The questions raised by social scientists, then, are designed to generate information about groups and recurrent situations. Typical studies seek to answer questions like these:

1. What is the correlation between event or condition X and event or condition Y within population Z?
2. What are the norms and values shared by a particular population?
3. What concept or theory will explain a particular form of behavior?

38.2C Natural Sciences—Focus on Physical Properties

When we turn from the social sciences to the natural sciences, the focus shifts from social groups to physical properties. While social scientists try to answer a question about a group of human beings by observing or interviewing sample members of the group, physical scientists try to answer a question about the human body or the physical properties of the natural world. The kind of question that a scientific researcher sets out to answer will call for observation, experiment, or both.

Suppose, for instance, that a biologist wants to know whether hair condition in humans tells anything about protein or calorie deficiencies. This is the kind of question that can be answered by observation and comparison—specifically by comparing hair samples taken from persons who don't have those deficiencies with hair samples taken from persons who do. Or suppose a neurologist wants to know whether or not minor head injuries in children produce any special long-term effects. This question too can be answered by observation and comparison, as shown by the article from which passage no. 3 is quoted above.

Like the authors of that article, physical scientists typically make controlled comparisons. To learn how one particular event or condition affects a certain population, they establish a control group that matches the group being tested in all but one respect—the one being studied. Controlled comparison allows researchers to focus on just one variable at a time and thus to see its effects clearly.

One other feature of the article typifies scientific writing: the frequent use of the passive voice. It appears twice in the introductory passage we quote *(these abnormalities have been established, All children were followed prospectively by telephone interviews)*, and often thereafter. Scientists use the passive voice in order to sound as objective as possible: to keep the focus on what was done rather than on who did it. (Even if the study was conducted by a team of researchers, reports do not usually say which member of a team did anything in particular.) Also, by separating the action from the agent, the passive voice underscores the point that scientific experiments and procedures are repeatable: anyone who is properly trained should be able to do them.

In general, then, physical scientists try to answer questions like these:

1. What are the effects or causes of a particular physical condition or event?
2. What is the correlation between event or condition A and event or condition B?
3. If such a correlation may exist, what kind of experiment will confirm or disprove it?

38.3 Writing on Specialized Topics for Non-Specialists

Like good teachers, good specialists in any subject generally know how to explain it to non-specialists, and—just as importantly—how to show why it matters to all of us. In the following paragraph the author explains why some babies born with spina bifida are denied corrective surgery:

> The single most common cause of mental retardation in children with spina bifida is infection of the brain: either infection of the chambers of the brain (ventriculitis) or of the linings and substance of the brain (meningoencephalitis). Such infection is most likely in those infants from whom corrective surgery is withheld. The parents of Baby Jane Doe, a child born with spina bifida, were told she would inevitably be severely retarded. For that reason they decided not to allow a

surgeon to treat her. Because she was not treated, she acquired a brain infection which means she is likely to be retarded. *This becomes a self-fulfilling prophecy.*
—David G. McLone, "The Diagnosis, Prognosis, and Out-
come for the Handicapped: A Neonatal View"

The author of this paragraph is a pediatric neurosurgeon who has treated hundreds of infants born with spina bifida. But since he is writing for a journal of general interest, he wants to reach more than just an audience of fellow specialists. So he explains such technical terms as *ventriculitis* and *meningoencephalitis*. He also explains—in language we can readily understand—exactly how the threat of retardation is used to justify the withholding of surgery from infants who need it.

This explanatory point serves a persuasive end. Elsewhere in his essay, McLone shows that no one can predict the life of an infant born with spina bifida until that infant has been treated. Here he shows what happens when a prediction of retardation is used to justify the withholding of corrective surgery: the with-holding of surgery leads to infection and retardation, and the pre-diction becomes "self-fulfilling." Thus McLone converts his specialized knowledge into writing that can reach and persuade a general reader to accept his main point, which is that *all* infants born with spina bifida should be treated.

38.4 Organizing a Research Paper in the Humanities

The interpretive essay in section 10.2F illustrates one way of orga-nizing a humanistic paper focused on a single primary source—a work of literature. A research paper on one or more works of lit-erature, art, music, or philosophy normally includes secondary as well as primary sources, and in general, you should organize this material as follows.

1. In the *introduction* you identify the particular work or works you will consider in the paper and formulate the question that will guide your investigation: Why is Thoreau so concerned with mea-suring time in *Walden?* How does Hume's *Treatise on Human Nature* undermine the principle of causality? Why does Mary Wollstonecraft attack Rousseau in *Vindication of the Rights of Women?* Why does Velázquez' *Las Meninas* include a self-portrait of the artist himself at work? How does the hard-boiled hero of the

American detective novel reflect American notions of heroism? Here, for instance, is the introduction to a research paper by a first-year college student:

> Individual identity is a cherished ideal, and when institutions threaten to deny it, they provoke resentment. Nevertheless, in order to function in a society, individuals must be willing to compromise their personal moralities and assume certain prescribed roles. This conflict between the rights of the individual and those of society produces a sense of frustration, creating the need for an outlet. Consequently, we look to heroes, to strong individuals who will never compromise their values or surrender their identities. To nineteenth-century individuals, America offered a vast and challenging frontier—a place where individuals could preserve their identities. The question I want to answer is how the values of these frontier heroes survive in the hard-boiled heroes of American detective novels.

2. In the *body* of the paper, you develop an answer to the basic question in terms of individual works, supplemented by comments drawn from secondary sources. Secondary sources—books and articles—help you to clarify the meaning of the works you discuss, to explain the connections between them, and to sharpen the edge of your argument. But the works themselves should be the prime source of evidence for your argument.

> Dashiell Hammett's first novel, *Red Harvest,* pits the Continental Op against a town totally controlled by three mobs and a corrupt police force. As Robert Parker notes, Personville (pronounced "Poisonville") is the ultimate "symbol of the end of the frontier . . . a western city, sprung up on the prairie in the wake of the mines" (Parker 95). When the Op arrives in response to a call for his services, he discovers a dead client. At this point he could have left, since he had already received all the pay he would get. But in leaving, he would have sacrificed his heroic stature, so he stays to fight for what he sees as justice.
>
> He wins only a limited victory. Though he eventually cleans up the town by turning the various mobs against each other, the novel lets us see that evil will return. When the Op leaves, Personville is "nice and clean and ready to go to the dogs again" (Hammett 178). Nevertheless, the detective has endured and upheld his own personal code of morality.

3. In the *conclusion,* you restate the main point of your argument and indicate what it contributes to our understanding of the works you have discussed.

> The demand for an individual who will not compromise on questions of morality produced the wilderness hero, a man who fled the corrupting influence of society for the freedom and challenge of the frontier. When the frontier closed, this man no longer had a refuge; he was forced to fight to retain his individuality and preserve his moral integrity. With a value system rooted in the nineteenth-century frontier, the hero of the detective novel must often confront the twentieth-century city. The reaction is often violent, and the hero can never impose his values on society. Yet he is personally victorious, for he always leaves uncorrupted, and he continually restores our faith in what Sisk calls "the American as rugged individualist and shaper of his own destiny" (368).

38.5 Documenting Sources in the Humanities

The author of the paragraphs quoted above uses the MLA style of parenthetical citation. Chapter 35 explains this style, which is commonly used in research papers on humanistic subjects. The MLA note style, which may also be used in papers on these subjects, is explained in Appendix 1.

38.6 Organizing Research Papers in the Social Sciences

Research papers in the social sciences are commonly based on the observation of particular cases or groups. If you are asked to write a case study or to report your findings on an assigned question, your most important primary source will be the record of your own observations, including the results of interviews you may conduct and questionnaires you may distribute. Together with the published sources you consult, these will provide the material for your paper.

A report of findings in the social sciences normally includes five parts:

1. The *introduction* states the question you propose to answer and explains how the methods of a particular social science can help you answer it. Suppose the question is "Do handicapped children gain more confidence from competitive sports (such as the Special

Olympics) than from noncompetitive activities?" Having posed this question, the introduction explains how the methods of developmental psychology can help you find and interpret the data needed to answer it.

2. The *methods* section of the paper indicates how you gathered the data for your study. Here you describe the particular characteristics of the group you studied, your methods of study (observation, interview, questionnaire), the questions you asked, and the printed sources you consulted, such as previous studies of handicapped children engaged in competitive sports. You should describe your methods of gathering data in such a way that someone else can repeat your study and thus test its results.

3. The *results* section puts the raw data you have gathered into clearly organized form: into paragraphs, tabulated listings, illustrations, or graphs. (On figures and tables see section 38.10 below.)

4. The *discussion section* interprets the results of the study and explains its significance for an understanding of the topic as a whole. With reference to the sample question above, for instance, it could explain whether or not competitive sports actually benefit handicapped children. If competition threatens their confidence rather than strengthening it, then programs like the Special Olympics should be re-evaluated.

5. The *conclusion* briefly summarizes the main points of the study.

38.7 Documenting Sources in the Social Sciences— The APA Parenthetical Style

The APA style of parenthetical citation is recommended by the American Psychological Association (APA) for research papers in the social sciences. Though some social scientists (such as Shornack, quoted above on p. 591) use a different style of parenthetical citation, the APA style is widely accepted for research papers in the social sciences. Complete information on this style appears in the *Publication Manual of the American Psychological Association*, 3rd ed. (Washington: Psychological Association, 1983). Here we briefly explain how to use the APA style with some of the sources you are likely to cite in a research paper written for a college course. Each source cited parenthetically in this section is also shown as it would appear in the list of References at the end of the paper. We explain how to write this list in section 38.8B.

CITING SOURCES IN APA PARENTHETICAL STYLE

Material introduced without an author's name   602
Material introduced with an author's name   602
A work with two authors   603
A work with more than two authors   603

LISTING SOURCES IN APA PARENTHETICAL STYLE

A book with one author   604
A book with two or more authors   604
A book with an editor   604
An article in a journal   604

38.7A   Writing APA Parenthetical Citations

1. Material introduced without the author's name

Give in parentheses the author's last name, the publication date, and—if you are citing one or more specific pages—the letter "p." with the page number(s):

> One researcher has found that "marriages in which the parents share responsibilities equally tend to be the happiest" (Levine, 1976, p. 176).

> References
>
> Levine, J. A. (1976). Who will raise the children? Philadelphia: Lippincott.

2. Material introduced with the author's name

Give only the date and page number(s) in parentheses:

> Kamerman (1983, p. 36) reports that from 1967 to 1980, kindergarten enrollment rose by about a third, and from 1969 to 1980, nursery school enrollment more than doubled.

References

Kamerman, S. B. (1983). Child-care services: A national picture. Monthly Labor Review, 106 (12), 35–39.

3. A work with two authors

Give both names every time you cite the work:

For all their efforts to generalize about child behavior, psychologists recognize that "no two children are exactly alike" (Gesell and Ilg, 1949, p. 68).

References

Gesell, A. & Ilg, F. L. (1949). Child development: An introduction to the study of human growth. New York: Harper.

4. A work with more than two authors

Give all the names in the first citation only:

FIRST CITATION: Miller, Dellefield, and Musso (1980) have called for more effective advertising of financial aid programs.

In later citations give just the first author's name followed by "et al.," which means "and others":

LATER CITATION: Miller et al. (1980) have studied the institutional management of financial aid.

References

Miller, S., Dellefield, W., & Musso, T. (1980). A guide to selected financial aid management practices. Washington, D.C.: U.S. Department of Education.

38.7B Writing the Reference List—APA Style

Start the list on a separate sheet and alphabetize the entries by the authors' last names, with the date of publication immediately after each name. If you've cited two or more works by one author, list them chronologically by date of publication. If the works were published in the same year, list them alphabetically by title and use the letters a,b,c, etc., after the year, as shown below in the Astin entries.

References

Triple-space

Author's last name first, starting at margin

Astin, A. W. (1975a). Financial aid and student persistence. Los Angeles: Higher Education Research Institute.

←— *1"* —→ Astin, A. W. (1975b). Preventing students from

All lines after the first in each entry are indented 3 spaces.

dropping out. San Francisco: Jossey-Bass.

Cartwright, R. (1978, December). Happy endings for our dreams. Psychology Today, pp. 66—76.

Double-space between an within entries.

1. A book with one author

Date of publication

Erikson, E. H. (1964). Insight and responsibility: Lectures on the ethical implications of psychoanalytic insight. New York: Norton.

Place of publication and publisher

Capitalize only first word of title and subtitle

2. A book with two or more authors

Hall, C.S., & Nordby, V. J. (1972). The individual and his dreams. New York: New American Library.

3. A work with an editor

No quotation marks used with title of an article

El-Khawas, E. (Ed.) (1980). Special policy issues in management of student aid. Washington, DC: American Council on Education.

4. An article in a journal

Volume number underlined

Palvio, A. (1975). Perceptual comparisons through the mind's eye. Memory & Cognition, 3, 635—647.

No p. or pp. for page numbers

If each issue in the volume starts from page 1, give the issue number in parentheses after the volume number:

```
Kamerman, S. B. (1983). Child-care services: A
    national picture. Monthly Labor Review, 106
    (12), 35-39.
```

Use p. or pp. with page numbers only when you are citing a newspaper or magazine (as in the Cartwright reference on p. 604).

38.8 Organizing Research Papers in the Natural Sciences

Research papers in the natural sciences are generally of two kinds: *review papers*, which analyze the current state of knowledge on a specialized topic, and *laboratory reports*, which present the results of an actual experiment. Both kinds of papers normally begin with an *abstract*, a brief, one-paragraph summary of the paper's most important points. But the two kinds of papers differ in many respects.

The primary sources for a *review paper* are current articles in scientific journals, and the purpose of a review paper is not to make an argument or develop an original idea but to survey and explain what laboratory research has recently shown about the topic. A review paper normally does three things: 1) it introduces its topic by explaining why it is important and what questions about it have been raised by recent research; 2) it develops the topic by reviewing that research under a series of subheadings; and 3) it concludes by summarizing what has been discovered and stating what remains to be investigated.

A *laboratory report* explains how an experiment made in a natural science laboratory answers a question such as "How do changes in temperature affect the conductivity of copper?" Resembling in its format a report of findings in the social sciences, the lab report usually presents its materials as follows:

1. The *title* succinctly states what was tested. It might be, for instance, "The Effect of Temperature Changes on the Conductivity of Copper."
2. The *abstract* summarizes the report in about 200 words.
3. The *introduction* explains the question that the lab test is designed to answer.

4. A section on *methods and materials* explains how the experiment was made, what apparatus was used, and how data were collected.

5. A section on *results* puts the data into clearly organized form, using graphs, tables, and illustrations where necessary. (See section 38.10 on the presentation of tables and figures.)

6. The *conclusion* explains the significance of the results.

7. A *reference list* gives any published sources used, including any manuals or textbooks.

38.9 Documenting Sources in the Sciences

Each subject in the sciences has its own style of documentation, which is explained in one of the following style manuals:

BIOLOGY

Council of Biology Editors. Style Manual Committee. *Council of Biology Editors Style Manual: A Guide for Authors, Editors, and Publishers in the Biological Sciences.* 5th ed. Bethesda: Council of Biology Editors, 1983.

CHEMISTRY

American Chemical Society. *Handbook for Authors of Papers in American Chemical Society Publications.* Washington: American Chemical Soc. 1978.

GEOLOGY

United States Geological Survey. *Suggestions to Authors of the Reports of the United States Geological Survey.* 6th ed. Washington: GPO, 1978.

LINGUISTICS

Linguistic Society of America. *L.S.A. Bulletin,* Dec. issue, annually.

MATHEMATICS

American Mathematical Society. *A Manual for Authors of Mathematical Papers.* 7th ed. Providence: American Mathematical Soc., 1980.

MEDICINE

International Steering Committee of Medical Editors. "Uniform Requirements for Manuscripts Submitted to Biomedical Journals." *Annals of Internal Medicine* 90 (Jan. 1979): 95–99.

PHYSICS

American Institute of Physics. Publications Board. *Style Manual for Guidance in the Preparation of Papers*. 3rd ed. New York: American Inst. of Physics, 1978.

Your instructor will tell you which scientific style of documentation you are expected to use. What follows is a brief guide to the style recommended by the Council of Biology Editors (CBE). Complete information on this style will be found in the CBE manual cited above.

CITING SOURCES IN CBE STYLE

Single author mentioned in text 607
Two authors mentioned in text 607
Three or more authors mentioned in text 608
No author mentioned in text 608
Specific page or pages cited 608
Two or more sources cited in one reference 608

38.9A Citing Sources in the Natural Sciences—CBE style

Cite each source with a parenthesized number that refers to a reference list at the end of the paper. The form of citations varies, as shown here:

1. Single author mentioned in text

    According to Nagle (1), sunburn affects reproductive
    success only in rare instances.

The parenthetical reference comes immediately after the author's name.

2. Two authors mentioned in text

    Weiss and Mann (2) have shown that folate deficiency
    retards growth, causes anemia, and inhibits fertility.

3. Three or more authors mentioned in text

```
Holick et al. (3) exposed hypopigmented human skin to
simulated solar ultraviolet radiation for various times
and determined the photoproducts of 7-dehydrocholes-
terol.
```

The words "et al." mean "and others."

4. No author mentioned in text

```
This theory implies that ultraviolet radiation can
penetrate more easily into lightly pigmented skin and
will result in a greater production of vitamin D than
will a heavily melanated skin subjected to the same
light (4).
```

5. Specific page or pages cited

```
It is reasonable to assume that dark pigmentation was
prominent among the ancient human populations (5, p.
62).
```

6. Two or more sources cited in one reference

```
How is the distribution of skin color among indigenous
populations to be explained? One hypothesis is that
heavily melanated skin emerged in sundrenched coun-
tries as protection against sunburn (2,5).
```

38.9B Writing the Reference List—CBE style

Below is a reference list for all of the sources cited above in section 38.9A. Illustrating CBE style, the order of numbered sources follows the order in which they were first cited in the paper:

Use only initials for first and middle names of authors

References

Capitalize first word of title only, with no underlining italics, or quotation marks

Double space between and within entries

Name of periodical, volume number, and pages of article

1. Nagle, J.J. Heredity and human affairs. St. Louis: C.V. Mosby; 1974.

2. Weiss, M.A.; Mann, A.E. Human biology and behaviour: an anthropological perspective. Boston: Little Brown; 1985.

3. Holick, M.F.; MacLaughlin, J.A.; Doppelt, S.H. Regulation of cutaneous previtamin D3 photosynthesis in man: skin pigment is not an essential regulator. Science 211: 589–595; 1981.

4. Loomis, W.F. Skin-pigment regulation of vitamin-D biosynthesis in man. Science 157; 1967.

5. Kottack, C.P. Anthropology: the exploration of human diversity. New York: Random House; 1978.

38.10 Tables and Figures in Research Papers

Research papers in the social and physical sciences often require tables (tabular data) or figures (graphs and illustrations). Tables and figures should be numbered consecutively (Table 1, Table 2; Figure 1, Figure 2) and accompanied by a descriptive caption, as shown below.

38.10A Presenting Tables

Put the caption for a table above it as a heading:

Table 1. Percent of Traffic Exceeding 55 MPH

HIGHWAY SYSTEM	1980	1981	1982	1983	PERCENT CHANGE 1982–1983[a]
Urban Interstate	51.2	51.0	58.4	60.5	3.6
Rural Interstate	65.9	67.6	73.1	73.6	0.7
Other freeways	–[b]	47.1	53.8	56.6	5.2
Urban arterials	–[b]	30.2	32.4	34.3	5.8
Rural arterials	–[b]	43.2	46.2	47.5	2.8
Rural collectors	–[b]	32.7	34.8	36.6	5.2
All statewide highways polled at 55 mph	49.0	48.5	52.6	54.1	2.8

[a]Percentage change calculated for 1982–1983 because these are the only 2 years with consistent speed measurement in all states.

[b]Data not available.

Source: Edythe Traylor Crump, ed. 55: A Decade of Experience. Transportation Research Board Special Report 204. (Washington, DC: National Research Council, 1984) 137.

Use lower case letters (a,b,c) for footnotes to a table, and put the footnotes at the bottom of the table—not at the bottom of the page or the end of the paper. If the table is photocopied from a printed source, put a source note under it. (For a paper documented in MLA style—parenthetical or not—the source note follows the MLA note style explained in Appendix A1.4.)

38.10B Presenting Figures

Put the caption for a figure—a graph or an illustration—just below the figure:

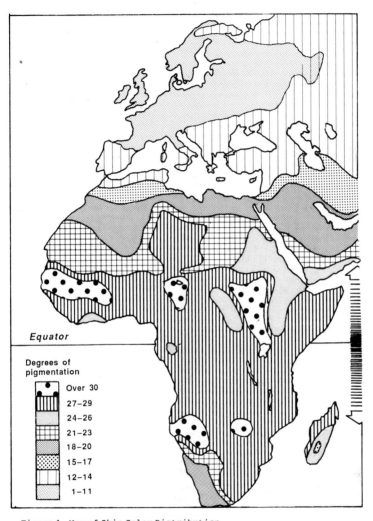

Figure 1. Map of Skin Color Distribution

Source: Weiss, M.L.; Mann, A.E. Human biology and behaviour: an anthro-

pological perspective. Boston: Little, Brown; 1985 (p. 433).

Except for the parenthetical page reference, the source note for a figure or table used in a paper on one of the sciences or social sciences may be written the same way as an entry in the reference list would be. (This note follows CBE style.)

Glossaries

Glossary of Usage

a, an   Use *a* before a word starting with a consonant, and *an* before a word starting with a vowel.

> *A* fool and his money are soon parted
> *An* empty bag cannot stand upright.   —Ben Franklin

accept, except   *Accept* means "receive" or "agree to."

> Medical schools accept less than half the students who apply.

As a preposition, *except* means "other than."

> I can resist anything except temptation.   —Oscar Wilde

As a verb *except* means "exclude," "omit," "leave out."

> If you except Eisenhower and Reagan, no U.S. president since Roosevelt has served two full terms in office.

A.D., B.C.   A.D. stands for *anno Domini,* "in the year of our Lord." It designates the period since the birth of Christ, and precedes the year number.

> The emperor Claudius began the Roman conquest of England in A.D. 43.

B.C. designates the period before the birth of Christ, and follows the year number. For this period, the lower the number, the more recent the year.

> Alexander the Great ruled Macedonia from 336 B.C. to his death in 323.

advice, advise   *Advice* is a noun meaning "guidance."

> When a man is too old to give bad example, he gives good advice.
> —La Rochefoucauld

Advise is a verb meaning "counsel," "give advice to," "recommend," or "notify."

> Shortly before the stock market crash of 1929, Bernard Baruch advised investors to buy bonds.

affect, effect   *Affect* means "change," "disturb," or "influence."

> The rising cost of gas has drastically affected the automobile industry.

It can also mean "feign" or "pretend to feel."

> She knew exactly what was in the package, but she affected surprise when she opened it.

As a verb, *effect* means "bring about," "accomplish," or "perform."

> With dazzling skill, the gymnast effected a triple somersault.

As a noun, *effect* means "result" or "impact."

> His appeal for mercy had no effect on the judge.

afraid   *See* frightened.

aggravate, irritate   *Aggravate* means "make worse."

> The recent bombing of a school bus has aggravated racial hostilities.

Irritate means "annoy" or "bring discomfort to."

> His tuneless whistling began to irritate me.

all   *See* almost.

all ready, already   Use *all ready* when *all* refers to things or people.

> At noon the runners were all ready to start. [The meaning is that *all* of the runners were *ready*.]

Use *already* to mean "by this time" or "by that time."

> I reached the halfway mark, but the front-runners had already crossed the finish line.

all right, * alright   *All right* means "completely correct," "safe and sound," or "satisfactory."

> My answers on the quiz were all right. [The meaning is that *all* of the answers were *right*.]
> The car was demolished, but aside from a muscle bruise in my shoulder and a few minor cuts, I was all right.

In formal writing, do not use *all right* to mean "satisfactorily" or "well."

> * In spite of a bruised shoulder, Ashe played all right.
> EDITED: In spite of a bruised shoulder, Ashe played well.

In formal writing, do not use *all right* to mean "very good" or "excellent."

> * Her performance was all right.
> EDITED: Her performance was excellent.

Do not use * *alright* anywhere; it is a misspelling of *all right.*

all together, altogether   Use *all together* when *all* refers to things or people.

> The demonstrators stood all together at the gate of the nuclear power plant.

Use *altogether* to mean "entirely" or "wholly."

> Never put off till tomorrow what you can avoid altogether. (Preston's Axiom)

allude, refer *Allude* means "call attention indirectly."

> When the speaker mentioned the "Watergate scandal," he alluded to a chain of events that led to the resignation of President Richard Nixon.

Refer means "call attention directly."

> In the Declaration of Independence, Jefferson refers many times to England's mistreatment of the American colonies.

allusion, delusion, illusion An *allusion* is an indirect reference.

> Prufrock's vision of his own head "brought in upon a platter" is an allusion to John the Baptist, whose head was presented that way to Salome, Herod's daughter.

A *delusion* is a false opinion or belief, especially one that springs from self-deception or madness.

> A megalomaniac suffers from the delusion that he or she is fabulously rich and powerful.

An *illusion* is a false impression, especially one that springs from false perception (an optical illusion, for example) or from wishful thinking.

> The sight of palm trees on the horizon proved to be an illusion.
> The so-called "free gifts" offered in advertisements feed the illusion that you can get something for nothing.

almost, most, mostly, all, * most all *Almost* means "nearly."

> By the time we reached the gas station, the tank was almost empty.
> Almost all the Republicans support the proposed amendment.

As an adjective or noun, *most* means "the greater part (of)" or "the majority (of)."

> Most birds migrate in the fall and spring.
> Most of the land has become a dust bowl.

As an adverb, *most* designates the superlative form of long adjectives and adverbs.

> Truman thought MacArthur the most egotistical man he ever knew.

Mostly means "chiefly," "primarily."

> Milk is mostly water.

All means "the whole amount," "the total number of," or "entirely."

> All art is useless. —Oscar Wilde
> The manufacturer has recalled all (of) the new models.
> The new buildings are all finished.

In formal writing, do not use * *most all*. Use *almost all* or *most.*

> * Most all of the plants looked healthy, but two of the roses were dying.
> EDITED: Almost all of the plants looked healthy, but two of the roses were dying.
> * Most all of the refugees suffered from malnutrition.
> EDITED: Most of the refugees suffered from malnutrition.

a lot, * alot, *See* lots of.

already *See* all ready.

* alright *See* all right.

altogether *See* all together.

alumnus, alumni; alumna, alumnae Use *alumnus* for one male graduate of a school, college, or university, and *alumni* for two or more male graduates or for a predominantly male group of graduates.

> Dartmouth alumni are extraordinarily loyal to their college.

Use *alumna* for one female graduate, and *alumnae* for two or more female graduates or for a predominantly female group of graduates.

> Vassar's alumnae include Mary McCarthy and Meryl Streep.

If you can't cope with all those Latin endings, use *graduate* for an individual of either sex, and just remember that *alumni* designates a male group, *alumnae* a female group. Do not refer to any one person of either sex as an *alumni.*

> * He is an alumni of Florida State.
> EDITED: He is an alumnus [*or* a graduate] of Florida State.

among, between Use *among* with three or more persons, things, or groups.

> There is no honor among thieves.

In general, use *between* with two persons, two things, or two groups.

> Political freedom in America means the right to choose between a Democrat and a Republican.

amoral, immoral *Amoral* means "without morals or a code of behavior," "beyond or outside the moral sphere."

> Rich, riotous, and totally amoral, he lived for nothing but excitement and pleasure.

Immoral means "wicked."

> The Roman emperor Nero was so immoral that he once kicked a pregnant woman to death.

amount, number Use *amount* when discussing uncountable things.

> No one knows the amount of damage that a nuclear war would do.

Use *number* when discussing countable things or persons.

> The store offered a prize to anyone who could guess the number of marbles in a large glass jug.

anxious, eager *Anxious* means "worried" or "fearfully desirous."

> The long silence on the other end of the line made her anxious.
> He took the long street at a dead run, anxious to reach home before the midnight curfew began.

Eager means "strongly desirous."

> After all I had heard about it, I was eager to see what remained of the famous prison on Alcatraz Island.

anyone, any one *Anyone* is an indefinite pronoun (like *everyone, everybody*).

> Anyone who hates dogs and children can't be all bad. —W.C. Fields

Any one means "any one of many."

> I felt wretched; I could not answer any one of the questions on the test.

apt *See* likely.

as, as if, like Use *as* or *as if* to introduce a subordinate clause.

> As I walked up the driveway, a huge dog suddenly leaped out at me.
> Susan looked as if she had just seen a ghost.

Use *like* as a preposition meaning "similar to."

> At first glance the organism looks like an amoeba.

Do not use *like* to mean "as if," "as," or "that."

> * Pat looked like he had just won the sweepstakes.
> EDITED: Pat looked as if he had just won the sweepstakes.
> * The hinge didn't work like the instructions said it would.
> EDITED: The hinge didn't work as the instructions said it would.
> * I felt like he resented me.
> EDITED: I felt that he resented me.

assure, ensure, insure *Assure* means "state with confidence to."

> The builders of the *Titanic* assured everyone that it could not sink.

Ensure means "make sure" or "guarantee."

> There is no way to ensure that every provision of the treaty will be honored.

Insure means "make a contract for payment in the event of specified loss, damage, injury, or death."

> I insured the package for fifty dollars.

awfully *See* very.

bad, badly *Bad* is an adjective meaning "not good," "sick," or "sorry."

> We paid a lot for the meal, but it was bad.
> In spite of the medicine, I still felt bad.
> She felt bad about losing the ring.

Badly is an adverb meaning "not well."

> Anything that begins well ends badly. (Pudder's Law)

Used with *want* or *need, badly* means "very much."

> The fans badly wanted a victory.

Do not use *bad* as an adverb.

> * We played bad during the first half of the game.
> EDITED: We played badly during the first half of the game.

B.C. *See* A.D.

because, since, * being that Use *since* and *because* to introduce clauses. Do not use * *being that.*

> Since fossil fuels are becoming scarce, scientists are working to develop synthetic forms of energy.
> The soldiers could not advance because they had run out of ammunition.

because of *See* due to.

* being that *See* because.

beside, besides *Beside* means "next to."

> A little restaurant stood beside the wharf.

As a preposition, *besides* means "in addition to."

> Besides working with the sun and the wind, engineers are seeking to harness the power of tides.

As a conjunctive adverb, *besides* means "moreover" or "also."

> Randy's notion of bliss was a night at the disco, but discos made me dizzy; besides, he stepped on my toes whenever we danced.

between *See* among.

can hardly, * can't hardly *Can hardly* means virtually the same thing as *cannot* or *can't.* Do not use * *can't hardly.*

> * We can't hardly bomb Moscow without getting bombed in return.
> EDITED: We can hardly bomb Moscow without getting bombed in return.

capital, capitol *Capital* means the seat of government of a country or state, the type of letter used at the beginning of a sentence, or a stock of accumulated wealth.

> Paris is the capital of France.
> This sentence begins with a capital *T.*
> What does capital consist of? It consists of money and commodities. —Karl Marx

Capitol means the building that houses the state or federal legislature. Remember that the *o* in *capitol* is like the *o* in the dome of a capitol.

> The new governor delivered his first official speech from the steps of the capitol.

censor, censure As a verb, *censor* means "expurgate."

> Television networks usually censor X-rated movies before broadcasting them.

As a noun, *censor* means "one who censors."

> Censors cut the best part of the film.

As a verb, *censure* means "find fault with" or "reprimand."

> In the 1950s, Senator Joseph McCarthy was censured for publicly questioning the integrity of President Eisenhower.

As a noun, *censure* means "disapproval" or "blame."

> Ridicule often hurts more than censure.

childish, childlike *Childish* means "disagreeably like a child."

The childish whining of a chronic complainer soon becomes an unbearable bore.

Childlike means "agreeably like a child."

Picasso's brilliant canvases express his childlike love of color.

cite *See* sight.

compare, comparison, contrast *Compare* means "bring together in order to note similarities and differences."

In *A Stillness at Appomattox*, Bruce Catton compares Lee and Grant not only to show the difference between a Virginia aristocrat and a rough-hewn frontiersman but also to show what these two men had in common.

Use *compare to* to stress similarities.

Lewis Thomas compares human societies to ant colonies, noting that individuals in each of these groups sometimes work together as if they were parts of a single organism.

Use *compare with* to stress differences.

Compared with Texas, Rhode Island is a postage stamp.

Comparison means "act of comparing."

Catton's comparison of Lee and Grant shows the difference between the South and the frontier.

In comparison with Texas, Rhode Island is a postage stamp.

As a transitive verb, *contrast* means "to show one or more differences."

In *Huckleberry Finn*, Twain contrasts the peaceful, easy flow of life on the river with the tense and violent atmosphere of life on shore.

As an intransitive verb, *contrast* means "show one or more differences."

In *Huckleberry Finn*, the peaceful flow of life on the river contrasts vividly with the violent atmosphere of life on shore.

As a noun, *contrast* means "striking difference."

To drive across America is to feel the contrast between the level plains of the Midwest and the towering peaks of the Rockies.

complement, compliment As a verb, *complement* means "bring to perfect completion."

A red silk scarf complemented her white dress.

As a noun, *complement* means "something that makes a whole when combined with something else" or "the total number of persons needed in a group or team."

Experience is the complement of learning.

Without a full complement of volunteers, a small-town fire department cannot do its job.

As a verb, *compliment* means "praise."

The teacher complimented me on my handwriting but complained about everything else.

As a noun, *compliment* means "expression of praise."

 Cheryl's compliment made my day.

conscience, conscious   *Conscience* is a noun meaning "inner guide or voice in matters of right and wrong."

 A pacifist will not fight in any war because his or her conscience says that all killing is wrong.

Conscious is an adjective meaning "aware" or "able to perceive."

 Conscious of something on my leg, I looked down to see a cockroach crawling over my knee.
 I was conscious during the whole operation.

consul   *See* council.

continual, continuous.   *Continual* means "going on with occasional slight interruptions."

 I grew up next to an airport. What I remember most from my childhood is the continual roaring of jet planes.

Continuous means "going on with no interruption."

 In some factories the assembly line never stops; production is continuous.

contrast   *See* compare.

could care less, couldn't care less   Don't use the first expression when you mean the second:

   * Carol likes hard rock, and could care less about Beethoven and Brahms.
   EDITED: Carol likes hard rock, and couldn't care less about Beethoven and Brahms.

council, counsel, consul   *Council* means "a group of persons who discuss and decide certain matters."

 The city council often disagrees with the mayor.

As a verb, *counsel* means "advise."

 President John F. Kennedy was badly counseled when he approved the American attack on Cuba at the Bay of Pigs.

As a noun, *counsel* means "advice" or "lawyer."

 Camp counselors tend to give orders more often than counsel.
 When the prosecution showed a picture of the victim's mangled corpse, the defense counsel vigorously objected.

A *consul* is a government official working in a foreign country to protect the interests of his or her country's citizens there.

 If you lose your passport in a foreign country, you will need to see the American consul there.

credible, credulous   *Credible* means "believable."

 A skillful liar can often sound highly credible.

Credulous means "overly ready to believe."

> Some people are credulous enough to believe anything they read in a newspaper.

See also incredible, incredulous.

criterion, criteria   A *criterion* is a standard by which someone or something is judged.

> In works of art, the only criterion of lasting value is lasting recognition.

Criteria is the plural of *criterion.*

> What criteria influence voters in judging a presidential candidate?

data   *Data* is the plural of the Latin *datum,* meaning "something given"—that is, a piece of information. *Data* should be treated as plural.

> The data transmitted by space satellites tell us much more about distant planets than we have ever known before.

delusion   *See* allusion.

different from, *different than   In formal writing do not use *than* after *different.* Use *from.*

> An adult's idea of a good time is often very different from a child's.

differ from, differ with   *Differ from* means "be unlike."

> Black English differs from Standard English not only in its sounds but also in its structure.   —Dorothy Z. Seymour

Differ with means "disagree with."

> Jung differed with Freud on the importance of the sex drive.

disinterested, uninterested   *Disinterested* means "impartial," "unbiased," "objective."

> Lawyers respect Judge Brown for his disinterested handling of controversial cases.

Uninterested means "indifferent," "not interested."

> Some people are so uninterested in politics that they do not even bother to vote.

due to, because of   *Due to* is adjectival and means "resulting from" or "the result of."

> Home-insurance policies sometimes fail to cover losses due to "acts of God," such as hurricanes and tornadoes.
> The senator's failure to win reelection was largely due to his lackluster campaigning.

Because of is adverbial and means "as a result of."

> Fighting persists in Northern Ireland because of animosities nearly three hundred years old.

Do not use *due to* to mean *because of.*

> * Due to a sprained ankle I had to drop out of the race.
> EDITED: Because of a sprained ankle I had to drop out of the race.

eager *See* anxious.

effect *See* affect.

emigrate *See* immigrate.

eminent, imminent, immanent *Eminent* means "distinguished," "prominent."

> An eminent biologist has recently redefined the concept of evolution.

Imminent means "about to happen."

> The leaden air and the black, heavy clouds told us that a thunderstorm was imminent.

Immanent means "inherent," "existing within."

> Pantheists believe that God is immanent in all things.

ensure *See* assure.

envelop, envelope *EnVELop* (second syllable accented) is a verb meaning "cover" or "enclose."

> Fog seemed to envelop the whole city.

ENvelope (first syllable accented) is a noun meaning "container used for mailing."

> The small white envelope contained a big check.

* etc., et al. The abbreviation * *etc.* stands for *et cetera,* "and other things." You should avoid it in formal writing. Instead, use *and so on,* or tell what the other things are.

> * Before setting out that morning, I put on my hat, mittens, etc.
> EDITED: Before setting out that morning, I put on my hat, mittens, scarf, and boots.

The abbreviation *et al.* stands for *et alia,* "and others." Use it only in a footnote or bibliography when citing a book written by three or more authors.

> Maynard Mack et al., eds., *World Masterpieces,* 3rd ed. (New York: Norton, 1973) 73–74.

everyday, every day *Everyday* means "ordinary" or "regular."

> The governor has a common touch; even in public speeches he likes to use everyday words.

Every day means "daily."

> While in training, Mary Thomas commonly runs at least ten miles every day.

except *See* accept.

factor *Factor* means "contributing element" or "partial cause." It can be used effectively, but far too often it simply clutters and obscures the sentence in which it appears. In general, you should avoid it.

> * One factor in the decay of the cities is the movement of middle-class families to the suburbs.

EDITED: One reason for the decay of the cities is the movement of middle-class families to the surburbs.

farther, further *Farther* means "a greater distance."

The trail went farther into the bush than the hunter had expected.

As an adjective, *further* means "more."

After high school, how many students really need further education?

As a conjunctive adverb, *further* means "besides."

Lincoln disliked slavery; further, he abhorred secession.

As a transitive verb, *further* means "promote" or "advance."

How much has the federal government done to further the development of solar energy?

fatal, fateful *Fatal* means "sure to cause death" or "resulting in death."

Even a small dose of cyanide is fatal.

In a fruitless and fatal attempt to save the manuscript that he had spent ten years to produce, the novelist rushed back into the burning house.

Fateful means "momentous in effect," and can be used whether the outcome is good or bad.

In the end, Eisenhower made the fateful decision to land the Allies at Normandy.

few, little, less Use *few* or *fewer* with countable nouns.

Few pianists even try to play the eerie music of George Crumb.

Use *little* (in the sense of "not much") or *less* with uncountable nouns.

A little honey on your hands can be a big sticky nuisance.

In spite of his grandiloquent title, the vice-president of the United States often has less power than a congressman.

former, formerly, formally As an adjective, *former* means "previous."

When we moved in, the apartment was a mess. The former tenants had never even bothered to throw out the garbage.

As a noun, *former* refers to the first of two persons or things mentioned previously.

Muhammad Ali first fought Leon Spinks in February 1978. At the time, the former was an international celebrity, while the latter was a twenty-four-year-old unknown.

Formerly means "at an earlier time."

Most of the men in the tribe were formerly hunters, not farmers.

Formally means "in a formal or ceremonious manner."

The president is elected in November, but he does not formally take office until the following January.

frightened, afraid   *Frightened* is followed by *at* or *by.*

> Many people are frightened at the thought of dying.
> As I walked down the deserted road, I was frightened by a snarling wolfhound.

Afraid is followed by *of.*

> Afraid of heights, Sylvia would not go near the edge of the cliff.

fun   Use *fun* as a noun, but not (in formal writing) as an adjective before a noun.

> As soon as Mark arrived, the fun began.
> * We spent a fun afternoon at the zoo.
> EDITED: We spent an enjoyable afternoon at the zoo.

further   *See* farther.

good, well   Use *good* as an adjective, but not as an adverb.

> The proposal to rebuild the chapel sounded good to many in the congregation.
> * She ran good for the first twenty miles, but then she collapsed.
> EDITED: She ran well for the first twenty miles, but then she collapsed.

Use *well* as an adverb when you mean "in an effective manner" or "ably."

> Fenneman did so well in practice that the coach decided to put him in the starting lineup for the opening game.

Use *well* as an adjective when you mean "in good health."

> My grandfather hasn't looked well since his operation.

* **got to**   *See* has to.

hanged, hung   *Hanged* means "executed by hanging."

> The prisoner was hanged at dawn.

Hung means "suspended" or "held oneself up."

> I hung my coat on the back of the door and sat down.
> I hung on the side of the cliff, frantically seeking a foothold.

Do not use *hung* to mean "executed by hanging."

> * They hung the prisoner at dawn.
> EDITED: They hanged the prisoner at dawn.

has to, have to, * got to   In formal writing, do not use * *got to* to denote an obligation. Use *have to, has to,* or *must.*

> * Anyone who wants to win the nomination has got to run in the primaries.
> EDITED: Anyone who wants to win the nomination has to run in the primaries.

hopefully   Use *hopefully* to modify a verb.

> As the ice-cream truck approached, the children looked hopefully at their parents. [*Hopefully* modifies *looked,* telling how the children looked.]

Do not use *hopefully* when you mean "I hope that," "we hope that," or the like.

> * Hopefully, the company will make a profit in the final quarter.
> EDITED: The stockholders hope that the company will make a profit in the final quarter.

human, humane   *Human* means "pertaining to human beings."

> To err is human.

Humane means "merciful," "kindhearted," or "considerate."

> To forgive is both divine and humane.

illusion   *See* allusion.

immanent, imminent   *See* eminent.

immigrate, emigrate   *Immigrate* means "enter a country in order to live there permanently."

> Professor Korowitz immigrated to the United States in 1955.

Emigrate means "leave one country in order to live in another."

> My great-great-grandfather emigrated from Ireland in 1848.

immoral   *See* amoral.

imply, infer   *Imply* means "suggest" or "hint at something."

> The manager implied that I could not be trusted with the job.

Infer means "reach a conclusion on the basis of evidence"; it is often used with *from*.

> From the manager's letter I inferred that my chances were nil.

in, into, in to   Use *in* when referring to a direction, location, or position.

> Easterners used to think that everyone in the West was a cowboy.

Use *into* to mean movement toward the inside.

> Before he started drilling, the dentist shot Novocain into my gum.

Use *in to* when the two words have separate functions.

> The museum was open, so I walked in to look at the paintings.

incredible, incredulous   *Incredible* means "not believable."

> Since unmanned exploration of Mars has revealed no signs of life there, the idea that "Martians" could invade the earth is now incredible.

In formal writing, do not use *incredible* to mean "amazingly bad," "compelling," "brilliant," or "extraordinary." In speech, you can indicate the meaning of *incredible* by the way you say it, but in writing, this word may be ambiguous and confusing.

> * Marian gave an incredible performance. [The reader has no way of knowing just how good it was.]
> EDITED: Marian gave a brilliant performance.

Incredulous means "unbelieving" or "skeptical."

> When Columbus argued that his ship would not fall off the edge of the earth, many of his hearers were incredulous, for they believed the earth was flat.

infer   *See* imply.

inferior to, * inferior than   Use *to* after *inferior*, not *than*.

> * America once led the world in its technology, but now many of its products—including the automobile—are inferior than those made elsewhere.
> EDITED: America once led the world in its technology, but now many of its products—including the automobile—are inferior to those made elsewhere.

insure   *See* assure.

* irregardless   *See* regardless.

irritate   *See* aggravate.

its, it's   *Its* is the possessive form of *it*.

> We liked the house because of its appearance, its location, and its price.

It's means "it is."

> It's a pity that we seldom see ourselves as others see us.

kind of, sort of   In formal writing, do not use *kind of* or *sort of* to mean "somewhat" or "rather."

> *When I got off the roller coaster, I felt sort of sick.
> EDITED: When I got off the roller coaster, I felt rather sick.

later, latter   Use *later* when referring to time.

> Russia developed the atomic bomb later than the United States did. During our century, aerospace technology has progressed with astounding speed. In 1903 the Wright brothers invented the first successful airplane; sixty-six years later, America put a man on the moon.

Use *latter* when referring to the second of two persons or things mentioned previously.

> Muhammed Ali first fought Leon Spinks in February 1978. At the time, the former was an international celebrity, while the latter was a twenty-four-year-old unknown.

lay   *See* lie.

lead, led   *Lead* (rhymes with *seed*) is the present-tense and infinitive form of the verb meaning "cause," "guide," or "direct."

> Deficit spending leads to inflation.
> An effective president must be able to lead Congress without bullying it.

Led is the past-tense form and past participle of *lead.*

> During the Civil War, General Robert E. Lee led the Confederate forces.
> Some buyers are led astray by simple-minded slogans.

learn, teach *Learn* means "gain knowledge, information, or skill." *Teach* means "give lessons or instructions."

> If you want to know how well you have learned something, teach it to someone else.

leave, let *Leave* means "go away from" or "put in a place."

> I had to leave the house at 6:00 A.M. in order to catch the bus.
> Just as I got to the bus station, I suddenly realized that I had left my suitcase at home.

Let means "permit," "allow."

> Some colleges let students take courses by mail.

led *See* lead.

less *See* few.

let *See* leave.

let's, *let's us Use *let's* before a verb. Do not follow *let's* with *us;* that would mean "let us us."

> *Let's us finish the job.
> EDITED: Let's finish the job.

liable *See* likely.

lie, lay *Lie (lie, lying, lay, lain)* is an intransitive verb meaning "rest," "recline," or "stay."

> I love to lie on the sand in the hot sun.
> Lying on the sand, I watched the clouds and listened to the pounding of the surf.
> After she lay in the sun for three hours, she looked like a boiled lobster.
> On April 26, 1952, workers digging peat near Grueballe, Denmark, found a well-preserved body that had lain in the bog for fifteen hundred years.

Lay (lay, laying, laid) is a transitive verb meaning "put in a certain position."

> "Lay down your weapons," shouted the captain. "We have you surrounded."
> A good education lays the foundation for a good life.
> The workers were laying bricks when an earthquake struck.
> He laid the book on the counter and walked out of the library.
> The earthquake struck after the foundation had been laid.

like *See* as.

likely, apt, liable   *Likely* indicates future probability.

> As gas becomes scarcer and more expensive, battery-powered cars are likely to become popular.

Apt indicates a usual or habitual tendency.

> Most cars are apt to rust after two or three years.

Liable indicates a risk or adverse possibility.

> Cars left unlocked are liable to be stolen.

little   *See* few.

loose, lose   *Loose* (rhymes with *moose)* means "free" or "not securely tied or fastened."

> The center grabbed the loose ball and ran for a touchdown.
> From the rattling of the door, I could tell that the catch was loose.

Lose (sounds like *Lou's)* means "fail to keep" or "fail to win."

> In some cultures, to lose face is to lose everything.
> The hard truth about sports is that whenever somebody wins, somebody else loses.

lots of, a lot of, *alot of   *A lot of* and *lots of* are colloquial and wordy. In formal writing, use *much* for "a great amount" and *many* for "a great number." Do not use **alot* anywhere; it is a misspelling of *a lot.*

> Lots of students come to college with no clear notion of what they want to do.
> BETTER: Many students come to college with no clear notion of what they want to do.

many, much, *muchly   Use *many* with countable nouns.

> Many hands make light work.

Use *much* with uncountable nouns.

> Much of the work has been done.

Use *much* or *very much,* not **muchly,* as an adverb.

> *The long sleep left me muchly refreshed.
> EDITED: The long sleep left me much [for "very much"] refreshed.

maybe, may be   *Maybe* means "perhaps."

> Maybe all cars will be electric by the year 2000.

May be is a verb phrase.

> Before the year 2000, the president of the United States may be a woman.

might have, *might of   Use *might have,* not **might of.*

> *Oklahoma might of won the game if it had lasted just two minutes longer.
> EDITED: Oklahoma might have won the game if it had lasted just two minutes longer.

moral, morale   *MORal* (first syllable accented) is an adjective meaning "ethical" or "virtuous."

> To heed a cry for help is not a legal duty but a moral one.
> Piety and morality are two different things: a pious man can be immoral, and an impious man can be moral.

MoRALE (second syllable accented syllable accented) is a noun meaning "spirit," "attitude."

> Eisenhower's habit of mixing with his troops before a battle kept up their morale.

most, mostly, *most all   *See* almost.

much, *muchly   *See* many.

not very, none too, *not too   In formal writing, use *not very* or *none too* instead of *not too.

> *Not too pleased with the dull and droning lecture, the students filled the air with catcalls, spitballs, and paper planes.
> EDITED: None too pleased with the dull and droning lecture, the students filled the air with catcalls, spitballs, and paper planes.

nowhere, *nowheres   Use *nowhere,* not *nowheres.

> *The child was nowheres to be seen.
> EDITED: The child was nowhere to be seen.

number   *See* amount.

OK, O.K., okay   Avoid all three in formal writing. In business letters or informal writing, you can use *OK* as a noun meaning "endorsement" or "approval," or *okay* as a verb meaning "endorse," "approve."

> The stockholders have given their OK.
> Union negotiators have okayed the company's latest offer.

only   Place *only* carefully. It belongs immediately before the word, phrase, or clause it modifies.

> *At most colleges, students only get their diplomas if they have paid all their bills.
> EDITED: At most colleges, students get their diplomas only if they have paid all their bills.
> *Some busy executives only relax on Sundays.
> EDITED: Some busy executives relax only on Sundays.

For more on the placement of *only,* see section 12.17.

ourselves, ourself   Use *ourselves,* not *ourself,* when the antecedent is plural.

> Nearly an hour after the front-runners had come in, Sally and I dragged ourselves across the finish line.

passed, past   *Passed* means "went by" or "threw."

> The idiot passed me on the inside lane.
> Conversation ground to a painful halt, and minutes passed like hours.
> Seymour passed to Winowski, but the ball was intercepted.

As a noun, *past* means "a certain previous time" or "all previous time."

> Prehistoric monuments like Stonehenge speak to us of a past that we can only speculate about.

As an adjective, *past* means "connected with a certain previous time" or "connected with all previous time."

> Past experience never tells us everything we want to know about the future.

As a preposition, *past* means "beyond."

> The space probe *Pioneer 10* will eventually travel past the limits of the solar system.

persecute, prosecute   *Persecute* means "pester" or "harass."

> As Nero persecuted the Christians, Hitler persecuted the Jews.

Prosecute means "bring charges against someone in a formal, legal way."

> Al Capone ran his criminal empire so shrewdly that authorities took years to prosecute him.

personal, personnel   *PERsonal* (first syllable accented) is an adjective meaning "private" or "individual."

> In writing or speaking, you can sometimes use a personal experience to illustrate a general point.

PersonNEL (last syllable accented) is a noun meaning "persons in a firm or a military group."

> If you want a job with a big company, you normally have to see the director of personnel.

phenomenon, phenomena   *Phenomenon* means "something perceived by the senses" or "something extraordinary."

> A rainbow is a phenomenon caused by the separation of sunlight into various colors as it passes through raindrops.
> Old Barney is a phenomenon. At eighty years of age he still swims five miles every day.

Phenomena is the plural of *phenomenon.*

> The Northern Lights are among the most impressive phenomena in nature.

poor, poorly   Use *poor* as an adjective.

> The poor man stood waiting in the rain.

Use *poorly* as an adverb.

> Mayhew ran the last mile poorly.

Do not use *poor* as an adverb:

> *The car starts poor in cold weather.
> EDITED: The car starts poorly in cold weather.

Do not use *poorly* as an adjective.

> *Heather looked poorly after the operation.
> EDITED: Heather looked poor after the operation.

precede, proceed, proceeds, proceedings, procedure   To *precede* is "to come before or go before in place or time."

> A dead calm often precedes a hurricane.

To *proceed* is "to move forward or go on."

> With the bridge washed out, the bus could not proceed, so we had to get out and take a ferry across the river.
> The bishop proceeded toward the cathedral.
> After the judge silenced the uproar, he told the prosecutor to proceed with her questioning.

Proceeds are funds generated by a business deal or a money-raising event.

> The proceeds of the auction went to buy new furniture for the Student Center.

Proceedings are formal actions, especially in an official meeting.

> During a trial, a court stenographer takes down every word of the proceedings for the record.

A *procedure* is a standardized way of doing something.

> Anyone who wants to run a meeting effectively should know the rules of parliamentary procedure.

principal, principle   As a noun, *principal* means "administrator" or "sum of money."

> The school principal wanted all of us to think of him as a pal, but none of us did.
> The interest on the principal came to $550 a year.

As an adjective, *principal* means "most important."

> In most American households, television is the principal source of entertainment.

Principle means "rule of behavior," "basic truth," or "general law of nature."

> Whenever we officially recognize a government that abuses its own citizens, we are tacitly accepting the principle that might makes right.

proceed   *See* precede.

proceeds, proceedings, procedure   *See* precede.

prosecute   *See* persecute.

quote, quotation   *Quote* means "repeat the exact words of."

> In his "Letter from Birmingham Jail," Martin Luther King, Jr., quotes Lincoln: "This nation cannot survive half slave and half free."

Do not use *quote* to mean "refer to" or "paraphrase the view of." Use *cite.*

> In defense of his stand against segregation, King cites more than a dozen authorities, and he quotes Lincoln: "This nation cannot survive half slave and half free."

Do not use *quote* as a noun to mean "something quoted." Use *quotation.*

> *A sermon usually begins with a quote from Scripture.
> EDITED: A sermon usually begins with a quotation from Scripture.

GLOSSARY OF USAGE   633

Quotation means "something quoted," as in the preceding example. But you should not normally use it to mean something *you* are quoting.

> *In a quotation on the very first page of the book, Holden expresses his opinion of Hollywood. "If there's one thing I hate," he says, "it's the movies." [Holden is not quoting anybody. He is speaking for himself.]
>
> EDITED: Holden states his opinion of Hollywood on the very first page of the book: "If there's one thing I hate," he says, "it's the movies."

raise, rise   *Raise (raise, raising, raised, raised)* is a transitive verb—one followed by an object.

> Moments before his hanging, Dandy Tom raised his hat to the ladies.
> My grandmother has raised ten children.

Rise (rise, rising, rose, risen) is an intransitive verb—one that has no object.

> Puffs of smoke rose skyward.
> The farmhands rose at 5:00 A.M. Monday through Saturday.
> Have you ever risen early enough to see the sun rise?

rational, rationale, rationalize   *Rational* means "able to reason," "sensible," or "logical."

> Can a rational person ever commit suicide?
> Is there such a thing as a rational argument for nuclear warfare?

Rationale means "justification," "explanation," or "underlying reason."

> The rationale for the new bypass is that it will reduce the flow of traffic through the center of town.

Rationalize means "justify with one or more fake reasons."

> He rationalized his extravagance by saying that he was only doing his part to keep money in circulation.

real, really   *Real* means "actual."

> The unicorn is an imaginary beast, but it is made up of features taken from real ones.

Really means "actually."

> Petrified wood looks like ordinary wood, but it is really stone.

In formal writing, do not use *real* to modify an adjective.

> *In parts of the country, synthetic fuels have met real strong resistance.
>
> EDITED: In parts of the country, synthetic fuels have met really strong resistance.
>
> FURTHER REVISED: In parts of the country, synthetic fuels have met strong resistance. [This version eliminates *really*, which—like *very*—often weakens rather than strengthens the word it modifies.]

reason . . . is that, * reason . . . is because   Use *reason* with *that*, not with *because*, or use *because* by itself.

> *The reason many college freshmen have trouble with writing is because they did little or no writing in high school.

EDITED: The reason many college freshmen have trouble with writing is that they did little or no writing in high school. [or] Many college freshmen have trouble with writing because they did little or no writing in high school.

refer *See* allude.

regardless, *irregardless Use *regardless,* not *irregardless.*

*Irregardless of what happens to school systems and public services, some cities and towns have voted to cut property taxes substantially.
EDITED: Regardless of what happens to school systems and public services, some cities and towns have voted to cut property taxes substantially.

respectively, respectfully, respectably *Respectively* means "in turn" or "in the order presented."

The college presented honorary degrees to Harriet Brown and Emanuel Lee, who are, respectively, an Olympic medalist and a concert pianist.

Respectfully means "with respect."

Parents who speak respectfully to their children are most likely to end up with children who speak respectfully to them.

Respectably means "presentably" or "in a manner deserving respect."

She ran respectably but not quite successfully for the Senate.

rise *See* raise.

set, sit *Set (set, setting, set, set)* means "put" or "place."

I filled the kettle and set it on the range.
When daylight saving changes to standard time, I can never remember whether to set my watch forward or back.

Sit (sit, sitting, sat, sat) means "place oneself in a sitting position."

On clear summer nights I love to sit outside, listen to crickets, and look at the stars.
Grandfather sat in an easy chair and smoked his pipe.

sight, cite, site As a verb, *sight* means "observe" or "perceive with the eyes."

After twenty days on the open sea the sailors sighted land.

As a noun, *sight* means "spectacle," "device for aiming," or "vision."

Some travelers care only for the sights of a foreign country; they have no interest in its people.
The deadliest weapon of all is a rifle with a telescopic sight.
Most of us take the gift of sight for granted; only the blind know how much it is worth.

Cite means "refer to," "mention as an example or piece of evidence."

Anyone opposed to nuclear power cites the case of Three Mile Island. But just how serious was the accident that occurred there?

As a verb, *site* means "locate" or "place at a certain point."

> The architect sited the house on the side of a hill.

As a noun, *site* means "location" or "place," often the place where something has been or will be built.

> The site of the long-gone Globe Theatre, where Shakespeare himself once trod the boards, will soon be occupied by a reconstructed version of the Globe.

since *See* because.

sit *See* set.

site *See* sight.

so *See* very.

sometimes, sometime *Sometimes* means "occasionally."

> Sometimes I lie awake at night and wonder what I will do with my life.

As an adjective, *sometime* means "former."

> In the presidential campaigns of 1952 and 1956, Eisenhower twice defeated Adlai Stevenson, sometime governor of Illinois and later U.S. ambassador to the United Nations.

As an adverb, *sometime* means "at some point."

> A slot machine addict invariably thinks that he or she will sometime hit the jackpot.

somewhere, *somewheres Use *somewhere,* not **somewheres.*

> *Somewheres in that pile of junk was a diamond necklace.
> EDITED: Somewhere in that pile of junk was a diamond necklace.

sort of *See* kind of.

stationary, stationery *Stationary* means "not moving."

> Before you can expect to hit a moving target, you need to practice with a stationary one.

Stationery means "writing paper," "writing materials."

> Since my parents sent me off to college with a big box of personalized stationery, I feel obliged to write to them occasionally.

statue, statute *Statue* means "sculpted figure."

> The Statue of Liberty in New York harbor was given to America by France.

Statute means "law passed by a governing body."

> Some people are upset by the new statute governing the registration of motorcycles.
> Though the Supreme Court has ruled that abortion is legally permissible, some state legislatures have enacted statutes restricting the conditions under which it may be performed.

such a   Do not use *such a* as an intensifier unless you add a result clause beginning with *that*.

> WEAK: The commencement speech was such a bore.
> BETTER: The commencement speech was such a bore that I fell asleep after the first five minutes.

supposed to, *suppose to   Use *supposed to* when you mean "expected to" or "required to." Do not use **suppose to*.

> *Truman was suppose to lose when he ran against Dewey, but he surprised almost everyone by winning.
> EDITED: Truman was supposed to lose when he ran against Dewey, but he surprised almost everyone by winning.
> *I was suppose to get up at 5:30 A.M., but I overslept.
> EDITED: I was supposed to get up at 5:30 A.M., but I overslept.

teach   *See* learn.

than, then   Use *than* when writing comparisons.

> Many people spend money faster than they earn it.

Use *then* when referring to time.

> Lightning flashed, thunder cracked, and then the rain began.

that, which, who   Use *which* or *that* as the pronoun when the antecedent is a thing.

> There was nothing to drink but root beer, which I loathe.
> Any restaurant that doesn't serve grits ought to be closed.

Use *who* or *that* as the pronoun when the antecedent is a person or persons.

> I like people who can do things.   —R. W. Emerson
> Anyone that smokes a pack a day is living dangerously.

themselves, *theirselves, *theirself   Use *themselves*, not **theirselves* or **theirself*.

> *Fortunately, the children did not hurt theirselves when they fell out of the tree.
> EDITED: Fortunately, the children did not hurt themselves when they fell out of the tree.

then   *See* than.

there, their, they're   Use *there* to mean "in that place" or "to that place," and in the expressions *there is* and *there are*.

> I have always wanted to see Las Vegas, but I have never been there.
> There is nothing we can do to change the past, but there are many things we can do to improve the future.

There is and *there are* should be used sparingly, since most sentences are tighter and better without them.

> We can do nothing to change the past, but many things to improve the future.

Use *their* as the possessive form of *they.*

> The immigrants had to leave most of their possessions behind.

Use *they're* when you mean "they are."

> I like cats because they're sleek, quiet, and sly.

thus, therefore, *thusly   Use *thus* to mean "in that manner" or "by this means." In formal writing, do not use *thusly.*

> Carmichael bought a thousand shares of IBM when it was a brand-new company. Thus he became a millionaire.

Do not use *thus* to mean "therefore," "so," or "for this reason."

> A heavy storm hit the mountain. *Thus the climbers had to take shelter.
> EDITED: A heavy storm hit the mountain, so the climbers had to take shelter.

to, too   Use *to* when writing about place, direction, or position, and with infinitives.

> We drove from Cleveland to Pittsburgh without stopping.
> Like many before him, Fenwick was determined to write the great American novel.

Use *too* when you mean "also" or "excessively."

> In spite of the cast on my foot, I too got up and danced.
> Some poems are too confusing to be enjoyable.

try to, *try and   Use *try to,* not *try and.*

> *Whenever I feel depressed, I try and lose myself in science fiction.
> EDITED: Whenever I feel depressed, I try to lose myself in science fiction.

two   *See* to.

-type   Do not attach *-type* to the end of an adjective.

> *He had a psychosomatic-type illness.
> EDITED: He had a psychosomatic illness.

uninterested   *See* disinterested.

unique   *Unique* means "one of a kind."

> Among pop singers of the fifties, Elvis Presley was unique.

Do not use *unique* to mean "remarkable," "unusual," or "striking."

> *She wore a unique dress to the party.
> EDITED: She wore a striking dress to the party.

used to, *use to   Write *used to,* not *use to,* when you mean "did regularly" or "was accustomed to."

> *She use to run three miles every morning.
> EDITED: She used to run three miles every morning.

very, awfully, so   Use *very* sparingly, if at all. It can weaken the effect of potent modifiers.

> The very icy wind cut through me as I walked across the bridge.
> BETTER: The icy wind cut through me as I walked across the bridge.

Do not use *awfully* to mean "very."

> *We were awfully tired.
> EDITED: We were very tired.
> FURTHER REVISED: We were exhausted.

Do not use *so* as an intensifier unless you add a result clause beginning with *that.*

> *They were so happy.
> EDITED: They were so happy that they tossed their hats in the air.

wait for, wait on   To *wait for* means "to stay until someone arrives, something is provided, or something happens."

> The restaurant was so crowded that we had to wait half an hour for a table.

To *wait on* means "to serve."

> Monica waited on more than fifty people that night. When the restaurant closed, she could barely stand up.

way, ways   Use *way*, not *ways*, when writing about distance.

> *A short ways up the trail we found a dead rabbit.
> EDITED: A short way up the trail we found a dead rabbit.

well   *See* good

were, we're   Use *were* as a verb or part of a verb phrase.

> The soldiers were a sorry sight.
> They were trudging across a wheat field.

Use *we're* when you mean "we are."

> We're trying to build a telescope for the observatory.
> Most Americans have lost the urge to roam. With television scanning the world for us, we're a nation of sitters.

which, who   *See* that.

whose, who's   *Whose* means "of whom."

> Whose property has been destroyed?

Who's means "who is."

> Who's deceived by such claims?

would have, *would of   Use *would have*, not *would of*.

> *Churchill said that he would of made a pact with the devil himself to defeat Hitler.
> EDITED: Churchill said that he would have made a pact with the devil himself to defeat Hitler.

Have, not *of*, is also customary after *may, might, must,* and *should.*

Glossary of Grammatical Terms

absolute phrase A modifier usually made from a noun or noun phrase and a participle. It can modify a noun or pronoun or the whole of the base sentence to which it is attached.

> *Teeth chattering,* we waited for hours in the bitter cold.
> Who is the best person for the job, *all things considered?*

active voice *See* voice.

adjective A word that modifies a noun or pronoun, specifying such things as what kind, how many, and which one.

> For a *small* crime, he spent *seven* years in a *tiny* cell of the *old* prison.
> She is *funny.*

adjective phrase A phrase that modifies a noun or pronoun.

> A *long, thin* scar was visible on his back.
> On the table was a vase *with red roses.*
> It was a *once-in-a-lifetime* opportunity.

adjective (relative) clause A subordinate clause used as an adjective within a sentence. It normally begins with a relative pronoun—a word that relates the clause to a preceding word or phrase.

> Pablo Picasso, *who learned to paint by the age of twelve,* worked at his art for nearly eighty years.

adverb A word that modifies a verb, an adjective, another adverb, or a clause. It tells such things as how, when, where, why, and for what purpose. It often ends in *-ly.*

> She *seldom* spoke.
> The road was *extremely* bumpy.
> The cyclists were breathing *very heavily.*
> *Fortunately,* no one was injured.

640

adverb clause A subordinate clause used as an adverb within a sentence. It begins with a subordinator, a term like *because, if, when,* or *although.*

> We canceled the deal *because the buyer could not get a loan.*
> *If the temperature falls below freezing,* roads will become unsafe.
> Smiling *when the guests arrived,* she was miserable *when they left.*

adverb phrase A phrase that modifies a verb, an adjective, another adverb, or a clause.

> The fox hid *under the hedge.*
> Wary *at first,* we approached *in silence.*
> The children were eager *to see the clowns.*

agent The source of the action in a passive voice construction.

> The preamble was written by *Alice Harvey.*
> The launching of the space shuttle will be viewed by *millions.*

agreement of pronoun and antecedent Correspondence in gender and number between a pronoun and its antecedent.

> Nellie Bly, the American journalist, was noted for *her* daring. [*Her* is feminine and singular.]
> Ms. Sterns handed Mr. Nichols *his* briefcase. [*His* is masculine and singular.]
> You can't tell a book by *its* cover. [*Its* is neuter and singular.]
> The Andrews Sisters sang some of *their* best-known songs during World War II. [*Their* is plural and used for all genders.]

agreement of subject and verb Correspondence in number between the form of a verb and its subject. In most cases, the subject affects the form of the verb only in the present tense; when the subject is a singular noun or a third-person singular pronoun, the present tense is made by the addition of *-s* or *-es* to the bare form.

> Jerry *paints* houses.
> He *fishes* every summer.

When the subject is not a singular noun or a third-person singular pronoun, the present tense is normally the same as the bare form.

> I *paint* houses.
> The men *fish* every summer.

The verb *be* has special forms in the present and the past, as shown on p. 365.

antecedent The word or word group that a pronoun refers to.

> *Oliver* said that he could eat a whole pizza.
> *The police,* who have surrounded the building, expect to free the hostages tonight.
> A *snake* sheds its skin several times a year.

appositive   A noun, noun phrase, or series of nouns used to identify another noun, noun phrase, or a pronoun.

> The blackjack player, *an expert at counting cards in play,* was barred from the casino.
> They were denied their favorite foods—*ice cream, pizza, and peanut butter.*
> He and she—*brother and sister*—opened a record store.

article   A short word *(a, an* or *the)* commonly used before a noun or noun equivalent.

> *The* bombing of *a* village provoked *an* outcry of protest.

auxiliary (helping verb)   A verb used with a base verb to make a verb phrase.

> I *have* seen the Kennedy Library.
> It *was* designed by I. M. Pei.
> People *do* find it impressive.

bare form   The verb form used in the present tense with every subject except a singular noun and a third-person singular pronoun.

> When the children *laugh,* we *laugh* too.

base (bare-bone) sentence   A sentence without modifiers.

> Prices rose.
> Orders dropped.
> Customers saved money.

base verb   The principal verb in a verb phrase made with an auxiliary.

> She has *earned* a promotion.
> She will be *supervising* all overseas operations.

case   The form that a noun or pronoun takes as determined by its role in a sentence. The **subject case** is used for a pronoun that is the subject of a verb.

> The dog was far from home, but *he* still wore a leather collar.

The **object case** is used for a pronoun that serves as an object *(See* object) or that immediately precedes an infinitive.

> I found *him* trailing a broken leash behind *him.*
> I wanted *him* to come home with *me.*

The **possessive case** of a noun or pronoun indicates ownership of something or close connection with it.

> The *dog's* hind feet were bleeding, and *his* coat was muddy.

The **reflexive/emphatic case** of a pronoun indicates a reflexive action—an action affecting the one who performs it. This case is also used for emphasis.

> The dog hurt *himself;* I *myself* saw him do so.

clause   A word group consisting of a subject and a predicate.

> S   P
> We / bought an old house. [one clause]

$$\overset{S}{\text{After we}} / \overset{P}{\text{bought the house,}} \overset{S}{\text{we}} / \overset{P}{\text{found a crack in the foundation.}}$$
[two clauses]

$$\text{Furthermore, the } \overset{S}{\text{roof}} / \overset{P}{\text{leaked, the }} \overset{S}{\text{floors}} / \overset{P}{\text{sagged,}}$$

$$\text{and the } \overset{S}{\text{furnace}} / \overset{P}{\text{was out of order.}} \text{ [three clauses]}$$

collective noun   A noun naming a collection of people, animals, or things treated as an entity. Examples include *team, committee, herd, flock,* and *family.*

comma splice (comma fault)   The error of trying to link two independent clauses with nothing but a comma.

>*Sir Richard Burton failed to find the source of the Nile, John Hanning Speke discovered it in 1862.
>EDITED: Sir Richard Burton failed to find the source of the Nile; John Hanning Speke discovered it in 1862.

You could also separate the clauses with a period. That would give you two sentences.

common and progressive forms   Forms of the verb. The **common form** indicates a momentary, habitual, or completed action.

>They *take* excursions on weekends.
>He *opened* the door and *entered* the room.
>She *will finish* by dark.

The **progressive form** indicates a continuing action or one that was in progress when something else occurred.

>They *are taking* an excursion right now.
>He *was opening* the door when the cat scratched him.
>She *will be working* on the design throughout the day.

The progressive consists of some form of the auxiliary *be* followed by a present participle—a verb with *-ing* on the end.

comparative, positive, and superlative   Forms of the adjective and adverb. The **positive** form describes a person or thing without drawing a comparison.

>This lemonade tastes sour.
>Ms. Berkle talks loudly.

The **comparative** is used to compare one person, thing, or group with another person, thing, or group.

>Los Angeles is *bigger* than Sacramento.
>Cal was *more ambitious* than his classmates.
>Sheila argued *less persuasively* than Susan did.
>In general, women live *longer* than men.

The **superlative** is used to compare one person, thing, or group with all others in its class.

>Joan's quilt was the *most colorful* one on display.
>Whales are the *largest* of all mammals.
>Gold is the *most eagerly* sought mineral in the world.

gl/t

complete subject *See* subject.

complex sentence A sentence consisting of one independent clause and at least one subordinate clause. The independent clause in a complex sentence is usually called the main clause.

> Although Frank pleaded with Ida [subordinate clause], she would not give him the money [main clause].

compound-complex sentence A sentence consisting of two or more independent clauses and one or more subordinate clauses.

> When I moved to Chicago [subordinate clause], I first applied for a job [main clause], and then I looked for an apartment [main clause].

compound phrase Words or phrases joined by a conjunction, a comma, or both.

> The plan was *simple but shrewd.*
> We saw an *old, rough-skinned, enormous* elephant.
> The kitten was *lively, friendly, and curious.*
> You must *either pay your dues on time or turn in your membership card.*

compound sentence A sentence consisting of two or more independent clauses.

> Jill made the coffee, and Frank scrambled the eggs.
> He practiced many hours each day, but he never learned to play the piano well.

conditional sentence A sentence normally consisting of an *if* clause, which states a condition, and a result clause, which states the result of that condition.

> If it rains on the Fourth of July, the fireworks will be canceled.
> If Social Security were abolished, millions of retirees would be destitute.

conjunction (coordinating conjunction) A word used to show a relation between words, phrases, or clauses. The conjunctions are *and, yet, or, but, nor,* and—for joining clauses only—*for* and *so.*

> The tablecloth was red, white, *and* blue.
> Small *but* sturdy, the cabin had withstood many winters.
> Al *and* Joan walked to the meeting, *for* they liked exercise.

conjunctive adverb A word or phrase used to show a relation between clauses or sentences. Conjunctive adverbs include *nevertheless, as a result, therefore, however,* and *likewise.*

> The ship was supposed to be unsinkable; *nevertheless,* it did not survive its collision with an iceberg.
> The lawyer spoke for an hour; the jury, *however,* was unimpressed.

coordinating conjunction *See* conjunction.

coordination An arrangement that makes two or more parts of a sentence equal in grammatical rank.

Martha *took the script* home and *read it* to her husband.
The fight ended, and *the crowd dispersed.*
A porcupine or *a raccoon* had raided the garbage can.

correlatives Words or phrases used in pairs to join words, phrases, or clauses. Correlatives include *both . . . and, not only . . . but also, either . . . or neither . . . nor,* and *whether . . . or.*

He was *both* rich *and* handsome.
She *not only* got the part *but also* played it brilliantly.
Either they would visit us, *or* we would visit them.

dangling modifier A modifier without a headword—a word or phrase that it can modify.

Running angrily out the back way, a couple of milk bottles were overturned.
EDITED: Running angrily out the back way, he overturned a couple of milk bottles.

declarative sentence A sentence that makes a statement and ends with a period.

The earth orbits around the sun.
Americans spend millions of dollars on Japanese products every year.

definite pronoun *See* pronoun.

dependent clause *See* subordinate clause.

direct object *See* object.

direct and indirect reporting Two ways of reporting spoken or written statements and questions. A **direct report** reproduces within quotation marks the words someone spoke or wrote.

"He that cannot obey, cannot command," writes Benjamin Franklin.

An **indirect report** turns the original statement into a subordinate clause usually starting with *that.*

Franklin writes that anyone who cannot obey is unable to command.

double negative The error of using two negative words to make one negative statement.

*We *didn't* need *no* guide.
EDITED: We *didn't* need a guide. [or] We needed *no* guide.

expletive A word used before a linking verb when the linking verb is followed by the subject.

There was no food in the house.
It was exciting to see the bald eagles.

faulty comparison The omission of one or more words needed to make a comparison clear.

> *The neighborhood is more violent than five years ago.
> EDITED: The neighborhood is more violent than it was five years ago.

faulty parallelism A construction in which two or more elements are parallel in meaning but not in form.

> *He wants to write *with clarity, power, and logically.*
> EDITED: He wants to write *clearly, powerfully,* and *logically.*

faulty predication Using words after a linking verb that are not compatible with the subject.

> *A necessary step in any campaign to lose weight is *eating habits.*
> EDITED: A necessary step in any campaign to lose weight is *to change one's eating habits.*

faulty shift in tense An unjustified shift from one tense to another, or an inconsistency between the tense of a subordinate verb and the tense of the main verb.

> *I lit a candle, but the darkness *is* so thick I saw nothing.
> EDITED: I lit a candle, but the darkness was so thick I saw nothing.
> *Though he *blows* as hard as he could, the drummer drowned him out.
> EDITED: Though he blew as hard as he could, the drummer drowned him out.

fragment *See* sentence fragment.

fused sentence *See* run-on sentence.

future perfect tense *See* tense.

future tense *See* tense.

gender The form of a pronoun as determined by the sex of its antecedent, which may be masculine, feminine, or neuter.

> Bill [antecedent] brought *his* fishing rod, and Sally [antecedent] brought *her* paints.
> The sun [antecedent] shed *its* rays over the lake.

gerund A verbal noun made with the present participle.

> *Gambling* takes nerve.
> Fawn hated *washing dishes.*

headword A word or phrase modified by another word, phrase, or clause.

>   M   H
> A black leather *wallet* was found in the men's room.
>   M   H
> Running for the elevator, *Pritchett* nearly knocked over Mr. Givens.
>   M   H   M
> The *breeze* that refreshes us comes from the ocean.

helping verb *See* auxiliary.

imperative   *See* mood.

indefinite pronoun   *See* pronoun.

independent clause   A clause that can stand by itself as a simple sentence.

>   The roof leaks.

It can be combined with one or more other independent clauses in a compound sentence.

>   The roof leaks, and the floor sags.

And it can serve as the main clause in a complex sentence.

>   Whenever it rains, the roof leaks.

indicative mood   *See* mood.

indirect object   *See* object.

indirect report   *See* direct and indirect reporting.

infinitive   A form usually made by the placing of *to* before the bare form of a verb.

>   Some say that politicians are born *to run.*
>   The prisoners of war refused *to continue* their forced march.

After some verbs the *to* in the infinitive is omitted. Compare:

>   Jack wanted the little boy *to feed* the ducks.
>   Jack watched the little boy *feed* the ducks.

infinitive phrase   A phrase formed by an infinitive and its object, its modifiers, or both.

>   She hates *to see horror movies.*
>   It was beginning *to rain furiously.*
>   I hope *to find a job soon.*

interrogative pronoun   A pronoun that begins a question.

>   *What* is making that noise?

interrogative sentence   A sentence that asks a question and ends with a question mark.

>   Do whales have lungs?

intransitive verb   *See* transitive and intransitive verbs.

irregular verb   *See* regular and irregular verbs.

linking verb   A verb followed by a word or word group that identifies or describes the subject.

>   This machine *is* a drill press.
>   I *feel* good today.
>   That perfume *smells* sweet.

main clause   The independent clause in a complex sentence.

>   Since there was no food in the house, *we went to a restaurant.*

main verb   The verb of the independent clause in a complex sentence.

> I *cut* the grass before the storm came.
> Since the store was closed, we *drove* away.

misplaced modifier   A modifier that does not clearly point to its headword—the word or phrase it modifies.

> * *Crawling slowly up the tree,* the elderly Mrs. Cartwright spotted a bright green worm.
> EDITED: The elderly Mrs. Cartwright spotted a bright green worm crawling slowly up the tree.

mixed construction   Any combination of words that do not fit together grammatically or meaningfully.

> * Fearful of punishment caused the boy to stutter.
> EDITED: Fear of punishment caused the boy to stutter.
> EDITED: Fearful of punishment, the boy stuttered.

modal auxiliary   A helping verb that indicates the subjunctive mood.

> The children *should* be here on Father's Day this year.
> I'm not so sure that the average citizen *can* fight City Hall.

Besides *should* and *can,* the modal auxiliaries include *would, could, may, might, must,* and *ought.*

modifier   A word or word group that describes, limits, or qualifies another word or word group in a sentence.

> Pat smiled *winningly.*
> I *rarely* travel *anymore.*
> The big gray cat seized *the little* mouse *as it ran up the stairs.*
> *Polished to a high gloss,* the mahogany table *immediately* drew *our* attention.

mood   The form of a verb that indicates the writer's attitude toward a particular statement as it is made. The **indicative** is the mood used in statements of actuality or strong probability.

> He always *lingers* over his second cup of coffee.
> We *will sleep* well tonight.

The **imperative** is the mood of commands and requests made directly.

> *Be* quiet!
> Please *go* away.
> *Let us pray.*
> *Stop!*

The **subjunctive** is the mood used in statements of hypothetical conditions or of wishes, recommendations, requirements, or suggestions. Normally the subjunctive requires either a modal auxiliary or a subjunctive verb form.

> I wish I *could* go. [modal auxiliary expressing a wish]
> I wish I *were* a rock star. [subjunctive verb form expressing a wish]
> Each member *must* pay her dues by December 1. [modal auxiliary expressing a requirement]
> The rules require that each member *pay* her dues by December 1. [subjunctive verb form expressing a requirement]

nonrestrictive modifier   *See* restrictive and nonrestrictive modifiers.

noun   A word that names a person, creature, place, thing, activity, condition, or idea.

noun clause   A subordinate clause that is used as a noun within a sentence. It serves as subject, object, predicate noun, or object of a preposition.

> *Whoever contributed to the office party* deserves many thanks.
> I said *that I was hungry.*
> You are *what you eat.*
> He did not know *how he could start the engine.*

noun equivalent   A verbal noun or a noun clause.

noun marker   A word that marks the presence of a noun or noun equivalent.

> *The* soup was cold.
> *This* problem has never been solved.
> *Her* haircut turned heads.
> *His* singing electrified the audience.

noun phrase   A phrase formed by a noun and its modifiers.

> She floated happily on *a big, fat, black inner tube.*
> *The eighteenth-century building* was declared a landmark last week.

number   The form of a word as determined by the number of persons or things it refers to. Most nouns and many pronouns may be singular or plural.

> A *carpenter* [singular] works hard.
> *Carpenters* [plural] work hard.
> Jeff said that *he* [singular] would give the party.
> All *his* [singular] friends said that *they* [plural] would come.

object   A word or word group naming a person or thing affected by the action that a verb, a participle, an infinitive, or a gerund specifies.

> I hit *the ball.*
> Sighting *the bear,* he started to aim *his rifle.*
> Splitting *wood* is hard work.

An **direct object** names the person or thing directly affected by the action specified.

> The accountant prepared *my tax return.*

An **indirect object** names the person or thing indirectly affected by the action specified.

> I gave *Joe* a bit of advice.
> She bought *her father* a shirt.

Objects also include any word or word group that immediately follows a preposition.

> For *her,* the meeting was crucial.
> I found the sponge under *the kitchen sink.*

object case   *See* case.

object complement   A word or word group that immediately follows a direct object and identifies or describes it.

> I found the first chapter *fascinating.*
> Many sportswriters consider Greg Louganis *the best diver in the world.*

parallel construction   The arrangement of two or more elements of a sentence in grammatically equivalent patterns: noun lined up with noun, verb with verb, phrase with phrase, and clause with clause.

> *Sink or swim, live or die, survive or perish,* I give *my hand* and *my heart* to this vote.   —Daniel Webster
> We must *take the risk* or *lose our chance.*

participle   A term usually made by the addition of *-ing, -d,* or *-ed* to the bare form of a verb.

present participle:	calling	living	burning	lifting
past participle:	called	lived	burned	lifted

A **perfect participle** is made by the combination of *having* or *having been* with the past participle.

> having called   having been lifted

participle phrase   A phrase formed by a participle and its object, its modifiers, or both. Usually it modifies a noun or pronoun:

> *Screaming the lyrics of its hit song,* the rock group could hardly be heard above the cheers of the crowd.
> *Wearied after their long climb,* the hikers were glad to stop and make camp.
> She picked at the knot, *loosening it gradually.*

passive voice   *See* voice.

past participle   *See* participle.

past perfect tense   *See* tense.

past tense   *See* tense.

perfect infinitive   The form of the infinitive made with *have* and the past participle.

> I was glad *to have finished* the project by the deadline.

perfect participle   *See* participle.

person   In English grammar the term *person* designates the following system of classification.

	SINGULAR	PLURAL
first person	I, me, mine, my	we, us, ours, our
second person	you, yours, your	you, yours, your
third person	he, him, his	
	she, her, hers	they, them, theirs, their
	it, its	
	and singular nouns	*and* plural nouns

phrase   A sequence of two or more words that serves as a unit within a clause.

> *A bright red kimono* caught my eye.
> *Encouraged by her friends*, Helen bought the house.
> I hurried *to reach the post office*.

possessive case   *See* case.

predicate   A word or word group that normally follows the subject of a sentence and tells what it does, has, or is, or what is done to it.

> The strong man *can lift 450 pounds.*
> The pastry chef *makes doughnuts, napoleons, and éclairs.*
> Venice *is a golden city interlaced with canals.*

A **base predicate (simple predicate)** is a predicate without its modifiers.

> Simon and Garfunkel *sang* for a crowd of almost half a million.
> The little boys *threw snowballs* at all of the passing cars.
> They *were* soon *punished.*

predicate adjective   An adjective or adjective phrase that follows a linking verb and describes the subject.

> Velvet feels *soft.*
> Henry seemed *upset by the vote.*

predicate noun   A noun or noun phrase that follows a linking verb and identifies the subject.

> Bill Gorham is *treasurer.*
> "Ma Bell" is *a nickname for AT&T.*
> Time was our only *enemy.*
> Children eventually become *adults.*

preposition   A word used to show the relationship of a noun, pronoun, or noun equivalent to another word or word group in a sentence.

> The table was set *under* a tree.
> Hounded *by* his creditors, he finally declared himself bankrupt.

Besides *under* and *by*, prepositions include *with, at, of, in,* and *on.*

prepositional phrase   A phrase that starts with a preposition. Phrases of this type are regularly used as adjectives or adverbs.

> Helen admired women *with strong ambition.*
> Have you ridden *on the Ferris wheel?*

present participle   *See* participle.

present perfect tense   *See* tense.

present tense   *See* tense.

principal parts   The following parts of a verb.

PRESENT (BARE FORM)	PRESENT PARTICIPLE	PAST	PAST PARTICIPLE
see	seeing	saw	seen
work	working	worked	worked

progressive form   *See* common and progressive forms.

pronoun   A word that commonly takes the place of a noun or noun phrase. Pronouns may be definite or indefinite. A **definite pronoun** refers to an antecedent, a noun or noun phrase appearing before or shortly after the pronoun.

> As soon as Grant [antecedent] saw the enemy, *he* ordered his men to fire.
> Janis Joplin [antecedent] was only twenty-seven when *she* died.
> Though *he* won the battle, Nelson [antecedent] did not live to savor the victory.

An **indefinite pronoun** refers to unspecified persons or things. It has no antecedent.

> *Everyone* likes Marvin.
> *Anything* you can do, I can do better.
> *Nobody* around here ever tells me anything.

An **interrogative pronoun** introduces a question.

> *What* did the policeman say?
> *Who* is pitching for the Blue Jays tomorrow?

pronoun-antecedent agreement   *See* agreement of pronoun and antecedent.

reflexive/emphatic case   *See* case.

regular and irregular verbs   A **regular verb** is one for which the past and past participle are formed by the addition of *-d* or *-ed* to the present.

PRESENT (BARE FORM)	PAST	PAST PARTICIPLE
work	worked	worked
tickle	tickled	tickled
walk	walked	walked

An **irregular verb** is one for which the past, the past participle, or both are formed in other ways.

sew	sewed	sewn
have	had	had
eat	ate	eaten

relative clause   *See* adjective clause.

relative pronoun   A pronoun that introduces an adjective clause.

> Women *who* like engineering are hard to find.
> Some companies now make furnaces *that* burn wood as well as oil.

The relative pronouns are *which, that, who, whom,* and *whose.*

restricter   An adverb that limits or restricts the meaning of the word immediately after it.

> On the first day, we hiked *nearly* thirty miles.
> Walking along the beach, she *almost* stepped on a crab.

Restricters include *almost, hardly, just, only,* and *nearly.* When used at the end of a sentence, a restricter limits the meaning of the word just before it.

Tickets were sold to adults *only.*

restrictive and nonrestrictive modifiers   A **restrictive modifier** restricts or limits the meaning of its headword.

All taxpayers *who fail to file their returns by April 15* will be fined.

A restrictive modifier is essential to the meaning of a sentence. Without the modifier, the meaning of the preceding sentence would be fundamentally different.

All taxpayers will be fined.

A **nonrestrictive modifier** does not restrict or limit the meaning of its headword.

Daphne, *who loves football,* cheered louder than anyone else.

A nonrestrictive modifier is not essential to the meaning of a sentence. Without the modifier, the meaning of the preceding sentence remains basically the same.
Daphne cheered louder than anyone else.

run-on sentence (fused sentence)   Two or more independent clauses run together with no punctuation or conjunction between them.

* Mosquitoes arrived at dusk they whined about our ears as we huddled in our sleeping bags.
EDITED: Mosquitoes arrived at dusk, and they whined about our ears as we huddled in our sleeping bags.

sentence   A word group consisting of at least one independent clause. A sentence begins with a capital letter and closes with a period, a question mark, or an exclamation point.

The telephone was ringing.
By the time I got out of the shower, the caller had hung up.
I was furious!
Was the call important?

sentence fragment   A part of a sentence punctuated as if it were a whole one.

The plant drooped. *And died.*
I could not get into the house. *Because I had forgotten my key.*

sequence of tenses   The relation between the tenses of the verbs in a sentence that contains more than one verb, or in a passage of several sentences.

By the time I *arrived,* everyone else *had left.*
When the parade *goes* through town, all the townspeople *come* to see it.

simple sentence   A sentence consisting of just one independent clause.

The problem was complex.
It challenged the skill of experts.
For months there was no solution.

Then a solution was found by two veterans in the decoding department.

simple subject *See* subject.

split infinitive An infinitive in which one or more words are wedged between *to* and the verb.

The purchasing department is going *to carefully check* each new order.
BETTER: The purchasing department is going to check each new order carefully.

squinting modifier A modifier placed so that it could plausibly modify either the word(s) before it or the word(s) after it.

* Cutting classes frequently leads to low grades.
EDITED: Frequent cutting of classes leads to low grades.
EDITED: Frequently, cutting classes leads to low grades.
[or]
EDITED: Cutting classes leads frequently to low grades.

subject A word or word group that tells who or what performs or undergoes the action named by a verb, or that is described or identified in a linking verb construction.

Gossip fascinates me.
Morgan hit one of Johnson's best pitches.
Piccadilly Circus is the Times Square of London.
Does *your allergy* cause a rash?
Jan and I were pelted by the rain.
There was *a snake* under the chair.

A **simple subject** is a subject without its modifiers.

The old dusty *volumes* fell to the floor.

A **complete subject** is a subject with its modifiers.

The old dusty volumes fell to the floor.

subject case *See* case.

subject complement A word or word group that immediately follows a linking verb and identifies or describes the subject:

Blue is *my favorite color.*
The house was *enormous.*

subject-verb agreement *See* agreement of subject and verb.

subjunctive mood *See* mood.

subordinate (dependent) clause A clause that normally begins with a subordinator or a relative pronoun. Such a clause cannot stand alone as a sentence. It must be connected to or included in a main clause.

Because Mrs. Braithwaith was writing her memoirs, she reviewed all her old diaries and correspondence.
The essay *that won the prize* was written by a freshman.
I didn't know *where she had left the key.*

subordinate verb   The verb of a subordinate clause in a complex sentence.

> I cut the grass before the storm *came.*
> Since the door *was* open, I walked in.

subordinating conjunction   *See* subordinator.

subordination   An arrangement that makes one or more parts of a sentence secondary to and dependent upon another part.

> WITHOUT SUBORDINATION: The dog ate his dinner, and then he took a nap.
> WITH SUBORDINATION: *After the dog ate his dinner,* he took a nap.

subordinator (subordinating conjunction)   A word or phrase regularly used to introduce a subordinate clause.

> *Before* we left, I locked all the doors.
> They can do nothing *if* the drought continues.
> No one knew *when* the bus was scheduled to arrive.

superlative   *See* comparative, positive, and superlative.

tense   The form of a verb that helps to indicate the time of an action or condition.

> PRESENT: I jump.
> PAST: I jumped.
> FUTURE: I will jump.
> PRESENT PERFECT: I have jumped.
> PAST PERFECT: I had jumped.
> FUTURE PERFECT: I will have jumped.

transitive and intransitive verbs   A **transitive verb** names an action that directly affects a person or thing specified in the predicate.

> He *struck* the gong.
> Water *erodes* even granite.
> Did you *mail* the letters?
> We *elected* Sloan.

An **intransitive verb** names an action that has no direct impact on anyone or anything specified in the predicate.

> Wilson *smiled* at the comedian's best efforts, but he did not *laugh.*

verb   A word or phrase naming an action done by or to a subject, a state of being experienced by a subject, or an occurrence.

> Cavanaugh *runs* every day.
> Pandas *eat* bamboo.
> My aunt *has lived* in Chicago.
> President Reagan *was reelected* by a landslide.

verbal noun   A word or phrase formed from a verb and used as a noun.

> *Hunting* was once the sport of kings.
> I want *to travel.*
> *Fixing bicycles* keeps me busy.
> *To sacrifice his rook* would have been Gilman's best move.

verb phrase   A phrase formed by two or more verbs—a base verb and at least one auxiliary.

> Richard *may complete* his experiment by July.
> Alison *would have come* earlier if you *had called* her.

voice   The aspect of a verb that indicates whether the subject acts or is acted upon. A verb is in the **active voice** when the subject performs the action named by the verb.

> She *raised* her hand.
> He *painted* the ceiling.
> They *built* a house.

A verb is in the **passive voice** when the subject undergoes the action named by the verb.

> I *was told* to do it that way.
> The operation *was performed* by a famous surgeon.
> *Is* this form *preferred?*

Appendices

Appendix 1
Citing with
Notes—MLA
Style

Complete information on the MLA note style appears in the *MLA Handbook for Writers of Research Papers*, 3rd ed., by Joseph Gibaldi and Walter B. Achtert (New York: Modern Language Association, 1988). In what follows here, we explain how to use the MLA note style with the kinds of sources you are likely to use in a research paper written for a college course.

A1.1 Writing Footnotes and Endnotes

To cite a source by means of a note, put a slightly raised number in your text and, at the foot of the page or on a page of endnotes, a corresponding number followed by your identification of the source. Since careful measurements are needed to fit footnotes on the bottom of a page, endnotes are much easier to use. But footnotes are easier for the reader to find. Ask your teacher which format you are expected to follow.

Whether you use footnotes or endnotes, you should number your notes consecutively throughout the paper. Do not start with number 1 on each new page of your text.

Put the note number at the end of the sentence or group of sentences in which you have used a source. Avoid the awkwardness of putting a number in the middle of a sentence:

While Jung says that children's dreams are complex and frightening,[2] Foulkes's research has led him to conclude that children's dreams are "rather simple and unemotional."[3]

Every number you insert draws the reader away from your text to a note, and no reader wants to be interrupted in the middle of a sentence. If you

Placement of Footnotes

Raised numbers in text

Double-space between and within notes

Jung cites the dreams of an eight-year-old girl as evidence, suggesting they put her in touch with primordial images foretelling her own death.² But Foulkes questions this view. His own research has led him to conclude that children's dreams are "rather simple and unemotional."³

Quadruple-space between text and first note

²Carl G. Jung, "Approaching the Unconscious," Man and His Symbols, ed. Carl G. Jung and M.-L. von Franz (Garden City, NY: Doubleday, 1964) 69–75.

Number indented 5 spaces and raised

³David Foulkes, "Dreams of Innocence," Psychology Today Dec. 1978: 78.

Sample Endnotes

Walsh 10

Double-space

Notes

Number indented 5 spaces and raised

¹Erich Fromm, The Forgotten Language (1951; New York: Grove, 1957) 17.

²Carl G. Jung, "Approaching the Unconscious," Man and His Symbols, ed. Carl G. Jung and M.-L. von

Double-space between and within notes

refer to two or more sources in one sentence, use one number at the end of the sentence and one note to identify them all; within the note, use a semicolon between one reference and another:

While Jung says that children's dreams are complex and frightening, Foulkes's research has led him to conclude that children's dreams are "rather simple and unemotional."²

²Carl G. Jung, "Approaching the Unconscious," Man and His Symbols, ed. Carl G. Jung and M.-L von Franz (Garden City, NY: Doubleday, 1964) 69–75; David Foulkes, "Dreams of Innocence," Psychology Today Dec. 1978: 78.

A1.2 Writing Explanatory Notes

Besides documenting a source, a note can give an explanation that cannot be easily fitted into the text:

Psychologists disagree about the content and significance of children's dreams.¹ Jung believed that children's dreams could be rich, complex, and

¹I refer to children old enough to talk about their dreams. Though measurement of REM may tell us how long and how often infants dream, we have no way of knowing just what they dream about.

Explanatory notes are sometimes necessary, but before you write one, try to see whether you can fit the explanation into your text.

A1.3 Writing Notes—First and Later References

1. The first note for any source gives detailed information:

¹Lawrence Durrell, Bitter Lemons (New York: Dutton, 1957) 138–42.

The author's name in the normal order (surname last) is followed by a comma, the full title and subtitle (if any), the facts of publication in parentheses, the page numbers without p. or pp., and a period. The facts of a publication include the place, the publisher, and the copyright date. Use a colon after the place and a comma after the publisher.

2. Later references to a source normally include just the author's name, the page number(s), and a period:

²Durrell 197.

If you are citing more than one work by an author, use a short form of the title in references after the first:

⁸Durrell, Bitter 80.
⁹Durrell, Reflections 138-40.

CITING SOURCES IN MLA NOTE STYLE

(numbers refer to entries in A1.4)

A book with one author   1

A book with one author and an editor   2

A second or later edition   3

A book with two or three authors   4

A book with more than three authors or editors   5

A book with a corporate author   6

A work in more than one volume   7

A book in a numbered series   8

A short work from a collection   9

A reprint   10

A translation   11

An anonymous book   12

An article in a reference book   13

The first reference to *Reflections* would give the full title: *Reflections on a Marine Venus.*

A1.4   Writing Notes for Various Sources

1. A book with one author

> [1]Robert Hartman, Credit for College: Public Policy for Student Loans (New York: McGraw-Hill, 1971) 45.

2. A book with one author and an editor

> [2]Theodore Dreiser, Sister Carrie, ed. Kenneth S. Lynn (New York: Rinehart, 1959) 145.

Put the author's name first when you are citing the author's text. To cite material written by the editor, start with the editor's name and the uncapitalized title of the material.

> Kenneth S. Lynn, introduction, Sister Carrie, by Theodore Dreiser (New York: Rinehart, 1959) xvi.

An article in a journal   14

An article in a periodical published monthly, weekly, or daily   15

An unsigned article   16

Newspaper article   17

An editorial   18

An interview   19

A personal letter to the researcher   20

A government publication   21

A document from an information service   22

Computer software   23

A television program   24

A recording   25

A film   26

A live performance   27

A work of art   28

3. A second or later edition

> [4]Robert E. Ornstein, The Psychology of Consciousness, 2nd ed. (New York: Harcourt, 1977) 104—15.

The abbreviation "2nd ed." means "second edition."

4. A book with two or three authors

> [5]Nathan Dickmeyer, John Wessels, and Sharon L. Coldren, Institutionally Funded Student Financial Aid, (Washington: American Council on Education, 1981) 8.

The name of each author is given in full in ordinary word order.

5. A book with more than three authors or editors

Give the name of the first author listed and add the abbreviation "et al.," which means "and others."

> [6]Robert H. Fenske et al., eds., Handbook of Student Financial Aid (San Francisco: Jossey-Bass, 1983) 22.

6. A book with a corporate author

> [7]Sloan Study Consortium, Paying for College:
> Financing Education at Nine Private Institutions
> (Hanover, NH: UP of New England, 1974) 30.

7. A work in more than one volume

> [8]Page Smith, A New Age Now Begins, 2 vols. (New
> York: McGraw-Hill, 1976) 2: 15—25.

The number of volumes in the work follows the title, and the volume cited appears at the end, followed by a colon and the page numbers.

8. A book in a numbered series

> [9]Joe B. Henry, ed., The Impact of Student Finan-
> cial Aid on Institutions, New Directions for Institu-
> tional Research 25 (San Francisco: Jossey-Bass) 12—20.

The name of the series and the number of the book follow the title.

9. A short work from a collection

> [10]Robert Frost, "The Death of the Hired Man," The
> Poetry of Robert Frost, ed. Edward Connery Lathem (New
> York: Holt, 1969), 39—40.

> [11]Ernest Hemingway, "The Short Happy Life of
> Francis Macomber," The Short Stories of Ernest Hem-
> ingway (New York: Scribner's, 1938) 3—37.

> [12]Samuel Taylor Coleridge, "The Rime of the Ancient
> Mariner," The Norton Anthology of English Literature,
> ed. M. H. Abrams et al., 2 vols. (New York: Norton,
> 1962) 2: 181—97.

> [13]George E. Dimock, Jr., "The Names of Odysseus,"
> Essays on The Odyssey: Selected Modern Criticism, ed.
> Charles Taylor (Bloomington: Indiana UP, 1963) 54—72.

Note above what happens to the title of a book *(The Odyssey)* when it appears within the title of another book: it is not underlined.

10. A reprint

> ^{14}Jessie L. Weston, From Ritual to Romance (1920; Garden City, NY: Anchor-Doubleday, 1957) 32–45.

The date of the original publication comes first, followed by a semicolon. The date of the reprint follows the name of the publisher.

11. A translation

> ^{15}Gustave Flaubert, Madame Bovary, trans. Francis Steegmüller (New York: Random House, 1957) 46–52.

To cite material from the translator's introduction or notes, use this form:

> ^{16}Francis Steegmüller, trans., Madame Bovary, by Gustave Flaubert (New York: Random House, 1957) v–xv.

12. An anonymous book

> ^{17}College Cost Book, 1982–83 (New York: College Entrance Examination Board, 1983) 23.

13. An article in a reference book

In citing articles from familiar reference works, give the name(s) of the author(s), the title of the article, the title of the book, and the year of the edition. If the articles are alphabetically arranged, you don't need volume or page numbers:

> ^{18}Edward S. Kilma, "Phonetics," Funk & Wagnalls New Encyclopedia, 1973 ed.

The initials usually given at the end of the article will lead you to the name(s) of the author(s) in a reference list commonly given at the beginning of the book. If the article is unsigned, start with its title:

> ^{19}"Pollution," The Columbia Encyclopedia, 1963 ed.

If the edition is numbered, give the edition number before the year(s) of publication:

> ^{20}"Martha Graham," Who's Who of American Women, 13th ed., 1983–84.

If the book is specialized or has appeared in only one or two editions, give full information about its publication:

> [21]Kurt Weinberg, "Romanticism," Princeton Ency-
> clopedia of Poetry and Poetics, ed. Alex Preminger,
> Frank J. Warnke, and O. B. Hardison, Jr., enl. ed.
> (Princeton: Princeton UP, 1974).

Note that even here you need no page numbers so long as the article has been alphabetized.

14. An article in a journal

> [22]Max Delbrück, "Mind from Matter?" The American
> Scholar 47 (1978): 345.

The name of the journal is followed by the volume number, date, and pages. If each issue in the volume starts from page 1, give the volume and issue number with a period between:

> [23]Sheldon I. Posen and Joseph Sciorra, "Brook-
> lyn's Dancing Tower," Natural History 92.6 (1983): 30–
> 37.

15. An article in a periodical published monthly, weekly, or daily

> [24]Jane Stein, "The Bioethicists: Facing Matters
> of Life and Death," Smithsonian Jan. 1979: 107–09.
> [25]Richard L. Strout, "Another Bicentennial,"
> Christian Science Monitor 10 Nov. 1978: 27.

Abbreviate the name of the month (except May, June, and July) and put the day of the month first when the day is given.

16. An unsigned article

> [26]"The Vietnam War: The Executioner," Newsweek 13
> Nov. 1978: 70.

When the article is unsigned, begin with the title.

17. A newspaper article

> [27]Jane E. Brody, "Multiple Cancers Termed on Increase," New York Times 10 Oct. 1976: sec. 1: 37.

18. An editorial

> [28]"How to End Watergate," editorial, New York Times 10 Jan. 1979, city ed.: A22.

You should identify an editorial as such to distinguish it from a news report. If the editorial is signed, begin the entry with the writer's name. Otherwise begin with the title of the article.

19. An interview

> [29]Harland W. Hoisington, Jr., Director of Financial Aid at Dartmouth College, personal interview, 3 May 1985.

20. A personal letter to the researcher

> [30]Walter S. Achtert, letter to the author, 2 Nov. 1984.

21. A government publication

> [31]United States, National Commission on Student Financial Assistance, Access and Choice: Equitable Financing of Postsecondary Education, Rept. 7 (Washington: GPO, 1983) 10—15.

"GPO" is a standard abbreviation for "Government Printing Office."

22. A document from an information service

> [32]National Commission on Student Financial Assistance, Access and Choice: Equitable Financing of Postsecondary Education, Rept. 7 (ERIC, 1983) (ED 234 734).

The initials ERIC stand for Educational Resources Information Center. If the document was originally published by someone other than ERIC, cite the original publisher in the usual way before giving the ERIC data:

[33]Paul Franklin, Beyond Student Financial Aid: Issues and Options for Strengthening Support Service Programs under Title IV of the Higher Education Act (Washington: College Entrance Examination Board, 1980) (ERIC ED 185 913).

23. Computer software

[34]Wayne Holder, The Word Plus, computer software, Oasis Systems, 1982.

24. A television program

[35]"The Enlightened Machine," The Brain, narr. George Page, PBS, WETK, Burlington, VT, 10 Oct. 1984.

25. A recording

[36]Robert Frost, "The Road Not Taken," Robert Frost Reads His Poetry, Caedmon, TC 1060, 1956.

26. A film

[37]Way Down East, dir. D. W. Griffith, with Lillian Gish, Creighton Hale, and Burr McIntosh, D. W. Griffith, Inc., 1920.

If your reference is to a particular individual involved in the film, begin with his or her name:

[38]John Guare, screenwriter, Atlantic City, dir. Louis Malle, with Burt Lancaster, Kate Reid, and Susan Sarandon, Paramount, 1980.

27. A live performance

> ³⁹William Shakespeare, Much Ado about Nothing, dir.
> Terry Hands, with Derek Jacobi and Sinead Cusack,
> Gershwin Theatre, New York, 19 Oct. 1984.

28. A work of art

> ⁴⁰J. M. W. Turner, Snow Storm: Hannibal and His
> Army Crossing the Alps (1812), The Tate Gallery, Lon-
> don.

A1.5 Writing the Bibliography

The bibliography for a paper documented with notes in the MLA style
should follow the general and specific rules given for the list of Works
Cited in section 35.2, pp. 545–64.

EXERCISE 1 Citing Notes—The MLA Style

Take the information given on each source in Chapter 35, exercise
1, pp. 564–65, and use it to write two entries in the MLA note style:
one on the source as it would appear in a note and the other on the
source as it would appear in the bibliography.

EXAMPLE

IN A NOTE

> Paul Fussell, The Great War and Modern Memory (NY: Oxford
> UP, 1975) 96–97.

IN THE BIBLIOGRAPHY

> Fussell, Paul. The Great War and Modern Memory. NY: Oxford
> UP, 1975.

A1.6 Sample Explanatory Research Paper with MLA Note Style

Erica Berl

Professor Stephen Jones

English 101

November 10, 1989

Options for the Working Mother

Everyone knows that women are no longer staying at home. They have gone out into the world of
work, filling not only such traditionally feminine
roles as secretary and clerk, but also such typically masculine roles as lawyer, doctor, stockbroker, business executive, United States senator,
and even candidate for the vice presidency. At the
same time, statistics show that a growing percentage of working women are mothers of preschool children. While less than a third of these mothers held
jobs outside the home in 1970, the figure rose to
nearly a half by 1978 and is expected to keep on
rising into the 1990s.[1] A crucial question of our
time, therefore, is how these women can reconcile
the demands of a career with the responsibilities
of childrearing. By examining various answers to
this question, we can understand the options open
to American women.

The cheapest solution to this problem is for
the working mother to find a relative willing to
supervise her children while she works. But aside

from the children's father, who may not be living
with her and who in any case usually has a job of
his own, she may not have relatives near enough or
free enough to serve as babysitters. The children's
grandparents, for instance, may live beyond commut-
ing distance, and even if they live nearby and are
willing to babysit regularly, they too may both be
holding jobs that make them unavailable during the
day. In any case, a census taken in 1982 showed
that less than half the working mothers of young
children had them supervised by a relative other
than their father.[2]

An obvious alternative to the babysitting relative is the professional babysitter who can be
hired to care for children alone or in small
groups, usually in the babysitter's home. But the
major drawback here is that professional babysitters cost money. Since a professional babysitter is
running a business, he or she must not only cover
expenses but also make a profit, which often means
consuming a substantial portion of the working
mother's paycheck.

The decreasing availability of relatives for
babysitting and the high cost of professional babysitters have together helped to increase the use of
preschools, where children are taught as well as

supervised. Kamerman reports that from 1967 to
1980, kindergarten enrollment rose by about a
third, and from 1969 to 1980, nursery school
enrollment of three- and four-year-olds more than
doubled.[3] Kindergartens are especially attractive
because 88 percent of them are public and therefore
free. But kindergartens do not take children under
five, and only 34 percent of nursery schools are
public.[4] As a result, the only kind of preschool
available for most three- and four-year-olds is the
private nursery school, which charges fees that not
all working mothers can afford.

Another kind of preschooling, however, is
absolutely free. Federally funded Head Start centers are designed to help poor women work so they
can escape from their poverty and shed their dependence on welfare.[5] In these centers, children of
poor parents get not only an education but also
medical care, dental care, and psychological coun-
seling. Furthermore, under Title XX of the Social
Security Act of 1975, the number of these centers
has grown from about eight thousand in 1977 to over
eleven thousand in 1981, and in quality they usually surpass federal guidelines.[6]

Nevertheless, besides the fact that funding
for the Title XX programs has recently been cut,

Head Start centers do not help working mothers of
the vast middle class.[7] In fact, as Norgren
observes, none of the current federal programs is
designed for them.[8] So where can they find day care
for their children? A number of private centers
have been established by churches, settlement
houses, social agencies, parent cooperatives, hospitals, and universities. But Feinstein notes that
because these centers have to meet federal guidelines in order to be licensed, they are costly to
run and expensive to use.[9]

   Given the cost of independent day-care centers, a growing number of companies have established day-care centers of their own. In 1982, the
National Employer-Supported Child-Care Project
reported that 240 employees provided child-care
facilities, which was twice the number provided in
1978.[10] And to promote the establishment of still
more company-sponsored centers, the Reagan administration revised the tax code so that employers no
longer have to pay taxes on child-care benefits.

   Though some companies have been slow to
respond to such inducements, many have taken decisive action. Business Week reported recently that
Corning Glass Wares bought a church across the
street from its main office in New York and turned

it into a day-care center where employees can leave
their children for just forty-three dollars a week
per child, which covers only two-thirds of the
total operating cost.[11] Companies that subsidize day
care in this way often reap more than tax benefits.
According to Business Week, Intermedics Inc., which
makes pacemakers with the aid of a 70 percent
female staff, established a center where employees
can leave their children for just fifteen dollars a
week per child--barely a fourth of the operating
cost. But since the center was established,
employee turnover has dropped by 23 percent and
absenteeism has dropped by fifteen thousand hours.
As a result, productivity has increased by quite
enough to cover the cost of subsidizing the new
center.[12]

    Day-care centers in the workplace benefit
employee and employer alike. The mother who can
take her child to work saves the time that would
otherwise be required to leave and pick the child
up elsewhere. Because she can easily see her child
during the day--on her lunch hour, for instance--
and can easily get to the child in case of emergency, she is free from worry. As a result, she can
concentrate better on her work, which benefits her
employer. In addition, Clarke-Stewart notes that

because day-care centers relieve the mother from
the strain of caring for her child all day long,
they can also improve the "quality of time" that
mother and child spend together.[13]

Another way in which companies are beginning
to meet the needs of working mothers is the system
of flextime--an alternative to the standard eight-
hour day. Under flextime, the employee must work for
certain specified periods each day, such as from
9:00 to 11:00 and from 2:00 to 4:00, but otherwise
she can choose her working hours to suit her convenience from one day to the next. This gives the
mother extra time when she needs it in the morning,
in the afternoon, or in the middle of the day.

Though companies rarely declare an official
policy on flextime, they have been led to see its
advantages for them as well as for working mothers.
Business Week reported that Elizabeth Carlson, manager of personnel systems and research at Continental Illinois National Bank & Trust Company of
Chicago, left the bank because she was denied flextime there and went to work for Bell and Howell,
where she was granted it. When other employees left
the bank for the same reason, the bank stopped
fighting flextime and rehired Ms. Carlson on her own
terms.[14] Clearly, women are gaining new respect on

the job, and employers have begun to recognize the importance of meeting their needs. Says Eugene Ricci, president of CIGNA Service Company: "You don't voluntarily lose key people. Brains are hard to come by."[15] Thus flextime may eventually win acceptance in the business world at large. Lynette and Thomas Long note that while it is now available in only 15 percent of private organizations employing more than fifty people, three independent surveys have found that a majority of respondents would welcome it.

For women who cannot work a full day, even on flextime hours, the obvious alternative is a part-time job. Though many women say that part-time work reduces their chances for advancement, most of them agree that even part-time work is better than none at all.[16] And some women can do part of their jobs at home. Randi Starr Savitzky, a production manager at McDougal Littell & Company in Northbrook, Illinois, divides her working day between the office and her own home, where she uses a computer.[17]

All of the options so far described are available to the single mother--whether unmarried, divorced, or separated. Yet no matter how the working mother arranges her schedule, she will seldom if ever find that she can easily resolve the conflicts involved in pursuing a career while raising one or more children by herself. This is why the most valuable thing that a working mother can have is a husband who not only lives with her but also fully cooperates with her. If women are going to work outside the home, men must be willing to share the jobs that have to be done inside it, to help not just with weekend chores but also with the daily tasks of preparing meals, washing dishes, making beds, and--most importantly--looking after the children. This arrangement offers a bonus to both partners, since Levine has found that "marriages in which the parents share responsibilities equally tend to be the happiest."[18]

It takes a gift for organization to manage both a job and a family. But given the variety of ways in which the demands of each can be met, a woman no longer needs to feel that she must sacrifice one for the other, must abandon her family for the sake of her job or give up her job for the sake of her family. Working women who happen to be mothers have made themselves an indispensable part of the work force, and they are here to stay.

A. 1

A. 1

Berl 9

Notes

[1] U.S. Bureau of Labor Statistics, Women in the Labor Force: Some New Data Series, Rept. 575 (Washington: GPO, 1979) 1.

[2] U.S. Bureau of Census, Child-Care Arrangements of Working Mothers: June 1982 (Washington: GPO, 1983) 9–10.

[3] Sheila B. Kamerman, "Child-Care Services: A National Picture," Monthly Labor Review 106.12 (1983): 36.

[4] Kamerman 37.

[5] Karen Wolk Feinstein, "Directions for Day Care," Working Women and Families, ed. Karen Wolk Feinstein (Beverly Hills: Sage, 1979) 182.

[6] Kamerman 37.

[7] Kamerman 38.

[8] Jill Norgren, "In Search of a National Child-Care Policy: Backgrounds and Prospects," Women, Power, and Policy, ed. Ellen Boneparth (New York: Pergamon, 1982) 134.

[9] Feinstein 187.

[10] "Child Care Grows as a Benefit," Business Week 21 Dec. 81: 63.

[11] "Child Care Grows" 60.

[12] "Child Care Grows" 60.

[13] Alison Clarke-Stewart, Child Care in the Family: A

<u>Review of Research and Some Propositions for Policy</u>, A
Carnegie Council on Children Monograph (New York: Academic
Press, 1977) 111.

[14]"Working Around Motherhood," <u>Business Week</u> 24 May
1982: 108.

[15]"Companies Start to Meet Executive Mothers Halfway," <u>Business Week</u> 17 Oct. 1983: 191—95.

[16]"Companies Start" 195.

[17]"Companies Start" 191.

[18]James A. Levine, <u>Who Will Raise the Children?</u>
(Philadelphia: Lippincott, 1976) 176.

Berl 11

Works Cited

"Child Care Grows as a Benefit." Business Week 21 Dec. 1981:
    60–63.

Clarke-Stewart, Alison. Child Care in the Family: A Review
    of Research and Some Propositions for Policy. A Carnegie
    Council on Children Monograph. New York: Academic Press,
    1977.

"Companies Start to Meet Executive Mothers Halfway." Busi-
    ness Week 17 Oct. 1983: 191–95.

Feinstein, Karen Wolk. "Directions for Day Care." Working
    Women and Families. Ed. Karen Wolk Feinstein. Beverly
    Hills: Sage, 1979. 177–94.

Kamerman, Sheila B. "Child-Care Services: A National Pic-
    ture." Monthly Labor Review 106.12 (1983): 35–39.

Levine, James A. Who Will Raise the Children? Philadel-
    phia: Lippincott, 1976.

Norgren, Jill. "In Search of a National Child-Care Policy:
    Backgrounds and Prospects." Women, Power, and Policy.
    Ed. Ellen Boneparth. New York: Pergamon, 1982. 124–43.

U.S. Bureau of Census. Child-Care Arrangements of Working
    Mothers: June 1982. Washington: GPO, 1983.

U.S. Bureau of Labor Statistics. Women in the Labor Force:

Some New Data Series. Rept. 575. Washington: GPO, 1979.

"Working Around Motherhood." Business Week 24 May 1982: 108.

Appendix 2 Beyond Freshman English

WRITING EXAMINATIONS, APPLICATIONS, AND LETTERS

Anyone who writes well is likely to succeed in almost any writing task. But the requirements for various kinds of writing differ in some respects, and you should know what these differing requirements are. Also, you should know what good writing can do for you in the world beyond freshman composition. So this chapter aims to show you how to use your writing skills for a variety of purposes both in and out of the classroom.

A2.1 Writing Examination Essays

The best way to start writing a good examination essay is to read the question carefully. On a final examination in a course on modern American history, for example, students were asked to "show how Lyndon Johnson's policies in Vietnam grew out of the policies pursued by his predecessors from 1941 on." The question was quite pointed. It asked not for general impressions of the Vietnam War but for a specific analysis of the succession of policies that led America into it.

After reading the question, one student made a single scratch outline inside the cover of his bluebook:

CONTAINMENT
1. FDR, Truman—Vietnam and Korea
2. Ike—1954, SEATO, South Vietnam
3. JFK—military buildup
Sum up Johnson's inheritance

With those few notes before him, the student then wrote the following essay:

American involvement in the Vietnam War did not begin with Johnson, or even with Kennedy. Rather, it began during World War II and was developed considerably during the years of containment of the Truman administration. As Stephen Ambrose puts it in his book, the U.S. was paying up on an insurance policy on containment that began with the Truman doctrine (1947), was extended to Korea (1950), and was applied finally to Vietnam (1954).

In 1941, Roosevelt supported the Vietnamese (specifically Ho Chi Minh), along with the French colonialists, against Japanese aggression. But after the Japanese were forced out, intense fighting broke out between the French and the Vietnamese, and in 1950 Truman signed a Mutual Defense Agreement with the French. From this point on, the U.S. had committed itself to support anyone against Ho Chi Minh and the communists of Hanoi. Truman was thus applying to Vietnam the containment policy he was also using in Korea. As in Korea, the U.S. aimed to halt the communism (in this case, of China) anywhere.

The next rung in the American ladder of involvement came in 1954. The Vietnamese defeat of the French at Dien Bien Phu signalled the end of French involvement and the official beginning of American involvement. In September 1954 the Eisenhower administration formed the Southeast Asia Treaty Organization (SEATO) and committed the United States to the defense of South Vietnam as a bulwark against the expansion of Communist China.

Kennedy inherited much of Eisenhower's policy toward Vietnam and added some of his own thinking, leaving Johnson an even larger legacy of involvement. While Kennedy did not commit troops, his military actions were significant. First, he increased dramatically (to 16,000) the number of American advisers in Vietnam. Second, he gave American air support to South Vietnam and allowed American advisers to shoot back if shot at. Third, he began military preparations within the Pentagon. As a result of all these actions, the first death of an American soldier occurred during Kennedy's first year in office, and American casualties increased considerably.

When Kennedy was assassinated in 1963, Johnson inherited the Vietnam quagmire, and his inheritance was a rich one. From Roosevelt, he got the beginning of a U.S. role in Vietnam. From Truman, the policy of containment—the pledge to stop communist expansion at the hands of Ho Chi Minh. From Eisenhower he got an official commitment to the defense of South Vietnam. And from Kennedy, finally, he got the beginnings of a substantial U.S. military involvement there.

So Johnson's decision to send troops to Vietnam in 1965 simply capitalized on the military preparations that Kennedy had made. Though Johnson imposed his own personality on Vietnam policy, he was strongly influenced by what Truman, Eisenhower, and Kennedy gave him: the need to succeed in Vietnam—militarily—along the lines of containment.

Like most examination essays, this one shows some signs of haste, such as the sentence fragment in the next to last paragraph. But no one taking a one- or two-hour exam has much time to worry about the finer points of diction and sentence structure. What we do find here are the three things essential to a good examination essay: (1) a response focused sharply and consistently on the question, (2) a substantial quantity of specific detail, and (3) strong organization.

From beginning to end, the author consistently focuses on the development of the policies Johnson inherited. In the opening paragraph, he introduces the key idea of containment; in the concluding paragraph, after summarizing what Johnson inherited from each of his predecessors, he reaffirms the influence of this idea. In between, he traces its evolution through a succession of stages, with one paragraph for each major stage: Truman's application of containment to Vietnam, Eisenhower's commitment of U.S. support to South Vietnam, and Kennedy's military actions there. Throughout the essay, the author keeps his eye on the task of answering the question: of explaining what Johnson received from his predecessors and how that inheritance shaped his actions in Vietnam.

Now consider what another student did with a question on a sociology exam. Asked to "define 'economic-opportunity structure' and describe its relation to the traditional nuclear family," the student wrote this:

The "economic-opportunity structure" (EOS) refers to the "working world" and is most often associated with the practical aspect of marriage. Traditionally, males have had superior access to this structure and still do today.

In the traditional nuclear family, the male is the mediator between the family and the EOS. Such a position gives him considerable "power" within the family unit. If members of a family are totally dependent on the man for economic survival, they must concede all power and authority to him. He is the "king of the family." He brings home the fruits of the EOS, the production (usually monetary), and the family consumes these products, investing in various material possessions which in turn give them social status and prestige.

The man's degree of success in the EOS highly affects his relation to his wife and family. In the traditional family, if the man fulfills his "duty" as chief economic supporter, the wife "rewards" him with more attention to his needs and to her traditional duties—keeping a house and raising children.

The husband then rewards her in various ways, with a car of her own, perhaps, or a fur coat, or a bigger house. It's an ongoing cycle. The higher-status wives are also more likely to concede that the husband should have the "upper hand" in the marriage.

This whole cycle works in reverse in lower-status families where the husband is unsuccessful as a breadwinner, causing resentment among the wives and unwillingness to submit to his authority.

If the wife in the traditional nuclear family decides to enter the EOS, her commitment to a career is usually far less than that of her husband. Her primary duty is still to her family and husband. The husband remains chief economic provider. But the woman gains more marital power because now she actually brings income into the house. Her occupation gives her self-esteem, and the marriage moves toward an egalitarian relation.

All of these cases show how economic power outside the family affects the balance of power within it. A successful breadwinner is rewarded with attention; an unsuccessful one has to put up with resentment; and the status of a wife within the family improves when she takes a job. Thus the power of any one member of a nuclear family seems to depend a lot on his or her performance in the "economic-opportunity structure"—the working world.

The question calls for a definition of a phrase and an explanation of a relationship. The answer provides both. It defines the phrase and explains the relationship of the "EOS" to the traditional nuclear family, showing how the husband's power to make money affects his power within the family and how the status of the wife is affected by her decision to take a job. This essay has no introduction because it needs none; in effect, it is introduced by the question. But it does have a conclusion. Its final paragraph sums up its principal points, and its final sentence clearly states the essential point of the whole essay. (For more on conclusions, see section 3.6, pp. 67–70.)

To write a good examination essay, then, you should go directly to the point of the question. You should deal with the question as specifically as possible, and you should keep it continually in sight. Finally, you should end by summarizing your chief points and reaffirming the main point of the essay as a whole.

A2.2 Applying for Admission to a School of Business, Law, Medicine, or Graduate Study—The Personal Statement

Applying for admission takes more than simply filling out an application form. Most schools ask you to write a personal statement in which you explain why you plan to go into business, medicine, law, or an academic field. Your chances of getting admitted will of course depend considerably on your college grades, your letters of recommendation, and your performance on examinations like the LSAT. But a personal statement often tells more about you than anything else can. That is why it may well determine whether or not you are admitted to a particular school.

What kind of statement do admissions officers want? They want to know as specifically as possible what has led you to choose a particular career, what you hope to accomplish in it, and what you have already done to prepare yourself for it. The more specific you can be about your motivation, your experience, and your long-range plans, the more persuasive your statement will be. To see how this kind of information can be effectively presented, consider this statement made by an applicant to medical school:

> A major turning point in my life occurred following my second year in college, when I was hired as a research assistant in pediatric hematology at the New England Medical Center. During the sixteen months I spent in Boston, I gained valuable insights into the practice of medicine and found that I had a special aptitude for research. I returned to college determined to become a doctor and quite motivated in my academic work.
>
> At New England Medical Center I worked with very little supervision and was expected to be resourceful and creative in carrying out my lab responsibilities. I found that I had a talent for working out technical problems and the intellectual ability to design my own procedures. In addition to my laboratory work, I took the initiative to learn about the diseases seen by the department and about the treatment programs that were employed.
>
> I learned a great deal about terminal illness through my job, and also through the death, from leukemia, of the young son of close friends of mine. During the last months of this child's life, I spent a considerable amount of time with his family, helping them to cope with their impending loss. I found I was able to offer types of support other friends and family members could not. I matured and grew from this experience. I learned that I could be open and responsive when faced with difficult and painful situations. I also realized that a need existed for people who could assist the terminally ill and their families.
>
> In January 1989 I joined Hospice of Santa Cruz, where I was trained as a volunteer visitor and was assigned to the family of a man with stomach cancer. I feel that my involvement with the family is of benefit both to them and to me. I can support them by serving as a catalyst to get feelings expressed, and from them I am learning to be a compassionate listener. I am convinced my experience with Hospice will help me, as a medical worker, to be understanding and open in dealing with death.
>
> My academic work during the past two years, has, for the most part, been of outstanding quality. I chose to complete a chemistry major, with emphasis in biochemistry, and

will be graduating in December 1989. I have worked for the past year and a half on a senior research project in cryoenzymology. Laboratory work presents numerous technical and intellectual challenges, and I have become quite skilled and competent in approaching these problems. I have been attracted to research because it serves to ground the theory one learns in the classroom in practical day-to-day applications. Whereas I do not expect to pursue a career in research, my laboratory experience has given me a good perspective into the nature of scientific study, has helped me develop critical thinking skills, and has offered the pleasure and satisfaction that comes with the successful completion of a project.

This past academic year I have encountered for the first time the challenge of teaching. I have been a tutor in organic chemistry, introductory chemistry, and biochemistry. To be a good tutor one not only needs to have a solid command of the subject matter but must also look at the material from the student's perspective and seek creative methods to convey information in a way that can be grasped by the student. I have found that I can do this quite effectively, both at the very basic introductory level and at the more sophisticated level of biochemistry. Through tutoring I have discovered that I love teaching. I now realize that one of the compelling attractions that medicine offers me is the opportunity to be a teacher to all kinds of people, from patients to other physicians.

I am grateful to have had in these past five years a rich variety of experiences that have prepared me for the diversity I expect to encounter in a medical career. Research, teaching, the direct care of people who are sick, and encounters with death are all part of the practice of medicine. I have gained insights, limited though they may be, into all of these. As a result I am confident that I know what I will be facing as a doctor and that I have the skills and ability to be a creative and supportive physician.

This statement bristles with detail. It tells exactly how the writer discovered her interest in medicine and what she has already done to prepare herself for a career in it. By specifically describing her experiences in laboratory research, college courses, teaching, and working with the families of the terminally ill, she convincingly shows that she has both the ability and the sensitivity to make a career in medicine.

Furthermore, this statement is very well organized. Introduced with a paragraph on the particular experience that led the writer to a medical career, the statement concludes with a paragraph on the net effect of all her experiences. In between these two paragraphs, she tells in chronological order the story of her development, and each of her paragraphs is written to develop a point about what she learned. Altogether, it is not hard to see why she was admitted to medical school.

Obviously, this applicant had plenty of experience to write about.

But if you take the time to recall the various kinds of work that you yourself have probably done, you may discover that you too have had a good deal of experience. In any case, the fact that you have had experience will not by itself make your statement effective. You have to organize your account of that experience, to present it in such a way that the reader can see how it led to a specific end. The statement just discussed is organized in exactly this way, clearly showing how the stages of the writer's experience led to her desire for admission to medical school. To see what a difference organization makes, compare her statement with one made by an applicant to a graduate school of business:

> Represented a Cable TV association in a twelve-million dollar public financing. Responsibilities included fostering a marketable image of our client and their objictives for the benifet of the underwriters and potential investors. This also involved making numerous decisions and analyses in regard to our interface with FCC requirements.
>
> The more significint factors impacting my long-range development from this experience include that I learned the coordination of financing needs and federal requirements. Throughly mastered quality control. Discovered how to identify areas of agreement and difference among the participants. Who eventually reached agreement through my involvement. Developed methods of meeting and turning around objections. And developed the ability to state my opinions in spite of intense pressure from various individules in a high-demand environment situation.

The writer has obviously had a good deal of experience in business, but he has failed to describe it effectively. First of all, he has confused a personal statement with a résumé (see below, section A2.3). In a résumé, statements about what the applicant has done sometimes start without a subject, so that instead of saying, "I represented X," the applicant might simply say, "Represented X." But a personal statement requires complete sentences. The lack of subjects in the first two sentences of the opening paragraph and the vagueness of *This* in the third sentence make the paragraph incoherent. Instead of an organized summary of the writer's experience, we get a string of disconnected remarks.

Second, the language is at once pretentious and sloppy. The writer uses pretentious jargon in phrases like *fostering a marketable image, in regard to our interface,* and *impacting my long-range development.* At the same time, he makes a number of spelling errors: *objictives* for *objectives, benifet* for *benefit, significint* for *significant,* and *individules* for *individuals.* In the second paragraph the writer claims to have *throughly mastered quality control,* but he has not yet mastered the spelling of *thoroughly.*

These two examples show what makes the difference between a bad statement and a good one, or—to put it bluntly—between rejection and acceptance. If you want to be rejected, put a lot of high-sounding words and phrases together without bothering to check your organization, sentence construction, or spelling, and without bothering to provide any clear and telling detail about what you have done. If you want to be accepted, write clearly, honestly, and specifically about your own experience and goals; take the time to see that your statement is well organized, that every sentence is complete and correct, and that every word is spelled right. Sloppy writing makes a bad impression; careful writing makes a good one. If you write carefully and explain specifically what has led you to choose a particular career, your statement will carry the kind of commitment and conviction that admissions officers want to see.

A2.3 Applying for a Job—The Resumé and the Covering Letter

The most important thing you need when applying for a job is a resumé—a list of your achievements and qualifications. The resumé should give all the essential facts about the position you seek, the date of your availability, your education, your work experience (with informative details), your extracurricular activities, and your special interests. You may include personal data, but you do not have to. The resumé should also list the names and addresses of your references—persons who can write to a prospective employer on your behalf; before listing their names, of course, you should get their permission to do so. The sample resumé on p. 690 shows the format we recommend.

The resumé alone, however, will seldom get you a job or even an interview. With the resumé you must send what a hiring officer expects to see first: a covering letter. Since the resumé will list all the essential facts about you, the covering letter may be brief. But it should nonetheless be carefully written. If the letter makes a bad first impression, you will have one strike against you even before your résumé is seen. With some company offices getting over a thousand applications a month, you need to give yourself the best possible chance, and your covering letter can make a difference in the way your resumé is read.

What do hiring officers want in a covering letter? They look for a capsule summary of the resumé itself, and also for things that resumés don't often tell them: how much you know about the company you hope to work for, what kind of work you hope to do, where you want to work, and what special skills you may have that need to be emphasized. The resumé defines your past; the covering letter can define your future, indicating what you hope to do for the company if you are hired.

To see what a difference a covering letter can make, compare these two, both sent to the same company:

> Dear Ms.———:
> In January, 1989, you were interviewing at the———
> College campus. I was schedule to see you but I had just
> accepted a position with———Stores and canceled my inter-
> view.
> At the present time I am working as an assistant buyer
> in Tulsa, Oklahoma. I have been commuting every two weeks
> to see my family in Chicago. I am seeking employment in the
> Chicago area.
> Enclosed is my resumé for your consideration again.
> Thank you for your attention. I will look forward to hearing
> from you in the near future.
> Sincerely,

Sample Resumé

Harold B. Rivers
44 Buell Street
Faribault, Minnesota 55021
(507) 555-6789

<u>Job Objective</u>

Marketing or advertising trainee
(Date available: July 1, 1990)

<u>Education</u>

1986-90

Monmouth College, Monmouth, Illinois
Degree: B.A. (expected in June 1990)
Major: Business administration

1982-86

Faribault Senior High School, Faribault,
Minnesota
Academic degree

<u>Work Experience</u>

Summer 1989

Acting Assistant Manager, Brown's
Department Store, Faribault, Minnesota.
Responsibilities included checking
inventory, handling complaints, and
processing special orders.

Summer 1988

Salesclerk, Brown's Department Store,
Faribault, Minnesota

Summers 1986
and 1987

Waiter, The Village Pub, Northfield,
Minnesota

<u>Extracurricular
Activities</u>

Undergraduate Council, Monmouth College
Debate Forum (President, 1988-89),
Monmouth College
Drama Club (President, 1985-86),
Faribault Senior High School

<u>Special Interests</u>

Photography, public speaking, drama

<u>References</u>

For academic references:
Office of Student Placement
Monmouth College
Monmouth, Illinois 61462

Mr. George C. Hazen
Manager, Brown's Department Store
300 Main Street
Faribault, Minnesota 55021

Mrs. Nancy Wright
Manager, The Village Pub
24 Harris Street
Northfield, Minnesota 55057

Dear Ms.———:

I am seeking a challenging position in marketing and consumer relations with a company in the Chicago area. I am particularly drawn to your firm because it is a utility, and utilities must maintain a proper balance between serving the public and protecting their own corporate interests. The challenge of maintaining this balance strongly appeals to me.

I have studied both marketing and consumer relations. At Monmouth College, from which I will shortly receive a B.A. in business administration, I took courses in such subjects as Consumer Attitudes, Marketing Strategies, and Principles of Retail Management.

Along with my education, I have had job experience that has given me frequent contact with the public. Working in a small business for two summers, I learned firsthand how to deal with consumers, and in the second summer I was promoted from salesclerk to acting assistant manager.

I hope you will review the attached resumé. Although a position in my field of interest may not be open at this time, I would appreciate your consideration for future management or marketing opportunities.

Yours truly,

These two letters make quite different impressions. The first writer opens by misspelling *scheduled* and by recalling that he once canceled an interview with the woman to whom he is now writing for a job; the second writer opens with a clear-cut statement of her ambition. The first writer tells almost nothing about his interest in the company; the second tells exactly what makes the company appealing. The first writer asks to be hired because he wants to see more of his family; the second asks to be hired because her studies in marketing and consumer relations and her experience in selling will enable her to help the company. Which of these two applicants do you think the hiring officer will want to see?

If you can answer that question, you know the difference between a weak covering letter and a strong one. A weak letter speaks of what the company can do for the writer; a strong letter speaks of what the writer can do for the company. If your own covering letter can at least begin to indicate how your experience and qualifications will help the company, the hiring officer will probably read your resumé with more than usual interest.

(For the format of a covering letter, which is a kind of business letter, see the next section.)

A2.4 Writing a Business Letter—The Proper Format

The covering letter that accompanies a resumé is just one example of a business letter—a letter designed to initiate or transact business. Such a letter should be concise and forthright. In relatively short paragraphs it should accurately state all the information that the writer needs to convey.

Format of a business letter

Return address   14 Sunset Drive
Interlaken, N.J. 08074
October 1, 1990

Date

inside address
Mr. Roy A. Blodgett
Director, Research Division
Baker Games, Inc.
502 Broad Sreeet
Buffalo, N.Y. 14216

Salutation → Dear Mr. Blodgett:

Body
I am writing at the suggestion of Ms. Grace Smith, owner of the Nifty Novelty Shop in Interlaken, N.J. She has carried your games for more than fifteen years.

Ms. Smith thinks you would be interested in a game I have invented. It resembles backgammon but requires the two players to use mini-computers rather than dice when making a move. This step reduces the element of chance and rewards the players' skill. Friends tell me the game is more exciting than backgammon or chess.

If you would like to see the game, I would be glad to give a demonstration when you come to New York City for a meeting with your buyers in the area. I can be reached at the following number: 1-609-555-2468.

Complimentary close ⟶ Sincerely yours,

Signature ⟶ *George A. Andrews*

Typed name ⟶ George A. Andrews

Format of a business envelope

George A. Andrews
14 Sunset Drive
Interlaken, N.J. 08074

Mr. Roy A. Blodgett
Director, Research Division
Baker Games, Inc.
502 Broad Street
Buffalo, N.Y. 14216

The format of a business letter is shown on p. 692. For a business letter you normally use medium-weight typing paper of standard size (8½ by 11 inches). Center the letter as well as you can, leaving side margins of at least 1½ inches. Unless the body of the letter is extremely short, use single-spacing and block form; type the paragraphs without indentation, and separate one from the next by a double space. Also leave a double space between the inside address and the salutation, between the salutation and the body, and between the body and the complimentary close. Leave at least four spaces for your signature between the complimentary close and the typed name.

Fold the completed letter in two places—a third of the way down from the top and up from the bottom—and insert it in a business envelope (4⅛ by 9½ inches) addressed as shown.

A2.5 Writing for Your Rights—The Letter of Protest

We live in a world of huge and increasingly impersonal corporations. Most of the bills and probably most of the letters you get come not from human beings but from machines. Bills are processed automatically; letters are clacked out by computers that know your address and your social-security number and have been taught to use your name in every other sentence, but nonetheless have not the faintest idea who you are or what your problems might be. How do you shout back at all this machinery? When you have a problem that can't be solved by a computerized explanation, how do you make yourself heard?

In a word, write. Do not accept the computerized explanation. Do not accept the words of a machine. If you think you have been overcharged or incorrectly billed or stuck with defective goods or shoddy service, don't keep silent. Fight back. Write a letter to the company or the institution, and demand to have your letter answered by a live human being. If the facts are on your side and you state them plainly, you may win your case without ever going to court or spending one cent for legal advice.

A friend of ours was billed $46.00 for an emergency service that he thought his medical insurance should cover. When the insurance company denied the claim, he phoned the company, got the name of the president, and wrote this letter directly to him:

> Dear Sir:
>
> In connection with the enclosed bill for emergency-room service provided to my son Andrew on October 15, I write to ask for an explanation for your company's refusal to pay for this service.
>
> Your company's statement for October indicates that the charge for emergency-room service is not covered because "use of emergency room is covered when in connection with accident or minor surgery." Does this mean that use of the emergency room is covered *only* when in connection with accident or minor injury? Andrew had neither of these, but his condition was a genuine emergency, and I don't see why you refuse to cover treatment for it.
>
> Andrew has asthma. He has long been treated for it by Dr.———, who is an allergy specialist, but from time to time

he has severe respiratory attacks that require emergency treatment—or rather, that require adrenalin, which is available *only* at the emergency room of———Hospital. If Andrew could have received adrenalin anywhere else, I could understand your denial of our claim, but so long as the hospital dispenses adrenalin *only* to emergency-room patients, we have to take him there. If we hadn't taken him there on October 15, he might have stopped breathing.

I can fully understand why you stop short of reimbursing all visits to the emergency room, since that would be an open invitation for your subscribers to use the emergency room for any and all ailments. But I believe you must distinguish between genuine emergencies and routine problems. I therefore expect your company to pay this particular bill in full.

Yours truly,

This letter got fast results. The president of the company referred it to the vice-president in charge of claims, and within a week the vice-president wrote to say that an asthma attack was indeed a genuine emergency, so the company would pay the bill in full. Thus the letter writer saved himself $46.00—not bad pay for the half hour he took to write the letter.

To see the effect that a letter of protest can have is to discover the power of the written word. Whether you realize it or not right now, the way you write can make a real difference in the life you lead after you have completed freshman English. In a composition course, you are writing for a grade. But when you write a statement for an admissions officer, you are writing for a place in a school, and getting that place may determine the rest of your career. When you write a letter of application to a hiring officer, you are writing for a job. And when you write a letter of protest, you are writing for your rights.

What writing ability finally gives you, then, is the power to express yourself on paper for any purpose you choose. The more you write, the better you will write; and the more kinds of writing you do, the more you will discover what writing can do for you. If you care about your writing, you will continue to refine and develop it long after the composition course is over. Very few things that college can give you will be more important to you afterward than the ability to put your thoughts and feelings into words.

Index

a, an, 482, 615
abbreviations, 487–90
  for geographic entities, 487, 489
  misuse of, 488–90
  for organizations, 488
  periods in, 449–50, 488
  plural forms of, 474, 478
  possessive forms of, 478
  for time and dates, 487, 488
  of titles, 487
  for units of measurement, 489
absolute phrases, 285–86, 640
Academic American Encyclopedia,
    504
accept, except, 615
acronyms, 449–50
active voice, 397–404
  defined, 260, 397, 656
  editing for, 89–90
  passive voice changed to, 399
  style invigorated by, 399, 423
  use of, 399
A.D., B.C., 615
addition:
  conjunctive adverbs indicative of,
    298
  words indicative of, 178
addresses:
  commas in, 439–41
  numbers in, 490
ad hominem argument, 158
adjective (relative) clauses, 315–22
  antecedents in, 315
  defined, 315, 640
  nonrestrictive, 317, 319, 435
  overuse of, 321
  placement of, 318–19
  pronoun case in, 357
  punctuation of, 319–20
  relative pronouns in, 315, 316–17
  restrictive, 320, 435, 436
  wordiness of, 223
adjective phrases, 272, 640
adjectives:
  commas with, 438
  comparative, 275–77
  coordinate, 438
  defined, 272, 640
  misused as adverbs, 275
  nouns as, 272–73
  predicate, 258, 651

prepositional phrases replaced
    with, 223
  proper, 481
  special forms of, 276
  superlative, 275–77
adverb clauses, 322–28
  in comparisons, 327–28
  defined, 322, 641
  nonrestrictive, 306
  placement of, 325–26
  punctuation of, 326–27
  subordinators in, 322, 323–25
adverb phrases, 273–74, 641
adverbs:
  adjectives misused as, 275
  comparative, 275–77
  conjunctive, 297–301, 644
  defined, 273, 640
  in infinitive phrases, 284
  prepositional phrases replaced
    with, 223
  special forms of, 276
  superlative, 275–77
advice, advise, 615
affect, effect, 616
afraid, frightened, 626
agent, 641
aggravate, irritate, 616

agreement, *see* pronoun-antecedent
    agreement; subject-verb
    agreement
aim, 34–38
  directed freewriting and, 37–40
  self-expression in, 35–37
  thesis in, 40–41, 47–48
  thinking about, 34–35
  tone in, 42–47
all, almost, most, mostly, most all,
    617
all ready, already, 616
all right, alright, 616
all together, altogether, 616
allude, refer, 617
allusion, delusion, illusion, 617
a lot of, alot of, lots of, 630
alumnus, alumni, alumna, alumnae,
    618
Americana, 504
among, between, 618
amoral, immoral, 618
amount, number, 618

analogies:
definition by, 122
in essay development, 115–16
in fallacies, 157–58
in pre-writing, 28–29
analysis, 124–27
by classification and division, 124–27
definition by, 122
analytical response, 227, 235–51
and, 294–95, 350
antecedents:
in adjective clauses, 315
defined, 345, 641
gender of, 351
indefinite pronouns as, 346
pronoun agreement with, 93, 346–56, 641
anxious, eager, 618
anyone, any one, 619
APA style of citation, *see* parenthetical citation, APA style of
apostrophes, 478–80
in contractions, 479
editing for, 94–95
with gerunds, 270–479
misuse of, 479–80
in possessive nouns and pronouns, 95, 478–79
in time and measurement phrases, 479
applications:
employment, 689–91
school admission, 685
appositives, 277–78, 642
apt, likely, liable, 630
argument, 137–71, 495–96
argumentative words in, 161–62
assumptions in, 142, 147–55
claims as origin of, 141
concessions in, 162–63
conclusions in, 148–49, 150–51, 153
construction of, 167–71
deductions in, 147–50, 153–55
defined, 138, 139
emotional persuasion vs., 139–40, 165–66
evidence for, 141, 142–47
exposition vs., 140–41
facts and examples in, 142–45
fallacies in, 156–61
figures and statistics in, 145

general claims vs. specific evidence in, 142
induction in, 147–48, 150–52, 153–55
opposing position in, 162–65
reader in, 137–41, 142
sources and authorities in, 145
articles:
defined, 642
in titles, 485
as, as if, like, 619
ASI (American Statistics Index), 510
assumptions, 147–55
assure, ensure, insure, 619
auxiliary (helping) verbs:
defined, 260, 642
modal, 406–8, 648
tenses formed with, 377
awfully, so, very, 639

bad, badly, 619
bare form of verbs, 642
base predicate, 651
base sentence, 642
base verb, 642
B.C., A.D., 615
be, 365, 366, 370
because, being that, since, 620
because of, due to, 623
beside, besides, 620
between, among, 618
Bible, citation of, 556
biographical guides, 505
book-and-article bibliographies, 501–2
Book Review Digest, 506–7
Book Review Index, 507
books:
reference, *see* reference books
source cards for, 515–16
brackets, 459–60
Bulletin of the Public Affairs Information Service (PAIS), 510
business letters, 691–93
but, 332

Canadian Encyclopedia, The, 504
can hardly, can't hardly, 620
capital, capitol, 620
capitalization, 481–83
editing for, 94, 95
for first word of sentence, 481
within parentheses, 466

of proper nouns and adjectives, 95, 481
in quotations, 454
of titles, 95, 482
card catalogs, 511–14
author cards in, 513
on-line catalogs vs., 512
subject cards in, 514
title cards in, 513
case forms, 93, 316–17, 357–62
defined, 357, 642
misuse of, 360–62
object, 357, 358
possessive, 357, 358–59, 478–49
reflexive/emphatic, 357, 359
subject, 357, 358
cause and effect:
conjunctive adverbs indicative of, 298
in essay development, 130–32
in progression, 84
subordinators and, 324
words indicative of, 179
CBE style of citation, *see*
parenthetical citation, CBE style of
censor, censure, 620
chain structure, 183–86
advantages of, 184
list structure combined with, 185–86
Chambers's Biographical Dictionary, 505
childish, childlike, 621
CIS, 510
citation:
APA style, 601–5
CBE style, 607–9
MLA note style, 659–81
MLA parenthetical style, 545–65
cite, sight, site, 635–36
classics, 621
classification, as analytical method, 124–27
clauses:
adjective, 315–22, 357
adverb, 322–28
defined, 642–43
independent, 94, 294–95, 296–305, 431, 432–33, 444, 647
nonrestrictive, 306, 317, 319, 435–36
noun, 329–30, 370, 649
restrictive, 320, 436–37

subordinate, 314–31, 445, 655
clichés, 92, 214–15
coherence, 181–87
chain structure for, 183–84
combination structure for, 185
connections strengthened for, 186–87
defined, 181
lead sentence and, 182, 184
list structure for, 182–83
collective nouns, 353, 372, 643
colons, 446–48
lists introduced by, 446
misuse of, 447
quotations introduced by, 446, 454
after salutations, 446
in time of day, 447
Combined Retrospective Index to Book Reviews in Scholarly Journals, 507
commas, 431–41
with addresses, 439–41
in adjective clauses, 319–20
with adjectives, 438
in adverb clauses, 326
appositives set off by, 277–78
in compound sentences, 296
with conjunctions, 94, 296, 431–32, 438
after conjunctive adverbs, 299, 434
with coordinate items, 438
with dates, 439–41
in greetings, 439–40
between independent clauses, 94, 431, 432–33
after introductory elements, 433–35
with large numbers, 439–40
misreadings prevented by, 439
with names, 439–40
with nonrestrictive elements, 435–36
in parenthetical citations, 548
participles set off by, 279–80
quotations introduced by, 441, 454
with restrictive elements, 94, 436–37
to separate sentence parts, 94
in series, 431, 436
between subject and predicate, 441
between verbs and objects, 441
comma splices, 301–3
avoidance of, 301–3, 432
defined, 432, 643

common forms, 643
comparatives, 275–77, 643
compare, comparison, contrast, 621
comparison:
  adverb clauses used in, 327–28
  alternating structure for, 117–18
  block structure for, 117–18
  definition by, 122
  in essay development, 116–21
  figurative, 211–14
  in parallel constructions, 307
  subordinators used for, 325
  words indicative of, 179
complement, compliment, 621–22
complements:
  object, 260, 650
  subject, 258, 654
complete subject, 654
complex sentences:
  defined, 315, 644
  main clause in, 648
  tense sequence in, 389–91
compound-complex sentences, 644
compound phrases, 265–67
  in coordination, 332–33
  defined, 265, 644
compound sentences, 294–305
  and overused in, 296–97
  comma splices in, 301–3
  conjunctions in, 295–96
  conjunctive adverbs in, 297–301
  coordination in, 332–33
  defined, 294, 644
  independent clauses in, 294–95
  punctuation of, 296, 297, 299, 301
  run-on sentences vs., 303–5
  semicolons in, 297
  tense sequence in, 389
compound words, 474–75, 476–77
comprehensive plot summary, 244
computerized indexes, 502–3
computer programs, *see* word
  processing
conclusions:
  in arguments, 148–49, 150–51, 153
  course of action recommended in,
    68
  in deduction, 148–49
  for essays, 67–70
  findings summarized in, 543
  in induction, 150–51
  paragraphs ended with, 188
  placement of, 153, 188
  questions answered in, 68

for research papers, 543
  thesis reaffirmed in, 67–70, 76,
    543
conditional sentences, 409–11, 644
conjuctions:
  commas with, 94, 431–32, 438
  in compound sentences, 295–96
  defined, 644
  semicolons with, 444
  in titles, 485
conjunctive (sentence) adverbs,
    297–301
  commas with, 299, 434
  defined, 644
  punctuation of, 299
connotation, 206–8
  defined, 206
  editing for, 90–92
conscience, conscious, 622
consul, council, counsel, 622
Contemporary Authors, 505
continual, continuous, 622
continuity:
  defined, 75
  revising for, 75–76
contractions, 480
contrast:
  alternating structure for, 117–18
  block structure for, 117–18
  in compound phrases, 266
  with conjunctive adverbs, 298
  definition by, 122
  in exposition, 120–21
  in parallel constructions, 307
  subordinators used for, 324
  words indicative of, 178
contrast, compare, comparison, 621
coordinating conjunctions, *see*
  conjunctions
coordination, 332–37
  defined, 438, 645
  in parallel constructions, 90,
    306–11
  subordination combined with,
    312–13, 332–37
  untangling sentences with, 336–37
correlatives:
  defined, 645
  in parallel constructions, 308
could care less, couldn't care less,
    622
council, counsel, consul, 622
countries, abbreviations for, 488
covering letters, 689, 691

format for, 659
résumés accompanied by, 689, 691
credible, credulous, 622
criterion, criteria, 623
Cumulative Book Index, 506
Current Index to Journals in
Education (CIJE), 510–11
Current Review Citations, 507

dangling modifiers, 290–91
defined, 290, 645
editing for, 93
dashes, 464–68
appositives set off by, 277–78
in dialogue, 465
overuse of, 465
phrases set off by, 464–65
series set off by, 464
data, 623
dates:
abbreviations for, 488
commas in, 439–41
numbers in, 490
declarative sentences, 645
deduction, 147–50
advantage of, 153
defined, 148, 150
induction combined with, 153–154
induction vs., 150
persuasive, 149–50
premises in, 149–50
syllogisms in, 148–49
valid vs. invalid conclusions in,
148–49
definite pronouns, *see* pronouns
definitions of words, 122–24, 461
by analogy, 122
by analysis, 122
by comparison and contrast, 122
dictionary as guide to, 202–5
in essay development, 122–24
by etymology, 123–24, 204
by example, 123
by function, 122
by synonym, 122
delusion, illusion, allusion, 617
denotation, 205–6
defined, 205
dictionary as guide to, 205–6
editing for, 90–92
dependent clauses, *see* subordinate
clauses
description, 106–9
analytical, 107

defined, 106
in essay development, 106–9
evocative, 108–9
external, 106–7
narration combined with, 112–13
technical, 107
development of essays, 105–36
analogies in, 115–16
analysis in, 124–27
cause and effect explained in,
130–32
combining methods in, 112–13,
132–36
comparison and contrast in,
116–21
defined, 105
definitions in, 122–24
description in, 106–9, 112–13
examples in, 113–14
exposition in, 128–36
narration in, 110–13
processes explained in, 128–29
dialects, 365–67
dialogue:
dashes in, 465
extended, 414
paragraphing of, 458
punctuation of, 453–54
diction, 198–202
defined, 198
dictionary as guide to, 203–4
editing for, 91
high level of, 199–200
low level of, 200
middle level of, 198–99
mixed levels of, 200–201
usage labels in, 203–4
dictionary, use of, 202–5
Dictionary of American Biography,
505
Dictionary of American Negro, 505
Dictionary of Canadian Biography,
The, 505
Dictionary of National Biography,
The, 505
different from, different than, 623
differ from, differ with, 623
direct objects:
defined, 649
faulty predication and, 269
noun clauses as, 329
transitive verbs and, 259
direct reporting of discourse, 413–19
defined, 645

extended dialogue in, 414
of poetry and prose, 415
questions in, 416–18
quotation marks in, 413–14
use of, 413
verb tenses in, 414
disinterested, uninterested, 623
division, as analytical method,
124–27
documentation, 544–65
see also citation
double negatives, 274, 645
drama, 243
due to, because of, 623

each, 354
eager, anxious, 618
editing, 88–103
to activate verbs, 89–90
for choice of words, 90–92
for faulty predication, 268–70
for grammar, 92–93
of mixed constructions, 267–68
for punctuation, 94
revising vs., 71
for rhetorical effectiveness, 88–90
for spelling, 94–95
for wordiness, 90
effect, affect, 616
ellipsis dots, 459–61
for omissions in quotations,
459–60
emigrate, immigrate, 627
eminent, imminent, immanent, 624
emotional persuasion, 139–40
emphasis, 187–89
arrangement for, 188–89
exclamation points for, 451
indicative mood for, 405
italics for, 187
repetition for, 187–88
subordination for, 88–89, 312–14
underlining for, 187, 483
emphatic/reflexive case, 357, 359,
642
Encyclopedia of Education, The, 504
Encyclopedia of World Art, 504
encyclopedias, 496, 504
endmarks, *see specific endmarks*
endnotes, *see* notes, MLA style of
English, Standard, 4–6
cultural deviations from, 4–5
regional deviations from, 5–6
ensure, assure, insure, 619

envelop, envelope, 624
envelopes, format for, 692
Environment Index, 509
Essay and General Literature Index,
507–8
essays:
arranging points in, 53–56
comparison and contrast in,
116–21
conclusion for, 67–70
development of, 105–36
examination, 682–85
freewriting for, 37–40
interpretive, 219–22
introduction of, 59–64
major points of, 53–56
organization of, 49–70
outlines for, 56–59, 65, 682–83
paragraphing in, 65–67
pre-writing for, 13–33
reading audience of, 50–53
submitting final copy of, 98–105
thesis for, 38–42, 47–48
tone in, 42–47
topics for, 19–26, 29, 47–48
etc., et al., 624
etymology, 123–24, 204
euphemisms, 218–19
everyday, every day, 624
examination essays, 682–85
essential points in, 684
organization in, 682–85
outlines for, 682–83
example, definition by, 123
except, accept, 615
exclamation points, 451
for emphasis, 451
overuse of, 451
in quotations, 465
explanations, 128–32
of cause and effect, 130–32
of processes, 128–29
reporting in, 129
teaching in, 128–29
see also exposition
explanatory notes, 661
expletives, 263, 645
exposition, 495–96
argument vs., 140–41
of cause and effect, 130–32
combination of methods for,
132–36
defined, 139
reporting method of, 128–29

teaching method of, 128–29
factor, 624
Facts on File, 504–5
fallacies, logical, 156–61
  arguing *ad hominem*, 158
  arguing by association, 156
  begging the question, 156
  defined, 156
  false alternatives, 157
  false analogy, 157–58
  false causes, 158–59
  hasty generalizations, 159–60
  irrelevant conclusions, 159
  personal attacks, 158
  shifting meaning of key terms, 156
farther, further, 625
fatal, fateful, 625
faulty comparison, 646
faulty parallelism, 308–10, 646
faulty predication, 268–70, 646
faulty tense shifts, 93, 392–96, 646
few, little, less, 625
figurative language, 211–14
figures, in research papers, 609–10
first drafts, citing sources in, 535
flashbacks and flashforwards, 111–12
footnotes, *see* notes
foreign words or phrases, 363, 373,
  484
former, formerly, formally, 625
fractions, 467
fragments, *see* sentence fragments
freewriting, directed, 37–40
  defined, 37
  thesis discovered in, 38–40
frightened, afraid, 626
fun, 626
further, farther, 626
fused (run-on) sentences, 93, 303–4,
  653
future perfect progressive tense, 383
future perfect tense, 382–83, 390
future tense, 381–82, 390

gender:
  defined, 646
  pronoun-antecedent agreement in,
    351
generalizations, 76–78
  in argument, 142
  in induction, 150–51
General Science Index, 509
gerunds:
  defined, 263, 646

possessives before, 270
pronoun case and, 358–59
good, well, 626
got to, has to, have to, 626
government publications, 510–11
  note citations for, 667
guides to articles in books, 507–8
guides to books, 506–7
Guide to Reference Books (Sheehy),
  504

has, have, 364
has to, have to, got to, 626
headwords, 288, 646
helping verbs, *see* auxiliary verbs
homonyms, 472–73
hopefully, 626–27
human, humane, 627
humanities, research papers in:
  documenting sources in, 600
  example of, 590–91
  focus of, 593–95
  organization of, 598–600
Humanities Index, 510
hyphens, 476–77
  in compounds, 476
  in numbers, 477
  with prefixes, 477
  words divided by, 476

identifying tags, 453, 455
idioms, 216–17
illusion, allusion, delusion, 617
imitative response, 227, 251–53
immanent, imminent, eminent, 624
immigrate, emigrate, 627
immoral, amoral, 618
imperative mood, 406, 648
imply, infer, 627
in, into, in to, 627
incredible, incredulous, 627–28
indefinite pronouns, 652
indentation, 458–59
  of paragraphs, 567
  of quotations, 458–59
independent clauses, 294–95
  commas between, 94, 431, 432–33
  defined, 647
  semicolons between, 444
  subordinate clauses and, 314–15
indexes to periodicals, 508–10
indicative mood:
  in conditional sentences, 410
  defined, 405, 648

use of, 375, 405
indirect objects:
  defined, 649
  transitive verbs and, 259–60
indirect reporting of discourse,
    413–19, 449, 451, 645
  questions in, 417–18, 449, 451
  use of, 415
  verb tenses in, 415
induction, 147–48, 150–52
  advantages and disadvantages of,
    151–52
  deduction combined with, 153–54
  deduction vs., 150
  defined, 150
  persuasive, 151–52
infer, imply, 627
inferences, logical, 147–48
inferior to, inferior than, 628
infinitive phrases, 283–84, 647
infinitives, 283–84
  defined, 263, 647
  perfect, 650
  pronoun case with, 358
  split, 284, 654
  tenses of, 383–84
insure, assure, ensure, 619
interlibrary loan, 514
*International Encyclopedia of the
    Social Sciences*, 504
interpretive writing, 248–51
  aim of, 249
  organization in, 250
interrogative pronouns, 647
interrogative sentences, 647
interviews:
  arrangements for, 518, 519
  note citations for, 667
  questions asked in, 518–19
  for research papers, 517–20
intransitive verbs, 204, 259, 655
introductions:
  assumptions challenged in, 63
  in essays, 59–64
  general and particular in, 62
  method explained in, 62
  opposing position explained in, 63
  personal stories as, 61
  questions posed in, 61
  of research paper, 540–42
  in revising, 75
  thesis stated in, 60, 75
  topic established in, 540–41

introductory elements, 433–35
irony, 237
irregardless, regardless, 635
irregular verbs:
  defined, 647
  principal parts of, 384–87
irritate, aggravate, 616

it, 263, 347, 348–49
italics, 483–84
  for emphasis, 187, 483
  underlining as indication of, 483
its, it's, 628

jargon, 217–18
journals, *see* periodicals

kind of, sort of, 628

language, *see* words
later, latter, 628
lay, lie, 629
lead, led, 628–29
lead sentences, 176–77, 180
learn, teach, 629
leave, let, 629
less, little, few, 625
let's, let us, 629
letters:
  business, 691–93
  covering, 689, 691
  protest, 693–94
  punctuation in, 440, 446
  salutations in, 440, 446
liable, likely, apt, 630
libraries, 499–515
  bibliographies and indexes in,
    499–511
  card catalogs in, 511–14
  interlibrary loans in, 514
  microtexts in, 517
  on-line catalogs in, 499–501,
    511–12
*Library of Congress Subject
    Headings*, 512
lie, lay, 629
like, as, as if, 619
likely, apt, liable, 630
likeness, conjunctive adverbs
    indicative of, 298
linking verbs, 258–59, 647
lists:
  punctuation of, 435, 436

vertical, 440, 519
list structure, 182–83
  basic pattern in, 182
  chain structure combined with, 185–86
little, few, less, 625
logic, 147–48
  see also argument
loose, lose, 630
lots of, a lot of, alot of, 630

Magazine Index, 509
main clauses, *see* independent clauses
main point, 75–76
  as conclusion, 188–89
  emphasis of, 176–77
  identification of, 239–43
  supporting points and, 190, 192, 246–47
main verb, 648
many, much, muchly, 630
maybe, may be, 630
means-and-end relations, conjunctive adverbs indicative of, 298
measurement, abbreviations for units of, 489
mechanics, 481–91
  abbreviations, 449–50, 487–90
  capitalization, 94–95, 454, 466, 481–83
  italics, 187, 483–84
  numbers, 439–40, 450, 467, 477, 490–91
  titles, 485–87
  underlining, 187, 483–86
metaphors, 211–14
  defined, 212
  mixed, 214
  similes vs., 213
microtexts, 517
might have, might of, 630
misplaced modifiers, 288
  defined, 648
  editing for, 93
mixed constructions, 267–68, 648
mixed metaphors, 214
MLA Handbook for Writers of Research Papers (Gibaldi and Achtert), 545, 659
MLA International Bibliography, 502, 503, 507

MLA style of citation, *see* notes, MLA style of; parenthetical citation, MLA style of
modal auxiliary verbs, 406–8, 648
modifiers, 271–93
  absolute phrases as, 285–86
  adjectives and adjective phrases as, 272–73
  adverbs and adverb phrases as, 273–75
  appositives as, 277–78
  comparative, 275–77
  dangling, 93, 290–91
  defined, 264, 648
  functions of, 271–72
  headwords for, 288
  infinitives and infinitive phrases as, 283–84
  misplaced, 93, 288, 648
  nonrestrictive, 649, 653
  participles and participle phrases as, 278–80
  placement of, 286–93
  restrictive, 288–90, 653
  in simple sentences, 264
  squinting, 288, 654
  superlative, 275–77
modifying phrases, 267
Monthly Catalog of United States Government Publications, 510
mood, 405–12
  in conditional sentences, 409–11
  defined, 405, 648
  imperative, 406, 648
  indicative, 375, 405, 410, 648
  subjunctive, 406–9, 658
moral, morale, 631
most, mostly, most all, almost, all, 617
much, muchly, many, 630

names, capitalization of, 95
narration, 105, 110–12
  chronological order in, 110–12
  defined, 110
  description combined with, 112–13
  flashbacks and flashforwards in, 111–12
natural sciences, research papers in:
  documenting sources in, 606–9
  example of, 592–93
  figures in, 609–10
  focus of, 596–97

organization of, 605–6
tables in, 609–10
negatives, double, 275
New Columbia, 504
New Encyclopaedia Britannica, 504
newspapers, *see* periodicals
New York Times Index, 509
nonprint sources, citation of, 557–59
    in list of works cited, 563–64
    in notes, 668–69
nonrestrictive clauses:
    adjective, 317, 319
    adverb, 306
    commas with, 435–36
nonrestrictive modifiers, 649, 653
nor, 339
Notable American Women, 505
notes (footnotes and endnotes), MLA
        style of, 659–69
    for articles in periodicals, 666–67
    authors' names in, 662–64, 665,
        666
    bibliography of, 669
    for collections, 664
    editors' names in, 662–63
    explanatory, 661
    for first references, 661
    for later references, 661–62
    for multi-volume works, 664
    for nonprint sources, 628–30
    numbering of, 659
    placement of, 659–60
    punctuation of, 660
    for reference books, 665–66
    for reprints, 665
    for second or later editions, 663
    for translations, 665
note-taking, 523–32
    on index cards, 525–26
    outlines and, 533–34
    paraphrasing in, 526–29
    quotations in, 529–31
    researcher's reaction recorded in,
        525, 528
    summarizing in, 526–29
    thesis in, 531–32
    with word-processor, 523–25
not very, none too, not too, 631
noun clauses, 329–30
    defined, 329, 649
    as singular, 370
noun equivalents, *see* noun clauses;
        verbal nouns

noun markers 649
noun phrases, 262, 437, 649
nouns:
    in absolute phrases, 285
    as adjectives, 272–73
    as appositives, 277–78
    collective, 353, 372
    compound, 474–75
    defined, 262, 649
    of measurement, 372
    plural forms of, 352–54, 368–73,
        473–75
    possessive forms of, 95, 478–80
    predicate, 258, 269, 329, 651
    proper, 95, 481–82
    sentences cluttered with, 223
    simple, 473–74
    singular forms of, 368–73
    as subjects, 262–63
    verbal, 262–63, 370
nowhere, nowheres, 631
nuggets, working with, 29
number:
    defined, 649
    pronoun-antecedent agreement in,
        352–55
    pronouns fixed in, 369
number, amount, 618
numbers, 490–91
    in addresses, 490
    commas with, 439–40
    for dates, 490
    figures for, 490–91
    fractions, 467
    hyphens in, 477
    plural forms of, 474
    spell-out, 490–91
    for sums of money, 490
    for time of day, 490
    in vertical lists, 450
numerical order, words indicative of,
        179

object case, 357, 358, 642
object complements:
    defined, 650
    transitive verbs and, 260
objects:
    defined, 649
    direct, 259, 269, 329, 649
    indirect, 259–60, 649
    of prepositions, 358, 447
OK, O.K., okay, 631

on-line catalogs, 499–501, 511–12
    card catalogs vs., 511
    information in, 511–12
    subject headings in, 512
only, 631
onomatopoeia, 109
opposing points, 247
or, 339
organizations, abbreviations for, 479
ourself, ourselves, 631
outlines:
    for essays, 56–59, 65–67
    for examination essays, 652
    paragraphs shaped from, 65–67
    for research papers, 533–35
    tree diagrams, 56–58
    vertical lists, 58–59

paragraphs, 172–97
    chain structure in, 183–86
    coherence in, 181–87
    combination structure in, 185–86
    conclusions in, 189–90
    in dialogue, 458
    direction of, 176–81
    emphasis in, 187–89
    faulty tense shifts in, 394–96
    indentation of, 567
    length of, 172
    list structure in, 182–83, 185–86
    main point in, 75–76, 176–77
    outlines converted into, 65–67
    purpose of, 172–76
    rearranging sentences in, 189–93
    in revising, 182–83
    strengthening connections in,
        186–87
    tense sequence in, 391–92, 394–96
    thesis supported by, 75
    topic sentence in, 176–77
    transitional words within, 178–81
    transitions between, 75, 193–97
    unity in, 150–56
parallel construction, 306–11
    for coordination, 90
    correlatives in, 308
    defined, 306, 650
    faulty, 308–10
    grammatical form in, 307
    purpose of, 306–7
    types of, 307
paraphrasing, 245
    in note-taking, 526–29

plagiarism and, 524
parenthesis, 464–68
    around interruptions, 462, 466
    around numbers, 450
    for side comments, 465–66
parenthetical citation, APA style of,
        601–5
    authors' names in, 602–3
    reference list for, 603–5
parenthetical citation, CBE style of,
        607–9
    authors' names in, 607–8
    reference list for, 608–9
parenthetical citation, MLA style of,
        545–65
    for anonymous works, 552–53
    for articles, 559–61
    authors' names in, 547–52
    basic procedures of, 546–47
    for Bible, 556
    editors' names in, 547–52
    for indented material, 556–57
    lists of works cited in, 547
    for material not indented, 556–57
    for multiple volumes, 552
    for nonprint sources, 557–59
    placement of, 546
    for plays, 553–54
    for poetry, 554–55
    punctuation in, 546–47
    for quoted source material, 553
    use of, 531
participle phrases, 278–80, 435, 650
participles, 278–80
    in absolute phrases, 285
    defined, 278, 650
    infinitives and, 283
    of irregular verbs, 384–87
    misforming of, 280
    past, 279, 280, 650
    perfect, 279, 650
    present, 278, 650
    punctuation of, 279–80
    tenses of, 383–84
passed, past, 631–32
passive voice, 397–404
    active voice changed to, 398
    with adjective clauses, 319
    agents in, 397
    defined, 260, 656
    editing for, 89–90
    misuse of, 401
    use of, 399–401

past participles, 279, 280, 650
past perfect progressive tense, 381
past perfect tense, 381, 390
past progressive tense, 380
past tense, 377, 380, 390
perfect infinitives, 650
periodicals:
  indexes to, 508–10
  in list of works cited, 559
  note citations for, 666
  serials list for, 514–15
  source cards for, 516
periods, 449–51
  after abbreviations, 488
  within abbreviations, 449–50, 488
  in acronyms, 449–50
  at end of sentences, 449
  misuse of, 450–51
  with numbers, 450
  with parentheses, 450
  in quotations, 466
  in sentence fragments, 342
persecute, prosecute, 632
person, 650
personal, personnel, 632
personal statements, 685–89
  detail in, 687
  jargon in, 688
  organization in, 687
  purpose of, 685–86
  résumés vs., 688
persuasion, 106, 137–71
  in advertising, 138
  defined, 137
  emotional appeals in, 137–38,
    165–66
  see also argument
phenomenon, phenomena, 632
Philosopher's Index, 503
phrases:
  absolute, 285–86, 640
  adjective, 272, 640
  adverb, 273–74, 641
  compound, 265–67, 332–33, 644
  dashes in, 464–65
  defined, 651
  infinitive, 283–84
  modifying, 267
  noun, 262
  participle, 278–80, 435, 650
  prepositional, 223, 342, 651
  verb, 260–61, 656
plagiarism, 537–39

acknowledgment of sources and,
  539
  copying key word or phrase as, 538
  defined, 537
  paraphrasing without citation as,
    538
  word-for-word copying as, 538
plays, parenthetical citations for,
  553–54
plural forms:
  of abbreviations, 474
  of nouns, 352–54, 368–69,
    473–75, 479
  of numbers, 474
  of pronouns, 352–55
poetry:
  parenthetical citations for, 554–55
  quoting from, 415, 458–59, 466–67
poor, poorly, 632
positives, 643
possessive forms:
  of abbreviations, 478
  defined, 642
  gerunds and, 270
  of nouns, 95
  of pronouns, 95, 357, 358–59, 479,
    480
precede, proceed, proceeds,
  proceedings, procedure, 633
predicate adjectives, 258, 651
predicate nouns, 258
  defined, 651
  faulty predication and, 269
  noun clauses as, 329
predicates, 257–61
  base, 651
  defined, 651
  intransitive verbs in, 259
  linking verbs in, 258–59
  in sentence fragments, 341
  transitive verbs in, 259–60
  verb phrases in, 260–61
predication, faulty, 268–70, 646
prefixes, 472, 477
premises, 149–50
prepositional phrases:
  defined, 651
  in sentence fragments, 342
  in wordiness, 223
prepositions:
  defined, 651
  in idioms, 216–17
  objects of, 358, 447

present perfect tense, 379, 389
present progressive tense, 379
present tense, 376–77, 378–79, 389
pretentious words, 92, 218, 688
pre-writing, 13–33
  analogies used in, 28–29
  asking questions in, 24–27
  for assigned topics, 21–24
  branching in, 16–19
  choosing topics in, 19–20
  conflicts as stimulation for, 19–20,
    26–27
  inspiration and, 13
  nuggets in, 29
  pinpointing in, 22–23
  reading for, 29–31
  right brain in, 13–16
  soliciting reactions to, 27–28
  triple-viewing in, 23–24
  word processors in, 14–17
primary sources, 521
principal, principle, 633
principal parts, 376–78, 651
proceed, proceeds, proceedings,
    procedure, precede, 633
progression:
  in cause and effect, 84
  defined, 75
  revising for, 75–76
progressive forms of verbs, 377,
    379–80, 381–83, 643
pronoun-antecedent agreement, 93,
    351–55
  defined, 641
  in gender, 351
  inconsistencies in, 352–54
  in number, 352–55
pronoun reference, 93, 347–50
  ambiguous, 347
  broad, 347–48
  faulty shifts in, 93, 355–56
  free-floating *they* and *it*, 348–49
  indefinite *you* and *your*, 349
  muffled, 348
  remote, 349
pronouns, 345–62
  in adjective clauses, 315, 316–17,
    357
  with antecedents, 345–46
  without antecedents, 346, 652
  case forms of, 357–62
  defined, 262, 345, 652
  definite, 262, 346–47

editing for, 93
faulty shifts in reference in,
    355–56
fixed in number, 369
gender agreement in, 351
indefinite, 652
in indirect reporting of discourse,
    415
interrogative, 647, 652
number agreement in, 352–55
object case of, 357, 358
plural, 352–55
possessive case of, 95, 357,
    358–59, 479, 480
reflexive/emphatic case of, 357,
    359
relative, 315, 316–317, 340–41,
    354–55
subject case of, 357, 358
as subjects, 262
unclear reference of, 347–51
pronunciation, 202
proofreading, 96–97
proper adjectives, 481–82
proper nouns, 95, 481–82
prose:
  quotations from, 415, 453, 458
  quotations in, 418–19
prosecute, persecute, 632
protest letters, 693–94
punctuation, 431–91
  after abbreviations, 488
  of adverb clauses, 326–27
  apostrophes, 95, 478–80
  of appositives, 277
  brackets, 459–60, 530
  colons, 446–48, 454
  commas, 94, 277–78, 279–80, 296,
    299, 319–20, 326, 431–41,
    454–55
  of compound sentences, 296, 297,
    299, 301
  with conjunctive adverbs, 299
  dashes, 277–78, 464–68
  editing for, 94–95
  ellipsis dots, 459–61
  exclamation points, 451, 465
  of footnotes and endnotes, 660
  hyphens, 476–77
  parentheses, 464–68
  in parenthetical citations, 546–47
  of participles, 279
  periods, 342, 449–51

question marks, 451, 456, 465
quotation marks, 413–14, 453–63
semicolons, 297, 444–48, 660
slashes, 458–59, 464–68
word processing programs for, 650

question marks, 451, 465
in quotations, 456
questions:
indirect, 417–18, 449, 451
posed in introduction, 61
in pre-writing process, 24–27
pronoun case in, 357
punctuation of, 449, 451
quotation marks, 453–63, 484
for definitions, 461
in direct reporting of discourse,
413–14
double, 453–54
for familiar sayings, 462
misuse of, 462
with other punctuation, 454–57
for phrases not taken at face value,
462
single, 453–54
special uses of, 461–62
with titles, 485–86
quotations, 453–63
accuracy of, 529
adding emphasis in, 530
brackets in, 459–60, 530
capitalization of, 456
colons with, 446, 454
commas with, 454–55
commentary on, 530, 542
of dialogue, 444
ellipsis dots in, 459–61, 529–30
exclamation points with, 456
explanatory words within, 515
identifying tags in, 453
indentation of, 458, 459
misfitted, 418–19
note-taking for, 529, 31
overuse of, 542
in own prose, 418–19
periods with, 455
of poetry, 415, 458–59, 466–67
of prose, 415, 453, 458
punctuation of, 413–14, 454–57
question marks with, 456
within quotations, 454
for research papers, 529–31
semicolons with, 454

slashes in, 458–59
of spoken discourse, 453
quote, quotation, 633–34

raise, rise, 634
rational, rationale, rationalize, 634
*Reader's Guide to Periodical
Literature,* 508–9
reading, 227–53
analytical response to, 227, 235–51
critical, 523
detecting tone in, 235–39
finding main point in, 235–43
imitative response to, 227, 251–53
judging supporting points in,
246–47
paraphrasing and, 245
purposeful, 29–33
selective, 522
subjective response to, 227–35
summarizing and, 243–45
real, really, 634
*reason . . . is that, reason . . . is
because,* 634–35
redundancy, 221–22
refer, allude, 617
reference books, 501–11
for articles in books, 507–8
biographical guides, 505
for book reviews, 506–7
encyclopedias, 496, 504
for facts and statistics, 504–5
for government publications,
510–11
guides to, 501–3, 506–7
in lists of works cited, 560–61
note citations for, 665–66
for periodicals, 508–10
specialized, 504

reflexive/emphatic case, 357, 359,
642
regardless, irregardless, 635
regular verbs, 652
relative clauses, *see* adjective clauses
relative pronouns, 315, 316–17,
354–55
defined, 652
in sentence fragments, 340–41
repetition, 187–88, 222
for emphasis, 187–88, 222
as wordiness, 222
reporting method of exposition, 129

reprints, citations of, 665
research papers, 493–612
  audience of, 495
  choice of sources for, 520–22
  commentary in, 542–43
  composition of, 540–43
  conclusions for, 543
  documentation of, 544–65
  essays vs., 495
  examination of sources for, 522–23
  explanatory vs. argumentative,
    495–96, 543
  figures in, 609–10
  filling gaps in research for, 532
  final copy of, 566–68
  interviews for, 517–20
  introducing sources in, 535–36
  introductions for, 540–42
  library work for, 499–515
  microtext sources for, 517
  note-taking for, 523–26
  outlines for, 495, 533–35
  paraphrasing in, 526–29
  plagiarism in, 537–39
  preparation for, 495–532
  quotations in, 529–31
  reference books for, 501–11
  revision of, 495
  samples of, 569–88, 670–81
  source cards for, 515–17
  sources cited in, 535–36
  in specialized disciplines, 589–610
  summarizing in, 526–29
  tables in, 609–10
  thesis formulated for, 495, 531–32
  title page for, 567
  topics for, 495, 496–501
  writing of, 495, 533–43
respectively, respectfully,
  respectably, 635
restricters, 288–90, 652–53
restrictive clauses:
  adjective, 320
  commas with, 436–37
restrictive modifiers, 288–90, 653
résumés, 689–90
  covering letters for, 689, 691
  information included in, 689
  personal statements vs., 688
revising, 70–87
  to adjust aim, 72–73
  to develop texture, 76–77
  examples of, 78–86

first principle of, 71, 86
  with generalizations, 76–77
  to improve structure, 74–76
  as large-scale, 71, 86
  of mixed constructions, 240–42
  with specifics, 76–77
  for tone, 73–74
rhetoric, 6–7
RIE (Resources in Education), 507,
  510–11
rise, raise, 634
run-on (fused) sentences, 93, 303–4,
  653

salutations, 440
sayings, familiar, 462
secondary sources, 521
semicolons, 444–48
  in compound sentences, 297
  in footnotes and endnotes, 660
  between independent clauses, 444
  misuse of, 445
  in series, 445
sentence adverbs, *see* conjunctive
  adverbs
sentence fragments, 338–44
  common forms of, 340–42
  defined, 338–39, 653
  editing for, 92, 340–42
  periods in, 342, 450
  recognition of, 340–42
  use and misuse of, 339–40
sentences, 255–427
  arrangement of, 189–93
  basic parts of, 257–70
  capitalization of first word of, 481
  clauses in, 258
  commas in, 94
  complex, 315, 389–91, 644, 648
  compound, 294–305, 332–33, 389,
    644
  compound-complex, 644
  conditional, 409–11
  construction varied in, 88–89
  coordination in, 312–13, 332–37
  declarative, 263, 645
  defined, 653
  editing of, 88–90
  exclamation points after, 451
  faulty predication in, 268–70, 646
  faulty tense shifts in, 392–93
  interrogative, 647
  inversion in, 263

lead, 176–77, 180
length of, 89
mixed constructions in, 267–68
periods at end of, 449
rhetorically effective, 88–90
run-on, 93, 303–4, 653
simple, 257–70, 653–54
subjects of, 262–63
subordination in, 312–37
tangled, 90, 336–37
topic, 176–77
with two or more main clauses, 332
variation in, 421–22
sequence of tenses, 653
sequential plot summary, 243–44
series, punctuation of, 431, 464
set, sit, 635
sexist language, 219–21
shall, 382
sic, 460
sight, cite, site, 635–36
similes, 211–13
defined, 212
metaphors vs., 213
simple sentences, 257–70
compound phrases in, 265–67
defined, 653–54
modifiers in, 264–65
predicates in, 257–61
simple subjects, 654
since, because, being that, 620
sit, set, 635
site, sight, cite, 635–36
slang, 200–201
slashes, 464–68
alternative words indicated by, 466
in fractions, 467
between lines of poetry, 458–59, 466–67
so, very, awfully, 639
social sciences, research papers in:
documenting sources in, 601–5
example of, 590–91
figures in, 609–10
focus of, 595–96
organization of, 600–601
tables in, 609–10
Social Sciences Index, 507, 510
sometimes, sometime, 636
somewhere, somewheres, 636
sort of, kind of, 628
source cards, 515–17

for articles, 515–17
for books, 515–16
sources for research papers:
availability of, 497
bibliographies as, 522
choice of, 520–22
classics as, 521
critical reading of, 523
examination of, 522–23
filling gaps in, 532
in first draft, 535
frequently cited works as, 520–21
introduction of, 535–36
microtexts as, 517
note-taking from, 523–26
organized reading of, 522
overuse of quotations from, 542
paraphrasing from, 526–29
plagiarizing from, 537–39
primary, 521
quoting from, 529–31
recently published works as, 520
relevance of, 520
responsible treatment of, 522
secondary, 521
selective reading of, 522
summaries of, 526–29
topic selection and, 496–97
spatial order, words indicative of, 179–80
specialized research and writing, 589–610
examples of, 590–93
non-specialists as audience for, 597–98
organization of, 598–601, 605–6
questions asked in, 593–97
specifics, 76–78
in arguments, 142
speech, parts of, 202–3
spelling, 469–80
dictionary as guide for, 202, 469, 472
of homonyms, 472–73
hyphens and, 476–77
improvement methods for, 469–70
of pluralized nouns, 473–75
problem words in, 470
word processing programs for, 469–80
of words with apostrophes, 478–80
of words with prefixes, 472
of words with suffixes, 471

split infinitives, 284, 654
squinting modifiers, 288, 654
states, abbreviations for, 479
stationary, stationery, 636
Statistical Abstract of the United States, 505
statue, statute, 636
structure:
  complete, 654
  continuity and progression in, 75–76
  in revising, 74–76
  unity of, 74
style, invigoration of, 420–27
  action verbs in, 422–23
  active voice in, 423
  questions asked in, 423–24
  sentence variation in, 421–22
  wordiness eliminated in, 425
subject case, 357, 358, 642
subject complements, 258, 654
Subject Guide to Books in Print, 506
subjective response, 227–35
subjects:
  complete, 654
  defined, 654
  definite pronoun as, 262
  faulty predication and, 268–69
  noun as, 262
  noun clause as, 329
  noun phrase as, 262
  number of, 368–73
  placement of, 263
  in sentence fragments, 341–42
  simple, 654
  subject complements and, 258
  verb agreement with, 93, 363–74
  verbal noun as, 262–63
subject-verb agreement, 93, 363–74
  for *be,* 365, 366, 370
  for collective nouns, 372
  for compound subjects, 371–72
  defined, 363, 641
  dialectal mistakes in, 365–67
  finding the subject in, 368
  for foreign words, 363, 373
  for modified nouns and pronouns, 371
  for noun clauses, 370
  for nouns of measurement, 372
  for pronouns fixed in number, 369
  for pronouns variable in number, 370

recognizing number of subject and, 368–73
  rules for, 364
  for singular vs. plural nouns, 369, 372–73
  for verbal nouns, 370
subjunctive mood:
  in conditional sentences, 409–11
  defined, 406, 648
  modal auxiliaries in, 406–8
  special verb forms for, 408–9
subordinate clauses, 314–31
  adjective clauses as, 315–22
  adverb clauses as, 322–28
  defined, 314, 654
  independent clauses and, 314–15
  noun clauses as, 329–30
  placement of, 330
  semicolons with, 445
subordinate verb, 655
subordination, 312–31
  coordination combined with, 312–13, 332–37
  defined, 312, 655
  for emphasis, 88–89, 312–14
  modifiers in, 313
  purpose of, 312–13
  untangling sentences with, 336–37
  see also subordinate clauses
subordinators, 322–25
  adverb clauses introduced by, 322
  defined, 323, 655
  relations signalled by, 323, 655
  in sentence fragments, 340
such a, 637
suffixes, 471
summarizing, 243–45
  in note-taking, 526–29
superlatives, 275–77, 643
supporting points, 246–48
  facts vs. opinions in, 246
  fallacies in, 156–61, 247
  number of, 246–47
  opposing points vs., 247
supposed to, suppose to, 637
syllable division, 202
syllogisms, 148–49
synonyms:
  definition by, 122
  dictionary as guide to, 205

tables, in research papers, 609–10
teach, learn, 629

teaching method of exposition,
128–29
technical terms, 217–18
tense, 375–96
  auxiliaries in, 377
  common form of, 378–82
  defined, 375, 655
  in direct reporting of discourse,
    414
  faulty shifts in, 93, 392–96, 646
  future, 381–82, 390
  future perfect, 382–83, 390
  future perfect progressive, 383
  in indirect reporting of discourse,
    415
  of infinitives, 383–84
  of irregular verbs, 384–87
  misuse of, 383
  in paragraphs, 391–92, 394–96
  of participles, 383–84
  past, 377, 380, 390
  past perfect, 381, 390
  past perfect progressive, 381
  past progressive, 380
  present, 376–77, 378–79, 389
  present perfect, 379, 389
  present perfect progressive, 380
  present progressive, 379
  progressive forms of, 377, 379–80,
    381–83, 643
  sequence of, 388–96, 653
  time indicated by, 375–76, 383–84
texture, 76–78
than, then, 637
that, 347, 436
that, which, who, 637
the, 480
themselves, theirselves, theirself,
  637
then, than, 637
there, their, they're, 637–38
therefore, 161
therefore, thus, thusly, 638
thesis:
  aim expressed in, 72
  defined, 40
  freewriting for development of,
    37–40
  generalizations vs. specifics in, 62
  in introduction, 60, 75
  and main points of paragraphs, 75
  as one-sentence declaration, 40
  in outline, 533–35

  reaffirmed in conclusion, 67, 76,
    543
  for research papers, 531–32
  in revising, 75–76
  samples of, 47–48
  tone, 42, 73–74
they, 348–49
they're, there, their, 637–38
this, 347
thus, therefore, thusly, 638
time:
  subordinators and, 323–24
  tense and, 375–76, 383–84
  words indicative of, 178
time of day:
  abbreviations in, 487
  apostrophes in, 479
  colons in, 447
  numbers in, 490
title page, 98
titles, book and article, 485–87
  capitalization in, 485
  quotation marks for, 485–86
  underlining of, 485, 486
titles, personal:
  abbreviations for, 487
  capitalization of, 95, 485
  commas with, 440
to, too, two, 638
tone:
  as attitude toward topic, 42
  consistency in, 73–74
  detection of, 73, 235–39
  development of, 42–47
  diction in, 73–74
  impersonal, 44–45
  ironic, 46–47
  personal, 42–44
  straightforward, 45–46
topic sentence, 176–77
topics for essays, 19–26
  assigned, 21
  methods for development of, 19–33
  nuggets in, 29
  pinpointing, 22
  questions used in development of,
    24–28
  readers considered in development
    of, 50–53, 137–41, 142
  theses and, 47–48
  tone and, 42
topics for research papers, 495,
  496–501

interest in, 497
introduction of, 540–42
limiting size of, 497
questions used in development of,
    496–98
source availability and, 497
transitions:
    ideas expressed in, 178–80, 193–96
    between paragraphs, 75–76,
        193–97
    within paragraphs, 178–80
    voice and, 260
    words indicative of, 178–80, 193
transitive verbs, 204
    defined, 655
    direct objects and, 259
    indirect objects and, 259–60
    object complements and, 260
translations:
    in list of works cited, 562
    note citations for, 665
tree diagrams, for research paper
        outlines, 56–58
try to, try and, 638
two, to, too, 638
-type, 638
typing:
    of final copy, 98
    of research papers, 566

underlining, 483–84
    for emphasis, 187, 483
    for foreign words, 484
    italics indicated by, 483
    to set off words referred to as
        words, 483
    of titles, 484–86
uninterested, disinterested, 623
unique, 638
unity, *see* coherence
used to, use to, 638

verbal nouns, 262–63, 370, 655
verb phrases, 260–61, 656
verbs, 363–412
    of action, 422–23
    auxiliary, 260, 377, 406–8, 642
    base, 260
    colons with, 447
    defined, 655
    dictionary as guide to, 202–3
    faulty tense shifts in, 93, 392–96
    future perfect tense of, 382–83,
        390
    future tense of, 381–82, 390
    intransitive, 204, 259
    irregular, 384–87
    linking, 258–59
    main, 608
    mood of, 405–12
    participles of, 383–84
    passive voice of, 89–90, 260, 319,
        397–404
    past perfect tense of, 381, 390
    past tense of, 377, 380, 390
    placement of, 263
    present perfect tense of, 379, 389
    present tense of, 376–77, 378–79,
        389
    principal parts of, 376–78, 651
    progressive forms of, 377
    regular, 652
    subject agreement with, 93,
        363–74, 641
    subordinate, 655
    tense of, 375–96
    transitive, 204, 259–60, 655
    verb phrases, 260–61, 656
    voice of, 89–90, 260, 319, 397–404,
        423, 656
vertical lists, 451
very, awfully, so, 639
virgules, *see* slashes
voice:
    active, 89–90, 260, 397–404, 423,
        656
    defined, 656
    passive, 89–90, 260, 319, 397–404,
        656

wait for, wait on, 639
way, ways, 639
well, good, 626
were, we're, 639
which, 347
which, that, who, 637
*who, whom, whose, whoever,
    whomever*, 360
whose, who's, 639
Who's Who, 505
will, 381–82
wordiness, 221–25
    editing for, 90, 222
    specific sources of, 222–24
    style invigorated by elimination of,
        425

technique for elimination of, 222
word processing:
  for final copy, 98
  note-taking in, 523–25
  spelling programs in, 469–70
words, 198–226
  abstract vs. concrete, 91, 209–11
  argumentative, 161–62
  cliché, 214–15
  compound, 474–75, 476–77
  connotations of, 90–92, 206–8
  definitions of, 122–24, 202–5, 461
  denotations of, 90–92, 205–6
  dictionaries and, 202–5
  diction level and, 198–202
  divided at end of line, 476
  editing for choice of, 90–92
  euphemisms, 218–19
  figurative use of, 211–14
  forms of, 203, 205
  general vs. specific, 91, 209–11
  idiomatic, 216–17

  jargon, 217–18
  pretentious, 92, 218, 688
  related forms of, 205
  sexist, 219–21
  transitional, 178–80, 193
  usage labels for, 203–4
would have, would of, 639
writing:
  conscious learning in, 3
  descriptive, 106–9
  directed freewriting and, 37–40
  narrative, 110–12
  pre-writing and, 13–33
  readers considered in, 50–53,
    137–41, 142
  of research papers, 533–43
  rhetoric in, 6–7
  as solitary act, 3–4
  in specialized disciplines, 589–610
  talking vs., 3–4

you, your, 349

Introduction

Talking and Writing 3
Standard English 4
Grammar and Rhetoric 6
Using This Book 7

Part 1
Writing Essays

1. Pre-Writing *pre* 13

1.1 Your Right Brain 13
1.2 Branching 16
1.3 Choosing a Topic 19
1.4 Assigned Topics 21
1.5 Pinpointing the Topic 22
1.6 Triple-viewing 23
1.7 Dramatizing the Topic 24
1.8 Choosing a Basic Question 26
1.9 Get Reactions 27
1.10 Use Analogies 28
1.11 Work with a Nugget 29
1.12 Read with a Purpose 29

2. Finding Your Aim *aim* 34

2.1 Your Aim 34
2.2 Self-Expression 35
2.3 Directed Freewriting 37
2.4 Formulating a Thesis 40
2.5 Finding Your Tone 42
2.6 Sample Theses 47

3. Organizing Your Essay *org* 49

3.1 Thinking about Readers 50
3.2 Arranging Your Points 53
3.3 Outlines 56
3.4 Introducing Your Essay 59
3.5 Shaping Your Essay 64
3.6 Ending Your Essay 67

4. Revising Your Essay *rev* 71

4.1 Aim 72
4.2 Tone 73
4.3 Structure 74
4.4 Texture 76
4.5 Revising 78

5. Editing Your Essay *edit* 88

5.1 Effective Sentences 88
5.2 Words 90
5.3 Grammar 92
5.4 Punctuation 94
5.5 Spelling, Capitalization, and Apostrophes 94
5.6 Proofreading Your Essay 97
5.7 Proofreading Your Final Copy *ms* 98

6. Methods of Development *m / dev* 105

6.1 Description 106
6.2 Narration 110
6.3 Combining Description and Narration 112
6.4 Using Examples 113
6.5 Using Analogy 115
6.6 Using Comparison and Contrast 116
6.7 Using Definition 122
6.8 Explaining by Analyzing 124
6.9 Explaining a Process 128
6.10 Explaining Cause and Effect 130
6.11 Combining Methods 133

7. Persuasion and Argument *pers* 137

7.1 What Is an Argument? 138
7.2 Supporting Claims 142
7.3 Using Assumptions 147
7.4 Avoiding Fallacies *fal* 156
7.5 Argumentative Words 161
7.6 Reckoning with the Opposition 162
7.7 Appealing to the Emotions 165
7.8 Constructing an Argumentative Essay 167

8. Writing Paragraphs *par* 172

8.1 Why Use Paragraphs? ¶ 172
8.2 Direction ¶ *d* 176
8.3 Coherence ¶ *coh* 181
8.4 Emphasis ¶ *em* 187
8.5 Rearranging Sentences 189
8.6 Transitions between Paragraphs *trans / bp* 193

9. Choosing Words *w* 198

9.1 Levels of Diction *d* 198
9.2 The Dictionary 202
9.3 Denotation 205
9.4 Connotation 206
9.5 General and Specific Words 209
9.6 Using Words Figuratively *fig* 211
9.7 Avoiding Mixed Metaphor *mix met* 213
9.8 Controlling Clichés *cli* 214
9.9 Using Idioms 216
9.10 Avoiding Jargon, Pretentious Words, and Euphemisms 217
9.11 Using Gender-Inclusive Language *sxl* 219
9.12 Avoiding Wordiness *wdy* 221

10. Reading in Order to Write *read* 227

10.1 Subjective Response 227
10.2 Analytical Response 235
10.3 Imitative Response 251

Part 2
Writing Sentences

11. The Simple Sentence—Basic Parts *ss* 257

11.1 Subject and Predicate 257
11.2 Predicate 258
11.3 Subject 262
11.4 Subjects after Verb 263
11.5 Modifiers 264
11.6 Compound Phrases 265
11.7 Editing Mixed Constructions *mixed* 267
11.8 Editing Faulty Predication *pred* 268
11.9 Adding Possessives before Gerunds *poss/g* 270

12. Modifiers *mod* 271

12.1 What Modifiers Do 271
12.2 Adjectives and Adjective Phrases 272
12.3 Nouns as Adjectives 272
12.4 Adverbs and Adverb Phrases 273
12.5 Adjectives as Adverbs 275
12.6 Comparatives and Superlatives 275
12.7 Misusing Comparatives and Superlatives 277
12.8 Appositives 277
12.9 Participles and Participle Phrases 278
12.10 Misforming the Past Participle 280
12.11 Infinitives and Infinitive Phrases 283
12.12 Avoiding the Split Infinitive *si* 284
12.13 Absolute Phrases 285
12.14 Placing Modifiers 286
12.15 Misplaced Modifiers *mm* 288
12.16 Squinting Modifiers *sm* 288
12.17 Misplaced Restricters *mr* 288
12.18 Dangling Modifiers *dg* 290

13. Coordination 1— Compound Sentences *coor* 294

13.1 Making Compound Sentences 294
13.2 Compounding with Conjunctions 295
13.3 Overusing *and* 296
13.4 Compounding with the Semicolon 297
13.5 Compounding with Conjunctive Adverbs 297
13.6 Comma Splices *cs* 301
13.7 Run-On Sentences *run-on* 303

14. Coordination 2— Parallel Construction *pc* 306

14.1 Why Choose Parallelism? 306
14.2 Writing Parallel Constructions 307
14.3 Correlatives with Parallelism 308
14.4 Editing Faulty Parallelism *//* 308

15. Subordination— Complex Sentences *sub* 312

15.1 What Subordination Does 312
15.2 What Subordinate Clauses Are 314
15.3 Adjective Clauses 315
15.4 Relative Pronouns 316
15.5 Placing the Adjective Clause 318
15.6 Punctuating Adjective Clauses 319
15.7 Overusing Adjective Clauses 321
15.8 Adverb Clauses 322
15.9 Choosing Subordinators 323
15.10 Placing Adverb Clauses 325
15.11 Punctuating Adverb Clauses 326
15.12 Adverb Clauses in Comparisons 327
15.13 Noun Clauses 329
15.14 Placing Subordinate Clauses 330

16. Coordination and Subordination *coor / sub* 332

16.1 Coordination and Subordination Together 332
16.2 Untangling Sentences *tgl* 336

17. Complete Sentences and Sentence Fragments *sent* 338

17.1 What is a Sentence Fragment? 338
17.2 Using and Misusing Fragments 339
17.3 Spotting and Editing Fragments *frag* 340

18. Using Pronouns *pr* 345

18.1 With Antecedents 345
18.2 Without Antecedents 346
18.3 Using Pronouns Clearly 346
18.4 Avoiding Unclear Pronoun Reference *pr ref* 347
18.5 Gender Agreement *pr agr / g* 351